T0141848

Contemporary Empirical Methods in Software
Engineering

Michael Felderer • Guilherme Horta Travassos
Editors

Contemporary Empirical Methods in Software Engineering

 Springer

Editors
Michael Felderer
Department of Computer Science
University of Innsbruck
Innsbruck, Austria

Guilherme Horta Travassos
Department of Systems Engineering and
Computer Science, COPPE
Federal University of Rio de Janeiro
Rio de Janeiro, Brazil

ISBN 978-3-030-32491-9   ISBN 978-3-030-32489-6   (eBook)
https://doi.org/10.1007/978-3-030-32489-6

This Springer imprint is published by the registered company Springer Nature Switzerland AG.
The registered company address is: Gewerbestrasse 11, 6330 Cham, Switzerland

Foreword

As the name of the field suggests, software engineering is expected to be an engineering discipline. However, it is not governed, to the same extent, by underlying mathematical models as many other engineering disciplines, in particular, those addressing physical artifacts as in electrical engineering or mechanical engineering. Thus, mathematics is insufficient to conduct research and improve in software engineering, although it is vital for some sub-areas within software engineering. There are several reasons for this insufficiency.

First of all, the software is invisible (Brooks 1987). We can read the code, but we cannot see it in use. We can only observe the effect of the software being executed. Furthermore, software engineering is intrinsically complex since it is, to a considerable extent, dependent on the knowledge and capability of humans developing the software. Moreover, the ability of the individuals to work in a team contributing to the same software system is essential. The development is supported by different processes, methods, techniques, languages, and tools, which, in one way or another, are used by the organization developing the software. Thus, software engineering is an interplay between human knowledge, social networks of the individuals, and available assets in the organization developing the software (Wohlin et al. 2015).

To be able to study and improve the way software is engineered, many researchers have embraced and promoted software engineering as an empirical engineering discipline. Empirical studies were conducted early in the discipline, but they were quite rare. In 1986, an article describing experimentation in software engineering was published (Basili et al. 1986) outlining software engineering as an experimental science. The establishment of empirical software engineering was done to a large extent in the 1990s. At the beginning of the twenty-first century, two books on experimentation in software engineering were published (Wohlin et al. 2012; Juristo and Moreno 2001). The former book came in a second edition in 2012 (Wohlin et al. 2012), and it was published in Chinese in 2015.

In 2004, the concept of evidence-based software engineering was established in software engineering (Kitchenham et al. 2004). The evidence is most often generated from empirical studies, and hence, it was a natural continuation of the previous work on empirical software engineering. As the area of empirical software engineering became well established, the need for advances in our conduct of empirical studies grew (Shull et al. 2008). Given the applied nature of software engineering, the need to conduct empirical studies in a real-life context was strengthened by the publication of guidelines for conducting case studies (Runeson et al. 2012).

As a continuation concerning the focus on evidence in software engineering, a book on evidence-based software engineering was published in 2015 (Kitchenham et al. 2015). Furthermore, empirical software engineering has gone from being a sub-area of software engineering to be an integral part of software engineering. Nowadays, it is expected that research is evaluated and assessed using empirical methods. Thus, it is, in most cases, insufficient to present an idea or a solution without empirical evidence. In summary, software engineering has moved into truly being an engineering discipline.

The book *Contemporary Empirical Methods in Software Engineering*, edited by Prof. Michael Felderer and Prof. Guilherme Horta Travassos, takes the next step by including chapters on essential and timely topics in empirical software engineering. The chapters are written by some of the world's leading experts on empirical methods in software engineering. The editors have done an excellent job of attracting experts in the field who contribute with essential topics concerning the empirical software engineering of today.

The book follows up on the previous books and articles on empirical and evidence-based software engineering. As the title of the book suggests, the book takes a timely step in including a set of chapters addressing emerging areas in empirical software engineering. It provides an excellent combination of chapters addressing contemporary areas of interest for anyone conducting research in software engineering and in particular for those with a strong focus on empirical software engineering. The book is a highly recommended read for, in particular, Ph.D. students and researchers interested in conducting high-quality software engineering research aspiring to apply empirical research methods for today and the future.

Blekinge Institute of Technology   Claes Wohlin
Karlskrona, Sweden

References

Basili VR, Selby RW, Hutchens DH (1986) Experimentation in software engineering. IEEE Trans Softw Eng SE-12(7):733–743

Brooks FP Jr (1987) No silver bullet – essence and accidents of software engineering. IEEE Comput 20(4):10–19

Juristo N, Moreno AM (2001) Basics of software engineering experimentation. Springer, New York

Kitchenham BA, Dybå T, Jørgensen M (2004) Evidence-based software engineering. In: Proceedings of 26th international conference on software engineering, Edinburgh, pp 273–281

Kitchenham BA, Budgen D, Brereton P (2015) Evidence-based software engineering and systematic reviews. Chapman and Hall/CRC, Boca Raton

Runeson P, Höst M, Rainer A, Regnell B (2012) Case study research in software engineering – guidelines and examples. Wiley, Hoboken

Shull F, Singer J, Sjøberg DIK (eds) (2008) Guide to advanced empirical software engineering. Springer, London

Wohlin C, Runeson P, Höst M, Regnell B, Ohlsson MC, Wesslén A (2012) Experimentation in software engineering. Springer, Berlin

Wohlin C, Šmite D, Moe NB (2015) A general theory of software engineering: balancing human, social and organizational capitals. J Syst Softw 109:229–242

Contents

The Evolution of Empirical Methods in Software Engineering

Michael Felderer (iD) and Guilherme Horta Travassos (iD)

Abstract Empirical methods like experimentation have become a powerful means to drive the field of software engineering by creating scientific evidence on software development, operation, and maintenance, but also by supporting practitioners in their decision-making and learning. Today empirical methods are fully applied in software engineering. However, they have developed in several iterations since the 1960s. In this chapter we tell the history of empirical software engineering and present the evolution of empirical methods in software engineering in five iterations, i.e., (1) mid-1960s to mid-1970s, (2) mid-1970s to mid-1980s, (3) mid-1980s to end of the 1990s, (4) the 2000s, and (5) the 2010s. We present the five iterations of the development of empirical software engineering mainly from a methodological perspective and additionally take key papers, venues, and books, which are covered in chronological order in a separate section on recommended further readings, into account. We complement our presentation of the evolution of empirical software engineering by presenting the current situation and an outlook in Sect. 4 and the available books on empirical software engineering. Furthermore, based on the chapters covered in this book we discuss trends on contemporary empirical methods in software engineering related to the plurality of research methods, human factors, data collection and processing, aggregation and synthesis of evidence, and impact of software engineering research.

Guilherme Horta Travassos is a CNPq Researcher.

M. Felderer (✉)
Department of Computer Science, University of Innsbruck, Innsbruck, Austria

Department of Software Engineering, Blekinge Institute of Technology, Karlskrona, Sweden
e-mail: michael.felderer@uibk.ac.at

G. H. Travassos
Department of Systems Engineering and Computer Science, COPPE, Federal University of Rio de Janeiro, Rio de Janeiro, Brazil
e-mail: ght@cos.ufrj.br

1 Introduction

The term software engineering originated in the early 1960s (Hey et al. 2014). During the NATO Software Engineering Conferences held in 1968 and 1969, participants made explicit that engineering software requires dedicated approaches that are separate from those for the underlying hardware systems. Until that "software crisis," software-related research mostly focused on theoretical aspects, e.g., algorithms and data structures used to write software systems, or practical aspects, e.g., an efficient compilation of software for particular hardware systems (Guéhéneuc and Khomh 2019). Since then, these topics are investigated in computer science, which pertains to understanding and proposing theories and methods related to the efficient computation of algorithms, and differs from software engineering (research), which has become a very dynamic discipline on its own since its foundation in the 1960s. IEEE (1990, 2010) defines software engineering (SE) as: (1) The application of a systematic, disciplined, quantifiable approach to the development, operation, and maintenance of software, that is, the application of engineering to software, and (2) The study of approaches as in (1). Software engineering also differs from other engineering disciplines due to the immaterial nature of software not obeying physical laws and the importance of human factors as software is written by people for people. Software engineering is fundamentally an empirical discipline, where knowledge is gained applying direct and indirect observation or experience. Approaches to software development, operation, and maintenance must be investigated by empirical means to be understood, evaluated, and deployed in proper contexts. Empirical methods like experimentation are therefore essential in software engineering to gain scientific evidence on software development, operation, and maintenance, but also to support practitioners in their decision-making and learning (Travassos et al. 2008). The application of empirical methods makes software engineering more objective and less imprecise, facilitating the transfer of software technologies to the industry (Shull et al. 2001). Software engineers learn by observing, exploring, and experimenting. The level of learning depends on the degree of observation or intervention (Thomke 2003) promoted by the experiences and studies performed.

Traditionally, *empirical software engineering* (ESE) is the area of research that emphasizes the use of empirical methods in the field of software engineering. According to Harrison and Basili (1996), "Empirical software engineering is the study of software-related artifacts for the characterization, understanding, evaluation, prediction, control, management, or improvement through qualitative or quantitative analysis. The quantitative studies may range from controlled experimentation to case studies. Qualitative studies should be well-defined and rigorous." The role and importance of the different types of empirical methods in software engineering have evolved since the foundation of software engineering. In this chapter, we discuss the evolution of empirical methods in software engineering and especially also take key venues and books into account as they reflect that evolution.

The chapter is organized as follows: In Sect. 2, we provide background on empirical research methods in software engineering. In Sect. 3, we present the evolution of empirical software engineering by describing five iterations of its development. Based on that "historical" perspective on empirical software engineering, in Sect. 4 we describe current trends in empirical software engineering based on the chapters on contemporary empirical methods in software engineering covered in this book. In Sect. 5, we present the available books on empirical methods in software engineering in chronological order as recommended further reading. Finally, in Sect. 6, we conclude this chapter.

2 Empirical Research Methods in Software Engineering

The scientific approach typically consists of observation, measurement, and experimentation. Observation helps researchers to formulate essential questions about a phenomenon under study to build models and to derive hypotheses that can be tested through experimentation. Measurement is essential for both observation and experimentation. A scientific hypothesis must be refutable to be meaningfully tested. Tested hypotheses are compiled and communicated in the form of laws or theories. At the heart of the scientific approach are research methods in general and the empirical method in particular. Empirical methods leverage evidence obtained through observation, measurement, or experimentation to address a scientific problem. Evidence should be based on qualitative and quantitative research. In this section, we provide an overview of research methods in software engineering in general and empirical methods in particular.

2.1 Research Methods

To perform scientific research in software engineering, one has to understand the available research methods and their limitations. For the field of software engineering, Basili (1993) and Glass (1994) summarized four research methods: scientific, engineering, empirical, and analytical.

The so-called *scientific method* observes the world and builds a model based on the observations, e.g., a simulation model of the software process or product. The scientific method is inductive and tries to extract from the world some model that can explain a phenomenon and to evaluate whether the model is representative for the phenomenon under observation. It is a model-building approach.

The *engineering method* studies current solutions, proposes changes, and then evaluates them. It suggests the most appropriate solutions, develops, measures and analyzes, and repeats until no further improvement is possible. It is an evolutionary improvement-oriented approach that assumes the existence of some model of the software process or product. It modifies this model to improve the objects of study.

The *empirical method* proposes a model and evaluates it through empirical studies like case studies or experiments. The empirical method normally follows an iterative and incremental approach that can begin with an exploratory survey, followed by case studies in an industrial context to better understand specific phenomena and controlled experiments to investigate cause–effect relationships.

The *analytical method* proposes a formal theory, develops the theory, derives the results, and, if possible, compares it with empirical observations. It is deductive and provides an analytical basis for developing a model.

Traditionally, the analytical method is used in the more formal areas of electrical engineering and computer science, but is important for software engineering as well, e.g., when building mathematical models for software reliability growth (Lyu et al. 1996). The scientific method, inspired by natural science, is traditionally used in applied areas, such as the simulation of a sensors network to evaluate its performance. However, simulations are used as a means for conducting an experiment as well (Baros et al. 2004). The engineering method is dominating in industry (Wohlin et al. 2012). The empirical method, mainly using empirical strategies, has traditionally been used in social sciences and psychology, where one is unable to state any laws of nature but concerned with human behavior. The engineering and the empirical method can be seen as variations of the scientific method (Basili 1993). This overlap and an integrated view of the scientific, engineering, and empirical methods is also an underlying design principle of this book on empirical methods. It considers not only chapters on traditional empirical strategies like surveys (see chapter "Challenges in Survey Research"), but for instance, also a chapter on simulation-based studies (see chapter "The Role of Simulation-Based Studies in Software Engineering Research"), which are closer to the scientific method as defined above, or a chapter on design science (see chapter "The Design Science Paradigm as a Frame for Empirical Software Engineering"), which can tightly be linked to the engineering method. All of these investigation strategies refer to empirical methods.

2.2 Empirical Methods

Empirical methods rely on the collected data. Data collection methods may involve qualitative or quantitative data. Some widely used *qualitative data collection methods* in software engineering are interviews and participant observation (Seaman 1999). Some commonly used *quantitative data collection methods* are archival data, surveys, experiments, and simulation (Wohlin et al. 2012). Once data are collected, the researcher needs to analyze the data by using *qualitative analysis methods*, e.g., grounded theory, thematic analysis, or hermeneutics, and *quantitative analysis methods*, e.g., statistical analysis and mathematical modeling approaches.

In general, there are three widely recognized research processes called quantitative research, qualitative research, and semiquantitative research. An alternative option is the combination of both qualitative and quantitative research, denoted as mixed research (Creswell and Creswell 2018). The distinction between qualitative and quantitative research comes not only from the type of data collected, but also the objectives, types of research questions posed, analysis methods, and the degree of flexibility built into the research design as well (Wohlin and Aurum 2015). *Qualitative research* aims to understand the reason (i.e., "why") and mechanisms (i.e., "how") explaining a phenomenon. A popular method of qualitative research is case study research, which examines a set of selected samples in detail to understand the phenomenon illustrated by the samples. For instance, a qualitative study can be conducted to understand the impediments of automating system tests. *Quantitative research* is a data-driven approach used to gain insights about an observable phenomenon. Data collected from observations are analyzed using mathematical and statistical models to derive quantitative relationships between different variables capturing different aspects of the phenomenon under study. A popular method of quantitative research are controlled experiments to examine cause–effect relationships between different variables characterizing a phenomenon in a controlled environment. For instance, different review techniques could be compared via a controlled experiment. *Mixed research* collects quantitative and qualitative data. It is a particular form of *multi-method research*, which combines different research methods to answer some hypotheses, and is often used in empirical software engineering due to the lack of theories in software engineering with which we interpret quantitative data and due to the need to discuss qualitatively the impact of the human factor on any experiments in software engineering (Guéhéneuc and Khomh 2019). *Semiquantitative research* deals with approximate measurements to data rather than exact measurements (Bertin 1978). It looks for understanding the behavior of a system based on causal relations between the variables describing the system. Semiquantitative models allow one to express what is known without making inappropriate assumptions, simulating ranges of behavior rather than values of point (Widman 1989). It has many applications in both the natural and social sciences. Semiquantitative research supports cases where direct measurements are not possible, but where it is possible to estimate an approximated behavior. In other words, this type of study is applied in scenarios where the numerical values in the mathematical relations governing the changes of a system are not known. In this context, the direction of change is known, but not the size of its effect (Ogborn and Miller 1994). Simulation-based studies in software engineering can benefit from using semiquantitative research (Araújo et al. 2012).

The three major and well-established empirical methods in software engineering are: survey, case study, and experiment (Wohlin et al. 2012). Primary studies using such methods can be performed in vivo, in vitro, in virtuo, and in silico (Travassos and Barros 2003). In vivo studies involve participants and projects in their natural environments and contexts. Such studies are usually executed in software development organizations throughout the software development process under real working conditions. In vitro studies are performed in controlled environments, such as laboratories or controlled communities, under configured working conditions. In virtuo studies have the subjects interacting with a computerized model of reality. The behavior of the environment with which subjects interact is described as a model and represented by a computer program. In silico studies represent both subjects and real world as computer models. The environment is fully composed of computer models to which human interaction is reduced to a minimum.

A *survey* is a system for collecting information from or about subjects (people, projects, among others) to describe, compare, or explain their knowledge, attitudes, and behavior (Fink 2003). A survey is often an investigation performed in retrospect, when, for instance, a tool or technique has been in use for a while (Pfleeger 1995). The primary means of gathering qualitative or quantitative data are interviews or questionnaires. These are done through taking a sample that is representative of the population to which is generalized.

A *case study* in software engineering is an empirical inquiry that draws on multiple sources of evidence to investigate one or a small number of instances of a contemporary software engineering phenomenon within its real-life context, especially when the boundary between phenomenon and context cannot be clearly specified (Runeson et al. 2012).

An *experiment* is used to examine cause–effect relationships between different variables characterizing a phenomenon (Guéhéneuc and Khomh 2019). Experiments allow researchers to verify, refute, or validate hypotheses formulated about the phenomenon under study. In a controlled experiment, one variable of the study setting is manipulated, and based on randomization, different treatments are applied to or by different subjects while keeping other variables constant, and measuring the effects on outcome variables (Wohlin et al. 2012). A quasi-experiment is similar to a controlled experiment, where the assignment of treatments to subjects cannot be based on randomization, but emerges from the characteristics of the subjects or objects themselves (Wohlin et al. 2012). Replication experiments reproduce or quasi-reproduce previous experiments with the objectives to confirm or infirm the results from previous experiments or to contrast previous results in different contexts (Guéhéneuc and Khomh 2019).

Regardless of the applied empirical method, to acquire scientific evidence about the investigated software engineering phenomena involves observation, measurement, and experimentation of the world and existing solutions. It demands the proposition of models and theories describing the observed behavior, collecting and analyzing data, putting the hypotheses under proof, and repeating the overall process over time to strengthen the evidence on the observed phenomena. Based on several primary studies, in which direct observations and measurements about the objects of interest are made, whether by surveys, experiments, or case studies, which are there also called *empirical strategies*, one can perform secondary studies. A *secondary study* does not generate any data from direct observation or measurement, instead, it analyzes a set of primary studies and usually seeks to aggregate the results from these to provide stronger forms of evidence about a particular phenomenon (Kitchenham et al. 2015). Secondary studies typically appear as *systematic (literature) reviews*, which aim to provide an objective and unbiased approach to finding relevant primary studies, and for extracting, aggregating, and synthesizing the data from these (Kitchenham et al. 2015). A particular type of a systematic review is a *systematic mapping study* (Petersen et al. 2015), which classifies studies to identify clusters of studies (that could form the basis of a fuller review with more synthesis) and gaps indicating the need for more primary studies.

The scientific or industrial significance of empirical studies depends on their validity, i.e., the degree to which one can trust the outcomes of an empirical study (Kitchenham et al. 2015). Validity is usually assessed in terms of four commonly encountered forms of *threats to validity*: internal, external, construct, and conclusion validity (Shadish et al. 2002). *Internal validity* refers to inferences that the observed relationship between treatment and outcome reflects a cause–effect relationship. *External validity* refers to whether a cause–effect relationship holds over other conditions, including persons, settings, treatment variables, and measurement variables. *Construct validity* refers to how concepts are operationalized as experimental measures. *Conclusion validity* refers to inferences about the relationship between treatment and outcome variables.

The accomplishment of empirical studies relies on performing well-defined and evolutionary activities. The classical empirical study process consists of five phases: definition, planning, operation, analysis, and interpretation, as well as reporting and packaging (Juristo and Moreno 2001; Malhotra 2016). The definition phase makes the investigated problem and overall objectives of the study explicit. The planning phase covers the study design and includes the definition of research questions and hypotheses as well as the definition of data collection, data analysis, and validity procedures. In the operation phase, the study is actually conducted. In the analysis and interpretation phase, the collected data is analyzed, assessed, and discussed. Finally, in the reporting and packaging phase, the results of the study are reported (e.g., in a journal article, a conference paper, or a technical report) and suitably packaged to provide study material and data. The latter has become more critical recently due to the open science movement (see chapter "Open Science in Software Engineering").

3 Evolution of Empirical Software Engineering

The application of empirical methods in general and empirical software engineering in particular is well-established in software engineering research. Almost all papers published in major software engineering venues these days include an empirical study (Theisen et al. 2017). Furthermore, since 2000, research methodology has received considerable attention in the software engineering research community resulting in many available publications on empirical research methodology in software engineering. In a recent mapping study, Molléri et al. (2019) identified 341 methodological papers on empirical research in software engineering.

The application of empirical methods and the underlying research methodology has developed iteratively since the foundation of software engineering in the 1960s. Guéhéneuc and Khomh (2019) discuss landmark articles, books, and venues in empirical software engineering that indicate the iterative development of the field. Bird et al. (2015) distinguish four "generations" of analyzing software data, i.e., preliminary work, academic experiments, industrial experiments, and "data science everywhere." In this section, we present five iterations of the development of empirical software engineering from a methodological perspective. We additionally take articles and venues into account, which is needed for a holistic understanding of the field's development. We complement our presentation of the evolution of empirical software engineering by presenting the current situation and an outlook in Sect. 4 and the available books on empirical software engineering in chronological order in Sect. 5 on recommended further reading.

3.1 First Iteration: Mid-1960s to Mid-1970s

In the early years of software engineering, empirical studies were rare, and the only research model commonly in use was the analytical method, where different formal theories were advocated devoid of any empirical evaluation (Glass 1994). According to a systematic literature review of empirical studies performed by Zendler (2001), Grant and Sackman (1967) published the first empirical study in software engineering in 1967. The authors conducted an experiment that compared the performance of two groups of developers, one working with online access to a computer through a terminal and the other with offline access in batch mode. Another empirical study published early in the history of software engineering was an article by Knuth (1971), in which the author studied a set of Fortran programs to understand what developers do in Fortran programs. Akiyama (1971) describes the first known "size law" (Bird et al. 2015), stating that the number of defects is a function of the number of lines of code. The authors in these and other early studies defined the goal of the study, the questions to research, and the measures to answer these questions in an ad hoc fashion (Guéhéneuc and Khomh 2019). However, they were pioneers in the application of empirical methods in software engineering.

3.2 Second Iteration: Mid-1970s to Mid-1980s

In the second iteration, already more empirical studies, mainly in vitro experiments, were conducted. Prominent examples are experiments on structured programming (Lucas et al. 1976), flowcharting (Shneiderman et al. 1977), and software testing (Myers 1978). The second iteration is characterized by first attempts to provide a systematic methodology to define empirical studies in software engineering in general and experiments in particular. These attempts culminated in the definition of the Goal/Question/Metrics (GQM) approach by Basili and Weiss (1984). The GQM approach helped practitioners and researchers to define measurement programs based on goals related to products, processes, and resources that can be achieved by answering questions that characterize the objects of measurement using metrics.

The methodology has been used to define experiments in software engineering systematically.

In that iteration, empirical software engineering was also institutionalized for the first time. In 1976, the NASA Goddard Software Engineering Laboratory (NASA/SEL) was established at the University of Maryland, College Park (USA), aiming to support the observation and understanding of software projects (Basili and Zelkowitz 2007). The establishment of NASA/SEL provided the means to strengthen the importance of using basic scientific and engineering concepts in the context of software engineering (McGarry et al. 1994). The paradigm change provided by using GQM (Basili and Weiss 1984), including the ability of packaging knowledge on how to better build a software system, improved the way experiences could be organized and shared. The building and evolution of models at NASA/SEL pave the road for organizing the Experience Factory model (Basili et al. 1994) and the dissemination of initial good practices on empirical software engineering.

3.3 Third Iteration: Mid-1980s to End of the 1990s

In the third iteration, not only experiments but also surveys (for instance, by Burkhard and Jenster (1989) on the application of computer-aided software engineering tools) and case studies (for instance, by Curtis et al. (1988) on the software design process for large systems) were performed to some extent. Also, the explicit discussion of threats to validity appeared in that iteration. One of the first studies explicitly discussing its threats to validity was an article by Swanson and Beath (1988) on the use of case study data in software management research. From the late 1980s, researchers also started to analyze software data using algorithms taken from artificial intelligence research (Bird et al. 2015). For instance, decision trees and neural networks were applied to predict error-proneness (Porter and Selby 1990), to estimate software effort (Srinivasan and Fisher 1995) and to model reliability growth (Tian 1995).

In the third iteration, empirical studies began to attract the attention of several research groups all over the world, who realized the importance of providing empirical evidence about the developed and investigated software products and processes. The experiences shared by NASA/SEL and the participation of several researchers in conducting experiments together with NASA/SEL helped to strengthen the use of different experimental strategies and the application of surveys.

The interest in the application of the scientific method by different researchers, the identification of the need to evolve the experimentation process through sharing of experimental knowledge among peers as well as the transfer of knowledge to industry, among other reasons, led to the establishment of the International Software Engineering Research Network (ISERN) in 1992. ISERN held its first annual meeting in Japan in 1993 sponsored by the Graduate School of Information Science at the Nara Institute of Science and Technology.

The need to share the ever increasing number of studies and their results and the growing number of researchers applying empirical methods in software engineering lead to the foundation of suitable forums. In 1993 the IEEE International Software Metrics Symposium, in 1996, the Empirical Software Engineering International Journal, and in 1997, the Empirical Assessments in Software Engineering (EASE) event at Keele University were founded.

By the end of this iteration, several institutes dedicated to empirical software engineering were established. In 1996, the Fraunhofer Institute for Experimental Software Engineering (IESE) associated with the University of Kaiserslautern (Germany) was established. In 1998, the Fraunhofer Center for Experimental Software Engineering (CESE) associated with the University of Maryland, College Park (USA) began operations. Also, other institutions and laboratories, such as National ICT Australia as well as the Simula Research Laboratory and SINTEF (both located in Norway), among others, started to promote empirical studies in software engineering in the industry.

Finally, by the end of the 1990s, the publication of methodological papers on empirical methods in software engineering started. Zelkowitz and Wallace (1998) provided an overview of experimental techniques to validate new technologies, Seaman (1999) provided guidelines for qualitative data collection and analysis, and Basili et al. (1999) discussed families of experiments.

3.4 Fourth Iteration: The 2000s

Since 2000 research methodology has received considerable attention, and therefore the publication of methodological papers further increased. For instance, Höst et al. (2000) discuss the usage of students as subjects in experiments, Shull et al. (2001) describe a methodology to introduce software processes based on experimentation, Pfleeger and Kitchenham (2001) provide guidelines on surveys in software engineering, Lethbridge et al. (2005) provide a classification of data collection methods, Kitchenham and Charters (2007) provide guidelines for performing systematic literature reviews in software engineering, Shull et al. (2008) discuss the role of replication in empirical software engineering, and Runeson and Höst (2009) provide guidelines for case study research. In connection to the increased interest in research methodology, also the first books on empirical research methods in software engineering with a focus on experimentation written by Wohlin et al. (2000) and Juristo and Moreno (2001) appeared around 2000 (see Sect. 5 for a comprehensive overview of books on empirical software engineering). Also, combining research methods and performing multi-method research became more popular in the period. One of the first papers following a multi-method research methodology was published by Espinosa et al. (2002) on shared mental models, familiarity, and coordination in distributed software teams.

With the growing number of empirical studies, knowledge aggregation based on these primary studies became more crucial to understand software engineering phenomena better. No single empirical study on a software engineering phenomenon can be considered definitive (Shull et al. 2004) and generalized to any context. Therefore, the replication of studies in different contexts is of paramount importance to strengthen its findings. However, the existence of conclusive, no conclusive, contradictory, and confirmatory results about a particular software engineering phenomenon should be combined to strengthen the evidence on the software phenomena or to reveal the need for more primary studies on phenomenon of interest. In consequence, there arose a need for secondary studies that aim to organize, aggregate, and synthesize all relevant results from primary studies regarding a particular phenomenon under research. Kitchenham (2004) was the first who recommended the use of systematic literature reviews (SLRs) in software engineering and adapted respective guidelines, mainly from medical research, to software engineering. With the guidelines of Kitchenham (2004) and Biolchini (2005), the empirical software engineering community had a tool to systematically synthesize knowledge available in primary studies, which spread rapidly and enabled evidence-based software engineering (Kitchenham et al. 2004). In a systematic review of SLRs in software engineering, Kitchenham and Brereton (2013) identified 68 papers reporting 63 unique SLRs published in SE conferences and journals between 2005 and mid-2012. Petersen et al. (2008) clarify and expand upon the differences between SLRs and systematic mapping studies and provide guidelines for the latter. In their seminal paper on the future of empirical methods in software engineering research, Sjøberg et al. (2007) present the important role of synthesis of empirical evidence in their vision of software engineering research. The vision is that for all fields of software engineering, empirical research methods should enable the development of scientific knowledge about how useful different SE technologies are for different kinds of actors, performing different kinds of activities, on different kinds of systems to guide the development of new SE technology and important SE decisions in industry. Major challenges to the pursuit of this vision are more and better synthesis of empirical evidence, and connected to that building and testing more theories as well as increasing quality, including relevance, of studies.

One of the problems faced by the software engineering community has often been the scarcity of software data for conducting empirical studies (Malhotra 2016). The availability of (open) source code repositories and software process data due to automated or even continuous software engineering enabled new data mining approaches in software engineering in that period. In a seminal paper, Zimmermann et al. (2005) used association rule learning to find patterns of defects in a large set of open-source projects. Furthermore, also, software data from companies were analyzed. For instance, at AT&T, Ostrand et al. (2004) used code metrics to predict defects, and at Microsoft—which even founded an own Empirical Software Engineering (ESE) group in Microsoft Research (Bird et al. 2011)—Nagappan and Ball (2005) showed that data from that organization could predict software quality. In consequence, also repositories—like the PROMISE repository—that collect software data and make them publicly available were founded. The PROMISE repository was founded in 2005 and seeded with NASA data (Menzies et al. 2014).

The empirical evidence gathered through analyzing the data collected from the software repositories is considered to be an important support for the (empirical) software engineering community these days. There are even venues that focus on analysis of software data such as Mining Software Repositories (MSR), which was organized for the first time in 2004 in Edinburgh (UK) and Predictive Models and Data Analytics in Software Engineering (PROMISE), which was organized for the first time in 2005 in St. Louis (USA).

In general, the growing interest in empirical software engineering in that period resulted in projects such as the Experimental Software Engineering Research Network (ESERNET) in Europe from 2001 to 2003 and the foundation of several venues. In 2007, the first ACM/IEEE International Symposium on Empirical Software Engineering and Measurement (ESEM) was held in Madrid (Spain). ESEM is the result of the merger between the ACM/IEEE International Symposium on Empirical Software Engineering, which ran from 2002 to 2006, and the IEEE International Software Metrics Symposium, which ran from 1993 to 2005. In 2003, Experimental Software Engineering Latin American Workshop (ESELAW) was organized for the first time. Also, in 2003, the International Advanced School on Empirical Software Engineering (IASESE) performed its first set of classes in Rome (Italy). In 2006, the International Doctoral Symposium on Empirical Software Engineering (IDoESE) was founded. Today, the ISERN annual meeting, IASESE, IDoESE, and ESEM form the Empirical Software Engineering International Week (ESEIW), which is held annually.

3.5 Fifth Iteration: The 2010s

Since 2010 empirical studies are "everywhere" in software engineering. Almost all papers in major software engineering conferences like ICSE contain empirical studies. Also, more and more books dedicated to empirical research methodology in software engineering are published (see Sect. 5), and papers on empirical research methodology are published at a constant pace. For instance, Ivarsson and Gorschek (2011) present a model for evaluating the rigor and relevance of technology evaluations in industry, Arcuri and Briand (2014) provide a guide to statistical tests for assessing randomized algorithms in software engineering, Wieringa (2014a) discusses scaling up of empirical methods for technology validation in practice, Wohlin and Aurum (2015) provide a decision-making structure for selecting a research design, de Mello et al. (2015) provide probabilistic sampling approaches for large-scale surveys, Sharp et al. (2016) discuss the use and value of ethnographic studies in software engineering research, Stol et al. (2016) discuss the use of grounded theory and their reporting, Briand et al. (2017) discuss the importance of context and the overrating of generalizability in software engineering, and Stol and Fitzgerald (2018) provide a holistic framework for software engineering research. Furthermore, Harman et al. (2010) provide a comprehensive overview and guidance on the application of search-based optimization in software engineering.

Especially, in this period many papers presenting results on search-based software engineering, that generally (though not exclusively) fall in the category of empirical software engineering papers were published. Due to the potentially high computational complexity of optimization algorithms, some researchers have started to use high performance computing environments to support the execution of their studies (Farzat et al. 2019).

In this iteration, one can observe a growing interest in the role of theory within software engineering research to develop the field further as a scientific discipline. In December 2009, the Software Engineering Method and Theory (SEMAT) initiative was launched that aims towards the development of a general theory of software engineering. SEMAT organized several events, among others, a workshop series on a General Theory of Software Engineering (GTSE) between 2012 and 2015. Stol and Fitzgerald (2015) even argue for a theory-oriented software engineering research perspective, which can complement the recent focus on evidence-based software engineering. Also, several concrete theories have been developed in that iteration. For instance, Johnson and Ekstedt (2016) present a general theory of software engineering called Tarpit, Bjarnason et al. (2016) a theory of distances in software engineering, and Wagner et al. (2019) a theory on requirements engineering.

Today not only almost all papers in major software engineering conferences contain empirical studies, but also most software engineering conferences have explicitly integrated empirical software engineering into their program, e.g., as dedicated sessions or tracks. In addition, there are several workshops on conducting empirical studies in specific areas. For instance, at ICSE, there has been a collocated International Workshop on Conducting Empirical Studies in Industry (CESI) and at RE the International Workshop on Empirical Requirements Engineering (EmpiRE). The Experimental Software Engineering Latin American Workshop (ESELAW) joined the Ibero-American Conference on Software Engineering (CIbSE) in 2011 as a colocated workshop and became a dedicated track in 2013 due to the increased number of submissions.

ESEIW, including ESEM, and EASE are established as the two leading annual events to discuss methodological issues on empirical research in software engineering. Empirical methods have been an explicit topic in several summer schools including the annual LASER summer school (which hosted the topic empirical software engineering in 2010), PASED—Canadian Summer School on Practical Analyses of Software Engineering Data in 2011, the Empirical Research Methods in Software Engineering and Informatics (ERMSEI) in 2016 and 2017, the International Summer School on Software Engineering (SIESTA) in 2018 and 2019 as well as the 2019 Summer School in Empirical Software Engineering at Brunel (UK). In the context of ESEIW, the International Advanced School on Empirical Software Engineering (IASESE) has been organized annually since 2003 and helped to spread knowledge on current empirical methods in software engineering among junior and senior researchers. Figure 1 presents the IASESE timeline and its topics along the places and years. The topics taught over the years also reflect the evolution of empirical software engineering, as discussed in this section.

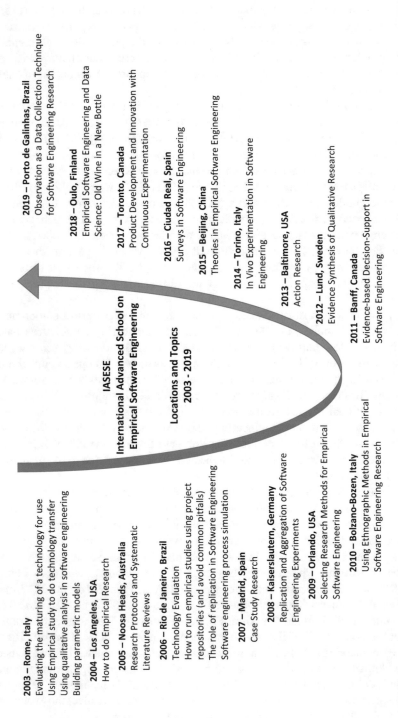

Fig. 1 International Advanced School on Empirical Software Engineering (IASESE) timeline and topics from 2003 to 2019

4 Current Situation and Outlook

Since the first empirical studies in the 1960s, the field of empirical software engineering has considerably matured in several iterations. However, the empirical methods resulting from the five iterations presented in the previous section are not the end of the story, and as in any scientific discipline, research methods develop further. The chapters of this book discuss contemporary empirical methods that impact the current evolution of empirical software engineering and form the backbone of its next iteration. For sure, the description of the current situation and future trends is never complete and always subjective to some extent. But we think that the chapters covered in this book show several interesting trends in contemporary empirical methods in software engineering, which we want to summarize here.

The evolution of empirical software engineering leads to the continuous adoption of empirical methods from other fields and the refinement of existing empirical methods in software engineering. The resulting plurality of research methods requires guidance in knowledge-seeking and solution-seeking (i.e., design science) research. The chapter "Guidelines for Conducting Software Engineering Research" presents guidelines for conducting software engineering research based on the *ABC framework*, where ABC represents the three desirable aspects of research generalizability over actors (A), precise control of behavior (B), and realism of context (C). Each empirical method has its strengths and weaknesses. It is beneficial to utilize a mix of methods depending on the research goal or even to combine methods. Case survey research combines case study and survey research, which rely primarily on qualitative and quantitative data, respectively. The chapter "Guidelines for Case Survey Research in Software Engineering" provides an overview of the *case survey method*. While being an important and often used empirical method, survey research has been less discussed on a methodological level than other types of empirical methods. The chapter "Challenges in Survey Research" discusses *methodological issues in survey research* for software engineering concerning theory building, sampling, invitation and follow-up, statistical analysis, qualitative analysis, and assessment of psychological constructs. Although software engineering is an engineering discipline, the design science paradigm has been explicitly adapted to software engineering relatively late by Wieringa (2014b), and the full potential of the design science paradigm has not been exploited so far in software engineering. The chapter "The Design Science Paradigm as a Frame for Empirical Software Engineering" uses the *design science paradigm* as a frame for empirical software engineering and uses it to support the assessment of research contributions, industry-academia communication, and theoretical knowledge building.

It is generally acknowledged that software development is a human-intensive activity as software is built by humans for humans. However, traditionally SE research has focused on artifacts and processes without explicitly taking human factors in general and the developer perspective in particular into account. If the perspective on how developers work was considered, then it was mostly measured from a subjective perspective, e.g., by interviews or opinion surveys, or a "black box" perspective by mining repository data or measuring the created development artifacts. The chapter "Biometric Measurement in Software Engineering" introduces *biometric sensors and measure* that provide new opportunities to more objectively measure physiological changes in the human body that can be linked to various psychological processes. These biometric measurements can be used to gain insights on fundamental cognitive and emotional processes of software developers while they are working, but also to provide better and more prompt tool support for developers. Another human-related issue is the involvement of humans in empirical studies, especially in experiments. On the one hand, it is normally difficult to recruit a significant number of professionals for an empirical study, and on the other hand, measurements are invasive. The chapter "Empirical Software Engineering Experimentation with Human Computation" explores the potential of *human computation methods*, such as crowdsourcing, for experimentation in empirical software engineering.

Empirical methods rely on the collected data. However, the volume, velocity, and variety of data in software products and processes have exploded during the last years. Therefore, the new scientific paradigm of *data science* has gained much attention, also within software engineering. The chapter "Data Science and Empirical Software Engineering" relates to traditional ESE and data science. It shows that both paradigms have many characteristics in common and can benefit from each other. Given large data sets, *optimization* is an important form of data analytics support of human decision-making. Empirical studies serve both as a model and as data input for optimization. The chapter "Optimization in Software Engineering: A Pragmatic Approach" provides an overview of optimization in software engineering in general and its value and applicability in ESE in particular. With increased automation, uncertainty (due to the application of statistical models), and monitoring capabilities in data-driven software engineering, also the role of *simulation* techniques becomes more important. The chapter "The Role of Simulation-Based Studies in Software Engineering Research" provides a guide to simulation-based studies in software engineering. *Bayesian data analysis* is a means to embrace uncertainty by using multilevel statistical models and making use of all available information at hand. The chapter "Bayesian Data Analysis in Empirical Software Engineering: The Case of Missing Data" provides an introduction to Bayesian data analysis and an application example to empirical software engineering dealing with common issues in ESE like missing data.

Extracting, aggregating, and synthesizing evidence from empirical studies is essential for the development of scientific knowledge and the field of software engineering. However, conducting secondary studies like systematic literature reviews and aggregating evidence is still challenging. Conducting systematic literature reviews (SLRs) is largely a manual and, therefore, time-consuming and error-prone process. The chapter "Automating Systematic Literature Review" provides strategies to *automate the SLR process*. Secondary studies often lack connection to software engineering practice, which is essential to software engineering. The chapter "Rapid Reviews in Software Engineering" presents the concept of *rapid reviews*, which are lightweight secondary studies focused on delivering evidence to practitioners on time. Another approach to link to practice is to take grey literature into account in empirical studies. The chapter "Benefitting from the Grey Literature in Software Engineering Research" discusses the concept of *grey literature* in software engineering and ways how to consider it in primary and secondary studies. Considering that secondary studies are often used to support the evidence-based paradigm, it is crucial to managing their threats properly. The chapter "Guidelines for Managing Threats to Validity of Secondary Studies in Software Engineering" provides guidelines for managing *threats to validity of secondary studies* in software engineering. Evidence in software engineering is often rare and produced in both quantitative and qualitative forms. It makes the synthesis of evidence, which is an essential element in scientific knowledge creation, a challenging task. The chapter "Research Synthesis in Software Engineering" provides an overview of research *synthesis methods* in software engineering.

Society in general and funding agencies in particular put a stronger focus on the impact of (software engineering) research. Therefore, open science and research transfer are becoming essential topics in (empirical) software engineering. *Open science* describes the movement of making any research artifact available to the public and includes open access, open data, and open source. The topic is natural and especially important in empirical software engineering to guarantee the replicability of empirical studies. The chapter "Open Science in Software Engineering" reflects upon the essentials in open science for software engineering to help to establish a common ground and to make open science a norm in SE. Industry-academia collaboration is one of the cornerstones of empirical software engineering. However, close and sustainable collaboration with industry are key issues in the field. The chapter "Third Generation Industrial Co-production in Software Engineering" presents a seven-step *industrial coproduction* approach that enables deep and long-term industry-academia collaboration.

5   Recommended Further Reading

Since 2000 research methodology has received considerable attention in the software engineering research community. Therefore, plenty of literature is available on empirical research methodology in software engineering. Molléri et al. (2019) identified in a recent systematic mapping study 341 methodological papers on empirical research in software engineering—and therefore, a complete overview would exceed the scope of this book chapter. However, following the style of this book chapter, we provide an overview of the available English text and special issue books explicitly dedicated to empirical research methodology in software engineering in chronological order of their publication.

Wohlin et al. (2000) published a book entitled "Experimentation in Software Engineering," which provides an overview of the core empirical strategies in software engineering, i.e., surveys, experimentation, and case studies and as its main content all steps in the experimentation process, i.e., scoping, planning, operation, analysis and interpretation as well as presentation and package. The book is complemented by exercises and examples, e.g., an experiment comparing different programming languages. Consequently, the book targets students, teachers, researchers, and practitioners in software engineering. In 2012 a revision of this popular book had been published with Springer (Wohlin et al. 2012).

Juristo and Moreno (2001) published a book entitled "Basics of Software Engineering Experimentation," which presents the basics of designing and analyzing experiments both to software engineering researchers and practitioners based on SE examples like comparing the effectiveness of defect detection techniques. The book presents the underlying statistical methods, including the computation of test statistics in detail.

Endres and Rombach (2003) published "A Handbook of Software and Systems Engineering. Empirical Observations, Laws, and Theories." The book presents rules, laws, and their underlying theories from all phases of the software development lifecycle. The book provides the reader with clear statements of software and system engineering laws and their applicability as well as related empirical evidence. The consideration of empirical evidence distinguishes the book from other available handbooks and textbooks on software engineering.

Juristo and Moreno (2003) edited "Lecture Notes on Empirical Software Engineering," which aims to spread the idea of the importance of empirical knowledge in software development from a highly practical viewpoint. It defines the body of empirically validated knowledge in software development to advise practitioners on what methods or techniques have been empirically analyzed and what the results were. Furthermore, it promotes "empirical tests," which have traditionally been carried out by universities or research centers, for application in industry to validate software development technologies used in practice.

Shull et al. (2007) published the "Guide to Advanced Empirical Software Engineering." It is an edited book written by experts in empirical software engineering. It covers advanced research methods and techniques, practical foundations, as well as knowledge creation, approaches. The book at hand provides a continuation of that seminal book covering recent developments in empirical software engineering.

Runeson et al. (2012) published a book entitled "Case Study Research in Software Engineering: Guidelines and Examples," which covers guidelines for all steps of case study research, i.e., design, data collection, data analysis and interpretation, as well as reporting and dissemination. The book is complemented with examples from extreme programming, project management, quality monitoring as well as requirements engineering and additionally also provides checklists.

Wieringa (2014b) published a book entitled "Design Science Methodology for Information Systems and Software Engineering," which provides guidelines for practicing design science in software engineering research. A design process usually iterates over two activities, i.e., first designing an artifact that improves something for stakeholders, and subsequently empirically validating the performance of that artifact in its context. This "validation in context" is a key feature of the book.

Menzies et al. (2014) published a book entitled "Sharing Data and Models in Software Engineering." The central theme of the book is how to share what has been learned by data science from software projects. The book is driven by the PROMISE (Predictive Models and Data Analytics in Software Engineering) community. It is the first book dedicated to data science in software and mining software repositories. Closely related to this book, Bird et al. (2015) published a book entitled "The Art and Science of Analyzing Software Data," which is driven by the MSR (Mining Software Repositories) community and focuses mainly on data analysis based on statistics and machine learning. Another related book published by Menzies et al. (2016) covers perspectives on data science for software engineering by various authors.

Kitchenham et al. (2015) published a book entitled "Evidence-based Software Engineering and Systematic Reviews," which provides practical guidance on how to conduct secondary studies in software engineering. The book also discusses the nature of evidence and explains the types of primary studies that provide inputs to a secondary study.

Malhotra (2016) published a book entitled "Empirical Research in Software Engineering: Concepts, Analysis, and Applications," which shows how to implement empirical research processes, procedures, and practices in software engineering. The book covers many accompanying exercises and examples. The author especially also discusses the process of developing predictive models, such as defect prediction and change prediction, on data collected from source code repositories, and, more generally the application of machine learning techniques in empirical software engineering.

ben Othmane et al. (2017) published a book entitled "Empirical Research for Software Security: Foundations and Experience," which discusses empirical methods with a special focus on software security.

Staron (2019) published a book entitled "Action Research in Software Engineering: Theory and Applications," which offers a comprehensive discussion on the use of action research as an instrument to evolve software technologies and promote synergy between researchers and practitioners.

In addition to these textbooks, there are also edited books available that are related to special events in empirical software engineering and cover valuable methodological contributions.

Rombach et al. (1993) edited proceedings from a Dagstuhl seminar in 1992 on empirical software engineering entitled "Experimental Software Engineering Issues: Critical Assessment and Future Directions." The goal was to discuss the state of the art of empirical software engineering by assessing past accomplishments, raising open questions, and proposing a future research agenda at that time. However, many contributions of that book are still relevant today.

Conradi and Wang (2003) edited a book entitled "Empirical Methods and Studies in Software Engineering: Experiences from ESERNET," which covers experiences from the Experimental Software Engineering Research NETwork (ESERNET), a thematic network funded by the European Union between 2001 and 2003.

Boehm et al. (2005) edited a book entitled "Foundations of Empirical Software Engineering: The Legacy of Victor R. Basili" on the occasion of V. R. Basili's 65th birthday, which covers reprints of 20 papers that defined much of his work.

Basili et al. (2007) edited proceedings from another Dagstuhl seminar in 2006 on empirical software engineering entitled "Empirical Software Engineering Issues. Critical Assessment and Future Directions."

Münch and Schmid (2013) edited a book entitled "Perspectives on the Future of Software Engineering: Essays in Honor of Dieter Rombach" on the occasion of Dieter Rombach's 60th birthday, which covers contributions by renowned researchers and colleagues of him.

6 Conclusion

In this chapter we presented the evolution of empirical software engineering in five iterations, i.e., (1) mid-1960s to mid-1970s, (2) mid-1970s to mid-1980s, (3) mid-1980s to end of the 1990s, (4) the 2000s, and (5) the 2010s. We presented the five iterations of the development of empirical software engineering mainly from a methodological perspective and additionally took key papers, venues, and books into account. Available books explicitly dedicated to empirical research methodology in software engineering were covered in chronological order in a separate section on recommended further readings. Furthermore, we discuss—based on the chapters in this book—trends on contemporary empirical methods in software engineering related to the plurality of research methods, human factors, data collection and processing, aggregation and synthesis of evidence, and impact of software engineering research.

Acknowledgements We thank all the authors and reviewers of this book on contemporary empirical methods in software engineering for their valuable contribution.

References

Akiyama F (1971) An example of software system debugging. In: IFIP congress (1), vol 71. North-Holland, Amsterdam, pp 353–359

Araújo MAP, Monteiro VF, Travassos GH (2012) Towards a model to support studies of software evolution. In: Proceedings of the ACM-IEEE international symposium on empirical software engineering and measurement (ESEM '12). ACM, New York, pp 281–290

Arcuri A, Briand L (2014) A hitchhiker's guide to statistical tests for assessing randomized algorithms in software engineering. Softw Test Verification Reliab 24(3):219–250

Baros MO, Werner CML, Travassos GH (2004) Supporting risks in software project management. J Syst Softw 70(1):21–35

Basili VR (1993) The experimental paradigm in software engineering. In: Experimental software engineering issues: critical assessment and future directions. Springer, Berlin, pp 1–12

Basili VR, Weiss DM (1984) A methodology for collecting valid software engineering data. IEEE Trans Softw Eng SE-10(6):728–738

Basili VR, Zelkowitz MV (2007) Empirical studies to build a science of computer science. Commun Assoc Comput Mach 50(11):33–37

Basili VR, Caldiera G, Rombach HD (1994) Experience factory. Encycl Softw Eng 1:469–476

Basili VR, Shull F, Lanubile F (1999) Building knowledge through families of experiments. IEEE Trans Softw Eng 25(4):456–473

Basili V, Rombach D, Schneider K, Kitchenham B, Pfahl D, Selby R (2007) Empirical software engineering issues. In: Critical assessment and future directions: international workshop, Dagstuhl Castle, June 26–30, 2006, Revised Papers, vol 4336. Springer, Berlin

ben Othmane L, Jaatun MG, Weippl E (2017) Empirical research for software security: foundations and experience. CRC Press, Boca Raton

Bertin E (1978) Qualitative and semiquantitative analysis. Springer, Berlin, pp 435–457

Biolchini MPNATG J (2005) Systematic review in software engineering: relevance and utility. Technical report

Bird C, Murphy B, Nagappan N, Zimmermann T (2011) Empirical software engineering at Microsoft research. In: Proceedings of the ACM 2011 conference on computer supported cooperative work. ACM, New York, pp 143–150

Bird C, Menzies T, Zimmermann T (2015) The art and science of analyzing software data. Elsevier, Amsterdam

Bjarnason E, Smolander K, Engström E, Runeson P (2016) A theory of distances in software engineering. Inf Softw Technol 70:204–219

Boehm B, Rombach HD, Zelkowitz MV (2005) Foundations of empirical software engineering: the legacy of Victor R. Basili. Springer, Berlin

Briand L, Bianculli D, Nejati S, Pastore F, Sabetzadeh M (2017) The case for context-driven software engineering research: generalizability is overrated. IEEE Softw 34(5):72–75

Burkhard DL, Jenster PV (1989) Applications of computer-aided software engineering tools: survey of current and prospective users. ACM SIGMIS Database Database Adv Inf Syst 20(3):28–37

Conradi R, Wang AI (2003) Empirical methods and studies in software engineering: experiences from ESERNET, vol 2765. Springer, Berlin

Creswell JW, Creswell JD (2018) Research design: qualitative, quantitative, and mixed methods approaches. SAGE, Los Angeles

Curtis B, Krasner H, Iscoe N (1988) A field study of the software design process for large systems. Commun Assoc Comput Mach 31(11):1268–1287

de Mello RM, Da Silva PC, Travassos GH (2015) Investigating probabilistic sampling approaches for large-scale surveys in software engineering. J Softw Eng Res Dev 3(1):8

Endres A, Rombach HD (2003) A handbook of software and systems engineering: empirical observations, laws, and theories. Pearson Education, Old Tappan

Espinosa A, Kraut R, Slaughter S, Lerch J, Herbsleb J, Mockus A (2002) Shared mental models, familiarity, and coordination: a multi-method study of distributed software teams. In: Proceedings of ICIS 2002, p 39

Farzat F, Barros MO, Travassos GH (2019) Evolving JavaScript code to reduce load time. IEEE Trans Softw Eng

Fink A (2003) The survey handbook. SAGE, Los Angeles

Glass RL (1994) The software-research crisis. IEEE Softw 11(6):42–47

Grant EE, Sackman H (1967) An exploratory investigation of programmer performance under on-line and off-line conditions. IEEE Trans Hum Factors Electron 1:33–48

Guéhéneuc YG, Khomh F (2019) Empirical software engineering. In: Cha S, Taylor RN, Kang KC (eds) Handbook of software engineering. Springer, Berlin, pp 285–320

Harman M, McMinn P, De Souza JT, Yoo S (2010) Search based software engineering: techniques, taxonomy, tutorial. In: Empirical software engineering and verification. Springer, Berlin, pp 1–59

Harrison W, Basili VR (1996) Editorial. Empir Softw Eng 1:5–10

Hey AJ, Hey T, Pápay G (2014) The computing universe: a journey through a revolution. Cambridge University Press, Cambridge

Höst M, Regnell B, Wohlin C (2000) Using students as subjects—a comparative study of students and professionals in lead-time impact assessment. Empir Softw Eng 5(3):201–214

IEEE (1990) 610.12-19919—IEEE standard glossary of software engineering terminology. IEEE, New York

IEEE (2010) ISO/IEC/IEEE 24765:2010 systems and software engineering—vocabulary. IEEE, Geneva

Ivarsson M, Gorschek T (2011) A method for evaluating rigor and industrial relevance of technology evaluations. Empir Softw Eng 16(3):365–395

Johnson P, Ekstedt M (2016) The Tarpit–a general theory of software engineering. Inf Softw Technol 70:181–203

Juristo N, Moreno AM (2001) Basics of software engineering experimentation. Springer, Berlin

Juristo N, Moreno AM (2003) Lecture notes on empirical software engineering, vol 12. World Scientific, New Jersey

Kitchenham B (2004) Procedures for performing systematic reviews. Technical report

Kitchenham B, Brereton P (2013) A systematic review of systematic review process research in software engineering. Inf Softw Technol 55(12):2049–2075

Kitchenham B, Charters S (2007) Guidelines for performing systematic literature reviews in software engineering. Technical report

Kitchenham BA, Dybå T, Jorgensen M (2004) Evidence-based software engineering. In: Proceedings of the 26th international conference on software engineering. IEEE Computer Society, Silver Spring, pp 273–281

Kitchenham BA, Budgen D, Brereton P (2015) Evidence-based software engineering and systematic reviews, vol 4. CRC Press, Boca Raton

Knuth DE (1971) An empirical study of Fortran programs. Softw Pract Exp 1(2):105–133

Lethbridge TC, Sim SE, Singer J (2005) Studying software engineers: data collection techniques for software field studies. Empir Softw Eng 10(3):311–341

Lucas J, Henry C, Kaplan RB (1976) A structured programming experiment. Comput J 19(2):136–138

Lyu MR, et al (1996) Handbook of software reliability engineering, vol 222. IEEE Computer Society Press, Los Alamitos

Malhotra R (2016) Empirical research in software engineering: concepts, analysis, and applications. Chapman and Hall/CRC, London

McGarry F, Pajerski R, Page G, Waligora S, Basili V, Zelkowitz M (1994) Software process improvement in the NASA software engineering laboratory. Technical report, CMU/SEI-94-TR-022. Software Engineering Institute/Carnegie Mellon University, Pittsburgh. http://resources.sei.cmu.edu/library/asset-view.cfm?AssetID=12241

Menzies T, Kocaguneli E, Turhan B, Minku L, Peters F (2014) Sharing data and models in software engineering. Morgan Kaufmann, Amsterdam

Menzies T, Williams L, Zimmermann T (2016) Perspectives on data science for software engineering. Morgan Kaufmann, Amsterdam

Molléri JS, Petersen K, Mendes E (2019) Cerse-catalog for empirical research in software engineering: a systematic mapping study. Inf Softw Technol 105:117–149

Münch J, Schmid K (2013) Perspectives on the future of software engineering: essays in honor of Dieter Rombach. Springer, Berlin

Myers GJ (1978) A controlled experiment in program testing and code walkthroughs/inspections. Commun Assoc Comput Mach 21(9):760–768

Nagappan N, Ball T (2005) Use of relative code churn measures to predict system defect density. In: Proceedings of the 27th international conference on software engineering. ACM, New York, pp 284–292

Ogborn J, Miller R (1994) Computational issues in modelling. The Falmer Press, Basingstoke

Ostrand TJ, Weyuker EJ, Bell RM (2004) Where the bugs are. In: ACM SIGSOFT software engineering notes, vol 29. ACM, New York, pp 86–96

Petersen K, Feldt R, Mujtaba S, Mattsson M (2008) Systematic mapping studies in software engineering. In: Ease, vol 8, pp 68–77

Petersen K, Vakkalanka S, Kuzniarz L (2015) Guidelines for conducting systematic mapping studies in software engineering: an update. Inf Softw Technol 64:1–18

Pfleeger SL (1995) Experimental design and analysis in software engineering. Ann Softw Eng 1(1):219–253

Pfleeger SL, Kitchenham BA (2001) Principles of survey research: part 1: turning lemons into lemonade. ACM SIGSOFT Softw Eng Notes 26(6):16–18

Porter AA, Selby RW (1990) Empirically guided software development using metric-based classification trees. IEEE Softw 7(2):46–54

Rombach HD, Basili VR, Selby RW (1993) Experimental software engineering issues: critical assessment and future directions. In: Proceedings of international workshop, Dagstuhl Castle, September 14–18, 1992, vol 706. Springer, Berlin

Runeson P, Höst M (2009) Guidelines for conducting and reporting case study research in software engineering. Empir Softw Eng 14(2):131

Runeson P, Höst M, Rainer A, Regnell B (2012) Case study research in software engineering. In: Guidelines and examples. Wiley, London

Seaman CB (1999) Qualitative methods in empirical studies of software engineering. IEEE Trans Softw Eng 25(4):557–572

Shadish WR, Cook TD, Campbell DT (2002) Experimental and quasi-experimental designs for generalized causal inference. Mifflin and Company, Boston, MA

Sharp H, Dittrich Y, De Souza CR (2016) The role of ethnographic studies in empirical software engineering. IEEE Trans Softw Eng 42(8):786–804

Shneiderman B, Mayer R, McKay D, Heller P (1977) Experimental investigations of the utility of detailed flowcharts in programming. Commun Assoc Comput Mach 20(6):373–381

Shull F, Carver J, Travassos GH (2001) An empirical methodology for introducing software processes. In: ACM SIGSOFT software engineering notes, vol 26. ACM, New York, pp 288–296

Shull F, Mendonça MG, Basili V, Carver J, Maldonado JC, Fabbri S, Travassos GH, Ferreira MC (2004) Knowledge-sharing issues in experimental software engineering. Empir Softw Eng 9(1–2):111–137

Shull F, Singer J, Sjøberg DI (2007) Guide to advanced empirical software engineering. Springer, Berlin

Shull FJ, Carver JC, Vegas S, Juristo N (2008) The role of replications in empirical software engineering. Empir Softw Eng 13(2):211–218

Sjøberg DI, Dybå T, Jorgensen M (2007) The future of empirical methods in software engineering research. In: 2007 Future of software engineering. IEEE Computer Society, Silver Spring, pp 358–378

Srinivasan K, Fisher D (1995) Machine learning approaches to estimating software development effort. IEEE Trans Softw Eng 21(2):126–137

Staron M (2019) Action research in software engineering: theory and applications. Springer, Berlin

Stol KJ, Fitzgerald B (2015) Theory-oriented software engineering. Sci Comput Program 101:79–98

Stol KJ, Fitzgerald B (2018) The ABC of software engineering research. ACM Trans Softw Eng Methodol 27(3):11

Stol KJ, Ralph P, Fitzgerald B (2016) Grounded theory in software engineering research: a critical review and guidelines. In: 2016 IEEE/ACM 38th international conference on software engineering (ICSE). IEEE, Piscataway, pp 120–131

Swanson EB, Beath CM (1988) The use of case study data in software management research. J Syst Softw 8(1):63–71

Theisen C, Dunaiski M, Williams L, Visser W (2017) Writing good software engineering research papers: revisited. In: Proceedings of the 39th international conference on software engineering companion. IEEE, Piscataway, pp 402–402

Thomke SH (2003) Experimentation matters: unlocking the potential of new technologies for innovation. Harvard Business Press, Boston

Tian J (1995) Integrating time domain and input domain analyses of software reliability using tree-based models. IEEE Trans Softw Eng 21(12):945–958

Travassos GH, Barros MO (2003) Contributions of in virtuo and in silico experiments for the future of empirical studies in software engineering. In: 2nd workshop on empirical software engineering the future of empirical studies in software engineering, pp 117–130

Travassos GH, dos Santos PSM, Mian PG, Neto ACD, Biolchini J (2008) An environment to support large scale experimentation in software engineering. In: 13th IEEE international conference on engineering of complex computer systems (ICECCS 2008). IEEE, Piscataway, pp 193–202

Wagner S, Fernández DM, Felderer M, Vetrò A, Kalinowski M, Wieringa R, Pfahl D, Conte T, Christiansson MT, Greer D, et al (2019) Status quo in requirements engineering: a theory and a global family of surveys. ACM Trans Softw Eng Methodol 28(2):9

Widman L (1989) Expert system reasoning about dynamic systems by semi-quantitative simulation. Comput Methods Prog Biomed Artif Intell Med 6(3):229–247

Wieringa R (2014a) Empirical research methods for technology validation: scaling up to practice. J Syst Softw 95:19–31

Wieringa RJ (2014b) Design science methodology for information systems and software engineering. Springer, Berlin

Wohlin C, Aurum A (2015) Towards a decision-making structure for selecting a research design in empirical software engineering. Empir Softw Eng 20(6):1427–1455

Wohlin C, Runeson P, Höst M, Ohlsson M, Regnell B, Wesslén A (2000) Experimentation in software engineering: an introduction. Kluwer Academic Publishers, Norwell, MA

Wohlin C, Runeson P, Höst M, Ohlsson MC, Regnell B, Wesslén A (2012) Experimentation in software engineering. Springer, Berlin

Zelkowitz MV, Wallace DR (1998) Experimental models for validating technology. Computer 31(5):23–31

Zendler A (2001) A preliminary software engineering theory as investigated by published experiments. Empir Softw Eng 6(2):161–180

Zimmermann T, Zeller A, Weissgerber P, Diehl S (2005) Mining version histories to guide software changes. IEEE Trans Softw Eng 31(6):429–445

Part I
Study Strategies

Guidelines for Conducting Software Engineering Research

Klaas-Jan Stol ⓘ **and Brian Fitzgerald** ⓘ

Abstract This chapter presents a holistic overview of software engineering research strategies. It identifies the two main modes of research within the software engineering research field, namely knowledge-seeking and solution-seeking research—the Design Science model corresponding well with the latter. We present the ABC framework for research strategies as a model to structure knowledge-seeking research. The ABC represents three desirable aspects of research—generalizability over actors (A), precise control of behavior (B), and realism of context (C). Unfortunately, as our framework illustrates, these three aspects cannot be simultaneously maximized. We describe the two dimensions that provide the foundation of the ABC framework—generalizability and control, explain the four different types of settings in which software engineering research is conducted, and position eight archetypal research strategies within the ABC framework. We illustrate each strategy with examples, identify appropriate metaphors, and present an example of how the ABC framework can be used to design a research program.

1 Introduction

Research methodology—the study of research methods—is receiving increasing attention from software engineering (SE) researchers. Numerous books and papers have been written on the topic (Easterbrook et al. 2008; Glass et al. 2002; Seaman 1999; Singer et al. 2000; Stol et al. 2016b; Wohlin et al. 2012). While these are very

K.-J. Stol (✉)
Lero—The Irish Software Research Centre and School of Computer Science and Information Technology, University College Cork, Cork, Ireland
e-mail: klaas-jan.stol@lero.ie

B. Fitzgerald
Lero—The Irish Software Research Centre and Department of Computer Science and Information Systems, University of Limerick, Limerick, Ireland
e-mail: bf@lero.ie

© Springer Nature Switzerland AG 2020
M. Felderer, G. H. Travassos (eds.), *Contemporary Empirical Methods in Software Engineering*, https://doi.org/10.1007/978-3-030-32489-6_2

27

useful reference works, there are several issues with the current state of literature on methodology. First, there is a strong emphasis on a limited set of specific methods, in particular experimentation, case studies, and survey studies. Although these are the three most used empirical methods (Stol and Fitzgerald 2018), many other methods exist that have not received the same level of attention. A second issue is that the field has no agreement on an overall taxonomy of methods, which is somewhat problematic as methods vary in terms of granularity and scope. This makes a systematic comparison of methods very challenging. Furthermore, new methods are being adopted from other fields. Grounded theory, for example, has gained widespread adoption within the SE literature in the last 15 years or so (Stol et al. 2016b). (We note that, like many other methods used in SE, grounded theory is not a "new" method, as it was developed in the 1960s by social scientists Glaser and Strauss—however, its application is relatively new to the SE domain.) Other techniques and methods that are relatively new to the software engineering field include the repertory grid technique (Edwards et al. 2009) and ethnography (Sharp et al. 2016). With new methods and techniques being adopted regularly, it becomes challenging to understand how these new methods compare to established approaches. Further, numerous sources present a range of research methods, but these presentations are limited to "shopping lists" of methods: definitions without a systematic comparison. Rather than maintaining a list of definitions of research methods, a more systematic approach is needed that allows us to reason and position existing methods, and new methods as they emerge. Hence, in this chapter we present a taxonomy of research strategies.

There is an additional challenge within the software engineering research community. Different methods have varying strengths and drawbacks, but it is quite common to see unreasonable critiques of studies due to the research methods employed. For example, a common complaint in reviews of case studies is that they do not allow statistical generalizability. Similarly, experiments are often critiqued on the basis that they involved computer science students solving "toy" problems, thus rendering them unrealistic, and therefore not worthy of publication. Not unreasonably, researchers may wonder which method, then, is the silver bullet that can address all of these limitations?

The answer is none.

Instead of discussing research methods, we raise the level of abstraction and have adopted the term *research strategy*. A research strategy can be considered a category of research methods that have similar trade-offs in terms of generalizability and the level of obtrusiveness or control of the research context—we return to these two dimensions in a later section in this chapter. Previously, we outlined what we have termed the ABC framework of research strategies and demonstrated how this taxonomy is suitable for software engineering research (Stol and Fitzgerald 2018). In this chapter we draw on this earlier work, elaborate on how the ABC framework is related to Design Science, and provide general guidance for researchers to select appropriate research strategies.

The remainder of this chapter is organized as follows. Section 2 starts with a discussion of research goals, dimensions, and settings. This section presents the two modes of research, namely knowledge-seeking and solution-seeking research. It outlines the ABC framework and positions it in relation to Design Science. Section 3 discusses the eight archetypal research strategies that are represented within the ABC framework. For each strategy, we discuss the essence of the strategy, identify a metaphor for the strategy, and provide high-level guidelines. Because research studies are never conducted in isolation, we discuss in Sect. 4 how the ABC framework can be used to design research programs. Section 5 offers a list of recommended readings. Finally, Sect. 6 concludes the chapter.

2 Foundations

This section introduces a number of concepts that together form the foundation for the ABC framework. We first introduce the two modes of research in software engineering: knowledge-seeking and solution-seeking research. These are two distinct modes representing different types of activities. This chapter focuses primarily on one mode, namely knowledge-seeking research, but contrasts it with solution-seeking research. In so doing, we draw a link to Design Science. Much has been written on Design Science, which is why we do not discuss it in this chapter. Instead, we refer interested readers to chapter "The Design Science Paradigm as a Frame for Empirical Software Engineering" of this book.

We then return our attention to knowledge-seeking research and introduce two key dimensions that are present in all knowledge-seeking studies: the level of obtrusiveness and generalizability. Each research strategy represents a unique combination along these two dimensions. This section ends with a discussion of research settings, which refers to the environment in which the research is conducted.

2.1 Knowledge-Seeking vs. Solution-Seeking Research

There are two modes of software engineering research: knowledge-seeking and solution-seeking research. These two modes address different types of questions; Wieringa (2009) has referred to these as knowledge questions and practical problems, respectively. Figure 1 presents how these two modes of research are positioned within the wider context of SE research, the real world, and the SE knowledge base.

Knowledge-seeking studies aim to learn something about the world around us by making observations in some type of environment—this includes the technologies, organizations, and people in natural, contrived, or simulated (virtual) settings. Knowledge-seeking research studies lead to new knowledge, which is typically reported in research papers and books, thereby contributing to the software engineering knowledge base, from which researchers may draw when designing new studies.

In solution-seeking studies, researchers design, create, or develop solutions for a given software engineering challenge. The outcome of these studies includes algorithms, models, and tools. Such solution-seeking studies may draw applicable knowledge from the SE knowledge base, which might have originated in either knowledge-seeking or solution-seeking research. Much research within the SE domain is solution-seeking with resulting design artifacts. These artifacts represent "design knowledge," in that they embody knowledge on how a particular engineering problem can be solved—and this knowledge is added to the SE knowledge base as well. Solution-seeking studies fit very well within a Design Science framework (March and Smith 1995; Simon 1996), as discussed in more detail in chapter "The Design Science Paradigm as a Frame for Empirical Software Engineering" of this book. Implemented solutions can be deployed into the real world and their effectiveness or utility can be studied using knowledge-seeking research. We note that the research process for Design Science as proposed by Hevner et al. (2004) does not align perfectly with solution-seeking research but claims a wider scope that includes evaluation studies—we categorize the latter firmly as knowledge-seeking studies.

As Wieringa (2009) has pointed out, knowledge-seeking and solution-seeking research can be interlinked—nested, even—because knowledge is needed to design solutions, and once designed, a researcher is interested in learning whether the solution works or how well it compares to other solutions. This linkage is represented by the two white arrows in Fig. 1. In this chapter we are primarily concerned with strategies to conduct knowledge-seeking research and refer readers interested in

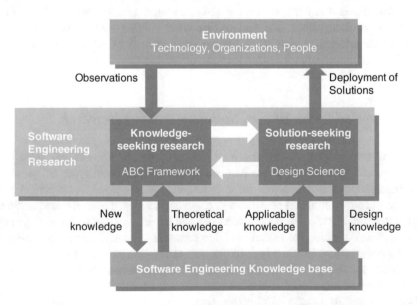

Fig. 1 Knowledge-seeking and solution-seeking research: positioning the ABC framework and Design Science

Design Science to chapter "The Design Science Paradigm as a Frame for Empirical Software Engineering".

2.2 Two Dimensions of Research: Obtrusiveness and Generalizability

In the remainder of this chapter we focus primarily on knowledge-seeking research. Numerous methods can be used to "seek knowledge," and as mentioned above, there are numerous sources in the software engineering literature that provide lists of methods. However, a systematic framework to position these methods in relation to one another has been lacking. To address this, we draw on McGrath (1981, 1984, 1995), who organized the most common methods in the social sciences into a methodological "circumplex" that positions eight research strategies. We operationalized the circumplex for a software engineering context and have labeled the result the "ABC framework" for reasons that will become clear. Below we explain the key concepts of this framework.

The framework is organized along two dimensions: obtrusiveness and generalizability (see Fig. 2). The first dimension is concerned with how obtrusive the research

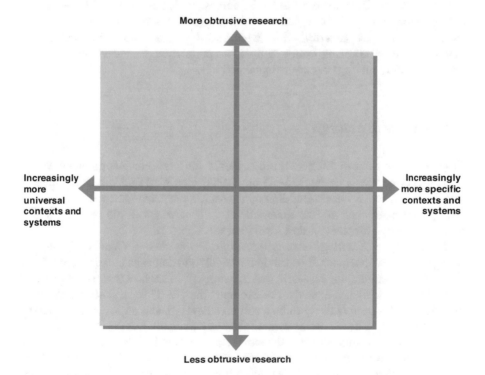

Fig. 2 Two dimensions in knowledge-seeking research

is: to what extent does a researcher "intrude" on the research setting, or simply make observations in an unobtrusive way. Research methods can vary considerably in the level of intrusion and resulting level of "control" over the research setting. Clearly, a study that seeks to evaluate the efficiency or performance of a tool requires a careful study set-up, whereas a case study that seeks to describe how agile methods are tailored at one specific company does not (Fitzgerald et al. 2013).

The second dimension is the level of generalizability of research findings. This is a recurring concern in software engineering research, in particular in the context of case studies. Indeed, exploratory case studies, and other types of field studies, are limited in that the researcher cannot draw any statistically generalizable conclusions from such studies. However, generalization of findings is not the goal of such studies—instead, exploratory case studies and other types of field studies aim to develop an understanding rather than generalization of findings across different settings. Exploratory case studies can be used to theorize and propose hypotheses about other similar contexts.

It is worth noting that a broader view of generalizability beyond that of the statistical sample-based one has also been identified (e.g., Yin 2014; Lee and Baskerville 2003). Yin identifies Level 1 inference generalizability which has two forms. The first is the widely known *statistical* generalizability from a representative sample to a population. He also identifies another Level 1 inference, namely from experimental subjects to experimental findings, which is also quite relevant to our research strategies. However, Yin also suggests a further Level 2 inference category of *analytic generalizability* which involves generalizing to theory. This could involve generalizing from a sample to a population, or, indeed, generalizing from field study findings or experimental findings.

2.3   Research Settings

Research takes place in different settings, that is, the environment or context within a researcher conducts research. McGrath (1984) identified four different types of settings to conduct research. Building on the two dimensions described above, these settings are positioned as four quadrants at a 45° angle with the main axes that represent the two dimensions described above (see Fig. 3).

The first type of settings is *natural settings*, represented as Quadrant I. Natural settings are those that naturally occur in the "field" and that exist independently from the researcher conducting research; that is, settings that are host to the phenomenon that a researcher wishes to study. For example, the "field" for a study on software process improvement is likely to be a software development organization, whereas the "field" can also be the online communication channels when the topic of study is a particular open source software development project (Mockus et al. 2000)—after all, for open source developers, these online channels are the (virtual) place where they communicate and do work. Natural settings are always specific and concrete, rather than abstract and general; hence, the quadrant representing natural settings is

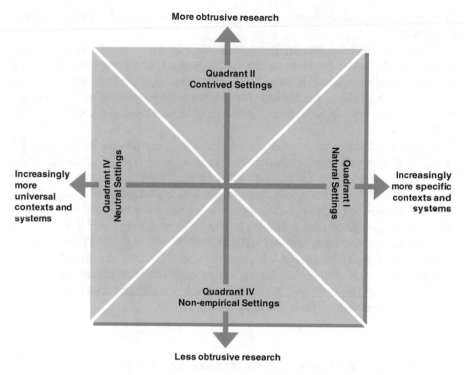

Fig. 3 Research settings in knowledge-seeking research

positioned on the right-hand side of Fig. 3. Researchers may still exert some level of control over a natural setting (Quadrant I, above the x axis) or may simply make empirical observations without manipulating the research setting (below the x axis).

In contrast to natural settings, *contrived settings* (represented as Quadrant II) are created by a researcher for the study. In a software engineering research context, contrived settings include laboratories with specific and dedicated equipment to conduct an experiment on some algorithm or software tool. Contrived settings are characterized by a significant degree of control by the researcher. This manifests as the set-up of specialized equipment and measurement instruments that facilitate the execution of a study. Many experimental studies within software engineering are conducted in such contrived settings, whereby algorithms and tools are evaluated for performance and precision. Contrived settings are created by a researcher to either mimic some specific or concrete class of systems (the right-hand side of Quadrant II), or a more abstract and generic class of systems (the left-hand side of Quadrant II). Either way, a contrived setting is always specifically set up by a researcher, implying the researcher has a high degree of control over the research—hence, Quadrant II is positioned at the upper half of the x axis. A contrived setting is essential to conduct the research—without measurement instruments and other tools such as the design of scenarios or tasks for human participants, the study could not be performed.

There are, however, also studies that do not rely on a specific setting. Some types of studies can take place in *any* setting, and so the setting is *neutral*—this is represented in Fig. 3 as Quadrant III. Researchers may or may not manipulate the research setting; in any case, because the research setting is neutral and not specific to any concrete or specific instance, Quadrant III is positioned at the left-hand side of the *x* axis.

Finally, the fourth type of setting is *non-empirical*, represented by Quadrant IV in Fig. 3. That is, this type of research does not lead to any *empirical* observations. Within software engineering, non-empirical research includes the development of conceptualizations or theoretical frameworks, and computer simulations. While software engineering as a field of study has not traditionally been strongly focused on the development of theory, several initiatives have emerged in recent years to address this (Stol and Fitzgerald 2015; Ralph 2015; Wohlin et al. 2015). Quadrant IV is positioned at the bottom of Fig. 3 because the researcher does not "intrude" on any empirical setting. Non-empirical research is typically conducted at the researcher's desk or in his or her computer, through the development of symbolic models and computer programs that mimic real settings.

2.4   The ABC of Software Engineering Research

Having laid the foundations for the ABC framework, we now populate the grid in Fig. 3 with eight archetypal research strategies. The result is what we have termed the ABC framework (see Fig. 4). Several of the research strategies will sound familiar; for example, field study, laboratory experiment, and sample study, which includes survey studies. Other terms such as experimental simulation may be less known within the SE field. Section 3 presents each of these eight strategies in detail. We now turn our attention to the last aspect of the framework, which are the markers A, B, and C.

The term "ABC" seeks to convey the fact that knowledge-seeking research generally involves actors (A) engaging in behavior (B) in a particular context (C). Within software engineering, actors include software developers, users, managers, and when seeking to generalize over a "population," can also include non-human artifacts such as software systems, tools, and prototypes. Behavior can relate to that of software engineers, such as coordination, productivity, motivation, and also system behavior (typically involving quality attributes such as reliability and performance). Context can involve industrial settings within organizations, open source communities, or even classroom or laboratory settings.

In the context of our discussion on obtrusiveness and generalizability above, researchers will want to maximize the generalizability of the evidence across actor populations (A), while also exercising precise measurement and control over behavior (B) being studied, in as realistic a context (C) as possible. However,

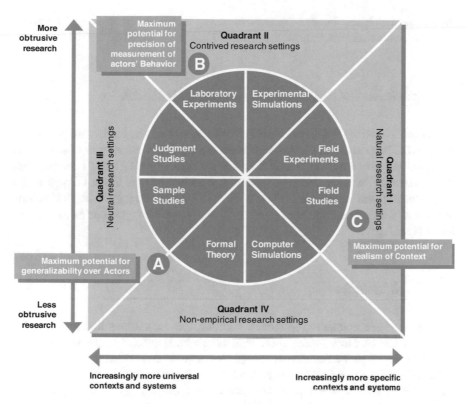

Fig. 4 The ABC framework positions eight archetypal research strategies along two dimensions: generalizability of findings and obtrusiveness of the research (adapted from McGrath 1984)

as McGrath (1981) pointed out, it is impossible to maximize all three goals simultaneously. Increasing precision of measurement and control of behavior (B), for example, inevitably intrudes on and reduces the naturalness and thus the realism of the context (C). Conversely, if one seeks to preserve the realism of context (C), this will reduce both the precision of measurement of behavior (B) and also the degree of generalizability over actors (A). This is reflected in Fig. 4 which identifies the research strategies that are best positioned to deliver for each of the A, B, and C. Sample studies can achieve high generalizability (A) but they sacrifice realism of context (C) and precision of behavior (B). Laboratory experiments allow precise measurement and control of behavior (B) but this comes at the expense of the realism of context (C) and generalizability (A). Field studies maximize the realism of context (C) but this is at the expense of control of behavior (B) and generalizability (A). Clearly, the full range of research strategies is required to deliver across all three research goals and these need to be planned and managed. The above also highlights the fact that certain strategies have inherent and intrinsic weaknesses which cannot be overcome—thus field studies can never provide generalizability, but that is neither their purpose nor strength, and this is not a limitation which can be overcome when using this research strategy. Therefore, research studies adopting that strategy should not be criticized on that basis.

3   Strategies for Software Engineering Research

In this section we outline the eight archetypal research strategies that are positioned in the ABC framework in Fig. 4. We discuss the research strategies as organized by the quadrants discussed in Sect. 2.3, starting in Quadrant I. Table 1 summarizes the discussion for each strategy, including a metaphor that might help in better understanding the nature and essence of the research strategy, how that setting manifests in software engineering research, and general suggestions as to when to use that strategy.

3.1   Field Studies

Field studies are conducted in natural settings; that is, settings that pre-exist the design of the research study. Field studies are best suited for studying specific instances of phenomena, events, people or teams, and systems. This type of research helps researchers to understand "what is going on," "how things work," and tends to lead to descriptive and exploratory insights. Such descriptions are useful because they provide empirical evidence of phenomena that are relevant to software engineering practitioners, students, and researchers. The findings may provide the basis for hypotheses, which can then be further studied using other strategies. Typical examples in software engineering research are the case studies of the Apache web-server (Mockus et al. 2000) and agile method tailoring (Fitzgerald et al. 2013).

Field studies are relatively unobtrusive with respect to the research setting. The setting for field studies is akin to a jungle, a natural setting that contains unexplained phenomena, unknown tribes, and secrets that the researcher seeks to discover and understand (see Fig. 5). Within a software engineering context, the researcher does not manipulate the research setting, but merely collects data to describe and develop an understanding of a phenomenon, a specific system, or a specific development team. This is why field studies are best suited to offer a high degree of realism of context as the researcher studies a phenomenon within its *natural* setting, and not one that the researcher manipulated.

Typical research methods include the descriptive or exploratory case study, and ethnography (Sharp et al. 2016), but archival studies of legacy systems also fall within the category of field studies, for example, Spinellis and Avgeriou's study of the evolution of Unix's system architecture (Spinellis and Avgeriou 2019). An alternative metaphor for such archival studies is an *archaeological site* rather than a jungle. Data collection methods for field studies include (but are not limited to)

Table 1 Research strategies in software engineering

Strategy	Metaphor	Setting in SE	When to use
Field study	Jungle: a natural setting that is ideally left untouched, where creatures and plants can be observed in the wild with a great level of detail	Software engineering phenomena in a natural context, such as pair programming in industry, open source software projects, etc.	To understand phenomena: How does it work? how and why do project teams do what they do? what are characteristics of a phenomenon? Maximum potential to capture a realistic context
Field experiment	Nature reserve: a natural setting that has some level of manipulation, e.g., fences, barriers, closed-off sections, sections treated with some intervention	Industry or open source software projects or teams with some level of researcher intervention; interventions could include different workflows, tools	To measure "effects" of some intervention in a natural setting, acknowledging lack of precision due to confounding factors that cannot be controlled for
Experimental simulation	Flight simulator: a contrived environment to let pilots train specifically programmed scenarios to evaluate their behavior and decisions. Realism varies depending on resources	Realism varies from classroom to industry settings designed by researchers with a specific set of tasks or scenarios which recruited participants are asked to process	To evaluate/measure behavior of participants on a set of tasks in a setting that seeks to resemble a real-world setting
Laboratory experiment	Cleanroom/test tube: highly controlled setting allowing a researcher to make measurements with high degree of precision	Classroom or research laboratory settings with a specific set-up and instrumentation to measure, e.g., performance of algorithms or tools	To make high-precision measurements, e.g., for comparing different algorithms and tools. Maximum potential for precision of measurement
Judgment study	Courtroom: neutral setting to present evidence/exhibits to a carefully selected panel, asking them for a response (e.g., guilty)	Online or offline setting to solicit input from carefully selected experts after presenting them with a question on a topic or an exhibit (e.g., a new tool)	To get input ("judgment") from experts on a given topic, which requires intense stimulus/response communication
Sample study	Referendum: a process to collect a sample of data to seek generalizability over the population. Unusable (invalid) data must be filtered out before analysis	Online surveys conducted among a population of (typically) developers, or data collected from a software repository. Data must be checked before analysis	To answer generalizability questions, incl. characterization of a dataset, correlation studies. Maximum potential for generalizability over findings
Formal theory	Jigsaw puzzle: attempt to make sense of, integrate, or fit in different pieces into a coherent "picture"	Given a set of related observations and evidence regarding a topic of interest, aim to find common patterns and codify these as a theory	To provide a framework that can describe, explain, or predict phenomena or events of interest, while remaining consistent (generalizable) across different events within some boundary
Computer simulation	Weather forecasting system: model of the real world is programmed, capturing as many parameters as possible. Scenarios are run to make informed predictions, but cannot anticipate events not programmed in the simulation	A computer program that simulates a real-world phenomenon, capturing as many important parameters as possible. Program different scenarios to "run" to explore ranges of, and interactions between, parameters of interest	To develop an understanding of phenomena and settings that are too complex or expensive to create in the real world

Fig. 5 Field studies are conducted in pre-existing settings that are not manipulated by a researcher, to study and observe natural phenomena and actors. *Image credits*: Public domain. Source: maxpixel.net (no date)

interviews, document and archival study, or mining repositories—Lethbridge et al. (2005) have discussed a variety of data collection methods and their trade-offs for field studies.

Guidelines for Field Studies
- Use the field study strategy to study phenomena in their natural setting, to understand "what is going on," or "how things work." They provide good opportunities to develop substantive theory. Typical methods include the exploratory case study, ethnography, and archival study.
- Field studies require a high level of attention and engagement with the subject and setting. Audio and video recording may help to capture details for later analysis, but these media may affect the behavior of human actors.
- Success of field studies depends on good access to the relevant people and artifacts, which can be particularly challenging within corporate settings. An internal "champion" or maintaining good relationships is key.
- To generalize findings from field studies, use complementary strategies such as formal theory and sample studies.

3.2   Field Experiments

Field experiments are also conducted in natural settings, but unlike field studies, this type of study involves some type of manipulation, thus imposing a greater degree of control. That is, the researcher introduces some form of experimental set-up by making changes to some variables of interest. After making such changes, the researcher may observe some effect. If field studies are conducted in a "jungle," then the setting for a field experiment is more like a *nature reserve*: a dedicated area that may be very similar to a jungle, but the researcher can introduce specific changes to study different aspects within the reserve. Figure 6 shows a jungle with specific patches of trees cut down; the purpose of this study was to study the effects of different types of forest fragmentation on wind dynamics and seed dispersal (Damschen et al. 2014).

It is important to remember that field experiments take place in *natural* settings, which should be clearly distinguished from *contrived* settings that provide the setting for experimental simulations and laboratory experiments, discussed later.

A range of methods are available to conduct field experiments. These are not limited to the traditional controlled experiment that separates a population of actors into two or more different groups so as to make comparisons. Experimentation also occurs when a researcher adopts the action research method; with action research, a researcher follows a recurring cycle of making changes and evaluating the results of those changes. While not a randomized controlled experiment, action research can still be considered a form of experimentation.

Ebert et al. (2001) conducted a field experiment to investigate three factors that might impact the cost of rework in distributed software development: (1) the effect

Fig. 6 Field experiments involve the manipulation of an otherwise pre-existing natural setting to facilitate observation and measurement in order to collect data. *Image source*: Damschen et al. (2014), used with permission

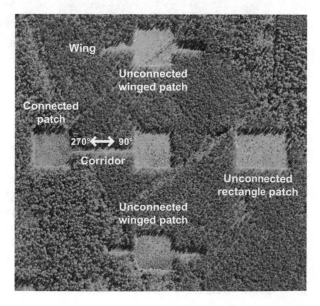

of co-location on the efficiency and effectiveness of defect detection; (2) the effect of coaching on software quality, and (3) the effect of changes to the development process on teamwork, and continuous build on management of distributed project. To evaluate these effects, Ebert et al. used project data that the company had gathered for several years.

Despite careful measurement of a range of parameters, certain factors are hard to measure, such as "culture." Ebert et al. divided the projects into different sets, e.g., "within one culture (i.e., Europe)." While we can certainly generalize that there are common attributes across different European cultures, there is no single Europe culture—each European culture is quite distinct, with significant changes even between neighboring countries such as Ireland and the UK, or the Netherlands and Germany. Furthermore, each of the projects in the data set used by Ebert et al. will undoubtedly have had specific obstacles, such as particularly challenging technology or changing requirements, and strengths such as particularly talented staff. These factors are very hard, if not impossible to capture, reducing the precision of measurement.

Guidelines for Field Experiments
- Use the field experiment strategy to evaluate the effects of manipulations within realistic settings.
- Field experiments require a high degree of prior investment in design and execution of data collection, typically in corporate settings.
- Contextual factors must be recorded carefully, so that they can be considered in the analysis.
- Use formal theory or sample studies to seek a higher degree of generalizability. Computer simulations can be used to model a complex real-world system to explore key parameters and their interactions when a field experiment would be too costly.

3.3 Experimental Simulations

Experimental simulations combine some elements of the field experiment strategy and laboratory experiments (discussed below). A key difference with field experiments is that experimental simulations take place in contrived settings. That is, the research environment is artificial and is purposely designed to conduct the study—before and beyond the study, it does not exist. While this makes the experimental simulation less realistic, it also gives the researcher opportunities to make more precise measurements and observations, because participants can be asked to do specifically designed tasks that may not be part of their daily routine. This increases the level of control even further with respect to field experiments. While we compared the field experiment to a nature reserve, the experimental simulation is

Fig. 7 Flight simulators are experimental simulations that facilitate training and study of the behavior of pilots in pre-programmed scenarios. *Image credits:* SuperJet International, distributed under CC BY-SA 2.0. Source: SuperJet International (2011)

more akin to a greenhouse, which mimics a warmer climate. The researcher is still interested in natural processes (e.g., how do flora flourish), but the setting in which that process is observed is artificially created for that purpose.

The greenhouse metaphor links well to the jungle and nature reserve metaphors, but another useful metaphor for the experimental simulation is a flight simulator (see Fig. 7). Within the flight simulator, specific events can be introduced, such as heavy storms and rainfall. Pilots in training would be asked to perform as they would in a real aircraft, but the research setting is considerably easier and cheaper to plan.

The level of realism that is achieved in experimental simulations can vary considerably, just like flight simulators. The latter can vary from low-cost set-ups consisting of a standard PC, a budget flight yoke, and rudder pedals to high-end, full motion flight simulators used by professional pilots that might cost millions of dollars. The tasks that participants are asked to perform in experimental simulation may also vary in realism. While such tasks are part of normal daily life of the participants in field experiments, in experimental simulations participants are recruited and invited to perform certain tasks designed by the researcher. The process that the researcher wishes to study is simulated, facilitating systematic measurement and comparison. The level of realism of the task can be very high, such as debugging a program within a professional setting (Jiang et al. 2017), or it can be as contrived as producing and trading colored shapes, such as blue squares and red circles (Bos et al. 2004).

Jiang et al. (2017) conducted an experimental simulation to investigate whether developers conduct impact analysis during debugging. Their contrived setting consisted of a specifically set-up work station, equipped with the SimpleScreen-Recorder recording software. Videos were captured of nine professional developers who had been given two bug reports. The bug reports had been identified by the researchers in two specific applications (PdfSam and Raptor) and were selected because these bugs had already been fixed at the time of the study. While the task at hand and the study setting were contrived (designed by the researchers), both were quite realistic. However, the realism of the study was reduced as the researchers set a time limit for some of the participants and offered a suggested fix to the defects.

In contrast, Bos et al. (2004) focused on collaboration between co-located and distributed individuals, and the task at hand was simply a mechanism to engage participants. The focus of the study was therefore on the emergent behavior of the participants, rather than how a specific task was performed as was the case for the Jiang et al. study described above. Therefore, to ensure that the participants understood the task at hand, and to minimize any distraction that might ensue from introducing complex tasks, the researchers chose to design trivial tasks.

Guidelines for Experimental Simulations
- Use experimental simulations to find an appropriate balance between measuring emergent behavior and achieving realism.
- Choose an appropriate level of realism of the research setting, balancing between cost and effort of setting up the research setting and the need for realism.
- If the research focus is on participant behavior that is not dependent on a specific type of task, then minimize the complexity of the task.
- If the research focus is on the behavior in relation to a specific type of task, then the task should exhibit a high level of realism.

3.4   Laboratory Experiments

The laboratory experiment is a strategy that offers maximum opportunity to control the research setting. Like experimental simulations, laboratory experiments take place in contrived settings that are created by the researcher. Laboratory experiments involve a careful manipulation or initialization of variables and settings that give the researcher the maximum opportunity to take precise measurements of actors' behavior, whether these are human participants or software systems.

If the experimental simulation is akin to a greenhouse, then we can compare the laboratory experiment to a test tube or cleanroom (see Fig. 8). Both a greenhouse and a test tube provide a contrived setting, but the difference lies in the compromise

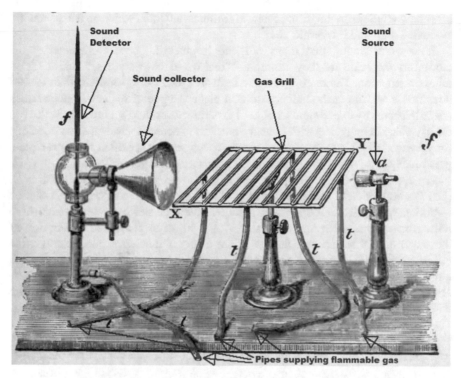

Fig. 8 Laboratory experiments are conducted in settings contrived by the researcher to allow for a maximum level of precision of measurement. *Image credits*: Public domain. Source: Tyndall (1896)

that the researcher makes between the level of control over the setting, on the one hand, and, the level of realism, on the other hand.

Laboratory experiments can be conducted with human participants or with programmed "actors": algorithms, prototype tools, etc. A laboratory experiment with human participants usually involves a treatment and a control group, and the researcher aims to measure with a high degree of precision to observe any differences. A good example of this is a study by Niknafs and Berry (2017), who investigated the impact of domain knowledge on the effectiveness of requirements engineering activities. Niknafs and Berry conducted two controlled experiments involving a total of 40 teams of three members each. The participants were all technological students (computer science, software engineering, and other technical areas). Their article offers a detailed presentation of the experimental set-up, procedures, and variables that they measured.

Programmed actors are systems running specific algorithms or other software applications that are experimentally evaluated. This approach is extremely common in software engineering research studies, because a significant portion of SE studies offer new solutions in the form of new algorithms and tools which are subsequently evaluated (Stol and Fitzgerald 2018).

It is worth noting that many software engineering papers characterize the laboratory experiments they report as "real-world case studies," but this is a misrepresentation. The mere fact that a realistic system or operational data is used does not mean that such studies exhibit a higher degree of realism—such studies are still laboratory experiments, not field experiments or field studies. While there is clearly value in engaging with industry partners to access their data or source code for an experimental study, we observe that such studies are often misrepresented, presumably to convince the reader of the relevance and rigor of the work.

An example of a laboratory experiment using programmed actors is Li et al. (2017)'s evaluation of search algorithms. Li et al. proposed a new fitness function to address an optimization problem and evaluated the newly proposed algorithm with commonly used search algorithms. Li et al. offer a detailed description of the experimental set-up and the statistical analyses that were conducted on the collected data. This study clearly took place in a setting specifically contrived, aiming to maximize the precision of measurement so as to be able to conclude which algorithm performed best. Such comparative studies are very common in software engineering and are sometimes referred as benchmarking studies (Sim et al. 2003).

Guidelines for Laboratory Experiments
- Use laboratory experiments to achieve a high level of precision in measuring variables.
- Laboratory experiments may involve either students or professionals; the use of professionals does not make a study a field experiment per se.
- Laboratory experiments may involve the use of data or systems that come from natural settings, but this does not make such studies field experiments.
- To address the limitation of a lack of realism, laboratory experiments can be complemented with experimental simulations and field experiments.

3.5 Judgment Studies

Judgment studies are positioned next to the laboratory experiment. The latter allow maximum precision of measurement in a research setting that is fully under the control of the researcher, who plans and introduces stimuli into the research setting. Judgment studies also involve stimuli introduced by the researcher, but rather than observing or measuring behavior, the researcher is interested in the *responses* of the participants. Judgment studies take place in neutralized settings—the researcher does not need a contrived setting, but can conduct the study in any setting that is available. The primary consideration is that participants are not distracted. For example, if a judgment study takes place in settings that make the participants

Fig. 9 Judgment studies are usually conducted in neutral settings so that participants can focus on the study—much like how a case is presented in a courtroom. *Image credits*: Fayerollinson CC BY-SA 3.0. Source: Fayerollinson (2010)

uncomfortable due to factors such as temperature or noise, then this may inhibit completion of the study. Hence, the researcher may actively seek to neutralize the setting—much like a *courtroom* (see Fig. 9). Rather than manipulating the study setting, the researcher conducts the study by carefully and systematically selecting appropriate participants (or "judges").

Judgment studies commonly include Delphi studies and focus group studies. These methods involve systematic and purposively selected experts whom the researcher deems to be suitable for the study. These studies usually do not involve a large number of participants—that is, judgment studies do not seek statistical generalizability over the population of which the experts are representatives, but rather generalizability over the experts' *responses* (McGrath 1984).

One example of a judgment study is Krafft's (2016) Delphi study that investigated how open source developers pick their tools when they contribute to a large project and thus where tools must be compatible. Krafft's study involved a systematic selection of 24 experts within the Debian open source community, which were asked for their input in three different rounds. Each round, the data were analyzed, aggregated, and sent back to the panel to solicit further input. The setting of this study was not important; in fact, the study was conducted mostly via email interaction, and so the experts were simply based in the comfort of their own home or office space. Rather than generalizing over the population of OSS developers, Krafft sought to develop a generalizable answer to his question, namely how do Debian developers select their tools.

There are of course studies that seek generalizability over a population. These are sample studies, and we discuss them next.

Guidelines for Judgment Studies
- Judgment studies represent a compromise between a sample study (generalizability) and a laboratory experiment (precision of measurement): use judgment studies to seek generalizability over participants' *responses*, not the participants themselves.
- Judgment studies rely on a systematic sampling rather than representative sampling; careful selection of experts is essential.
- Findings from a judgment study can be evaluated through large-scale sample studies, or categories of observed behavior or responses can be further studied in realistic settings through field studies.

3.6 Sample Studies

Sample studies involve the collection of data from a population, whether that population consists of human actors or of system artifacts. Surveys are useful to seek generalizability over a population by studying a sample of that population. For example, researchers who wish to learn more about open source software developers could conduct a sample study among developers active on public GitHub projects. Sample studies are also discussed in chapter "Challenges in Survey Research" of this book.

Like judgment studies, sample studies do not depend on a specific research setting that is set up by a researcher. The setting plays no role in the research; no specific setting is required to conduct sample studies.

We compare a sample study to a referendum or election (see Fig. 10), with the goal of collecting a relatively small number of data points from a large number of actors. We use the abstract term "actor" here, because actors may be human participants (as in a referendum), but sample studies are also widely used in SE research by collecting data from software repositories. In sample studies that collect data from human respondents, a critical issue is whether or not a sufficiently large sample can be collected, because response rates tend to be limited. Rates of less than 30% are not unusual and this can make survey research quite challenging. (We note that it is not possible to calculate a response rate if the size of the target group is unknown).

Sample studies have high potential to achieve generalizability of findings to a larger population of actors, whether they be software developers or software system artifacts such as bug reports. However, sample studies are inherently limited in that they offer limited precision in measuring behavior, either human or system behavior. The reason for this limitation is that the researcher collects whatever data he or she can get. For example, even a carefully designed survey instrument aimed at collecting data from software professionals may still be misinterpreted by respondents, or respondents may accidentally or deliberately skip questions.

Fig. 10 Sample studies with human participants are like referendums or elections; the amount of information gathered per participant is limited, and achieving a good response rate can be challenging if the population has low interest. *Image credits*: Australian Electoral Commission, distributed under CC BY 3.0. Source: Australian Electoral Commission (2016)

The researcher's control over this is limited. When collecting data from a software repository, the researcher can only gather the data that is stored, which is not always what the researcher would like to have. Furthermore, data in software repositories may not be consistent or correct. Indeed, many studies have investigated events on the popular GitHub.com development platform, but mining that repository is not free from perils (Kalliamvakou et al. 2016). In some cases, database tables and fields may be ambiguously named and labeled, leading to misinterpretations by the researcher relying on the data for analysis.

Sample studies are among the most common studies in software engineering (Stol and Fitzgerald 2018), though the type of data analysis can vary widely. Quantitative data analysis types vary from descriptive to inferential (Russo and Stol 2019). Storey et al. (2017)'s sample study of GitHub developers sought to understand developers' use of communication channels and used a descriptive analysis. An example of a sample study using inferential analysis is Sharma and Stol (2019)'s study of onboarding of software professionals that sought to understand what makes for a successful onboarding experience of new hires.

An example of a sample study of software development artifacts is Stol et al. (2017)'s analysis of crowdsourcing contests. This study investigated the potential influence of a number of factors on the interest and participation of members of the crowd in contests, based on a sample of over 13,000 crowdsourcing contests on the Topcoder platform.

Guidelines for Sample Studies

- Use sample studies to achieve maximum generalizability over a population, whether that is a population of human actors (e.g., software developers, managers) or software actors or artifacts (e.g., bugs and bug fixes, apps, projects).
- The number of data points per subject is usually limited, and so the questions must be carefully selected.
- As there is often no direct contact between the researcher and human respondents, questions must be unambiguous.
- When relying on archival data from software repositories, the data comes "as-is"; sanity checks must be conducted to ensure consistency.
- Generalizability is limited by the sample that is studied.

3.7 Formal Theory

Formal theory is a strategy that aims to seek generalizability, not through empirical methods, but rather through the specification of symbolic representations of variables and constructs (Runkel and McGrath 1972). Therefore, formal theory takes place in a non-empirical setting. Formal theory development typically involves extensive reviews of prior research in order to identify, distill, and codify recurring patterns. Thinking in terms of abstractions and aiming to identify theoretical relationships is one of the most important activities in research. However, the amount of prior research may be quite scarce, and indeed, theories can be proposed on little more than a rich imagination and mental models that develop over time. The importance of theory development is illustrated by Nisbett (2005, p. 4), who described how the early Mesopotamian and Egyptian civilizations made systematic (empirical) observations, but only the Greeks made significant progress by explaining their observations in terms of the principles underpinning them—that is, by reasoning what might link or cause those observations.

A major role of theory is to inform future research, as it motivates further studies to evaluate hypothesized relationships—this is true both for the periodic table of elements and for Einstein's theory of relativity. Both theories allowed predictions to be made which could only be empirically verified many decades later.

The process of formal theory is like making a jigsaw puzzle (see Fig. 11). When you first open up the box, there may be many pieces and it may not be readily clear as to how they all fit together.[1] This is the case in many areas of software engineering: much empirical research exists, but the field lacks theories

---

[1]This is also the point where the jigsaw puzzle metaphor breaks down, as jigsaw puzzles tend to come in a box with the solution printed on the cover—researchers do not have such luxury.

Fig. 11 Formal theory can be similar to making a jigsaw puzzle: lots of pieces, and a challenge to put it all together in a coherent way. *Image credits*: Public domain

that can explain and integrate these individual studies. Of course, theories may also be developed without much initial empirical evidence. Einstein's proposed theory of relativity was not grounded in any empirical observations, but rather through *"sheer genius, fully formed from the mind of the theorist"* (Hassan 2015). Empirical evidence for Einstein's theory has been gathered since.

Both the theory of relativity and the periodic table of elements are "general" or "grand" theories, as they are *"all embracing, unified theories"* that are relatively unbounded (Hassan 2015). Formal theory may refer to grand theory, but may also refer to middle range theories—those that are more limited in scope and context (Bourgeois 1979).

It is worth clarifying how grounded theory (GT) relates to formal theory as a research strategy. GT is an approach by which the researcher makes empirical observations, typically through field studies, and in parallel generates theory that is grounded in those observations. Barney Glaser, one of the two creators of GT together with Anselm Strauss (Glaser and Strauss 1967), explicitly refers to such theory as "substantive theory" distinguishing it from "formal grounded theory" (Glaser 1978). Glaser (1978, p. 52) describes the difference between substantive and formal grounded theory as:

> The former is about a specific area, e.g., route milkmen, the latter about a concept in its full generality: e.g., cultivating.

Thus, the distinction that Glaser draws here is that substantive theory explains some specific phenomenon (e.g., a milkman cultivating relationships with his customers), while formal theory is at a higher level of abstraction (e.g., the act of cultivating relationships in *any* type of setting).

Formal theory is positioned on the left-hand side of the ABC framework, because it refers to those theories that have a sufficient degree of generalizability and are not intrinsically linked to any substantive domain. Using the example above, a substantive theory of a milkman cultivating relationships with his customers would not exhibit sufficient generalizability, while a formal grounded theory explaining the general act of cultivating relationships would do so.

In software engineering, much "theory" is what we have termed "micro-theories" (Stol et al. 2016a)—and what Merton would call *"the minor but necessary working hypotheses that evolve in abundance during day-to-day research* (Merton 1968, p. 39). Other forms of theory can also be observed, such as theoretical frameworks, models, or other types of conceptualizations (Stol and Fitzgerald 2015). The traditional forms of theories found in the social sciences (variance, process theory) are less common in software engineering research, though this has started to change in recent years. While "formal theory" (i.e., general theory) by Glaser's description is not common in software engineering, we believe generalizable conceptualizations should still be an ambition of the community.

One example of what we would classify as formal theory is Ralph's theory of Sensemaking, Coevolution, and Implementation (SCI) (Ralph 2015). SCI seeks to *"replace lifecycle depictions of the development process"* because the latter suggest software design as a linear sequence of phases and label these phases as mutually exclusive activities. SCI offers a new perspective that researchers and educators may adopt to study and teach software development processes.

Arguably another form of substantive theory is design artifacts that are the result of the Design Science paradigm. Such products are also "vehicles" of knowledge. Runeson et al. discuss the Design Science paradigm in software engineering research in chapter "The Design Science Paradigm as a Frame for Empirical Software Engineering" of this book.

Guidelines for Formal Theory
- Develop formal theory when an area of interest attracts a high number of empirical studies without an overall framework to integrate the findings.
- Formal theory is also a useful starting point *before* conducting any empirical studies as it helps to focus and identify important research questions or hypotheses, or to predict observations (e.g., the periodic table of elements).
- Formal theory can be developed based on previous empirical observations (for example, through field studies), substantive theory (identified through, for example, literature reviews), and computer simulations.

3.8 Computer Simulations

A computer simulation is a fully closed system that implements a concrete theoretical model. One type of computer simulation that people living in rainy climates can appreciate is weather forecasting systems (see Fig. 12). Predicting the weather is done by means of highly complex computer models that are carefully configured and calibrated using a wide range of parameters. By considering a series of scenarios, the most likely scenario will then be the basis for any forecasts. These weather forecasting systems are completely closed, in that *all* parameters and equations are fully programmed. The values of these parameters may be based on values empirically observed through a range of sensors throughout the country, but once these are entered into the simulation, there is no further interaction with the outside world—computer simulations do not make any new *empirical* observations. Or, as McGrath stated succinctly: *"no new behavior transpires during the run of the simulation"* (McGrath 1995, p. 159). This is one key characteristic that sets computer simulations apart from experimental simulations.

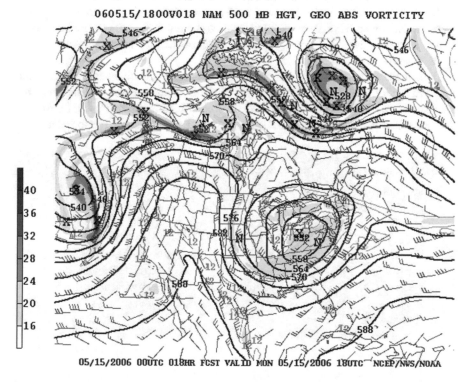

Fig. 12 Computer simulations are like weather forecasting systems. Computer models take empirical observations and a set of complex mathematical models to run scenarios. The result is a forecast: information, but not empirically gained, and may be imprecise. *Image credits*: Public domain

Because computer simulations do not make any empirical observations, the results from a simulation should be treated with care. Any predictions or results coming from a computer simulation might be wrong—while weather forecasting computers can make impressively precise predictions, occasionally they are still wrong. This is because computer simulations are based on models of reality, not reality itself.

A good example of the use of computer simulations is a study to evaluate task allocation strategies in distributed software development (Setamanit 2007; Setamanit et al. 2007). Software development tasks in distributed settings can be allocated following three strategies: Follow-the-Sun (FTS), phase-based, and module-based. Using FTS, one team may finish the workday, as another team located elsewhere may start the workday. The work continues potentially 24/7, depending on the number of teams and the time differences between them. Phase-based development means that each team takes responsibility for a particular phase of the development lifecycle. Module-based development implies that each development team has end-to-end responsibility for a given software module. By running a number of scenarios with computer simulations, Setamanit et al. found that by neutralizing any communication and cultural barriers, the FTS strategy led to a development cycle that was 70% shorter than a single-site development scenario. However, when these communication and cultural factors were introduced into the model, the FTS strategy performed considerably worse than single-site development.

It is important to realize that the scenarios are modeled based on formulas and assumptions, and that the outcome of these computer simulations may not correspond to reality. The chapter "The Role of Simulation-Based Studies in Software Engineering Research" discusses computer simulations in more detail.

Guidelines for Computer Simulations
- Use computer simulations to create a model of real-world systems or phenomena that cannot be easily or affordably set up in real life.
- Identify and model all parameters of interest, and which have relevance as suggested by prior literature.
- Be cautious in interpreting the results of computer simulations as they are necessarily simplified models of reality. It is important to remember that computer simulations do not generate *empirical* observations.
- Conduct empirical studies to confirm or disconfirm the results of computer simulations.

4 Applying the ABC Framework

Research studies are rarely conducted in isolation, but usually as part of a research program that seeks to investigate a phenomenon. This is true for PhD dissertations, but also for funded research programs, such as those funded by the US National Science Foundation (NSF), the European Committee's funding programmes such as Horizon 2020 and its follow-up Horizon Europe, or other funding programs. In order to study a phenomenon, it is useful to employ different research strategies— each strategy has potential strengths and inherent limitations, and by using different strategies to study the same topic, researchers can address such inherent limitations, and ultimately learn more about the topic of study. In our previous work, we discussed two scenarios (Stol and Fitzgerald 2018). To complement those, we discuss a recent research program that we were both involved in.

In Fig. 13 we present the positioning of strategies used by Dr. Ann Barcomb in her PhD dissertation, whom we co-supervised (together with Prof. Dirk Riehle at the Friedrich–Alexander University Erlangen–Nürnberg) (Barcomb 2019). Ann's dissertation, entitled *"Retaining and Managing Episodic Contributors in Free/Libre/Open Source Software Communities"* (Barcomb et al. 2019a), focused on episodic volunteers: those volunteers that may contribute intermittently.

The dissertation was designed as a set of three empirical studies. The first study was a qualitative survey that sought to document what episodic volunteering looks like in an open source software setting (Barcomb et al. 2019a). The study involved interviews with members of 13 different open source communities. The choice of an exploratory survey is interesting. While the field study strategy seems a

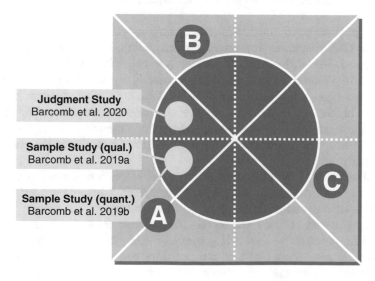

Fig. 13 Three studies of Ann Barcomb's PhD dissertation: two sample studies and one judgment study

straightforward choice for topics that have not been studied in great detail, this study sought a higher degree of generalizability to achieve the research goal. If only a single OSS project had been studied, for example, by means of a case study or ethnographic study, the findings would have been rather limited: we would have learned in great detail and enriched with great contextual detail how episodic volunteers behave or operate in one project, but this would not have answered the question *"what does episodic volunteering look like in OSS projects?"* Thus, a qualitative survey was deemed a more useful approach.

The second study drew on the general literature on volunteering and episodic volunteers (Barcomb et al. 2019b). Specifically, other researchers had developed a theoretical model that sought to explain reasons why episodic volunteers might return. Ann's second study, therefore, sought to test this theoretical model in the context of OSS episodic volunteers. This study consisted of a survey instrument implemented with SurveyMonkey; 101 usable responses analyzed using PLS structural equation modeling.

Having established (1) what episodic volunteering looks like in an OSS setting, (2) what reasons might help to retain episodic volunteers in OSS communities, Ann's next focus was on managing those episodic volunteers. Hence, the third study sought to identify practices that OSS community managers believe are useful to do so (Barcomb et al. 2020). Through a Delphi study, Ann carefully selected 24 community managers from a variety of communities and engaged them in three rounds of interaction (through email). The Delphi study is categorized as a judgment study: each of the panel members was asked to provide detailed responses to a set of carefully crafted questions. In each of the three rounds, responses were analyzed, anonymized, and collated. At the end of the three rounds, the analysis resulted in a set of practices, based on community experts' input, for managing episodic volunteers.

Together, these three studies add considerable insight to this nascent area within the larger OSS literature. The selected research strategies are all positioned on the left-hand side of the ABC framework (see Fig. 13), but still vary in certain aspects. While Ann conducted two sample studies, one was of qualitative nature, whereas the other was quantitative. The third study is a judgment study, which provides a higher degree of control of the conversation—indeed, the Delphi method facilitates interaction in several rounds, providing researchers an opportunity to clarify answers when needed; such flexibility was not available in the quantitative sample study.

It is interesting to reflect on the design of this research program (Table 2). The program did not involve any experimentation, nor did it involve any field studies. While one of the studies involved face-to-face interviews, the setting in which these took place was of no importance—the goal was not to focus on the context of a specific volunteer in a specific project. Arguably this is one limitation of the research program, which could be addressed in the future by conducting a case study or ethnographic study of episodic volunteers in a specific project. This could potentially lead to rich insights as to the reasoning process on a day-to-day basis of

Table 2 Summary of the three studies in Barcomb's dissertation

Study	Strategy	Description	Limitations
1	Sample study	Qualitative survey involving interviews with 20 informants from 13 OSS communities selected based on variety across two dimensions	Captures a range of perspectives on episodic volunteering in OSS communities, but does not establish any causal relationships or any specific context
2	Sample study	Cross-sectional, quantitative survey with 101 responses to evaluate a theoretical model	Seeks generalizability, but does not capture any causal relationships or any specific context
3	Judgment study	Delphi study involving a panel of 24 experts; documents a set of practices to manage episodic volunteers	Offers a trade-off between generalizability and precision of measurement; does not capture any specific context

episodic volunteers whether or not to contribute or return to the project they have been involved in before.

5 Recommended Further Reading

This chapter provides a high-level framework to help researchers in their selection of an appropriate knowledge-seeking research strategy. What this chapter does not offer is detailed guidance for each and every specific method and technique that can be positioned within the framework. References to a wide range of excellent resources are provided in a previous article (Stol and Fitzgerald 2018). In this section we list a number of recommended sources organized by theme or research strategy.

5.1 Empirical Studies in Software Engineering

Numerous sources discuss general matters regarding empirical studies which we cannot list all. We suggest the following as a starting point.

Glass et al. (2002) were among the first to reflect on the research methods used within the software engineering research community through an extensive literature review, and observed little variation in research approaches and methods. Much has changed in the two decades that have passed. Kitchenham has written extensively on empirical software engineering since the late nineties. She and her co-authors have primarily focused on quantitative methods, including survey research (Kitchenham and Pfleeger 2002) and experimentation (Kitchenham et al. 2002). In 2004, Kitchenham et al. (2004) published a seminal paper arguing for evidence-based software engineering, which borrows from the concept of evidence-based medicine, arguing that software engineering practice should be informed by evidence. A key source for many has been Easterbrook et al. (2008)'s guidelines for selecting empirical methods, which provides an overview of several widely used methods as well as a brief discussion of epistemology within software engineering. In the decade since, several other works have discussed the maturity of empirical software engineering—a recent article by Méndez Fernández and Passoth (2019) discusses the increasing focus on human-centric challenges and the need to establish interdisciplinary collaborations.

5.2 Field Studies

Numerous research methods fall within the scope of the field study strategy. Most common among those is the descriptive or exploratory case study. A widely cited resource is Yin (2014)'s book. Runeson et al. (2012) have tailored guidance for case studies to the software engineering domain. Lethbridge et al. (2005) have presented a taxonomy of data collection techniques for field studies, whereas Seaman (1999) presented a seminal paper on the use of qualitative methods, which are typically used in field studies. Besides the case study method, two other methods warrant brief discussion. The first is grounded theory, a method originally proposed by Glaser and Strauss (1967), and which has since seen more specific interpretations (Stol et al. 2016b). Grounded theory studies have become common in software engineering, though in many cases the term has been misused (Stol et al. 2016b). We note that grounded theory studies do not always focus on one specific research setting, but could also be used, for example, to investigate a range of different companies (cf. Hoda et al. 2013). Another method within the strategy of field studies is the ethnography; Sharp et al. (2016) have discussed its role within the software engineering domain.

5.3 Experimental Studies

There are numerous sources that provide advice for experimental studies. Besides Kitchenham et al. (2002)'s preliminary guidelines, we suggest interested readers consult Wohlin et al. (2012)'s discussion of experimentation in software engineering as well as Juristo and Moreno (2001)'s book on the same topic.

5.4 Judgment Studies and Sample Studies

Judgment studies, sometimes referred to as *user studies*, can be a useful way to evaluate a tool or get insights from a carefully selected set of experts. Focus group studies and Delphi studies are also methods that fit clearly within this strategy.

The Delphi method has been well documented by Dalkey and Helmer (1963) and Linstone and Turoff (2002). Kontio et al. (2008) offer guidance for focus group studies. Another method that fits well within this strategy is the repertory grid technique; Edwards et al. (2009) discuss its role within software engineering.

Sample studies are among the most common in software engineering (Stol and Fitzgerald 2018). Kitchenham and Pfleeger (2002) have published a six-part series of guidelines in ACM Software Engineering Notes. The chapter "Challenges in Survey Research" in this book also discusses sample studies. Studies that use samples of development artifacts from software repositories such as GitHub are extremely common as well. Kalliamvakou et al. (2016) offer useful guidance to address the many pitfalls in such studies.

5.5 Formal Theory and Computer Simulations

An important category of research that is often overlooked due to the strong focus on empirical methods is non-empirical research. The two strategies defined in the ABC framework, formal theory and computer simulations, are both useful approaches that can complement empirical methods in a variety of ways. In earlier work, we coined the concept of theory-oriented software engineering, emphasizing that research studies consist of elements from three different "domains": the substantive domain, representing some phenomenon of interest, the methodological domain, representing the variety of methods to study that phenomenon, and the conceptual domain, which represents any theoretical construct or framework to design a study or make sense of its findings. While most researchers are familiar with the so-called variance theories, which seek to link different measurable constructs, Ralph (2018) provides methodological guidelines for the so-called process theories. It is worth noting that grounded theory is often associated with theory development (as the name suggests), but as we pointed out earlier, grounded theory studies tend to result in substantive theories, rather than formal theories—the latter exhibiting a higher degree of generalizability (Glaser 1978). Several useful resources on computer simulation research are available. Müller and Pfahl (2008) provide a good starting point, and chapter "The Role of Simulation-Based Studies in Software Engineering Research" in this book provides additional details.

5.6 Solution-Seeking Research

The recommended sources listed above focus on knowledge-seeking research. For those researchers who seek to conduct solution-seeking research, we suggest the following sources as a good starting point.

Much of the research published in the flagship conference of our field, the International Conference on Software Engineering (ICSE) tends to present solution-seeking research, by means of a new tool, technique, algorithm, or process. Such papers also include an evaluation of the proposed solution using a knowledge-seeking strategy. Shaw (2003) presented an analysis of all submitted research papers to ICSE 2002 and sought to distill "patterns" of what constitutes good research in software engineering. Wieringa and Heerkens (2006) has discussed methodological soundness of papers within the requirements engineering domain and has offered a paper classification and evaluation criteria (Wieringa et al. 2006) to help researchers distinguish between different types of research. In later work, Wieringa (2009) linked this more explicitly to Design Science. Hevner et al. (2004) have discussed Design Science in Information Systems research, a field of research that has considerable overlap with software engineering closely. Design Science is also the topic of chapter "The Design Science Paradigm as a Frame for Empirical Software Engineering."

6 Conclusion

Issues to do with research methodology are receiving increased attention in SE research. However, the field suffers from inconsistent use of terminology and the lack of an integrated and holistic framework within which to categorize research strategies. We seek to provide both consistent terminology and a holistic and integrated framework—the ABC framework. While consistency in labeling research methods may remain challenging to achieve, the ABC framework (with origins in the social sciences (McGrath 1984)) offers useful terminology for what we have labeled *research strategies*.

In this chapter, we describe the two modes of software engineering research and position them within the wider context of conducting software engineering research (Fig. 1): knowledge-seeking and solution-seeking research. Whereas the ABC framework positions eight archetypal research strategies that can be used to conduct knowledge-seeking research, we link Design Science to solution-seeking research. Design Science is discussed in detail in chapter "The Design Science Paradigm as a Frame for Empirical Software Engineering" of this book, which is why we do not discuss this further. Design Science complements the ABC framework, as suggested in Fig. 1; hence, we suggest that the "ABC" is followed by a "D," with D for Design Science.

In addition to providing descriptions, metaphors, and references for each research strategy, we offer practical guidelines to help SE researchers select an appropriate research strategy.

The ABC framework is useful in several ways. First, it offers a systematic approach to explore the landscape of knowledge-seeking research, and as such it serves the purpose of a tutorial. Second, the ABC framework can be used to design a research program as illustrated in this chapter. Third, the ABC framework can also be used in a reflective manner, for example, by categorizing studies as part of a systematic literature review—most systematic reviews organize studies by their research method as *claimed* by the studies' authors. However, due to the confusion that exists within the software engineering field (we elaborate on this point elsewhere (Stol and Fitzgerald 2018)), in many cases studies are mischaracterized, which leads to a misrepresentation of a research area when presented in a systematic review. We hope the re-discovery of McGrath's circumplex and its introduction to the software engineering field help to address this issue.

Acknowledgements This work was supported, in part, by Science Foundation Ireland grant 15/SIRG/3293 and 13/RC/2094 and co-funded under the European Regional Development Fund through the Southern & Eastern Regional Operational Programme to Lero—the Irish Software Research Centre (http://www.lero.ie).

References

Australian Electoral Commission (2016) Australian Electoral Commission image library, 2016 federal election. Opening the house of representatives ballot papers (election night). https://upload.wikimedia.org/wikipedia/commons/9/93/AEC-Senate-election-night-opening.jpg, distributed under Creative Commons CC BY 3.0, https://creativecommons.org/licenses/by/3.0

Barcomb A (2019) Retaining and managing episodic contributors in free/libre/open source software communities. PhD thesis, University of Limerick

Barcomb A, Kaufmann A, Riehle D, Stol KJ, Fitzgerald B (2019a) Uncovering the periphery: a qualitative survey of episodic volunteering in free/libre and open source software communities. IEEE Trans Softw Eng (in press)

Barcomb A, Stol KJ, Riehle D, Fitzgerald B (2019b) Why do episodic volunteers stay in FLOSS communities? In: Proceedings of the 41st international conference on software engineering. ACM, New York, pp 948–954

Barcomb A, Stol KJ, Fitzgerald B, Riehle D (2020) Managing episodic volunteers in free/libre/open source software communities. IEEE Trans Softw Eng (in press)

Bos N, Sadat Shami N, Olson J, Cheshin A, Nan N (2004) In-group/out-group effects in distributed teams: an experimental simulation. In: Proceedings of the international conference on computer-supported cooperative work and social computing, CSCW'04. ACM, New York, pp 429–436

Bourgeois L (1979) Toward a method of middle-range theorizing. Acad Manag Rev 4(3):443–447

Dalkey N, Helmer O (1963) An experimental application of the Delphi method to the use of experts. Manag Sci 9(3):458–467

Damschen E, Baker D, Bohrer G, Nathan R, Orrock J, Turner JR, Brudvig L, Haddad N, Levey D, Tewksbury J (2014) How fragmentation and corridors affect wind dynamics and seed dispersal in open habitats. Proc Natl Acad Sci USA 111(9):3484–3489. https://doi.org/10.1073/pnas.1308968111

Easterbrook S, Singer J, Storey MA, Damian D (2008) Selecting empirical methods for software engineering research. In: Shull F, Singer J, Sjøberg DI (eds) Guide to advanced software engineering. Springer, Berlin

Ebert C, Parro C, Suttels R, Kolarczyk H (2001) Better validation in a world-wide development environment. In: Proceedings of the 7th international software metrics symposium (METRICS)

Edwards H, McDonald S, Young M (2009) The repertory grid technique: its place in empirical software engineering research. Inform Softw Tech 51(4):785–798

Fayerollinson (2010) The Victorian Civil Courtroom at the National Justice Museum. https://commons.wikimedia.org/wiki/File:Victorian_Civil_Courtroom_National_Justice_Museum_June_2010.jpg, distributed under Creative Commons BY-SA 3.0, https://creativecommons.org/licenses/by-sa/3.0)

Fitzgerald B, Stol KJ, O'Sullivan R, O'Brien D (2013) Scaling agile methods to regulated environments: an industry case study. In: Proceedings of the 2013 international conference on software engineering. IEEE Press, New York, pp 863–872

Glaser B (1978) Theoretical sensitivity. The Sociology Press, Mill Valley

Glaser B, Strauss A (1967) The discovery of grounded theory. AldineTransaction, Piscataway

Glass RL, Vessey I, Ramesh V (2002) Research in software engineering: an analysis of the literature. Inform Softw Tech 44(8):491–506

Hassan NR (2015) Seeking middle-range theories in information systems research. In: Proceedings of the 36th international conference on information systems, Fort Worth

Hevner A, March S, Park J, Ram S (2004) Design science in information systems research. MIS Q 28(1):75–105

Hoda R, Noble J, Marshall S (2013) Self-organizing roles on agile software development teams. IEEE Trans Softw Eng 39(3):422–444

Jiang S, McMillan C, Santelices R (2017) Do programmers do change impact analysis in debugging? Empir Softw Eng 22(2):631–669

Juristo N, Moreno A (2001) Basics of software engineering experimentation. Springer, Berlin

Kalliamvakou E, Gousios G, Blincoe K, Singer L, German D, Damian D (2016) An in-depth study of the promises and perils of mining GitHub. Empir Softw Eng 21(5):2035–2071

Kitchenham B, Pfleeger S (2002) Principles of survey research part 2: designing a survey. ACM Softw Eng Notes 27(1):18–20

Kitchenham B, Pfleeger S, Pickard L, Jones P, Hoaglin D, Emam KE, Rosenberg J (2002) Preliminary guidelines for empirical research in software engineering. IEEE Trans Softw Eng 28(8):721–734

Kitchenham B, Dybå T, Jørgensen M (2004) Evidence-based software engineering. In: Proceedings of the 26th international conference on software engineering. IEEE, Piscataway, pp 273–281

Kontio J, Bragge J, Lehtola L (2008) The focus group method as an empirical tool in software engineering. In: Guide to advanced empirical software engineering. Springer, Berlin

Krafft M, Stol K, Fitgerald B (2016) How do free/open source developers pick their tools? A Delphi study of the Debian project. In: Proceedings of the 38th ACM/IEEE international conference on software engineering (SEIP), pp 232–241

Lee A, Baskerville R (2003) Generalizing generalizability in information systems research. Inform Syst Res 14:221–243

Lethbridge T, Sim S, Singer J (2005) Studying software engineers: data collection techniques for software field studies. Empir Softw Eng 10:311–341

Li Y, Yue T, Ali S, Zhang L (2017) Zen-ReqOptimizer: a search-based approach for requirements assignment optimization. Empir Softw Eng 22(1):175–234

Linstone H, Turoff M (eds) (2002) The Delphi method techniques and applications. Addison-Wesley, Reading

March ST, Smith G (1995) Design and natural science research on information technology. Decis Support Syst 15(4):251–266

maxpixel.net (no date) Creative Commons CC0 1.0 Universal. https://www.maxpixel.net/Nature-Green-Jungle-Animals-Fauna-Forest-3828424

McGrath JE (1981) Dilemmatics: the study of research choices and dilemmas. Am Behav Sci 25(2):179–210

McGrath JE (1984) Groups: interaction and performance. Prentice Hall, Englewood

McGrath JE (1995) Methodology matters: doing research in the behavioral sciences. In: Baecker R, Grudin J, Buxton W, Greenberg S (eds) Readings in human computer interaction: toward the year 2000, 2nd edn. Morgan Kaufmann, Los Altos, pp 152–169

Méndez Fernández D, Passoth JH (2019) Empirical software engineering: from discipline to interdiscipline. J Syst Softw 148:170–179

Merton RK (1968) Social theory and social structure. Free Press

Mockus A, Fielding R, Herbsleb J (2000) A case study of open source software development: the Apache server. In: Proceedings of the international conference on software engineering. IEEE, Piscataway

Müller M, Pfahl D (2008) Simulation methods. In: Shull F, Singer J, Sjøberg DI (eds) Guide to advanced software engineering. Springer, Berlin

Niknafs A, Berry D (2017) The impact of domain knowledge on the effectiveness of requirements engineering activities. Empir Softw Eng 22(1):80–133

Nisbett R (2005) The geography of thought: how Asians and Westerners think differently and why. Nicholas Brealey Publishing, Boston

Ralph P (2015) The sensemaking-coevolution-implementation theory of software design. Sci Comput Program 101:21–41

Ralph P (2018) Toward methodological guidelines for process theories and taxonomies in software engineering. IEEE Trans Softw Eng 45(7):712–735

Runeson P, Höst M, Rainer A, Regnell B (2012) Case study research in software engineering: guidelines and examples. Wiley, London

Runkel PJ, McGrath JE (1972) Research on human behavior: a systematic guide to method. Holt, Rinehart and Winston, New York

Russo D, Stol K (2019) Soft theory: a pragmatic alternative to conduct quantitative empirical studies. In: Proceedings of the joint 7th international workshop on conducting empirical studies in industry and 6th international workshop on software engineering research and industrial practice, CESSER-IP@ICSE 2019, Montreal, pp 30–33

Seaman CB (1999) Qualitative methods in empirical studies of software engineering. IEEE Trans Softw Eng 24(4):557–572

Setamanit SO (2007) A software process simulation model of global software development (GSD) projects. PhD thesis, Portland State University

Setamanit SO, Wakeland W, Raffo D (2007) Using simulation to evaluate global software development task allocation strategies. Softw Process Improve Pract 12:491–503

Sharma G, Stol KJ (2019) Exploring onboarding success, organizational fit, and turnover intention of software professionals. J Syst Softw 159:110442

Sharp H, Dittrich Y, de Souza C (2016) The role of ethnographic studies in empirical software engineering. IEEE Trans Softw Eng 42(8):786–804

Shaw M (2003) Writing good software engineering research papers. In: Proceedings of the 25th international conference on software engineering, pp 726–736

Sim S, Easterbrook S, Holt R (2003) Using benchmarking to advance research: a challenge to software engineering. In: Proceedings of the 25th international conference on software engineering. IEEE Computer Society, Silver Spring

Simon H (1996) The sciences of the artificial, 3rd edn. MIT Press, Cambridge,

Singer J, Storey MA, Sim SE (2000) Beg, borrow, or steal: using multidisciplinary approaches in empirical software engineering research. In: Proceedings of the international conference on software engineering

Spinellis D, Avgeriou P (2019) Evolution of the Unix system architecture: an exploratory case study. IEEE Trans Softw Eng (in press)

Stol K, Fitzgerald B (2015) Theory-oriented software engineering. Sci Comput Program 101:79–98

Stol K, Fitzgerald B (2018) The ABC of software engineering research. ACM Trans Softw Eng Methodol 27(3):51

Stol K, Goedicke M, Jacobson I (2016a) Introduction to the special section—general theories of software engineering: new advances and implications for research. Inform Softw Tech 70:176–180

Stol K, Ralph P, Fitzgerald B (2016b) Grounded theory in software engineering research: a critical review and guidelines. In: Proceedings of the 38th International Conference on Software Engineering. ACM, New York, pp 120–131

Stol K, Caglayan B, Fitzgerald B (2017) Competition-based crowdsourcing software development: a multi-method study from a customer perspective. IEEE Trans Softw Eng 45(3):237–260

Storey MD, Zagalsky A, Filho FMF, Singer L, Germán DM (2017) How social and communication channels shape and challenge a participatory culture in software development. IEEE Trans Softw Eng 43(2):185–204

SuperJet International (2011) Full flight simulator. https://www.flickr.com/photos/superjetinternational/5573438825, distributed under Creative Commons CC BY 2.0, https://creativecommons.org/licenses/by-sa/2.0/legalcode

Tyndall J (1896) Fragment of science, volume one. Taken from an electronic copy of the book at Archive.Org (1896 edition of the book) and subsequently annotated in colored typeface. Public Domain, https://commons.wikimedia.org/w/index.php?curid=57653822

Wieringa R (2009) Design science as nested problem solving. In: Proceedings of the 4th international conference on design science research in information systems and technology, DESRIST '09. ACM, New York

Wieringa R, Heerkens M (2006) The methodological soundness of requirements engineering papers: a conceptual framework and two case studies. Requir Eng 11:295–307

Wieringa R, Maiden N, Mead N, Rolland C (2006) Requirements engineering paper classification and evaluation criteria: a proposal and a discussion. Requir Eng 11:102–107

Wohlin C, Runeson P, Höst M, Ohlsson M, Regnell B, Wesslén A (2012) Experimentation in software engineering, 2nd edn. Springer, Berlin

Wohlin C, Smite D, Moe NB (2015) A general theory of software engineering: balancing human, social and organizational capitals. J Syst Soft 109:229–242

Yin R (2014) Case study research design and methods, 5th edn. Sage Publications, Thousand Oaks

Guidelines for Case Survey Research in Software Engineering

Kai Petersen

Abstract This chapter presents guidelines for case survey research. The chapter includes a description of the research process and provides examples for each step of the process. The process comprises the following steps: (1) define research scope, (2) case identification and selection, (3) case extraction, (4) case analysis, and (5) reporting. In addition, we also present a checklist for the quality assessment of case surveys.

1 Introduction

The case survey method suggests a process describing how to identify, select, extract, and analyze a set of cases. Case surveys are review (i.e., secondary) studies. Case surveys emphasize analysis methods to synthesize the evidence provided by several cases. The research process of case surveys uses steps from case studies (Runeson and Höst 2009), surveys (Molléri et al. 2016; Linaaker et al. 2015), and also systematic literature reviews (Kitchenham and Charters 2007), however, only considering secondary data.

The purpose and also the strength of case study research is to gain an in-depth understanding of phenomena in software engineering (SE). Case studies rely primarily on qualitative data to gain understanding. They utilize triangulation considering multiple sources, observers, and types of data (qualitative and quantitative). Case studies are effort intensive. Therefore, only a limited number of cases may be obtained, which limits generalizability to a larger population.

K. Petersen (✉)
University of Applied Sciences, Flensburg, Germany

Blekinge Institute of Technology, Karlskrona, Sweden
e-mail: kai.petersen@hs-flensburg.de

© Springer Nature Switzerland AG 2020
M. Felderer, G. H. Travassos (eds.), *Contemporary Empirical Methods in Software Engineering*, https://doi.org/10.1007/978-3-030-32489-6_3

Surveys, on the other hand, aim for a large number of data points to generalize to a larger population. They are primarily quantitative. More responses can be obtained, but the detail and hence depth of information is less compared to case studies. Surveys are commonly analyzed using descriptive and inferential statistics.

No one research method is generally superior to others. The comparison of case studies and surveys is a good illustration. Instead, different methods have their strengths and weaknesses. It is beneficial for the research community to utilize a mix of methods depending on the goals of the research, or combine and find a compromise between methods.

One such effort is the case survey. Larsson (1993) highlights case surveys as a promising method that may help to

> overcome the problem of generalizing from a single case study and at the same time provide more in-depth analysis of complex organizational phenomena than questionnaire surveys.

With similar intentions Gable (1994) proposes to combine case study and survey research, i.e. conducting a case survey as a primary study, thus benefiting of the strengths of both methods and addressing their specific weaknesses.

In this chapter, we provide an overview of the case survey method (Sect. 2). Based on the guidelines and our own experience of using the case survey method we propose guidelines for case survey research in SE (Sect. 3). We propose to modify the original case survey method now considering primary and secondary data, while the traditional case survey only considered secondary data. We provide examples of the case survey method based on a recent case survey study focusing on the selection of sources for software assets (e.g., open source versus in-house) (Petersen et al. 2018). The example also considered primary as well as secondary data.

2 Related Work

In this section, first position case survey research relative to other methods. After that, we present and compare the existing guidelines for case survey research and summarize software engineering studies using the case survey method.

Jurisch et al. (2013) propose to classify methods according to the type of data (quantitative or qualitative) from two perspectives: input data and result. The classification as previously illustrated by Jurisch et al. is shown in Fig. 1. For example, the methods that are purely qualitative for input data and results (qualitative content analysis and narrative analysis) are placed in Quadrant 1 in the figure. Case surveys typically take qualitative data from cases as input. The analysis of case survey data typically results in quantitative data.

Further details regarding the methods related to case survey research (see Fig. 1) are provided by Jurisch et al. (2013), Cruzes et al. (2015), and Cruzes and Dybå (2011).

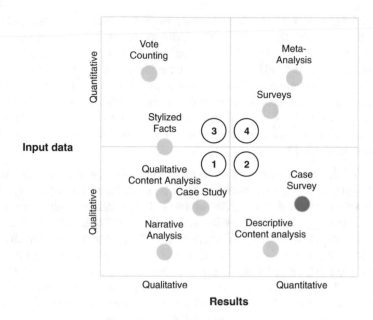

Fig. 1 Comparison of methods (adapted from Jurisch et al. 2013)

2.1 Case Survey Method

Lucas (1974) outlines a process for conducting case survey research. First, the research aims and questions are defined. These are used as inputs to drive the selection of cases. To analyze the cases a coding scheme is defined. Based on the coding scheme, the cases are coded. That is, qualitative information is transformed into quantitative information through coding. The quantitative information is then statistically analyzed. Overall, the processes of the various applications of the case survey method are similar (Larsson 1993). On the detailed level, some variations in the processes exist, which are discussed in the following.

Defining the Research Questions (RQs) The research questions may be of exploratory or confirmatory nature. In a first case survey Yin and Heald (1975) highlighted that case surveys are specifically suitable to test hypotheses (confirmatory RQs); however, as Larsson (1993) points out, previous case surveys have demonstrated that more complex processes may be understood and hence exploratory research questions may be answered (exploratory RQs). The research aims and questions are essential as they are the drivers for the identification of relevant cases (Yin and Heald 1975).

Case Identification and Selection The case selection requires criteria for the selection and an actual process of how to select the cases. Yin and Heald (1975) propose to define explicit inclusion as well as exclusion criteria. Having defined the criteria, the cases published in the literature need to be identified, e.g. through searches. After that, the identified literature has to be screened. Recent guidelines describe how to search (Zhang et al. 2011; Ali and Usman 2018) and screen relevant literature and to conduct the inclusion and exclusion process (Ali and Petersen 2014). Ali and Petersen (2014) demonstrate the importance of multiple researchers during the inclusion and exclusion. Wohlin et al. (2013) raised the concern that it may not be possible to identify all relevant studies (or cases), but instead one should aim for a good sample of existing studies. Defining a good sample is challenging as the population of studies is unknown, while some strategies are proposed by Badampudi et al. (2015).

Coding The coding scheme is used to code the qualitative data into quantitative variables (coding items)—the variables may be of different types (Larsson 1993), such as nominal (categorization) (Yin and Heald 1975), ordinal (Golembiewski et al. 1981), or Likert-type questions (Miller and Friesen 1977). As outlined earlier (see Fig. 1), the focus is only on quantitative results. Coding schemes may also be of varying complexity. For the case surveys reviewed by Larsson (1993) the number of coded variables ranged from 2 (Golembiewski et al. 1981) to 118 (Yin and Yates 1974). Larsson (1993) suggests using multiple reviewers when coding the cases. In order to assess the reliability of the coding, we assess interrater reliability. Discrepancies are then discussed and resolved among the coders.

Systematic reviews similarly conduct data extraction. A data extraction form is designed, encoding information into quantitative variables as well as qualitative results. Here, it is also recommended to involve multiple researchers and resolve conflicts among them systematically.

Statistical Analysis The statistical analysis serves multiple purposes in the context of case surveys.

First, it allows assessing the validity of the coding. The validity is important as complex coding schemes are prone to mistakes, as experienced by Yin and Yates (1974). One may correlate the coded data (secondary) with the data collected by the researchers conducting the case study (primary) to identify deviations. A sample of the cases may be used to check the consistency. Additionally, other studies not being part of the case survey and their findings are compared to those of the case survey. In order to assess the reliability of the coding, interrater reliability (e.g., Kappa statistics (Cohen 1960)) should be assessed. Discrepancies are then discussed and resolved among the coders. Systematic reviews and maps similarly conduct data extraction. A data extraction form is designed (Kitchenham and Charters 2007), encoding information into quantitative variables as well as qualitative results. Here, it is also recommended to involve multiple researchers and resolve conflicts among them systematically.

Second, the data of the case survey is statistically analyzed to answer the research questions. Bivariate statistics (associating one variable with another) or multivariate statistics (associating multiple variables with another) is possible to use. Examples are measures of association (correlation) and regression analysis (Bullock and Tubbs 1990). Furthermore, one may identify patterns in the case variables, e.g. using cluster analysis.

2.2 Case Surveys in Software Engineering

Software engineering research uses case studies widely, and the software engineering research community has a keen interest in case studies, which is evident by the impact of the guidelines proposed by Runeson and Höst (2009).

While looking at individual cases is intriguing, drawing more general conclusions by combining the information from multiple cases may lead to stronger conclusions in terms of generalizability. Cruzes et al. (2015) illustrate the application of different approaches to synthesize the findings for multiple case studies. The synthesis methods compared were cross-case analysis, thematic analysis, and narrative synthesis (see also chapter "Research Synthesis in Software Engineering"). The researchers found that similar overall conclusions were reached for cross-case analysis and thematic synthesis. At the same time, they highlight that the process of synthesis is affected by factors such as context and the research goal itself. Also, we have to take the experience of the researchers in using different methods into account. Finally, to increase reliability the use of multiple methods is suggested.

Recently the case survey method has been used in software engineering. For example, Petersen et al. (2018) investigated the choice of origins for software assets (such as components and systems). Klotins (2017) presented a research design on conducting a case survey to understand practices in software startups.

As mentioned earlier, the case survey method is using secondary data and thus can also be referred to as a case meta-analysis.

The studies differ in some steps from the above definition of the case survey method. Both studies (Petersen et al. and Klotins) elicited cases from primary data sources through interviews and questionnaires who have practical experiences and participated in relevant cases. Petersen et al. also used qualitative as well as quantitative data for both inputs and results, which contradicts the classification of case surveys presented in Fig. 1. Overall, the study by Petersen et al. follows the idea proposed by Gable (1994) to combine case studies and surveys as a series of subsequent studies.

3 Case Survey Guideline for Software Engineering Considering Primary and Secondary Data During Data Collection

The process proposed for case survey research in software engineering mainly took inspiration from various sources, namely:

- Our own experience of conducting a case survey (see Petersen et al. 2018).
- Guidelines and examples for conducting case surveys as presented in Sect. 2.1.

- Guidelines for methods strongly associated with case surveys, namely survey (Linaaker et al. 2015; Kitchenham and Charters 2007), case study (Runeson and Höst 2009), and review guidelines (Kitchenham and Charters (2007) for systematic reviews and Petersen et al. (2015) for systematic mapping studies).

In our proposed process we add a new mode of data collection to the case survey method. Originally, the method focused only on secondary data. We expand the method also taking primary data into account. We believe that primary data collection in the context of a case survey is highly valuable as the cases can be obtained using a shared data collection instrument based on the same research question. The shared instrument helps in obtaining a comprehensive coverage of the coding scheme. Besides, secondary studies or gray literature shall be considered as well.

The data obtained in our process is of both qualitative and quantitative nature, which is also true for the results. That is, our proposal for the case survey method would be located in the upper right corner of Fig. 1. We argue that using both quantitative and qualitative data representations during collection and in the results consistently over a broad set of cases enables us to strike a balance between survey and case study research, leveraging on the benefits of both methods and at the same time addressing their limitations. At the same time the analysis becomes more complex, which poses a challenge for the researchers.

The research process consists of five main activities. Each activity has several steps. Table 1 shows an overview of the process. The following section describes the activities and steps. We provide pointers to different ways of conducting the steps. Each activity is complemented with a description of how it was implemented in the case survey study by Petersen et al. (2018).

Table 1 Case survey: activities and steps

Activities	Steps
A1: Define research scope	**S1:** Define aim and objectives → **S2:** Define research questions → **S3:** Define propositions/ hypotheses
A2: Case identification and selection	**S4:** Define population and sample → **S5:** Identify case sources → **S6:** Define and pilot case selection criteria → **S7:** Identify cases → **S8:** Select cases → **S9:** Assess case selection quality
A3: Case extraction	**S10:** Define extraction form → **S11:** Pilot extraction form → **S12:** Elicit cases → **S13:** Assess elicitation quality
A4: Case analysis	**S14:** Data coding → **S15:** Synthesis → **S16:** Data partitioning → **S17:** Assess analysis quality
A5: Reporting	**S18:** Write report → **S19:** Assess report quality

3.1 A1: Define Research Scope

S1: Define Aim and Objectives The process starts with the definition of the research scope and is a step always needed in research studies. We need to determine the aim of the research and from that derive the research questions.

S2: Define Research Question The literature provides an input to the identification of relevant questions, though also problem descriptions from collaborating companies in research projects may be a driver. Different types of research questions are distinguished. Easterbrook et al. (2008) provides a good overview of the types of research questions we may ask.

S3: Define Propositions/Hypotheses In case the research aims to test a theory or proposition; these need to be explicitly formulated as well.

We also would like to highlight that it is important to contextualize the research when defining the scope: Are we focusing on answering a research question generally for all of software engineering, or for a specific context? Examples are specific life-cycle models, product types, etc. Various publications highlight the importance of contextualizing the research, such as Briand et al. (2017), Dybå (2013), and Petersen and Wohlin (2009).

> **Example (Petersen et al.)** The study **aimed** at understanding how decision-making took place in practice when deciding among component sourcing options (CSOs), such as open source versus in-house. The research was exploratory. Hence, we formulated no propositions. Two main **research questions** were phrased:
>
> (RQ1) How are CSOs chosen? The sub-questions were concerned with the CSO options considered (e.g., in-house, open source, or commercial off the shelf products); the stakeholders involved in the decision process; the decision criteria; the approach or model used for the decision.
> (RQ2) What was the decision outcome? The sub-questions were concerned with the effort invested in making the decision and the actual choice and evaluation of choice.

3.2 A2: Case Identification and Selection

S4: Define Population and Sample First we define the population and sample (Linaaker et al. 2015). In the context of surveys, it is essential to understand the target audience, based on which the population, sampling frame, and sample are defined. The target audience describes for whom the result of the survey is of interest. The description provides input to our selection criteria, as when we characterize the target audience we find the characteristics that our cases should have. A subset of the target audience is the population. The sampling frame is a subset of the population and comprises subjects that we could reach out to and that are accessible. The sample is a subset of the sampling frame. At this stage, we define the target audience and the population.

S5: Identify Case Sources After that, we identify the case sources. In the previous guidelines for case survey research (see Sect. 2.1) case surveys are considered a secondary research method. As argued earlier, a common coding scheme for primary data collection may allow for higher coverage of the questions to be answered in the coding scheme. Hence, we propose to utilize various sources in a case survey. Table 2 provides examples of possible sources. A similar question arises for systematic reviews and mapping studies. A classification of possible sources for literature is presented in Petersen et al. (2015).

S6: Define and Pilot Selection Criteria We define inclusion and exclusion criteria. The definition of the target audience drives the criteria and population and in the end, should guide the researcher during the sampling activity. If a case does not fit the target audience and population, it should not be included. However, as recommended by Larsson (1993), quality should not be considered at this stage as an exclusion criterion. Instead, we should account for different levels of quality during the analysis. After the selection criteria are defined, we propose to pilot them, similar to the procedure proposed for systematic reviews. There, we choose a sample of papers, and we apply the criteria. Two or more researchers conduct the paper selection based on the criteria and compare their findings to determine interrater reliability. If the reliability is low, then it may be needed to clarify and refine the criteria.

When applying the principle to experts, we may ask an expert to review the criteria in order to identify a case based on their own experience. They may ask clarification questions in order to identify the case, which enables us to improve the criteria. It is also helpful to provide examples for the criteria.

Table 2 Sources for cases

Source	Description and examples
Gray literature	Non-peer-reviewed results (blogs, white papers)
Peer-reviewed studies	Journal articles, conferences, workshops
Archival data	Data generated as part of software development activities in companies (such as documentation or datasets, e.g. ISBSG (see https://www.isbsg.org), as well as gray literature
Experts	People with insights and actual experience in the studied case

S7: Identify Cases The case identification requires to access the sources and from there to identify the potentially relevant cases. These are then filtered using the criteria (selection).

We first discuss the identification. Different strategies apply for literature (gray and peer-reviewed) and archival data as well as experts. In the case of literature the strategies from guidelines for gray literature (Garousi et al. 2019) and systematic reviews (Kitchenham and Charters 2007; Petersen et al. 2015) apply. In order to access documentation in a company, we may need experts that may guide and obtain the relevant documentation for us based on the criteria. When identifying the experts, we use our definition of the target audience, population, sampling frame, and sample to identify the experts. Depending on the sampling strategy (such as convenience sampling versus random sampling) the way we work with identification of the actual sample changes. In the case of random sampling, we need a well-defined sampling frame from which we randomly select the sample. When using convenience sampling, the frame would comprise the subjects we have easier access to (e.g., through personal networks, collaborations in joint research projects, etc.). Convenience sampling may be complemented with snowball sampling as subjects able to provide case information could point us to other subjects with relevant cases.

Additionally, we have to decide whether we consult one or more subjects (persons) per case. In order to increase the validity of the study, source triangulation is encouraged (e.g., at least two persons per case). However, with the inclusion of many cases, a trade-off has to be made, and not too many persons per case could be considered, as the data has to be collected.

S8: Select Cases For literature, a study (Ali and Petersen 2014) described and evaluated how to select cases using multiple researchers and alternative strategies of when to resolve conflicts. Kuhrmann et al. (2017) further elaborate on the process of selection. One of the challenges with literature will likely be that the data collection instrument (coding scheme) may be poorly covered by studies reported in the literature as each study had its research design and research questions. The same may be true also for documentation.

When selecting cases consulting experts with information about important cases, we propose to conduct the following steps:

1. Present the research questions and selection criteria to the expert.
2. Obtain a short narrative description of the cases the expert considers relevant.
3. Determine the degree of involvement of the expert in the case.

The last point is particularly important. If the experts were strongly involved, they are likely able to provide high coverage of the extraction scheme. If they were not strongly involved, they are still an excellent source to obtain the relevant persons.

S9: Assess Case Selection Quality In case of the literature various measures of quality are possible, such as assessing interrater reliability, checking the selected papers against a reference set of papers, or consulting experts to identify additional studies. In the case of experts, it is essential to be aware of the degree of involvement of the expert, and to strengthen the validity of the study it is desirable to check whether source triangulation has been utilized.

We propose to store the information regarding the cases in a spreadsheet or database, keeping track of the source as well as a narrative description of the case, and the rationale for including the case (e.g., describing why it fits the criteria).

Example (Petersen et al.) As mentioned earlier the study aimed to understand how decision-making for CSO options takes place in practice. We defined three **criteria for selection**. We focused the study on software-intensive system development. We were, for example, not interested in CSOs for tools used in the actual software development. In the study, we only stated inclusion criteria (e.g., initial criteria formulated as exclusion criteria were reformulated to inclusion criteria—such as cases should focus on software-intensive systems). We formulated the criteria (quotes from the study) as follows:

1. The case provides information on how the decision-making between at least two CSOs has been taking place where the component should become part of a software-intensive system. For example, a database component becomes part of the system, while the development environment does not.
2. The system for which the CSO decision is made is industrial (can involve academics if they are supporting the industry).
3. Cases should at least be explicit about the CSOs considered, the persons involved in the decision-making process, the CSO choice, the methods used in decision-making, and the criteria used when preparing and making the decision.
4. The source (person) reports the case based on his or her own experiences (e.g., as a consultant, participant in the decision-making process, etc.), or the case has been elicited from an industry representative through an interview.

The source itself was described as a criterion. In this study, it was an expert. To define what experts we are looking for we characterized the **target audience** and the **sample**. The target audience and populations were described as:

practitioners supporting or making the decision for CSOs for software-intensive systems.

The sampling strategy was **convenience sampling**. More specifically, the researchers of the ORION project (http://orion-research.se) either contributed cases where they took part in CSO decision processes or they interviewed practitioners in their contact network who were closely involved. In order to identify the subjects, the selection criteria were presented in the research project group and to the practitioners in the contact network. The contacts provided a brief description of the decision scenario and process, which allowed to the authors of the study to judge the relevance of the case. As an example, the following description was provided for one of the cases:

(continued)

The company needed to find a tool to be used when doing complex calibrations of embedded systems. It was a stand-alone tool, but many of the aspects were similar to what would have been the case for a component for similar use. The decision process was quite rigorous. I was in charge of preparing the decision material and spent considerable time first interviewing stakeholders about their concerns, and then transforming this to a list of decision criteria, expressed similarly as a requirements specification. There were two alternatives: one developed in-house in one decision, and one from a local company. The aim was to find a tool that could be used across several divisions of the company. Data was collected on both alternatives, by interviewing people from the organizations responsible for it. A Pugh analysis (decision matrix) was used, and it was quite clear that the in-house alternative was superior. The whole decision process was documented in a report.

The statement describes the asset, the context (industrial), considered the relevant decision options for CSOs, and the subject was closely involved. Hence, the case was clearly to be included.

3.3 A3: Case Extraction

S10: Define Extraction Form In order to extract the cases a data extraction form is needed, similar to what would be used to extract information from primary studies in systematic reviews (Kitchenham and Charters 2007). The extraction form comprises all the characteristics of the case that are relevant and needed to answer the research questions. We recommend to divide the form into the parts suggested in Table 3.

The data used as input may be either quantitative or qualitative. Various types of data are possible for each piece of information collected. Textual descriptions represent qualitative data. Measurement data may take the forms of typical data

Table 3 Main elements of the data extraction form

Characteristics	Description
Case metadata	Includes a case ID (unique identifier), the researcher working with the case, the name of the case (e.g., company name, project name), and the source (e.g., expert, blog)
Case abstract	Short narrative description of the case
Unit of analysis	Describe what the unit of analysis is (e.g., the case is the company and the unit of analysis is a project, process, etc., at that company)
Case context	Information related to the context, such as product information, market, methods and tools used, people involved, and organizational information (Petersen and Wohlin 2009)
Study data	Main data directly connected to answering the research questions. Information may be organized in groups (e.g., in a tree structure). For each characteristic, we should also record whether the characteristic represents a dependent or independent variable

types, such as nominal, ordinal, interval, and ratio data. We also distinguish between independent and dependent variables, representing the different characteristics. As an example, we may gather information on development practices as the independent variables and performance data related to flexibility, quality, etc., as dependent variables. Thereby, it is important that the variables represent the theoretical constructs. As an example, when we intend to capture the theoretical construct size of the software as Lines of Code, the theoretical construct may be not well represented due to various issues with the Lines of Code measure.

S11: Pilot Extraction Form When consulting literature at least two researchers should independently extract data and compare as well as discuss the extraction. In case of deviations, the conflicts need to be resolved and the extraction form should be improved to be more explicit. It is important to define the information that should be extracted and to provide a sufficiently detailed description, preferably with examples. When using the extraction form with experts, it should be piloted similarly as for surveys. Ways of piloting are focus groups discussing the form and the usage and discussion involving a small set of real subjects.

S12: Elicit Cases The extraction form is then used to extract the cases identified earlier. Literature and documentation are read and coded according to the extraction form. The cases provided by experts are elicited through interviews, questionnaires, or focus groups.

S13: Assess Elicitation Quality Finally, we assess the quality of the elicitation. Interrater reliability is a measure used to assess the consistency of the extraction of information from the literature. When gathering data from experts, interrater reliability may also be used to check the consistency of extraction when more than one person (source triangulation) provided the data for a single case and unit of analysis. In case of deviations, a meeting is needed to discuss and resolve the deviations. It is also essential to review the data set for missing data. Missing data may lead to the exclusion of cases if the number of missing data is too high, or the fact of having missing data has to be accounted for when discussing the validity and interpreting the findings.

Example (Petersen et al.) The **extraction form** was divided into the categories of meta information, case abstract, and context information. The main focus was on CSO decision-making. For this we identified the following high-level categories:

- Stakeholders: Roles with interest in the decision. We distinguished here between decision initiator and people involved in preparing the decision.
- Decision criteria: The criteria used for decision-making.
- Decision method: The method used for decision-making (e.g., expert based, type of models used for decision-making).

(continued)

- Decision result: The decision outcome in terms of CSOs chosen, the effort invested in making the decision, and an evaluation of the decision.
- Other information: The possibility to provide additional comments.

Table 4 shows an excerpt of the extraction form. Each characteristic was mapped to a research question. We also indicated for which variables coding was needed (e.g., item 32 in Table 4), as those variables were presented in the form of textual descriptions. A total of 33 variables were coded.

Please note that the case abstract is not shown in this table but was collected for every case. The unit of analysis for all cases was CSO decision.

The **piloting** of the form took place taking the input of the members of the research project providing their cases. A document for commenting was shared among the researchers, where each could enter their comments. In total 21 comments were given. For each comment, a response and an action proposal were formulated and reviewed within the group. The group agreed on the changes and they were implemented in the extraction form.

The cases were **elicited** through a Google form. Researchers entered their cases directly. In the instances where practitioners from the researchers' contact networks were involved, the Google form was used as the interview guide, and the researcher provided the information they collect in the interviews through the form. A total of 22 cases were obtained.

The **quality of the elicitation was assessed** through a review of the filled in extraction form and the coding done for textual descriptions. Two researchers reviewed the extraction form.

3.4 A4: Case Analysis

S14: Data Coding and S15: Synthesis We combine the discussion of the steps of coding and synthesis as they are both strongly tied. In the extraction form some data could be directly encoded into variables, on various measurement levels, such as nominal, ordinal, interval, and ratio. Here, the input data and the results are represented as quantitative data. Qualitative data needs to be coded, e.g. using open and axial coding used in grounded theory, or using a thematic analysis. Hence, the input data is qualitative and the output may be either qualitative or quantitative (e.g., when counting occurrences in themes across cases). Table 5 provides an overview of data types used for inputs and results for quantitative (Q_N) and qualitative (Q_L) data and presents ways of representing the data. Also, examples of key statistics (e.g., measures of central tendency) are stated. The table shows that, according to our use of the case survey method, the inputs, as well as results, can be both quantitative and qualitative in a single case survey. A comprehensive overview is presented in Cruzes and Dybå (2011). Additionally, in another study Cruzes et al. (2015) provided a

Table 4 Extraction scheme for the case elicitation

Item ID	Category	Item	Description	Type	RQ	Comments
1	Meta	Code	Unique identifier for case	Integer	X	X
2	Meta	Author	ORION research participant providing the case	String	X	X
3	Meta	Company	Case company	String	X	X
...	...	...	...	...	...	...
6	Context	Domain	Domain in which the decision was taken (e.g., automotive, avionics)	String	X	X
7	Context	Application type	Type of the application developed (e.g., embedded, information system)	String	X	X
...	...	...	...	...	...	...
11	CSOs	CSOs considered in the decision	CSOs = In-house, COTS, OSS, Outsource, Services	Enumeration	RQ1.1	X
12	Stakeholders	Decision initiator	Stakeholders involved in the initiation of the decision (identification of the need to make a decision and formulation of the decision problem)	String	RQ1.2	Requires coding
...	...	...	...	...	...	...
15	Criteria	Performance	Response time, timing behavior of the system	Boolean	RQ1.3	X
16	Criteria	Maintainability	Ease of updating the system (corrective, enhancements)	Boolean	RQ1.3	X
...	...	...	...	...	...	...

27	Method	Decision model	Method used to make the decision	String	RQ1.4	Requires coding
28	Method	Property model	Method used to estimate the impact of the decision	String	RQ1.4	Requires coding
...	...	...	...	...	...	...
32	Evaluation	Evaluation of the decision and the decision impact	Important criteria of the decision and reflections on the success/failure	String	RQ2.3/RQ2.4	Requires coding
33	Other information	Noteworthy comments	Remarks considered important by the person extracting the case	String	X	Requires coding

Table 5 Representation and analysis (examples)

Input → result	Relevant data types	Representation	Analysis and synthesis methods
$Q_N \to Q_N$	Nominal, ordinal, interval, ratio	Segmentation and cross-tabulation, histograms, box-plots, scatter plots, dendrograms	Median (ordinal), mean and standard deviation (interval, ratio), standard deviation (interval, ratio), measures of association (regression, correlation), identification of patterns and groups (cluster analysis), meta-analysis
$Q_L \to Q_N$	Textual (input), nominal in the form of themes and categorizations (output)	Tabulation and narrative explanations	Descriptive content analysis
$Q_L \to Q_N$	Textual (input), textual, tabular, and theme counting (output)	Tabulation and narrative explanations, counting of frequencies in themes	Descriptive content analysis, thematic analysis
$Q_L \to Q_L$	Textual (input), textual (output)	Narrative summary and supporting tabulation	Narrative analysis, qualitative content analysis

detailed example of using alternative analysis methods when qualitative data is used as input.

S16: Data Partitioning With several cases, sub-groups may be analyzed and compared as is a common practice in surveys. For example, we compare the findings for companies of different sizes with each other. Hence, we code and synthesize for our sample as a whole and subsets of our sample. Contextual information plays an important role during data partitioning. Hence, during the design of the extraction form (Sect. 2) context needs to be considered. Another way of segmentation is to group the cases by quality. If a case is obtained from a high-quality study and the extraction form is covered, this study should be, for example, valued as high rigor. In an earlier study, we found that partitioning studies according to quality lead to different findings in the categories (Munir et al. 2014).

S17: Assess Analysis Quality The analysis of data is prone to bias and mistakes, especially when considering a high number of variables. As an example, the process of identifying codes and categorizing them into themes is influenced by experiences and preferences of the coders. To increase the reliability it is recommended to involve multiple researchers in the analysis (observer triangulation). Interrater reliability has been used to assess the reliability of the selection of cases but is also useful when assessing the reliability of coding. Care also has to be taken when analyzing quantitative data, only applying statistics suitable for the data type.

Example (Petersen et al.) To recall, the case survey aimed at answering two research questions, namely (1) How are CSOs chosen? and (2) What was the decision outcome? In the following, we present examples of the analyses done for each of the research questions. Before presenting the research questions, we first provided an overview of the case context, documenting company size, size of the development unit, domain, application type, and development methodology (see Table 6).

Thereafter, we answered the research questions and associated sub-questions.

(1) How Are CSOs Chosen? The first research question was concerned with understanding how the decision was made. All information collected in relation to RQ1 are considered as independent variables.

(2) What Were the Decision Outcomes? The second research question was looking into effort invested, the actual decision taken, and its evaluation. All information collected about RQ2 is considered dependent variables.

In the following, we provide examples for **coding and synthesis** of how the data of the case survey has been presented and analyzed, covering the alternatives presented in Table 5.

(continued)

Example (Q_N (Nominal) $\rightarrow$ Q_N (Ratio)) For the first research question (RQ1) we investigated how many criteria were considered when making a decision. The input was the nominal data, and we counted how many criteria were considered in each decision case. The data was presented in a tabular way and as a histogram. The table showed the criteria, the number of cases, and the % of cases (see Table 7). Additionally, the distribution of the number of criteria used in the cases was presented as a histogram.

Example (Q_L (Textual) $\rightarrow$ Q_L (Textual, Ordinal)) The evaluation of the outcome (RQ2) of the decision was described in a narrative form. From the narrative description, the outcome was categorized as positive ($\checkmark$), negative ($\dagger$), and indifferent (o). The decisions (independent variable) were summarized in a tabular form together with independent variables, such as the choice made and the criteria considered. Table 8 shows three examples, one positive, one negative, and one indifferent.

Associating Variables As we had both independent and dependent variables, it was interesting to analyze whether specific criteria were associated with the decision for a specific CSO, both variables are representing nominal data. For example, when reliability was considered, were people more likely to go for a specific option (such as in-house). Odds ratio is a measure that checks whether the presence or absence of one variable is associated with the presence or absence of another variable and has earlier been applied in software engineering (Badampudi and Wohlin 2016). The higher the odds ratio, the higher the association. As an example, we saw that the use of the criterion certification was more strongly associated with the choice for in-house (odds ratio of 6.86) compared to open source (odds ratio of 1.25), components off the shelf (odds ratio of 0.18), services and outsourcing (odds ratio of 0.78).

Clustering As we had 22 cases it was interesting whether we find patterns concerning the cases (e.g., groups with similar traits). In order to do so, we used hierarchical cluster analysis. The clusters were presented in the form of a dendrogram. We, for example, found that the cases were quite diverse and no clear pattern emerged to group them. Only four cases were identified as being similar based on the cluster analysis. Those four cases were presented in a table, naming the contextual variables, decision-making characteristics, and the outcome.

The **segmentation** of data to present subsets of cases has been used various times in the study. Two examples where segmentation was used were:

- The grouping of the evaluations of the decision (see Table 8) made by the decision options. For example, four cases were in the group "in-house,"

(continued)

four in the group "commercial off the shelf," three in "open source," and five in "outsource." Additionally, a segment for combinations of options was created.

- The cross-tabulation of roles involved in the decision and the different decision activity including the roles.

In order to **assess the quality of the analysis,** observer triangulation was used. The interpretation and findings were reviewed by the researchers.

3.5 Reporting

We propose that researchers use the following guidelines when reporting their case surveys.

1. Introduction
   Describe the background and position of the research. Identify the research problem and the gap. Describe the main contributions and how they relate to the problem and the gap. Explicitly state that a case survey has been conducted and briefly explain how the process has been applied. Also, state whether the case survey is of exploratory or confirmatory nature.
2. Related work
   Present related studies. Derive theories and propositions from these studies, which may be tested when the case survey is confirmatory.

Table 6 Overview of the cases (excerpt from Petersen et al.)

Case ID	Company size	Size dev. unit	Domain	Appl. type	Development methodology
Case 1	100,000	5000	Automotive	Embedded systems	Iterative development, lean manufacturing
Case 2	1200	350	Utilities	Embedded + Software + Apps	Agile SCRUM variant
⋮	⋮	⋮	⋮	⋮	⋮
Case 17	100,000	30	Automotive	Embedded control system	Each of the department uses its own development methodology but there is a global process (V model). The components used SCRUM
⋮	⋮	⋮	⋮	⋮	⋮

Table 7 Criteria for decision-making considered (frequency)—excerpt from Petersen et al.

Group	Criterion	Cases	%
Product	Performance	17	77.27
	Reliability	13	59.09
	Maintainability	13	59.09
	⋮	⋮	⋮
Financial	Cost—general (time, effort, resources)	17	86.36
	Cost—buy/rent	3	1.62
	Cost—acquisition	1	4.55
	Cost—adaptation	1	4.55
	⋮	⋮	⋮
Project	Level of support	5	22.73
	Familiarity with technology	1	4.55
Business	Ecosystems	1	4.55
	Market trend	1	4.55
	time to market	1	4.55
Total		158	

Table 8 Evaluation of decisions made

Case	Outcome of the decision	Attributes considered in preparation	Attributes considered important in decision-making (subset of preparation)	Attributes considered important in decision-making (new)	Evaluation of the final decision $\sqrt{}$ = positive, o = indifferent, † = negative)
	In-house				
Case 21	In-house over outsource	Performance, reliability, and certification	Performance, reliability		$\sqrt{}$: reliability was improved
Case 16	COTS over in-house	Maintainability, cost, fitness for purpose	Cost, fitness for purpose		o
Case 12	Outsource over in-house	Performance, maintainability, reliability, cost, functionality, compatibility, certification	Performance, cost, maintainability, functionality, compatibility, reliability		†: underestimated computing resources needed (performance) of the chosen solution

3. Case survey design

   For the reporting we suggest to follow the process presented in Table 1 to describe the method, namely defining the research scope, describing case identification and selection, case extraction, and the approach of analysis. In each of the sections, the steps presented in the figure should be described. Additionally, validity threats are described. Here it is important to focus on those threats that are open or only partially reduced by actions through the study design.

4. Results

   The results present the analyzed data. We propose to structure this section along with the research questions.

5. Discussion

   The discussion should contain three parts. First, the implications for practice are described. Describing the implications means to discuss how practitioners should act based on the findings. Second, the implications for research present which future directions the investigations should take, or whether the way we approach a research problem should change. As case surveys are not widely adopted yet, it is also of interest to present reflections on the research process using case surveys. Third, the findings should be compared with the findings of the related work, e.g. reflecting on theories and propositions of previous studies.

6. Conclusion

   In conclusion briefly summarize what has been done in the study (background, objectives, and case survey method). After that, answer each research question. Suggestions for future work are also presented.

Example (Petersen et al.) The study was having the following outline, which closely followed the suggestions stated above. Minor deviations exist in the wording, and the discussion included the validity threats instead of the method. As the case survey method is not widely known, we have also provided a comprehensive introduction to the method in Sect. 3.

1. Introduction
2. Related work

   (a) Choosing among CSOs
   (b) Choosing vendors and suppliers
   (c) Choosing components

3. Method

   (a) Research questions
   (b) The case survey method

(continued)

      (i) Select the cases of interest
     (ii) Design data extraction scheme for data elicitation
   (iii) Conduct the coding
   (iv) Analysis

4. Results

  (a) Overview of cases and context
  (b) RQ1: How are CSOs chosen?

      (i) RQ1.1: Which CSOs (a) were considered and (b) which CSOs among those considered were chosen?
     (ii) RQ1.2: Which stakeholders were involved in the decision process?
   (iii) RQ1.3: Which criteria (a) were considered for making the decision and (b) which criteria initially considered ended up as significant for the final decision?
   (iv) RQ1.4: Which decision-making approach/model was used?

  (c) RQ2: What was the result of the decision-making process?

      (i) RQ2.1: What was the effort invested in the decision-making process?
     (ii) RQ2.2: Were the chosen CSOs considered the "right" choice retrospectively?

5. Discussion

  (a) Reflections with respect to the research questions
  (b) Characterization of decisions
  (c) Comparison with the general traits of decision-making from related work
  (d) Validity threats

6. Conclusion

3.6 Validity Threats

There exist different views of how to categorize validity threats, for example, focusing on positivist research (Campbell and Cook 1979), interpretivist (Guba and Lincoln 1982), and participatory (Greenwood and Levin 2006). Maxwell (1992) provides a comprehensive framework for validity that does, for example, not clearly distinguish between quantitative and qualitative approaches, but aims to find a typical frame of reference for them. Petersen and Gencel (2013) propose to use the categories proposed by Maxwell (1992) in software engineering research and chapter "Guidelines for Managing Threats to Validity of Secondary Studies in Software Engineering" discusses validity threats of secondary studies. The categories are descriptive validity (factual accuracy), theoretical validity (ability to capture what we intend to capture), generalizability (degree to which we can generalize findings to other contexts), and interpretive validity (objectiveness of the researcher when drawing conclusions), and evaluative validity (evaluating and assigned a value to the objects of study). Maxwell acknowledges that all five types are relevant for qualitative research. We discuss four of the validity threats to illustrate that case surveys, case studies, surveys, and experiments have different levels of difficulty mitigating the four types of threats.

Having used different research methods such as surveys, experiments, case studies as well as case surveys, we positioned these methods concerning the difficulty to control the threats mentioned above (see Fig. 2). The positioning of the studies is an approximation based on own experiences and may change based on the specific study context (e.g., number of subjects, size of the company, online vs. offline experiment).

Below we briefly discuss the main differences between the methods and the specific difficulties when mitigating the threats.

Experiments are based on well-defined constructs and measures (for example, in controlled experiments the number of defects detected is measured). They are also conducted in a controlled environment and deviations from the experimental process can be controlled for. This contributes positively to descriptive validity. However, it has been acknowledged that it is difficult to reproduce a realistic environment for various reasons (Sicgmund et al. 2015), as subjects, instrumentation, and context are often not all industrial at the same time. Theoretical validity is also mitigated more easily compared to other methods due to the controlled environment, we can, for example, account more easily for contextual factors. The interpretation of the data to draw conclusions is also difficult with quantitative data, though less compared to qualitative data as previous experiences and biases may strongly influence coding and categorization.

In contrast, case studies provide mechanisms for achieving in-depth insights based on qualitative and quantitative data and data triangulation. Using data triangulation from various perspectives (e.g., using multiple data sources and observers) helps in achieving descriptive validity. Generalizability, however, is difficult to

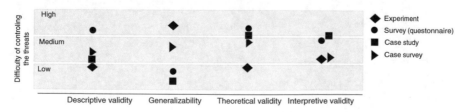

Fig. 2 Validity threats and how difficult they are to mitigate for different methods

achieve as case studies require a high degree of effort and are often conducted investigating a single or small set of cases. Theoretical validity is difficult to achieve as we may not control for confounding factors easily and measures collected in the industry may be sparse representations of the constructs investigated. As case studies to a large degree rely on qualitative data, interpretive validity is an issue.

In surveys, specifically questionnaires, descriptive validity is difficult to achieve. This is due to the reason that today the research community does not share a common vocabulary, and the industry does not either (see, e.g., Runeson 2006), which is not only a challenge specific to surveys. However, it is more critical here compared to case studies as in an online questionnaire targeting a large number of persons, we may not have the opportunity to ask follow-up questions. We also may not be able to provide detailed explanations of concepts used in the survey (e.g., the definition of a development practice) due to extensive questionnaire lengths. Surveys provide mechanisms to systematically derive a sampling strategy given a target audience and population. Surveys also allow gathering a high number of data points. We face challenges concerning theoretical validity when defining measures to be specified. It is furthermore difficult to account for confounding factors in a survey. The survey, similar to an experiment, relies to a large degree on quantitative analysis, which in comparison to qualitative methods reduces the threat to interpretive validity.

When positioning the case survey to the other methods, we can say that in comparison to the case study the generalizability is accounted for as we systematically analyze target audience and population and devise a sampling strategy. It is also more challenging to achieve a high degree of descriptive validity as we cannot go as in-depth compared to a full case study. Otherwise, a large number of cases is infeasible to collect.

Overall the above analysis shows that the case survey is a trade-off between case studies and surveys. When discussing validity in ones papers, it is however important to also consider validity threats associated with quantitative research (e.g., internal validity); see Petersen and Gencel (2013) for an overview of threat categories. The reason is that the case survey method proposed in this chapter utilizes both quantitative and qualitative data.

Example (Petersen et al.) The study used the classification by Maxwell as proposed by Petersen and Gencel (2013). We briefly present the main threats reported for the study.

Descriptive Validity The main threat here was missing data, as not all subjects could answer the questions related to all items in the extraction form. Specifically, effort data was missing for six cases.

Generalizability The main threat to generalizability was the bias in the data set as convenience sampling was used.

(continued)

Theoretical Validity When relating independent and dependent variables (decision-making approaches to decision outcomes) the main threat was confounding factors. Context also played an important part, and only a limited set of a potentially very large set of contextual variables could be collected.

Interpretive Validity The conclusions drawn from the data were not drawn by an individual researcher. Hence, during the study, we focused on observer triangulation to reduce this threat.

3.7 Quality Assessment

Checklists are used to assess the quality of different studies. Runeson and Höst (2009) included checklists for case study research. Molléri et al. (2019) proposed a checklist to support the design of surveys. In this section, we propose one checklist used to support the design of case surveys. The questions list the reflections to be made during the research design. These reflections also should then be reported to be able to assess the quality of the case survey. Each item evaluates to "yes," "partially," and "no." When reviewing, it is important to state a rationale for the assessment.

1. **Research scope**

   (a) Was the study positioned relative to other studies?
   (b) Were the research objective and research questions stated?
   (c) Was the type of case survey (exploratory or confirmatory) defined? If confirmatory, were propositions or hypotheses stated?
   (d) Was the study motivated by practical or research relevance?

2. **Research set-up**

   (a) Were guidelines followed when designing the case survey?
   (b) Was a risk analysis performed on whether the research team is able to (a) obtain a sufficient number of cases and (b) analyze and process the data collected?

3. **Population and sampling plan**

   (a) Were inclusion and exclusion criteria for the cases defined?
   (b) Were the criteria clearly linked to the research objective and questions?
   (c) Was the target audience of the research determined?
   (d) Was the population defined?
   (e) Was the sampling frame and the sample defined?
   (f) Was the sampling strategy (e.g., convenience vs. random sampling) described?
   (g) Was the case selection quality assessed?

4. **Case extraction**

   (a) Did the design of the extraction form consider case metadata, case abstract, units of analysis, case context, and study data?
   (b) Was the mode of data collection (primary versus secondary source and data collection method) for each case specified?
   (c) Was the feasibility of data collection considered in relation to the number of variables to be extracted?
   (d) Did the variables represent the theoretical constructs?
   (e) Were multiple sources considered (literature, experts, documentation, or a combination)?
   (f) Was data triangulation (e.g., two interviews per case) practiced?
   (g) Was the data extraction form piloted and the pilot assessed (e.g., member checking with expert, interrater reliability when using literature or documentation)?
   (h) Was an instrument defined to reliably record the data (e.g., online form, audio recording) determined?
   (i) Was the quality of the extracted data verified (completeness, rigorously collected)?
   (j) Was the elicited data assessed with respect to its reliability (interrater reliability, member checking)?

5. **Analysis**

   (a) Was the method for data analysis identified?
   (b) Was the analysis suitable to answer the research questions?
   (c) Was the method capable of providing reliable results for the given data (type, distribution, etc.)?
   (d) Was qualitative synthesis across cases performed using multiple observers?
   (e) Was the reliability of the qualitative synthesis evaluated?

6. **Discussion and conclusion**

   (a) Did the discussion provide practical implications to answers of the research questions?
   (b) Did the discussion provide research implications to answers of the research questions?
   (c) Were the implications and conclusions valid given the data?
   (d) Were the results compared against propositions, hypotheses, and findings in the related work?

7. **Assessment of research validity**

   (a) Did the study discuss validity threats?
   (b) Did a self-evaluation take place (e.g., using a checklist)? Was the outcome reported?

Example (Petersen et al.) We applied the checklist to our study to determine the possibilities of how the study could have been improved.

Research Scope Concerning research scope we found that all questions could be answered with "yes." As an example, related literature supported us in the view that it is vital to understand the industrial processes of selecting components and highlighted limited evidence (yes). Also, it was explicitly stated that the study is exploratory (yes).

Research Set-up The guideline has been specified (Larsson 1993). Also, the research team was quite large (10 authors) in order to achieve the goals of the research. Though, this has not been explicitly motivated in the paper (i.e., partially fulfilled).

Population and Sampling Plan The criteria have been explicitly defined and motivated. The population has been presented, though no distinction between the target audience and population has been made (partially). No sampling frame has been explicitly stated, though a sample was defined. The sampling strategy was named as convenience sampling. The quality of elicitation was ensured through peer review.

Case Extraction The extraction form missed units of analysis (partially). The mode of data collection was specified (project members, experts was defined). An explicit thought and motivation in relation to feasibility were not discussed (no). We only covered specific aspects of the decision, e.g. details of the decision process steps were not considered. Hence, the constructs may not be fully represented (partially). We decided a-priori to base the findings on primary data, the consideration of additional sources (literature, documentation, blogs) could have further improved the study (partially). No triangulation through multiple interviews was done (no). The extraction form has been piloted (yes). Google forms were used that allow to quickly grasp whether the desired information has been captured (yes). Member checking has not been conducted (no).

Analysis The data analysis methods have been described (yes) and were suitable for answering the questions (yes). We used methods that were suitable for the types of data (e.g., odds ratio, i.e., yes). Multiple researchers were involved in the interpretation of the data (yes) and evaluated its quality through the review (yes).

Discussion and Conclusions The discussion focused on the research questions, though it mainly focused on practical implications (yes) and research implications were only represented in future work (partially). The conclusions, having the limitations raised in the validity threats in mind, follow a red threat from research questions to conclusions and are traceable, i.e. they

(continued)

are considered valid (yes). The results have been systematically compared to related work (yes).

Quality Assessment The study discusses validity threats (yes), a self-evaluation (i.e., internal review) was conducted, though not based on a checklist to systematically determine flaws (partially).

4 Recommended Further Reading

To gain an in-depth understanding of case study research we recommend to read the guidelines by Runeson et al., including the guideline paper (Runeson 2006) as well as the book (Runeson et al. 2012).

Larsson (1993) provides a detailed account of how to conduct case surveys using secondary data. This includes a description of the process steps and a reflection on how to conduct them.

Molléri et al. (2016) aggregated guidelines for survey research and summarized the main steps for conducting surveys. The chapter "Challenges in Survey Research" discusses challenges of survey research.

5 Conclusion

In this chapter, we presented guidelines for case survey research. Originally the guidelines for case survey research classified the method as secondary research. The aim was to find a trade-off between case studies and surveys. In the guideline presented in this paper, the case survey research is modified to also incorporate primary data.

We believe that the case survey research method may be useful for both developing generalizable results while also supporting the study of individual cases. We believe that a prerequisite is to assemble a research team that uses its networks to collect the cases. This way we will have comparable cases based on the same research question and data collection instruments.

The chapter presents the initial version of the guidelines. In future work, the guidelines need to be applied and evaluated. This will hopefully lead to mature and beneficial ways of conducting large-scale case surveys within the empirical research community.

References

Ali NB, Petersen K (2014) Evaluating strategies for study selection in systematic literature studies. In: 2014 ACM-IEEE international symposium on empirical software engineering and measurement, ESEM '14, Torino, pp 45:1–45:4

Ali NB, Usman M (2018) Reliability of search in systematic reviews: towards a quality assessment framework for the automated-search strategy. Inform Softw Tech 99:133–147. https://doi.org/10.1016/j.infsof.2018.02.002

Badampudi D, Wohlin C (2016) Bayesian synthesis for knowledge translation in software engineering: method and illustration. In: 2016 42th Euromicro conference on software engineering and advanced applications (SEAA). IEEE, Piscataway, pp 148–156

Badampudi D, Wohlin C, Petersen K (2015) Experiences from using snowballing and database searches in systematic literature studies. In: Proceedings of the 19th international conference on evaluation and assessment in software engineering, EASE 2015. Nanjing, pp 17:1–17:10

Briand LC, Bianculli D, Nejati S, Pastore F, Sabetzadeh M (2017) The case for context-driven software engineering research: generalizability is overrated. IEEE Softw 34(5):72–75

Bullock R, Tubbs ME (1990) A case meta-analysis of gainsharing plans as organization development interventions. J Appl Behav Sci 26(3):383–404

Campbell DT, Cook TD (1979) Quasi-experimentation: design and analysis issues for field settings. Rand McNally College Publishing, Chicago

Cohen J (1960) A coefficient of agreement for nominal scalcs. Educ Psychol Meas 20(1):37–46

Cruzes D, Dybå T (2011) Research synthesis in software engineering: a tertiary study. Inform Softw Tech 53(5):440–455

Cruzes DS, Dybå T, Runeson P, Höst M (2015) Case studies synthesis: a thematic, cross-case, and narrative synthesis worked example. Empir Softw Eng 20(6):1634–1665

Dybå T (2013) Contextualizing empirical evidence. IEEE Softw 30(1):81–83

Easterbrook S, Singer J, Storey MA, Damian D (2008) Selecting empirical methods for software engineering research. In: Guide to advanced empirical software engineering. Springer, Berlin, pp 285–311

Gable GG (1994) Integrating case study and survey research methods: an example in information systems. Euro J Inform Syst 3(2):112 126

Garousi V, Felderer M, Mäntylä MV (2019) Guidelines for including grey literature and conducting multivocal literature reviews in software engineering. Inform Softw Tech 106:101–121

Golembiewski RT, Proehl CW, Sink D (1981) Success of od applications in the public sector: toting up the score for a decade, more or less. Public Adm Rev 41(6):679–682

Greenwood DJ, Levin M (2006) Introduction to action research: social research for social change. SAGE, Thousand Oaks

Guba EG, Lincoln YS (1982) Epistemological and methodological bases of naturalistic inquiry. ECTJ 30(4):233–252

Jurisch M, Wolf P, Krcmar H (2013) Using the case survey method for synthesizing case study evidence in information systems research. In: 19th Americas conference on information systems, AMCIS 2013. Chicago

Kitchenham B, Charters S (2007) Guidelines for performing systematic literature reviews in software engineering. Ver. 2.3 EBSE Technical report. EBSE

Klotins E (2017) Using the case survey method to explore engineering practices in software start-ups. In: 2017 IEEE/ACM 1st international workshop on software engineering for startups (SoftStart). IEEE, Piscataway, pp 24–26

Kuhrmann M, Fernández DM, Daneva M (2017) On the pragmatic design of literature studies in software engineering: an experience-based guideline. Empir Softw Eng 22(6):2852–2891

Larsson R (1993) Case survey methodology: quantitative analysis of patterns across case studies. Acad Manag J 36(6):1515–1546

Linaaker J, Sulaman SM, Höst M, de Mello RM (2015) Guidelines for conducting surveys in software engineering v. 1.1. Technical report, Department of Computer Science, Lund University

Lucas WA (1974) The case survey method. Tech. rep., Rand Corporation, report R-1515-RC

Maxwell J (1992) Understanding and validity in qualitative research. Harv Educ Rev 62(3):279–301

Miller D, Friesen PH (1977) Strategy-making in context: ten empirical archetypes. J Manag Stud 14(3):253–280

Molléri JS, Petersen K, Mendes E (2016) Survey guidelines in software engineering: an annotated review. In: Proceedings of the 10th ACM/IEEE international symposium on empirical software engineering and measurement. ACM, New York, pp 58:1–58:6

Molléri JS, Petersen K, Mendes E (2019) An empirically evaluated checklist for surveys in software engineering. http://arxiv.org/abs/1901.09850

Munir H, Moayyed M, Petersen K (2014) Considering rigor and relevance when evaluating test driven development: a systematic review. Inform Softw Tech 56(4):375–394

Petersen K, Gencel Ç (2013) Worldviews, research methods, and their relationship to validity in empirical software engineering research. In: 2013 joint conference of the 23rd international workshop on software measurement and the 8th international conference on software process and product measurement. Ankara, pp 81–89

Petersen K, Wohlin C (2009) Context in industrial software engineering research. In: Proceedings of the third international symposium on empirical software engineering and measurement, ESEM 2009. Lake Buena Vista, pp 401–404

Petersen K, Vakkalanka S, Kuzniarz L (2015) Guidelines for conducting systematic mapping studies in software engineering: an update. Inform Softw Tech 64:1–18

Petersen K, Badampudi D, Shah SMA, Wnuk K, Gorschek T, Papatheocharous E, Axelsson J, Sentilles S, Crnkovic I, Cicchetti A (2018) Choosing component origins for software intensive systems: in-house, cots, OSS or outsourcing? A case survey. IEEE Trans Softw Eng 44(3):237–261

Runeson P (2006) A survey of unit testing practices. IEEE Softw 23(4):22–29

Runeson P, Höst M (2009) Guidelines for conducting and reporting case study research in software engineering. Empir Softw Eng 14(2):131–164

Runeson P, Höst M, Rainer A, Regnell B (2012) Case study research in software engineering—guidelines and examples. Wiley, London

Siegmund J, Siegmund N, Apel S (2015) Views on internal and external validity in empirical software engineering. In: Proceedings of the 37th international conference on software engineering, vol 1. IEEE Press, New York, pp 9–19

Wohlin C, Runeson P, da Mota Silveira Neto PA, Engström E, do Carmo Machado I, de Almeida ES (2013) On the reliability of mapping studies in software engineering. J Syst Soft 86(10):2594–2610

Yin RK, Heald KA (1975) Using the case survey method to analyze policy studies. Adm Sci Q 1:371–381

Yin RK, Yates D (1974) Street-level governments: assessing decentralization and urban services (an evaluation of policy related research)

Zhang H, Babar MA, Tell P (2011) Identifying relevant studies in software engineering. Inform Softw Tech 53(6):625–637. https://doi.org/10.1016/j.infsof.2010.12.010

Challenges in Survey Research

Stefan Wagner ⓘ, Daniel Mendez ⓘ, Michael Felderer ⓘ, Daniel Graziotin, and Marcos Kalinowski

Abstract While being an important and often used research method, survey research has been less often discussed on a methodological level in empirical software engineering than other types of research. This chapter compiles a set of important and challenging issues in survey research based on experiences with several large-scale international surveys. The chapter covers theory building, sampling, invitation and follow-up, statistical as well as qualitative analysis of survey data and the usage of psychometrics in software engineering surveys.

1 Introduction

Empirical software engineering started with a strong focus on controlled experiments. It widened only later to case studies and similar research methods. Both methodologies have been discussed extensively for software engineering (Wohlin et al. 2012; Runeson et al. 2012). While survey research has been used to capture

S. Wagner (✉) · D. Graziotin
University of Stuttgart, Stuttgart, Germany
e-mail: stefan.wagner@iste.uni-stuttgart.de; daniel.graziotin@iste.uni-stuttgart.de

D. Mendez
Technical University of Munich, Munich, Germany

Blekinge Institute of Technology, Karlskrona, Sweden

fortiss GmbH, Munich, Germany
e-mail: mendezfe@acm.org

M. Felderer
Department of Computer Science, University of Innsbruck, Innsbruck, Austria

Blekinge Institute of Technology, Karlskrona, Sweden
e-mail: michael.felderer@uibk.ac.at

M. Kalinowski
Pontifical Catholic University of Rio de Janeiro, Rio de Janeiro, Brazil
e-mail: kalinowski@inf.puc-rio.br

© Springer Nature Switzerland AG 2020
M. Felderer, G. H. Travassos (eds.), *Contemporary Empirical Methods in Software Engineering*, https://doi.org/10.1007/978-3-030-32489-6_4

93

a broader sample for mostly cross-sectional studies, the methodological issues have rarely been discussed.

The aim of this chapter is to complement existing more general literature on survey research and questionnaire design as well as the existing software-engineering-specific literature. Therefore, this is not a tutorial to survey research, but it provides a compact description of important issues and lessons learned that any empirical software engineering research can make use of in their next surveys.

To not only discuss pure methodology and theory, we provide concrete examples of our experiences with the methodologies based on two lines of survey research: First, the project *Naming the Pain in requirements engineering*[1] (NaPiRE) has the goal to provide an empirical basis for requirements engineering research by capturing the state of the practice and current problems and challenges with requirements engineering. We have already made three rounds of surveys in this project over seven years and over ten countries. In these, we developed a theory as basis for the questionnaire, several variations on questions for similar concepts, and also experimented with different methodological options (Méndez Fernández and Wagner 2015; Wagner et al. 2019; Méndez Fernández et al. 2017). We will discuss these variations and experiences in the following.

We complement the NaPiRE experiences with a study that aimed to assess the happiness of software developers and targeted GitHub developers with a psychometrically validated test (Graziotin and Fagerholm 2019; Graziotin et al. 2018, 2017). This example described in Sect. 7.3 is different in the target population and how the questionnaire was created. Hence, it gives us even more possibilities to discuss.

The chapter is organized so that we discuss different areas that we consider interesting and challenging. We start with a discussion on how survey research can be integrated with theory building, then explain what we need to consider when using psychometric tests in our questionnaires and why we need to consider psychometric properties. We then discuss the limited possibilities in evaluating the sample of a survey study including a short discussion of ethics. We continue with the closely related issue of how and whom to invite to a survey and how to manage follow-ups. The last two sections discuss issues in quantitative statistical and qualitative analysis of the data from a survey.

2 Survey Research and Theory Building

The ultimate goal of empirical software engineering is, in one way or another, to build and evaluate scientific theories by applying empirical research methods (Méndez Fernández and Passoth 2018). Survey research is one such means to contribute to theory development (Malhotra and Grover 1998) as the main objective for

---

[1] http://napire.org.

conducting a survey is either of the following (Wohlin et al. 2012; Pinsonneault and Kraemer 1993): *explorative*, *descriptive*, or *explanatory*. Explorative surveys are used as a pre-study to a more thorough investigation to assure that important issues like constructs in a theory like requirements elicitation techniques are not foreseen. Descriptive surveys can be conducted to enable assertions about some population like the distribution of certain attributes (e.g., usage of requirements elicitation techniques). The concern is not why the observed distribution exists, but instead what that distribution is. Finally, explanatory surveys aim at making explanatory claims about the population (e.g., why specific requirements elicitation techniques are used in specific contexts).

A theory provides explanations and understanding in terms of basic constructs and underlying mechanisms, which constitute an important counterpart to knowledge of passing trends and their manifestation (Hannay et al. 2007). The main aim of a theory is to *describe*, *explain*, or even *predict* phenomena, depending on the purpose of the theory (Gregor 2006). A theory can be defined as a statement of relationship between units observed or approximated in the empirical world (Malhotra and Grover 1998), i.e., we capture a pattern in real world phenomena. Theories may have further quality criteria, such as the level of support or practical and/or a scientific utility (Stol and Fitzgerald 2015).

From the practical perspective, theories should be useful and explain or predict phenomena that occur in software engineering. From a scientific perspective, theories should guide and support further research in software engineering. The main building blocks of a theory according to Sjøberg et al. (2008) are constructs, relationships, explanations, and a scope. Constructs describe what the basic elements are, propositions how the constructs interact with each other, explanations why the propositions are as specified, and the scope elaborates what the universe of discourse is in which the theory is applicable.

The five steps of theory building of Sjøberg et al. (2008) are:

1. defining the constructs,
2. defining the propositions,
3. providing explanations to justify the theory,
4. determining the scope, and
5. testing the theory (or, more precisely, to test its consequences via hypotheses, i.e., testable propositions) through empirical research

For the last steps, mainly controlled experimentation is typically considered. In general, the relationship of theory building and experiments has been well investigated in software engineering (Hannay et al. 2007), whereas the relationship to survey research has not. Theory building and evaluation can guide the design and analysis of surveys, and surveys can also be applied to test theories. In the following, we discuss the interplay between theory building and survey research based on examples taken from NaPiRE.

In the early stages of studying a phenomenon, concepts of interest need to be explored and described in a conceptual framework or theory defining basic constructs and relationships, which also corresponds to the initial steps of theory building, i.e., definition of constructs and propositions. In later phases, a phenomenon can be explained and finally predictions based on cause–effect relationships can be drawn. Survey research can support all these phases of theory building. Both activities, survey research and theory building, are strongly interrelated. The concrete relationship between survey research and theory building depends on whether the theory is descriptive, explanatory, or predictive.

Initial theories, that is to say theories for which the level of evidence is yet weak, can be drawn from observations and available literature. An initial theory can be a taxonomy of constructs (Usman et al. 2017) or a set of statements relating constructs. Inayat et al. (2015) provide, for instance, an initial taxonomy on practices adopted in agile RE according to published empirical studies. Also common terminology as, for instance, provided by the Software Engineering Body of Knowledge (SWEBoK) by Bourque et al. (2014), which covers a taxonomy of requirements elicitation techniques, can be considered as an initial descriptive theory. For NaPiRE, we followed a similar strategy where we elaborated a set of constructs and propositions based on available literature and expert knowledge, thus, unifying isolated studies to a more holistic but initial (descriptive) theory on contemporary practices in RE (Méndez Fernández and Wagner 2015). One such example was how practitioners tend to elicit requirements. Exemplary statements for the requirements elicitation were *Requirements are elicited via workshops* or *Requirements are elicited via change requests*. These two statements relate the concept requirements elicitation to the concepts workshops and change requests, respectively. The survey is designed to test the theory and find next statements to extend the theory. The statements on requirements elicitation resulted in the closed multiple-choice survey question "If you elicit requirements in your regular projects, how do you elicit them?" with the additional option "Other." The responses were that 80% use workshops and discussions with the stakeholders, 58% use change requests, 44% use prototyping, 48% refer to agile approaches at the customer's site, and 7% use other approaches. The two statements from the theory about requirements elicitation via workshops and change requests, respectively, were supported by respective null-hypothesis tests (see Sect. 5.2).

Subsequent survey runs were then designed to test that initial theory and make further observations to further extend, refine, and improve the initial theory to an explanatory theory.

In principle, the more advanced theories are, the better explanations for the propositions they provide. The core issue of this is to provide explicit assumptions and logical justifications for the constructs and propositions of the theory. Table 1 shows propositions and explanations for requirements elicitation as formulated in the theory presented by Wagner et al. (2019). The presentation follows the tabular schema for presenting explanatory theories as suggested by Sjøberg et al. (2008).

The first run, however, showed that other elicitation techniques are also widely in use. This resulted in the propositions stated in Table 1. P 1, P 2, P 3, and P 5 are new. P 4 was already supported in the first run and included in the initial theory. The used terminology in the propositions was also aligned with elicitation techniques as described in the SWEBoK. The answer possibilities in

Table 1 Propositions about elicitation with explanations after the survey (Wagner et al. 2019)

No.	Propositions
P 1	Requirements are elicited via interviews
P 2	Requirements are elicited via scenarios
P 3	Requirements are elicited via prototyping
P 4	Requirements are elicited via facilitated meetings (including workshops)
P 5	Requirements are elicited via observation

No.	Explanations	Propositions
E 1	Interviews, scenarios, prototyping, facilitated meetings, and observations allow the requirements engineers to include many different viewpoints including those from nontechnical stakeholders	P1–P5
E 2	Prototypes and scenarios promote a shared understanding of the requirements among stakeholders	P2, P3

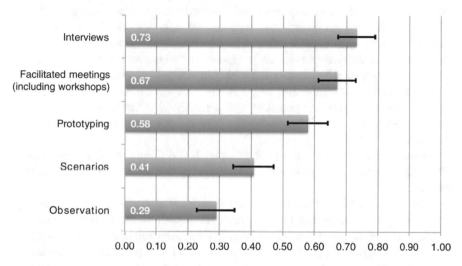

Fig. 1 Proportions with confidence intervals for the question "How do you elicit requirements?" (Wagner et al. 2019)

the questionnaire correspond directly to the propositions and resulted in the closed multiple-choice survey question "If you elicit requirements in your regular projects, how do you elicit them?" with the choices "Interviews," "Scenarios," "Prototyping," "Facilitated meetings (including workshops)," "Observation," and "Other." The answers of the respondents together with an error bar that represents the 95% confidence interval (CI) are shown in Fig. 1. The confidence intervals of all response types, even from the least frequently used elicitation technique Observations with $P = 0.29[0.23, 0.35]$ are still larger than the threshold of 0.2. We therefore have support for all corresponding propositions P 1–P 5. Additional answers for "others" included "Created personas and presented them to our stakeholders," "Questionnaires"/"Surveys," "Analysis of existing system," and "It depends on the client." Especially some kinds of surveys/questionnaires are mentioned several times. This could be a candidate for an additional proposition for the refined theory of the next iteration.

The explanations E 1 and E 2 are for the five propositions P 1–P 5. The difference between a proposition and an explanation is that the former is a relationship among constructs, and the latter is a relationship among constructs and other categories, which are not central enough to become constructs (Sjøberg et al. 2008). For explanations of the propositions, we do not have any additional insights from the open answers, which would be of value. However, explanations can be backed up by literature. For instance, Sommerville et al. (1998) state that it is important to include different viewpoints during requirements elicitation, which supports E 1. Mannio and Nikula (2001) developed an iterative requirements elicitation method combining prototypes and scenarios, which supports E 2.

Predictive theories are geared towards predicting what will happen. The key underlying principle is finding cause–effect relationships among variables. This is typically performed via quantitative statistical models like correlation and regression. Correlation quantifies the degree to which variables are related. Regression quantifies the relationship between independent and dependent variables. In any case, causal quantitative relationships should always be backed up by theory-based expectations on how and why variables should be related. Gregor (2006) even considers integrated explanatory and predictive theories as a separate type of theory. Therefore, qualitative methods also play an important role even in predictive theories.

Based on the survey results of the second NaPiRE run, we developed cause–effect relationships with different degrees of quantification to support predictive theories.

Méndez Fernández et al. (2017) developed initial cause–effect relationships between top ten causes, top ten RE problems as well as the project impact, i.e., whether projects failed or were completed. The resulting relationships are shown via an Alluvial diagram in Fig. 2. This diagram enables initial predictions of the project impact based on available causes like lack of time or missing direct communication to customer and problems like incomplete and/or hidden requirements.

The predictive model was created based on the survey in the following way. After selecting the five most critical RE problems in the survey, we asked our respondents to provide what they believe to be the main causes and effects for each of the problems. They provided the causes and effects in an open question format, with one open question for the cause and another for the effect for each of the previously selected RE problems. For analyzing the answers given to the open questions on what causes and effects the RE problems have, we applied qualitative data analysis techniques as recommended in the context of Grounded Theory (see Sect. 6). For each answer given by a participant, we applied open and axial coding until reaching a saturation in the codes and relationships, and we allocate the codes to previously defined subcategories, i.e., Customer, Design/Implementation, Product, Project, and Verification/Validation for the effect. The procedure finally delivers triples of causes, problems, and effects that are visualized in the Alluvial diagram shown

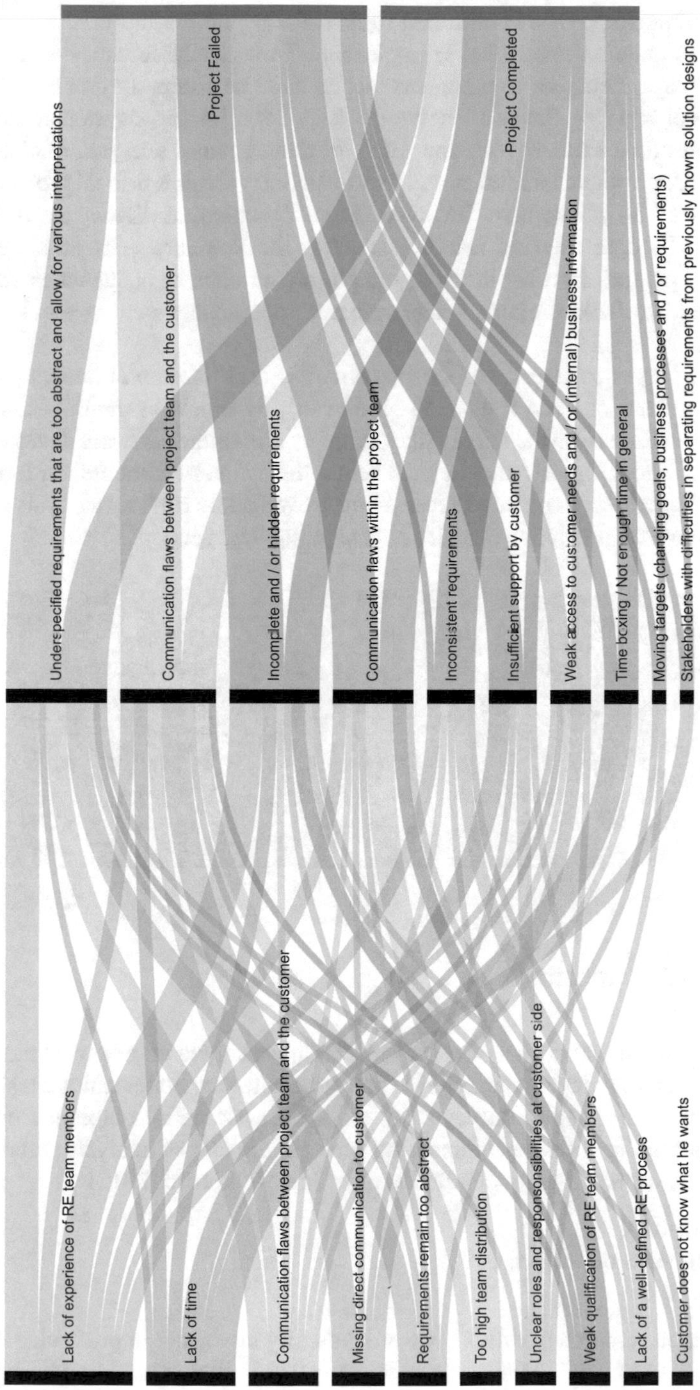

Fig. 2 Cause–effect relationship between top ten causes, top ten RE problems, and effects in terms of project impact (Méndez Fernández et al. 2017)

in Fig. 2. Dynamically implemented Alluvial diagrams, which support highlighting and hiding elements, provide additional support for predictive analysis.

Méndez Fernández et al. (2018) implemented the available cause–effect relationships in dependency of two context factors such as company size or software process model used as Bayesian networks (see Sect. 5.4 for Bayesian analysis). We did so based on similar work done also for defect causal analyses (Kalinowski et al. 2017). Our implementation allowed us to quantify the conditional probabilistic distributions of all phenomena involved. More precisely, it allows us to, based on the NaPiRE data used as learning set, use the Bayesian network inference to obtain the posterior probabilities of certain phenomena to occur when specific causes are known. This supports evidence-based risk management in requirements engineering.

So in the Bayesian approach, we performed a cross-sectional analysis of the NaPiRE data from one run (i.e., the second run), by blocking the data based on specific information from the survey like company size or the software development process used. Blocking can also help to refine the scope of a theory. In future, if NaPiRE will have been replicated several times, even a longitudinal analysis will be possible to develop predictive theories by analyzing time series.

Takeaways
- Survey research and theory building are strongly interrelated. The exact relationship depends on whether the theory is descriptive, explanatory, or predictive.
- Survey data supports the definition or refinement of constructs, relationships, explanations, and the scope of a theory as well as testing of a theory.
- Theories are of high value to guide the design of surveys.

3 Issues in Sampling

At the beginning of any design of survey research, we should clarify what the target population is that we try to characterize and generalize to. Statistical analysis (see Sect. 5), which we apply to survey data, relies on systematic sampling from this target population. In software engineering surveys, the unit of analysis that defines the granularity of the target population is often (de Mello et al. 2015)

- an organization,
- a software team or project, or
- an individual.

For common research questions, we are typically interested in producing results related to all organizations that develop software in the world or all software developers in the world. Sometimes, this is reduced to certain regions of the world such as all requirements engineers in Europe or Brazil. The reason for this large aim in the target population is that we want to find theories that have a scope as wide as possible.

This brings us, however, to the problem that in most cases, we have no solid understanding about the target population. How many software developers are there in the world? Which companies are developing software? What are the demographics of software engineers in the world? This is a hard question that nobody has a certain answer to. Yet, without answering this question precisely, we face enormous difficulties to discuss representativeness of a sample, the needed size of the sample and, therefore, to what degree we can generalize our results. We will first introduce a way for investigating representativeness; second, discuss the issue of sample size estimation for contexts where we can estimate the size of the target population; and, third, providing a note on the ethics in sampling.

3.1 Representativeness

For other types of survey research, scientists often rely on demographic information published by governmental or other public bodies such as statistical offices of countries, the EU, or the United Nations. These bodies are, so far, rather unhelpful for our task, because they do not provide a good idea about software-developing companies. These bodies scatter software engineering over various categories. For example, the EU's Statistical classification of economic activities in the European Community (NACE REv. 2) has different categories for software publishing, developing software for games or application hosting. More difficult, however, is that software development occurs in many other companies as well. For example, data from the German statistical office[2] on the usage of information and communication technologies shows that in 2018, 13% of *all* German companies stated that they develop business information systems internally. For web-based software solutions, even 17% stated that they build them internally. Put together, this means that we do not have a good estimate for the number and properties of organizations that develop some kind of software.

There are possibilities to approach the demographics of software engineers in the world. There are commercial providers of data from large surveys such as Evans Data Corporation.[3] Evans Data Corporation estimated for 2018 the number of developers worldwide to be 23 million. They include information on different roles, genders, used development processes and technologies. An open alternative is the Stack Overflow Annual Developer Survey.[4] They have the bias that only people registered at Stack Overflow can be sampled. Yet, this could be tolerated

---

[2] Table 52911-0001 in https://www-genesis.destatis.de.
[3] https://evansdata.com/.
[4] https://insights.stackoverflow.com/survey/.

in light of the popularity of the platform among software developers. They provide demographic information, for example, on whether developers are professionals, their roles, experiences, and education.

With this demographic information, we can design our survey in a way that we collect comparable data as is available in the distributions for the total population. Then, we can compare the distributions in our survey and the larger surveys to estimate representativeness. This comparison should primarily be part of the interpretation and discussion of the results. This comparison prevents us from overclaiming but at the same time gives more credibility in case we cover the population well.

3.2 Sample Size Estimation

Having the estimate of the total number of developers worldwide, we can now ask, what would be a good size for our sample? In other contexts, we might even have better information on the population size, for example, when we want to survey GitHub developers. This is an information we can extract from GitHub itself.

There is a large body of existing work that discusses sampling techniques and suitable sample sizes. A simple way, for example, is to follow Yamane (1973). He proposed to use this equation to calculate a suitable sample size n:

$$n = \frac{N}{1 + Ne^2} \qquad (1)$$

In the equation, N is the population size and e is the level of precision. This level of precision is often set to 0.05 or 0.01. For the estimate of 23 million developers worldwide, how large would our sample need to be?

$$n = \frac{23,000,000}{1 + 23,000,000 \cdot 0.05^2} = 400 \qquad (2)$$

So, for most intents and purposes, with a sample size of more than 400, we could claim a strong generalizability given that we also checked the representativeness as described above. Of course, most survey will fall short of this. Yet, a clear discussion comparing the sample size and representativeness with these figures makes it easy to evaluate the strength and weaknesses of a particular survey study.

For the happiness study we described in Sect. 7.3, we assessed how happy are software developers that have GitHub accounts. We needed to contact these developers; therefore, we queried the GitHub Archive for public events providing e-mail addresses. We obtained almost 456,283 unique e-mail addresses. We needed to find a way to sample these addresses properly. First, we conducted three pilot studies with $N = 100$ randomly sampled e-mail addresses. From the studies we could estimate that roughly 98% of the e-mails were delivered, and that the response rate was rather low, between 2% and 4%. After deducting the 300 entries from the three pilot samples, our new population size was 455,983. With Yamane's formula, with $e = 0.05$, we found out that we required $N = 400$ complete responses. On the other hand, the formula by Cochran (1977), which uses a desired value α for significance, suggested us to aim for $N = 664$ responses with a significance level of $\alpha = 0.01$. We opted for the more conservative value of $N = 664$ for our desired sample. That meant that we needed to send out 33,200 e-mails assuming a 2% response rate.[5]

3.3 Ethics

Sampling in survey research today almost always means soliciting answers via e-mail or social media. In a recent paper, Baltes and Diehl (2016) discuss that the common practice of sending unsolicited e-mails to GitHub developers could be ethically problematic. In software engineering, there is yet no established standard or guidelines on how to conduct surveys ethically. They report that in their own surveys, the received feedback from developers on GitHub being "spammed" with research-related e-mails. They conclude that researchers in software engineering should discuss this issue further and create their own guidelines.

For happiness study of Sect. 7.3, as described in the previous subsection, we had to contact more than 30,000 software developers via e-mail. Even though the developers provided a publicly listed e-mail address, we were aware that our e-mails were unsolicited and might have disturbed their daily activities. There were no available guidelines for the situation or even portals to gather volunteers for software engineering research. All we could do was to design a short and cordial invitation e-mail that, besides acting as informed consent form including ethical and privacy considerations, was of *opt-in* nature. We believe that the consideration worked to a certain extent, but we also add to the experience of Baltes and Diehl (2016) of receiving feedback from potential participants who were annoyed by this. While the number of complaints was not excessive, a very annoyed participant asked GitHub to check on us. After inquiring with us on the nature of the study and after inspecting our invitation e-mail, GitHub concluded that our study did not break any of their terms of services and kindly asked us to be advised before starting research activities, in the future, as they might want to check on the research design, invitation, and compliance with their terms. This last information might help future research in our field.

The *Insight Association* provides ethical guidelines that consider unethical sampling, among other practices: "Collection of respondent emails from Web sites, portals, Usenet or other bulletin board postings without specifically notifying

---

[5]More information on the sampling methodology can be found in our paper Graziotin et al. (2017).

individuals that they are being 'recruited' for research purposes."[6] Hence, using
GitHub or Stack Overflow information of users would not be an ethical way to
contact potential survey participants.

There is no easy way out of this. We agree with Baltes and Diehl that we will
probably need flexible rules and guidelines to keep developers in social media from
being spammed by study requests while still allowing research to take place. In any
case, we should all consider thoughtfully how and whom we contact for a survey
study.

Takeaways
- There is no suitable official data on the number and properties of software-
  developing companies in the world.
- For individual software engineers, existing demographic studies can be
  used to assess a survey's representativeness.
- For the estimate of 23 million developers worldwide, a good sample size
  would be 400 respondents.
- Ethics needs to be considered before contacting potential survey participants.

---

4 Invitation and Follow-Up

Depending on the target population, there are essentially two strategies to approach
this population having both very distinct implications on the survey design and the
recruitment approaches:

1. *Closed invitations* follows the strategy of approaching known groups or individuals to participate in a survey per invitation-only and restrict the survey access
   only to those being invited.
2. *Open invitations* follows the strategy of approaching a broader, often anonymous
   audience via open survey access; i.e., anyone with a link to the survey can
   participate.

The first strategy allows to accurately choose the respondents based on predefined characteristics and the suitability to provide the required information, and it
also allows to accurately calculate the response rate and control the participation
along the data collection, e.g., by targeting those who did not respond yet via specific
requests. This increase of control by inviting subjects individually typically comes
at the cost of a lower number of total responses.

---

[6]https://www.insightsassociation.org/issues-policies/best-practice/imro-guidelines-best-
practices-online-sample-and-panel-management.

The second strategy allows to spread the invitation broader, e.g., via public forums, mailing lists, social media, or at venues of conferences and workshops. This strategy is often preferred as it does not require to carefully select lists of subject candidates and to approach them individually, but it also comes at the cost of control in who provides the responses, thus, causing further threats that need to be carefully addressed in the survey design already. In that strategy, we need to define proper demographic questions that allow us to analyze the extent to which the respondents are eventually suitable to provide the required information (see also Sect. 3).

In the NaPiRE project, for example, we started our initial runs with closed invitations. To this end, we drafted a list of subject candidates based on contacts from industry collaborations. Criteria for their inclusion were their roles and responsibilities in their respective project settings and their knowledge about not only requirements engineering, but also about how their processes were continuously improved. That is to say, we were particularly interested in surveying experienced requirements engineers which dramatically narrowed down the list of suitable candidates. The survey was then password protected and the invitation was individualized with a clear explanation of the scope of the survey and the contained questions. When inviting our candidates, we asked them also to report to us in case they had passed the invitation to a colleague allowing us to calculate the response rates. We repeated this strategy during the first two NaPiRE runs, the second one being conducted in ten countries in parallel and via independent invitation lists administrated individually by the respective researchers in those countries.

For the follow-up runs, we changed our instrument to focus more on current practices and problems in requirements engineering at project level taking also into account a broader spectrum of project roles (e.g., developers and architects). We further decided to open the survey and added more demographic questions that allowed us to better understand the respondents' roles and backgrounds in their projects. The distribution was then done using software engineering-related mailing lists, distribution channels of associations, such as the International Requirements Engineering Board (IREB), social media, such as Twitter, but also, again, personal contacts. We further published an IEEE Software blog post. The idea was to increase the visibility of the survey project. At the same time, we were not able to calculate the response rate and also noticed a significant drop-out rate (i.e., participants entering the survey out of curiosity and dropping out on the first survey page already). Above all, it further required an analysis of making sure that the responding population is the one of the target population and, respectively, to remove those answers from the data set clearly unrelated to the target population (e.g., respondents with no insights into the projects' requirements engineering).

Regardless of the strategy followed, it is often the case that invitees cannot participate in the survey the moment they receive an invitation despite being otherwise willing to participate. In both surveys, we therefore implemented a follow-up invitation roughly 2 weeks before closing the survey. To this end, we formulated, regardless of the strategy, a reminder message thanking all participants and reminding them that there is still the possibility of engaging in case they did not already.

For the happiness study (Sect. 7.3) we decided to not adopt any follow-up. Ethical reasons (see the previous section) made us decide for an opt-in mechanism. We contacted possible participants only once, at invitation time.

Takeaways
- Both strategies to approach the target population (closed and open invitations) can be applied, but have distinct implications on the survey design and the recruitment approaches.
- Closed invitations are suitable in situations in which it is possible to precisely identify and approach a well-defined sample of the target population. They may also be required in situations where filtering out participants that are not part of the target population would be difficult, harming the sample representativeness.
- Open invitations allow reaching out for larger samples. However, they typically require more carefully considering context factors when designing the survey instruments. These context factors can then be used during the analyses to filter out participants that are not representative (e.g., applying the blocking principle to specific context factors).

5 Alternative Approaches for Statistical Analysis

Although surveys can be qualitative (see Sect. 6 for more details on that analysis), most often a majority of the questionnaires are composed of closed questions that have quantitative results. Even for yes/no questions, we can count and calculate proportions of the answers. Therefore, and with the often large number of participants in surveys, we usually aim at a statistical analysis of the survey results. So, which kind of statistical analysis is reasonable for surveys?

Before we go into the different options we have for the statistical analysis, we want to discuss another important issue that is sometimes neglected: To know what we can analyze, we need to be clear what we asked for. In a survey, we can either ask for the opinions of the participants on topics ("Automated tests are more effective than manual tests.") or for specific facts that they experienced ("In my last project, I found more defects in the software using automated tests than manual tests.") (Torchiano et al. 2017). In the former case, we can only make an analysis of the *opinion* that, for example, most people hold. Only in the latter case, we can try to analyze about facts. But even then, we need to discuss in the threats to validity that the participants' answers might be biased.

With that out of the way, we can start with the first option of statistical analysis that is always reasonable: *descriptive statistics*. Afterwards, we will discuss three alternative approaches to do inference statistics which will help us to interpret the sample results for the whole population. We will cover null-hypothesis significance testing, bootstrapping confidence intervals, and Bayesian analysis.

5.1 Descriptive Statistics

The goal of descriptive statistics is to characterize the answers to one or more questions of our specific sample. We do not yet talk about generalizing to the population.

Which descriptive statistic is suitable depends now on what we are interested in most and the scale of the data. Most often, we come across nominal, ordinal, and interval scales in survey data. Nominal data are names or categories that have no order and can simply be counted. Ordinal data is what we often have in surveys where we can order the data but cannot clearly say if each point on the scale has the same distance to the next point.

An example are the famous Likert items that range from "I fully agree" to "I fully disagree." If we have clearly defined distances, we have interval data. Only for the latter, we can employ the full range of statistical tests.

For dichotomous variables, where the participants can check an answer option or not, we can calculate the proportion of the participants that checked a particular answer option. A proportion can be stated as a number between 0 and 1 or in percentages. A useful addition to giving the number is a visualization as bar chart that allows us to quickly compare many answer options. An example from the NaPiRE survey is shown in Fig. 3.

Quite common are also answers in an ordinal scale such as Likert items ("I fully agree," "I somewhat agree"...) or frequencies ("Always," "Often," "Sometimes"...). There are various descriptive statistics that we can calculate for this data. For the central tendency, we can safely use the *mode*, which is simply the most frequent answer, as well as the *median*, which is the middle answer when sorting all answers (Freedman et al. 2007). To give a better understanding of the spread and dispersion of the data, we usually add the *minimum* and *maximum* as well as the

Fig. 3 The proportion of respondents giving a particular answer to the question "If you elicit requirements in your regular projects, how do you elicit them?" Visualized as bar chart (Méndez Fernández and Wagner 2015)

Table 2 Descriptive statistics for ordinal data coded as 1–5 (Méndez Fernández and Wagner 2015)

Statement	Mode	Med.	MAD	Min.	Max.
The standardization of requirements engineering improves the overall process quality	5	4	1	1	5
Offering standardized document templates and tool support benefits the communication	5	4	1	1	5

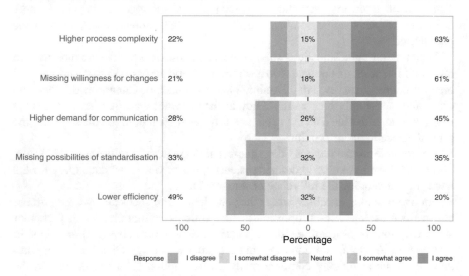

Fig. 4 Stacked bar chart showing all answers to a Likert item about barriers to requirements engineering standards (Wagner et al. 2019)

median absolute deviation (MAD) or the *interquartile range* (IQR). In Table 2, we see a table from (Méndez Fernández and Wagner 2015) that used these statistics to describe answers to Likert items about various aspects of requirements engineering. The answers were coded from 1: I disagree to 5: I agree. In addition or alternatively, it is also quite easy to show the whole distribution of ordinal data in a stacked bar chart as shown in Fig. 4. This particular chart was created using the *Likert* package[7] in R.

It is rather rare that we get data in interval scales or higher. We may get data on an interval scale when we ask for specific numbers such as the length of the last project of the participants in months. Those data can be analyzed with all available descriptive statistics such as the *mean* for central tendency and *variance* or *standard deviation* for dispersion in addition to the ones we already have for ordinal data. A very useful visualization for such data is a boxplot, because it visualizes the distribution and allows us to identify outliers.

---

[7]https://CRAN.R-project.org/package=likert.

5.2 Null-Hypothesis Significance Testing

Now that we have a good understanding of our sample—and possibly are able to answer our research questions specifically about the sample—we want to analyze whether and what we can say about the population we are actually interested in. This is the area of *inference statistics*. To be able to analyze something about the population, we first need hypotheses to evaluate. In our experience, unless we are conducting an exploratory study, the survey should be guided by a theory (see Sect. 2). The theory should provide propositions that can be operationalized into hypotheses to be tested with the survey data.

The classical way to do that is to use null-hypothesis significance testing (NHST). This is the usual way one is taught in statistics classes and has been used for numerous experiments and surveys. In surveys, we most often have two types of hypotheses:

- Point estimate hypotheses for answers to single questions
- Hypotheses on correlations between answers to two questions

For an example, we look again at Méndez Fernández and Wagner (2015). There, we tested several hypotheses on the experience of the participants with requirements engineering in their projects. Let us look at the hypothesis H 76: *Communication flaws between project team and customer are a problem.* The question in the questionnaire was "Considering your personal experiences, how do the following problems in requirements engineering apply to your projects?" The corresponding statement was "Communication flaws between us and the customer" with five answer options from "I disagree" to "I agree." As above, we coded these answers as numbers from 1 to 5.

We operationalized the hypothesis so that the median of the data needs to be larger than 3 (the neutral answer) so that we see the hypothesis as true. The corresponding null hypothesis is than that the median is smaller or equal to 3. To then test this, we employed the Wilcoxon signed rank test implemented in R. We used the rank test as we have ordinal data which breaks the assumptions of, for example, a t-test. The result of the test is a p-value that we need to compare with our previously specified significance level (usually 0.05). This then gives us a dichotomous answer whether we have to reject the null hypotheses and, therefore, have support for our alternative hypothesis or not. Similarly, there are statistical tests to give us p-values for which we can consider a correlation to hold true in the population.

In both cases, point estimates and correlation analysis, it is also informative and important to look at the effect sizes. A NHST only tells us whether the observed data is unlikely given the null hypothesis not how large the effect is. Especially in survey research, it is rather easy to achieve large sample sizes. The larger the sample, the more likely we get significant effects. Then the effect sizes can help us interpret the results. For correlation analysis, the correlation coefficient is already a useful effect size. For point estimates, we need an effect size that fits to the data and the used statistical test. For the Wilcoxon signed rank test above, it is often suggested to divide the test statistic z by the square root of the sample size N to the standardized effect size r:

$$r = \frac{z}{\sqrt{N}} \tag{3}$$

This can then be interpreted as 0.1 being a small effect up to 0.5 and larger as being a large effect.

There are various problems with NHST in general such as the dichotomous nature of its result (Levine et al. 2008; Amrhein et al. 2019). Yet, in our survey context, there is even one more: As discussed in Sect. 3, it is in most cases very difficult to obtain a sample that is representative of the population, we want to generalize to. In such cases, it is unclear what the result of a NHST actually means. How can we generalize from nonrepresentative data? Therefore, we need to look at alternatives.

5.3   Alternative 1: Bootstrapping Confidence Intervals

An approach that has seen considerable attention as an alternative to null-hypothesis significance testing is to use confidence intervals. The basic idea is instead of a point estimate of a p-value and a fixed threshold in the form of a significance level, we rather estimate a confidence interval around a metric we are interested in. We then rather interpret what the confidence interval means in terms of, for example, how large it is or how strongly confidence intervals of methods to compare overlap. Hence, the interpretation is not as easy as comparing the p-value with the significance level but it allows us to avoid a too simplistic dichotomous result.

To address the problem of the unclear representativeness of the sample because the population is unknown, we can further support the estimation of confidence intervals by using a resampling method. In particular, bootstrapping is helpful as it gives us asymptotically more accurate results than intervals estimated with the standard assumption of normality (DiCiccio and Efron 1996). The idea of bootstrapping is that we repeatedly take samples with replacement and calculate the statistic we are interested in. This is repeated a large number of times and, thereby, provides us with an understanding of the distribution of the sample.

Wagner et al. (2019) applied this approach to evaluate our theory without the use of null-hypothesis significance testing. For that, we ran 1000 times resampling for bootstrapping confidence intervals for proportions and means of the answers to the survey questions. This works particularly well for proportions. It is problematic for questions that have answers on an ordinal scale. We discussed above that for those, we should use the median instead of the mean. As, so far, there are no established methods for bootstrapping confidence intervals for medians, we decided to work with the confidence intervals of the means but report the medians alongside of them.

In Fig. 1, we see the visualization of answers to a survey question as bar chart. Each bar shows the mean proportion of answers with additional black bars showing the confidence interval both derived from bootstrapping. We had a proposition for each of the answer possibilities in our theory. As we wanted to characterize what techniques are *commonly* used in practice, we decided that common use should imply a proportion above 20%. Hence, only when the confidence interval is above 20%, we consider it as support for a positive proposition.

If we wanted a dichotomous decision on the propositions in the example, we would see that all confidence intervals are above 20% and, hence, we have support for all propositions. Yet, we can also clearly see and discuss that interviews and facilitated meetings are much more common in practice than scenarios or observation.

An alternative use of bootstrapping is for the estimation of true population means when the obtained data is not normally distributed. In the happiness study we obtained 1318 questionnaire responses contributing to the SPANE-B happiness score (explained in Sect. 7.3). Our example showed strong evidence of non-normality in its distribution. Therefore, we used bootstrapping to estimate the population true mean and its confidence interval (or, how confident we are on how much developers are happy).

Bootstrapping confidence intervals has, however, also disadvantages. One problem is that it can easily be interpreted as dichotomous and would bring us back to null-hypothesis significance testing. Another problem is that it is less clear what a confidence interval means for hypotheses. When should we see support for the hypothesis, when should we not? Furthermore, there is no clear way how to integrate different sets of data, for example, from different survey runs or independent surveys.

Finally, one might argue that a disadvantage is that it is a frequentist statistical technique that interprets probabilities as relative frequencies. This brings along various assumptions (Kass 2011) that have been criticized and could, for example, be overcome by a Bayesian analysis as discussed in the following.

5.4 Alternative 2: Bayesian Analysis

In Bayesian statistics, probability is understood as a representation of the state of knowledge or belief. It acknowledges the uncertainty in our knowledge by assigning a probability to a hypothesis instead of an accept/reject decision. Furthermore, it allows us to easily integrate existing evidence and accumulate knowledge. It does so by defining a *prior* distribution. This is the distribution that describes our certainty of a hypothesis before we collected new data. The Bayes theorem allows us then to describe the probability of a hypothesis given the prior and new evidence. This is called the *posterior* distribution.

A major difficulty with employing Bayesian data analysis instead of classical null-hypothesis significance testing or classical confidence intervals is that there is not just one Bayesian technique. It is a completely different way of thinking and, thereby, there is a plethora of techniques that can resemble what we did in the frequentists methods. The most general way would be, as stated above, to calculate a probability for a hypothesis. Yet, there are many alternatives: For example, there is the concept of the *Bayes factor* that can be calculated and there are standard interpretations on how strong the support for a hypothesis is. This is close to the way we approach the evaluation of hypothesis in NHST. Moreover, and that is the method we will describe in an example in more detail, we can also calculate confidence intervals using Bayesian methods.

For Bayesian confidence intervals, we only need three inputs: a prior distribution, data, and the level of confidence we want to have for the confidence intervals. Data we should have from the survey. The confidence level is commonly set to 0.95 but could be different if you have specific needs. The problem is usually the prior. This is one aspect of Bayesian analysis that draws a lot of criticism, because there is no mechanical way to get to it unless you have prior data. If you have prior data, for example from a previous survey, you can calculate the prior from that data. In all other cases, you have to decide on a prior. In case there is no reasonable argument for something else, the uniform distribution should be used. If another argument from theoretical considerations can be made, however, it is legitimate and useful to put in another prior. Given all inputs, there are many ways to calculate the confidence intervals. One way is, for example, to use the *binom.bayes* function of the *binom* R package.

When we go to the NaPiRE example, we have not yet published a Bayesian data analysis. Yet, there is data from a third run, where we apply the Bayesian confidence interval approach at the moment of writing this chapter. Here, it comes in very handy to be able to combine the data of more than one run. We do have many similarities between the second and third run. Using Bayesian analysis, we do not throw away the second run but build on it. We will look at the proposition again that workshops are commonly used in practice for eliciting requirements.

We use the data from the second run from this question to calculate a posterior distribution given a uniform prior distribution. Commonly, beta distributions are used for that. Our R analysis gives us a posterior of beta(154, 76). Now, we can use this posterior distribution from the second run as prior for the third. Figure 5 shows graphically how this turned out. From the second run, we had an estimation used as prior between 60 and 80% for the proportion of practitioners using workshops. The data from the third run gives us an estimate more between 40 and 60% (Likelihood). From that, we calculate the posterior that lies in between and is somewhat narrower with an estimate roughly between 50 and 60%.

With the *binom.bayes* package, we can make this more precise. When we calculate 95% confidence intervals, it gives us a mean of 0.54 with a lower estimate of 0.51 and an upper estimate of 0.58. For interpreting this according to the hypothesis, we can again use the 20% threshold and confidently state that we are closer but still far away from it. We have support for the hypothesis. By using Bayesian analysis, we strengthened the evaluation of the hypothesis by including the data from two surveys and probably corrected the estimate to a range not as low as the data from the third run would suggest.

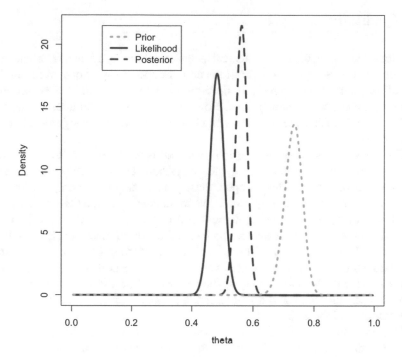

Fig. 5 Graphical summary of the distribution of the used statistics in the Bayesian analysis

There are also disadvantages in the Bayesian approach. As for confidence intervals, we do not have a standard way of interpreting the results of the analysis. Furthermore, the tool support is not as mature as it is for the frequentist methods and, thereby, sometimes rather confusing. Furthermore, reviewers in scientific venues often know Bayesian methods less and that brings the risk of misinterpretations on their side.

The more general issues in using Bayesian data analysis in empirical software engineering are discussed in the chapter "Bayesian Data Analysis in Empirical Software Engineering: The Case of Missing Data."

Takeaways
- Always make clear whether you aim at analyzing opinions or facts.
- Descriptive statistics are always helpful.
- Bootstrapping confidence intervals helps to deal with uncertain sampling.
- Bayesian analysis allows us to directly integrate prior knowledge.

6 Qualitative Analysis

Besides the common focus on statistical analyses, surveys can also be qualitative and contain open questions. Open questions do not impose restrictions on respondents and allow them to more precisely describe the phenomena of interest according to their perspective and perceptions. However, they can lead to a large amount of qualitative data to analyze, which is not easy and may require a significant amount of resources.

The answers to such open questions can help researchers to further understand a phenomenon eventually including causal relations among theory constructs and theoretical explanations. Hence, open questions can help generating new theories. A research method commonly employed to support such qualitative analyses is Grounded Theory (Glaser 1992; Strauss and Corbin 1990; Charmaz 2014). This method involves inductively generating theory from data (Glaser and Strauss 1967). While specific considerations for conducting and reporting grounded theory can be found from Stol et al. (2016), we hereafter describe the experience and challenges of conducting the qualitative analysis in the context of the NaPiRE initiative. NaPiRE involved open questions and a large amount of data from respondents of different countries around the globe.

The first issue faced in this context was the need to translate the questionnaires into the respondents' native languages to assure that they would precisely understand the meaning of each survey question. The translations were conducted by native speakers that were part of the NaPiRE team. All translations were validated by piloting the survey with independent team members that were also native speakers. Moreover, respondents also answered in their native language. We believe that this decision allowed avoiding any confounding factor related to difficulties with the language. On the other hand, it required us a significant team coordination effort to conduct the analyses appropriately. We had to translate all the answers to English and validate the translations before starting with the analysis. The strategy that we employed was exporting all answers into a spreadsheet, creating a separate column for each answer with an automatic Google translation, and then having the team validating and adjusting all translations as needed.

The main open questions concerned causes and effects of RE problems. We asked our respondents to provide what they believe to be the main causes and effects for each of the previously selected RE problems, with one open question for the cause and another for the effect. We applied the following Grounded Theory steps on this data:

1. Open coding to analyze the data by adding codes (representing key characteristics) to small coherent units in the answers, and categorizing the developed concepts in a hierarchy of categories as an abstraction of a set of codes— all repeatedly performed until reaching a state of saturation. We define the (theoretical) saturation as the point where no new codes (or categories) are identified and the results are convincing to all participating researchers (Birks and Mills 2011).

2. Axial coding to define relationships between the concepts, e.g., "causal conditions" or "consequences."
3. Internal validation as a form of internal quality assurance of the obtained results.

Please note that we deviated from the Grounded Theory approach as introduced by Glaser and Strauss (1967) in two ways. First, given that we analyzed data from an anonymously conducted survey after the fact, we were not able to follow a constant comparison approach where we iterate between the data collection and the analysis. This also means that we were not able to validate our results with the participants, but had to rely on internal validation procedures. Second, we did not inductively build a theory from bottom-up, as we started with a predefined conceptual model (i.e., the problems) whereby we did not apply selective coding to infer a central category. In our instrument, we already had a predefined set of RE problem codes for which we wanted to know how the participants see their causes and effects. For this reason, we rely on a mix of bottom-up and top-down approach. That is, we started with our predefined core category, namely RE problems and a set of codes each representing one key RE problem, and subcategories regarding the causes and effects, which then group the codes emerging from the free text answers provided by the participants. We believe that similar decisions could be taken in the context of other anonymously conducted surveys relying on a predefined conceptual model. Most importantly, we highlight the importance of precisely describing the approach that has been followed and the deviations from it.

Within the causes and effects, we again predefined the subcategories. These subcategories were as follows:

- For the causes, we used the subcategories Input, Method, Organization, People, Tools suggested in our previous work on defect causal analysis (Kalinowski et al. 2012) as we wanted to know from where in the socioeconomic context the problems stem.
- For the implications, we use the subcategories Customer, Design or Implementation, Product, Project or Organization, and Verification or Validation as done in our previous work (Méndez Fernández et al. 2015) as we wanted to know where in the software project ecosystem the problems manifest themselves.

For each answer given by the participants, we then applied open coding and axial coding until reaching a saturation in the codes and relationships and allocated the codes to the previously defined subcategories. For coding our results, we first coded in a team of two coders the first 250 statements to get a first impression of the resulting codes, the way of formulating them, and the level of abstraction for capturing the codes. After having this overview, we organized a team of five coders within Germany and Brazil. Each of the coders then coded approx. 200 statements for causes and additional 200 statements for effects while getting the initial codes from the pilot phase as orientation. In case the coder was not sure how to code given statements, she marked the code accordingly for the validation phase. During that validation phase, we formed an additional team of three independent coders who then reviewed those codes marked as "needs validation" as well as an additional sample, comprising 20% of the statements assigned to each coder, selected on their own. After the validation phase, we initiated a call where we discussed last open issues regarding codes which still needed further validation, before closing the coding phase. The overall coding process took in total 3 months. Despite of this huge effort, we emphasize the importance of validating qualitative analysis procedures to enhance the reliability of the results.

As a result we had information on how often a certain cause was mentioned as mechanism triggering a specific RE problem. Similarly, on how often a consequence was mentioned as a result of an RE problem. This allowed us to analyze the occurrence of certain RE problem cause and effect patterns, which are reported in further detail by Méndez Fernández et al. (2017).

Takeaways
- When preparing your survey, always invest effort in avoiding confounding factors that may interfere in having respondents focusing mainly on the survey question when providing their answers (e.g., language issues). A good strategy that helps to check if this goal is properly achieved involves piloting the survey and discussing it afterwards with the pilot participants to assure that questions were easily and correctly understood.
- Applying coding and analysis techniques from Grounded Theory can help to understand qualitative data gathered through open questions.
- When reporting the qualitative analysis of your survey, explicitly state your research method, providing details on eventual deviations.
- To avoid researcher bias and improve the reliability of the results, qualitative analyses should be conducted in teams and make use of independent validations. Also, ideally the raw and analyzed data should be open to enable other researchers to replicate the analysis procedures.

7   Issues When Assessing Psychological Constructs

Often, we are interested in assessing psychological constructs of survey participants. Psychological constructs are theoretical concepts to model and understand human behavior, cognition, affect, and knowledge (Binning 2016). Examples include happiness, job satisfaction, motivation, commitment, personality, intelligence, skills, and performance. These constructs can only be assessed indirectly. We cannot take out a ruler to measure the motivation of people. Yet, we need ways to proxy our measurement of a construct in robust, valid, and reliable ways.

This is why, whenever we wish to investigate psychological constructs and their variables, we need to either develop or adopt measurement instruments that are psychometrically validated. Researchers in the behavioral and social sciences refer to these validated measurements instruments as *psychometrically validated psycho-*

logical tests (Cohen et al. 1995). Scientists have investigated issues of validity, reliability, bias, and fairness of psychological tests. These aspects are reflected by the word *psychometrics*, which is both the act of constructing valid and reliable psychological tests as well as the branch of psychology and statistics devoted to the construction of these tests (Rust 2009). Psychometrics is an established field, but software engineering has, most of the times, ignored it so far.

In this last section, we build the case for software engineering research to favor psychometric validation of tests, we introduce the very basic concepts of validity and reliability as seen by psychometric theory, which is different to how we see reliability and validity in software engineering research, and we finally describe the happiness study that we often refer as an example in the previous sections.

7.1 Software Engineering Questionnaires for Human Participants Should Focus on Psychometrics

Lenberg et al. (2015) have conducted a systematic literature review of behavioral software engineering studies. They found that software engineering research still has several knowledge gaps when conducting behavioral studies, and that there have been very few collaboration between software engineering and social science researchers. This missed collaboration has likely resulted in the issue that software engineering research lacks maturity when adopting or developing questionnaires to assess psychological constructs.

Graziotin et al. (2015) have echoed a previous call by Feldt et al. (2008) to adopt measurement instruments that come from psychology, but they argued that much research in software engineering has adopted wrong or non-validated psychological tests, and when the right test is adopted, most of the times the test items are modified towards the destruction of the test reliability and validity. Research in software engineering also fails to report on thorough evaluations of the psychometric properties of the chosen instruments. An instance of such misconduct was found by Cruz et al. (2015) in their systematic literature review of 40 years of research in personality in software engineering. Although not directly mentioned by the authors, the results showed that almost half of personality studies in software engineering use the Myers–Briggs type indicator (MBTI), which has low to none validity and reliability properties (Pittenger 1993) up to being called as "little more than an elaborate Chinese fortune cookie" (Hogan 2017).

As argued by Gren (2018), there is a need for a culture change in software engineering research to shift from "seeing tool-constructing as the holy grail of research and instead value validation studies higher." We agree with his stance and add that the culture shift should also be from developing ad hoc measurement instruments or tinkering with established ones to properly develop or adopt them. It is our hope, with this section, to provide motivation and background information to start this shift.

We will now provide a short overview of psychometric reliability and validity so that it becomes clearer that researchers in software engineering, when designing questionnaires that assess psychological constructs, should pay extra care when selecting tests and also when modifying existing ones. For a deeper understanding of these issues, we direct the reader to the work of Gren (2018), who has offered a psychological test theory lens for characterizing validity and reliability in behavioral software engineering research, our seminar works on qualitative and quantitative methodologies for behavioral software engineering, and the major textbooks and standards on this topic (e.g., AERA et al. 2014; Cohen et al. 1995; Rust 2009; Kline 2015; Coaley 2014).

7.2 Reliability and Validity in Psychometrics

Reliability can be seen either as the consistency of a questionnaire score in repeated instances of it (also known as reliability/precision; for example, does a questionnaire that reveals I am extrovert tell the same if I take the same questionnaire 1 week from now?) or as a coefficient between scores on two equivalent forms of the same test (also known as reliability/coefficients; for example, do two different tests on personality reveal that I am extrovert to the same or very similar degree?) (AERA et al. 2014). The reliability/coefficients can be further divided into three categories, namely alternate-form (derived by administering alternative forms of test), test–retest (derived by administering the same test on different times), and internal-consistency (derived by computing the relationship between scores derived from individual test items during a single session).

Both forms of reliability are interesting and should be kept high when developing and validating a measurement instrument. The Standards for Educational and Psychological Testing (AERA et al. 2014) reports that several factors influence the reliability of a measurement instrument, especially adding or removing items, changing test items, causing variations in the constructs to be measured (for example, using a test for mood to assess motivation of software developers), and administering a test to a different population than the one originally planned.

Validity in psychometrics is seen a little bit differently to what we usually mean with validity in software engineering research (see, for example, the work of Wohlin et al. (2012)). Validity in psychometrics is "the degree to which evidence and theory support the interpretation of test scores for proposed uses of tests" (AERA et al. 2014). What that means is that we need to ensure that any meaning we provide to the values obtained by a measurement instrument needs to be validated. Rust (2009) has summarized six facets of validity in the context of psychometric tests, which we now summarize. Gren (2018) has offered an alternative lens on validity and reliability of software engineering studies, also based on psychology, that we advise to read.

Face validity concerns how the items of a measurement instrument are accepted by respondents. This is mostly about wording and meaning of the test questions and how they are perceived by participants. If you promise a questionnaire on software reliability but then deliver one about software testing, participants will likely feel confused or offended. Face validity is usually assessed qualitatively.

Content validity (also known as criterion validity or domain-referenced validity) reflects how a test fits the purposes for which it was developed. If you develop a test on job satisfaction of software developers and assessed their mood instead, you have issues of content validity. Content validity is also evaluated qualitatively, because the form of deviation matters more than the degree of deviation.

Predictive validity is assessed with the correlation between the score of a measurement instrument and a score of the degree of success in the real world. For example, a high number of years in experience in software testing is expected to have a positive correlation with ability in writing unit tests. If the correlation between these two items is higher than 0.5, the criterion for predictive validity is met and the item for years of software testing experience is retained in the test.

Concurrent validity is defined as the correlation of a new measurement instrument and already existing measurement instruments for the same construct. If we develop a test for assessing how developers feel motivated when at their job, we should compare the results of our test with established tests for motivation on the job. Concurrent validity assessment is very common in psychometric studies; its importance, however, is relatively secondary as the old, established measurement instruments might have low overall validity. Assessing it is, on the other hand, important for detecting issues of low validity.

Construct validity is a major validity criterion. Constructs are not directly measurable; therefore, one way to assess how valid a measurement instrument is is to observe the relationship between the test and the phenomena that the test attempts to represent. For example, a questionnaire to assess high motivation and commitment of software developers should correlate with instances of observable high motivation and commitment of developers. It is quite difficult to assess construct validity in psychometrics, and its nature is that it is cumulative over the number of available studies.

Differential validity assesses how scores of a test correlate with measures they should be related to, and how scores of a test do not correlate with measures they should not be related to. Campbell and Fiske (1959) have differentiated between two aspects of differential validity, called convergent and discriminant (also called divergent) validity. Convergent validity is about correlations between constructs that are supposed to exist. A test assessing logical reasoning is supposed to correlate positively with a test assessing algorithm development. Discriminant ability is on the opposite side. A test assessing reading comprehension abilities is not supposed to strongly correlate positively with a test on algorithm development, because the two constructs are not the same. Differential validity is overall empirically demonstrated by a discrepancy between convergent validity and discriminant validity.

We have so far reported how measurement instruments implemented with questionnaires, when they are about human behavior, cognition, affect, and knowledge, face several issues of reliability and validity. Researchers in the social and behavioral sciences and statistics have spent considerable effort on developing strong methodologies and theory for implementing valid and reliable tests. Software engineering needs a cultural shift to observe and respects these issues, both when adopting and when implementing a measurement instrument. As a running example, we will now briefly summarize an experience report on adopting a psychometrically validated measurement instrument.

7.3 An Experience Report on Adopting a Psychometrically Validated Instrument

For a project on the happiness of software developers (Graziotin and Fagerholm 2019; Graziotin et al. 2018, 2017) one of our goals was to estimate the distribution of happiness among software developers or, in other words, find out how happy developers are. We had a further requirement: the related questionnaire had to be as short as possible.

The first step in finding a psychometrically validated instrument to assess happiness was to find out what happiness is. We discovered two main definitions of happiness in the literature, one of which sees happiness as a sequence of experiential episodes. If we face frequent positive experiences, we are led to experiencing positive emotions and moods and appraise our existence to be a happy one. The reverse happens with negative experiences, which lead to negative affect and unhappiness. Happiness overall is the difference, or balance, between positive and negative experiences.

Once agreed on a definition, we searched for happiness and related words in academic search engines. Reading more papers led to finding new keywords and enriching our sample of candidates, which was not small at all. We then inspected all possible candidates to retain those that were short to be completed. The sample of candidates was further reduced.

We then searched all candidate names in academic search engines to look for validation studied (particular keywords here are validation, reliability, and psychometric properties). Some measurement instruments did not have any validation study beyond the one which introduced the instrument itself.

We eventually decided to adopt the Scale of Positive and Negative Experience (SPANE), which we explain in Graziotin et al. (2017), as it is a short scale, 12 Likert items in total, on how frequently participants experience affect in the last 4 weeks. The introductory paper explained very carefully why and how the scale was implemented, as well as the choice of limiting the recall of experiences in the last 4 weeks (in short, accuracy of human memory recalling and ambiguity of people's understanding of the items themselves).

We found out that SPANE has been validated to provide high validity and reliability coefficients in (at the time) nine very large-scale psychometric studies with samples coming from different nations and cultures. Furthermore, the scale converges to other similar measurements (concurrent validity). Finally, the scale was found to be consistent across full-time workers and students. These aspects were important because the target population was sampled on GitHub, which hosts projects of developers from all around the world (indeed, we had responses from 88 different countries) and having different backgrounds and job experiences (75% were professionals ranging from freelancing to large industries, and 15% were students).

There was enough evidence for us to be confident in including SPANE in our studies. As we respect the hard work of those who developed and validated the scale, we included the scale verbatim in our studies. We introduced the scale using the recommended instructions, we presented the items in the same order, and we used the same Likert items as recommended.

There are several advantages of adopting a psychometrically validated scale. One of them is that we can be confident about the reliability and validity of the way we interpret the scores. In our research endeavor, we found out that software engineers have a SPANE-B (the overall SPANE score, or "the happiness score") centered around the values of 9–10 over a range of −24 and +24. The interpretation of this scoring is that developers are, on average, a slightly happy population. Moreover, relying on validated scales also means that often we can compare our scores with *norm scores*, which are *standardized scores* of several groups or populations. As many other research projects have used SPANE, we can add to our interpretation that software developers even are (just a little bit) happier than other groups of people.

A big disadvantage in adopting psychometrically validated scales lies in the complete lack of flexibility of the items, as it follows an "all or nothing" approach. We either include a validated scale or we do not, as changing any aspect of the items will likely invalidate the scale. SPANE has got 12 items related to emotional and affective experiences, 6 of which are positive and 6 negative. We can provide a granularity of analysis of these 12 items but nothing more than that.

Takeaways
- Representing and assessing constructs on human behavior, cognition, affect, and knowledge is a difficult problem that requires psychometrically validated measurement instruments.
- Software engineering research should either adopt or develop psychometrically validated questionnaires.
- Adoption or development of psychometrically validated questionnaires should consider psychometric reliability and validity issues, which are diverse and very different from the usual and common validity issues we see in "Threats to Validity" sections.
- Software engineering research should introduce studies on the development and validation of questionnaires.

8   Recommended Further Reading

We recommend several further book chapters and articles to complement this chapter: Fowler (2013) provides a solid general discussion on survey research in general including sampling, questions, and instruments and ethics. Kitchenham and Pfleeger (2008) provided an earlier book chapter that focuses on collecting opinions by surveys but provided also more general issues relevant for survey research in software engineering. They provided more details in an older series of publications (Pfleeger and Kitchenham 2001; Kitchenham and Pfleeger 2002a,b,c,d). Ciolkowski et al. (2003) provide a more comprehensive process for planning and analyzing a survey in software engineering. Ghazi et al. (2019) conducted a systematic literature review and interviews to identify common problems in software engineering surveys and also provide mitigation strategies. For more details and methodological support on sampling, de Mello et al. (2015) are a good source. General guidelines for designing an effective survey are available from the SEI (Kasunic 2005). Molléri et al. (2019) found 39 papers with methodological aspects of surveys in software engineering that can be used as a starting point for issues not discussed (in enough depth) in this chapter. Furthermore, the chapter "Guidelines for Case Survey Research in Software Engineering" provided specific guidelines for case surveys.

9   Conclusion

Survey research is becoming more and more an elementary tool in empirical software engineering as it allows to capture cross-sectional snapshots of current states of practice, i.e., they allow to describe and explain contemporary phenomena in practice (e.g., opinions, beliefs, or experiences). Survey research is indeed a powerful method and its wide adoption in the software engineering community is also steered, we believe, by the prejudice of that it is easy to employ while there exist, in fact, many nontrivial pitfalls that render survey research cumbersome. In response to this problem, the community has started to contribute hands-on experiences and lessons learnt contributions, such as by Torchiano et al. (2017).

In this chapter, we have complemented existing literature on challenges in survey research by discussing more advanced topics. Those topics range from how to use survey research to build and evaluate scientific theories over sampling and subject invitation strategies to data analysis topics considering both quantitative and qualitative data, and we complemented it with specialized use cases such as using surveys for psychometric studies. To this end, we drew from our experiences in running a globally distributed and biyearly replicated family of large-scale surveys in requirements engineering. While we are certainly aware of that our own journey in learning from own mistakes and slips is not done yet. We hope that by reporting and discussing these lessons we learnt over the past years, we already support other members of our research community in further improving their own survey projects.

Acknowledgement We are grateful to all collaborating researchers in the NaPiRE initiative.

References

AERA, APA, NCME (2014) Standards for educational and psychological testing. American Educational Research Association, Washington

Amrhein V, Greenland S, McShane B (2019) Retire statistical significance. Nature 567:305–307

Baltes S, Diehl S (2016) Worse than spam: issues in sampling software developers. In: Proceedings of the 10th ACM/IEEE international symposium on empirical software engineering and measurement, ESEM '16. ACM, New York, pp 52:1–52:6. http://doi.acm.org/10.1145/2961111.2962628

Binning JF (2016) Construct. https://www.britannica.com/science/construct

Birks M, Mills J (2011) Grounded theory: a practical guide. Sage, Thousand Oaks

Bourque P, Fairley RE et al (2014) Guide to the software engineering body of knowledge (SWEBOK): version 3.0. IEEE Computer Society Press, Washington

Campbell DT, Fiske DW (1959) Convergent and discriminant validation by the multitrait-multimethod matrix. Psychol Bull 56(2):81–105

Charmaz K (2014) Constructing grounded theory. Sage, Thousand Oaks

Ciolkowski M, Laitenberger O, Vegas S, Biffl S (2003) Practical experiences in the design and conduct of surveys in empirical software engineering. In: Conradi R, Wang AI (eds) Empirical methods and studies in software engineering, experiences from ESERNET, vol 2765. Lecture notes in computer science. Springer, Berlin, pp 104–128. https://doi.org/10.1007/978-3-540-45143-3_7

Coaley K (2014) An introduction to psychological assessment and psychometrics. Sage, Thousand Oaks

Cochran WG (1977) Sampling techniques. Wiley, New York

Cohen RJ, Swerdlik ME, Phillips SM (1995) Psychological testing and assessment: an introduction to tests and measurement. Mayfield Publishing, California

Cruz S, da Silva FQ, Capretz LF (2015) Forty years of research on personality in software engineering: a mapping study. Comput Hum Behav 46:94–113

de Mello RM, da Silva PC, Travassos GH (2015) Investigating probabilistic sampling approaches for large-scale surveys in software engineering. J Softw Eng Res Dev 3(1):8. https://doi.org/10.1186/s40411-015-0023-0

DiCiccio TJ, Efron B (1996) Bootstrap confidence intervals. Stat Sci 11(3):189–228

Feldt R, Torkar R, Angelis L, Samuelsson M (2008) Towards individualized software engineering: empirical studies should collect psychometrics. In: Cheng L, Sillito J, Storey MD, Tessem B, Venolia G, de Souza CRB, Dittrich Y, John M, Hazzan O, Maurer F, Sharp H, Singer, J, Sim SE (eds) Proceedings of the 2008 international workshop on cooperative and human aspects of software engineering, CHASE 2008, Leipzig. ACM, New York, pp 49–52. https://doi.org/10.1145/1370114.1370127

Fowler FJ (2013) Survey research methods. Sage, Thousand Oaks

Freedman D, Pisani R, Purves R (2007). Statistics. Norton, New York

Ghazi AN, Petersen K, Reddy SS, Nekkanti H (2019) Survey research in software engineering: problems and mitigation strategies. IEEE Access 7:24703–24718

Glaser BG (1992) Basics of grounded theory analysis: emergence vs. forcing. Sociology Press, Mill Valley

Glaser BG, Strauss AL (1967) Discovery of grounded theory: strategies for qualitative research. Aldine de Gruyter, New York

Graziotin D, Fagerholm F (2019) Happiness and the productivity of software engineers. In: Rethinking productivity in software engineering. Apress, Berkeley, pp 109–124

Graziotin D, Wang X, Abrahamsson P (2015) Understanding the affect of developers: theoretical background and guidelines for psychoempirical software engineering. In: Proceedings of the 7th international workshop on social software engineering, SSE 2015. ACM, New York, pp 25–32. http://doi.acm.org/10.1145/2804381.2804386

Graziotin D, Fagerholm F, Wang X, Abrahamsson P (2017) On the unhappiness of software developers. In: Mendes E, Counsell S, Petersen K (eds) Proceedings of the 21st international conference on evaluation and assessment in software engineering. ACM Press, New York, pp 324–333

Graziotin D, Fagerholm F, Wang, Abrahamsson P (2018) What happens when software developers are (un)happy. J Syst Softw 140:32–47

Gregor S (2006) The nature of theory in information systems. MIS Q 30(3):611–642. http://misq.org/the-nature-of-theory-in-information-systems.html

Gren L (2018) Standards of validity and the validity of standards in behavioral software engineering research. In: Standards of validity and the validity of standards in behavioral software engineering research. ACM Press, New York

Hannay JE, Sjøberg DI, Dybå T (2007) A systematic review of theory use in software engineering experiments. IEEE Trans Softw Eng 33(2):87–107

Hogan R (2017) Personality and the fate of organizations. Erlbaum, Mahwah

Inayat I, Salim SS, Marczak S, Daneva M, Shamshirband S (2015) A systematic literature review on agile requirements engineering practices and challenges. Comput Hum Behav 51:915–929

Kalinowski M, Card DN, Travassos GH (2012) Evidence-based guidelines to defect causal analysis. IEEE Softw 29(4):16–18

Kalinowski M, Curty P, Paes A, Ferreira A, Spínola RO, Fernández DM, Felderer M, Wagner S (2017) Supporting defect causal analysis in practice with cross-company data on causes of requirements engineering problems. In: Proceedings of the 39th IEEE/ACM international conference on software engineering: software engineering in practice track, ICSE-SEIP 2017, Buenos Aires. IEEE Computer Society, Silver Spring, pp 223–232. https://doi.org/10.1109/ICSE-SEIP.2017.14

Kass RE (2011) Statistical inference: the big picture. Stat Sci Rev J Inst Math Stat 26(1):1

Kasunic M (2005) Designing an effective survey. Technical report, Carnegie-Mellon University, Pittsburgh, PA and Software Engineering Institute

Kitchenham BA, Pfleeger SL (2002a) Principles of survey research part 2: designing a survey. ACM SIGSOFT Softw Eng Notes 27(1):18–20. https://doi.org/10.1145/566493.566495

Kitchenham BA, Pfleeger SL (2002b) Principles of survey research: part 3: constructing a survey instrument. ACM SIGSOFT Softw Eng Notes 27(2):20–24. https://doi.org/10.1145/511152.511155

Kitchenham, BA, Pfleeger SL (2002c) Principles of survey research part 4: questionnaire evaluation. ACM SIGSOFT Softw Eng Notes 27(3):20–23. https://doi.org/10.1145/638574.638580

Kitchenham BA, Pfleeger SL (2002d) Principles of survey research: part 5: populations and samples. ACM SIGSOFT Softw Eng Notes 27(5):17–20. https://doi.org/10.1145/571681.571686

Kitchenham BA, Pfleeger SL (2008) Personal opinion surveys. In: Guide to advanced empirical software engineering. Springer, Berlin, pp 63–92

Kline P (2015) A handbook of test construction (psychology revivals): introduction to psychometric design. Routledge, London

Lenberg P, Feldt R, Wallgren LG (2015) Behavioral software engineering: a definition and systematic literature review. J Syst Softw 107:15–37

Levine TR, Weber R, Hullett C, Park HS, Massi Lindsey LL (2008) A critical assessment of null hypothesis significance testing in quantitative communication research. Hum Commun Res 34:171–187

Malhotra MK, Grover V (1998) An assessment of survey research in POM: from constructs to theory. J Oper Manag 16(4):407–425

Mannio M, Nikula U (2001) Requirements elicitation using a combination of prototypes and scenarios. Technical report, Telecom Business Research Center Lappeenranta

Méndez Fernández D, Passoth J-H (2018) Empirical software engineering: from discipline to interdiscipline. J Syst Softw 148:170–179

Méndez Fernández D, Wagner S (2015) Naming the pain in requirements engineering: a design for a global family of surveys and first results from Germany. Inform Softw Tech 57:616–643

Méndez Fernández D, Wagner S, Kalinowski M, Schekelmann A, Tuzcu A, Conte T, Spinola R, Prikladnicki R (2015) Naming the pain in requirements engineering: comparing practices in Brazil and Germany. IEEE Softw 32(5):16–23

Méndez Fernández D, Wagner S, Kalinowski M, Felderer M, Mafra P, Vetrò A, Conte T, Christiansson M-T, Greer D, Lassenius C et al. (2017) Naming the pain in requirements engineering—contemporary problems, causes, and effects in practice. Empir Softw Eng 22(5):2298–2338

Méndez Fernández D, Tießler M, Kalinowski M, Felderer M, Kuhrmann M (2018) On evidence-based risk management in requirements engineering. In: International conference on software quality. Springer, Berlin, pp 39–59

Molléri JS, Petersen K, Mendes E (2019) CERSE-catalog for empirical research in software engineering: a systematic mapping study. Inform Softw Tech 105:117–149

Pfleeger SL, Kitchenham BA (2001) Principles of survey research: part 1: turning lemons into lemonade. ACM SIGSOFT Softw Eng Notes 26(6):16–18. https://doi.org/10.1145/505532.505535

Pinsonneault A, Kraemer K (1993) Survey research methodology in management information systems: an assessment. J Manag Inform Syst 10(2):75–105

Pittenger DJ (1993) Measuring the MBTI. . . and coming up short. J Career Plan Employ 54(1):48–52

Runeson P, Höst M, Rainer A, Regnell B (2012) Case study research in software engineering. Wiley, London

Rust J (2009) Modern psychometrics: the science of psychological assessment. Routledge, Hove, East Sussex New York

Sjøberg DI, Dybå T, Anda BC, Hannay JE (2008) Building theories in software engineering. In: Guide to advanced empirical software engineering. Springer, Berlin, pp 312–336

Sommerville I, Sawyer P, Viller S (1998) Viewpoints for requirements elicitation: a practical approach. In: Proceedings of the 3rd international conference on requirements engineering (ICRE '98), Putting requirements engineering to practice, Colorado Springs. IEEE Computer Society, Silver Spring, pp 74–81. https://doi.org/10.1109/ICRE.1998.667811

Stol K-J, Fitzgerald B (2015) Theory-oriented software engineering. Sci Comput Program 101:79–98

Stol K, Ralph P, Fitzgerald B (2016) Grounded theory in software engineering research: a critical review and guidelines. In: Dillon LK, Visser W, Williams L (eds) Proceedings of the 38th international conference on software engineering, ICSE 2016, Austin. ACM, New York, pp 120–131. https://doi.org/10.1145/2884781.2884833

Strauss A, Corbin J (1990) Basics of qualitative research. Sage, Thousand Oaks

Torchiano M, Fernández DM, Travassos GH, de Mello RM (2017) Lessons learnt in conducting survey research. In: Proceedings of the 5th IEEE/ACM international workshop on conducting empirical studies in industry, CESI@ICSE 2017, Buenos Aires. IEEE, Piscataway, pp 33–39. https://doi.org/10.1109/CESI.2017.5

Usman M, Britto R, Börstler J, Mendes E (2017) Taxonomies in software engineering: a systematic mapping study and a revised taxonomy development method. Inform Softw Tech 85:43–59

Wagner S, Méndez Fernández D, Felderer M, Vetrò A, Kalinowski M, Wieringa R, Pfahl D, Conte T, Christiansson M-T, Greer D, Lassenius C, Männistö T, Nayebi M, Oivo M, Penzenstadler B, Prikladnicki R, Ruhe G, Schekelmann A, Sen S, Spínola R, Tuzcu A, De La Vara JL, Winkler D (2019) Status quo in requirements engineering: a theory and a global family of surveys. ACM Trans Softw Eng Methodol. 28(2):9:1–9:48

Wohlin C, Runeson P, Höst M, Ohlsson MC, Regnell B, Wesslén A (2012) Experimentation in software engineering. Springer, Berlin

Yamane T (1973) Statistics: an introductory analysis. Longman, New York

The Design Science Paradigm as a Frame for Empirical Software Engineering

Per Runeson, Emelie Engström, and Margaret-Anne Storey

Abstract Software engineering research aims to help improve real-world practice. With the adoption of empirical software engineering research methods, the understanding of real-world needs and validation of solution proposals have evolved. However, the philosophical perspective on what constitutes theoretical knowledge and research contributions in software engineering is less discussed in the community. In this chapter, we use the *design science paradigm* as a frame for articulating and communicating prescriptive software engineering research contributions. Design science embraces *problem conceptualization, solution (or artifact) design*, and *validation* of solution proposals, with recommendations for practice phrased as *technological rules*. Design science is used in related research areas, particularly information systems and management theory. We elaborate the constructs of design science for software engineering, relate them to different conceptualizations of design science, and provide examples of possible research methods. We outline how the assessment of research contributions, industry–academia communication, and theoretical knowledge building may be supported by the design science paradigm. Finally, we provide examples of software engineering research presented through a design science lens.

1 Introduction

Software engineering research aims to develop and validate practically useful methods, technologies, and tools to help industry improve software engineering practice. This practical aspect was discussed when the term "software engineering"

P. Runeson (✉) · E. Engström
Lund University, Lund, Sweden
e-mail: per.runeson@cs.lth.se; emelie.engstrom@cs.lth.se

M.-A. Storey
University of Victoria, Victoria, BC, Canada
e-mail: mstorey@uvic.ca

© Springer Nature Switzerland AG 2020
M. Felderer, G. H. Travassos (eds.), *Contemporary Empirical Methods in Software Engineering*, https://doi.org/10.1007/978-3-030-32489-6_5

was coined by Margaret Hamilton in the late 1960s,[1] and later put in print in a NATO conference report (Naur and Randell 1969, p. 13).

> The phrase 'software engineering' [implied] the need for software manufacture to be based on the types of theoretical foundations and practical disciplines that are traditional in the established branches of engineering.

Numerous solutions to software engineering problems have been proposed and published during the past few decades—these include development methods and processes, tools, frameworks, taxonomies, or languages—but few involve systematic investigations of real-world problem instances and validation by large-scale software practice.

With the advent of empirical software engineering (Basili et al. 1986) and evidence-based software engineering (Kitchenham et al. 2004), the research focus has shifted towards an empirically informed understanding of practice and solution proposals. Empirical methods have been inherited and adapted from other research fields, particularly medicine and the social sciences. Applying these methods, the software engineering knowledge base has been systematically extended through families of experiments (Basili et al. 1999) and systematic literature reviews (Kitchenham et al. 2015). However, the introduction of new research methods is rarely framed in a research paradigm explicitly, and as a consequence it is debated what constitutes a research contribution and how to assess it (Briand et al. 2017).

A *research paradigm* refers to "the combination of types of research questions asked, the research methodologies allowed to answer them, and the nature of the pursued research products" (Van Aken 2004). The goal of this chapter is to assist with the identification of theoretical research contributions, help assess these contributions, and communicate them to researchers and practitioners. We propose the *design science paradigm* as a frame to present and analyze software engineering research, rather than a prescription of methods on how to conduct it. Design science is elaborated by Hevner et al. (2004) for information systems, extended by Wieringa (2014a) into software engineering, which sources we here merge with perspectives from Van Aken (2004) in management theory. Software engineering is a socio-technical field, which integrates technical and managerial perspectives. As a consequence, this chapter is influenced from both perspectives, acknowledging the interdisciplinary characteristics of software engineering (Méndez Fernández and Passoth 2019).

The design science paradigm comprises *problem conceptualization, solution design*, and *validation*. We demonstrate how this paradigm fits as a frame for empirical software engineering research in order to provide theoretical knowledge about practical solutions for real-world software engineering challenges. In particular, multiple case studies are proposed as the typical research methodology to

---

[1] https://publications.computer.org/software-magazine/2018/06/08/margaret-hamilton-software-engineering-pioneer-apollo-11/.

gain design knowledge under the design science paradigm (Van Aken 2004), which aligns with the widespread use of case studies in software engineering (Garousi et al. 2019).

We provide an overview of the design science paradigm in Sect. 2, and a more in-depth elaboration of design science concepts in Sect. 3. In Sect. 4, we discuss how design science can be used to frame software engineering research and present a visual abstract template to help identify and assess theoretical contributions in software engineering. Section 5 explores some references to work with complementary views on design science, and Sect. 6 concludes this chapter.

2 Design Science: An Overview

There are three major research paradigms, according to Van Aken (2004):

- *formal sciences*
- *explanatory sciences*
- *design sciences*

A research paradigm is a philosophical perspective on the knowledge produced within a research field, using different research methodologies to answer research questions (Van Aken 2004). The *formal sciences* (e.g., philosophy and mathematics) focus on building internally consistent systems of knowledge. They are empirically void as the systems are not related to any empirical observation or validation. The *explanatory sciences* (e.g., the natural sciences and most of the social sciences) aim to describe and explain phenomena that exist, without and before any intervention. *Design sciences* (e.g., engineering sciences and medical sciences) aim to understand and improve human-made designs in an area of practice. The boundary between explanatory sciences and design sciences is not always clear as a research endeavor may contain elements explaining a naturally occurring phenomenon for which a proposed intervention is later designed and validated.

In this chapter, we view design science as a research paradigm that helps frame research and aims to improve an area of practice. In our case, the engineering of software is the practice area in focus. The software itself, the tools designed to support the engineers, as well as the organizations developing it, are human-made constructs. This speaks for design science being a feasible research paradigm for software engineering. On the other hand, some of the human behavior of software engineers and their stakeholders are related to intrinsic human capabilities and characteristics, which would speak for the explanatory science research paradigm. Still, we argue that many of the studied phenomena in software engineering are designed artifacts, and thus the research would benefit from being framed as design science.

The practice is not homogeneous over all kinds of software engineering research, neither are the potential improvements the same for all instances of practice. Thus, design science addresses general problems by studying specific *problem instances* in practice, which constitute the *research contexts*, and where the research activities of *problem conceptualization*, *solution design*, and *validation* take place, see Fig. 1. The cyclic process resembles basic engineering or quality improvement models like the Deming cycle (Deming 1986) and the quality improvement paradigm by Basili (1992).

The theoretical contributions of design science research, i.e., the prescriptions for practice, are context dependent. The scientific knowledge emanating from design science research consists of prescriptive recommendations typically captured in *technological rules*, i.e., "field-tested and grounded" exemplars of how a problem can be solved (Van Aken 2004). It is not claimed to be an optimal solution, but since it is field-tested and grounded, it is a feasible solution. As a consequence, the validation must be done in either a real-world context or an artificial context resembling aspects of the real one (Wieringa 2014a).

Other than the relation to context, design science does not prescribe specific method steps to be conducted in a research study. The above mentioned research activities (visualized in Fig. 1) are constituents of a research process that may be instantiated in different ways, using different research methods.

Further, a single study or research paper may or may not contain all the constituents of the design science paradigm. For example, one study may focus on problem conceptualization, whereas another may report the complete chain from problem conceptualization to a validated solution. Studies that focus on one aspect of design science may contain research contributions that build on, or constitute, the basis for other research under the design science paradigm.

Design science research aims to address real practice problems, and thus *problem conceptualization* is a core constituent of the research. This is typically, but not necessarily, the first step in a design science research endeavor. Understanding a general problem in terms of one or more concrete problem instances is a basis for understanding how this general problem may be solved. During the exploration of a specific problem instance, it may become clearer what the core of the problem is, thus focusing the potential solution design to these areas.

While problem conceptualization is a basis for the research activity, it is not a pure description of the problem. Under the design science paradigm, problems need to be conceptualized in terms of an envisioned solution. Thus, problem

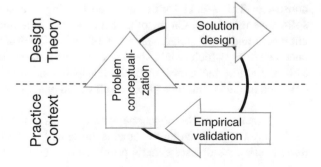

Fig. 1 A visualization of the types of research activities that take place in design science research. These activities may be instantiated in different ways

conceptualization is often intertwined with the creative activity of *solution design*, where alternative solutions and previous research are considered.

The primary goal of *empirical validation* is to assess whether the solution proposal is feasible for the problem instance. The scope of the design knowledge gained in a study can be extended by systematically extending the scope of the validation in subsequent studies. Thereby, the knowledge base of the research area is extended.

Design science is a paradigm used in many different research fields and it is instantiated in many different variants. The above summary reflects what we have found prevalent in software engineering. Some of our rationale and alternative instantiations are discussed below.

3   A Model of Design Science Research

Design science spans two major dimensions: the *problem–solution* dimension and the *theory–practice* dimension. To guide our in-depth elaboration of the design science paradigm, we extend the research activities model (Fig. 1) with design science contributions, see Fig. 2, where research activities under the design science paradigm can be expressed as transitions across this two-dimensional space.

The *practical* contribution of the research (i.e., the actual problem solving) is visualized by the boxes in the two bottom quadrants as instances of both the *problem* and the *solution*. The *theoretical* contribution (i.e., generalization and scope definition) is visualized in the two top quadrants in terms of the *technological rule(s)* and the corresponding *constructs*. The arrows in Fig. 2 illustrate knowledge creating activities that can be performed by both practitioners and researchers.

- *Problem conceptualization* refers to the activity of describing the problem;
- *Solution design* refers to the activity of mapping a problem to a general solution;
- *Abstraction* refers to the activity of identifying the key design decisions for a defined scope of validity of a solution;
- *Instantiation* refers to the activity of implementing the solution in context; and
- *Empirical validation* refers to an evaluation of how well the implemented solution addresses the problem.

These activities are performed iteratively across the theory–practice and problem–solution dimensions. Below we explore the contributions and activities of the design science model.

3.1   Technological Rules and Its Constructs

A technological rule captures generalized knowledge about mappings between instances of problems and solutions (i.e., in-context validations), and thus is a

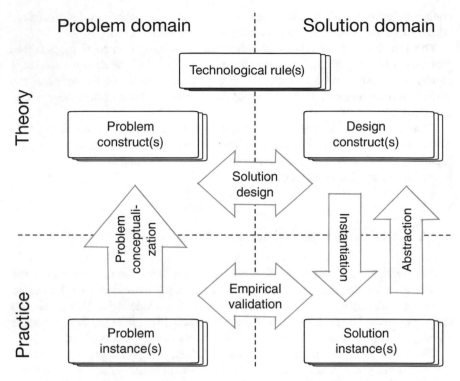

Fig. 2 Model of design science contributions in software engineering (Engström et al. 2020). The boxes represent theoretical and practical *contributions* of design science research, and the arrows represent *knowledge creating activities* that can be performed by both practitioners and researchers

means to transfer knowledge between contexts. The technological rule spans both a problem domain and a solution domain and is formulated based on constructs in both domains.

The scope of validity of the solution is described in terms of a *desired effect* of a *proposed intervention* in a particular *context*. Thereby, it frames the research outcome in terms of effects of interventions, rather than in terms of a solution to a problem. A technological rule can typically be expressed in the form:

To achieve <Effect > in <Context > apply <Intervention>.

The design knowledge within the technological rule aims to help software engineering professionals design customized solutions to their specific problems. Ideally it is a general recommendation based on current state of the art, including new research contributions.

The notion of technological rules comes from Bunge (1998), while different instantiations of design science name the theoretical contributions differently. Gregor and Hevner (2013) discuss them in terms of design theory and Wieringa (2009) defines them as "theories of artifacts in context." A thorough reflection about the role, nature, and need for technological rules in design science research is provided by Van Aken (2004).

In a technological rule, a class of software engineering problems is generalized to a stakeholder's desired effect of applying a potential intervention in a specified context. Making this problem generalization explicit helps the researcher identify and communicate the different value-creating aspects of a research study or program.

How the intervention in a technological rule is formulated may vary. It could, for example, refer to the use of a tool, articulate abstractions of the knowledge embedded in the tool, or even advise not to use the tool. It could also refer to the application of a practice, a technique, a framework, or a set of guidelines. We extracted 38 examples of technological rules from a set of distinguished ICSE-papers from 2014–2018 (Engström et al. 2020); these examples demonstrate the breadth of knowledge that can be represented using technological rules. These technological rules are available online in the visual abstracts for each distinguished paper at http://dsse.org.

One single instance of a problem–solution pair can generate multiple technological rules that are hierarchically related to each other. For example, an abstract rule may recommend using a general type of technology, while several more detailed rules may specify the use of technology, embedded in a specific tool. Similarly, there are hierarchical relationships with prior related technological rules to which a specific contribution is compared. However, technological rules expressed at a very high abstraction level (e.g., "To produce software of high quality, apply good software engineering practices") tend to be either trivial or too bold (easy to debunk), while rules at very low abstraction levels have a narrow scope, and thus lack relevance for most software engineers.

Thus, it is important to explicitly formulate the technological rule when presenting design science research and to be consistent with it, both when arguing for its relevance and its novelty, as well as when presenting the empirical (or analytical) support for the claims. A research contribution may refine any of the three constituents of an existing technological rule, add empirical support for the rule as a whole, or present a new rule.

Another type of theoretical knowledge produced in design science is the constructs on which we build technological rules. That is, the conceptualization of the problem domain and the solution domain, respectively. A construct can, for example, be a taxonomy that is used to articulate a technological rule or classify a set of technological rules in a research review. Taxonomies provide the means to relate different technological rules to each other. The different constituents of a technological rule may belong to different taxonomies. A construct can also be a conceptual model or a conceptualization approach that helps describe a problem in terms of an envisioned solution.

3.2 Problem Conceptualization and Solution Design

In a mature research field, existing theory may help practitioners design solutions for their specific problems. Problem conceptualization is then an act of the practitioner, as is the instantiation of the solution in a specific context. In fields where the theoretical foundation is less mature, such as software engineering, researchers and practitioners may work together to advance and extend the scope of the theory.

Above, we described how design knowledge is first obtained and later matures through observations of real-life instances of problem–solution pairs. For each such instance, the problem needs to be formulated (understood) according to a conceptual lens. Such problem conceptualization can take place in collaboration between practitioners and researchers in, for example, action research or case study research, or by researchers observing software engineering practice.

The outcome of the problem conceptualization is expressed in terms of problem constructs, matching corresponding constructs of an envisioned solution. If, for example, the proposed solution is to design a visualization system, the problem should typically be described in terms of a group of target users, their questions and tasks, and their measurements or data (Meyer et al. 2015). Thus, the problem conceptualization is tightly connected to the solution design and cannot be performed in isolation.

Depending on the type of solution, problem conceptualization may need to be repeated at several abstraction levels, starting with the stakeholder's problem description and, in case of a tool, reaching to the level of implementation details (such as choice of algorithm). If this is the case, different types of technological rules are used and validated at different abstraction levels. It is important to be aware of what these technological rules are, and to ensure that the validation of a solution takes place at all these levels and that the validations are mapped to the correct technological rules. Further, while solution design is a creative activity, the design knowledge it produces can be made more accessible and trustworthy if critical design decisions are clearly reported together with considerations about alternative solutions.

Finally, problem conceptualization is, to a large extent, in the eye of the beholder. A behavioral scientist would, for example, make a different problem conceptualization of a software project, compared to a software engineering researcher. Similarly, different software engineering researchers may be influenced by their background, emphasizing how problem conceptualization is intertwined with solution design.

3.3 Validation, Instantiation, and Abstraction

To validate a technological rule it must be instantiated, preferably in multiple cases of problem–solution pairs that instantiate the rule where each case adds to the validity strength of the rule. Alternatively, a new technological rule may be abstracted from an observed implemented solution applied to a real-life problem. The constituents of the technological rule implicitly specify the validation activities if expressed in the form of: *To achieve <Effect > in <Context > apply <Intervention>*.

The *intervention* is the object of the validation study, the *context* refers to where the research is conducted, and the expected *effect* defines the validation criteria. This points to real software engineering contexts as the ultimate validation context for design science research. Consequently, multiple case studies are brought forward as the natural research methodology in design science (Van Aken 2004). However, for some design problems, the characteristics of the real context may be very similar to the artificial context settings for the validation. For example, a tool which has no human–tool interaction can be evaluated with real or realistic data in an offline setting. In other cases, practical and economical limitations can prevent the research endeavor from taking place in real operational environments, and thus scaled down validation contexts may be used in the research.

The risks related to validating interventions in business critical contexts may be high. If the intervention does not deliver the effect as expected, the outcome of the software engineering activity as a whole may be endangered. Furthermore, the costs related to implementing the intervention may also be high (e.g., changing a work flow or adapting the information infrastructure to a new tool). Thus the validation procedures should gradually extend the validation scope for the intervention to manage these risks. However, reducing the scope and complexity of the validation context too much may reduce the realism, which is essential for addressing a relevant problem with a feasible solution. Studies in artificial contexts may be useful to validate specific mechanisms, but they are not feasible for complex systems studies.

Stol and Fitzgerald adapted Runkel and McGrath's framework for research strategies to guide balancing generalizability, precision, and realism in designing validation studies, see chapter "Guidelines for Conducting Software Engineering Research". This framework may be useful in choosing research strategies in relation to the goals of the research endeavor. The framework defines two dimensions: (1) universality/specificity of context and systems and (2) level of obtrusiveness, which have to be balanced, as discussed above.

The specific choice of methods for the validation depends on the research question. Easterbrook et al. (2008) provide guidance to the selection of methods for types of research question and conclude for the philosophical stance behind design science: "Pragmatists use any available methods, and strongly prefer mixed methods research, where several methods are used to shed light on the issue under study." This recommendation fits well with the design science paradigm and its pragmatist viewpoint.

Furthermore, the choice of validation methods depend on the abstraction level of the validation. Munzner (2009) illustrates this in a nested model for visualization design and validation, see Fig. 3. This model shows how one design science project must respond to validity questions at several levels of abstraction, and that it is important to be consistent when selecting validation methods to avoid a mismatch

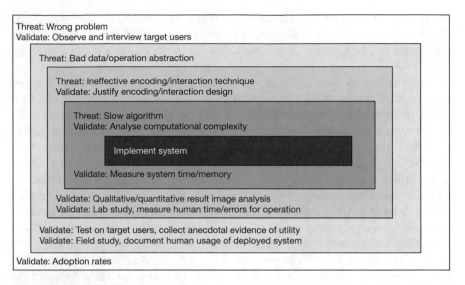

Fig. 3 Nested model for visualization design and validation (Munzner 2009). At each level there is a "black-box" to be tested. Above the box, validity threats are specified and examples of validation strategies for the problem conceptualization are proposed for that abstraction level, while validation strategies for the instantiation of the solution are proposed below the box

between levels. As discussed in Sect. 3.1, technological rules may be defined at all these different levels, and the scope of validity of each technological rule is defined by the context in terms of the conceptualization of the problem at the current abstraction level.

The design science paradigm primarily builds on theoretical/analytical generalizations, in contrast to explanatory sciences, which mostly rely on statistical generalizations (Runeson et al. 2012). Extending the scope of validity for a technological rule (i.e., creating a new, more general technological rule) is done by applying the intervention to new contexts, or by reasoning about the validity to another context by comparing key characteristics of the contexts. This is referred to as case-based generalization (Wieringa and Daneva 2015). Technological rules may also develop from the general to the specific. The research may start with a general technological rule which is refined as new knowledge is gained through the instantiation of the technological rule in multiple contexts.

3.4 Design Science Research in Practice

The design science paradigm may embrace the use of a multitude of research methods. For *problem conceptualization* and *validation* of technological rules, empirical research methods are used; however, methods supporting natural settings are preferred as the problem in context is a focus for design science research.

In a survey of 101 industry–academia collaboration projects, Garousi et al. (2019) found 75 that were characterized as case studies. Further, they note that "industrial case studies usually apply either the 'exploratory' or the 'improving' type, or both, rather than other case study types (descriptive, explanatory)." Methods for data collection and analysis can be selected from the rich plethora of options available for such studies, for example, interviews, focus groups, observational studies, archival data analysis, and software metric analysis.

Action research is another way of producing and validating technological rules. 41 of the 101 industry–academia collaboration projects surveyed by Garousi et al. (2019) were labeled as action research. However, action research does not explicitly aim to develop knowledge that can be transferred to other contexts, but rather to make a change in one specific local context. Nevertheless, both Wieringa and Moralı (2012) and Johannesson and Perjons (2014) discuss action research as one of several empirical methods that can be used to produce design knowledge.

Gorschek et al. (2006) define a "model for technology transfer in practice" focusing on industry–academia collaboration, which has some elements of design science. The model, which prescribes conceptual steps in solving a problem in an industry–academia collaboration setting, has elements of problem identification and conceptualization. The design of solutions involve studying the literature (state of the art) and selection of a candidate solution. This solution is validated in three steps, in academia, statically, and dynamically, before it is released into operations.

The elements of this model fit the design science frame, although it (by intention) focuses primarily on the intervention in the specific context rather than the generalized knowledge and technological rule, which are significant elements of design science research. Further, when the generalization of knowledge and iterative knowledge building is stressed, it becomes clear that industry–academia collaboration is not a one-way transfer of technology, but a mutual interaction between the two.

4   Using the Design Science Frame in Software Engineering

We designed a *visual abstract template* as a tool to analyze design science constructs in software engineering research (Sect. 4.1). We suggest three direct uses of the design science paradigm as a frame for software engineering research, which we illustrate through an example (Sect. 4.2). First, it can help in assessing contributions in research, both for the research community and during the planning and design of a research project (Sect. 4.3). Second, design science, particularly the technological rule, can be used in knowledge building, synthesizing and advancing the theoretical knowledge in the software engineering field (Sect. 4.4). Third, the design science frame may help in communicating research across the research community and with industry (Sect. 4.5).

4.1 A Template to Highlight Design Science Constructs

The design science perspective is rarely used explicitly to design and present software engineering research (Engström et al. 2020). We therefore designed a *visual abstract template* to help identify the design science constructs in software engineering research (Storey et al. 2017), see Fig. 4. We further extended the template with survey questions to help analyze software engineering literature from a design science perspective (Engström et al. 2020). The template aims to capture the key takeaway from a research study to help researchers assess the research contribution, build knowledge iteratively, and communicate research to practitioners.

Our design science template covers the main constructs of design science research: the theoretical contribution in terms of a *technological rule*; its instantiation in terms of a real *problem–solution* pair; the empirical or theoretical support for *problem* conceptualization and the *solution* design. Further, the bottom three boxes address the *relevance* of the research, the *rigor* of the research activities, and a statement about what makes the technological rule *novel* in relation to the underpinning research, be it with focus on a refined problem conceptualization, or a new or improved solution design, or a validation of the technological rule in a new context.

4.2 Design Science Example

To illustrate the use of the design science lens for software engineering research, we present and discuss an example by Jonsson et al. (2016), introducing automated bug assignment to handle a large inflow of bug reports. We have used the same example to illustrate our visual abstract (Storey et al. 2017), see Fig. 5.

The automated bug assignment research was not originally presented within the design science frame. However, like much software engineering research, it is implicitly conducted as design science research (Engström et al. 2020). The scientific knowledge gained from the work can be phrased as a *technological rule*:

> To achieve more effective assignment of bugs to teams in large scale industrial contexts, use ensemble-based machine learning to automate bug assignment.

The general *problem* of inefficient bug assignment is observed in the literature as well as in the specific industrial contexts where this research was conducted. With the solution in mind (to use machine learning techniques to assign bugs to teams), the characteristics of the defect data and the organizational context were explored, and thus identifying the characteristics of the *problem instance*. Related work on bug classification as well as on machine learning techniques was identified (Borg et al. 2014), which underpinned the *design decisions* for the

Fig. 4 Visual abstract template including the core constructs in the design science paradigm

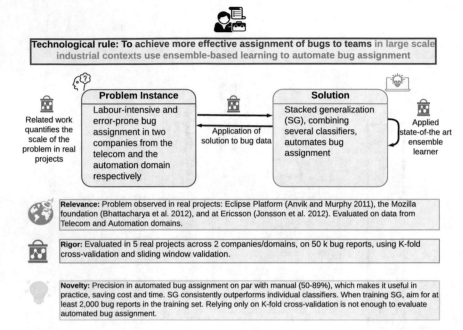

Fig. 5 Visual abstract for the paper on automated bug assignment (Jonsson et al. 2016)

proposed solution. The machine learning solutions were implemented and trained using the Weka framework (Hall et al. 2009). Several alternative solution instances were *validated* on real data (50,000 bug reports) from five projects across two companies/domains. For the specific companies, a design artifact was produced, namely the bug assignment tool built on top of Weka.

4.3 Assessment of Contributions

Hevner (2007) presents three research cycles in the conceptual model of design science, namely the *relevance*, the *rigor*, and the *design* cycles. We propose that the contributions of design science research be assessed accordingly with respect to *relevance, rigor*, and *novelty*. Assessment of research contributions can be conducted proactively (when relevance may be a primary concern for consideration, and before the research is executed), prospectively (as the research is ongoing and when rigor should be carefully considered), or retrospectively (where novelty of the design knowledge produced may become more evident). Below, we discuss assessments of contributions and refer to the example we described above.

4.3.1 Relevance

The relevance of a research contribution can be viewed from two perspectives: (1) from other practitioners that may benefit from the design knowledge produced and (2) from the research community.

From an individual practitioner's point of view, the relevance of a research contribution may be assessed by comparing its specific context with the study context described in the research report. Practitioners may need to consider whether the design knowledge can be applied to their specific context as is, or if it should be customized in some way, or if the knowledge does not apply to their context or problem at all. In the example by Jonsson et al. (see Fig. 5) a practitioner, that faces the challenge of manually assigning bugs to teams, could benefit from using ensemble-based machine learning to automate bug assignment (or not).

From the research community perspective, relevance is often considered in terms of how common the studied problem is, and how generalizable the produced design knowledge may be. Jonsson et al. (2016) report 20 previous studies on machine learning-based bug assignment, with different models for various bug report sets. To enable both types of assessments, relevant context factors need to be reported. Not all context factors are helpful in making this assessment, but only those that are critical for either the applicability of the solution or for the potential gain of applying the solution (Petersen and Wohlin 2009).

4.3.2 Rigor

Rigor of a design science study refers to the strength of the added support for the technological rule. It may be assessed in all of the three knowledge creating activities (problem conceptualization, design, and validation). Rigor should be considered when the research project is designed, as well as throughout and after the project to reflect on possible threats to validity. It is worth noting that the solution design activity is by nature a creative process and does not necessarily have to add to the rigor of the overall research.

One aspect of rigor in the design activity could be the extent to which a solution builds on prior design knowledge, or whether alternative solutions have been taken into account. In the case by Jonsson et al., they choose alternative classifiers from the Weka tool by reasoning about their properties and combined them into ensembles of classifiers for evaluation.

Rigor with respect to problem conceptualization and validation is based on common empirical methods that support relevant validity criteria, such as using structured and transparent research methods and using realistic data. For example, the study by Jonsson et al. can be considered high in rigor as the proposed solution is validated by its application to five defect datasets from two large software systems, comprising 50,000 bugs. Furthermore, they found that the precision in the automated bug assignment was on par with manual industry processes, which makes it scalable to practice.

4.3.3 Novelty

Novelty of a design science study is expressed in terms of new or refined technological rules. Technological rules may be expressed at several abstraction levels, thus it is always possible to identify an abstraction level at which a research contribution is novel, may it be at the cost of general relevance. In the research by Jonsson et al., novelty of the intervention proposed in the technological rule is not straightforward to assess, as there already exist 20 studies on machine learning to automate bug assignment. The novel contribution here is the systematic design and evaluation of a machine learning approach, applied to a real-world context, as expressed in the technological rule.

However, novelty may not always be a priority in a given research effort. To optimize rigor, novelty, and relevance of reported research, one should strive to express the technological rule at the highest possible abstraction level at which it is novel, the provided evidence gives strong support, and the technological rule is not debunked by previous studies (or common sense). However, adding empirical support for existing, but under-validated, technological rules has a value of its own (replication), which makes novelty less important than the rigor and relevance criteria.

4.4 Knowledge Building

Articulating the knowledge produced by our research in a more uniform way may help in building and synthesizing related knowledge in our community. The technological rules that emerge can at best be considered as theory fragments that prescribe and predict how a certain intervention for a particular context will lead to a proposed change. Our hope is that linking technological rules that are related (perhaps in hierarchical form) may help our community arrive at more general theories that can be refined and improved over time.

For example, Jonsson et al.'s research on automated bug assignment is related to previous bug assignment research, although it is hard to compare due to a lack of detail and inconsistent (or lack of) phrasing of technological rules. If the contributions were clearly expressed as technological rules with corresponding validation, the outcomes together would be more generalizable.

4.5 Research Communication

As we discussed above, building design knowledge in software engineering requires close partnership with practitioners. Practitioners may play a participatory role in our research by confirming and eliciting the problems to be solved, as well as by designing practical solutions using design knowledge and then validating them in context (on real problem instances). Consequently, how we communicate design knowledge to practitioners is critical to this participatory research approach.

We feel that technological rules will be valuable in communicating our findings to industry, and that the visual abstract may also appeal to those practitioners wanting to quickly gain a bigger picture of the research behind the design knowledge embodied by a technological rule. At the time of writing this chapter, we are in the process of evaluating our visual abstracts and in the future hope to evaluate them with practitioners.

Other initiatives for research communication include the SERP taxonomy architecture framework by Petersen and Engström (2014), which includes the constructs of a technological rule to support the mapping of practical problems with research. The SERP framework provides a taxonomy that establishes a common understanding between practitioners and researchers in software testing (Engström et al. 2017) and may support practitioners in their reviews of regression testing literature from a relevance point of view (Ali et al. 2019), which may lead to generalized recommendations in terms of technological rules.

Another attempt to make evidence available to practitioners is presented by Cartaxo et al. (2016). They present the concept of "evidence briefings," which is a way to summarize systematic literature reviews in a one-page format. They used accepted information design principles to design the structure of the one-page briefing. The format and content were positively validated by both practitioners and researchers. While evidence briefings may provide an effective way to synthesize evidence from several studies, our visual abstract template provides a means to effectively summarize the contribution of one study or research program from a design science perspective.

5   Recommended Further Reading

Several fields of research have explicitly framed their work under the design science paradigm. This chapter is based on critically appraising these fields and adopting what we have found feasible for software engineering. We present the main literature sources and recommend them for further reading to advance software engineering under the design science paradigm.

Hevner et al. (2004) and Hevner and Chatterjee (2010) have conceptualized design science for *information systems research*, combining behavioral science and design science research. The philosophical stance behind design science is what is characterized as pragmatism (Easterbrook et al. 2008), referring to a view that all knowledge is approximate and valued by its usefulness for solving practical problems. Hevner et al. (2004) express this in terms of *utility*:

> That is the essence of design science. Contribution arises from utility. If the artifact does not solve the problem (search, implementability), it has no utility. If utility is not demonstrated (evaluation), then there is no basis upon which to accept the claims that it provides any contribution.

Gregor and Hevner (2013) also refer to design science as a paradigm. Johannesson and Perjons (2014) disagree with this view and argue that design science refers to the objective of changing the world—in contrast to describing it—and that this is done primarily by creating artifacts, not knowledge. Johannesson and Perjons' view emphasizes design science as action research. Wohlin and Aurum (2015) also present design science as a methodology. As a consequence, they focus on the activities (how to conduct the research) rather than on the theoretical contributions of the research (how to theorize from the research), which is the case when it is considered a paradigm. However, there is a strong connection between the paradigm and the methodologies used. Our stance is that design science is a paradigm for software engineering research, and as researchers our primary goal is to create knowledge to be applied by practitioners in the field. Furthermore, we consider artifacts as embedding design knowledge.

Hevner (2007) adds three research cycles to the conceptual model of design science, namely the *relevance*, the *design*, and the *rigor* cycles. The relevance cycle connects the environment with the design science activities, the design cycle iterates between designing and evaluating the interventions, while the rigor cycle connects the research with the theoretical foundation of the research. We were inspired by Hevner's work when we added assessment criteria to the visual abstract template.

Van Aken (2005) explored the design science paradigm for management science, with a focus on theoretical contributions captured as technological rules. In the field of research with organizations as their study objects, Van Aken (2004) proposed making a distinction between explanatory and design sciences by dividing the research into two fields:

- Organization theory as description-driven research under the explanatory research paradigm, observing how organizations behave "naturally"; and
- Management theory as prescription-driven research under the design sciences paradigm, designing interventions to manage organizations.

We do not propose a corresponding distinction for software engineering, but rather call researchers to awareness of the existence of these different paradigmatic perspectives and their implications on the choice of research methodology and knowledge building.

The Nobel Prize laureate in Economics, Herbert A. Simon, used other terms for the distinction between explanatory and design sciences paradigms (Simon 1969). Design sciences are referred to as the "science of the artificial," in contrast to explanatory science as the "science of the natural." The latter refers not only to natural sciences in the narrow sense, but to other phenomena that seem to appear "naturally." In this broader sense, we may find both "natural" and "artificial" phenomena in software engineering, and thus may frame the research in different paradigms depending on the phenomenon under study.

Wierenga promoted design science for software engineering and information systems research in the concept of technical action research, including an engineering cycle and an empirical research cycle, which combine research with real-world consultancy projects (Wieringa and Daneva 2015; Wieringa and Moralı

2012; Wieringa 2014a). Further, to address the distinction between descriptive and prescriptive research, he introduces two types of research questions: *knowledge* questions and *improvement* questions (Wieringa 2009). He also discusses scaling up research to practice (Wieringa 2014b).

Munzner (2009) reviewed design science research in the field of visualization design and introduced a four-level nested model of design and validation, see Fig. 3. She divides the design process into four distinct stages and emphasizes the importance of distinguishing between these levels when claiming contributions at more than one level. The nested model is a good example of a design construct in the solution domain, i.e., visualization, providing a lens for problem conceptualization. Although not all software engineering problems are solved with visualization approaches, the model may inspire similar thinking in other design processes.

6 Conclusion

The design science paradigm is used in many fields of research that aim to understand and improve some area of practice. Software engineering researchers rarely use design science to frame their research explicitly, although our analysis showed that it resonates well with the aims of and research practice in software engineering (Engström et al. 2020).

There are many flavors of design science in related fields of research. In this chapter, we propose an instantiation of design science that we find suitable for the characteristics of software engineering research. We also present our visual abstract template, derived to help assess and communicate design science research (Storey et al. 2017).

We hope that the community will adopt the design science framework for software engineering research to provide better tools for researchers to define and assess relevance, rigor, and novelty of research, to assist communication between researchers and with practitioners, and to support continuous theoretical knowledge building in software engineering.

References

Ali NB, Engström E, Taromirad M, Mousavi MR, Minhas NM, Helgesson D, Kunze S, Varshosaz M (2019) On the search for industry-relevant regression testing research. Empir Softw Eng 24(4):2020–2055

Basili VR (1992) The experimental paradigm in software engineering. In: Rombach HD, Basili VR, Selby RW (eds) Proceedings of experimental software engineering issues: critical assessment and future directions, international workshop, Dagstuhl Castle, September 14–18, 1992. Lecture notes in computer science, vol 706. Springer, Berlin, pp 3–12

Basili VR, Selby RW, Hutchens DH (1986) Experimentation in software engineering. IEEE Trans Softw Eng 12(7):733–743

Basili VR, Shull F, Lanubile F (1999) Building knowledge through families of experiments. IEEE Trans Softw Eng 25(4):456–473

Borg M, Runeson P, Ardö A (2014) Recovering from a decade: a systematic map of information retrieval approaches to software traceability. Empir Softw Eng 19(6):1565–1616

Briand LC, Bianculli D, Nejati S, Pastore F, Sabetzadeh M (2017) The case for context-driven software engineering research: generalizability is overrated. IEEE Softw 34(5):72–75

Bunge M (1998) Philosophy of science: volume 2, from explanation to justification, 1st edn. Routledge, New Brunswick

Cartaxo B, Pinto G, Vieira E, Soares S (2016) Evidence briefings: towards a medium to transfer knowledge from systematic reviews to practitioners. In: Proceedings of the 10th ACM/IEEE international symposium on empirical software engineering and measurement, pp 57:1–57:10

Deming WE (1986) Out of the crisis. Massachusetts Institute of Technology, Center for Advanced Engineering Study, Cambridge

Easterbrook S, Singer J, Storey M-A, Damian D (2008) Selecting empirical methods for software engineering research. In: Shull F, Singer J, Sjøberg DIK (eds) Guide to advanced empirical software engineering. Springer, London, pp 285–311

Engström E, Petersen K, Ali NB, Bjarnason E, (2017) SERP-test: a taxonomy for supporting industry–academia communication. Softw Qual J 25(4):1269–1305

Engström E, Storey M-A, Runeson P, Höst M, Baldassarre M (2020) How software engineering research aligns with design science: a review. Empir Softw Eng. http://dx.doi.org/10.1007/s10664-020-09818-7

Garousi V, Pfahl D, Fernandes JM, Felderer M, Mäntylä MV, Shepherd D, Arcuri A, Coşkunçay A, Tekinerdogan B (2019) Characterizing industry-academia collaborations in software engineering: evidence from 101 projects. Empir Softw Eng 24(4):2540–2602

Gorschek T, Garre P, Larsson S, Wohlin C (2006) A model for technology transfer in practice. IEEE Softw 23(6):88–95

Gregor S, Hevner AR (2013) Positioning and presenting design science research for maximum impact. MIS Q 37(2):337–356

Hall M, Frank E, Holmes G, Pfahringer B, Reutemann P, Witten IH (2009) The WEKA data mining software: an update. ACM SIGKDD Explor Newsl 11(1):10–18

Hevner AR (2007) A three cycle view of design science research. Scand J Inf Syst 19(2):87–92

Hevner AR, Chatterjee S (2010) Design research in information systems: theory and practice. Springer, New York

Hevner AR, March ST, Park J, Ram S (2004) Design science in information systems research. MIS Q 28(1):75–105

Johannesson P, Perjons E (2014) An introduction to design science. Springer, Berlin

Jonsson L, Borg M, Broman D, Sandahl K, Eldh S, Runeson P (2016) Automated bug assignment: ensemble-based machine learning in large scale industrial contexts. Empir Softw Eng 21(4):1579–1585

Kitchenham BA, Dybå T, Jørgensen M (2004) Evidence-based software engineering. In: Finkelstein A, Estublier J, Rosenblum DS (eds) 26th international conference on software engineering (ICSE). IEEE Computer Society, Edinburgh, pp 273–281

Kitchenham BA, Budgen D, Brereton P (2015) Evidence-based software engineering and systematic reviews. Chapman and Hall/CRC, London

Méndez Fernández D, Passoth J-H (2019) Empirical software engineering: from discipline to interdiscipline. J Syst Softw 148:170–179

Meyer M, Sedlmair M, Quinan PS, Munzner T (2015) The nested blocks and guidelines model. Inf Vis 14(3):234–249

Munzner T (2009) A nested model for visualization design and validation. IEEE Trans Vis Comput Graph 15(6):921–928

Naur P, Randell B (1969) Software engineering: report on a conference sponsored by the NATO science committee. Technical report, Scientific Affairs Division, NATO, Brussels

Petersen K, Engström E (2014) Finding relevant research solutions for practical problems: the SERP taxonomy architecture. In: Proceedings of the 2014 international workshop on long-term industrial collaboration on software engineering. ACM, New York, pp 13–20

Petersen K, Wohlin C (2009) Context in industrial software engineering research. In: Proceedings of the third international symposium on empirical software engineering and measurement, ESEM 2009, October 15–16, 2009, Lake Buena Vista. IEEE Computer Society, Silver Spring, pp 401–404

Runeson P, Höst M, Rainer A, Regnell B (2012) Case study research in software engineering—guidelines and examples. Wiley, New York

Simon HA (1969) The sciences of the artificial. MIT Press, Cambridge

Storey M-A, Engström E, Höst M, Runeson P, Bjarnason E (2017) Using a visual abstract as a lens for communicating and promoting design science research in software engineering. In: ACM/IEEE international symposium on empirical software engineering and measurement (ESEM), pp 181–186

Van Aken JE (2004) Management research based on the paradigm of the design sciences: the quest for field-tested and grounded technological rules. J Manag Stud 41(2):219–246

Van Aken JE (2005) Management research as a design science: articulating the research products of mode 2 knowledge production in management. Br J Manag 16(1):19–36

Wieringa RJ (2009) Design science as nested problem solving. In: Proceedings of the 4th international conference on design science research in information systems and technology. ACM, New York, pp 8:1–8:12

Wieringa RJ (2014a) Design science methodology for information systems and software engineering. Springer, Berlin

Wieringa RJ (2014b) Empirical research methods for technology validation: scaling up to practice. J Syst Softw 95:19–31

Wieringa RJ, Daneva M (2015) Six strategies for generalizing software engineering theories. Sci Comput Program 101:136–152

Wieringa RJ, Moralı A (2012) Technical action research as a validation method in information systems design science. In: Peffers K, Rothenberger M, Kuechler B (eds) Design science research in information systems. Advances in theory and practice. Springer, Berlin, pp 220–238

Wohlin C, Aurum A (2015) Towards a decision-making structure for selecting a research design in empirical software engineering. Empir Softw Eng 20(6):1427–1455

Part II
Data Collection, Production, and Analysis

Biometric Measurement in Software Engineering

Fabian Fagerholm and Thomas Fritz

Abstract Biometric sensor technology provides new opportunities to measure physiological changes in the human body that can be linked to various psychological processes. In software engineering, these biometric measurements can be used to gain insights on fundamental cognitive and emotional processes of software developers while they are working. In addition, biometric measures may be used to provide better and more instantaneous tool support for developers, for instance, by preventing defects from being introduced in the code or supporting focused work. In this chapter, we motivate the use of biometric measurements, introduce common types of biometric sensors and measures, discuss how to choose the right set of them and considerations for analyzing the collected data. We also discuss work in the area of software engineering and recommend further reading.

1 Introduction

Software is built by humans. Software developers are the ones who develop and evolve code, who elicit requirements, test the software, and talk to their teammates to coordinate. Yet, traditionally, research has focused to a large extent on normative approaches to creating processes and artefacts–how developers ought to develop software–and on measuring output variables that are visible in the process and the development tools. While this focus on ideal work processes and developers' output can provide interesting and relevant insights, it falls short when the goal is to better understand the humans in the process, such as the cognitive demands and

F. Fagerholm (✉)
Aalto University, Espoo, Finland

Blekinge Institute of Technology, Karlskrona, Sweden
e-mail: fabian.fagerholm@aalto.fi

T. Fritz
Department of Informatics, University of Zürich, Zürich, Switzerland
e-mail: fritz@ifi.uzh.ch

© Springer Nature Switzerland AG 2020
M. Felderer, G. H. Travassos (eds.), *Contemporary Empirical Methods in Software Engineering*, https://doi.org/10.1007/978-3-030-32489-6_6

emotions they experience, and the individual differences between developers while they create and evolve the output data. Especially since these human aspects can have a significant effect on the output and its quality, such as a higher cognitive load leading to a higher error rate (Sweller 1988; Ayres 2001), the better we understand the human in the process, the better we can support the software development endeavour, and the better software quality we can achieve.

There are many ways we can measure the cognitive and emotional processes that are active while humans develop software. Some of these provide indirect means to gain more understanding, such as self-report measurements of happiness (Graziotin et al. 2018) or objective performance on cognitively demanding tasks. Recent advances in biometric (*aka.* psycho-physiological) sensor technology offer new opportunities to collect and examine a wide variety of direct, detailed data on a human and her cognitive and emotional states while she is working and developing software. The underlying idea is that a human's psychological states are linked to her physiological processes and that these physiological processes can be measured using biometric sensors. Research in psychology and other fields has already investigated and correlated certain biometric measures, including skin-, heart-, eye-, and brain-related metrics, with a human's cognitive and emotional states. For instance, researchers have found that pupil size and electrodermal activity (EDA) can be linked to cognitive load (Wilson 1992; Richter et al. 1998; Setz et al. 2010; Haapalainen et al. 2010; Iqbal et al. 2004).

Research in software engineering is also starting to take advantage of biometric measurements using a variety of sensor technology to examine cognitive processes among software developers. These studies range from the use of an eye tracker to capture a developer's eye fixations when reading or navigating code (Crosby and Stelovsky 1990; Bednarik and Tukiainen 2006; Sharif et al. 2012; Kevic et al. 2015), EDA wristbands, EEG sensors, or chest straps to capture skin conductivity as well as brain- and heart-related metrics to assess mental load and the experienced difficulty of the code (Nakagawa et al. 2014; Fritz et al. 2014; Müller and Fritz 2016), all the way to the use of functional magnetic resonance imaging (fMRI) and near-infrared spectroscopy (NIRS) to examine brain activation patterns during program comprehension (Siegmund et al. 2014; Ikutani and Uwano 2014).

As biometric sensor technology becomes less invasive, easier to integrate into the developer's work, cheaper, and more accurate, we are now able to capture more fine-grained biometric data of software developers in real-time and in real-life environments. These advances will not only allow us to better understand a developer while working, but also to develop and provide more instantaneous support to developers. For instance, by monitoring when a developer is experiencing a high cognitive load, we might be able to reduce interruptions by other co-workers at inopportune moments, or be able to intervene before a developer introduces a defect. Moreover, we will be able to gain a more fundamental understanding of software development that could lead to advances that we cannot imagine today.

Overall, the research results on the use of biometric measurements in software engineering already demonstrate the potential of this data. At the same time, there are still a lot of challenges to address before the use of biometric data can become widely accepted. These challenges range from the exact interpretation of the data, its noisiness, sensor limitations and invasiveness, to privacy concerns of the developers. For instance, low heart rate variability can generally be linked to a person's stress and high cognitive load, yet, when a low heart rate variability is detected, it is not straightforward to differentiate whether this is due to stress, a high cognitive load, or both. Another example is the limitation and noisiness of current low-invasive heart rate sensors that use optical sensing. Since an optical sensor is affected by movements or changes in the environmental lighting, it is difficult to accurately and reliably capture heart rate variability data with such sensors, especially when they are integrated into wristbands and users move around a lot.

This chapter introduces some common types of biometric sensors and measures that have been used in software engineering research, discusses some of the challenges involved in such research, and gives examples of research in the area. Throughout the chapter, we use a motivating example to illustrate how the information in the chapter could be applied in real-life software development.

2 Motivating Example

To illustrate the potential value of biometric data, we will sketch out and highlight a few scenarios of a team developing software. This team, which is part of a larger software development organisation, has three developers: *Mary*, a senior developer with 10 years of professional experience in Java backend development; *Joe*, an experienced developer with 5 years of professional experience on full stack development including JavaScript and Java amongst others; and *Sam*, a new hire fresh out of school with some experience in Java and JavaScript development. All three developers are working together to finish the next version of their software application within a month. While the first 2 weeks were pretty much free of any time pressure, now that they are a week away from the milestone, the time pressure is slowly picking up a bit. This may influence some important psychological processes:

Stress.   Joe's eighth-month-old son has had a fever for the past week and has not been sleeping well. Since Joe and his wife alternate nights to take care of their son, Joe has been getting a lot less sleep at home than usual and therefore is feeling more and more stressed about the approaching milestone at work and getting everything done. As studies in psychology have shown, increased stress often leads to an increased error rate, and the lack of sleep additionally makes it harder for Joe to concentrate and work for extended periods of time.

Stress generally evokes a physiological response, such as higher blood pressure, an increase in perspiration (also known as sweating), or a decrease in the variability of the heart rate. Biometric sensor technology can be used to capture these physiological responses, such as a wristband to measure electrodermal activity or a chest strap to measure heart rate variability. By using such sensors, one might be able to continuously monitor the stress level of a person and then use this information to support them in their work. Some possible ways of supporting could be to suggest taking more breaks, reassigning tasks, or recommending additional code reviews to lower the chances of errors being committed to the project.

Cognitive Load. Due to the time pressure in the current iteration cycle, each developer is supposed to help with any open tasks. Therefore, it happened that Sam picked up a task that requires changes to the Java backend. While Sam is working on the task, he experiences a high cognitive load due to the lack of expertise in Java development and the backend as well as the complexity of the existing code that he has to change.

As studies in psychology have shown, a high cognitive load is often linked to certain physiological responses, such as a higher pupil dilation, less eye blinks, and a lower heart rate variability (HRV). By using an eye tracking sensor or a HRV sensor, we might be able to track the cognitive load and determine when the developer is experiencing difficulties and intervene before he introduces a defect. At the same time, by measuring the difficulty that all developers on the team have when they are working on specific parts of the code, we might be able to determine which parts of the code base are more or less challenging, hinting at where the technical debt is higher and where refactoring might provide the biggest benefits.

Availability for Interruptions. As in all office environments, the developers of this team are often interrupted by their co-workers from both their own team and teams from other parts of the organisation. When these interruptions happen at inopportune moments, such as a developer being very focused on the task and memorising a lot of relevant context for the task in her head, or the developer being very engaged in the task, the interruptions can lead to a steep increase in the time needed to complete the tasks, heightened frustration for the developer, and an increased error rate, as studies have shown (Bailey et al. 2001; Czerwinski et al. 2000; Mark et al. 2008).

Similarly to cognitive load and stress, this focus on and engagement in the task might express itself in physiological responses that can then be measured using biometric sensor technology. By continuously monitoring the relevant biometric measure, we might be able to indicate to co-workers the developer's availability for interruptions (*aka.* interruptibility) and thereby help to shift the interruptions to more opportune moments.

Common to all of these scenarios is that there are individual differences between the developers that influence the process of developing software and the end result of it. These range from individual characteristics—such as temperament and personality, how the individual is affected by time pressure, and their level of expertise—to social characteristics—such as the overall stress level at work and at home, the amount of support received by co-workers and the organisation at large, and the consequences of success and failure. By only focusing on the output, it is difficult to detect these individual differences that influence both the developers' experience and the outcomes of the development endeavour. By using biometric measurements that can be captured in real-time, we might be able to intervene earlier and better support the human in the process.

3 Biometrics or Psychophysiology

Biometric data generally denotes measurements made on some part of the human body. These measurements could, for example, be used to identify and authenticate an individual, such as a fingerprint, a voice, or a DNA sample. In this chapter, we focus more specifically on measurements made on some part of the human body that are linked to various psychological processes, such as performing cognitive tasks or experiencing emotions. This type of biometric data is also often referred to as psycho-physiological data. In the following, we will use the term biometric data and psycho-physiological data interchangeable to denote this kind of data.

Biometric data is usually structured as time-series data and is analysed for changes in response to a stimuli, such as a task, a piece of code, a diagram, an emotion inducing picture, or something else that has relevance for what is being studied.

3.1 Examples of Biometric Sensors and Measures

Many different physiological measurements are used in research today due to their ability to reveal more about what goes on in a person's mind. In software engineering research, such measures have commonly been used to determine what a person is paying attention to in a cognitively demanding task, how much the task occupies their mental capacity, or to what extent the task triggers an emotional response. Physiological measurements can roughly be categorised by the origin of the measurement: eye-, skin-, brain-, heart-, and breathing-related measurements. Table 1 presents an overview of some of these measures and the psychological states and processes they have been linked to in previous research, predominantly in psychology. In the following we briefly discuss how a few selected physiological measurements and sensors work in principle.

3.1.1 Eye-Related Measurements

The inner workings of the mind can be probed by measuring how various eye muscles contract. By taking advantage of this psycho-physiological fact, eye tracking hardware and software have developed to a level where accurate and fine-grained measurements of the eye can be made in a minimally invasive way.

Table 1 Overview of several physiological measures and previously linked states and processes (see also Fritz and Müller 2016)

Measure	Previously linked to
Eye-related	
Eye gaze	Cognitive load (Ikehara and Crosby 2005); valence (Carniglia et al. 2012)
Pupillary response	Cognitive and mental load (Haapalainen et al. 2010; Iqbal et al. 2004); excitement (Muldner et al. 2010)
Eye-blink rate	Mental workload (Brookings et al. 1996); frustration, stress, anxiety (Kapoor et al. 2007; Doehring 1957)
Skin-related	
Electrodermal activity (EDA)	Valence, arousal, engagement (Haag et al. 2004; McDuff et al. 2012); frustration (Freeman 1940; Kapoor et al. 2007); stress and cognitive load (Setz et al. 2010)
Skin temperature	Task difficulty (Anthony et al. 2011); valence, arousal (Haag et al. 2004); boredom, engagement, anxiety (Chanel et al. 2008)
Brain-related	
EEG frequency bands	Mental workload (Brookings et al. 1996); valence, arousal (Sammler et al. 2007; Reuderink et al. 2013; Lin et al. 2010); happiness and sadness (Li and Lu 2009); task engagement (Kramer 1991)
Heart-related	
Heart rate (HR)	Mental load and effort (Richter et al. 1998; Veltman and Gaillard 1998); valence, arousal (Haag et al. 2004; Sammler et al. 2007); positive/negative affect (Drachen et al. 2010); happiness (Steptoe et al. 2005)
Heart rate variability (HRV)	Mental effort (Veltman and Gaillard 1998); task difficulty (Walter and Porges 1976); anxiety (Rani et al. 2004); various emotional states (McCraty and Tomasino 2006)
Blood volume pulse (BVP)	Cognitive load (Peper et al. 2007); various emotions (Picard et al. 2001); valence, arousal (Haag et al. 2004)
Breathing-related	
Respiratory rate	Mental effort (Veltman and Gaillard 1998); task difficulty (Kuznetsov et al. 2011)

Eye tracking can be divided into three common measurements: eye gaze, pupillary responses, and eye-blink rate. Each of these provides information on what the human mind is doing, and when combined with specific tasks in carefully designed study set-ups, they can be used to gain understanding of where the person is focusing their attention and how their mind is processing the information that the eye sees.

Eye gaze contains information on what a person is looking at. Many studies corroborate the fact that a person's eyes are generally directed towards the object that their attention is directed to. This means that to some extent, knowing what a person is looking at gives hints about what they are thinking about.

Eye gaze is commonly measured by an infrared camera that detects reflections on the outermost surface of the eye—the so-called corneal reflections. Automatic analysis of the reflection allows the eye tracking device to determine which direction the eye is looking in, to calculate the angle of the eye, and, with the correct calibration, to determine what the eye is looking at.

Eye gaze may be used to calculate *gaze points*, which are the individual samples of what the eye looks at, and which form the base unit of eye gaze measures. If the gaze is held for a long enough duration, this can be interpreted as a *fixation* where the eyes are locked on towards a specific object—giving indications of things like attention and the time required to process what is seen. While fixations are the periods of time when the eye is fixated on a specific object, *saccades* refer to the quick moving of the eye gaze between fixations. Gaze point data may be combined to yield information on the eye gaze sequences used when performing a task. A correctly designed study protocol can use such sequences to infer how properties of the task influence what visual information the study participant focuses on and how she processes it—for example, in terms of how long the person looks at different parts of the visual stimuli.

Pupillary responses or changes in pupil size are caused by two muscles in the eye. One of these, the contracting muscle, receives input from brain systems that respond to light. However, both muscles also receive inputs from areas that are involved in cognitive and autonomic functions. This means that cognitive and autonomic activities influence pupil diameter, and it is possible to gain information on these processes by measuring the pupil. In simple terms, mental exertion leads to dilatation of the pupil, and so the pupil response can be used to infer the level of mental effort.

Pupillary response is commonly measured by an infrared camera that takes into account the distance to the person's eyes. Pupil tracking is already necessary to obtain eye gaze information, and the same algorithms that detect and track the pupil in the overall image are used here.

Eye-blink rate, meaning the frequency at which the eyelids spontaneously open and close, is an indirect measure of dopamine activity in the central nervous system. Dopamine is an important neurotransmitter that is involved in many cognitive and affective functions, such as learning, working memory, and goal-oriented behaviour. The eye-blink rate thus provides clues on what is going on in a person's mind in terms of controlling impulses, maintaining long-term goals, and flexibly adapting to changing rules in the environment.

When the eye is closed, an eye tracker cannot determine the eye gaze or pupillary response. Modern eye trackers include functionality that allows to distinguish eye blinks from other kinds of data loss—such as head movements that prevent the tracker from detecting the eyes.

Eye tracking has several advantages as a research instrument. Sampling rates of commercially available eye tracking devices range from 25 to 2000 measurements per second, meaning that very accurate timing information is available. Eye tracking devices can be completely non-invasive, being attached to a computer monitor, or minimally invasive, in the form of special eye glasses worn by study participants. This means that participants can be observed in quite natural environments and can freely move around. The portability of the devices also means that they can be brought to participants in their own environment rather than having participants visit a lab. Although eye tracking devices have become much more sophisticated in recent years, eye tracking data must always be carefully examined to rule out errors due to changing light conditions, miscalibration, and other sources of errors.

3.1.2   Skin-Related Measurements

Commonly used skin-related measurements are skin temperature and electrodermal activity (EDA). We will focus on EDA in the following.

Electrodermal activity (EDA) is a property of the human skin that causes a continuous variation in its electrical characteristics. More specifically, the ability of the skin to conduct electricity varies and is linked to the level of psychological or physiological arousal of a person. By measuring electrical properties such as resistance, it is possible to infer, e.g., the level of stress experienced by a person. Since EDA is not under voluntary control, it offers a degree of direct insight into the autonomous regulation of emotions. However, measuring EDA at different locations of the body yields different results, and EDA responses are delayed 1–3 s, meaning that it is not straightforward to determine mental activity from an EDA signal. The EDA signal can generally be split into two parts: the slowly changing, low frequency, tonic part and the fast adapting, high frequency, phasic part (Schmidth and Walach 2000). Commonly used metrics for the tonic part are the mean value or the area under the curve (AUC), while commonly used features for the phasic part are related to the peaks in the signal.

3.1.3   Brain-Related Measurements

Measuring activity of the brain can be done in various ways and the measurements that can be captured depend heavily on the device that is being used. These devices vary in the kind, accuracy, and granularity of the data they capture, but also in their invasiveness which limits the kinds of studies that can be performed.

Electroencephalography (EEG) is a method to record electrical activity in the brain. Electrodes placed on the scalp of a participant measure voltage fluctuations that reflect neural activity. When the electrodes are placed correctly, the multiple signals from the many electrodes can be analysed to provide information on activity in different brain regions. This information may be used to investigate cognitive processes. Commonly used measures retrieved from an EEG are brain wave frequency bands that are called alpha (α), beta (β), gamma (γ), delta (δ), and theta (θ). Each of these brain wave frequency bands has a specific frequency range and amplitude and exhibits more or less activity under different stimuli. For example, alpha waves can typically be observed when an individual is in a relaxed state, but the alpha waves either disappear or their amplitude decreases significantly as soon as the physical or mental activity increases (Andreassi 2007).

EEG has a low spatial resolution, meaning that it can only provide rough information on activations in different brain regions. However, it has high temporal resolution, is less invasive than other sensor technologies, and can be quite mobile and therefore used in situations where participants are moving.

Functional magnetic resonance imaging (fMRI) provides information on the brain activity by measuring changes in blood flow in the brain. When an area of the brain is in active use, blood flow in that area increases. Using fMRI, it is possible to investigate which areas are activated by a stimulus. This may be used to gain knowledge of how participants process the stimulus.

fMRI requires sophisticated equipment and fMRI devices are large and not portable, meaning that participants must visit a research lab to take part in studies. In addition, fMRI generally requires the person to lay still without moving much, and the display that study participants in an fMRI study can look at is also quite small, which limits the kinds of tasks that can be studied with an fMRI significantly.

Functional near-infrared spectroscopy (fNIRS) uses electrical signals close to the infrared wavelengths to detect the composition of materials. As a biosensor, fNIRS works by detecting oxygen saturation in brain tissue. As with fMRI, when a brain region is in active use, blood flow in that region increases, and fNIRS detects this as increased oxygen saturation. A fNIRS device provides more mobility than an fMRI device, but while fMRI can monitor activity in the entire brain, fNIRS is limited to the cortical areas.

3.1.4 Heart-Related Measurements

Commonly used heart-related measurements are the *heart rate (HR)*, the *heart rate variability (HRV)*, and the *blood volume pulse (BVP)*. The heart rate refers to the number of contractions of the heart each minute and the heart rate variability represents the variation in the time interval between two consecutive heart beats. The blood volume pulse measures the blood flow through specific parts of the body and may change when the sympathetic nervous system increases its activity, for instance, because of stress (Andreassi 2007). Common features of these measurements are the mean heart rate, the mean and the standard deviation of the time between two heart beats, and features that capture the peaks of the BVP signal.

Today, there are various ways to capture heart-related measurements that again vary in the kind, granularity, and accuracy of the data captured. The devices range from commonly used wrist watches, such as the Apple Watch,[1] that capture heart rate using an optical sensor, to chest straps or arm bands, all the way to

---

[1] https://www.apple.com/watch/.

electrocardiograms that use specific electrodes. Especially the kind of sensor used and the location of the sensor(s) affect the accuracy of the measurements. For instance, capturing accurate HRV data with a wrist watch using an optical sensor is difficult at best: first the wrist is generally used and moved a lot and second, wrist watches are often not tightly fixated to the wrist such that the optical sensor moves around a lot.

Electrocardiography An electrocardiogram (EKG) is a recording of the electrical activity of the heart over time. Electrodes placed on the skin measure small electrical changes that occur when the heart is beating. EKG data may be used to measure physiological arousal connected to a stimulus. If the stimulus increases heart rate, it may be inferred that they are experiencing an emotion—but to determine which emotion, more information is needed, such as a self-report instrument.

3.2 Biometric Sensing

Physiological measurements captured by biometric sensors have the potential to tell us more about the human in the process of developing software and to do so in real-time. Yet, there are several points to be considered before using biometrics for studying or supporting software developers. Some of the most prominent of these points are the choice of the biometric sensor or the physiological measurement, the individual differences in the measurements, the processing of the data, and how to best use them for a study or in the field.

3.2.1 Choosing the Right Measurement and Sensor

Gaining insight into the minds of software developers requires careful selection of research instruments. However, picking a biometric sensor will not automatically result in new insights or practically applicable methods. Everything begins with the formulation of research questions or hypotheses informed by existing research and theory, as with any other kind of empirical research (see, for example, chapters "The Evolution of Empirical Methods in Software Engineering", "Guidelines for Conducting Software Engineering Research", and "Data Science and Empirical Software Engineering"). Without these, the collected data cannot answer any specific questions and is likely to be useless.

The right measurement must thus be informed by an understanding of psychophysiology. In our example, we can observe that Joe is experiencing a state of heightened stress and sleep deprivation, which likely decreases his performance at work. His body will show physiological signs of stress, which can be measured, e.g., by heart sensors or EDA. This could be the basis of a study that tries to associate physiological measures of stress with software development outcomes such as error rate or problem-solving ability.

There are other factors weighing in on the selection of biometric sensors, including the environment and scenario the sensors should be used for, the invasiveness and comfort of the sensor, privacy concerns with the collected data, the required accuracy and granularity of the measurements, and the accessibility of the data and sensor. First, the *environment and scenario* that the sensors should be used in limits the choices of sensors. For example, if the study set-up requires an authentic workplace environment the mobility of the sensors plays an important role. So while an fMRI sensor is perfectly reasonable for running precise lab studies and provides very fine-granular data, it is not possible to be used in a realistic setting within open office of a software development company. An eye tracker attached to a computer monitor, on the other hand, can be easily installed even in the workplace without restricting the developer's work, but will also only capture when the developer looks at the screen and not when she might be sketching out some design ideas on a sheet of paper.

Second, and closely related to the first is the *invasiveness and comfort* of the sensor. Sensors placed on the fingers might disturb the normal use of a keyboard and mouse, and may be unsuitable for many software development study tasks. EEG sensors will not disturb the normal use of a keyboard and mouse, but usually require time to set up, be properly placed, might require the user to not walk around too much, and can also cause discomfort to the participants, which is a problem both from an ethical perspective and in terms of potentially biasing the study results.

Third, *privacy concerns* should be taken into account—biometric data is considered to be among the most sensitive types of data about a person, and steps should be taken to carefully protect study participants. Responsible researchers should think ahead about whether their research leads to greater insights and beneficial applications, or if there is a possibility of misusing the data or results for purposes that put humans at risk.

Fourth, the *accuracy and granularity* of the measurements plays an important role. While there is already a large number of sensors to capture a variety of physiological measurements, many of them might not provide the accuracy and granularity that is required for the specific research question under investigation and that was linked to cognitive states and processes in previous research. For instance, there was and is a number of wristbands to capture heart-related measures that use an optical sensor. However, due to the often loose placement of the wristband and the sensor, the captured data can be very noisy and while that might be sufficient for measuring heart rate, it is often not accurate enough to measure heart rate variability.

Finally, *accessibility* of the data provided by the sensor technology also affects the choice of the sensor. For instance, while some biometric sensors might capture the data with the required granularity and sampling rate, the data that researchers have access to can be more limited in terms of the granularity or also the timeliness. Some of the reasons for this limited data access are the goal to reduce the data that needs to be stored and transferred from the often wireless sensor to another device, or the original purpose for the design of the sensor and the limitations in the provided API. An additional factor to keep in mind when choosing a sensor is the continuous support for these sensors. While the market for these technologies is increasing, we are still in the earlier stages of biometric sensing technologies and not all sensor technologies survive, such as the Microsoft Band, to take a prominent example.

3.2.2 Dealing with Noisy Data and Individual Differences

Biometric sensors are by nature *noisy and prone to data loss*. Most devices do some basic filtering of the raw physical signals, but the digital data collected is not ready for analysis as such. Every sensor is susceptible to calibration errors, missing data, noise, or even the weather (Cacioppo et al. 2007). As far as possible, it makes sense to try to minimise error sources already while collecting data. This might mean placing some restrictions on how the participant can move or reducing the amount of disturbances in the environment.

Having the raw digital data potentially poses a need for noise reduction. Often, the biometric sensor manufacturer has instructions and recommendations for how to obtain a cleaner signal. This may include a correction factor that is provided with the digital output of the device itself, or there may be averaging or algorithmic filtering approaches that should be used.

Physiological measures are also inherently *individual*. While this characteristic of physiological measures allows us to measure and focus on the individual, we also have to pay more attention when comparing data across individuals since the physiological response to certain stimuli can vary significantly across individuals. Let us take heart rate as an example: an individual that is athletic and does sports several times a week most likely has a lower base heart rate than an individual who is sedentary most of the week and additionally the range of the heart rate values will be different. In this case, we cannot directly compare the heart rate with each other. Instead, we have to independently capture a baseline for each individual's heart rate, and then for the periods of interest calculate the difference between the individual's heart rate and her baseline. However, even that is not enough since the range of the heart rate values can vary a lot and we often have to capture the range of individual's heart rate (at least for the states of interest) and then use this to normalise the data to better compare it between individuals. Also, when we measure individuals on a controlled and short task, we might have to take into account and control for certain characteristics, such as their daily rhythm and the participant being a morning or evening person (Levandovski et al. 2013), that can have an impact on the captured measures. Finally, for certain individuals it might not be possible to capture certain physiological measures.

3.3 Analyzing Biometric Data

Since a lot of biometric data comes in the form of time-series data, appropriate time-series analysis methods should be used. Here, the study design will inform the selection and application of analysis methods. In the following, we will discuss some of the usual steps; however, the concrete steps and order depends on the usage scenario of the biometric data.

One step performed frequently in addition to the cleaning of the data is *data segmentation and labelling*. In case of an explicit stimuli in the study design, one often requires an external timing source, such as a video or screen recording or an automatic signal, that can be used to determine when the stimuli has been displayed, changed, or appeared during the study. This way, there is an objective anchor point in time that can be used to segment and label the data, and that allows to compare the biometric data with and without (or with a different) stimuli. If the study design does not rely on synchronised presentation of a stimuli, other means of analysis are necessary. One approach that is often used is to collect self-reports from individuals for certain points in time or time periods that can then be used for segmentation and data labelling. Another approach is to use objective task data and have participants perform multiple tasks, in which case the task periods can be used for segmentation and the objective measures can be used for labelling.

A further step in the analysis is *feature extraction*. Generally, we are only interested in specific features of the physiological data. For instance, for heart rate data, we might be interested in the mean and the standard deviation, for EDA data one might be more interested in features related to the peaks in the signal. Previous literature, especially in psychology, can help to determine which feature might be best for a specific use case. In addition, we have to choose specific time windows for extracting and calculating features. The time window choice depends on the kind of physiological measure, the stimuli, and other factors and can be quite challenging, especially since the optimal time window for extracting a feature might even vary across participants.

In many cases, biometric data is used to *build a machine learning model* that can be used to determine which biometric features are best to classify or predict certain states. For this step, the data has to be split into training and test data and depending on the evaluation, e.g., cross-validation or leave-one-out, different methods for splitting have to be considered. It is thereby important to ensure that the training and test data, and in general the individual data points, do not overlap and are independent of each other. For biometric data, we have to pay special attention to this independence since physiological features of an individual can be affected for a long time by a certain stimuli. Therefore, we might have to consider adding periods of rest or longer breaks in between tasks or time segments to ensure that the effect of the stimuli has worn off. As with non-biometric data, another challenge in training a machine learning classifier for a specific use case is the selection of the features to be used. Depending on the machine learning method applied, different feature selection methods can be chosen. Given the often large number of possible biometric features (also based on the various time windows that can be used to extract the features), it can be challenging to determine an optimal set of features.

Ultimately, using biometric measurements in software engineering requires an understanding of phycho-physiology, operational knowledge of the biometric devices, data analysis skills, skills in study design, and an understanding of the real-life tasks that software developers carry out in their work.

4 Work in the Area

Biometric sensor data has been used in software engineering research for various purposes. Some of this research addresses questions that contribute to an improved understanding of the individual in the process of developing software, while other research explores how biometric sensor data could be used to build new tools and support the developer. Yet other research explores the sensor data itself and tries to understand what type of sensor data or combination thereof works best for detecting certain states of a developer or for studying specific types of tasks. In the following, we will focus on three areas of research: using eye tracking to understand developer's code comprehension, examining developers' brains with fMRI or EEG, and more general sensing of specific aspects of developers, such as experienced task difficulty or their emotions.

Overall, the research in this area is increasing and is helping to better understand software developers in their activities which can then be used to improve tool design. Furthermore, the real-time measurement and prediction of aspects such as a developer's cognitive load when reading code can be used to build novel tool support, for instance, to predict code difficulty and which code to refactor, to avoid bugs from being committed, and to signal the interruptibility to co-workers and avoid expensive interruptions.

4.1 Tracking Developers' Eyes in the Code

Some long-standing questions in software engineering research have to do with source code and how developers read and comprehend source code. Since developers spend significant amounts of time on reading and writing source code, various methods have been used to study developers during these activities, and more recently with the help of eye tracking.

Several studies have used eye tracking to examine how developers read algorithms and source code, what they focus on most when reading code snippets, and how the reading of code compares to reading natural text, e.g., Crosby and Stelovsky (1990), Busjahn et al. (2015), Rodeghero et al. (2014), Uwano et al. (2006). One of the interesting findings is that reading natural text happens largely linearly, in western languages, left-to-right and top-to-bottom. For source code, eye tracking has revealed that the reading is different and that experts read source code in a less linear manner than novices (Busjahn et al. 2015). Another finding is that initial code segments (e.g., in a function) are read more times and receive more focus, while later parts may only be skimmed (Jbara and Feitelson 2017).

Eye tracking has also been used to investigate how developers perform change tasks (Kevic et al. 2015), code reviews (Chandrika et al. 2017; Begel and Vrzakova 2018), and to trace requirements through the software life cycle (Sharif et al. 2017). These examples show the great diversity of research topics that may be addressed with eye tracking.

4.2 Examining Developers' Brains

Recently, researchers have started to look deeper into the brain using fMRI to investigate program comprehension. For example, in a study using fMRI, researchers found that that program comprehension was associated with a specific activation pattern in five brain regions related to working memory, attention, and language processing (Siegmund et al. 2014; Peitek et al. 2018). In another fMRI study, Siegmund et al. found evidence of semantic chunking during bottom-up code comprehension—when a developer has to interpret every individual program statement to form an understanding of the program—and found that semantic cues, such as method signatures and common programming idioms, ease comprehension (Siegmund et al. 2017). Floyd et al. further used fMRI to examine the difference between reviewing code and English prose and found that the neural representations of programming and natural language are distinct and that they are affected by expertise (Floyd et al. 2017).

The high spatial resolution of fMRI allows researchers to pinpoint precise areas that are activated in the brain. In contrast, EEG measurements are less invasive to collect and have lower spatial resolution but much higher temporal resolution, allowing studies to be more precise in terms of timing. In one EEG study, it was shown that brain measures of cognitive load could quantify programming experience among students—in terms of the state of progression through an undergraduate computer science program—and self-reported experience level (Crk et al. 2015). Code comprehension has also been investigated using EEG. A study identified EEG signatures specific to code comprehension and found neural correlates of subjective difficulty during code comprehension by using study participants' ratings of the tasks they had to perform in the study (Kosti et al. 2018).

4.3 Sensing Developers

One of the earliest approaches in the software engineering domain mentioning biometric sensing is the Ginger2 environment by Torii and colleagues that talked about the use of an eye tracking and a skin resistance level sensor to empirically study developers (Torii et al. 1999). Since then, there is an increasing amount of studies that examine further aspects of developers and/or combine various physiological measures and sensors. Several studies focused on the *difficulty* of the task or the cognitive load that developers experience during a change task or when reviewing or comprehending small code snippets. One study, for instance, examined the use of various physiological measurements to predict difficulty of small code snippets (Fritz et al. 2014). In another study on short code comprehension and bug localisation tasks, the researchers used a combination of fNIRS and eye tracking and found that linguistic antipatterns—poor practices in naming, documentation, and choice of identifiers—in the source code significantly increased the developers' cognitive load (Fakhoury et al. 2018). In a longer term study conducted over the course of a week, a combination of heart-, breathing-, and skin-related measurements from two different sensors was captured in combination with computer interaction data to predict the difficulty of code elements and the quality of the code produced. Using a machine learning approach, the different biometric readings were used to construct a prediction model that was able to outperform a model based only on traditional (non-biometric) measurements (Müller and Fritz 2016).

Research has also looked into the use of biometric sensors to investigate developers' *emotions*. These studies can also benefit from using multiple sensors, since emotions manifest in several physiological responses. A study combining non-invasive, low-cost EEG, EMG, and GSR (EDA) sensors found that it was possible to obtain accurate classification of emotional valence and arousal using machine learning classifiers on the sensor data (Girardi et al. 2017). A study using a variety of biosensor data (EEG, EDA, skin temperature, heart rate, blood volume pulse, eye tracking) to build a machine learning model found that it was possible to distinguish between positive and negative emotions and low and high progress during software change tasks (Müller and Fritz 2015). In general though, predicting arousal—the amount of activation associated with an emotion—is easier than predicting valence—the positive or negative character of an emotion—as several studies in other fields have also shown.

Finally, studies have also investigated other aspects, such as interruptibility—the availability of a developer for an interruption. One study, for instance, investigated how biometric and interaction data could be used to predict interruptibility in an office setting (Züger et al. 2018). Computer interaction data was shown to be more accurate than biometric data alone, but a combination of both yielded the best results.

5 Recommended Further Reading

The literature on using biometric measurements in software engineering is growing, and a few years from now, we expect there to be a large body of research on the subject. However, there is already a larger body of literature in areas such as psychology or human–computer interaction, in which physiological measures have been explored in a variety of settings and tasks, such as car driving, physical exercise, specific cognitive skills tasks, and more.

In the previous sections, we have already listed quite a few of the relevant articles and books that can help you to gain a better understanding on the different types of physiological measures and which cognitive and emotional states they have been linked to especially based on previous work in psychology (see Sect. 3), but also on the types of studies that have been conducted in software engineering using biometrics (see Sect. 4). Many of the referenced literature as well as the research on biometrics in human–computer interaction and psychology can be a valuable source for understanding which measures best to use for which scenario, the challenges involved in the use of certain biometric sensors, how to analyse the data and how to design studies, and sometimes even provide the code for the analysis.

There is a range of further readings that, depending on the type of study and the biometric sensor(s) to be used, can be of relevance. For instance, for eye tracking there are several articles by Sharif et al. on the use of eye tracking metrics and the mapping of eye gazes to areas of interest in the code, as well as a tool that can help with the mapping (Sharif and Shaffer 2015; Sharif et al. 2016). Other papers look at and compare the use of low-cost EEG devices (e.g., Das et al. 2014), discuss the invasiveness of various sensors to detect emotions (e.g., Wrobel 2018), or also summarise some of the work in the area of using biometrics to increase developer productivity (Fritz and Müller 2016).

Due to the cross-disciplinary nature of this type of research, literature relevant for research in the area is not confined to the software engineering domain. There are various other domains that are relevant, such as psychology, human–computer interaction, but also conference proceedings or journals about sensor technology and more. We therefore strongly recommend that in addition to the software engineering literature, you also look outside the field, since there is much to be learnt from previous studies. Finally, sensor technology is rapidly changing and the companies that provide these technologies as well, so it is worthwhile to regularly explore what kind of sensors are available to measure certain physiological features.

6 Conclusion

Biometric or psycho-physiological measurement is an emerging and promising source of information that can help researchers and practitioners to better understand and support developers in their work. Biometric sensors provide a direct way of measuring physiological correlates of psychological processes that are active as developers conduct their work. When used correctly, biometric data can yield information that is not possible to obtain using other means and that allows us to capture more about an individual in real-time.

So far, research using biometric sensor data in the software engineering domain is in its early stages, yet there is a huge potential as previous work has already shown. Research in the area ranges from the use of eye tracking to examine code comprehension, to the use of fMRIs to detect brain activation patterns for code reviewing tasks, all the way to the use of less invasive heart-related sensors in the field to detect code difficulty and the likelihood of a developer to create a bug. Initial results in the area already demonstrate the potential that biometric data has for measuring a developer's cognitive and emotional states in real-time; however, there are also still several challenges to be addressed in the future.

By leveraging biometric data in the software engineering domain and by having real-time measures of a developer's cognitive and emotional processes during work, there are many new opportunities that open up to better understand a developer in the process and to train and support developers for and in their work. The possible developer support ranges from preventing developers from creating or committing a bug, to detecting difficult areas in a code base (areas with high technical debt), to helping software developers to stay focused and take breaks, regulating the amount of information available to the developer at a given point in time and avoiding stress, to actually assisting the developer in their decision-making tasks as well as in signalling to co-workers when a developer is available for an interruption or not. Future software development tools could be collaborative agents that are informed not only by models of the system being developed, but also by information on the developers and potentially other stakeholders and thus provide better and more tailored support. Especially with the fast advances in sensor and data analysis technology, we might soon all be wearing smart wearable devices with biometric sensors integrated that will already be accurate enough to provide some of this support.

To understand software development, you must understand software developers. Biometric measurements have the potential to significantly help us a lot in this regard and thereby not just change our understanding but also our way of developing software.

References

Andreassi JL (2007) Psychophysiology: human behavior and physiological response. Lawrence Erlbaum Associates, Mahwah

Anthony L, Carrington P, Chu P, Kidd C, Lai J, Sears A (2011) Gesture dynamics: features sensitive to task difficulty and correlated with physiological sensors. Stress 1418(360):312–316

Ayres P (2001) Systematic mathematical errors and cognitive load. Contemp Educ Psychol 26(2):227–248

Bailey BP, Konstan JA, Carlis JV (2001) The effects of interruptions on task performance, annoyance, and anxiety in the user interface. In: Proceedings of interact, vol 1, pp 593–601

Bednarik R, Tukiainen M (2006) An eye-tracking methodology for characterizing program comprehension processes. In: Proceedings of the symposium on eye tracking research and applications, pp 125–132

Begel A, Vrzakova H (2018) Eye movements in code review. In: Proceedings of the workshop on eye movements in programming (EMIP '18). ACM, New York, pp 5:1–5:5. https://doi.org/10.1145/3216723.3216727

Brookings JB, Wilson GF, Swain CR (1996) Psychophysiological responses to changes in workload during simulated air traffic control. Biol Psychol Psychophysiol Workload 42(3):361–377

Busjahn T, Bednarik R, Begel A, Crosby M, Paterson JH, Schulte C, Sharif B, Tamm S (2015) Eye movements in code reading: relaxing the linear order. In: 2015 IEEE 23rd international conference on program comprehension, pp 255–265. https://doi.org/10.1109/ICPC.2015.36

Cacioppo J, Tassinary LG, Berntson GG (2007) The handbook of psychophysiology. Cambridge University, Cambridge

Carniglia E, Caputi M, Manfredi V, Zambarbieri D, Pessa E (2012) The influence of emotional picture thematic content on exploratory eye movements. J Eye Mov Res 5(4):1–9

Chandrika KR, Amudha J, Sudarsan SD (2017) Recognizing eye tracking traits for source code review. In: 2017 22nd IEEE international conference on emerging technologies and factory automation (ETFA), pp 1–8. https://doi.org/10.1109/ETFA.2017.8247637

Chanel G, Rebetez C, Bétrancourt M, Pun T (2008) Boredom, engagement and anxiety as indicators for adaptation to difficulty in games. In: Proceedings of the 12th international conference on entertainment and media in the Ubiquitous Era, pp 13–17. https://doi.org/10.1145/1457199.1457203. http://doi.acm.org/10.1145/1457199.1457203

Crk I, Kluthe T, Stefik A (2015) Understanding programming expertise: an empirical study of phasic brain wave changes. ACM Trans Comput-Hum Interact 23(1):2:1–2:29. https://doi.org/10.1145/2829945

Crosby ME, Stelovsky J (1990) How do we read algorithms? A case study. Computer 23(1):25–35. https://doi.org/10.1109/2.48797

Czerwinski M, Cutrell E, Horvitz E (2000) Instant messaging: effects of relevance and timing. In: People and computers XIV: proceedings of HCI, British Computer Society, vol 2, pp 71–76

Das R, Chatterjee D, Das D, Sinharay A, Sinha A (2014) Cognitive load measurement—a methodology to compare low cost commercial EEG devices. In: 2014 International conference on advances in computing, communications and informatics (ICACCI), pp 1188–1194. https://doi.org/10.1109/ICACCI.2014.6968528

Doehring DG (1957) The relation between manifest anxiety and rate of eyeblink in a stress situation. Technical report, Central Institute for the Deaf, St Louis

Drachen A, Nacke LE, Yannakakis G, Pedersen AL (2010) Correlation between heart rate, electrodermal activity and player experience in first-person shooter games. In: Proceedings of the 5th symposium on video games, pp 49–54

Fakhoury S, Ma Y, Arnaoudova V, Adesope O (2018) The effect of poor source code lexicon and readability on developers' cognitive load. In: Proceedings of the 26th conference on program comprehension (ICPC '18). ACM, New York, pp 286–296. https://doi.org/10.1145/3196321.3196347

Floyd B, Santander T, Weimer W (2017) Decoding the representation of code in the brain: an fMRI study of code review and expertise. In: 2017 IEEE/ACM 39th international conference on software engineering (ICSE), pp 175–186. https://doi.org/10.1109/ICSE.2017.24

Freeman GL (1940) A method of inducing frustration in human subjects and its influence upon palmar skin resistance. Am J Psychol 53(1):117–120

Fritz T, Müller SC (2016) Leveraging biometric data to boost software developer productivity. In: 2016 IEEE 23rd international conference on software analysis, evolution, and reengineering (SANER), vol 5, pp 66–77

Fritz T, Begel A, Müller SC, Yigit-Elliott S, Züger M (2014) Using psycho-physiological measures to assess task difficulty in software development. In: Proceedings of the 36th international conference on software engineering (ACM, ICSE 2014), pp 402–413. https://doi.org/10.1145/2568225.2568266

Girardi D, Lanubile F, Novielli N (2017) Emotion detection using noninvasive low cost sensors. In: 2017 Seventh international conference on affective computing and intelligent interaction (ACII), pp 125–130. https://doi.org/10.1109/ACII.2017.8273589

Graziotin D, Fagerholm F, Wang X, Abrahamsson P (2018) What happens when software developers are (un)happy. J Syst Softw 140:32–47. https://doi.org/10.1016/j.jss.2018.02.041

Haag A, Goronzy S, Schaich P, Williams J (2004) Emotion recognition using bio-sensors: first steps towards an automatic system. Affect Dialogue Syst Lect Notes Comput Sci 3068:36–48

Haapalainen E, Kim S, Forlizzi JF, Dey AK (2010) Psycho-physiological measures for assessing cognitive load. In: Proceedings of the 12th international conference on ubiquitous computing, pp 301–310

Ikehara CS, Crosby ME (2005) Assessing cognitive load with physiological sensors. In: Proceedings of the 38th Hawaii international conference on system sciences, p 295a

Ikutani Y, Uwano H (2014) Brain activity measurement during program comprehension with NIRS. In: Proceedings of the international conference on software engineering, artificial intelligence, networking and parallel/distributed computing, pp 1–6

Iqbal ST, Zheng XS, Bailey BP (2004) Task-evoked pupillary response to mental workload in human-computer interaction. In: CHI '04 extended abstracts on human factors in computing systems, pp 1477–1480

Jbara A, Feitelson DG (2017) How programmers read regular code: a controlled experiment using eye tracking. Empir Softw Eng 22(3):1440–1477. https://doi.org/10.1007/s10664-016-9477-x

Kapoor A, Burleson W, Picard RW (2007) Automatic prediction of frustration. Int J Hum Comput Stud 65(8):724–736

Kevic K, Walters BM, Shaffer TR, Sharif B, Shepherd DC, Fritz T (2015) Tracing software developers' eyes and interactions for change tasks. In: Proceedings of the 2015 10th joint meeting on foundations of software engineering (ESEC/FSE 2015). ACM, New York, pp 202–213. https://doi.org/10.1145/2786805.2786864

Kosti MV, Georgiadis K, Adamos DA, Laskaris N, Spinellis D, Angelis L (2018) Towards an affordable brain computer interface for the assessment of programmers' mental workload. Int J Hum Comput Stud 115:52–66. https://doi.org/10.1016/j.ijhcs.2018.03.002

Kramer AF (1991) Physiological metrics of mental workload: a review of recent progress. In: Multiple-task performance, pp 279–328

Kuznetsov NA, Shockley KD, Richardson MJ, Riley MA (2011) Effect of precision aiming on respiration and postural-respiratory synergy. Neurosci Lett 502(1):13–17

Levandovski R, Sasso E, Hidalgo MP (2013) Chronotype: a review of the advances, limits and applicability of the main instruments used in the literature to assess human phenotype. Trends Psychiatry Psychother 35(1):3–11

Li M, Lu BL (2009) Emotion classification based on gamma-band EEG. In: Conference proceedings of the annual international conference of the IEEE engineering in medicine and biology society, pp 1323–1326

Lin YP, Wang CH, Jung TP, Wu TL, Jeng SK, Duann JR, Chen JH (2010) EEG-based emotion recognition in music listening. IEEE Trans Biomed Eng 57(7):1798–1806. https://doi.org/10.1109/TBME.2010.2048568

Mark G, Gudith D, Klocke U (2008) The cost of interrupted work: more speed and stress. In: Proceedings of the SIGCHI conference on human factors in computing systems. ACM, New York, pp 107–110

McCraty R, Tomasino D (2006) Stress in health and diseases. In: Chap emotional stress, positive emotions, and psychophysiological coherence. Wiley-VCH, New York

McDuff D, Karlson A, Kapoor A, Roseway A, Czerwinski M (2012) AffectAura: an intelligent system for emotional memory. In: Proceedings of the 2012 ACM annual conference on human factors in computing systems, pp 849–858

Muldner K, Burleson W, VanLehn K (2010) "Yes!": using tutor and sensor data to predict moments of delight during instructional activities. In: Proceedings of the 18th international conference on user modeling, adaptation, and personalization, pp 159–170

Müller SC, Fritz T (2015) Stuck and frustrated or in flow and happy: sensing developers' emotions and progress. In: 2015 IEEE/ACM 37th IEEE international conference on software engineering, vol 1, pp 688–699. https://doi.org/10.1109/ICSE.2015.334

Müller SC, Fritz T (2016) Using (bio)metrics to predict code quality online. In: 2016 IEEE/ACM 38th international conference on software engineering (ICSE), pp 452–463. https://doi.org/10.1145/2884781.2884803

Nakagawa T, Kamei Y, Uwano H, Monden A, Matsumoto K, German DM (2014) Quantifying programmers' mental workload during program comprehension based on cerebral blood flow measurement: a controlled experiment. In: Companion proceedings of international conference on software engineering

Peitek N, Siegmund J, Apel S, Kästner C, Parnin C, Bethmann A, Leich T, Saake G, Brechmann A (2018) A look into programmers' heads. IEEE Trans Softw Eng. https://doi.org/10.1109/TSE.2018.2863303

Peper E, Harvey R, Lin IM, Tylova H, Moss D (2007) Is there more to blood volume pulse than heart rate variability, respiratory sinus arrhythmia, and cardiorespiratory synchrony? Biofeedback 35(2):54–61

Picard RW, Vyzas E, Healey J (2001) Toward machine emotional intelligence: analysis of affective physiological state. IEEE Trans Pattern Anal Mach Intell 23(10):1175–1191

Rani P, Sarkar N, Smith CA, Kirby LD (2004) Anxiety detecting robotic system—towards implicit human-robot collaboration. Robotica 22(1):85–95

Reuderink B, Mühl C, Poel M (2013) Valence, arousal and dominance in the EEG during game play. Int J Autom Adaptive Commun Syst 6(1):45–62

Richter P, Wagner T, Heger R, Weise G (1998) Psychophysiological analysis of mental load during driving on rural roads—a quasi-experimental field study. Ergonomics 41(5):593:609

Rodeghero P, McMillan C, McBurney PW, Bosch N, D'Mello S (2014) Improving automated source code summarization via an eye-tracking study of programmers. In: Proceedings of the 36th international conference on software engineering (ICSE 2014), pp 390–401. https://doi.org/10.1145/2568225.2568247

Sammler D, Grigutsch M, Fritz T, Koelsch S (2007) Music and emotion: electrophysiological correlates of the processing of pleasant and unpleasant music. Psychophysiology 44:293–304. https://doi.org/10.1111/j.1469-8986.2007.00497.x

Schmidth S, Walach H (2000) Electrodermal activity (EDA)—state-of-the-art measurements and techniques for parapsychological purposes. J Parapsychol 64(2):139:163

Setz C, Arnrich B, Schumm J, Marca RL, Tröster G, Ehlert U (2010) Discriminating stress from cognitive load using a wearable EDA device. IEEE Trans Inf Technol Biomed 14(2):410–417

Sharif B, Shaffer T (2015) The use of eye tracking in software development. In: Schmorrow DD, Fidopiastis CM (eds) Foundations of augmented cognition. Springer, Cham, pp 807–816

Sharif B, Falcone M, Maletic JI (2012) An eye-tracking study on the role of scan time in finding source code defects. In: Proceedings of the symposium on eye tracking research and applications (ETRA '12). ACM, New York, pp 381–384. https://doi.org/10.1145/2168556.2168642

Sharif B, Clark B, Maletic JI (2016) Studying developer gaze to empower software engineering research and practice. In: Proceedings of the 2016 24th ACM SIGSOFT international symposium on foundations of software engineering. ACM, New York, pp 940–943. https://doi.org/10.1145/2950290.2983988

Sharif B, Meinken J, Shaffer T, Kagdi H (2017) Eye movements in software traceability link recovery. Empir Softw Eng 22(3):1063–1102. https://doi.org/10.1007/s10664-016-9486-9

Siegmund J, Kästner C, Apel S, Parnin C, Bethmann A, Leich T, Saake G, Brechmann A (2014) Understanding understanding source code with functional magnetic resonance imaging. In: Proceedings of the 36th international conference on software engineering, pp 378–389

Siegmund J, Peitek N, Parnin C, Apel S, Hofmeister J, Kästner C, Begel A, Bethmann A, Brechmann A (2017) Measuring neural efficiency of program comprehension. In: Proceedings of the 2017 11th joint meeting on foundations of software engineering (ESEC/FSE 2017). ACM, New York, pp 140–150. https://doi.org/10.1145/3106237.3106268

Steptoe A, Wardle J, Marmot M (2005) Positive affect and health-related neuroendocrine, cardiovascular, and inflammatory processes. Proc Natl Acad Sci 102(18):6508–6512

Sweller J (1988) Cognitive load during problem solving: effects on learning. Cogn Sci 12(2):257–285

Torii K, Matsumoto Ki, Nakakoji K, Takada Y, Takada S, Shima K (1999) Ginger2: an environment for computer-aided empirical software engineering. IEEE Trans Softw Eng 25(4):474–492

Uwano H, Nakamura M, Monden A, Matsumoto Ki (2006) Analyzing individual performance of source code review using reviewers' eye movement. In: Proceedings of the symposium on eye tracking research and applications. ACM, San Diego, pp 133–140

Veltman J, Gaillard AW (1998) Physiological workload reactions to increasing levels of task difficulty. Ergonomics 41(5):656–669

Walter GF, Porges SW (1976) Heart rate and respiratory responses as a function of task difficulty: the use of discriminant analysis in the selection of psychologically sensitive physiological responses. Psychophysiology 13(6):563–571

Wilson GF (1992) Applied use of cardiac and respiration measures: practical considerations and precautions. Biol Psychol 34(2–3):163–178

Wrobel MR (2018) Applicability of emotion recognition and induction methods to study the behavior of programmers. Appl Sci 8(3):323. https://doi.org/10.3390/app8030323

Züger M, Müller SC, Meyer AN, Fritz T (2018) Sensing interruptibility in the office: a field study on the use of biometric and computer interaction sensors. In: Proceedings of the 2018 CHI conference on human factors in computing systems (CHI '18). ACM, New York, pp 591:1–591:14. https://doi.org/10.1145/3173574.3174165

Empirical Software Engineering Experimentation with Human Computation

Marta Sabou ⓘ, Dietmar Winkler ⓘ, and Stefan Biffl ⓘ

Abstract *Empirical software engineering* (ESE) focuses on gathering evidence through measurements and experiments involving humans and software systems (software products, processes, and resources). While empirical studies often include considerable human effort for study planning, execution, and data analysis, *human computation* (HC) methods, such as crowdsourcing, are increasingly used to address human input intensive tasks in software engineering and beyond. Therefore, in this chapter, we explore the use of HC techniques to support ESE experiments. We address researchers from both research communities and provide (1) introductory notions into both fields, (2) an analysis of ESE experiment requirements and HC capabilities that could match those, and (3) a concrete example of an ESE experiment that compares the effects of using HC in software inspection with respect to a traditional inspection process preformed using pen and paper. Our focus is on software inspection for detecting defects in software engineering models (namely, extended entity relationship models). This chapter will enable ESE researchers to apply HC in their work and HC researchers to explore ESE as a new application area to further improve their methods and tools.

1 Introduction

Ever since the notion of the *wisdom of crowds* was coined in 2004 by Surowiecki, research has intensified on solving complex problems by involving large numbers of contributors (Surowiecki 2004). A concrete example is the field of *human*

M. Sabou (✉) · S. Biffl
Institute for Information Systems Engineering, Technische Universität Wien, Vienna, Austria
e-mail: marta.sabou@ifs.tuwien.ac.at; stefan.biffl@tuwien.ac.at

D. Winkler
Institute for Information Systems Engineering, Technische Universität Wien, Vienna, Austria

Christian Doppler Research Laboratory for Security and Quality Improvement in the Production System Life-cycle (CDL-SQI), Vienna, Austria
e-mail: dietmar.winkler@tuwien.ac.at

© Springer Nature Switzerland AG 2020   173
M. Felderer, G. H. Travassos (eds.), *Contemporary Empirical Methods in Software Engineering*, https://doi.org/10.1007/978-3-030-32489-6_7

computation and crowdsourcing (HC), which relies on collective intelligence methods to harvest human intelligence at scale for solving problems that cannot yet be reliably solved by computers. HC methods found their successful application in a wide range of domains ranging from natural language processing to database systems.

One of the fields, where this paradigm shift had an impact, is *software engineering* (SE). As pointed out by LaToza and van der Hoek (2016), the approach of collaboratively solving complex problems goes back to *peer production* in collaborative open-source software creation in software projects, such as Linux or Apache. However, the most recent paradigm of *microtasking* enabled by crowdsourcing platforms, such as *Amazon Mechanical Turk (*www.mturk.com/*)*, has seen an intensification of distributed software engineering, which has been applied to address tasks in many stages of the SE life-cycle (Mao et al. 2017) to solve these tasks more cheaply, faster, and at similar quality compared to traditional SE approaches. Microtasking focuses on splitting larger tasks into smaller pieces of work, executing them by a group of workers, and aggregating individual results into the results of the overall larger task.

This increased popularity of HC methods in software engineering opens interesting research avenues both for *empirical software engineering* (ESE) and *human computation*. On the one hand, for ESE, two important challenges emerge. Firstly, ESE researchers might be interested to study the effects of using HC methods on SE tasks, for example, in terms of effectiveness and efficiency, with respect to traditional approaches to achieve the same task. We illustrate such an endeavor by reporting on setting up an ESE experiment for comparing traditional (pen and paper) software inspection with inspection supported through HC. Secondly, ESE researchers might use HC methods to support certain stages of the ESE study process itself, in particular related to data collection and cleaning. On the other hand, HC researchers can benefit from the results of empirical research to further develop HC concepts, methods, and tools and to increase the awareness of HC application in the software quality assurance domain for which there is still limited support compared to other stages in the software life-cycle (Mao et al. 2017).

Therefore, this chapter aims to provide an introductory material about the research at the intersection of ESE and HC that is interesting to *both* communities. To that end, the chapter is structured into three increasingly detailed thematic areas that build on each other as follows.

Introductory and preparatory notions are covered for the benefit of researchers from both communities. In particular, we:

1. *Provide an introduction to the field of HC*, including the typical HC process and the involved stakeholders in Sect. 2.
2. *Clarify which stages of the ESE experiment process can benefit* the *most from HC*, based on a generic ESE process, as well as their concrete requirements that could be satisfied by HC (Sect. 3).

Requirements and Capabilities Analysis Building on the introductory notions, we deepen our analysis by providing an overview of ESE requirements for HC on the one hand and available HC capabilities on the other. Concretely, we:

1. *Elicit ESE requirements for HC*, with a dual focus (Sect. 4). First, we discuss *requirements for HC support for ESE experiment steps.* While several SE methods have been solved with HC (Mao et al. 2017), these traditional SE methods required adaptation to benefit from HC capabilities. Therefore, ESE experiments may compare the characteristics of HC-enabled and of traditional SE methods to better understand the impact of HC on SE method performance, e.g., task effectiveness and efficiency. We focus on requirements for the HC support of such ESE experiments as derived from the ESE experiment steps. Accordingly, we derive (a) tasks that may require HC support (Table 1) and (b) requirements for HC support (Sect. 4, requirements R1 to R5). Second, we identify *typical challenges in ESE experiments for which HC methods and technology could provide support.* Independently of the SE method investigated, some ESE experiment tasks, such as data cleaning and aggregation, typically take considerable effort for the research team to conduct as they are hard to automate. These tasks could be supported with HC contributors, who bring in the required skills and motivation through expert sourcing. We analyzed the tasks in the ESE experiment steps with standard HC capabilities to derive ESE tasks that are likely to benefit from HC support.
2. *Discuss HC capabilities relevant to address ESE requirements* grouped along the ESE experiment steps detailed in Sect. 4. For that, we rely on lessons learned from the literature and from our experience with HC-enabled model quality assurance (Sabou et al. 2018b) (Sect. 5).

Concrete Example of Using HC for ESE In Sect. 6, we report on a case study that illustrates how we adapted a generic ESE experiment process to the concrete context of an experiment on HC-enabled software inspection.

Concretely, we describe recent empirical work on using HC concepts to support software inspection (Fagan 1986) for detecting defects in software engineering models (Winkler et al. 2017a, b). In software inspection, the main goal is to identify defects in inspection artifacts, such as software engineering models, often in the context of reference documents, such as requirements specifications and use cases. Main steps may include the identification of model building blocks, such as expected model elements in the reference document, identifying candidate defects in the inspection artifact, such as the model, and analyzing and aggregating candidate defects. As these steps typically include considerable human effort of inspection teams, HC could help to overcome limitations of traditional (pen-and-paper-based) inspections. These limitations typically include the size of inspection artifacts, available effort for inspection execution, and inspection control.

We report on setting up an ESE experiment for comparing traditional (pen-and-paper) inspection with inspection supported through HC. We discuss how the experiment setup was affected by the use of HC both at a conceptual level (e.g.,

Table 1 Experiment process steps with HC roles

Role/Study stage	Experiment planning (E2)	Experiment operation (E3)	Experiment analysis (E4)
ESE researcher (HC requester)	Define experiment treatment Design experiment Define study groups (e.g., size) Define SE tasks Define task data input and output Define measurement in experiment	Execute experiment plan Audit experiment execution Collect experiment data Validate experiment data	Validate experiment data Aggregate experiment data
HC technical expert (HC task designer; HC platform configurator and operator)	Configure HC platform Define contributor groups Design and implement HC tasks Define HC data input and output Operate and monitor platform	Configure HC platform Schedule and monitor HC tasks Collect HC/experiment data Validate HC/experiment data Aggregate HC/experiment data	Validate HC/experiment data Aggregate HC/experiment data
Study participant (HC contributor)	Pilot with selected HC contributors	Take part in experiment Perform qualification tests Solve HC tasks Provide feedback	Solve tasks (validation, aggregation)

inclusion or modification of experiment steps) and on a technical level (e.g., use of the HC platform *Figure Eight*[1]). We discuss (1) the evaluation of an HC-enabled SE method in comparison to a traditional pen-and-paper approach and (2) the HC support for the ESE research team.

Section 7 discusses benefits and limitations regarding HC capabilities in ESE research. This chapter concludes with Sect. 8 providing recommended further reading and Sect. 9 which summarizes the chapter.

The chapter is aimed to and will benefit both ESE and HC researchers. *ESE researchers* will firstly benefit from an introduction and overview on HC methods and technology (e.g., the use of the *Figure Eight* HC platform to replicate an ESE experiment) as well as a discussion of their capabilities and their limitations in the context of an ESE experiment. Secondly, they will acquire an understanding of what topics to consider for planning and conducting an ESE experiment with HC method and technology support, based on an illustrative example experiment. Thirdly, the example implementation of a controlled experiment for model quality assurance with inspection can be seen as blueprint for the study process with HC support. It provides valuable insights into topics to be considered due to the use of HC as well as lessons learned on the benefits and limitations of the HC approach in general, and a concrete platform used for experimentation, in particular.

HC researchers will firstly get a better understanding of what ESE researchers require from HC methods and technology support for ESE experimentation. They will be introduced to relevant ESE notions that allow them to derive requirements to improve HC concepts, methods, and tools. Secondly, they will gain insight into lessons learned on what worked (or did not work) for HC with a specific, but typical, HC platform, *Figure Eight*, thus leading to ideas for new research in the HC field. Furthermore, HC researcher can use this example implementation as foundation for evaluating HC concepts, methods, and mechanisms.

2   Human Computation and Crowdsourcing (HC)

This section introduces basic notions related to human computation including its definition (Sect. 2.1), the typical HC process and stakeholders (Sect. 2.2), various HC genres (Sect. 2.3), as well as application areas (Sect. 2.4).

2.1   Definition

Human computation (HC) is a computational paradigm where human participation is directed by a computational system in order to (mostly) solve problems that

---

[1] *Figure Eight*: www.figure-eight.com

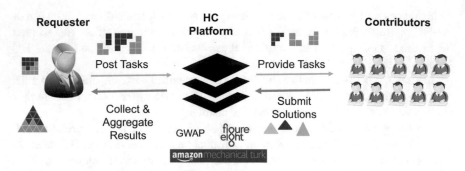

Fig. 1 A blueprint of the HC process (adapted from Mao et al. 2017)

cannot yet be solved by computer programs or which are still challenging to (fully) automate (Quinn and Bederson 2011; Barowy et al. 2016). HC is often achieved through *crowdsourcing* approaches, which leverage the *wisdom of the crowd* by engaging large numbers of online contributors (Howe 2006) to accomplish tasks, which cannot be easily automated, faster, at larger scale, and by benefiting from the diversity of a distributed online workforce (Snow et al. 2008). Therefore, in this chapter, we use the abbreviation HC to refer to HC tasks addressed with collaborative approaches such as *crowdsourcing*. Furthermore, we cover a range of topics related to HC, namely (1) the HC *method*, which refers to the conceptual process steps for conducting HC projects; (2) HC *technology* as available in terms of the *Figure Eight* crowdsourcing platform, and (3) HC *capabilities*, which refer to the functionalities provided by the concrete crowdsourcing platform.

2.2   Stakeholders and Process

HC projects typically involve the following *stakeholders* (see Fig. 1). On the one hand, the HC *requester* is a problem owner that seeks to solve a (complex) problem, for example, the translation of a document corpus or the annotation of an image collection. On the other hand, HC *contributors* have the capability to jointly solve the problem at hand. An HC *platform* mediates between requesters and contributors. Typically, this includes crowdsourcing marketplaces, such as *Amazon Mechanical Turk* (AMT) or *Figure Eight*, as well as problem-specific platforms and interfaces such as the *Zooniverse*[2] citizen science platform and *Games With A Purpose* (GWAP) (von Ahn and Dabbish 2008). A commercial crowdsourcing platform is maintained by a *platform operator* company, which charges a percentage of the transaction costs between requesters and contributors.

[2]*Zooniverse*: https://www.zooniverse.org/

In this setting, an *HC process* typically consists of the following steps: A *requester* defines the problem to be solved (e.g., she selects the data to be annotated, she decides on the annotation tags to be assigned) and subsequently splits the complex problem into small *tasks* that can be solved in parallel by contributors (e.g., the problem of translating a document is split into the smaller task of translating a sentence of a document). These tasks are then posted to an *HC platform*, which typically manages a large base of contributors with capability profiles, takes over the advertisement of tasks to contributors, and assigns the tasks to contributors. *Contributors* then solve and submit individual small task results (e.g., the translation of a sentence to a target language). These results are collected by the *HC platform*, which often offers dashboards and management interfaces, where requesters can follow the completion rate of their tasks. To benefit from the wisdom of the crowds, each task is solved by multiple contributors. Their responses are then aggregated in order to reflect the majority's opinion (e.g., the most often provided translation of a sentence is considered as correct translation). The aggregation of individual solutions to solve the original problem is performed either by the *HC platform* or by the *requester*.

Depending on the complexity of the problem that is solved, a *requester* might need the support of an *HC designer*, i.e., an *HC platform expert*, who performs the technical implementation and configuration of the tasks on the HC platform.

Simple tasks include the transcription of text from images or the classification of images in predefined categories. Such tasks require limited context or instructions, make use of the existing knowledge and capabilities of contributors, and lead to an unambiguous result such as a short text, a selection from a given set of items, or a number. For a family of such tasks, most HC platforms already offer task templates that can be easily reused and configured to create tasks populated with the requester's data, even without technical expertise.

A requester might also need to solve more complex problems, where it is unclear how to best split these into HC tasks. In such cases, the requester typically requires support by an *HC designer* to iteratively explore the possible types of HC tasks. A good example of a complex problem is the verification of model elements in an EER diagram with respect to a textual specification. This problem requires elaborate explanation of complex context (e.g., scenarios and models) to the contributor. One alternative would be that contributors are asked to verify one element in the EER diagram based on the entire system specification. This would result in cognitively complex HC tasks, as contributors would be faced with reading the entire specification over and over again. The number of tasks would however be low, that is, equal to the number of (M) elements in the EER model (M refers to the number of model elements). As an alternative, the requester could split the problem along (N) paragraphs within the specification text, asking contributors to focus on one paragraph at a time (N is the number of paragraphs to be inspected). This would result in HC tasks that could be performed much faster and with lower cognitive effort, but would result in NxM tasks to be crowdsourced. An HC designer can help the requestor to decide on a suitable splitting approach based on project priorities.

Complex problems are often split into nonstandard HC task types where no predefined templates are available and new interfaces need to be implemented on the HC platform (e.g., to allow an annotation directly on a picture representing a model). Another challenge is a tool chain with HC tasks, i.e., when the HC platform is part of a tool chain and support is needed to transform inputs from other tools into HC tasks, and to transform results from the HC platform into output for other tools. Programmatic support from the HC designer might be required for establishing such a tool chain.

An HC platform offers interfaces (both visual and programmatic) to requesters, contributors, and the *HC designer*. This platform typically offers the following functionalities: configuration of contributor groups, definition of HC tasks including instructions, input data (often text or pictures), questions to ask, and data to collect. During HC execution, the platform configures tasks with input data sets for contributor groups, schedules tasks, and monitors their completion (including start/end time, effort, completion, and results). The HC platform keeps records on (1) tasks and their results, including the quality of the results, and (2) contributors, their qualifications, work (open, done), quality of work, and performance level.

2.3   HC Genre

Figure 1 illustrates a blueprint of HC process steps that are at the core of a variety of HC genres, which primarily differ by the incentive mechanisms used to entice contributors to perform work. The key crowdsourcing genres according to Quinn and Bederson (2011) and de Boer et al. (2012) are:

Mechanized labor (MLab), a.k.a., *microtasking* is a type of paid-for HC genre, where *contributors* choose to carry out small tasks (known also as *microtasks*) and are paid a small amount of money in return (referred to as micro-payments). Therefore, this genre is characterized by extrinsic, economic incentives. Popular platforms for mechanized labor include *Amazon's Mechanical Turk* (AMT) and *Figure Eight*, which allow a *requester* to post microtasks—also known as *human intelligence tasks* (HITs, or units)—to a large population of micro-workers.

Games with a purpose (GWAPs) (von Ahn and Dabbish 2008) enable human contributors to carry out computation tasks as a side effect of playing online games. The main motivational factor for GWAPs is intrinsic, namely allowing participants to have fun while playing games. GWAPs are the results of a *gamification* process which is a way of designing tasks and exercises (e.g., learning a language) in a way that they have elements of a game and hence result more engaging. An example from the area of computational biology is the *Phylo* game[3] that disguises the problem of multiple sequence alignment as a puzzle-

---

[3] *Phylo Game*: phylo.cs.mcgill.ca/

like game thus *"intentionally decoupling the scientific problem from the game itself"* (Kawrykow et al. 2012). The challenges in using GWAPs are designing appealing gaming interfaces and attracting a critical mass of players.

Altruistic crowdsourcing refers to cases, where a task is carried out by a large number of volunteer contributors, typically motivated by altruistic reasons, such as the willingness to contribute to the advancement of science or a worthwhile cause. To reduce the incentive to cheat (e.g., for money or glory), altruistic crowdsourcing approaches leverage the intrinsic motivation of a community interested in a domain. The *Galaxy Zoo*[4] project, for example, seeks volunteers with a latent desire to help with scientific research for classifying *Hubble Space Telescope* galaxy images. The project has attracted more than 250 K volunteers which provided over 150 M galaxy classifications. The resounding success of this project prompted the generalization of the infrastructure created for *Galaxy Zoo* into a platform, named *Zooniverse*, where similar *citizen science* projects can be deployed. To date the platform offers a range of astronomy-related projects and boasts a base of over 430 K volunteers.

Expert sourcing (also known as *niche sourcing*) refers to the enrolling of a population of *"amateur experts rather than the "faceless" crowd [...] gathered from either distributed experts on a specific topic or from an existing network centered around the same culture, location, or topic"* (de Boer et al. 2012) in order to solve problems, where specialized knowledge is required that is typically not widespread among a generic crowd. Another motivation for *expert sourcing* is the case of organizations/companies that are reluctant to share data with crowds outside their boundaries. Examples of *expert sourcing* projects include acquiring high-quality image annotation on the cultural heritage domain by addressing a group of hobbyists; annotating rainfall images from Africa by members of the African diaspora (de Boer et al. 2012); technology forecasting by a group of experts (Fye et al. 2013); and public health surveillance (Berrang-Ford and Garton 2013).

2.4   Application Areas

HC techniques have greatly reduced the duration and cost of tasks that cannot be reliably automated in domains ranging from databases (Franklin et al. 2011) to image analysis (Quinn and Bederson 2011). Behrend et al. (2011) investigate the use of HC platforms to support collecting data for surveys in behavioral research. In the area of *Semantic Web* research, HC has been adopted for solving human-centric tasks (Sabou et al. 2018a; Sarasua et al. 2015), especially related to knowledge acquisition and evaluation (Acosta et al. 2018; Mortensen et al. 2015; Wohlgenannt et al. 2016). Another field that benefited from HC is *natural language processing*, e.g., Snow et al. (2008), Poesio et al. (2013), and Sabou et al. (2014).

---

[4]*Galaxy Zoo*: www.zooniverse.org/projects/zookeeper/galaxy-zoo/

In *software engineering*, crowdsourcing techniques are widespread and support many stages of the software engineering life-cycle (LaToza and van der Hoek 2016; Mao et al. 2017), including also tasks that are typical for *empirical software engineering*. Stolee and Elbaum (2010) report on lessons learned when adapting a study on the effect on code smells to be performed by using crowdsourcing through *Amazon Mechanical Turk*. Several authors also attempt to use crowdsourcing as support during *Systematic Literature Reviews*, a core ESE technique, both during the paper screening phase (Brown and Allison 2014; Mortensen et al. 2016) and during the data extraction step (Sun et al. 2016). Finally, in our earlier work (Sabou et al. 2018a; Biffl et al. 2018; Neto et al. 2019a), we conducted an experiment family with HC methods and tool support, to study the effects of expert sourcing on model quality assurance, in which participants verified EER diagrams with respect to a systems specification.

Therefore, HC concepts, methods, and tool support are relevant for improving tasks that are hard to automate (a) in SE methods or (b) in ESE studies. As HC approaches are increasingly used for enabling SE methods (Mao et al. 2017), ESE researchers should study the characteristics of HC-enabled SE methods. ESE researchers should be aware of typical HC characteristics when investigating HC-supported SE tasks in ESE studies. In addition to serving as an ESE study object, HC methods and technologies could also support aspects of ESE studies. In this chapter, we focus on using HC in ESE experiments in particular.

3   ESE Experiment Steps Related to HC

Major ESE study types, see also the evolution of ESE methods in chapter "The Evolution of Empirical Methods in Software Engineering," include *surveys* (see Ciolkowski et al. (2003); Molléri et al. (2016), and chapter "Challenges in Survey Research," in this book) *case studies* (see Runeson and Höst (2009); Runeson et al. (2012), and chapter "Guidelines for Case Survey Research in Software Engineering," in this book) and *experiments* (see Wohlin et al. (2012); Juristo and Moreno (2013); Ko et al. (2015)). While ESE study types may be investigating HC-enabled SE methods or consider using HC methods and technologies, we will focus in this chapter, due to space limitations, on the considerations of HC capabilities regarding ESE experiments.

In this section, we build on the background of HC stakeholders and process steps introduced in Sect. 2 and aim to identify (a) where the study of HC-enabled SE methods may make a difference for an ESE experiment step and (b) which typical ESE experiment steps are likely to benefit from HC method support. To emphasize the impact of considering HC methods and technology, we use a concrete non-HC experiment example and discuss HC issues to consider as foundation for the discussion of investigating ESE requirements for HC in Sect. 4, HC methods capabilities for experimentation in Sect. 5, and the concrete example of an ESE experiment using HC methods and technology in Sect. 6. Accordingly, in this section, we

- Summarize the main stages of the ESE experiment process based on Wohlin et al. (2012).
- Exemplify these stages for an example experiment on software inspection with different reading techniques in teams (Biffl and Halling 2003). That experiment used *pen and paper*[5] (P&P) to distribute and process the experiment materials and to collect data from the participants.
- Discuss, for each stage, issues that could be relevant for planning and conducting an experiment on or with HC methods and technologies.

Figure 2 shows the experiment process steps (E1 to E5) with their input, outputs, and main roles for each step, as discussed next. For each step, we describe (1) the general ESE experiment step, (2) a specific pen-and-paper example to exemplify typical experiment considerations without HC, and (3) HC considerations for ESE and HC experts, such as additional skills, tasks, and effort required, as background for the case study in Sect. 6.

E1. Experiment Scoping Based on an experiment idea, researchers define the experiment goal, scope, and hypotheses.

P&P Experiment. In their pen-and-paper experiment, Biffl and Halling (2003) studied the effectiveness and efficiency of inspectors, who used a reading technique, a checklist, or a scenario-based viewpoint, to detect defects in a requirements document and in design models. In this experiment, the participants received all materials, e.g., the experiment information, requirements and models to inspect, and data collection forms, on paper.

Experiment with HC. For scoping an experiment that investigates an SE method enabled with HC, such as inspection using HC methods and technology, researchers have to be aware of the impact of the HC methods and technology, as a phenomenon to be investigated or as a factor that may influence the experiment outcome, in the definition of the goal, scope, and hypotheses of the experiment.

E2. Experiment Planning Based on the experiment goal and hypotheses, the researchers determine the context of the experiment, including the personnel and the environment, and formalize the experiment hypothesis and variables, and the experiment design, considering the validity of the results. Based on the experiment design, the researchers have to prepare experiment materials and the instrumentation for data collection.

P&P Experiment. In Biffl and Halling (2003), the materials included experiment information, requirements, and models to inspect. The instrumentation for data collection included forms to fill in by the research staff and by the participating subjects. The preparation of the experiment materials may take considerable effort, e.g., for running pilot studies to ensure validity of data collection, and supporting

---

[5]Paper is used synonymous to pdf; easy to share and present, hard to analyze.

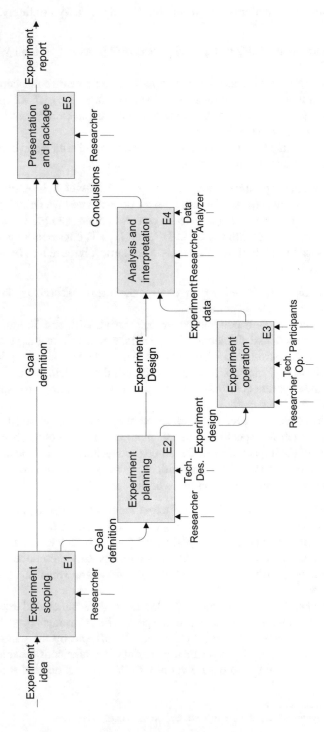

Fig. 2 Experiment process steps with roles (adapted from Wohlin et al. 2012)

research staff. For an experiment with a high number of participants, researchers have to consider how to organize the experiment to ensure the valid collection of data and of context factors that may influence the experiment results, e.g., if data are collected in different settings.

Experiment with HC. For planning an experiment that uses HC methods and technology, the researchers have to be aware of the strengths and limitations of the HC methods in general and of the specific HC technology used. A relevant issue may be scale, which is often much larger in experiments with HC than in traditional experiments. Therefore, different trade-offs may be leveraged in this case than in the case of more traditional controlled experiments involving human subjects. Further, a *technical HC designer* on the research staff may be required for designing and implementing the experiment materials for the specific HC technology, taking extra effort for communication and exploration of implementation options.

E3. Experiment Operation Based on the experiment design and materials, the researchers prepare the participating subjects and materials, execute the experiment according to the plan, and validate the collected data.

P&P Experiment. In Biffl and Halling (2003), the experiment subjects received training and conducted an individual inspection and a team meeting, from which defect data were collected on paper and in a web-based tool. Research staff supervised the participants, validated the collected data, and classified reported defects according to a list of true defects. For the more than 150 participants, it took considerable effort to recruit and train the research staff to ensure the supervision and documentation for valid data collection.

Experiment with HC. For conducting an experiment that uses HC methods, a *technical operator* on the research staff may be required for configuring and monitoring the specific HC technology to ensure valid data collection.

E4. Analysis and Interpretation Based on the collected data, the researchers analyze the data using descriptive statistics, data reduction, and hypothesis testing, and interpret the results regarding acceptance or rejection of the hypothesis. This step is similar for experiments that collect data using pen and paper or HC.

E5. Presentation and Package Based on the conclusions reached from interpreting the experiment data, the researchers document and report the results (Jedlitschka et al. 2008), often as a research paper, as a lab package for replication, or as knowledge in an experience base. This step is similar for both experiment types.

Building on the introduction to HC (Sect. 2) and to the main steps of the ESE process (Sect. 3), we continue with a more detailed analysis of ESE requirements for HC capabilities (Sect. 4) and sum up HC capabilities (Sect. 5).

4   Requirements in ESE Experiments for HC Capabilities

This section defines requirements in ESE experiment steps for HC capabilities. To that end, we analyzed the ESE experiment steps (Sect. 3), for experiment tasks, which are likely to require understanding HC capabilities, with HC roles, introduced in Sect. 2, to derive (a) tasks that may require HC support (see Table 1), and (b) requirements for HC support (see requirements R1 to R5). The experiment steps (E1) scoping and (E5) presentation and package are not likely to depend on HC support. Therefore, we focus on the experiment steps (E2) *planning*, (E3) *operation*, and (E4) *analysis*.

Experiment Roles and Process Steps Table 1 identifies the following roles from the perspectives *experiment process* and *HC support*: *ESE researcher*, *HC technical expert*, and *study participant*. These roles provide candidate requirements for HC support in the experiment process and may require HC expertise.

- *ESE researcher.* Regarding the experiment process, the ESE researcher defines the research method that the HC methods and tools should support and analyzes the data coming from the HC platform. Regarding the HC process, the ESE researcher is the HC requester.
- *HC technical expert.* In the experiment process, the HC technical expert is part of the research team to support the ESE researcher with technical expertise and resources. In the HC process, he designs the HC tasks, and configures and operates the HC platform.
- *Study participant* takes part in the experiment as an HC contributor.

Table 1 shows the experiment steps *planning*, *operation*, and *analysis*, in which researchers may take the role of an *HC requester* to support experimentation tasks with HC methods that are executed on an *HC platform*, with study participants in the role *HC contributors* qualified for the respective HC tasks. Table 1 describes for each HC role selected contributions to an experiment step. These contributions typically require the iterative interaction (a) between the HC requester and HC technical expert to design and configure the HC platform and (b) between the HC technical expert via the HC platform with the HC contributor to test or run the HC tasks.

E2. Experiment Planning Based on the goal for an experiment, the ESE researchers design the experiment, the hypotheses, and the detailed experiment tasks to collect valid data for analysis. Therefore, the ESE researcher needs to understand in sufficient detail the capabilities of the HC methods and platform to define the HC tasks and the HC data to be collected.

Interaction of ESE researcher as HC requester with HC technical expert. The researcher and the HC expert discuss iteratively research idea candidates and HC platform capabilities to explore the opportunities and risks of research design options, e.g., the number of participants required, and the estimated duration of HC tasks, and calculate the approximate cost of experiment options. Further, they translate the experiment design into an HC design, including data model, process model, and user interface for splitting SE tasks into HC tasks and aggregating HC results into SE results (see the case study example in Sect. 6). The HC design allows us to assess the complexity of HC tasks and the number of HC task types and contributions required as foundation for assessing the feasibility and cost of the experiment. An important part of the experiment design is to understand threats to validity coming from the HC method and technology, if basic assumptions of the experiment design and the HC method do not fit together, e.g., regarding the control of the experiment setting or regarding the traceability and validity of collected data.

Interaction of HC technical expert via *HC platform with HC contributor.* Based on the HC task design, the HC technical expert configures the platform and pilots the tasks with selected contributors to assess issues for a contributor, e.g., missing or too much information, or high task complexity.

E3. Experiment Operation The HC platform enables monitoring the experiment operation much better than a paper-based experiment environment.

Interaction of ESE researcher as HC requester with HC technical expert. The HC expert can provide the ESE researcher with information from the experiment operation, including the validation and aggregation of HC results, to enable the researcher spotting issues that have to be addressed during the experiment operation. During experiment operation, the platform allows monitoring the work on tasks and the HC results for assessing their quality.

Interaction of HC technical expert via *HC platform with HC contributor.* Via the HC platform, the HC expert can interact with contributors to address technical or procedural issues in the training, qualification, or experiment task phases.

E.4 Experiment Analysis The HC platform provides capabilities for validating and aggregating HC and experiment data.

Interaction of ESE researcher as HC requester with HC technical expert.

In addition to HC-enabled SE tasks, the researcher can define and run HC tasks for validating and aggregating HC results and experiment data that may be hard to validate and aggregate automatically (see the case study example in Sect. 6).

Interaction of HC technical expert via *HC platform with HC contributor.* Via the HC platform, the HC expert can schedule a sufficient number of HC tasks for validating and aggregating HC data until a defined level of data quality or the resource limit is reached.

ESE Requirements From the experiment and HC tasks identified in Table 1, we derive the following *ESE requirement* toward the HC method and platform regarding support for basic experiment principles, e.g., valid measurement.

R1 Definition of experiment plan. The architecture of the HC tasks and platform, e.g., regarding splitting of large tasks and aggregating small results in a chain of tasks, has to be compatible with the experiment goal and tasks. The HC method and platform have to support the definition of participant groups and tasks with context information, instructions, input data, and output data as required for fulfilling experimental requirements.

R2 Control during experiment operation. The HC platform has to provide capabilities for implementing the experiment plan and for monitoring experiment tasks during operation. It should provide capabilities for in-process control to enable dynamic scheduling of tasks and input data for participants according to the HC task result quality level achieved, e.g., sufficient agreement on whether a defect report is a true defect or a false positive.

R3   Measurement during experiment operation. The HC platform has to provide capabilities for collecting experiment data as defined in the experiment plan and for auditing the execution of the experiment operation process.

R4   Validation of data. The HC platform has to provide capabilities for validating the quality of measured and aggregated experiment data.

R5   Aggregation of data. The HC platform has to provide capabilities for aggregating HC task results, such as decisions taken or text entered, to experiment plan results, such as defects found per task, per scenario, or per defect class.

Experiment Challenges *For which typical challenges in ESE experiments may HC methods and technology provide support?* ESE experiments require valid data collection and classification, which may take considerable effort. Independent of the SE method investigated, some ESE experiment tasks, such as data cleaning and aggregation, typically take considerable effort for the research team to conduct as they are hard to automate but could be supported with HC contributors, who bring in the required skills and motivation.

Experiment challenges, which HC methods and technology could help automate, include (a) the qualification of experiment participants by assessing which participants are sufficiently motivated and capable of conducting the necessary HC tasks; (b) the monitoring of HC task execution during experiment operation; (c) the auditing of experiment operation; (d) validating and aggregating experiment data (as input to experiment data analysis); and (e) in-process control of experiment runs (if planned in the experiment plan).

5   HC Method Capabilities for ESE Experiments

We build on the requirements derived in the previous section to identify relevant HC capabilities that can address these requirements. We rely on lessons learned from the literature as well as from our experience with *expert sourcing* for model quality assurance (Sabou et al. 2018b).

As discussed in Sect. 2, HC methods follow a general pattern of problem decomposition into smaller tasks and of parallel execution of these tasks by a group of participants. Yet, the implementations of this problem-solving pattern are so diverse that it is challenging to agree on one particular HC methodology. Such methodologies (or guidelines) can emerge, however, but only in well-scoped application domains and problem types, for example, for the annotation of *corpora* in *natural language processing* (NLP) (Sabou et al. 2014). Nevertheless, general tooling to implement HC tasks is available, widely used, and a natural choice for newcomers to the use of HC techniques. Therefore, in this section we discuss capabilities offered by typical HC platforms (in particular, the example platform *Figure Eight*).

We discuss typical capabilities of HC platforms grouped by the experiment process steps depicted in Fig. 2. We synthesize these capabilities primarily based on our experience with HC platforms in previous work (Sabou et al. 2018b) for solving problems in the areas of NLP, Semantic Web, and software engineering. In addition, we refer to studies that highlight the same capabilities. Experiment steps E1 and E5 are not substantially supported by HC capabilities and not discussed.

E2. Experiment Planning The following capabilities support requirement R1 related to the definition of the experiment plan:

Support for task interface design. Visual task design interfaces make the creation of task interfaces fast. Simple interfaces, which collect choices, texts, and numbers, do not require programming knowledge. Task templates optimized for task types, such as annotating text or rating websites, facilitate efficient reuse.

Participant recruitment. Stolee and Elbaum (2010) point out the major ESE challenge of *obtaining a large number of adequate subjects* to participate in an experiment. To that end, a highly valued capability of HC platforms is assisting in subject recruitment, by making it possible to reach out to a large, diverse, and 24/7 available pool of study participant candidates, depending on the required participant qualifications. Behrend et al. (2011) observe that the participant population recruited via crowdsourcing tools is more diverse than a study pool recruitment from university students in terms of age, ethnicity, and work experience, thus being better suited to support organizational studies. HC platforms can advertise available tasks to their large participant pool, thus significantly reducing the effort for participant recruitment in a general crowd. In addition, should a study require the participation of a predefined pool of participants, as in *expert sourcing*, there is the possibility to make tasks available only to these participants through direct invitation and hide these tasks from the general crowd.

Participant screening. Most platforms offer built-in mechanisms for screening participants based on generic characteristics such as their geographic location and the quality level of their contributions (deduced from requester feedback). In addition, screening based on custom criteria (e.g., familiarity with the topic of the task) can be easily implemented with a *qualification questionnaire*, i.e., only workers that successfully answer questionnaire questions are given access to the tasks.

Participant training. A major difference, with respect to traditional studies, is the difficulty to incorporate training for performing the task at hand. Instructions are typically provided with all tasks, but reading these instructions cannot be enforced. Alternative testing mechanisms use *on-the-job training*, where workers are given feedback on their work as they complete it. This is possible in HC by injecting known answers into the data set, so-called *gold units*. When workers answer one of these units, the platform will offer the known answer as feedback and allow training the workers. Workers, who consistently give wrong answers, can be denied access to the rest of the tasks after a predefined number of failures.

Ensuring participant privacy. The platform acts as an intermediator, preventing requesters to access or record personal details of the participants, thus ensuring the privacy of the workers (Stolee and Elbaum 2010).

E3. Experiment Operation Requirements R2 (control during the experiment process) and R3 (measurement of experiment data) are enabled by these capabilities.

Dynamic task assignment. Once tasks are defined, the HC platform automates the dynamic distribution of these tasks to participants, making sure that each participant receives the same task only once. The platform optimizes assigning individual tasks to collect the required number of contributions quickly.

Collection of task results. The HC platform collects inputs from the participants in a table (*csv*) containing a wealth of details including the input data, participant data (e.g., the city of residence based on IP address), and the duration of performing each task.

Job completion monitoring. For management purposes, tasks are often grouped into jobs. The HC platform offers management interfaces to monitor the completion rate of the jobs and the expected time till their finalization, and to monitor the participants (e.g., their number, how many were excluded due to poor performance on test tasks). Job monitoring is useful for the requester to identify early potential issues. For example, if a high number of workers fail the competency test, this could be an indication that the task is not sufficiently clearly formulated and should be revised. High disagreement between responses (i.e., if workers provide very different responses to tasks thus making majority voting difficult) might be caused by unclear task design or because the data presented in the tasks are of poor quality (e.g., images that need to be annotated are blurred). Such in-process control of experiments is often not possible in traditional studies but a valuable benefit in case of HC-supported studies.

Participant feedback collection. When workers decide to finish working on the tasks of a job, they are asked to provide feedback about the ease of the task, the clarity of the instructions, and the fairness of the payment. Aggregated values of these ratings are available in real time, allowing requesters to identify exceptionally low ratings and act on those by stopping the experiment in order to refine it as needed. Such feedback is also useful for piloting studies during experiment design.

Payment distribution to participants can also be handled by the platform, which further lowers the associated management effort (Stolee and Elbaum 2010).

E4. Data Analysis and Interpretation Requirements R4 and R5 are addressed by the following capabilities.

(Semi-)Automatic data aggregation. A core element of the HC paradigm, especially of crowdsourcing, is benefiting from the *wisdom of the crowd* (Surowiecki 2004). Hence, for most problems solved with an HC method, the aggregated value of individual judgments is of key interest, as opposed to individual judgments. Therefore, an HC platform provides as an output of the HC task both the detailed data collected from individual workers and an aggregated version of this data. Aggregation depends on the type of data: *averages* are used for numeric data, while *majority voting* helps select the most frequent category in categorical data.

Some data, such as open-ended comments collected with a text-input box, cannot be aggregated and are simply collected. Generally, an HC platform tends to aggregate data in ways that identify the most agreed answer. Nevertheless, an experiment owner can implement custom aggregation functions based on their access to all the data. For example, some aggregation methods such as *CrowdTruth* (crowdtruth.org/) focus on computing *disagreement* rather than agreement in order to identify low-performing workers, and data items that lead to most disagreement (probably due to low-quality data rather than spammers).

We built on these HC capabilities to plan and conduct a line of experiments on HC-enabled software inspection methods. The following section illustrates the ESE experiment steps with a report on issues to consider when using HC methods and technologies in an ESE experiment context.

6   Case Study on Applying HC to a Line of Experiments

This section reports on an illustrative case study on applying HC to a line of experiments regarding *Software Model Inspection* with HC. In the case study, we describe individual aspects for planning and conducting the experiment (labeled with *Experiment Description*) and provide some reflections on the use of HC concepts, methods, and mechanisms in the ESE case study (labeled with *HC Reflection*). We introduce the case study in Sect. 6.1, discuss its stages E1–E5 (Sects. 6.2–6.6), and conclude with considerations about scaling up from a single experiment to a line of experiments in Sect. 6.7.

6.1   Illustrative Use Case: Software Model Inspection with HC

Experiment context and motivation. Models play an important role in software and systems engineering as they represent the foundation for engineering activities that depend on the correctness of these models in follow-up phases in the software engineering life-cycle (e.g., implementation phases that build on design models) or for more detailed planning activities (e.g., different levels of detail for architecture diagrams). Thus, there is the need for carefully evaluating these underlying models to minimize risks of defects and avoidable repair effort in later development phases. *Software Design Inspections* (Fagan 1986) are established approaches for effective and efficient defect detection. However, design inspections are often based on human expert effort and include limitations, such as the number of available human experts and resources as well as the size and complexity of inspection artifacts. Therefore, concepts from HC can help overcome these limitations by opening up new options regarding method and tool support for distributed and scalable model inspections with *expert sourcing* (Winkler et al. 2018).

In the following, we report on our experiences when applying and adapting HC methods and technology in an experiment process. We focus both on (a) the experiment setting (*Experiment Description*) and (b) experiment implementation with reflections on HC application in the study context (*HC Reflection*).

Experiment Description The *study goal* was to evaluate an adapted defect detection (inspection) process approach for structural models, such as the *extended entity relationship (EER) diagrams*, with concepts, methods, and technology from HC to facilitate distributed and scalable inspection processes for model inspection with *expert sourcing*. The EER diagrams extend the basic *entity relationship (ER)* diagram by providing more detailed concepts for database design, e.g., including aggregation and specialization (Gogolla 2008). Main investigated task was to check the correctness of the representation of concepts coming from a scenario, i.e., a textual requirements description as a reference document, in a structural model, such as an EER diagram. Figure 3 illustrates the concept for model analysis with (a) *Traditional Software Inspection* and (b) *HC-Supported Software Model Inspection* aligned with basic ESE study process steps.

For *evaluation purposes*, we followed the process steps of a *controlled experiment* (Wohlin et al. 2012) to investigate requirements for and capabilities of HC approaches for planning, execution, and data analysis of a controlled experiment. Building on Sect. 3, we follow the steps of the experiment process (see Fig. 3) with focus on (a) a traditional, pen-and-paper-based, approach and (b) an adapted inspection approach with HC concepts. Note that we focus on the methodological approach for experiment planning, execution, and data analysis to show potential support of HC concepts. Results of individual experiment runs have been reported, e.g., in Biffl et al. (2018), Sabou et al. (2018b), and Winkler et al. (2017a, b, 2018). First study results showed the feasibility of the HC-supported inspection process with a comparable defect detection effectiveness (i.e., share of reported defects) but increased defect detection efficiency (i.e., defects found per time interval). Note that first reported results did not consider scoping of the inspection material. More recent study reports showed increased effectiveness and efficiency when considering inspection material scoping (Neto et al. 2019b).

HC Reflection We report how the experiment setup was affected by the use of HC, both on a conceptual level (e.g., modification of experiment steps) and on a technical level (e.g., using a concrete HC platform, such as *Figure Eight*). ESE researchers, who consider using HC methods in their empirical studies, can benefit from lessons learned on the benefits and limitations of HC methods and technologies in the case study context. HC researchers can also benefit from lessons learned to further improve HC concepts, methods, and mechanisms to support (a) quality assurance in the SE life-cycle and (b) ESE research by providing improved platforms and support for HC application in the empirical study stages.

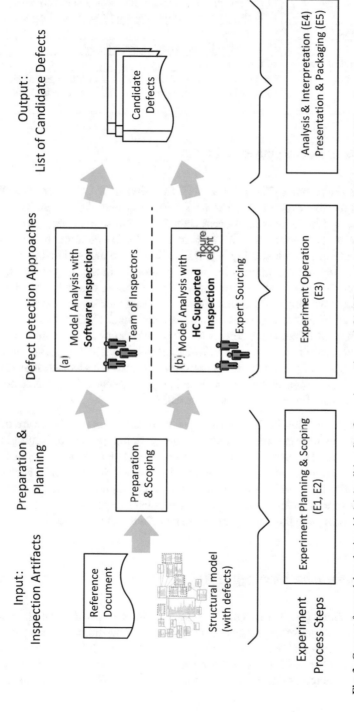

Fig. 3 Concept for model analysis with (**a**) (traditional) software inspection and (**b**) HC-supported inspection aligned with ESE study steps

Table 2 Experiment goal definition, based on the GQM approach (van Solingen et al. 2002)

Analyze	Defect detection performance of structural models (such as an EER diagram) using traditional and HC-supported inspection
For the purpose of	Comparison
With respect to	Defect detection effectiveness and efficiency
From the point of view of	ESE researchers
In the context of	Traditional design inspection based on a valid requirements specification when compared to an HC-supported inspection approach

6.2 Experiment Scoping (E1)

Experiment Description The process step *Experiment Scoping (E1)* (see Fig. 3) takes as input the experiment idea (see Sect. 6.1) and defines the experiment goal, scope, and hypothesis as process output. The *Goal Question Metric (GQM)* approach (van Solingen et al. 2002) can help researchers in defining the goals, scope, and hypotheses. In the illustrating experiment, we define the goal in Table 2.

We use a well-known application domain, typical restaurant processes, which cover important and easy-to-follow steps for reservation, order, kitchen handling, and payment. We use a requirements specification, which is considered to be correct and an EER data model of the database structure. The EER data model was seeded with a set of common defects that typically occur in software engineering practice. The study treatment is the HC-supported inspection process; the control group applies a traditional (pen-and-paper-based) software inspection approach. The initial hypotheses focuses on defect detection performance, i.e., defect detection effectiveness and efficiency (Winkler et al. 2018).

HC Reflection For the illustrating example, researchers need to be aware of effort required in the experiment preparation and planning phase for setting up the experiment with HC support. There was no explicit HC support applicable for the initial experiment definition phase, i.e., *Experiment Scoping* (E1), because this phase is similar for experiments with and without HC support. However, researchers should be aware of technological aspects (and related expertise and efforts) needed for implementing and conducting the experiment with and without HC support.

6.3 Experiment Planning (E2)

Experiment Description According to Table 1 in Sect. 4, three main roles are required in the experiment process with focus on the experiment planning step (E2): (a) *ESE researcher (HC requester)*, (b) *technical expert* for HC supporting activities approaches (*HC expert*), and (c) *study participant (HC contributor)*. The first author of this chapter acted as technical expert for HC support (*HC expert*), while the other two authors represent ESE researchers (and *HC requestors*). In the context of the example experiment, students represent *HC contributors*.

For the *ESE researcher*, the experiment planning step included (1) experiment treatment definition (e.g., HC-supported inspection), (2) experiment design (e.g., cross-over design of treatment and control groups, material preparation, study group definition, definition of measurement and data, and threats to validity considerations), and (3) definition of the study process (e.g., scheduling and sequence of study tasks). *HC technical experts* focused on (1) the configuration of the HC platform (e.g., setting up individual tasks, contributor groups, and data input/output) and (2) operation and monitoring of the platform. *Study participants* (HC contributors) mainly took part in pilot runs to ensure the correctness and completeness of the study design and the feasibility of the study operation in terms of scheduling.

ESE researchers defined the *experiment treatment* (see Fig. 4). Inputs were the *Inspection Artifacts*, i.e., the reference document and the *Structural Model*, i.e., the EER diagram (label 1, Fig. 4). Furthermore, the research team used the concept of *expected model elements* (EMEs) that represent building blocks of the model (label 2, Fig. 4), coming from the reference scenarios for checking their representation in the structural model. In case of an EER diagram, EMEs include entities, attributes, relations, and relation attributes (Winkler et al. 2018). ESE researchers derived these EMEs from the inspection artifacts. The HC management (label 3, Fig. 4) prepared the HC platform, in our case *Figure Eight*, by designing small-scale tasks for model inspection, for collecting defect reports from study participants, and for aggregating these reports for further analysis, i.e., defect validation, which was conducted manually by ESE researchers (label 5, Fig. 4). In the *model analysis* task (label 4, Fig. 4), individual study participants received small tasks, provided by the HC platform, checked the model for correctness, and reported defects or declared that they found no defect. These reports represent the input for the defect validation tasks (label 5, Fig. 4), executed by ESE researchers.

Study Process To compare HC-supported inspection and traditional inspection, the research team designed the basic study process in three groups (Fig. 5). Groups A and B represented HC treatment groups with a cross-over design and group C represented the control group applying traditional software inspection using the pen-and-paper (P&P) approach. Groups A and B received a *tutorial* (30 min) that presented the approach, introduced to the HC platform, including an experience questionnaire followed by an HC qualification process step. P&P participants (group C) received a *tutorial* that introduced a traditional software inspection process and included an experience questionnaire to capture background knowledge and skills. The *experiment phase* was structured into two sessions (60 min each): For HC participants, each session focused on two different main tasks: (a) identification of EMEs (HC Task 1) and (b) defect detection (HC Task 2). Group A started with EME identification followed by defect detection; group B executed similar tasks but in reverse order. Assigned tasks for individual groups included half of the application (controlled by the HC platform) to minimize bias and learning effects. The research team collected feedback on each task after task completion.

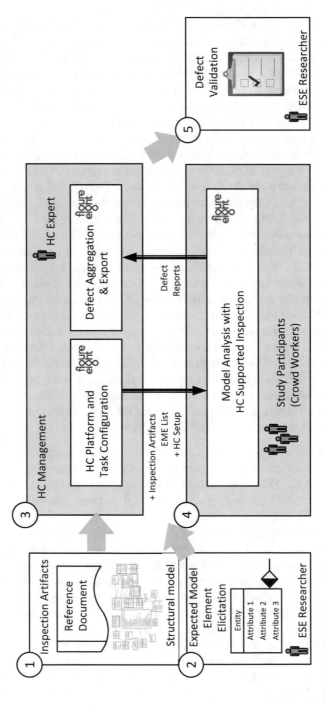

Fig. 4 HC-supported inspection process

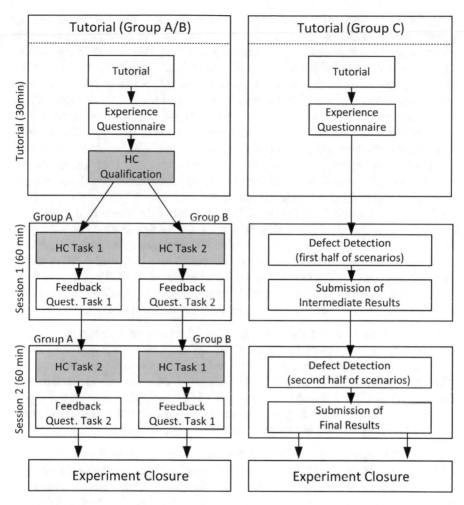

Fig. 5 Study process

The control group (group C) executed traditional inspection by focusing on the first half of the application in the first session and on the second half of the application in the second session. *Experiment Closure* included the submission of the material and a check if all tasks had been completed.

Materials included an *experience questionnaire* to capture background and skills of study participants. Although the HC platform supported questionnaires, the research team used *Google.forms* to keep questionnaires separated from the platform in the first step for simplicity reasons. Furthermore, the researchers captured participant feedback *(feedback questionnaire)* to gain experience on how the HC platform (and the P&P approach) was perceived by participants and to collect additional feedback, such as estimated numbers of remaining defects. For this step, the researchers applied *Google.forms*. Although it is possible to incorporate questionnaires in the HC platform, we decided to keep them separated to enable usage of similar questionnaires for all study groups (i.e., P&P and HC participants). Other materials included the *reference document*, i.e., a requirements specification (including four pages in English language, consisting of seven scenarios), the *model under inspection*, i.e., the EER diagram (consisting of 9 entities, 13 relationships, and 32 attributes) including 33 *seeded defects*. These defects were introduced by the experiment team, i.e., the authors, based on defects that typically occurred during software development processes such as missing, incomplete, ambiguous, superfluous, or wrong entities, relations, or attributes. The P&P group did not receive a list of *expected model elements (EMEs)* because they had to identify these elements in the first step of the inspection process.

P&P participants received the guideline, one-half of the requirements specifica- tion and scenarios, and the defective EER model for the first session and the second half of the scenarios for the second session. *HC participants* received microtasks via the platform and related scenarios for each task. Depending on the HC tasks, the participants received (a) a sentence (as a microtask) to elicit EMEs (HC Task 1) or (b) a sentence and the model for identifying whether or not the EME exists in the model and whether or not it is represented correctly in the model (HC Task 2).

Study Participants and Group Assignment The study was embedded within a course on *Software Quality Assurance* at TU Wien, where participants already had some experience on software development and quality assurance, especially on soft- ware inspection. In addition, the research team provided a tutorial as introduction to the study. For HC participants, a small task was implemented to measure participant qualification. Prior to the study, we used a *sort-card algorithm* for group assignment to ensure a balanced and randomized distribution of participants.

Data and Measurement We defined independent and dependent variables. Inde- pendent variables included seeded defects, defect types, tool configuration, and study treatments. Dependent variables were effort for task execution, reported and true defects, effectiveness (i.e., share of seeded defects and identified true defects) and efficiency (i.e., defects found per hour), and false positives (reported candidate defects that do not match a true defect). Data collection was organized via an *Experiment Management System (EMS)*[6] (P&P participants had to upload their results to the EMS), via the HC platform (for HC participants), and via *Google.forms* (all study groups). We transferred questionnaire data as well as data from P&P and HC (after some cleanup activities to exclude data management overhead) into an SQL database for analysis and interpretation.

Threats to Validity Based on the study design, several limitations needed to be considered. In the example experiment, we introduced a set of seeded defects based on typical defects in software engineering. Additional true defects, which came up

---

[6]TUWeL (tuwel.tuwien.ac.at.) is a learning platform for course organization/administration.

during the experiment, were added to the list of true defects. Issues regarding the application domain were addressed by using an application domain that was familiar to the prospective participants, scenarios in a restaurant. The experiment material had been reviewed and improved by experts. Furthermore, we conducted several pilot runs in small groups to ensure the feasibility and quality of the experiment materials and plan. The experiment was conducted in a classroom setting to avoid the unplanned communication of participants. Breaks were allowed and recorded. The experiment was carried out in university courses; the authors are aware of limitations of student experiments (Runeson 2003).

Tooling We used an *Experiment Management System (EMS)* to provide the relevant information to the participants: For *P&P participants*, we provided the guideline, links to the questionnaires, defect collection sheets, requirements specifications and scenarios in two parts, and the defective model. This material was available in electronic form via the EMS and as hardcopy. After experiment completion, P&P participants had to upload their results to the EMS and hand over all materials to the experiment team. For HC participants, we used the EMS for providing relevant information (similar to P&P participants) and links to the HC platform for individual HC-related tasks. The HC platform manages all related HC tasks.

HC Reflection HC Experts are responsible for the configuration of the HC platform and for setting up the administrative environment. HC tasks were managed via the *Figure Eight* platform. For HC qualification (in the context of the tutorial), EME identification (HC Task 1), and defect detection (HC Task 2), the participants were guided by the HC platform. In collaboration with the *ESE researcher*, the *HC expert* built on the inspection material to design and prepare the HC tasks. In the context of the HC qualification process step (within the tutorial), the researchers used a different simple application domain, typical scenarios of a parking garage use case, to measure the basic capabilities of participant candidates on working with the HC platform and on reporting defects. For the experiment, the researchers focused on processes of a restaurant. Main tasks of the HC expert included (a) analyzing and identifying small and manageable tasks, such as sentences of a requirements specification, (b) selecting related scenarios, (c) and preparing the related scope of the model (applicable for the defect detection task).

For the *EME identification task* (HC Task 1), the HC expert used the requirements specification to split this specification into sentences as foundation for a set of microtasks. Based on these microtasks, the HC expert prepared batches of tasks to be completed by study participants; see a sample task design in (Sabou et al. 2018b). For the model defect detection task (HC Task 2), HC experts used the set of EMEs as guidance for task design, i.e., defect detection. We used a predefined set of EMEs, prepared by the authors, as a stable baseline for defect detection. Furthermore, HC experts prepared the scenario (as reference document), the EER model (inspection artifacts), and guidance to enable participants to classify defect candidates. Figure 6 presents a set of screenshots from an experiment run, including:

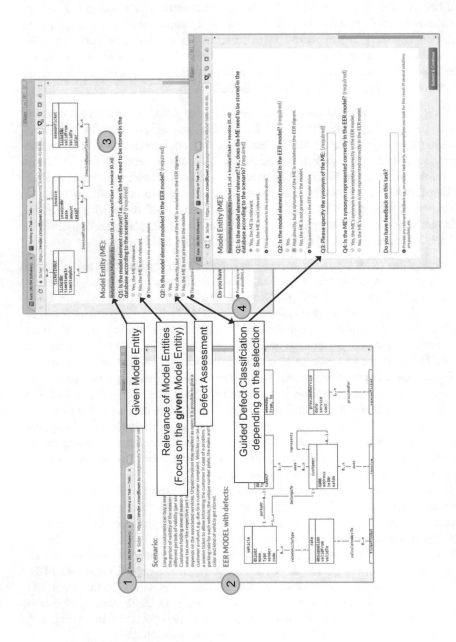

Fig. 6 Sample screenshots of a microtask for model analysis

1. *Scenario descriptions* based on the analysis of the requirements specification. Note that this scenario was considered to be correct (i.e., represents a snapshot of a part of the reference document).
2. *EER Model.* We presented the EER model that included 33 defects. This model could also be subset of the inspection artifact to be inspected, as input to tasks for scoping and selecting relevant model elements.
3. *Expected Model Element (EME).* Based on the task description, a selected model element guided the HC participant to identify defects. This is comparable to P&P where the participants had to identify EMEs in the first inspection step. Note that the first HC task also focused on the identification of EMEs, which were not directly used for defect detection in the same experiment but as input to a follow-up experiment in a family of experiments.
4. The *Defect Assessment* part guided HC participants in classifying a defect candidate. In an initial task pilot, we had not provided any guidance, but captured candidate defects in textual form. As the free form of measured data led to high effort for analyzing these reports, we changed toward a more guided approach, which makes it more efficient to aggregate and analyze candidate defects. This approach also facilitated immediate feedback to the participants.

To enable this structured defect detection approach, considerable effort was needed for the configuration of the HC platform, aggregating small tasks to related task groups and assigning these task groups to contributor groups, i.e., study participant groups. Furthermore, HC experts had to define input data, to provide mechanisms for data transformation (as input for the HC platform), and to provide data transformation approaches for data (defect) analysis and aggregation. These tasks strongly depend on the applied platform, e.g., *Figure Eight*. During the experiment run, the HC expert was responsible for operating and monitoring the platform, e.g., if participants were close to running out of tasks, the HC expert was able to assign further tasks to individual participants.

Based on the example experiment, identified ESE requirements, and HC capabilities for *the experiment planning phase* (E1), we see HC promising for supporting ESE research. Main benefits are (a) *participant recruitment* (e.g., by using qualification tasks, designing HC tasks, and supporting cognitive human tasks by providing guidance within the defect detection task); (b) *experiment organization* (e.g., generation, organization, distribution of tasks and inputs, and the collection of task results); (c) *experiment execution* (e.g., by distributing tasks to a group of experts); and (d) the *analysis and aggregation* of task results.

6.4   Experiment Operation (E3)

Experiment Description The *experiment operation* concerns the execution of the experiment run according to the experiment plan. While for the P&P experiment research staff supervised the participants, validated the collected data, and classified reported defects according to a list of true defects, for HC-supported experiments, an *HC expert* is required for configuring, monitoring, and managing the specific HC technology to ensure valid data collection. In this section, we focus on main process steps with HC roles.

Main tasks of *ESE researcher* focus on the *execution of the experiment* according to the experiment plan. In the example experiment, the ESE researcher provided the tutorial and supervised the P&P participants (due to the nature of pen-and-paper experiments), while the HC participants were efficiently guided by the HC platform without the need for supervision by ESE researchers. However, some supervision was provided to ensure that participants followed the experiment guidance, to provide answers to questions related to the inspection artifacts, and to observe the experiment environment (e.g., to avoid communication between participants). In collaboration with the HC expert, an ESE researcher observed the experiment execution *(audit experiment execution)* in terms of checking samples of incoming data from the experiment run in the HC platform. In our context, we provided questionnaires via *Google.forms*, and hard copy handouts. Thus, a task of the ESE researcher was to *collect* the *experimental material and data* that was not available via the HC platform. Although HC platforms can handle questionnaires and collect data, they may be more complex to set up for simple cases in comparison to specific survey tools. In addition, the ESE researcher conducted basic *experiment data validation* tasks in cooperation with the HC expert such as the availability and correctness of submitted data from individual microtask assignments.

The *HC technical expert* is responsible for the configuring and operating the HC platform, such as maintaining the platform in case of technical problems during operation and for configuring HC tasks for upcoming experiment process steps. In the context of the example experiment, the HC technical expert could execute consistency checks and aggregation tasks after the EME identification step (HC Task 1) as preparation for the defect detection task, i.e., model analysis. In the example experiment, researchers applied a predefined set of EMEs for the defect detection tasks to avoid issues from carrying over data between experiment sessions. Furthermore, one version of the implementation of HC tasks required considerable time for the manual setup of the defect detection task, which could be risky in the context of given time constraints. Therefore, tool support for the configuration was an issue with high priority (see Sect. 6.7).

HC contributors, i.e., study participants, (a) participate in the study by executing assigned HC tasks and (b) provide feedback on the tasks to be solved via the HC platform. After the HC experiment, researchers added a section to collect feedback on the task and the HC platform to enable participants to report observations and issues and to suggest improvements. Therefore, this feedback cycle can be used for HC technical experts to adjust HC platform capabilities as required.

HC Reflection An important benefit of applying HC technologies includes the opportunity for *in-process control* based on monitoring ongoing activities or based on results of previous experiment steps. Examples include monitoring participant activities to see whether or not they follow the experiment process correctly (and act accordingly), the re-assignment of tasks in case of deviations (e.g., contradicting results, incomplete or missing results), automated feedback to study participants (an important aspect for the motivation of participants), in-process data validity checks, or the re-assignment and/or extension of selected task assignments, e.g., if an HC participant might run out of tasks during experiment operation. Therefore, important tasks of HC technical experts include the scheduling and monitoring of the HC tasks (during experiment operation) and the monitoring, validation, and initial aggregation of data collection (*in-process control*). This initial validation focuses on monitoring incoming results for completeness and correctness from the HC platform perspective. Data aggregation addresses the issue of immediate feedback to participants on the task performance, i.e., defect detection performance.

6.5   Analysis and Interpretation (E4)

Beyond *in-process control* of the experiment during operation, analysis, and interpretation processes are conducted after the operation phase. These tasks represent the main responsibilities of *ESE researchers* who focus on the validation, aggregation, analysis, and interpretation of experiment data by following guidelines for reporting empirical study results, such as Jedlitschka et al. (2008).

Experiment Description While for P&P the data evaluation, especially the assignment of reported defects to true defects, was executed manually, the HC platform supported the automated classification of defect reports based on majority voting from several participants, typically 3 to 7, depending on the level of (dis)agreement. In the experiment context, the EMEs represented building blocks of the model and were used to locate defect candidates. Therefore, the analysis feature of the HC platform was able to support the classification of candidate defects reported for an EME and to aggregate defect reports. Thus, the effort of assessing and classifying defect reports was reduced for ESE researchers, who could focus on resolving contradicting results from several participants. We used this basic functionality as foundation for further analysis.

In the example experiment, experimental data was collected on various platforms, such as *Google.forms* (e.g., questionnaires), paper-based or as spreadsheet solutions (for P&P participants), and via the HC platform (for HC participants). Although the HC platform enables the collection, initial validation, analysis, and aggregation of data, heterogeneous sets of data needed to be organized and managed with considerable care and effort. Thus, researchers used SQL-based data storage to collect the materials for the analysis phase. The database represented the foundation for the analysis process using descriptive statistics, data reduction, and hypothesis testing for data validation and analysis and for the interpretation of the results regarding the acceptance or rejection of stated hypotheses. This database held all information, both from the traditional inspection process and from the HC-supported inspection including questionnaire results.

HC Reflection The HC platform provides some basic aggregation mechanisms as foundation for data analysis and aggregation. However, additional information, such as personal data and organizational information for managing HC tasks, is of limited interest for ESE researcher and, thus, should be removed before further analysis. The SQL database focused on experimental data that were relevant for analysis and interpretation. ESE researchers had to define beforehand which data were required for analysis as input for data preparation, a main task of the HC technical expert.

The *HC technical expert* has to (a) execute some basic consistency checks within the HC platform to ensure the correctness and completeness of experimental data based on assigned tasks and (b) maintain experimental raw data. This data maintenance step includes the removal of irrelevant data sets (such as organizational data needed for HC task execution, but not relevant to the experiment) and the removal of data from participants, who did not follow the experiment process properly or did not complete the experiment. After the maintenance step, the HC platform holds valid data usable for further analysis, such as initial aggregation of results for grouping defect reports as foundation for assigning them to true defects. In the last step of data maintenance, the HC technical expert needed to extract data (as required by ESE researcher) as input for the SQL database. This step required interfaces for data transformation from the HC platform to the SQL database. Finally, the HC expert provided interfaces to include external sources, such as *Google.forms* data and experimental data, captured in spreadsheet solutions (P&P participants), and made the data from external sources available in the SQL database.

In empirical studies, the feedback to participants is important for the acceptance of usefulness of the study for participants. Often this feedback is hard to provide or can be provided only later, after manual analysis steps. HC capabilities enable *immediate feedback to participants* and thus help increase the acceptance and the motivation of study participants. Therefore, during the experiment analysis phase, the *HC contributor* (i.e., study participant) receives feedback on their defect detection performance for improving their inspection skills. In the context of the example experiment, the participants received feedback on their performance within a couple of hours after the study, which was received well by many participants.

6.6   Presentation and Package (E5)

Based on the conclusions reached from analyzing and interpreting the experiment data, the researchers document and report the results (Jedlitschka et al. 2008). This step is similar for experiments that collect data using pen-and-paper (P&P) or HC technology.

Experiment Description In the context of the example experiment, we planned a *family of experiments* with variations that benefited from a high degree of reusing the material on and configurations of the HC platform in various experiment runs (Winkler et al. 2017a, b; Sabou et al. 2018b).

HC Reflection While experiments without HC allow reusing the material by manually assessing and adapting experiment settings and materials (e.g., in the context of replications), HC-supported experiments can go beyond this basic level of reuse by also reusing task organizations, strategies for the distribution of tasks and inputs, mechanisms for data collection, analysis, and aggregation.

6.7 Toward a Family of Experiments

Experiment Description The example experiment represents a snapshot of an experiment with HC-supported inspection with focus on defect detection. However, HC capabilities can enable a longer tool chain that supports individual experimental steps, which are usually done manually or with limited tool support. Biffl et al. (2018) presented a concept of a family of experiments for HC-supported inspection enabling the application of HC on various steps of the inspection process.

HC Reflection Figure 7 illustrates extensions of HC-supported inspection processes including (a) *Expected Model Element (EME) identification*, (b) *Model Analysis and Defect Detection* (as illustrated by the example experiment), and (c) *Defect Validation* (Biffl et al. 2018).

- *Inspection Artifacts* (label 1, Fig. 7). Similar to the illustrating example, inspection artifacts, such as reference documents and the model under inspection, represent the starting point for inspection scoping and for experiment scoping.
- *Expected Model Element (EME) Identification* (label 2, Fig. 7). The first step of the inspection process focuses on *EME* identification. This process step has been introduced in the example experiment (HC Task 1) without considering these results in the following steps, i.e., defect detection, of the experiment (we used a predefined set of EMEs for defect detection). However, inputs for EME identification were the requirements specification and the model. The HC platform (label 3a in Fig. 7) provided sentences to identify building blocks of the model (for an EER diagram: entities, relations, and attributes) and collects, analyzes, and aggregates expected model elements as input for defect detection.
- *Model Analysis and Defect Detection* (label 3b and 4, Fig. 7). The defect detection process step (managed by the HC platform) takes as input a set of EMEs, scenarios, and the model under inspection. Note that we used a predefined set of EMEs instead of an EME list created in the previous step. However, the HC platform (label 3c, Fig. 7) collects all reported candidate defects, provided by the participants, and executes some initial evaluation (see Sect. 6.4). After this process step, the HC platform holds an aggregated list of EMEs and a list of reported defects.

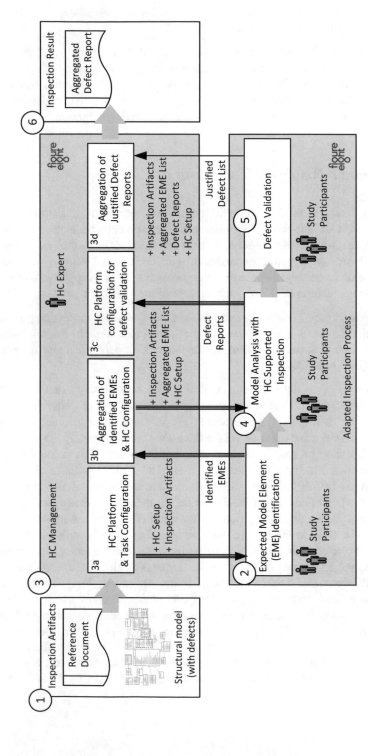

Fig. 7 Extensions of the HC-supported inspection process with EME identification and defect validation steps

Table 3 Experiment variants in the context of an experiment family (*TA* Text analysis for EME identification, *MA* model analysis for defect detection, *DV* defect validation)

Different usage of HC in a family of experiment	TA	MA	DV
Focus on eliciting EMEs	X		
Focus on model analysis/defect detection (i.e., our example experiment)		X	
Focus on EME identification and model analysis	X	X	
Focus on model analysis and defect validation		X	X
Complete HC-supported inspection process	X	X	X

- *Defect Validation* (label 5, Fig. 7). The third step focuses on the validation of defects based on EMEs, scenarios, and defect reports. The HC platform (label 3d in Fig. 7) provides microtasks for defect classification and assessment for participants and collects individual assessments of defect reports. Result is a set of classified defect reports (including voting and an initial mapping to seeded defects). We provided several options via the HC platform that supported participants in defect assessment (one of the options is the true defect if applicable). This process step is typically executed manually by ESE researchers after experiment completion. With HC support, HC contributors can contribute to solving these ESE tasks.
- *Defect Report* (label 6, Fig. 7). The final result after the defect validation process step includes a set of classified defects with voting as input for data analysis and interpretation. The set of defects can include agreements if several participants assessed the defect report in a similar way and some defect reports may include contradicting results. Contradicting results represent the input for ESE researcher for a more detailed manual analysis. However, the amount of these unclear assessments is limited.

Introducing all HC-supported inspection steps into an experiment at once might incur considerable risk because of several confounding factors. Therefore, we planned a family of experiments with variation points that focus on a defined set of HC capabilities in the context of the overall HC-supported inspection process (Biffl et al. 2018). Table 3 presents an overview of candidate combinations of HC-supported inspection tasks in the context of an experiment line. Furthermore, we highlight the core contributions of HC in the context of an experiment line. Note that other tasks are still needed but remain to be considered by the ESE researchers who execute these manually.

There are several published reports on the results of controlled experiments with focus on model analysis/defect detection (such as Biffl et al. 2018; Sabou et al. 2018b; Winkler et al. 2017a, b, 2018), with promising results regarding scalable defect detection performance, i.e., defect detection efficiency, and effectiveness, for inspector groups in the context of a defined model scope.

7   Benefits and Limitations

We hereby discuss a number of benefits and limitations of HC as emerged from other studies in the literature and our own work.

Benefits   The typical benefits of using HC in general (Snow et al. 2008; Behrend et al. 2011), and in software engineering in particular, relate to:

- Cost reductions by obtaining free (in the case of games) or cheap input from contributors (on average, the completion of one task on crowdsourcing marketplaces is in the range of US\$0.3–0.5)
- Time reductions by benefiting for a larger workforce that is typically available 24/7
- While typically obtaining results with high-quality rivaling what can be obtained from a small number of experts (provided using a proper setup of the HC task and appropriate quality assurance methods)

In addition, when used in scientific or teaching contexts, HC has the potential to promote learning and science among participants. Learning and self-improvement through participation in crowdsourcing projects are major opportunities and powerful incentive mechanisms. For example, the *Duolingo* (duolingo.com) game both trains contributors in a new language and helps with translation tasks. Participants in open-source software projects reportedly are motivated by learning new skills (LaToza and van der Hoek 2016). Within our experiment families (Winkler et al. 2017a, b; Sabou et al. 2018b), participating students benefited from an assessment of their model analysis skills: they received detailed feedback on each of their contributions (whether they were correct or not based on a comparison to a gold standard, that is, a set of model defects identified by the experiment team), as well as general statistics on how their performance compared to that of their peers in the group, both in terms of the quantity and the quality of their contributions.

Limitations   Although the use of HC reduces the overall duration needed to perform experiments, typically HC requires an effort from the experiment team to learn the approach and the intricacies of the HC platform used. We discuss further limitations grouped by the experiment steps that the limitations affect most.

E2. Experiment Planning
Splitting study tasks into small, individual tasks can be a challenge. A key characteristic of the HC method is splitting an overall problem into several independent tasks that can be (easily) performed in parallel by the participant pool. Yet, given the very nature of software as a highly complex and interconnected set of artifacts, such a task composition is challenging in general (LaToza and van der Hoek 2016; Mao et al. 2017), and in ESE experiments in particular (Stolee and Elbaum 2010). For the model analysis task we reported (Sabou et al. 2018b), decomposition was also a challenge and addressed by decomposing the EER model into individual model elements, and collecting defects at model element level.

The (demographic) composition of the study population is hard to predetermine. Although there are several methods to screen and select the study participants, the composition of the final population cannot be controlled prior to running the study. This is a drawback for studies where the balanced representation of certain groups is important (Stolee and Elbaum 2010). The population composition can, however, be determined by administering a post-study questionnaire to participants. In *expert sourcing* settings, this limitation is circumvented as the participant pool can be selected prior to the study.

Task interface design is limited by crowdsourcing platform capabilities. While crowdsourcing platforms allow easily building task interfaces, their capabilities are limited to a set of interface elements that are used by the majority of problems solved on these platforms, i.e., typical form-based questionnaires. Creating specialized interfaces that go beyond question answering is challenging and can often be realized only outside the platform with additional programming effort. In our case, for example, we aim at creating a task interface within the *Figure Eight* platform which allows workers to directly annotate (a picture of) an EER model.

Legal and ethical aspects need to be observed. An increasing number of institutions have introduced ethics boards to approve studies involving human participants, for example through HC. Therefore, ESE experiment teams may need to consider issues of ethical and legal nature, as discussed next. *Acknowledging the participating crowd's contributions*, i.e., listing *the Crowd* as an author. While there are no clear guidelines about this issue, some volunteer projects (e.g., *Foldit, Phylo*) already include contributors in the authors' list (Kawrykow et al. 2012). *Ensuring contributor privacy and well-being* by implementing appropriate safeguards and warnings to ensure that no personal data is stored or transmitted and that prolonged, potentially health-damaging engagement, addiction, or unethical exploitation of users is prevented. In some cases, the unknown age of the volunteers/gamers could also be of concern (many teenagers and younger children are avid gamers). Another issue is *licensing and consent*, i.e., making it clear to contributors that by carrying out some tasks they are contributing knowledge for scientific purposes and agree to a well-defined license for sharing and using their work. We also recommend that crowdsourcing projects adopt an open license, clearly stated and used as a motivating factor in recruiting contributors.

E3. Experiment Operation

Difficult to enforce task execution order. Although the dynamic and randomized assignment of tasks to participants is a key capability of crowdsourcing platforms, this aspect can be seen as a limitation for studies that need to control the order in which the tasks should be performed (Stolee and Elbaum 2010).

Difficult to guarantee that each participant performs all tasks. As participants join and leave the HC project at different times, it is very hard to ensure that a participant performs all tasks: some may leave without having seen all tasks, while others might join late, when all required inputs already have been collected for some tasks (Stolee and Elbaum 2010).

Difficult to assess and ensure similar experiment contexts and setups. If participants perform tasks in their own context with their own setup, it is challenging for the experiment team to ensure that these context/setups are similar (Stolee and Elbaum 2010). Diversity of user setups is, however, beneficial for crowdsourced testing (e.g., of apps) where this diversity ensures the reliability of results. In our *expert sourcing* experiment (Winkler et al. 2017a, b; Sabou et al. 2018b), we circumvented this issue by restricting participation from a controlled lab environment with the same setup for all participants.

E4. Data Analysis and Interpretation
Dealing with multiple, possibly low-quality contributions. A direct consequence of working with a diverse and unknown workforce is that the collected contributions are also likely to contain low-quality inputs introduced inadvertently (i.e., because of lack of needed skills or experience) or intentionally by spammers (Stolee and Elbaum 2010; Mao et al. 2017). *Quality assurance* (QA) is therefore a key aspect of using HC successfully. QA involves a set of measures that can be taken during task design (e.g., providing clear, example-based instructions, including *gold units* that help filter out spammers during task execution) and after the data collection process. In the later stage, aggregation methods should also take into consideration the overall performance of the contributors and attempt to minimize the influence of low-quality contributors. There is a large body or research on *truth inference mechanisms* as surveyed by Zheng et al. (2017).

Dealing with imprecise measurements of task duration. For studies that need exact information on how much time participants spend on performing a task, a challenge lies in collecting this duration information in a reliable manner: indeed, crowdsourcing platforms report the time during which a task was open in the browser, which does not necessarily correspond to the time that was dedicated to performing the task itself (Stolee and Elbaum 2010).

Lessons Learned We have already reported on preliminary results or parts of the family of experiments with focus model analysis and defect detection (Biffl et al. 2018; Sabou et al. 2018b; Winkler et al. 2017a, 2018) and received promising results in the context of model scoping. Up to now we have executed the experiment four times since 2016 and derived a set of lessons learned from previous experiment runs, involving 100+ participants during experiment runs. Thus, we have implemented several improvements:

Task design. In the first experiment run, tasks were designed in order to capture textual information from participants (for EME identification and defect reports). The research team experienced a considerable effort for manual aggregation of EME results (HC Task 1) and defect reports (HC Tasks 2) because it was hard to extract and analyze different spellings, acronyms, and free text information automatically via the HC platform. Thus, we introduced a so-called output language, i.e., informal grammars for reporting EMEs and for reporting defects. Although this change has improved the analysis process to some extent, manual effort was required to analyze the results because some participants did not follow the reporting grammars. Therefore, we introduced a defect reporting user interface that guides participants in reporting defects (e.g., by selecting relevant options). Although this setup requires additional effort for the HC technical experts, this change pays off during the analysis phase because the output can be analyzed automatically.

Participant feedback. In the first experiment runs, we received participant feedback on wanting to know their individual performance during defect detection, i.e., their effectiveness. At the beginning, it required several weeks for data analysis to deliver this feedback to participants. By introducing guided defect detection, we were able to inform participants via E-Mail on initial results within a couple of hours. This fast feedback was received positively and increased the motivation for taking part in the experiments.

Defect Validation. While we had to analyze defects with high human effort manually in the first two experiment runs, we implemented a defect validation task (another HC-related activity) to gain benefits of HC for defect classification and aggregation. To keep the experiment duration similar, we skipped the EME identification part as we use the predefined set of EMEs for the experiment runs. Note that this additional defect validation step is based on voting of participants (and only a subset of reported defects require manual analysis); therefore, the analysis process was more efficient and effective.

Evaluation Platform (SQL database). All HC-related data were captured via the HC platform including a large amount of organizational data required for HC management, not directly relevant for analysis and interpretation. Thus, we introduced an evaluation platform that holds relevant experimental data and external sources (such as *Google.forms* questionnaire results). However, the HC technical experts need to provide transformation and querying mechanisms to retrieve relevant experiment information for further analysis.

8   Recommended Further Reading

Interested readers could find interesting the papers on the following topics:

- *HC and related topics*: An excellent introductory paper of the HC field is Quinn and Bederson (2011), while O. Alonso (2019) presents practical considerations for designing and implementing large-scale HC tasks. A recent overview of truth inference mechanisms and their comparison is presented in Zheng et al. (2017). Ethical issues related to the use of crowdsourcing platforms are discussed in Fort et al. (2011).
- *HC and its impact on scientific research in other research communities.* In our own work, we have surveyed the use and impact of HC to support research in the communities of natural language processing (Sabou et al. 2012) and Semantic Web (Sabou et al. 2018a, b).
- *HC in software engineering.* The surveys of LaToza and van der Hoek (2016) and especially Mao et al. (2017) provide a valuable overview of crowdsourcing to support software engineering tasks in both industrial praxis and research.

9   Conclusion

This chapter is motivated by the recent, intensified use of HC methods to solve a variety of SE tasks (Mao et al. 2017) which implies that the traditional SE methods are adapted to benefit from HC capabilities. Therefore, two interesting research lines emerge for ESE. Firstly, to better understand the impact of HC on SE task performance, e.g., task effectiveness and efficiency, there is a need for ESE studies that compare HC-enabled SE tasks to traditional alternatives, such as illustrated in this chapter in the area of software inspection. Secondly, HC could provide useful capabilities for those steps in ESE studies (especially experiments) that deal with large-scale data processing tasks (collection, cleaning, and aggregation) and are currently hard to automate. HC seems to be mostly relevant to consider for ESE experiments, as the tool support for case studies and surveys is likely to benefit from HC, in general, only to a limited extent. Therefore, in this chapter, we focused on HC as a collaboration technology mainly used during study operation and data analysis of ESE experiments, which requires the consideration of HC methods and tools during the experiment design. We hereby summarize the main conclusions from the three thematic areas of the chapter.

Section 3 analyzed those ESE experiment steps that might benefit the most from HC. We concluded that, in general, the ESE study steps experiment scoping (E1), experiment planning (E2), and presentation and packaging (E5) are tasks that require the close collaboration of a small group of ESE researchers and are *not likely to benefit considerably* from the strengths of HC methods. However, for using HC methods and tools during experiment operation (E3), ESE study design has to consider HC-related aspects regarding HC method selection and HC technology strengths and limitations. Contrary to steps E1 and E2, experiment operation (E3) steps, such as data collection, cleaning, and aggregation, may benefit from involving a large number of distributed online contributors that may be pre-selected to ensure the necessary skills and motivation for these tasks. Therefore, experiment operation (E3) can benefit significantly from HC methods and tool support both for (a) the investigation of HC-enabled SE tasks and for (b) HC-enabled data collection.

In terms of ESE *requirements*, when performing an ESE experiment to compare a traditional SE task to its HC-enabled version, the underlying HC technology should provide capabilities for (R1) definition of the experiment plan; (R2) control of the SE task during the experiment; (R3) measurement during experiment operation; (R4) validation; and (R5) aggregation of experimental data. These requirements are met by *key capabilities of HC methods and technologies* such as the *efficient organization of study subjects and efficient data collection*. Further, HC methods are, in general, well suited for *data cleaning and aggregation*. Data aggregation with HC enables achieving better higher-level results at the cost of a higher number of lower-level contributions, e.g., building confidence in the classification of a defect report based on the classification results of several subjects on this defect report. Using HC technology may require effort to provide input to HC tasks and to organize HC tasks and integrate HC results. In an ESE experiment design, this means to consider how to collect, clean, and aggregate data using HC, in particular, the number of HC tasks resulting from an experiment design and the associated resources required to conduct these HC tasks. Data interpretation will remain the work of research experts. Therefore, it is important for an ESE researcher to understand which ESE processes and tasks are likely to benefit from HC method and tool support.

The core part of the chapter describes an ESE experiment for studying the effects of HC on a model quality assurance task, showing promising results regarding scalable defect detection performance, i.e., defect detection efficiency, and effectiveness. In this chapter, we reflect on the changes needed to the ESE experiment steps in order to perform this analysis. In particular, the experiment team needs to design and implement specific tasks and the associated data, e.g., the tasks the HC contributors should conduct, the data required to show task-specific texts to contributors, and the data to collect during a task. HC requires the configuration of HC tasks and workers to design and document the distribution of tasks to workers. While HC could, in principle, be used to support many different tasks in a distributed group, the strengths and benefits should be compared to alternative collaboration technologies for working on the task in a distributed group. Alternative collaboration technologies include collaborative editors in distributed office tools (e.g., Google Docs, MS Office 365), shared databases, or file systems (e.g., Dropbox).

Acknowledgments This work was supported by the Christian Doppler Forschungsgesellschaft, the Federal Ministry of Economy, Family and Youth, and the National Foundation for Research, Technology and Development in Austria. We thank Marcos Kalinowski and his team for collaboration on HC-enabled inspection.

References

Acosta M, Zaveri A, Simperl E, Kontokostas D, Flock F, Lehmann J (2018) Detecting linked data quality issues via crowdsourcing: a DBpedia study. Semantic Web J 9(3):303–335

Alonso O (2019) The practice of crowdsourcing, vol 11. Morgan & Claypool, San Rafael, p 1

Barowy DW, Curtsinger C, Berger ED, McGregor A (2016) AutoMan: a platform for integrating human-based and digital computation. Commun ACM 59(6):102–109

Behrend TS, Sharek DJ, Meade AW (2011) The viability of crowdsourcing for survey research. Behav Res Method 43:800

Berrang-Ford L, Garton K (2013) Expert knowledge sourcing for public health surveillance: national tsetse mapping in Uganda. Soc Sci Med 91:246–255

Biffl S, Halling M (2003) Investigating the defect detection effectiveness and cost benefit of nominal inspection teams. IEEE Trans Softw Eng 29(5):385–397

Biffl S, Kalinowski M, Winkler D (2018) Towards an experiment line on software inspection with human computation. In: Proceedings of the 6th international workshop on conducting empirical studies in industry. ACM, pp 21–24

Brown AW, Allison DB (2014) Using crowdsourcing to evaluate published scientific literature: methods and example. PLoS One 9:7

Ciolkowski M, Laitenberger O, Vegas S, Biff S (2003) Practical experiences in the design and conduct of surveys in empirical software engineering. In: Conradi R, Wang AI (eds) Empirical methods and studies in software engineering. Springer, Berlin, pp 104–128

de Boer V, Hildebrand M, Aroyo L, De Leenheer P, Dijkshoorn C, Tesfa B, Schreiber G (2012) Niche sourcing: harnessing the power of crowds of experts. In: ten Teije A et al (eds) EKAW 2012. Springer, Heidelberg

Fagan ME (1986) Advances in software inspections. IEEE Trans Softw Eng 12(7):744–751

Fort K, Adda G, Cohen KB (2011) Amazon mechanical Turk: gold mine or coal mine? Comput Linguist 37(2):413–420

Franklin MJ, Kossmann D, Kraska T, Ramesh S, Xin R (2011) CrowdDB: answering queries with crowdsourcing. In: Proceedings of the international conference on management of data, pp 61–72

Fye SR, Charbonneau SM, Hay JW, Mullins CA (2013) An examination of factors affecting accuracy in technology forecasts. Technol Forecast Soc Change 80(6):1222–1231

Gogolla M (2008) An extended entity-relationship model: fundamentals and pragmatics. Lecture notes in computer science, vol 767. Springer, Berlin

Howe J (2006) The rise of crowdsourcing. Wired Mag 14(6):06

Jedlitschka A, Ciolkowski M, Pfahl D (2008) Reporting experiments in software engineering. In: Shull E et al (eds) Guide to advanced empirical software engineering. Springer, London, pp 201–228

Juristo N, Moreno AM (2013) Basics of software engineering experimentation. Springer Science & Business Media, New York

Kawrykow A, Roumanis G, Kam A, Kwak D, Leung C, Wu C, Zarour E (2012) Phylo players. Phylo: a citizen science approach for improving multiple sequence alignment. PLoS One 7(3):e31362

Ko AJ, LaToza TD, Burnett MM (2015) A practical guide to controlled experiments of software engineering tools with human participants. Empir Softw Eng 20(1):110–141

LaToza TD, van der Hoek A (2016) Crowdsourcing in software engineering: models, motivations, and challenges. IEEE Softw 33(1):74–80

Mao K, Capra L, Harman M, Jia Y (2017) A survey of the use of crowdsourcing in software engineering. J Syst Softw 126:57–84

Molléri JS, Petersen K, Mendes E (2016) Survey guidelines in software engineering: an annotated review. In: Proceedings of the 10th ACM/IEEE international symposium on empirical software engineering and measurement, p 58

Mortensen JM, Minty EP, Januszyk M, Sweeney TE, Rector AL, Noy NF, Musen MA (2015) Using the wisdom of the crowds to find critical errors in biomedical ontologies: a study of SNOMED CT. J Am Med Inf 22(3):640–648

Mortensen ML, Adam GP, Trikalinos TA, Kraska T, Wallace BC (2016) An exploration of crowdsourcing citation screening for systematic reviews. Res Synth Methods. RSM-02-2016-0006.R4

Neto AA, Kalinowski M, Garcia A, Winkler D, Biffl S (2019a) A preliminary comparison of using variability modeling approaches to represent experiment families. In: Proceedings of the evaluation and assessment on software engineering. ACM, pp 333–338

Neto CG, Neto AA, Kalinowski M, de Oliveira DCM, Sabou M, Winkler D, Biffl S (2019b) Using model scoping with expected model elements to support software model inspections: results of a controlled experiment. In: Proceedings of ICEIS, pp 107–118

Poesio M, Chamberlain J, Kruschwitz U, Robaldo L, Ducceschi L (2013) Phrase detectives: utilizing collective intelligence for internet-scale language resource creation. ACM Trans Interact Intell Syst 3(1):1–44

Quinn AJ, Bederson BB (2011) Human computation: a survey and taxonomy of a growing field. In: Proceedings of conference on human factors in computing systems. ACM, pp 1403–1412

Runeson P (2003) Using students as experiment subjects – an analysis on graduate and freshmen student data. In: Proceedings of the 7th EASE conference

Runeson P, Höst M (2009) Guidelines for conducting and reporting case study research in software engineering. Empir Softw Eng 14(2):131

Runeson P, Host M, Rainer A, Regnell B (2012) Case study research in software engineering: guidelines and examples. Wiley, New York

Sabou M, Bontcheva K, Scharl A (2012) Crowdsourcing research opportunities: lessons from natural language processing. In: Proceedings of the international conference on I-KNOW

Sabou M, Bontcheva K, Derczynski L, Scharl A (2014) Corpus annotation through crowdsourcing: towards best practice guidelines. In: Proceedings of the international conference on language resources and evaluation (LREC), pp 859–866

Sabou M, Aroyo L, Bozzon A, Qarout RK (2018a) Semantic web and human computation: the status of an emerging field. Semantic Web J 9(3):1–12

Sabou M, Winkler D, Penzenstadler P, Biffl S (2018b) Verifying conceptual domain models with human computation: a case study in software engineering. In: AAAI conference on human computing and crowdsourcing

Sarasua C, Simperl E, Noy N, Bernstein A, Leimeister JM (2015) Crowdsourcing and the semantic web: a research manifesto. Hum Comput 2(1):3–17

Snow R, O'Connor B, Jurafsky D, Ng AY (2008) Cheap and fast—but is it good?: evaluating non-expert annotations for natural language tasks. In: Proceedings of the conference on empirical methods in NLP, pp 254–263

Stolee KT, Elbaum S (2010) Exploring the use of crowdsourcing to support empirical studies in software engineering. In: Proceedings of the interantional symposium on empirical software engineering and measurement

Sun Y, Cheng P, Wang S, Lyu H, Lease M, Marshall I, Wallace BC (2016) Crowdsourcing information extraction for biomedical systematic reviews. In: 4th AAAI conference on human computation and crowdsourcing (HCOMP): works-in-progress track

Surowiecki J (2004) The wisdom of crowds: why the many are smarter than the few and how collective wisdom shapes business, economies, societies and nations. Doubleday, New York

van Solingen R, Basili V, Caldiera V, Rombach HD (2002) Goal question metric (GQM) approach. In: Encyclopedia of software engineering

von Ahn L, Dabbish L (2008) Designing games with a purpose. Commun ACM 51(8):58–67

Winkler D, Sabou M, Petrovic S, Carneiro G, Kalinowski M, Biffl S (2017a) Improving model inspection processes with crowdsourcing: findings from a controlled experiment. In: European conference on software process improvement. Springer, Cham, pp 125–137

Winkler D, Sabou M, Petrovic S, Carneiro G, Kalinowski M, Biffl S (2017b) Improving model inspection with crowdsourcing. In: International workshop on crowdsourcing in software engineering (CSI-SE), pp 30–34

Winkler D, Kalinowski M, Sabou M, Petrovic S, Biffl S (2018) Investigating a distributed and scalable model review process. CLEI Electron J 21(1)

Wohlgenannt G, Sabou M, Hanika F (2016) Crowd-based ontology engineering with the uComp Protégé plugin. Semantic Web J 7(4):379–398

Wohlin C, Runeson P, Höst M, Ohlsson MC, Regnell B, Wesslén A (2012) Experimentation in software engineering. Springer Science & Business Media, New York

Zheng Y, Li G, Li Y, Shan C, Cheng R (2017) Truth inference in crowdsourcing: is the problem solved? VLDB Endow 10(5):541–552

Data Science and Empirical Software Engineering

Ezequiel Scott, Fredrik Milani, and Dietmar Pfahl

Abstract Empirical Software Engineering (ESE) roots back to the 1970s and has since then gained growing recognition as the standard approach to scientific inquiry in the context of software engineering. Many different quantitative and qualitative research methods have been described and supplied with guidelines and checklists and several books have been written about good practice in ESE. With the emerging amount of data being produced during software development, a new paradigm of scientific inquiry has gained much attention, i.e., Data Science (DS). The goal of this chapter is to discuss whether DS could replace traditional ESE or, if it does not replace it, how traditional ESE could benefit from adopting DS practices—and vice versa. In this chapter, we first give some general background information about ESE and DS, then we describe in more detail how both paradigms are typically used in the context of software engineering research and what are their respective strengths and weaknesses. Finally, we illustrate with the help of an industry-driven case example how both paradigms, ESE and DS, could benefit from each other if used in combination.

1 Introduction

The term "Empirical Software Engineering" (ESE) has been popularized by a community of researchers in academia and industry that roots back to the 1970s when Vic Basili at the University of Maryland started a long-term research program that resulted in methods and frameworks such as the Goal-Oriented Measurement (GQM) (Basili et al. 1994) method for designing and using proper measurement systems, the Experience Factory (EF) (Basili et al. 2001) for systematic reuse of products, processes, and models, and the Quality Improvement Paradigm (QIP) (Basili 1985) for systematic improvement of processes and products. Much of

E. Scott · F. Milani · D. Pfahl (✉)
Institute of Computer Science, University of Tartu, Tartu, Estonia
e-mail: ezequiel.scott@ut.ee; fredrik.milani@ut.ee; dietmar.pfahl@ut.ee

© Springer Nature Switzerland AG 2020
M. Felderer, G. H. Travassos (eds.), *Contemporary Empirical Methods in Software Engineering*, https://doi.org/10.1007/978-3-030-32489-6_8

the work inspired by Basili and his colleagues worldwide focused on quantitative approaches (Boehm et al. 2010).

A broader view on what constitutes empirical research was introduced into the ESE community under the label "Evidence-Based Software Engineering" (Kitchenham et al. 2004) by promoting the idea that qualitative methods constitute an important complement to purely quantitative methods. This led to an advanced and broader understanding of the essence of ESE (Shull and Singer 2007) and triggered the publication of several related guidelines (Kitchenham et al. 1995; Kitchenham and Charters 2007; Petersen et al. 2008; Runeson and Höst 2009; Seaman 1999).

While the view on ESE has become more comprehensive and inclusive during the past 20 years, a new science has emerged, i.e., "Data Science" (DS). There exists no agreement on how exactly the field of DS is defined. In this chapter, we use a definition given by Chikio Hayeshi as one possible point of reference. According to Hayeshi, DS is a "concept to unify statistics, data analysis, machine learning and their related methods" in order to "understand and analyze actual phenomena" with data (Hayashi 1998). With the new capabilities of modern computer hardware, the emergence of cloud computing, and its capabilities of handling large volumes of data, DS has become key to many fields of research, for example, in medicine and bioinformatics, in natural language processing, in robotics, and in image recognition. In particular in the field of medicine, DS has shown to be useful in the context of DNA analysis, interpretation of CT scans, personalized healthcare, and many other applications. This made software engineers wonder whether DS could not be similarly successfully applied to improve software engineering practice.

The goal of this chapter is to discuss whether DS could replace traditional ESE or, if it does not replace it, how traditional ESE could benefit from adopting DS practices—and vice versa. In Sect. 2, we first give some general background information about ESE and DS. Then, in Sect. 3, we describe in more detail how both paradigms are typically used in the context of software engineering research and what are their respective strengths and weaknesses. In Sect. 4 of this chapter we describe with the help of a case study how we think ESE and DS could benefit from each other when used in proper combination in a typical research setting of an industry-driven case study. Finally, in Sect. 5 we provide pointers for further reading and, in Sect. 6, we conclude the chapter.

2 Background

While the view on ESE has broadened during the past 20 years, all approaches that are usually subsumed under this label have one crucial aspect in common, i.e., goal-orientation. The reason for the strong focus on goal-orientation in the ESE community originally resulted from the problem that either there was no data at all available to understand and analyze real-world phenomena or the data that had been collected was useless, e.g., due to lack of quality, lack of completeness, or lack of consistency, in order to address a problem of interest. If clear goals for an understanding, evaluation, improvement, or problem-solving activity are defined, it is much easier to decide what data should be collected, how this data should be collected, and when it should be collected, in order to keep the collection effort low and focused. If, instead, existing data was used to answer a question related to a newly defined goal, typically, it turned out that a proper analysis was not feasible due to the fact that the collection of available data had been done in an overly opportunistic way (i.e., whatever was easy/cheap to collect was collected) and thus resulted in useless data cemeteries.

In order to guide data collection, goal-oriented methods such as Goal/Question/Metric (GQM), Quality Improvement Paradigm (QIP), and the Experience Factory (EF) organization were introduced. In particular, the process of setting up measurement (or rather, data collection) programs following the GQM method were precisely described and applied in industry despite its cost and administrative overhead (Briand et al. 1996). What is interesting about GQM is its flexibility with regard to the definition of goals (i.e., understanding, evaluation, prediction, improvement) and its strong demand for combining top-down definition of metrics, starting out from the defined goals, with bottom-up development of models from the collected data used to answer the questions related to the defined goals. One could argue that this combination of first top-down data definition and collection and then bottom-up data analysis and interpretation is the essence of ESE.

In the past 20 years, the situation with regard to availability of data has dramatically changed. Data is everywhere and can be collected automatically and cheaply.

Therefore, it is not surprising that DS has moved into the focus. One characteristic of DS is that it starts out with data. Often, data is simply explored in order to detect "interesting" phenomena using a constantly growing machinery of sophisticated machine learning techniques. Exploration is the standard case when unsupervised learning is employed. When supervised learning is employed, often prediction is the goal. What is similar for both supervised and unsupervised learning is that data is not specifically searched for or created but existing data is being used and models are built using advanced feature identification/selection processes to build best performing models. The question is now: Can DS achieve the same or even better results than ESE? If this is the case, can it do so at a lower cost? Is there perhaps not even a need to first define precise and measurable goals and then select the data and do an analysis to achieve the defined goal? In order to prepare the ground for answering this question, we present in the next section a framework that we will use to illustrate how we think a sensible combination of ESE and DS could look like.

3 Combining ESE with DS

Analyzing data in order to discover new insights can be cumbersome, especially if we are dealing with real-life datasets. For this reason, the Knowledge Discovery from Data (KDD) process (Fayyad et al. 1996) has been proposed as an iterative methodology to extract knowledge from data. The workflow includes several phases, ranging from data selection to interpretation and evaluation of the results. One can argue that this workflow is related to an inductive approach to research. In this approach, a researcher starts with first setting a goal or research interest, and then continues with the collection of data that is relevant to that goal. Once data have been collected, the researcher will then start the analysis and look for patterns in the data. The ultimate goal of the researcher is then to develop a theory that could explain those patterns. Basically, this approach involves moving from data to theory, or from the specific to the general (Blackstone 2012). Typically, this is what is done in DS.

When researchers use the opposite approach, i.e., the deductive approach, they start with a theory that they find compelling and select a set of hypotheses to be tested. During this process, researchers study what others have done and read existing theories of the phenomena they are studying. Then, researchers can either select hypotheses that emerge from those theories or elaborate new ones based on certain assumptions. In a next step, researchers collect the data that will allow them to test the selected hypotheses. That is, they move from a more general level to a more specific one (Blackstone 2012). While the deductive approach to scientific inquiry has a long tradition in science, it is rarely used in its pure form in ESE. This might be due to the fact that the field of software engineering still seems to have a lack of theories (Hannay et al. 2007). Nevertheless, there exist cases where specific goals might have been derived from theory, the theory often coming from another field, e.g., organization science or management science. Due to the underlying mindset one could argue that ESE at least mimics the deductive approach to research inquiry.

In general, there is not one single way to do research, and many examples of research exist that have successfully applied one or another approach. Usually, it is recommended to use a complementary approach (Blackstone 2012). This complementary approach has been used in many fields of science, and software engineering should not be the exception. Although it might seem to be oversimplifying reality, in the rest of this chapter, we treat ESE as a representative of a predominantly deductive approach, while we treat DS as a representative of a predominantly inductive approach. Our main goal is to demonstrate that the two approaches can benefit from each other if combined properly.

Before we illustrate with the help of an example how we experienced the advantage of using the complementary approach to research, i.e., combining induction (DS) with deduction (ESE), in the next section, we would like to provide a framework that will help us discuss our example case.

In 1971, W. L. Wallace published a book titled "The Logic of Science in Sociology" (Wallace 1971). This book presented the so-called Wallace Wheel of the scientific method.

The "Wallace Wheel" contains four key elements, i.e., theories, hypotheses (research questions), observations, empirical generalizations (laws). The interesting aspect is that there is no specific starting point for scientific inquiry. For example, a deductive approach would start out with a theory, then derive hypotheses, then make observations in the empirical world, analyze these to derive laws, and then integrate the laws into the theories that were used as a starting point. Integration of a law could mean that it is added to a theory (i.e., complementing the existing laws), or that it is replacing an existing law, or that it is used to update/correct/evolve an existing law.

The inductive approach, on the other hand, would start out with observations, then generate laws, then form a theory, and only then come up with hypotheses that would trigger a new round of data collection and analysis.

In the upper part of Fig. 1 we present a simplified version of the "Wallace Wheel," only showing the four key elements in the upper part of the figure, and added simple decision-tree that is supposed to help understand better the possibilities that a researcher may encounter when starting to analyze empirical observations.

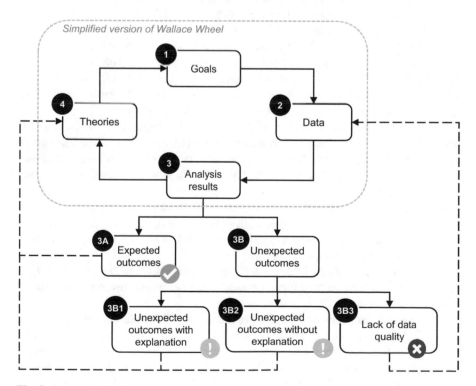

Fig. 1 Proposed steps for analyzing data

In order to adapt the vocabulary used by Wheeler to the context of software engineering, we use the following terminology in Fig. 1: "goals" (replacing "hypotheses/research questions"), "data" (replacing "observations"), and "analysis results" (replacing "laws/empirical generalizations"). We keep the term "theories." The numbers next to the key elements of the cycle only indicate the order in which the elements play a role in a scientific inquiry. That "goal" is labeled with "1" does not necessarily mean that a scientific inquiry starts with a goal. It might as well start with a theory (induction) or with data (deduction).

A goal (1) helps to focus the scientific inquiry and thus helps define the scope and direction of a study. In addition, a goal has to be defined precisely enough that it is possible to decide, after data analysis, whether it has been achieved or not. In other words, ideally, a proper goal is defined in such a way that it can be expressed in terms of variables that are measurable. Ideally the goals would have been derived from a theory (and stated in the form of hypotheses) but, as stated above, a theory might not always be readily available in the field of software engineering and its subfields. Once one or several goals have been set, researchers define the kind of data (2) they need to analyze in order to tackle the goal. In case data is not yet readily available, this may require the definition of data collection procedures. If data already exists, procedures for selecting and extracting the appropriate data may have to be defined and applied. Once the appropriate data is available, researchers must analyze the data. If the data is quantitative, this may involve the creation of descriptive statistics and follow-up in-depth analyses. If the data is qualitative, this may involve coding and follow-up analyses. Whatever analyses are applied, there will be results (3). Often the scientific inquiry stops at the point when analysis results are found and can be used to check whether the goals have been achieved. Ideally, however, one goes one step further and tries to generate a theory (4) from the results or, at least, uses the results to confirm, refute, or modify an existing theory.

What are now the characteristics of ESE and DS approaches to scientific inquiry? ESE typically starts out with clearly defined goals (1), then collects the appropriate data (2), and then conducts the analyses producing results (3) that will help to decide whether the goals have been achieved. This cycle may be conducted once, several times, or continuously.

DS typically starts out with a given set of data (2). There may or may not exist a precisely defined (measurable) goal. In the case where there is no measurable goal defined, the task is often to explore the data in order to find "something interesting" as a proxy for results related to a specific goal (3).

For both ESE and DS in the context of software engineering, theories do not yet play a big role although they have attracted more attention during the last 10–15 years (Hannay et al. 2007).

Once the data has been analyzed, there are two possible outcomes (items 3A and 3B in 1). Either the results are as expected or they are unexpected. Typically, an explicit expectation exists when a goal has been formulated as a precise hypothesis that can be tested statistically using the available data. There might also be weaker forms of expectations of a specific result of the data analysis. Even if the goal of the analysis is simply to understand or describe a phenomenon, researchers often expect at least to find something interesting. If the outcome of the data analysis is not confirming a stated hypothesis or an explicit (or even implicit) expectation, then we speak of an unexpected result. Unexpected results can be of different nature. An unexpected result might either come with an explanation from the analysis and thus help evolve an existing theory (3B1) or without explanation (3B2). In the latter case, it is most probably that the next round in the scientific inquiry would try to find an explanation and thus help establish a new or evolving an existing theory. Another possibility is that the analysis result is not as expected because it turns out that the data quality is not sufficient (3BC) to achieve an (explicit or implicit) goal, e.g., because the data is incorrect, incomplete, inconsistent, or simply insufficient.

Reflecting upon the different mindsets in ESE and DS, i.e., with ESE essentially being goal-driven while DS being essentially data-driven, one could argue that the goal-driven approach has the advantage of having control over the data that is been collected and analyzed but the disadvantage of high planning and data collection cost, while the data-driven approach has the advantage of small data-preparation cost but the disadvantage of a higher risk that data is not suitable for specific goals.

In order to take advantage of the new analysis techniques available in DS, and to balance out the disadvantages of each individual approach, we suggest to combine the goal-driven (ESE) with the data-driven (DS) approach, and thus the predominantly deductive mindset with the predominantly inductive mindset. We illustrate with the help of an example study how this could work.

4 Example Study

In the following, we describe an illustrative example of how the goal-driven (ESE) and the data-driven (DS) approach can be combined. The example is based on preliminary results taken from an ongoing collaboration project with a software company in Estonia. The project started when we were given a dataset containing information about the execution of developers' tasks. This dataset was directly extracted from the issue tracker and contains two sources of information. On the one hand, it describes 1 year of issue reports stored in the issue tracker. On the other hand, the dataset contains a log of the sequence of tasks (linked to the issue reports) performed by the developers and the time they spent on each one. In total, the dataset describes 2501 issues reported by 92 different developers.

As the project evolved, we went through different steps that have been organized in iterations. In the following, we describe each iteration and their main components and how they are related to the proposed steps for analyzing data (see Fig. 1). Finally, Table 1 summarizes the iterations.

Table 1 Summary of the steps applied during the example case study

	Iteration 1	Iteration 2	Iteration 3
1. Goal	?	Precise	Precise
2. Data	Yes*	Yes	Yes
3. Analysis result	Descriptive statistics	Task-switching vs. bugs	Task-switching vs. productivity
4. Theory	x	Seven wastes in lean software development*	Operational waste task-switching*

The starting point of each iteration is marked with (*)

4.1 First Iteration

At the beginning of the project, there was no precisely defined (measurable) goal to guide the research to be done. We had just a generic vision about providing insights from the data that might help to improve the company's software development process. Therefore, the project started with a set of observations (raw data) (see Fig. 1, element 2). These observations were directly extracted from the popular JIRA[1] issue tracker, without any specific data collection procedure driven by goals or hypotheses to test.

During the analysis phase of the dataset (see Fig. 1, element 3), we described the data using descriptive statistics. The dataset consists of 1 year of issue reports that were created from 02 Jan 2018 to 28 Dec 2018. In total, 2501 issue reports with their title, descriptions, metadata, and change records are included in the dataset. The issue reports were created by 92 different developers and the most important issue types are Improvement (1110; 44.38%), Bug (732; 29.27%), Task (419; 16.75%), New Feature (188; 7.52%), and Other (52; 2.08%).

In addition, the dataset contains records of the time spent on the issue reports. These records are self-reported by the developers and stored in a log (i.e., worklog) by using a JIRA plugin named Tempo.[2] Tempo allows developers to track the amount of time they spend on each task, which complements the existing information of the issue reports.

1945 of 2501 issue reports have entries in the worklogs. These entries were recorded by 50 developers. In total, the worklogs had 26,710 entries. The mean tracked time per entry is 1.98 h with values ranging from 0.004 to 13 h. Figure 2 shows the distribution of the tracked working hours, where it can be seen that most of the entry values are lower than 1 h.

Once the data was described, we discussed how to make the most of it. Since the dataset contains a reasonable amount of information about the tasks (issues) executed by the developers and the time spent, we decided to investigate if there is waste involved in the execution of those tasks. This decision was partly driven by

---

[1] JIRA web site—https://www.atlassian.com/software/jira.
[2] Tempo website—https://www.tempo.io/.

Fig. 2 Histogram of the working hours recorded in the worklog

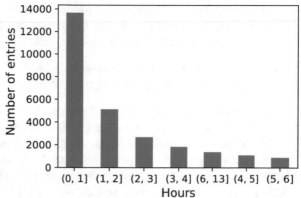

the fact that the company in general tries to follow a lean development approach. We will cover the selection of a suitable theory related to waste in the following section.

4.2 Second Iteration

The starting point of the second iteration corresponds to the element 4 in Fig. 1: Theories.

We sought for a theory, bearing in mind the characteristics of the company and the software development process that the teams said they were using. We were interested in waste analysis in lean software development processes. The theory of lean development (or rather production) originally introduced seven types of wastes that have been adapted for software development (Poppendieck and Poppendieck 2003; Morgan and Liker 2006). The seven wastes, *tasks switching*, *defects*, *waiting*, *motion*, *extra-processes*, *partially done-work*, and *extra-features*, exist in most organizations and therefore should be reduced to improve efficiency.

We decided to measure waste with the goal to identify where it originates in the software development process and, thereby, help us find starting points to reduce waste in the future. Having measurements showing the current status is important to determine potential improvement potential, i.e., opportunities where the waste can be reduced/eliminated. However, these measurements are not commonly measured and tracked by companies. In a multiple case study, Alahyari et al. (2019) asked 14 companies if they measure waste and found that the majority do not have any measurements in place and does not measure waste.

Among the different sources of waste, task-switching is considered to be the most important (Alahyari et al. 2019). Every time developers switch between tasks, a significant switching time is incurred before they get their thoughts into the flow of the new task. This amount of time is considered as waste that should be eliminated or, at least, reduced.

Once the theoretical background for our analysis had been determined, the definition of the goals and hypotheses to test (see Fig. 1, element 1) become much easier. We defined the following measurable goal:

Goal: To measure developers' context switching and determine if it is positively correlated with the number of reported bugs.

Correlation is calculated using the Spearman's correlation coefficient (r), where $r > 0.5$ indicates a correlation meriting further investigation.

Measuring context switching is not trivial since it requires to operationalize the concept. For example, the temporal resolution (e.g., days, weeks, months) and the dimension of analysis (e.g., project, tasks) are important factors to be considered (Vasilescu et al. 2016). In this project, we decided to focus on daily temporal resolution and the task dimension in order to get insights at the finest level of granularity. Then, the worklog collected from Tempo represents the sequence of ongoing tasks of each developer. We proposed three alternatives to measure context switching by analyzing this data:

1. Every time a developer changes tasks, there is a context switch involved that generates waste.
2. Every time a developer changes tasks and the developer is already worked on the task (repeated task), there is a context switch involved that generates waste.
3. Every time a developer changes tasks and the developer did not complete the task (incomplete task), there is a context switch involved that generates waste.

After performing a preliminary analysis of the data by following the first alternative, we observed that developers incur in context switching on a daily basis. Figure 3 shows the average number of daily switches per developer, which ranges from 2 to 6 task switches. In addition, we calculated the maximum number of task switches per day and developer, and we observed that it can reach a value of 16 switches per day.

When analyzing the distribution of context switching over time by considering the three alternatives, one can see that there is no relevant difference among the different values obtained: the three different measurements follow the same pattern over time. Figure 4 illustrates this by showing the average number of

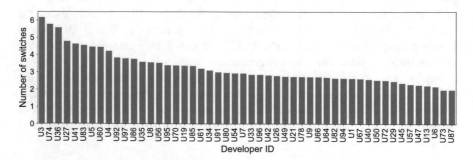

Fig. 3 Average number of daily switches per developer

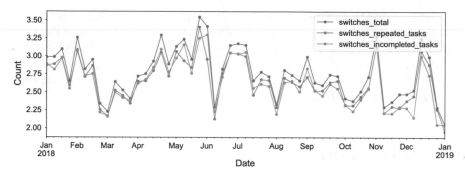

Fig. 4 Average number of daily switches per developer

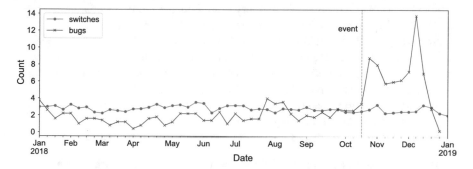

Fig. 5 Average number of daily switches per developer vs. average number of bugs

context switching per developer over time. In order to simplify the analysis and the visualization, we use weekly samples to calculate the average, which is represented by the dots in the figure. We concluded that using the three metrics for calculating context switching does not add any practical value. Therefore, we opt to use the simplest one: every time a developer changes tasks, there is a context switch involved that generates waste.

During the analysis phase (see Fig. 1, element 3), we analyzed task-switching with regard to the reported bugs. Figure 5 shows the number of task switches and the number of reported bugs over time. For simplicity, we aggregated the results using the weekly average number of occurrences (bugs or switches). It can be seen from the figure that the number of bugs reported increased sharply in October. This clearly indicates that a relevant event occurred at that time but the current data is not enough to tell us what happened.

We analyzed the correlation between both time series by calculating the Spearman rank-order correlation coefficient (r). There was no correlation between the weekly average number of task switches and the weekly average number of reported bugs ($r = -0.04$). Moreover, if we only consider the period before the number of bugs peaked (from Jan to Oct 2018), the variables are not correlated ($r = 0.06$). These results are then unexpected (see Fig. 1, element 3B), since we expected a correlation $r > 0.5$.

We concluded that we should go back to the data collection due to the lack of data quality of the dataset (see Fig. 1, point 3B3). The current dataset does not have enough information to explain the increased number of bugs in October. We decided that we should define new strategies that would help us explain the current situation. For example, interviews with the developers could be conducted to get a better understanding of the observed results.

4.3   Third Iteration

The starting point of the third iteration is element 4 in Fig. 1. During this iteration, another theory was explored. This theory complements the one studied during the second iteration by increasing the understanding of task-switching.

According to Clark and Wheelwright (1993), the time individuals (i.e., developers) spend on value-adding tasks drops rapidly when the individual works on more than two tasks. Figure 6 shows the described effect. The same idea was explored by McCollum and Sherman (1991). In their work, the authors arrived to similar conclusions that working on two tasks at the same time seemed to be optimal, while working on one or three tasks may still not be problematic.

In this context, we defined the following goal (see Fig. 1, element 1):

Goal: to measure productivity in terms of value-adding tasks (issues).

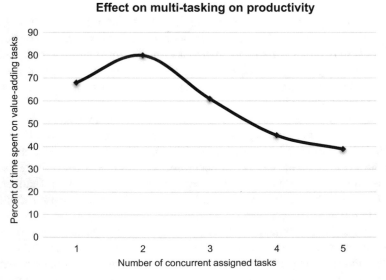

Fig. 6 Effect of multitasking on productivity as reported by the experimental results of Clark and Wheelwright (1993). Illustration adapted from Michael Cohn's book "Agile Estimating and Planning" (Cohn 2005)

Hypothesis: The percentage of time spent on value-adding tasks reaches their
                optimal value when the number of tasks is between two and three.

As for the data collection phase (see Fig. 1, element 2), we used the same dataset
with information about issues and worklogs. There was no additional data collection
performed in this iteration.

During the analysis phase (see Fig. 1, element 3), we analyzed context switching
with regard to productivity in terms of value-adding tasks (issues). The concept of
value-adding tasks was operationalized as follows: value-adding tasks are tasks that
were completed (e.g., their status is 'Closed'). That is, if a developer worked on a
task on a given day and the task was not closed, then the task is not adding value. In
contrast, if a developer worked on a task and the task was closed the same day, then
the task is consider as value-adding.

On average, each developer works on 2.65 tasks every day, spending 5.45 h in
total. Out of those tasks, each developer resolve 0.14 tasks every day, which means
that 0.28 h are spent on value-adding tasks every day. The percentage of time spent
on value-adding tasks is calculated as the total time spent on value-adding tasks over
the total working time. On average, the percentage of daily time spent on value-
adding tasks is 5.13%.

Figure 7 shows the results obtained from the analysis. We observed that the
highest percentage of time spent on value-adding tasks is obtained by developers
having between 3 and 4 daily task switches on average. Although these results are
not exactly the same than the reported by Clark and Wheelwright (1993), the results
are similar: the percentage drops rapidly when developers works on more than four
tasks.

These results are subject to certain limitations. Among them, we can mention
two as the most important ones. Firstly, there can be more value-adding tasks that
were not added to the issue tracker. Secondly, developers may spend more than 1
day working on it. These limitations indicate that, at this point, our results are still
preliminary and further studies are needed to mitigate these issues.

Fig. 7 Results of the effect
of task-switching on
productivity for the case
study. The line shows the
percentage of time spent on
value-adding tasks, whereas
the bars indicate the number
of developers on each bin.
The bins in the x-axis show
the range of task-switching
that developers have on a
daily average

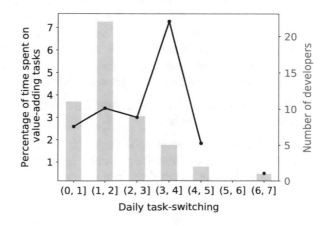

Takeaways

- The process of analyzing data can be described as an iterative process.
- Descriptive statistics can help us to understand the underlying properties of the data and to limit the scope of analysis.
- Theories and related work are fundamental to motivate the research, define research goals, and contribute to the body of knowledge.
- Often, there are several alternatives to operationalize the constructs we are interested in. We must be aware that each alternative involves a set of assumptions, and in consequence, threats to construct validity are introduced.
- When several alternatives to operationalize constructs are considered, it is recommended to apply the one that requires the smallest number of assumptions (Occam's razor).
- The lack of data quality in a dataset can lead to misleading conclusions. Different strategies (e.g., having interviews with the involved developers) are recommended to support quantitative results.

5 Recommended Further Reading

Other chapters in this book that are tightly related to this chapter include the following:

- In their chapter titled "The Evolution of Empirical Methods in Software Engineering," Michael Felderer and Guilherme Travasso describe the various flavors of empirical software engineering research and discuss challenges such as the lack of an agreed taxonomy and an unclear research agenda within the community of empirical software engineers (see chapter "The Evolution of Empirical Methods in Software Engineering").
- In their chapter titled "Guidelines for Conducting Software Engineering Research," Klaas-Jan Stol and Brian Fitzgerald describe the ABC framework as a means to structure knowledge seeking research (see chapter "Guidelines for Conducting Software Engineering Research"). This chapter evolves an older publication by the same authors (Stol and Fitzgerald 2018).

Good introductory sources describing the methods and discussing the evolution of ESE are the following books:

- Although already more than 10 years old, the book titled "Empirical Software Engineering Issues—Critical Assessment and Future Directions" edited by Basili et al. provides an interesting summary of discussions conducted by leading researchers of the empirical software engineering community during a workshop held at Dagstuhl Castle in June 2006 (Basili et al. 2007).

- The book titled "Guide to Advanced Empirical Software Engineering" edited by Shull et al. provides an overview of the most important research methods used in empirical software engineering (Shull and Singer 2007).

To get an introduction into the wide field of DS, we recommend the following literature as a starting point:

- An introduction into the basic concepts of DS can be found in the paper titled "What is Data Science? Fundamental Concepts and a Heuristic Example" by Hayashi. The paper is contained in a conference proceeding that in spite of its age gives a multi-facetted introduction into standard problems of DS with special focus on classification problems (Hayashi et al. 1998).
- While there exist many books on various topics of DS we recommend to the reader the book series written by Menzies et al. (2014), Bird et al. (2015), and Menzies et al. (2016) as their books not only describe DS techniques in an easy-to-understand way but also provide many application examples in the context of software engineering.

There does not exist any specific literature that would discuss the combination of or relationship between ESE and DS. However, in a recent article, Fitzgerald and Stol coin the term "continuous software engineering" (Stol and Fitzgerald 2017). The authors describe a road map and agenda towards creating software development systems that continuously self-improve based on a constant stream of feedback in the form of data. In our opinion, their vision is a good example of creating synergy from a smart combination of ESE and DS.

6 Conclusion

In this chapter we discussed whether DS could replace traditional ESE or, if it does not replace it, how traditional ESE could benefit from adopting DS practices—and vice versa. Our main assumption was that the most critical disadvantage of ESE is its potentially high data collection cost, while the disadvantage of DS is that, in a typical case, goals are not stated precisely enough to serve as a yardstick for deciding whether the conducted data analyses actually helped in achieving the vaguely stated goal. While it is not always true that ESE and DS have the stated downsides in a specific research situation, we think that it is often enough the case to spend some thinking on how to combine the two paradigms in order to generate synergy. With the help of an industry-driven case study we illustrated the ever more frequently occurring situation that a company has data but no clear (or rather precise) goals of what exactly the data analysis should achieve. In such a situation, we suggest that one starts out with the vague goal and does some descriptive data analysis which is fed back to the case stakeholders using the results to sharpen the goal definition to a degree that it allows to define more precise research questions (or even hypotheses derived from an existing theory) for which some deeper analysis is conducted on the given data. It may or may not turn out that additional data needs to be collected or another round of goal refinement or adjustment must be conducted.

In conclusion, we believe that ESE and DS have many characteristics in common. Both paradigms should not be considered as contradictory but rather constitute complementary approaches that can benefit from each other in cases where much data is available and specific research goals have not yet been formulated.

Acknowledgements This research was partly supported by the institutional research grant IUT20-55 of the Estonian Research Council and the Estonian Centre of Excellence in ICT Research (EXCITE).

References

Alahyari H, Gorschek T, Svensson RB (2019) An exploratory study of waste in software development organizations using agile or lean approaches: a multiple case study at 14 organizations. Inf Softw Technol 105:78–94

Basili VR (1985) Quantitative evaluation of software methodology. In: Keynote address, proceedings of the first pan pacific computer conference, Melbourne, pp 379–398

Basili VR, Caldiera G, Rombach DH (1994) The goal question metric approach. Wiley, Hoboken, pp 528–532

Basili VR, Caldiera G, Rombach HD (2001) The experience factory. In: Marciniak J (ed) Encyclopedia of software engineering. Wiley, Hoboken

Basili VR, Rombach HD, Schneider K, Kitchenham B, Pfahl D, Selby RW (2007) Empirical software engineering issues. Critical assessment and future directions. In: International workshop, Dagstuhl Castle, June, 2006. Revised Papers. LNCS 4336, Springer, Berlin, pp 26–30

Bird C, Menzies T, Zimmermann T (2015) The art and science of analyzing software data. Elsevier, Amsterdam

Blackstone A (2012) Principles of sociological inquiry–Qualitative and quantitative methods. BC open textbook collection, Open Textbook Library

Boehm B, Rombach HD, Zelkowitz MV (2010) Foundations of empirical software engineering: the legacy of Victor R, 1st edn. Springer; Basili Publishing Company, Berlin

Briand LC, Differding CM, Rombach HD (1996) Practical guidelines for measurement-based process improvement. Softw Process Improv Prac 2:253–280

Clark KB, Wheelwright SC (1993) Managing new product and process development: text and cases. The Free Press, New York

Cohn M (2005) Agile estimating and planning. Pearson Education, London

Fayyad U, Piatetsky-Shapiro G, Smyth P (1996) From data mining to knowledge discovery in databases. AI Mag 17:37–37

Hannay J, Sjøberg D, Dybå TA (2007) Systematic review of theory use in software engineering experiments. IEEE Trans Softw Eng 33:87–107

Hayashi C (1998) What is data science? Fundamental concepts and a heuristic example. In: Hayashi C, Yajima K, Bock H-H, Ohsumi N, Tanaka Y, Baba Y (eds) Data science, classification, and related methods. Studies in classification, data analysis, and knowledge organization. Springer, Berlin, pp 40–51

Hayashi C, Yajima K, Bock H-H, Ohsumi N, Tanaka Y, Baba YDS (eds) (1998) Classification, and related methods, studies in classification, data analysis, and knowledge organization. Springer, Berlin

Kitchenham B, Charters S (2007) Guidelines for performing systematic literature reviews in software engineering. Technical report, EBSE-2007-01, School of Computer Science and Mathematics, Keele University

Kitchenham B, Pickard L, Pfleeger SL (1995) Case studies for method and tool evaluation. IEEE Softw 12(4):52–62

Kitchenham BA, Dybå T, Jorgensen M (2004) Evidence-based software engineering. In: Proceedings of the 26th international conference on software engineering (ICSE '04), pp 273–281

McCollum JK, Sherman JD (1991) The effects of matrix organization size and number of project assignments on performance. IEEE Trans Eng Manag 38(1):75–78

Menzies T, Kocaguneli E, Turhan B, Minku L, Peters F (2014) Sharing data and models in software engineering. Morgan Kaufmann, Burlington

Menzies T, Williams L, Zimmermann T (2016) Perspectives on data science for software engineering. Morgan Kaufmann, Burlington

Morgan JM, Liker JK (2006) The Toyota product development system: integrating people, process and technology. Productivity Press, New York

Petersen K, Feldt R, Mujtaba S, Mattsson M (2008) Systematic mapping studies in software engineering. In: Visaggio G, Baldassarre MT, Linkman S, Turner M (eds) Proceedings of the 12th international conference on evaluation and assessment in software engineering (EASE'08). BCS Learning & Development Ltd., Swindon, pp 68–77

Poppendieck M, Poppendieck T (2003) Lean software development: an agile toolkit: an agile toolkit. Addison Wesley, Boston

Runcson P, Höst M (2009) Guidelines for conducting and reporting case study research in software engineering. Empir Softw Eng 14(2):2009

Seaman CB (1999) Qualitative methods in empirical studies of software engineering. IEEE Trans Softw Eng 25(4):1999

Shull FJ, Singer J (2007) Sjøberg, i. In: 'K', guide to advanced empirical software engineering. Springer, Berlin

Stol K, Fitzgerald BC (2017) Continuous software engineering: a roadmap and agenda. J Syst Softw 123:176 189

Stol K, Fitzgerald B (2018) The ABC of software engineering research. ACM Trans Softw Eng Methodol 27:3

Vasilescu B, Blincoe K, Xuan Q, Casalnuovo C, Damian D, Devanbu P, Filkov V (2016) The sky is not the limit: multitasking across GitHub projects. In: IEEE/ACM 38th international conference on software engineering (ICSE). IEEE, Piscataway, pp 994–1005

Wallace WL (1971) The logic of science in sociology. Aldine, New York

Optimization in Software Engineering: A Pragmatic Approach

Günther Ruhe

Abstract Empirical software engineering is concerned with the design and analysis of empirical studies that include software products, processes, and resources. Optimization is a form of data analytics in support of human decision-making. Optimization methods are aimed to find best decision alternatives. Empirical studies serve both as a model and as data input for optimization. In addition, the complexity of the models used for optimization triggers further studies on explaining and validating the results in real-world scenarios. The goal of this chapter is to give an overview of the *as-is* and of the *to-be* usage of optimization in software engineering. The emphasis is on a pragmatic use of optimization, and not so much on describing the most recent algorithmic innovations and tool developments. The usage of optimization covers a wide range of questions from different types of software engineering problems along the whole life cycle. To facilitate its more comprehensive and more effective usage, a checklist for a guided process is described. The chapter uses a running example *Asymmetric Release Planning* to illustrate the whole process. A Return-on-Investment analysis is proposed as part of the problem scoping. This helps to decide on the depth and breadth of analysis in relation to the effort needed to run the analysis and the projected value of the solution.

1 Introduction

The famous Aristotle (384 to 322 BC) is widely attributed with saying *It is the mark of an educated mind to rest satisfied with the degree of precision which the nature of the subject admits and not to seek exactness where only an approximation is possible* (Lucas and McGunnigle 2003). Applying Aristotle's saying to software engineering means that we need to understand the problem first, its nature and

G. Ruhe (✉)
Department of Computer Science, University of Calgary, Calgary, AL, Canada
e-mail: ruhe@ucalgary.ca

© Springer Nature Switzerland AG 2020
M. Felderer, G. H. Travassos (eds.), *Contemporary Empirical Methods in Software Engineering*, https://doi.org/10.1007/978-3-030-32489-6_9

degree of uncertainty, before we start running any sophisticated solution algorithm. In this chapter, we explore the usage and usefulness of optimization techniques in software engineering. We take a pragmatic perspective and propose a model looking at the Return-on-Investment and provide directions for future research in this field.

The purpose of optimization is insight rather than numbers (Geoffrion 1976). What counts is utilizing insight for making decisions. Software development and evolution are full of decisions to be made on processes, resources, artifacts, tools, and techniques occurring at the different stages of the life cycle. Some of these decisions have a strong impact on the success of the project. However, the information available for doing that is typically incomplete, imprecise, and even contradictory.

The paradigm of software engineering decision support (Ruhe 2002) emphasizes the decision-centric nature of software engineering. It outlines how different methods including modeling, measurement, simulation as well as analysis and reasoning can be used to support human decision-making. Optimization is another piece of that decision support agenda. Looking for the best possible item, artifact, process, action, or plan is tempting and a natural desire, but it is not automatically clear what that actually means. Part of the difficulty is that decisions typically are in the space of multiple criteria: Improving in one direction typically requires compromising against another criteria. In other cases, the data and information available are vague or even contradictory. Finally: To what extent decisions are based on rationality? Software development is a creative and human-centered process, and humans do not necessarily act based on rational arguments. So, another question arises: How valuable and how practical is optimization for the area of (Empirical) Software Engineering?

This chapter shows all the many opportunities of optimization in the various areas of software engineering (Sect. 2) and how to avoid pitfalls in its application. Optimization is not something that creates value automatically and easily. It is data intensive and requires time and effort investment. Optimization includes the whole process starting from the problem analysis, followed by modeling, running solution algorithms, understanding and interpreting data, likely modifying data and/or the underlying model, and rerunning algorithms. In this chapter, we take a process view and provide a checklist for how to perform this process (Sect. 3). Its implementation is illustrated by a case study addressing asymmetric release planning (Sect. 4). Usage and usefulness of optimization is the key concern of Sect. 5. The chapter is completed by recommendations for further reading (Sect. 6) and conclusions on the future usage of optimization in the context of software engineering (Sect. 7). A list of all abbreviations of the chapter is given in Table 1.

Table 1 List of abbreviations used in this chapter

Abbreviation	Full text
GA	Genetic Algorithm
NSGA-II	Non-dominated Sorting Genetic Algorithm II
MOEAs	Multi-Objective Evolutionary Algorithms
ACO	Ant Colony Optimization
ILP	Integer Linear Programming
QoS	Quality-of-Service
EAs	Evolutionary Algorithms
GSA	Genetic Simulated Annealing
SA/AAN	Simulated Annealing with Advanced Adaptive Neighborhood
CCEA	Cooperative Co-Evolutionary Algorithms
LSR	Least-Squares Linear Regression
CBR	Case-based reasoning

2 Software Engineering Optimization: What, How, and Where?

The Capability Maturity Model Integration (CMMI) (Chrissis et al. 2003) character-ized companies with the highest maturity CMMI level as *Optimizing*. This highest level of maturity refers to the application error analysis and process monitoring in order to optimize the current processes. While optimization is applicable to all types of questions, in software engineering it is primarily related to structured and semi-structured decisions on all technical and managerial aspects of software development and evolution.

The Software Engineering Body of Knowledge SWEBOK (Abran et al. 2004) lists technical and managerial areas to describe the field of software engineering:

- Software requirements
- Software design
- Software construction
- Software testing
- Software maintenance
- Software configuration management
- Software project management[1]
- Software engineering process
- Software engineering models and methods
- Software quality

---

[1]Replacing *Software Engineering Management* as used in SWEBOK.

Decisions are made during all stages of the software life cycle. Depending on their type of control and impact, decisions are classified into operational (short-term), tactical (midterm), and strategic (long-term) decisions (Aronson et al. 2005). As another dimension of their classification, decisions are classified, based on their input, into structured, semi-structured, or unstructured decisions. The emphasis of optimization is on tactical and strategic decisions based on structured or semi-structured information. In Table 2 we present a list of publications using optimization methods in software engineering. As it is impossible to present a complete list, we only selected papers published since 2000. Among the many papers found, we picked those having highest number of citations in Google Scholar (as of September 4, 2019).

Using the keywords of 84 optimization related papers published since 2000, a word cloud was created and is presented in Fig. 1. We found a diversity of algorithms and concepts. Overall, the highest number of publications is in testing, requirements engineering, and design. This does not imply that there is nothing to optimize in the remaining areas. Lack of proper data might be one reason, and uncertainty in formulating explicit objectives and constraints another one for these current deficits.

3 Recommended Process and Checklist for Applying Optimization

3.1 Recommended Process

Optimization is a form of prescriptive analytics, aimed to propose actions to the decision-maker. Different models for the process of data analytics exist (Kurgan and Musilek 2006). We adapted the widely accepted CRISP data mining process introduced by Shearer (2000) and integrated ideas of the engineering and the empirical cycle described by Wieringa (2014). The process model shown in Fig. 2 establishes a link between (1) iterative software development (object of study), (2) empirical studies (as a means to improve problem understanding, to create valid data, or to validate the research design), and (3) existing model and data repositories.

For iterative development, two sample iterations k and $k+1$ form the optimization context. Each iteration is assumed of having design, coding, and test activities, which result in a release version of the software product. Different parts of these processes might be optimized for higher efficiency. For example, there might be the problem of how to perform refactoring, to finding best test strategies and test cases, to perform scheduling and staffing, or to decide about the functionality of the

Table 2 Selected optimization studies in software engineering

Area	Problem	Optim. criteria	Optim. method	Year	Citations[a]	Ref
Requirements	Selecting optimal features for next release	Value	GA	2004	434	Greer and Ruhe (2004)
Requirements	Next release problem	Cost, value	Pareto optimal genetic algorithm, NSGA-II	2007	237	Zhang et al. (2007)
Requirements	Software release planning	Maximize the value of the product for each release	Hybrid intelligence	2004	125	Ruhe et al. (2004)
Requirements	Release planning for evolving systems	Value	GA	2005	109	Saliu and Ruhe (2005)
Requirements	Software release planning	Selection of highly coupled features in the same release	ILP	2007	103	Saliu and Ruhe (2007)
Requirements	Next release problem	Minimize cost and maximize customer satisfaction	GA, evolutionary strategy	2011	85	Durillo et al. (2011)
Requirements	Software release planning	Optimized resource allocation	ILP, GA	2009	58	Ngo-The and Ruhe (2008)
Design	Modularization	Cohesiveness	Pareto optimal genetic algorithm	2010	274	Praditwong et al. (2010)
Design	Refactoring	Search-based refactoring	Pareto optimality	2007	209	Harman and Tratt (2007)
Design	Performance of software	Genetic improvement	Genetic programming	2014	173	Langdon and Harman (2014)
Design	Modularization	Cohesiveness	GA	2002	163	Harman et al. (2002)
Design	Feature selection	Value	GA	2011	156	Guo et al. (2011)
Design	QoS-driven web service selection	Quick convergence	GA	2008	156	Ma and Zhang (2008)
Design	Optimal use of the hardware	Performance	Profiling, optimization	2003	134	Kistler and Franz (2003)

(continued)

Table 2 (continued)

Area	Problem	Optim. criteria	Optim. method	Year	Citations[a]	Ref
Design	Reassign methods and attributes to classes in a class diagram	Class coupling and cohesion	Multi-objective GA	2010	107	Bowman et al. (2010)
Design	Choosing the optimal architectural design alternative	Reduce development cost, improve quality	EAs	2006	80	Grunske (2006)
Design, maintenance	QoS-aware service composition	Concrete services combination	GA	2008	98	Wada et al. (2008)
Testing	Regression test prioritization	Quality	GA	2006	366	Walcott et al. (2006)
Testing	Regression test case selection	Code coverage, past fault-history detection and execution cost	GA	2007	333	Yoo and Harman (2007)
Testing	Test data generation	Multi-objective branch coverage	MOEAs	2007	160	Lakhotia et al. (2007)
Testing	Test case prioritization for regression testing	Fault coverage	ACO	2010	80	Singh et al. (2010)
Testing	Comparing different algorithms for test case generation	Coverage	GA, SA, GSA, SA/AAN	2007	76	Xiao et al. (2007)
Project management	Software effort estimate	Accurate effort estimation	GA with grey rational analysis	2008	238	Huang et al. (2008)
Project management	Staffing of software project	Value	Constraint satisfaction	2008	166	Barreto et al. (2008)
Project management	Software effort estimate	Input feature subset, parameters for machine learning	GA	2010	139	Oliveira et al. (2010)
Project management	Project task scheduling and human resource allocation	Flexibility	ACO	2012	138	Chen and Zhang (2013)

Project management	Comparing different techniques for planning resource allocation	Duration	GA, SA, hill climbing	2005	128	Antoniol et al. (2005)
Project management	Software project scheduling	Scheduling	GA	2008	121	Chang et al. (2008)
Project management	Assign features to releases	Value	ILP	2008	108	Van den Akker et al. (2008)
Project management	Comparing software effort prediction techniques	Accuracy of prediction	Expert judgment, LSR, CBR	2003	105	MacDonell and Shepperd (2003)
Project management	Software cost estimation	Feature selection with lower complexity	Mutual information based feature selection	2009	95	Li et al. (2009)
Project management	Deciding whether to buy or build a component	Cost and quality optimization	ILP	2008	93	Cortellessa et al. (2008)
Project management	Allocation of testing resource	Reliability and testing cost	MOEAs	2010	87	Wang et al. (2010)
Project management	Use of search-based optimization techniques for management activities	Staff and task allocation	GA, NSGA-II	2011	58	Di Penta et al. (2011)
Project management	Software project staffing and job scheduling	Team staffing and work package scheduling	CCEA	2011	51	Ren et al. (2011)
Process	Cloud computing deployment and reconfiguration	Response time and cost	GA	2013	125	Frey et al. (2013)
Quality	Software quality modeling	Cost	Genetic programming	2010	117	Liu et al. (2010)

[a]Google Scholar citations as of Sep. 5, 2019

Fig. 1 Word cloud for publications devoted to optimization in software engineering since 2000

upcoming releases. For any of these questions, optimization helps to find a good or even the (formally) best answer. The process to find these answers is composed of eight steps that are further outlined in Sect. 3.2 by providing checklist questions to each step.

3.2 Checklist

Checklists are a means to facilitate the application of the knowledge existing in a field (Gawande 2010). Similar to tools, applying checklists are no guarantee for success, but hopefully serve as filters or recommendations. They need continuous adaption to accommodate all the new directions and developments.

Checklists have been used in software engineering, e.g., for case studies, project risk analysis, and performing inspections. Here, we propose a checklist for the usage of optimization in software engineering. The checklist questions follow the key steps recommended in Sect. 3.1. The questions are classified in terms of their usage. M(andatory) questions need to be answered with "yes" to make optimization a valuable effort. C(larification) questions (What?) are aimed to qualify the setup of the whole process. TMTB questions (How? How much?) are the ones that benefit from "the more the better."

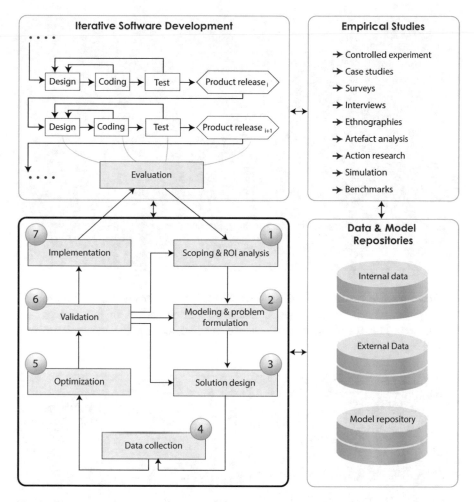

Fig. 2 Process of performing optimization in the context of empirical studies for iterative software development

1. Scoping and ROI Analysis Scoping defines the problem context and its boundaries. At this stage, performing an analysis of the potential *Return-on-Investment (ROI)* helps to determine the depth and the breadth of the investigation.

Questions	Type
How important is the problem?	TMTB
How much time and money can be invested to solve the problem?	TMTB
Can the problem not be solved easily without optimization?	M
What are alternative solution approaches?	C
How much is the optimization problem aligned with business objectives?	TMTB
How much impact an optimized solution has in the problem context?	TMTB
What is part of the investigation, what is not?	C
Who are the key stakeholders and decision-makers?	C

2. Modeling and Problem Formulation Modeling and formulation of the problem is the phase where the variables, constraints, and objectives of the problem are formulated. The formulation needs to be verified against the original problem statement.

Questions	Type
What are the key independent problem variables?	C
What is a reasonable granularity for problem formulation?	C
What are the dependent variables?	C
What are the human resource, budget, and time constraints?	C
What are the technological constraints?	C

3. Solution Design The design step includes an analysis of *what?* and *how much is enough?* Exploring possible solution alternatives and its related tools depends on the scope selected. The design depends on the size of the problem (and its subsequent computational effort), the nature of the problem (linear, integer, convex, non-convex), and its projected impact. The design also decides between the use of traditional methods (linear, integer programming) and one of the many existing bioinspired algorithms (Binitha et al. 2012).

Questions	Type
What baseline solution exists to compare with?	C
What are possible solution method alternatives and which ones have proven successful in similar context?	C
Which related tools exist?	TMTB
What are the expectations on optimization solutions (heuristic vs approximation vs exact)?	C
Is it search for just one (optimized) solution or for a set of solutions?	C
What scenarios are planned for running the algorithms?	C
How much would the optimization process benefit from interaction with the decision-makers?	TMTB

4. Data Collection Collect and prepare data needed to run optimization. While data is seldom complete, empirical studies can be used to improve the amount and quality of data. Goal oriented measurement (Van Solingen et al. 2002) is the established technique to guide the data collection and analysis.

Questions	Type
Is all necessary information available?	M
Is all available information also reliable?	TMTB
Is there a need for data cleaning?	M
Is there agreement between stakeholders on the data?	TMTB

5. Optimization Specify parameters for the tool and algorithm to execute optimization. How robust is the solution against changes on the input? What is the impact of adding or changing constraints?

Questions	Type
Which parameter settings are made and why?	C
Should the parameter settings be varied and if so, how?	C
For randomized algorithms (e.g., bioinspired algorithms), how many replications are needed to make sound conclusions?	C
Is there a time constraint for running the solution algorithm?	C
What are the termination criteria for the optimization algorithm?	C

6. Validation The solution of the mathematical optimization problem needs to be validated. How do the results compare to applying alternative algorithms? What do the results mean for the original problem? Possibly, the scope, the problem formulation, or the solution design needs to be adjusted.

Questions	Type
How much do the generated solutions make sense in the problem context?	TMTB
How much do stakeholders agree with the proposed solution(s)?	TMTB
In case of conflicts, how they can be resolved?	C
How robust is the proposed solution against changes of input data?	TMTB

7. Implementation The selected solution is implemented as a decision for the original problem.

Questions	Type
Are the additional considerations to select one solution for final implementation in the original problem context?	C
Is there any need to adjust the proposed solution to the actual problem context?	C

8. Evaluation The usefulness of the implemented solution is evaluated in the original problem context and with the stakeholders involved.

Questions	Type
How much does the implemented solution solve the original problem?	TMTB
How much the implemented solution is accepted by included stakeholders?	TMBM
How much the implemented solution improves the baseline?	TMTB

The checklist serves as a filter. In the case that the two M questions are not answered positive, optimization is not recommended. The more information is available on C questions, the more guidance is available to run the process. For the TMTB questions, the more they accumulate "more" evaluation, the more likely there is a positive return on the optimization investment.

4 Optimization Case Study: Asymmetric Release Planning

In this section, we go through a case study presented by Nayebi and Ruhe (2018). The purpose is to illustrate the steps of the process illustrated in Fig. 2.

4.1 Scoping and ROI Analysis

Release planning is a key part of iterative development. It is the process to decide about the functionality of upcoming releases of an evolving software product. Typically, a large number of requests for new or changing features as well as bug fixes are candidates to get implemented in each release. For simplicity, we call them features here. There are dependencies between the features that need to be considered for their implementation.

Implementation of features is expected to create value. However, there is an asymmetry in the sense that providing a feature does create satisfaction, but not providing it does not automatically create the same amount of dissatisfaction. This problem is called *Asymmetric Release Planning*. The ROI is supposed to be high, especially for products in a competitive market and when shipped in large quantities. The attractiveness of features is critical for success or failure of a product. Looking into the best release strategy in consideration of the asymmetry in value creation improves the traditional perspective of just looking at customer satisfaction as the single criterion.

4.2 Modeling and Problem Formulation

To run optimization, we need to model the problem and provide a formal problem description. Let $F = \{F(1)\ldots F(N)\}$ be a set of N candidate features for development during the upcoming K product releases. A feature is called *postponed* if it is not offered in one of the next K releases. Each release plan is characterized by a vector x with N components $x(n)(n = 1\ldots N)$ defined as:

$$x(n) = k \quad \text{if feature } F(n) \text{ is offered at release } k \tag{1}$$

$$x(n) = K + 1 \quad \text{if feature } F(n) \text{ is postponed} \tag{2}$$

The objective of the planning approach is to maximize stakeholder satisfaction and simultaneously minimize stakeholder dissatisfaction. These two objectives are independent and competing with each other. Pursuing each objective in isolation will create different release planning strategies.

To calculate stakeholder satisfaction $S(n)$ of feature F(n), all stakeholder responses related to satisfaction elements (Attractive and One-dimensional) are divided by the sum of the *Attractive, One-dimensional, Must-be*, and *Indifferent* portions of that feature:

$$S(n) = \frac{F_A(n) + F_O(n)}{F_A(n) + F_O(n) + F_I(n) + F_M(n)} \tag{3}$$

Similarly, $DS(n)$ is calculated by adding all responses with dissatisfaction elements (One-dimensional and Must-be) and dividing it by the total amount of relevant responses:

$$DS(n) = \frac{F_M(n) + F_O(n)}{F_A(n) + F_O(n) + F_I(n) + F_M(n)} \tag{4}$$

For modeling of the total satisfaction objective, we follow the proven concepts of the EVOLVE based algorithms, in particular, the more recent EVOLVE II (Ruhe 2010). For a given time horizon of K releases, there is a discount factor making the delivery of a feature less satisfactory when it is offered later. While using a weighting (discounting) factor $w(k)$ for all releases $k = 1\ldots K$, we assume that $w(K + 1) = 0$, $w(1) = 1$, and

$$w(k) > w(k + 1) \quad (k = 1\ldots K - 1) \tag{5}$$

This assumption implies that the value of delivering a feature will be the higher the earlier it is delivered. For a plan x assigning features to releases, *Total Satisfaction* $TS(x)$ is defined based on the summation of the discounted feature values $S(n)$ taken over all assigned features and all releases.

$$TS(x) = \sum_{k=1...K} \sum_{n:x(n)=k} w(k) \times S(n) \rightarrow Max! \tag{6}$$

Total Dissatisfaction $TDS(x)$ of a plan x follows the same idea as just introduced for satisfaction. The longer a feature is not offered, the higher the dissatisfaction. Similar to satisfaction, we introduce factors describing the relative degree of dissatisfaction between releases. $z(k)$ is the dissatisfaction discount factor related to release k. As dissatisfaction of nondelivery increases over releases, we assume $z(1) = 0, z(K + 1) = 1$, and

$$z(k) < z(k+1) \quad (k = 1 \dots K) \tag{7}$$

If plan x would not offer any features at all, total dissatisfaction $TDS(x)$ would be the summation of all feature dissatisfaction values. More generally, if a feature is offered in release k, then this creates a dissatisfaction of $z(k) \times DS(n)$. If it is offered in the next release, no dissatisfaction is created at all. Total dissatisfaction $TDS(x)$ created by a plan x is modeled as the summation of all adjusted feature values $DS(n)$, and this function needs to be minimized:

$$TDS(x) = \sum_{k=1...K+1} \sum_{n:x(n)=k} z(k) \times DS(n) \rightarrow Min! \tag{8}$$

Implementation of features is effort consuming. We make the simplifying assumption of just looking at the total amount of (estimated) effort needed per feature. The estimated effort for implementation of feature $F(n) (n = 1 \dots N)$ is denoted by *effort(n)*. When planning K subsequent releases, the consumed effort per release is not allowed to exceed a given release capacity. For all releases k ($k = 1 \dots K$), this capacity is denoted by $Cap(k)$.

More formally, a *feasible release plan* x needs to satisfy all constraints of the form:

$$\sum_{n:x(n)=k} effort(n) \leq Cap(k) \quad \text{for } k = 1 \dots K \tag{9}$$

In Eq. (9), effort consumption for release k is constrained by the given capacity $Cap(k)$. For each release k, the summation is done over all the features $F(n)$ that are assigned to this release, i.e., fulfilling $x(n) = k$.

Among all the plans fulfilling resource constraints (known as *feasible plans*), a plan x^* is called a *trade-off solution* if no other plan exists that is better on one criterion and at the same time not worse in the other. This means that we are looking for feasible plans x^* with the property that there is no other feasible plan x' (also called a *dominating plan*) such that is better in one dimension and not worse in all the others.

Asymmetric Release Planning ARP We consider a given set of features $F(n)$ with feature values $S(n)$ and $DS(n)(n = 1 \ldots N)$. Among all the plans fulfilling resource constraints, the ARP problem is to find trade-off solutions for concurrently maximizing $TS(x)$ and minimizing $TDS(x)$. That means, ARP is the problem of finding trade-off release plans that are balancing satisfaction and dissatisfaction.

4.3 Solution Design

Software release planning can be solved by a variety of algorithms. For a more recent analysis, we refer to Ameller et al. (2016). In its simplest form, greedy heuristics could be applied. The general greedy principle is to select the best local features at each iteration, where the definition of "locally best" varies between the heuristics (Cormen et al. 2001). With no backtracking, greedy solutions are fast and often "good enough." The quality of the solutions depends on the problem structure and the instance of the problem. It can be quite far from the optimum in specific instances.

Integer linear programming was used by Veerapen et al. (2015) to solve the single and bi-objective Next Release Problem. While there has been a dominance of search-based techniques in the past (starting with the genetic algorithm of Greer and Ruhe (2004)), the authors have shown that integer linear programming-based outperforms the NSGA-II (Deb et al. 2002) genetic approach on large bi-objective instances. For the bi-objective asymmetric release problem, we propose a method of solving a sequence of single-criterion optimization problems, each of them generating a new or an existing trade-off solution. The step-size for varying the parameter can be selected by the concrete problem. For the implementation, we apply the (mixed) integer linear programming optimizer *Gurobi (2012), version 6.4* and its interface *MATLAB* to manage data.

4.4 Data Collection

Data collection covered towards elicitation of features, effort estimation, and feature evaluation by stakeholders.

Stakeholders We invited 24 software engineering graduate students to serve as stakeholders. Even though students were not a direct customer of the company, they were familiar with the domain and were considered to be representative for the purpose of this case study.

Weight of Stakeholders The survey participants provided a self-evaluation in terms of their familiarity with Over-the-Top (OTT) services and mobile applications. At the beginning of the survey, stakeholders stated their domain expertise on a Likert scale ranging from one to nine. We used this value as the weight of stakeholders for the planning process.

Features The pool of candidate app features was extracted from the description of 261 apps, all of them providing media content over the internet without the involvement of an operator in the control or distribution of the OTT TV services. A commercial text analysis tool was used to retrieve 42 candidate features. Domain experts evaluated the meaningfulness of extracted features and eliminated the phrases which did not point into any OTT feature. Feature extraction itself was managed by the case study company and resulted in 36 features further investigated.

Feature Value To predict the impact of offering versus missing features, we applied the Kano analysis (Kano et al. 1984). We performed a survey with a continuous Kano design and asked the two types of questions (functional and dysfunctional). For each feature, each of the stakeholders expressed the percentages that the feature matches one of the five possible answers per question.

Effort The effort for developing each feature was estimated by domain experts within the company. A product manager and two senior developers estimated the effort needed (in person hours) to develop each feature. They applied a triangular (three point) effort estimation to estimate the optimistic, pessimistic, and most-likely effort amount needed to deliver a feature. The three estimates were combined using a weighted average.

Capacity To show the impact of tight, medium, and more relaxed resource availability, we ran three concurrent scenarios with three varying release capacities Cap(1) of 112.7 (lower bound), 367.4 (most probable), and 625.5 (upper bound) person hours, respectively.

4.5   Optimization

We were running the optimization solver for three defined optimization scenarios in correspondence to three varying capacity levels. Each time, a set of alternative solutions is generated. In total, 14 structurally trade-off solutions (plans) were generated. Each plan represents one possible way to balance between satisfaction and dissatisfaction of stakeholders. Based on the equivalence between parametric and multi-objective optimization (Clímaco et al. 1997), each solution set is received from running a sequence of single-criterion problems.

4.6 Validation

We performed a comparison between the quality of the optimized solutions in comparison to those obtained from (1) random search and (2) heuristic search. Using random search is selecting a feature randomly as long as the effort for implementing that feature is less than the available capacity. The results showed that optimized solutions strongly dominate all the 1000 solutions generated by random searching.

We also compared the results against running eight different heuristics. 66.7% of the heuristic plans were dominated with at least one of the fully optimized solutions. This demonstrates that heuristics are fast and conceptually easy, but often not good enough. The comprehensiveness of solutions generated from the optimization in conjunction with their guaranteed quality is considered a strong argument in favor of the proposed approach.

4.7 Implementation and Evaluation

We conducted a survey to understand stakeholders preference among the various plans generated. The survey included 20 stakeholders. Using Fleiss Kappa test (Sheskin 2003) for measuring inter-rater agreement showed a slight to poor agreement between the 20 participants.

By comparing plans per stakeholder, among stakeholders, and between criteria, we found that:

- One plan does not fit all: For both planning objectives, there is substantial variation between stakeholders in terms of what they consider their preferred solution.
- One criterion is not enough: Six of the 20 stakeholders have a varying top preference when comparing plans selected from satisfaction and dissatisfaction perspective.

5 Usage and Usefulness of Optimization

5.1 Limits of Optimization Models

As any model, even the most detailed models lack some details in comparison to the real-world ecosystem. This means that the representation of real world always lacks some details and contains inaccuracies. Meignan et al. (2015) described four types of potential optimization model limitations:

- Approximation of complex problem's aspects: Formulation of real-world problems might be difficult because of the lack of quantifying constraints or objectives. Human involvement, as being the case in software engineering, often requires to use approximations of the phenomena.

- Simplification for model tractability: Even if the phenomena under investigation are quantifiable, simplification of the model is needed to apply a computational optimization approach. For example, linear models are often used for that purpose.
- Limited specifications: In some cases, the problem is not (yet) well defined. This might be caused by the lack of problem and domain knowledge.
- Lack of resources: Optimization is not for free but consumes time and cost. This implies making compromises and simplifications.

5.2 Difficulties Which Are Specific to the Discipline of Software Engineering

Software engineering differentiates from other disciplines by a number of factors (Ruhe and Wohlin 2014). Among those factors, some of them are critical for deciding and running optimization:

- High degree of uncertainty in the software project and product scope.
- Planning and estimating of software projects is challenging because these activities depend on requirements that are often imprecise or based on lacking information.
- Software development is nondeterministic. The data received from observations are incomplete and sometimes contradictory.
- Objective measurement and quantification of software quality is difficult.

As a conclusion of the above, we need to check more carefully which type of optimization is most appropriate and in which situation and how much we should pursue this pathway. Is it always "The more the better"? The following subsection proposes three attributes to answer this question.

5.3 How Much Is Enough?

There is a very broad spectrum of decision problems that potentially benefit from running optimization. But which technique to apply in what situation? Both the problems under investigation and the techniques available have characteristics that are relevant to decide which one is used for what. Along with this understanding goes the question *How much is enough?*. In the sequel, we define three key dimensions which have shown to have substantial impact on the breadth and depth of analytics of optimization. The key motivation for doing this is the statement attributed to Aristotle mentioned in the introduction.

5.3.1 Validity: How Valid Is the Problem Definition?

There is no easy way to measure validity of a model (being always wrong and sometimes useful), but some possibilities to verify its behavior from running through some scenarios with an outcome already known. Validity can also relate to wickedness (Rittel and Webber 1974) which refers to the difficulty to find a proper formulation of the problem and a termination criterion for its solution.

5.3.2 Cost: How Much Effort Is Needed to Run the Whole Optimization Process?

The cost of performing the process outlined in Fig. 1 is mainly determined by the resources consumed in it. The cost might vary substantially between the cases. For example, the effort for data collection is highly influenced by the amount and quality of data already available and the effort needed to elicit additional information. Once the problem is defined, the notion of computational complexity (Garey and Johnson 2002) guides the effort estimation to determine a solution with a proven quality. This effort typically depends on the size (small, medium, or large number of variables involved), difficulty (low, medium, or high in terms of number of constraints, objectives), the linearity versus non-linearity, and the continuous versus discrete nature of the variables included.

5.3.3 Value: How Valuable Is It to Find an Optimized Solution?

How much value is added to the real-world problem when an optimized and carefully analyzed solution is applied versus an ad hoc one suggested by the domain expert? This value is associated with the impact of the decision to be made. Operational decisions are in the day-to-day business with typically short-term impact on a company. Tactical ones are concerned with work assignments, selection of tools, reuse of artifacts. Strategic decisions have the longest impact, but are also based on the strongest degree of uncertainty.

5.4 Return-on-Investment

Comparing the investment made into something with the potential return achieved from this investment is a common question, mainly triggered from economical considerations. As an example, Erdogmus et al. (2004) analyzed the ROI of quality investment. The authors state that "We generally want to increase a software product's quality because fixing existing software takes valuable time away from developing new software. But how much investment in software quality is desirable? When should we invest, and where?"

The same idea could be used to the application of optimization. More precisely, evaluating the impact of decisions made based on optimization versus the baseline decision-making approach, typically some form of relying on intuition. There are at least three prerequisites for doing that: (1) Characterization of the context, (2) Characterization and quantification of the investment (cost), and (3) Projection of the value added from implementing an optimized solution.

For the characterization of context, Dybå et al. (2012) introduced a template that has the two main dimensions called *omnibus context* and *discrete context*. The first dimension includes the 5 W's: What? Who? Where? When? and Why? The second one is along the technical, social, and environmental aspects of the context which are likely vary in detail from case to case. Specifying the context attributes allows to related specific empirical results to the characteristics where they are coming form. It also helps to provide more specific recommendations about when and how well certain things work.

Software development and evolution is a value-creating process. However, there seems to be a "disconnect" between the decision criteria that guide software engineers and the value creation criteria of an organization (Boehm and Sullivan 2000). Projecting the impact of an improvement in decision-making against a technical parameter (e.g., test coverage) in terms of its impact can be expressed as *Net Present Value* (NPV) but is a challenging task. If analyzing a project over a period of n time periods, the formula for the net present value of a project is

$$\text{NPV} = \sum_{t=0}^{n} \frac{R(t)}{(1+d)^t} \tag{10}$$

Therein, $R(t)$ denotes the difference between net cash inflow and net cash outflow during a single period t. The model assumes a discount rate d to transfer future value to the today value. The added NPV that is from applying an optimized versus a baseline solution is the difference between their respective NPVs.

$$\text{NPV}_{\text{Improvement}} = \text{NPV}_{\text{OptimalSolution}} - \text{NPV}_{\text{Baseline}} \tag{11}$$

The cost of analytics is determined from both the depth and the breadth of investigations. The *depth* can be exemplified by the extent of running optimization algorithms to achieve close to optimal results. Another example refers to the level of details included in visualization. The extent of applying multiple analytical techniques to data from multiple sources to achieve results refers to *breadth*. Solving a problem by looking for data from different sources and/or performing method triangulation is of clear value but also of clear additional cost. The variation of perspectives in visualization is an example for breadth.

Figure 3 shows a ROI curve of technology usage. Following some phase of increase, there is a saturation point. After that, further investment does not further pay off. We hypothesize that a similar behavior applies in principle for the usage of optimization and analytics in general.

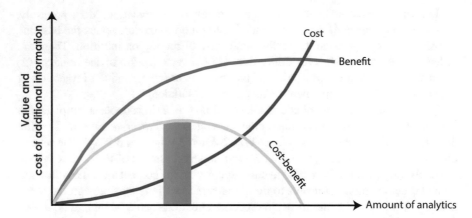

Fig. 3 Expected ROI curve from technology investment

5.5 ROI of Asymmetric Release Plan Optimization

It is difficult to quantify the ROI. The value of providing the right features at the right time depends on the competitiveness of the market the product is related to, the number of product instances sold, and maturity of data collection and decision-making processes the organization is in. For the running example, additional effort was needed to elicit the information related to stakeholder satisfaction and dissatisfaction. We performed a survey with six company managers and asked: To what extent do you think the additional effort (from answering ten questions per feature based on Kano) is worthwhile? In response, five managers agreed or strongly agreed, and one manager was neutral about the efficiency of the Kano model.

6 Recommended Further Reading

Optimization is an established discipline with roots going back to names such as Leonid Kantorovich, George Dantzig, and John von Neumann. Its applications range through all disciplines of Science, Engineering, and Economics. There are numerous models, methods, and tools. The encyclopedia of optimization (Floudas and Pardalos 2001) gives an overview. In its essence, optimization is the process of searching for the best out of a pool of alternatives. What means *best* is described by one or multiple criteria. The alternatives are explicitly or implicitly described (by constraints). For the actual optimization step in the whole problem-solving process (Step 5 in Fig. 1), different alternatives can be considered, ranging from simple heuristics to meta- and hyper-heuristics to exact common purpose solvers. In the sequel, we provide guidance for further reading for three emerging directions of using optimization in the context of (empirical) software engineering.

6.1 Meta- and Hyper-Heuristics

In the area of software engineering, the term *Search-based Software Engineering (SBSE)* was coined by a paper of Harman and Jones (2001), who argued that software engineering is ideal for the application of meta-heuristic search techniques, such as genetic algorithms, simulated annealing, and tabu search. In November 2017, the SBSE repository at University College London (edited by [Zhang, Harman, Mansouri]) counted 1727 relevant publications. More recently, the portfolio of techniques has been enlarged by other bioinspired algorithms that are designed and following the behavior of biological systems. These algorithms are intuitive and have proven successful in many occasions including software engineering (Kar 2016).

Independently, hyper-heuristics have been designed; Burke et al. (2013) have performed a state-of-the art survey regarding this. The key characteristic is that these algorithms operate on a search space of heuristics (or heuristic components) rather than directly on the search space of solutions to the underlying problem that is being addressed (Burke et al. 2013). For the area of testing, Balera and de Santiago (2019) performed a systematic mapping study on hyper-heuristics. For the multi-objective next release problem and analyzing ten real-world data sets, Zhang et al. (2018) have shown that hyper-heuristics are particularly effective.

6.2 Bioinspired Algorithms

Bioinspired optimization is an emerging paradigm which encompasses the principles and inspiration of the biological evolution of nature to develop new and robust optimization techniques (Binitha et al. 2012). These algorithms are drawing attention from the scientific community due to the increasing complexity of the problems, increasing range of potential solutions in multidimensional hyperplanes, dynamic nature of the problems and constraints, and challenges of incomplete, probabilistic, and imperfect information for decision-making.

Not much exploration has happened in the true application space for the rest of these algorithms, probably due to the recency of some of these developments or due to the lack of availability of pseudo-codes which can be used directly. There is a need for studies highlighting the preferred application for algorithms like artificial bee colony algorithm, bacterial foraging algorithm, firefly algorithm, leaping frog algorithm, bat algorithm, flower pollination algorithm, and artificial plant optimization algorithm in actual problem contexts.

6.3   Interactive Optimization

Interactive optimization approaches acknowledge existing limits to modeling and parameter settings and value the user's expertise in the application domain (Meignan et al. 2015). They maintain the human expert in the problem-solving loop and distinguish between problem-oriented interaction and search-oriented interaction. For the first one, the user can either adjust or enrich the optimization problem, e.g., by adjusting existing constraints or objectives or by defining new ones. For search-oriented interaction, the user actively influences the search procedure, e.g., by parameter tuning.

7   Conclusions

Optimization is an important means to improve software development and evolution. Optimizing processes is the ultimate goal of most mature CMMI level 5 organizations. Practically, there is almost no limit to consider optimization in software engineering. But as for any technology, its usage needs to be guided. Besides the opportunity to enlarge the scope of optimization, this chapter emphasizes the need to take a closer look at the ROI of optimization. Taking into account the perceived validity of the problem formulation, the ROI model serves as justification for investing into optimality. In the language of the CMMI model, it is unlikely that a specific part of the software development landscape is highly optimized if the whole surrounding is immature. The ROI estimation servers as a guidance in this decision process of deciding *How much optimization is needed and how much is enough?*

Optimization by no means is a silver bullet. We are not fascinated just by numbers but are more interested in insight, especially actionable insight. If designed and performed properly (for example, as guided in the recommended process of Fig. 2), it is a valuable part of decision support. Its pragmatic usage means to understand the scope and degree of its usage. Furthermore, it often means searching not for just one ultimate solution but for a diversity of alternative solutions which is formulated as the *diversification principle* (Ruhe 2010):

> A single optimal solution to a cognitive complex (optimization) problem is less likely to serve the original problem when compared to a portfolio of optimized solutions being qualified AND structurally diversified.

Acknowledgements This research was supported by the Natural Sciences and Engineering Research Council of Canada, Discovery Grant RGPIN-2017-03948. The literature analysis of the study was mainly done by Debjyoti Mukherjee. The author is grateful to discussions with and comments received from Maleknaz Nayebi and Julian Harty.

References

Abran A, Moore JW, Bourque P, Dupuis R, Tripp LL (2004) Software engineering body of knowledge. IEEE Computer Society, Angela Burgess, Washington

Ameller D, Farré C, Franch X, Rufian G (2016) A survey on software release planning models. In: Product-focused software process improvement: 17th international conference, PROFES 2016, Trondheim, November 22–24, 2016, Proceedings 17. Springer, Berlin, pp 48–65

Antoniol G, Di Penta M, Harman M (2005) Search-based techniques applied to optimization of project planning for a massive maintenance project. In: 21st IEEE international conference on software maintenance (ICSM'05). IEEE, Piscataway, pp 240–249

Aronson JE, Liang T-P, Turban E (2005) Decision support systems and intelligent systems, vol 4. Pearson Prentice-Hall, Upper Saddle River

Balera JM, de Santiago VA Jr (2019) A systematic mapping addressing hyper-heuristics within search-based software testing. Inf Softw Technol 114:176–189

Barreto A, de O Barros M, Werner CML (2008) Staffing a software project: a constraint satisfaction and optimization-based approach. Comput Oper Res 35(10):3073–3089

Binitha S, Sathya SS, et al (2012) A survey of bio inspired optimization algorithms. Int J Soft Comput Eng 2(2):137–151

Boehm, BW, Sullivan KJ (2000) Software economics: a roadmap. In: Proceedings of the conference on the future of Software engineering. ACM, New York, pp 319–343

Bowman M, Briand LC, Labiche Y (2010) Solving the class responsibility assignment problem in object-oriented analysis with multi-objective genetic algorithms. IEEE Trans Softw Eng 36(6):817–837

Burke EK, Gendreau M, Hyde M, Kendall G, Ochoa G, Özcan E, Qu R (2013) Hyper-heuristics: a survey of the state of the art. J Oper Res Soc 64(12):1695–1724

Chang CK, Jiang H-y, Di Y, Zhu D, Ge Y (2008) Time-line based model for software project scheduling with genetic algorithms. Inf Softw Technol 50(11):1142–1154

Chen WN, Zhang J (2013) Ant colony optimization for software project scheduling and staffing with an event-based scheduler. IEEE Trans Softw Eng 39(1):1–17

Chrissis MB, Konrad M, Shrum S (2003) CMMI guidelines for process integration and product improvement. Addison-Wesley Longman Publishing Co., Inc., Boston

Clímaco J, Ferreira C, Captivo ME (1997) Multicriteria integer programming: an overview of the different algorithmic approaches. In: Multicriteria analysis. Springer, Berlin, pp 248–258

Cormen TH, Leiserson CE, Rivest RL, Stein C (2001) Introduction to algorithms, vol 6. MIT Press, Cambridge

Cortellessa V, Marinelli F, Potena P (2008) An optimization framework for "build-or-buy" decisions in software architecture. Comput Oper Res 35(10):3090–3106

Deb K, Pratap A, Agarwal S, Meyarivan T, Fast A (2002) A fast and elitist multiobjective genetic algorithm: NSGA-II. IEEE Trans Evol Comput 6(2):182–197

Di Penta M, Harman M, Antoniol G (2011) The use of search-based optimization techniques to schedule and staff software projects: an approach and an empirical study. Softw Pract Exp 41(5):495–519

Durillo JJ, Zhang Y, Alba E, Harman M, Nebro AJ (2011) A study of the bi-objective next release problem. Empir Softw Eng 16(1):29–60

Dybå T, Sjøberg DIK, Cruzes DS (2012) What works for whom, where, when, and why?: on the role of context in empirical software engineering. In: Proceedings of the ACM-IEEE international symposium on empirical software engineering and measurement. ACM, New York, pp 19–28

Erdogmus H, Favaro J, Strigel W (2004) Return on investment. IEEE Softw 21(3):18–22

Floudas CA, Pardalos PM (2001) Encyclopedia of optimization, vol 1. Springer Science & Business Media, Berlin

Frey S, Fittkau F, Hasselbring W (2013) Search-based genetic optimization for deployment and reconfiguration of software in the cloud. In: 2013 35th international conference on software engineering (ICSE). IEEE, Piscataway, pp 512–521

Garey MR, Johnson DS (2002) Computers and intractability, vol 29. W. H. Freeman, New York

Gawande A (2010) Checklist manifesto, the (HB). Penguin Books India, New Delhi

Geoffrion AM (1976) The purpose of mathematical programming is insight, not numbers. Interfaces 7(1):81–92

Greer D, Ruhe G (2004) Software release planning: an evolutionary and iterative approach. Inf Softw Technol 46(4):243–253

Grunske L (2006) Identifying good architectural design alternatives with multi-objective optimization strategies. In: Proceedings of the 28th international conference on software engineering. ACM, New York, pp 849–852

Guo J, White J, Wang G, Li J, Wang Y (2011) A genetic algorithm for optimized feature selection with resource constraints in software product lines. J Syst Softw 84(12):2208–2221

Gurobi (2012) Gurobi optimizer reference manual. http://www.gurobi.com

Harman M, Jones BF (2001) Search-based software engineering. Inf Softw Technol 43(14):833–839

Harman M, Tratt L (2007) Pareto optimal search based refactoring at the design level. In: Proceedings of the 9th annual conference on genetic and evolutionary computation. ACM, New York, pp 1106–1113

Harman M, Hierons RM, Proctor M (2002) A new representation and crossover operator for search-based optimization of software modularization. In: GECCO 2002: Proceedings of the genetic and evolutionary computation Conference, New York, vol 2, pp 1351–1358

Huang S-J, Chiu N-H, Chen L-W (2008) Integration of the grey relational analysis with genetic algorithm for software effort estimation. Eur J Oper Res 188(3):898–909

Kano N, Seraku N, Takahashi F, Tsuji S (1984) Attractive quality and must-be quality. J Jan Soc Qual Control 14(2):39–48

Kar AK (2016) Bio inspired computing–a review of algorithms and scope of applications. Expert Syst Appl 59:20–32

Kistler T, Franz M (2003) Continuous program optimization: a case study. ACM Trans Program Lang Syst 25(4):500–548

Kurgan LA, Musilek P (2006) A survey of knowledge discovery and data mining process models. Knowl Eng Rev 21(1):1–24

Lakhotia K, Harman M, McMinn P (2007) A multi-objective approach to search-based test data generation. In: Proceedings of the 9th annual conference on genetic and evolutionary computation. ACM, New York, pp 1098–1105

Langdon WB, Harman M (2014) Optimizing existing software with genetic programming. IEEE Trans Evol Comput 19(1):118–135

Li Y-F, Xie M, Goh TN (2009) A study of mutual information based feature selection for case based reasoning in software cost estimation. Expert Syst Appl 36(3):5921–5931

Liu Y, Khoshgoftaar TM, Seliya N (2010) Evolutionary optimization of software quality modeling with multiple repositories. IEEE Trans Softw Eng 36(6):852–864

Lucas TW, McGunnigle JE (2003) When is model complexity too much? Illustrating the benefits of simple models with Hughes' salvo equations. Nav Res Logist 50(3):197–217

Ma Y, Zhang C (2008) Quick convergence of genetic algorithm for QoS-driven web service selection. Comput Netw 52(5):1093–1104

MacDonell SG, Shepperd MJ (2003) Combining techniques to optimize effort predictions in software project management. J Syst Softw 66(2):91–98

Meignan D, Knust S, Frayret J-M, Pesant G, Gaud N (2015) A review and taxonomy of interactive optimization methods in operations research. ACM Trans Interact Intell Syst 5(3):17

Nayebi M, Ruhe G (2018) Asymmetric release planning – compromising satisfaction against dissatisfaction. IEEE Trans Softw Eng 45(9):839–857

Ngo-The A, Ruhe G (2008) Optimized resource allocation for software release planning. IEEE Trans Softw Eng 35(1):109–123

Oliveira ALI, Braga PL, Lima RMF, Cornélio ML (2010) GA-based method for feature selection and parameters optimization for machine learning regression applied to software effort estimation. Inf Softw Technol 52(11):1155–1166

Praditwong K, Harman M, Yao X (2010) Software module clustering as a multi-objective search problem. IEEE Trans Softw Eng 37(2):264–282

Ren J, Harman M, Di Penta M (2011) Cooperative co-evolutionary optimization of software project staff assignments and job scheduling. In: International symposium on search based software engineering. Springer, Berlin, pp 127–141

Rittel HWJ, Webber MM (1974) Wicked problems. Man-Made Futures 26(1):272–280

Ruhe G (2002) Software engineering decision support–a new paradigm for learning software organizations. In: International workshop on learning software organizations. Springer, Berlin, pp 104–113

Ruhe G (2010) Product release planning: methods, tools and applications. CRC Press, Boca Raton

Ruhe G, Wohlin C (2014) Software project management: setting the context. In: Software project management in a changing world. Springer, Berlin, pp 1–24

Ruhe G, et al (2004) Hybrid intelligence in software release planning. Int J Hybrid Intell Syst 1(1–2):99–110

Saliu O, Ruhe G (2005) Supporting software release planning decisions for evolving systems. In: 29th annual IEEE/NASA software engineering workshop. IEEE, Piscataway, pp 14–26

Saliu MO, Ruhe G (2007) Bi-objective release planning for evolving software systems. In: Proceedings ESEC/FSE. ACM, New York, pp 105–114

Shearer C (2000) The CRISP-DM model: the new blueprint for data mining. J Data Warehouse 5(4):13–22

Sheskin DJ (2003) Handbook of parametric and nonparametric statistical procedures. CRC Press, Boca Raton

Singh Y, Kaur A, Suri B (2010) Test case prioritization using ant colony optimization. ACM SIGSOFT Softw Eng Notes 35(4):1–7

Van den Akker M, Brinkkemper S, Diepen G, Versendaal J (2008) Software product release planning through optimization and what-if analysis. Inf Softw Technol 50(1–2):101–111

Van Solingen R, Basili V, Caldiera G, Rombach HD (2002) Goal question metric (GQM) approach. Encycl Softw Eng 2:578–583

Veerapen N, Ochoa G, Harman M, Burke EK (2015) An integer linear programming approach to the single and bi-objective next release problem. Inf Softw Technol 65:1–13

Wada H, Champrasert P, Suzuki J, Oba K (2008) Multiobjective optimization of SLA-aware service composition. In: 2008 IEEE congress on services-part I. IEEE, Piscataway, pp 368–375

Walcott KR, Soffa ML, Kapfhammer GM, Roos RS (2006) TimeAware test suite prioritization. In: Proceedings of the 2006 international symposium on software testing and analysis. ACM, New York, pp 1–12

Wang Z, Tang K, Yao X (2010) Multi-objective approaches to optimal testing resource allocation in modular software systems. IEEE Trans Reliab 59(3):563–575

Wieringa RJ (2014) Design science methodology for information systems and software engineering. Springer, Berlin

Xiao M, El-Attar M, Reformat M, Miller J (2007) Empirical evaluation of optimization algorithms when used in goal-oriented automated test data generation techniques. Empir Softw Eng 12(2):183–239

Yoo S, Harman M (2007) Pareto efficient multi-objective test case selection. In: Proceedings of the 2007 international symposium on software testing and analysis. ACM, New York, pp 140–150

Zhang Y, Harman M, Mansouri SA (2007) The multi-objective next release problem. In: Proceedings of the 9th annual conference on genetic and evolutionary computation. ACM, New York, pp 1129–1137

Zhang Y, Harman M, Ochoa G, Ruhe G, Brinkkemper S (2018) An empirical study of meta-and hyper-heuristic search for multi-objective release planning. ACM Trans Softw Eng Methodol 27(1):3

The Role of Simulation-Based Studies in Software Engineering Research

Breno Bernard Nicolau de França and Nauman Bin Ali

Abstract Several decades ago, inspired by other knowledge areas, simulation was introduced as a research method to Software Engineering. Motivated by potential benefits achieved in other areas, the software engineering community has used simulation-based studies for planning, controlling, and improving software development. However, unclear expectations from simulation-based studies, a lack of methodological support, as well as dispersed knowledge to support model building and calibration have hindered widespread adoption of simulation-based investigations. In this chapter, we delineate the role of simulation in software engineering research and compile processes and guidelines into a comprehensive life cycle. This chapter aims to guide software engineering researchers to conduct effective simulation-based studies in real-world settings.

1 Introduction

Computer simulation is used as a research tool in several areas, such as Medicine (Burton et al. 2006), Engineering (Babuska and Oden 2004), Social Sciences (Eck and Liu 2008), and others (Law and Kelton 2000). In Software Engineering (SE), the community presented several initiatives on simulating different kinds of phenomena, ranging from software products, processes to team behavior.

Among these different areas, the use of the term *simulation* varies substantially. To frame our perspective on simulation for this chapter, we have adopted the following definition from Banks (1999): "Simulation is the *imitation* of the operation of a real-world process or system *over time*. Simulation involves the generation of

B. B. N. de França (✉)
Universidade Estadual de Campinas, Campinas, SP, Brazil
e-mail: breno@ic.unicamp.br

N. B. Ali
Blekinge Institute of Technology, Karlskrona, Sweden
e-mail: nauman.ali@bth.se

© Springer Nature Switzerland AG 2020

M. Felderer, G. H. Travassos (eds.), *Contemporary Empirical Methods in Software Engineering*, https://doi.org/10.1007/978-3-030-32489-6_10

263

an *artificial* history of the system, and the observation of that artificial history to draw *inferences* concerning the operating characteristics of the real system that is represented."

In this chapter, empirical investigations of a system of interest are referred to as simulation-based studies (SBS) if they use simulation to numerically evaluate a mathematical model that imitates the real-world behavior of the system.

As a supporting tool for research in SE, SBS are not meant to replace other types of empirical investigations such as controlled experiments or case studies (we refer to chapter "Guidelines for Conducting Software Engineering Research" for a more comprehensive view on research methods). Rather, it is useful to support knowledge acquisition and decision-making during the research process. Simulation-based studies also require previous empirical knowledge from in vivo[1] or in vitro[2] studies for modeling SE phenomena or behavior (Travassos and Barros 2003). Such modeling fosters large-scale observations, using a controlled and computational environment (in virtuo[3] and in silico[4]), to understand better the phenomenon and possibly explain it through simulation traces and diverse scenarios that could be difficult to observe in an in vivo or in vitro environment. Therefore, simulations are recommended for studies involving a combination of many factors (with possible interactions) and alternatives, as well as long-term observations.

Besides modeling, SBS also require data for calibration, validation, and experimentation. Usually, such data come from observations and, consequently, are limited to their original context. When insufficient data and theories are available, simulation can still be used. In such cases, the role of simulation is limited to a tool that models our assumptions and approximations. The likely outcome of our proposed solutions is then judged objectively under these assumptions. However, we should be aware of the reliability of the results and take extreme care not to overinterpret the results.

Building on lessons learned from the existing literature on simulation in SE, this chapter proceeds in Sect. 2 with a discussion of the claimed benefits to motivate the adoption of simulation in SE. Then, in Sect. 3, we present what we understand are the actual benefits and describe the role of SBS in SE research. In Sect. 4, we motivate the need for methodological support for conducting SBS. Later, in Sect. 5, we present a comprehensive and consolidated life cycle for simulation-based studies in SE. Section 6 presents two practical examples of SBS conducted based on several of the recommendations presented in this chapter. Furthermore, additional readings are suggested in Sect. 7. Finally, we conclude the chapter in Sect. 8.

---

[1] In vivo studies are the ones occurring in real-life environments.

[2] In vitro studies are the ones occurring in controlled environments with human participants.

[3] In virtuo studies are the ones occurring in computational environments driven by human participants.

[4] In silico studies are the ones occurring completely in computational environments with no human intervention.

2 Motivation for Simulation-Based Studies

Software development is a dynamic activity that involves several people, working with various tools and technologies, guided by policies and processes to develop solutions that fulfill user requirements. The interaction and interdependence between human, technological, and organizational factors make it difficult to confidently assess the potential impact of a proposed change in software development. Furthermore, introducing a change in the development practice is a time and resource-intensive undertaking. Therefore, we want to have high confidence in the likely impact of a change before changing the actual process.

Figure 1 depicts several ways of studying the impact of introducing a change in a system. Broadly, we can (1) manipulate the actual system and investigate the effect of an intervention or (2) study the effects on a model of the system in controlled settings. The main trade-off between the two choices is that of realism vs. control in conducting the investigation. An additional concern is that of the cost of conducting the investigation and the risk if the introduced change does not produce the expected results or has unforeseen consequences.

Due to the cost of manipulating the actual system and the lack of control in real-world settings, we tend to rely on developing and manipulating models of the system. It is only after gaining more confidence in solution proposals that we begin moving towards changing the actual practice. Even in that case, the investigations in real-world settings (through case study or action research) often try to reduce the cost of such studies by incorporating change on a smaller scale. For example, investigating by introducing change in one of the teams or projects and observing the effects before adopting a change throughout the organization.

Simulation is proposed as an inexpensive (Wu and Yan 2009; Melis et al. 2006; Kellner et al. 1999; Madachy 2002) and proactive means to assess what will happen before actually committing resources for a change (Kellner et al. 1999). McCall et al. (1979) made the first suggestion for its use in SE in 1979. It has since been used to study various aspects of software development, e.g., effort estimation, project planning, risk assessment, and training. The simulation models developed over the

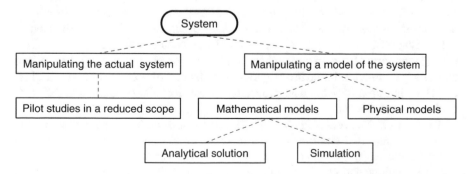

Fig. 1 Ways of studying a system (adapted from Law 2007)

years have varied in scope (from parts of the life cycle to long-term organizational evolution), purpose (including planning and training), and approach (e.g., system dynamics or discrete-event simulation) (Zhang et al. 2010).

3 Limitations of Simulation-Based Studies in SE

As discussed in the previous section, the range of claimed potential benefits coupled with occasional claims of industrial application and impact (Zhang et al. 2011) gives an impression that simulation is a panacea for problems in SE. However, in the following sections, we discuss the limitations of SBS in SE. This discussion draws on an analysis of the existing literature (Ali et al. 2014) and our experience of using simulation in industrial settings (Ali and Petersen 2012; Ali et al. 2015). In the SE literature, the use of simulation has two implied purposes, which are:

1. Simulation as a problem-solving tool for decision support for SE practitioners (Banks 1999).
2. Simulation as a means to conduct controlled experiments (Abdel-Hamid 1988) and as an alternative to industrial case study research (Müller and Pfahl 2008).

To scrutinize the above two claims, it is useful to assess the following two aspects of SBS: (a) the cost of conducting effective SBS and (b) the strength of evidence generated in SBS. Other limitations of SBS in SE are further discussed by Pfahl (2014).

3.1 Cost of Conducting SBS

SBS are certainly less risky than experimenting with a physical model of a system or the actual system (Fig. 1). Physical models in software engineering are very uncommon, so that is not considered as a feasible alternative unless embedded or robotics systems are into play. Similarly, the limitations of generalizability when experimenting with students as subjects and artifacts that are not representative of industrial-scale are well-documented (Feldt et al. 2018). However, the cost of conducting SBS for industrial cases should be accounted for, and will include, e.g.: (1) the cost of developing and calibrating a simulation model, (2) design and analysis of simulation-based investigations, (3) the cost of necessary data collection, or (4) setting up a measurement program that can feed the simulation model with sufficiently reliable data.

Pfahl and Lebsanft (2000) reported 18 months of calendar time for a simulation study. They reported an effort of one person-year in consulting and 0.25 person-years for the development part of the study. In another study, Pfahl et al. (2004) report the calendar time of 3 months for knowledge elicitation and modeling and four meetings with the client while conducting a simulation-based study. Shannon

(1986) predicted a high cost for simulation as well, "a practitioner is required to have about 720 h of formal classroom instruction plus 1440 h of outside study (more than one man-year of effort)."

3.2 Quality of Evidence from SBS

The role of SBS as a decision-support tool and an empirical method requires a consideration of the strength of evidence generated by SBS. Some limitations discussed below are general limitations of simulation, but they get aggravated in SBS because of the nature of software development.

Models Are Simplifications Simulation models are a simplification, abstraction, and approximation of the system of interest (Christie 1999). SBS in SE often require modeling the process or project dynamics. Fully capturing these complex dynamics of a real-world process or project in a simulation model is not possible, which raises questions about the validity of a simulation model.

Measurement Challenges SBS in SE deal with quantification of variables and their relationships. Often strict cause–effect relations with determined magnitudes of relations are not available in SE (Christie 1999). Therefore, the confidence in a simulation model depends on the verification and validation of both the structure and behavior of the model (Christie 1999). The lack of reliable measures and quantified relations (Jørgensen and Kitchenham 2012; Kitchenham 2010) also adds another degree of uncertainty in the simulation models used in SE.

Lack of Data Accurate data to use in an SBS is extremely important, as a model without supporting data cannot deliver adequate predictions, and such a model is essentially a visual metaphor (Olsen 1993). However, in SE, a lack of empirical data is a common challenge faced by researchers conducting SBS (Kellner et al. 1999). Launching a measurement program to feed a simulation model is often not feasible, and often existing SBS rely on the use of industrial averages, expert estimates, or values acquired from analytical models. The lack of accurate data also challenges the reliability of SBS results.

3.3 Simulation as a Problem-Solving, Decision-Support Tool for SE Practitioners

The vision to have practitioners using simulation as a decision-support tool in SE practice suggests a transfer of technology from academia to industry. As we are proposing a new tool or practice to the industry, it is important to have the following prerequisite information (Ali 2016):

- Cost of adoption.
- Effectiveness over the existing methods.

Apart from the cost of conducting an SBS, we should take into account the cost of required tool support and training and the effort required for the development and maintenance of a simulation model. Besides, frequent changes in technology, software development process, environment, and customer requirements require keeping the simulation model up to date. Given the high cost of simulation model development and maintenance, it is unlikely that practitioners will invest the required effort.

There is a need to identify the challenges when using simulation in a company. This includes the integration of simulation models with the existing decision-support systems used at the company (Balci 1990; Murphy and Perera 2001).

Contrary to the claims of impact on the software industry (Zhang et al. 2011), an extensive literature review on the industrial applications of simulation in SE found no evidence of adoption (Ali et al. 2014).

3.4 Simulation as an Alternative Empirical Method

In the past, some authors had suggested the use of simulation in SE research as an alternative to case study research. For example, "the usual way to analyze process behavior is to perform the actual process in a case study and observe the results. This is a very costly way to perform process analysis, because it involves the active participation of engineers. Furthermore, results from a particular case study cannot necessarily be generalized to other contexts. Another way of analyzing processes is to simulate them" (Müller and Pfahl 2008). Others have indicated its use as an alternative to expensive controlled experiments, e.g., "Simulation modeling provides a viable experimentation tool for such a task. In addition to permitting less costly and less time-consuming experimentation, simulation-type models make 'perfectly' controlled experimentation possible" (Abdel-Hamid 1988).

Given the strength of evidence generated in SBS (as we briefly summarized in Sect. 3.2), we do not see the use of simulation as an alternative to controlled experiments or case study research. Rather, we suggest the use of simulation to complement other empirical methods, which aligns with advice by Münch et al. (2003) and by Pfahl and Ruhe (2002).

The cost of conducting an SBS and the lack of the inclusion of simulation in CS/SE undergraduate or graduate curriculum are likely to prevent industry practitioners from designing and conducting SBS anytime soon. However, there is sufficient evidence (Ali et al. 2014) to show that researchers can use simulations to support empirical research.

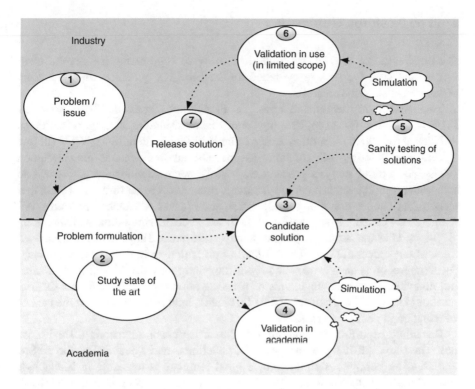

Fig. 2 The technology transfer model (adapted from Gorschek et al. 2006)

In our opinion, the use of simulation is most suitable as a means to *sanity test* solution proposals. Such SBS can be conducted both in academic and industrial settings, as shown in Fig. 2. Example 2 in Sect. 6 reports the use of simulation for supporting software process improvement decisions. Further use of simulation, with empirical evidence supporting its use, is for training and educational purposes (Pfahl 2014; Ali and Unterkalmsteiner 2014). Example 1 in Sect. 6 reports the use of simulation for training in an industrial setting.

Simulation Is Not a Silver Bullet
- Simulation is not free of cost, but there are contexts in which incurring this cost is worthwhile.
- Simulation results come with a certain degree of confidence. It is up to the experimenter to understand whether it has achieved the research goals.
- Simulation-based investigations do not mean to replace other empirical methods, but they can complement them in situations where the in loco observation is unfeasible.

4 The Need for Guidance

The conduction of SBS in the context of software engineering has several challenges, and here we present evidence on the need for guidance when adopting simulation to support research.

Two systematic literature reviews (De França and Travassos 2013; Ali et al. 2014) of SBS in software engineering found that these studies lack rigor. De França and Travassos (2013) identified lack of planning (study definition), V&V (before running simulation investigations) to assure minimal confidence in the simulation results, and output analysis procedures. Mainly, such activities are performed ad hoc, with particular studies using systematic procedures to perform one or another activity, but studies presenting a full systematic process or method are scarce. Ali et al. (2014) assessed the quality of software process simulation and modeling (SPSM) studies concerning rigor and practical relevance. They did not find reported cases of the successful transfer of SPSM to practitioners in the software industry. Furthermore, no studies were found reporting a long-term use of SPSM in practice and no evidence to back the claims of practical adoption and impact on industrial practice (Zhang 2012; Zhang et al. 2011). Finally, both reviews agree on the lack of information in simulation reports.

Regarding reporting of simulation studies in software engineering, De França and Travassos (2012) present general guidelines, and specifically for SPSM studies using continuous simulation, a good template is available in Madachy's book (Madachy 2008). Recently, Monks et al. (2019) proposed the STRESS checklist for reporting simulation studies.

Simulation can provide actual benefits when supporting software engineering research, and both simulation and SE literature have presented some guidance on conducting SBS. However, it is not an obvious decision for practitioners or researchers to select one process or a set of guidelines to follow, considering the little background in the area. For that, Ali and Petersen (2012) proposed a consolidated process for SPSM with supporting guidelines. Besides, De França and Travassos (2016) propose simulation guidelines for experimenting with dynamic models in SE. These contributions are the foundation for the life cycle presented in Sect. 5.

5 Simulation-Based Studies Life Cycle

When supporting a research process with simulations, researchers generally characterize the life cycle (process) for simulation studies as a knowledge-intensive and iterative process (Alexopoulos and Seila 1998; Balci 1990; Maria 1997; Banks 1999; Sargent 1999), including the following activities: study definition or phenomenon understanding (also called system observation); model design and development; verification and validation (V&V); performing simulation-based

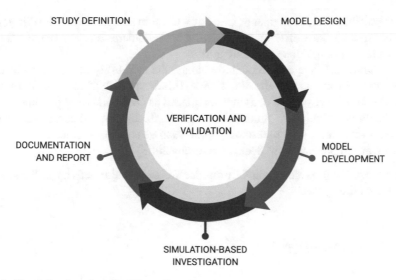

STUDY DEFINITION

MODEL DESIGN

VERIFICATION AND
VALIDATION

DOCUMENTATION
AND REPORT

MODEL
DEVELOPMENT

SIMULATION-BASED
INVESTIGATION

Fig. 3 Simulation-based studies life cycle

investigations, including experimental design and output analysis; and finally documentation and reporting.

The consolidated life cycle for SBS (Ali and Petersen 2012; Fig. 3) described in this section is based on processes identified both in general computer simulation and SE literature. For this, we adopt the following guiding principles:

- Start small and later on enhance the simulation model, looking for analogies to solve the problem rather than starting the model building from scratch and working over an extended period for developing the model in one go (Ahmed et al. 2008). It reinforces the iterative nature of the process.
- Involve and keep frequent contact with all stakeholders throughout the study (Murphy and Perera 2001; Ahmed and Robinson 2007; Ahmed et al. 2008). It is important to improve the utility and practical relevance for the simulation.
- Models are abstractions, and that imposes a trade-off between complexity and realism, so not pursuing a perfect model is recommended, but still critically analyzing the results (Madachy 2008).
- All models are incomplete, bounded by the behavior under study as much as it is required to answer the questions of interest (Madachy 2008). It highlights the need to constantly revisit the simulation goals and raises a question about the reuse of a model beyond its original intent.
- In industrial simulation studies, it is important to deliver results and recommendations quickly as the modeled system and its environment are likely to change (Ahmed and Robinson 2007; Murphy and Perera 2001).

- It is possible to model a phenomenon of interest in several ways. The differences may arise because of the perspective of stakeholders, level of detail, and the modeler's assumptions (Madachy 2008).
- Continually challenge the model to increase the credibility of the model through further verification and validation (V&V) (Madachy 2008; Ahmed and Robinson 2007). That is why V&V activities are placed as continuous and parallel.
- To facilitate effective communication, use simple diagrams to communicate with stakeholders until they seek more detail, such as equations, since it may not be necessary to present those details (Madachy 2008).

Next sections provide detailed discussion for each major activity in the simulation studies life cycle.

5.1   Study Definition

Simulation-based studies should present a definition including the research context, problem, goals, and questions. For the *context*, model users and audience should be taken into account, as well as organizational policies involved when conducting simulation studies in industry. There are two suggestions (Petersen and Wohlin 2009; Dybå et al. 2012) on how to identify and describe contextual information for software engineering research that we understand as useful for simulation studies. The motivating *problem* frames the SBS in a proper scope and can be used to define relevant usage scenarios. Ideally, simulation models answer questions based on a purpose that can be assessed. Therefore, research *goals* and derived *questions* should guide the whole life cycle so that the chances for practical acceptance are increased. Goal-Question-Metric (GQM) (Basili and Rombach 1988) goal template can support the study definition, also recommended in the IMMoS method (Pfahl 2001; Pfahl and Lebsanft 2000).

Kellner et al. (1999) mention common purposes for SPSM, such as strategic management; planning, control, and operational management; process improvement and technology adoption; understanding; and training and learning.

Before the simulation model development, technical feasibility should be checked (Pfahl and Ruhe 2002; Ahmed et al. 2005) considering prerequisites for model development and usages like adequacy of problem definition, availability of data, and process maturity (Pfahl 2001). For that, Balci (1990) proposed the following questions:

- Do the benefits of conducting a simulation-based study justify the cost?
- Is it possible to use simulation for the goal of the study?
- Is it possible to complete the study in the given time and resource constraints?
- Is the necessary information available, e.g., classified or not available?

Furthermore, we recommend questions to support this decision focusing on additional constraints regarding the model development and experimentation (De França and Travassos 2016):

- Are the risks of running the real system high, including loss or waste of money or time, reaching an irreversible state, or compromised safety?
- What are the available instruments and procedures for data collection?
- Is there enough data to support model calibration and validation, as well as statistical analysis?

5.2 Model Design

Simulation studies in SE span widely in terms of phenomena to simulate. Known behaviors like Brooks' law, process evaluation, and project estimation, as well as architectural issues such as performance and scalability assessment, are examples of objects of study. Mostly, software engineering simulations concentrate on software process and project issues (De França and Travassos 2013). In the following sections, we describe relevant aspects of simulation modeling and provide some specifics on software process and projects.

5.2.1 Input Parameters and Response Variables

Input parameters represent the independent variables for which users of a simulation model can define values that impact on the model state and, consequently, on the response variables. Inputs can be calibration or variable parameters. To identify these parameters, it is recommended to start designing the model early on (Kellner et al. 1999). Also, consider that it in case of unavailability of data it may not be practical to measure all relevant variables accurately.

In the case of stochastic simulation, select appropriate probability distributions for input parameters (Balci 1990). Law (2007) provides a detailed discussion of statistical methods to support this decision. Stochastic or not, the integrity of simulation data must be ensured by maintaining constant communication with stakeholders (Murphy and Perera 2001).

On the other side, to identify the response (output) response variables required for the model (Park et al. 2008; Kellner et al. 1999; Rus et al. 2003), one needs to address the problem statement by answering the key questions identified in the study definition. For that, it is recommended to use GQM to identify the response variables (metrics) that address the defined research goals (Madachy 2008; Rus et al. 2003). Additionally, to specify problematic or desired behaviors (called the reference behavior) (Müller and Pfahl 2008) can help to identify response variables.

Reference behaviors describe changes on variables by plotting their values over time (Madachy 2008), preferably using historical data (Pfahl 2001). However, it is also possible to consider behavioral patterns based on experience when actual data is not available (Madachy 2008; Pfahl 2001) and using relative measures instead of striving for absolute ones (Madachy 2008).

5.2.2 Conceptual Modeling

This activity requires both explicit and tacit knowledge about the phenomenon to be simulated. This way, modelers should identify constructs and behaviors (e.g., process elements, information flows, and decision rules) influencing the response variables and relevant to the simulation goal. In addition, it is essential to consult or interview domain experts as they have knowledge beyond the project or product documentation and can judge the relevance of the information to the problem under study (Müller and Pfahl 2008), avoiding missing important aspects and reducing the threat of misunderstanding (Pfahl and Lebsanft 1999).

At this stage, the creation of influence diagrams to describe the positive or negative influence of various parameters supports the identification of internal variables (Rus et al. 2003). In this sense, the researchers need to motivate the choice of cause–effect relationships with relevant data sources and evidence from the literature (Pfahl 2001). Besides, individual cause–effect relationships should be reviewed before introducing more combinations (Pfahl 2001).

In the case of SPSM, creating static process models helps to understand the flow of information and the transformation of artifacts in various activities (Rus et al. 2003).

The conceptual model should not capture the whole phenomenon at once, i.e., researchers should include only the constructs and relations necessary to generate the behaviors of interest, according to the goal and the scope of the model. For that, a top-down iterative approach provides additional details only when necessary (Madachy 2008).

As researchers gain more knowledge on model variables (explicitly described), the simulation feasibility should be assessed again, as described in Sect. 5.1.

5.3 Model Implementation

To develop a simulation model, it is required to understand the selected simulation approach, the conceptual model, including its variables, parameters, and associated metrics, as well as the underlying assumptions and calibration procedures. The lack of knowledge regarding any of these aspects may impose different types of threats to validity (De França and Travassos 2015).

In addition, the simulation model should be developed with high modularity (Ahmed et al. 2008), separating data from the model to support modification and experimentation (Murphy and Perera 2001), and always kept in a state that it could be simulated (or tested) (Madachy 2008).

5.3.1 Simulation Approach

An executable model is implemented from the conceptual model using a simulation language, which should be based on a simulation approach like system dynamics (SD), discrete-event simulation (DES), or agent-based simulation (ABS). The simulation approach abstracts the essential characteristics and behaviors the model has to fit in.

The choice of a proper simulation approach depends on the particular goal of the study (Madachy 2002; Kellner et al. 1999). One consequence of concentrating on software process and project issues is the focus on continuous and discrete simulation (De França and Travassos 2013). Madachy (2002) considers continuous simulation (e.g., SD) more suitable for strategic analysis, high-level perspectives, and long-term trends, while discrete simulations can make detailed process analysis, resource utilization, and relatively short-term analysis more convenient.

5.3.2 Simulation Environment and Tools

The simulation environment consists of all instruments needed to perform the study, encompassing the simulation model itself, data sets, data analysis tools (including statistical packages), and simulation tools/packages. This way, planning and reporting studies considering those aspects are very important (see chapter "Open Science in Software Engineering" for a broader discussion on making the experimental package available). Simulation packages often differ in how they implement the simulation engine mechanism. Therefore, it is possible to get different results depending on the engine implementation.

Also, a simulation package should support not only the underlying simulation approach, but also the experimental design and output data analysis. Several tools are available to facilitate this analysis, providing a graphical interface to support output visualization, walk-through, interactive simulation, sensitivity analysis, and integration with third-party applications.

Raw input data requires extra effort to understand its properties (e.g., data distribution and shape, trends, and descriptive stats) and perform the transformations (e.g., scale transformations and derived metrics) needed to fit the model parameters and variables. Similarly, the simulation output data needs specific analysis techniques such as statistical tests and accuracy analysis.

Madachy (2008) and Ahmed and Robinson (2007) list the price, ease of use, training, documentation and maintenance support, computer platform and user familiarity, and performance requirements as the criteria for choosing an appropriate simulation tool. This choice also depends on the fit of the research questions, assumptions, and the theoretical logic of the conceptual model with those of the simulation approach (Houston et al. 2001).

Another important perspective concerns the computational infrastructure. The simulation needs to be settled up and reported so that one can understand the details for replicating the study. This way, processor capacity, operating system, amount of data, and execution time interval are relevant characteristics to estimate schedule and costs for the study.

Finally, simulations involving multiple trials/runs often need to summarize information from each intermediate trial for the final output analysis. Mean and standard deviation are common measures for this purpose and determine confidence intervals, for instance. This way, the individual measures are stored in a database or external files.

5.3.3 Model Calibration

It is recommended to use actual data for model calibration (Madachy 2008; Kellner et al. 1999). Such data is used for the generation of equations and parameters and to determine the distribution of random variables. However, the lack of data for calibration and validation in real-world settings (Kellner et al. 1999) imposes some threats as the desired data is often poorly defined, inaccurate or missing altogether, considering it was not planned and collected to support a particular simulation-based study.

An alternative is to work with synthetic data (Ören 1981). However, it requires evidence on data validity, i.e., provide indications that the simulated data represents the real phenomenon. For that, statistical tests can be applied to verify how close both real and synthetic samples are. Additionally, modelers may consult domain experts to deduce the accuracy and relevance of data (Murphy and Perera 2001; Raffo and Kellner 2000).

Planning the data collection avoids measurement mistakes, promoting the collection of data as soon as they are made available for the target variables and tracking contextual information (including qualitative data), which provides better and accurate reasoning when performing output analysis by supporting the explanations.

After the collection, quality assurance procedures ought to take place to verify their consistency and accuracy, avoiding the inclusion of outliers or incomplete data. For instance, to avoid biased observations and exposure to risks (i.e., undetected seasonal periods in time series), the data collection period should represent both transient and steady states.

Data used for model calibration and setting model parameters in the investigations need to share the same context. Therefore, the values used for investigation have to be consistent, avoiding attempts to generalize behaviors to different contexts inappropriately. The use of cross-company data is an example of how it can impose a threat to internal validity on the simulation results.

5.4 Verification and Validation

As the phenomenon under investigation is essentially observed through the execution of a simulation model, validity aspects concentrate on both model and data validity. Besides, model validity is a relative matter (Madachy 2008), depending on the purpose of the study. This way, evidence regarding model (conceptual and implemented) validity means the researcher should be aware of all the initiatives of submitting the simulation model to V&V procedures and their results.

The list provided in Table 1 supports the identification of attempts to verify or validate a simulation model in existing reports. These procedures were identified both in the context of SE (De França and Travassos 2013) and general discrete simulation (Sargent 1999). Barlas (1989) presents general procedures for validating SD models. None of these V&V procedures can avoid all the potential threats to validity alone. However, properly combining some of them can increase the confidence in simulation results.

Face validity is a *white-box* procedure for reviewing both simulation model and I/O matching from the perspective of experts and it is a relevant indication that, in the face of the model representation and its generated behavior, it gives the impression of being valid. It enables the review of internal properties and behaviors of a simulation model like model variables, equations, and relationships, rather than dealing with it as black box, i.e., observing just the I/O matching. This way, domain experts may identify threats to construct validity in advance. Face validity sessions may happen on workshops, group or individual interviews. The main idea is to present the model by following a walk-through approach to show how the input values generate outcomes, exemplifying with real scenarios so that experts can realize the model behavior and validate the simulation results for a given set of inputs.

To have the causal relationships and assumptions supported by empirical evidence improves external validity (Davis et al. 2007). Besides, it reduces the modeler's bias, not relying exclusively on experts' opinions or ad hoc observations. This way, secondary studies may be performed to search for evidence. However, models with many causal relationships may impose a great effort into using this approach.

The verification of model assumptions increases the reliability of simulation results. Face validity can be combined with other procedures to compare empirical data/behavior (Sargent 1999) to assess explicit model assumptions. For instance, to use comparison with reference behaviors, historical validation, or predictive validation to understand if the model is capable of reproducing an empirical behavior in terms of internal variables and outcomes. The modelers make, even implicitly, some assumptions regarding the phenomenon. For instance, the increase in a response variable directly caused by the presence of a given parameter. If these assumptions are embedded in the model, it may represent a threat to internal validity, since this behavior should not be coded directly in the model, rather it should be treated as an effect of a chain of actions, events, and conditions generating such behavior in the output variable.

When performing sensitivity analysis, it is important to consider constraints from the real world to make sure that the model reflects real-world behavior (Madachy 2008).

Table 1 Verification and validation procedures (De França and Travassos 2016)

Procedure	Description
Face validity	Consists of getting feedback from individuals knowledgeable about the phenomenon of interest through reviews, interviews, or surveys, to evaluate whether the (conceptual) simulation model and its results (input–output relationships) are reasonable
Comparison with reference behaviors	Compare the simulation output results against trends or expected results captured from historical data or reported in the literature
Comparison with other models	Compare the results (outputs) of the simulation model being validated to the results of other valid (simulation or analytic) models. Controlled experiments can be used to arrange such comparisons
Event validity	Compare the events triggered during the simulation runs to those of the real phenomenon to determine if they are similar. This technique is applicable to event-driven models
Historical data validation	If historical data exists, part of the data is used to build the model, and the remaining data are used to compare the model behavior and the actual phenomenon. Such testing is conducted by driving the simulation model with either sample from distributions or traces, and it is likely used for measuring model accuracy
Rationalism	Use logic deductions from model assumptions to develop the correct (valid) model, by assuming that everyone knows whether the stated underlying assumptions are true
Predictive validation	Use the model to forecast the phenomenon behavior, and then compare this behavior to the model forecast to determine if they are similar (or equal). The data may be obtained by observing the real phenomenon or conducting experiments, e.g., field tests for provoking its occurrence. Also, data from the literature may be used when there is no complete data in hands
Internal validity	It is likely used for measuring model accuracy. Several runs of a stochastic model are made to determine the amount of (internal) stochastic variation. A large amount of variation (lack of consistency) may threat the model confidence, even if it is typical of the problem under investigation
Sensitivity analysis	Consists of systematically changing the values of the input and internal parameters of a model to determine the effect upon the model output. The same effects should occur in the model as in the real phenomenon. This technique can be used semi-qualitatively—trends only—and quantitatively—both directions and (precise) magnitudes of outputs
Testing model structure and behavior	Submit the simulation model to test cases, evaluating its responses and traces. Both model structure and outputs should be reasonable for any combination of values of model inputs, including extreme and unlikely ones. Besides, the degeneracy of the model behavior can be tested by appropriate selection of values of parameters
Based on empirical evidence	Collect evidence from the literature (empirical studies reports) to develop the model causal relationships (mechanisms)
Turing tests	Individuals knowledgeable about the phenomenon are asked if they can distinguish between real and model outputs

Performance measures such as bias, accuracy, coverage, and confidence intervals can be used as criteria to benchmark more accurate simulation models (Burton et al. 2006). For instance, if the outcomes have low accuracy or are in a wide confidence interval, these results may be distant from reality. This information also brings credibility to the simulation study.

Finally, modelers should avoid false expectations (e.g., perfect predictions on the first model run) by reviewing patterns for qualitative similarity (Madachy 2008).

5.5 Simulation-Based Investigation

The experimental design defines a causal model establishing relationships between parameters and response variables, based on research goals and questions. Balci (1990) mentions that different parameters (input variables), behavioral relationships, and auxiliary variables may represent model variants. Thus, during simulation execution, the model variables may be held constant or allowed to vary according to conditions established a priori.

To fully describe the experimental design, we suggest using a design matrix, in which every row is a design point or scenario, which is a combination of different alternatives for each factor (column). However, several designs can be generated for the same set of factors. Kleijnen et al. (2005) claim that the design of experiments for simulation is different since we are not limited by real-world constraints.

Factorial designs are the most common one for simulation as they include all possible combinations (scenarios) for a set of factors. For instance, a full factorial design for k factors using two alternatives per factor is denoted as 2^k design, meaning the number of scenarios required to determine effects from k factors and their interactions. In addition, there are variants for situations in which the simulation runs are time-consuming, as execution time grows exponentially with the number of factors and alternatives. Therefore, it is possible to reduce the number of scenarios by executing just a fraction of the scenarios (fractional factorial designs), but still having an effective estimator. In the following, we list (not exhaustively) important aspects to select an adequate design as suggested by De França and Travassos (2016):

- *Simulation goals*: designs for understanding or characterization are not the same for comparison or optimization;
- *Experimental frame*: whether the area of interest is local or global, and its impacts in the range of levels;
- *Number of factors and levels*: they exponentially increase the number of scenarios in full factorial designs;
- *Domain of admissible scenarios*: full factorial designs may generate inadmissible (unrealistic) scenarios;

- *Deterministic and stochastic components of the model*: they affect how to deal with variation in the experimental design;
- *Terminating conditions*: if it is a steady-state or a terminating simulation, with an event to specify the end of the experiment.

Sensitivity analysis is a useful technique to select interest factors and a range of alternatives. Furthermore, such a systematic approach reduces the bias and avoids the "fishing" for positive results. For characterization purposes, it is recommended to keep a low number of levels per factor, but covering a high region of interest (Montgomery 2017).

When designing a simulation-based investigation, researchers should consider as factors (and levels) not only the input parameters, but also internal parameters, different data sets and versions of the model, implementing alternative strategies to be evaluated (De França and Travassos 2016). For instance, Garousi et al. (2009) use a design with two distinct data sets as alternatives for calibration based on data from the technical literature to derive the scenarios and the simulation model remaining constant. This way, different calibrations representing the different simulation scenarios can be compared.

Ad hoc designs explore the use of scenarios. In this case, the modeler plans the scenarios of interest (Barros et al. 2000) and then derives the design. By adopting this strategy, the relevance and adequacy of each chosen scenario should be explained and tied to the study goals. Furthermore, the description of scenarios needs to be as precise as possible, clarifying all the relevant contextual information, as well as input parameters for them.

The main drawback of ad hoc designs is the possibility of introducing bias, with no opportunity to investigate side effects such as interactions between factors.

Selected scenarios and the nature of the model (deterministic or stochastic) drive the number of simulation runs. Each scenario consists of an arrangement of experimental conditions where possible alternatives are assigned to specific factors. The more scenarios involved, the more simulation runs are required.

Stochastic simulation models produce an inherent variation in the output due to the pseudorandom number generation. Therefore, running each scenario only once is not enough to reveal the amount of variation. On the other side, the higher the number of runs (replications), the closer one gets of the desired accuracy level. Replication is achieved by using different pseudorandom numbers to simulate the same scenario. In this case, each output is derived from auto-correlated observations (Kleijnen et al. 2005) that cannot be aggregated as they are not independent. Thus, given the required accuracy and a sample estimate from a few model runs, it is possible to determine the number of required runs and avoid threats to conclusion validity. Such a procedure for the calculation can be found in Law and Kelton (2000).

5.6   Threats to Simulation-Based Studies Validity

The SE community has discussed threats to validity, and most of the reported threats concerned with in vitro experimentation are described by Wohlin et al. (2012) and categorized under a positivist perspective as threats to construct, internal, external, and conclusion validity (Petersen and Gencel 2013). We consider this perspective is more suitable for considering and addressing threats to validity for SBS than other world-views. Therefore, most of the known threats to controlled experiments have to be considered when conducting simulation studies, especially considering in vitro experiments, in which the human subjects drive the simulations, which introduces additional risks to the validity of a study. Moreover, new situations emerge from in silico experiments, in which common types of experimental validity are closely related to the simulation model and data validity (De França and Travassos 2015). A list of categorized threats to simulation studies validity can be found in De França and Travassos (2015).

Garousi et al. (2009) and Raffo (2005), for instance, consider model validity in several perspectives, such as model structure, supporting data, input parameters and scenarios, and simulation output. We understand that these aspects are relevant, but researchers should not be limited to them (De França and Travassos 2015), also considering the simulation investigation design as well. This way, researchers should consider checking for threats to the simulation study validity before running the experiments and analyzing output data to avoid bias. Additionally, non-mitigated threats, limitations, and non-verified assumptions must be reported (De França and Travassos 2016).

The use of simulation promotes both the construct and internal validity as it demands accurately specifying and measuring constructs (and their relationships) and the theoretical logic that is enforced through the discipline of algorithmic representation in software, respectively (Davis et al. 2007). However, De França and Travassos (2015) identified threats to construct validity, such as inappropriate cause–effect relationship definitions, inappropriate real-world representation by model parameters and calibration data and procedure, hidden or invalid underlying assumptions regarding model concepts, and the simulation model not capturing the corresponding real-world building blocks and elements.

External and conclusion validity can be accomplished by reproducing empirical behaviors and applying adequate statistical analysis over the model outputs, respectively. However, conclusion validity also relates to design issues like sample size, the number of simulation runs, model coverage, and the degree of representation of scenarios for all possible situations.

Simulation Life Cycle Considerations
- A simulation-based study is about gaining knowledge and dynamically analyzing it. So, an iterative approach is fundamental to allow explication and reflection about the phenomenon under study.
- Keeping involved stakeholders when modeling and analyzing simulation results is as important as in software development.
- Verification and validation procedures play a fundamental role in the validity of a study.
- Mostly, this consolidated process is based on solid simulation literature, empirical evidence, and the authors' experience. This way, some recommendations may require a level of adaptation.

6 Practical Examples

To illustrate some potential uses of SBS, in the following sections, we briefly describe two practical scenarios where we have conducted SBS in industrial settings.

6.1 Example 1: Use of Simulation to Encourage Behavioral Change in a Company

We, together with the representatives from a case company, identified a need to illustrate the benefits of early integration. The intention was to highlight the consequences of missing a test iteration in the current way of working. Given the scale and complexity of the test process, it was not possible to demonstrate this with static process diagrams. The aim was to develop a simulation model that adequately represents the test process at the case company so that it is relevant and realistic for the developers. This realism made the results more relatable for them. Also, it provided the ability to show the consequences of various what-if scenarios in terms of the flow of requirements through the various stages of development, testing, and release.

We used interviews, process documentation, and guided walk-through of the testing process to develop a realistic process understanding. This understanding was modeled in a simulation model using system dynamics. The model was calibrated using data collected from various repositories in the company. For variables and relations where data was not available, we relied on expert opinion to estimate the missing values. For details, please see (Ali and Petersen 2012).

6.2 Example 2: Use of Simulation to Sanity-Check Process Improvement Ideas

We were supporting an organization in a process assessment and improvement initiative. Two main alternatives being considered were (a) changing the sprint length (particularly for testing) or (b) improving the flow. We conducted an SBS to assess the likely impact of the two improvement proposals. The simulation model represented both scenarios and was calibrated using the company data.

The use of a simulation model was received positively by the practitioners, and the results of the simulation study influenced the choice of improvement actions pursued by the company. For details, please see Ali et al. (2015).

7 Recommended Further Reading

7.1 Simulation Modeling and Approaches

The two most common approaches for simulation modeling are continuous and discrete-event simulation. Madachy's book (Madachy 2008) is an excellent resource when using system dynamics for continuous simulation of SE phenomena. For discrete-event simulation, Law and Kelton (2000) provide an excellent resource covering all technical steps in developing a simulation model. However, their focus is not on the modeling of SE phenomena.

7.2 Verification and Validation in SBS

For additional discussion on verification and validation in simulation-based studies, readers are encouraged to refer to the software engineering (De França and Travassos 2015) and general computer simulation literature (Sargent 1999; Babuska and Oden 2004).

7.3 Simulation-Based Investigations

For detailed instructions on designing simulation-based investigations or experiments using a simulation model, please see the works in De França and Travassos (2016), Kleijnen et al. (2005), and Houston et al. (2001).

7.4 Software Process and Project Simulation

For guidelines to investigate the software process and project using simulation, please see the guidelines from Ali et al. (2014), as well as the ones presented by Pfahl (2014).

8 Conclusion

This chapter summarizes a wide span of knowledge on computer simulations in the context of SE. We discussed, under several perspectives, the role of SBS in software engineering research and methodological aspects relevant for conducting this sort of study to support SE research.

Although we do not intend to discuss in detail each potential application of simulation, it is notable the need for systematic observation of the system or phenomenon to be simulated before developing and performing investigations based on simulation models. Moreover, the experimental basis is fundamental to benefit from simulation studies. Therefore, SBS should be considered as part of a greater research methodology, i.e., it should not be seen as an "end" or a sole research method, but a tool to achieve complementary evidence and to reduce risk before intervening on the target context or moving towards more focused observation.

Acknowledgements Breno has been supported by CNPq-Brazil (Grant 141152/2010-9) during the development of part of this work. Nauman has been supported by a research grant for the VITS project (reference number 20180127) by the Knowledge Foundation in Sweden and by ELLIIT, a Strategic Area within IT and Mobile Communications, funded by the Swedish Government. We would also like to thank the reviewers for their feedback that has helped us to improve the presentation and the contents of the chapter significantly.

References

Abdel-Hamid TK (1988) Understanding the "90% syndrome" in software project management: a simulation-based case study. J Syst Softw 8(4):319–330

Ahmed R, Robinson S (2007) Simulation in business and industry: how simulation context can affect simulation practice? In: Proceedings of the 2007 spring simulation multiconference, vol 3. Society for Computer Simulation International, pp 152–159

Ahmed R, Hall T, Wernick P, Robinson S (2005) Evaluating a rapid simulation modelling process (RSMP) through controlled experiments. In: 2005 International symposium on empirical software engineering. IEEE, Piscataway, p 10

Ahmed R, Hall T, Wernick P, Robinson S, Shah M (2008) Software process simulation modelling: a survey of practice. J Simul 2(2):91–102

Alexopoulos C, Seila AF (1998) Output data analysis. In: Banks J (ed) Handbook of simulation. Wiley, New York, pp 225–272

Ali NB (2016) Is effectiveness sufficient to choose an intervention?: considering resource use in empirical software engineering. In: Proceedings of the 10th ACM/IEEE international symposium on empirical software engineering and measurement, ESEM 2016, Ciudad Real, September 8–9, 2016, pp 54:1–54:6

Ali NB, Petersen K (2012) A consolidated process for software process simulation: state of the art and industry experience. In: 2012 38th Euromicro conference on software engineering and advanced applications. IEEE, Piscataway, pp 327–336

Ali NB, Unterkalmsteiner M (2014) Use and evaluation of simulation for software process education: a case study. In: European conference software engineering education (ECSEE), Shaker Verlag, Herzogenrath, pp 59–73

Ali NB, Petersen K, Wohlin C (2014) A systematic literature review on the industrial use of software process simulation. J Syst Softw 97:65–85

Ali NB, Petersen K, de França BBN (2015) Evaluation of simulation-assisted value stream mapping for software product development: two industrial cases. Inf Softw Technol 68:45–61

Babuska I, Oden JT (2004) Verification and validation in computational engineering and science: basic concepts. Comput Methods Appl Mech Eng 193(36):4057–4066

Balci O (1990) Guidelines for successful simulation studies. In: Proceedings of the winter simulation conference. IEEE Press, New Jersey, pp 25–32

Banks J (1999) Introduction to simulation. In: Proceedings of the 31st conference on Winter simulation: simulation – a bridge to the future, WSC 1999, Phoenix, December 05–08, 1999, vol 1, pp 7–13

Barlas Y (1989) Multiple tests for validation of system dynamics type of simulation models. Eur J Oper Res 42(1):59–87. https://doi.org/10.1016/0377-2217(89)90059-3

Barros M, Werner C, Travassos G (2000) Applying system dynamics to scenario based software project management. In: Proceedings of the 2000 international system dynamics conference

Basili VR, Rombach HD (1988) The TAME project: towards improvement-oriented software environments. IEEE Trans Softw Eng 14(6):758–773

Burton A, Altman DG, Royston P, Holder RL (2006) The design of simulation studies in medical statistics. Stat Med 25(24):4279–4292

Christie AM (1999) Simulation: an enabling technology in software engineering. CROSSTALK J Def Softw Eng 12(4):25–30

Davis JP, Eisenhardt KM, Bingham CB (2007) Developing theory through simulation methods. Acad Manag Rev 32(2):480–499

De França BBN, Travassos GH (2012) Reporting guidelines for simulation-based studies in software engineering. In: Proceedings of the 16th international conference on evaluation assessment in software engineering (EASE), pp 156–160

De França BBN, Travassos GH (2013) Are we prepared for simulation based studies in software engineering yet? CLEI Electron J 16(1):9

De França BBN, Travassos GH (2015) Simulation based studies in software engineering: a matter of validity. CLEI Electron J 18:5

De França BBN, Travassos GH (2016) Experimentation with dynamic simulation models in software engineering: planning and reporting guidelines. Empir Softw Eng 21(3):1302–1345

Dybå T, Sjøberg DI, Cruzes DS (2012) What works for whom, where, when, and why?: on the role of context in empirical software engineering. In: Proceedings of the ACM-IEEE international symposium on empirical software engineering and measurement. ACM, New York, pp 19–28

Eck JE, Liu L (2008) Contrasting simulated and empirical experiments in crime prevention. J Exp Criminol 4(3):195–213

Feldt R, Zimmermann T, Bergersen GR, Falessi D, Jedlitschka A, Juristo N, Münch J, Oivo M, Runeson P, Shepperd M, Sjøberg DIK, Turhan B (2018) Four commentaries on the use of students and professionals in empirical software engineering experiments. Empir Softw Eng 23(6):3801–3820. https://doi.org/10.1007/s10664-018-9655-0

Garousi V, Khosrovian K, Pfahl D (2009) A customizable pattern-based software process simulation model: design, calibration and application. Softw Process Improv Pract 14(3):165–180. https://doi.org/10.1002/spip.411

Gorschek T, Wohlin C, Garre P, Larsson S (2006) A model for technology transfer in practice. IEEE Softw 23(6):88–95

Houston DX, Ferreira S, Collofello JS, Montgomery DC, Mackulak GT, Shunk DL (2001) Behavioral characterization: finding and using the influential factors in software process simulation models. J Syst Softw 59(3):259–270. https://doi.org/10.1016/S0164-1212(01)00067-X

Jørgensen M, Kitchenham B (2012) Interpretation problems related to the use of regression models to decide on economy of scale in software development. J Syst Softw 85(11):2494–2503

Kellner MI, Madachy RJ, Raffo DM (1999) Software process simulation modeling: Why? What? How? J Syst Softw 46:91–105

Kitchenham B (2010) What's up with software metrics? – a preliminary mapping study. J Syst Softw 83(1):37–51

Kleijnen JPC, Sanchez SM, Lucas TW, Cioppa TM (2005) State-of-the-art review: a user's guide to the brave new world of designing simulation experiments. INFORMS J Comput 17(3):263–289. https://doi.org/10.1287/ijoc.1050.0136

Law AM (2007) Simulation modeling and analysis, vol 4. McGraw-Hill, New York

Law AM, Kelton WD (2000) Simulation modeling and analysis, vol 3. McGraw-Hill, New York

Madachy RJ (2002) Simulation. Wiley, New York

Madachy RJ (2008) Software process dynamics. Wiley-IEEE Press, New York

Maria A (1997) Introduction to modeling and simulation. In: Proceedings of the 29th conference on Winter simulation, WSC, pp 7–13

McCall JA, Wong G, Stone A (1979) A simulation modeling approach to understanding the software development process. In: Fourth annual software engineering workshop. Goddard Space Flight Center, Greenbelt

Melis M, Turnu I, Cau A, Concas G (2006) Evaluating the impact of test-first programming and pair programming through software process simulation. Softw Process Improv Pract 11(4):345–360

Monks T, Currie CS, Onggo BS, Robinson S, Kunc M, Taylor SJ (2019) Strengthening the reporting of empirical simulation studies: introducing the stress guidelines. J Simul 13(1):55–67

Montgomery DC (2017) Design and analysis of experiments. Wiley, Hoboken

Müller M, Pfahl D (2008) Simulation methods. In: Shull F, Singer J, Sjøberg DIK (eds) Guide to advanced empirical software engineering. Springer, London, pp 117–152

Münch J, Rombach D, Rus I (2003) Creating an advanced software engineering laboratory by combining empirical studies with process simulation. In: Proceedings of the international workshop on software process simulation and modeling (ProSim), pp 3–4

Murphy S, Perera T (2001) Key enablers in the development of simulation. In: Proceedings of the Winter simulation conference, pp 1429–1437

Olsen NC (1993) The software rush hour (software engineering). IEEE Softw 10(5):29–37

Ören TI (1981) Concepts and criteria to assess acceptability of simulation studies: a frame of reference. Commun ACM 24(4):180–189

Park S, Kim H, Kang D, Bae DH (2008) Developing a software process simulation model using SPEM and analytical models. Int J Simul Process Model 4(3–4):223–236. https://doi.org/10.1504/IJSPM.2008.023684

Petersen K, Gencel C (2013) Worldviews, research methods, and their relationship to validity in empirical software engineering research. In: 2013 Joint conference of the 23rd international workshop on software measurement and the 8th international conference on software process and product measurement. IEEE, Piscataway, pp 81–89

Petersen K, Wohlin C (2009) Context in industrial software engineering research. In: Proceedings of the 3rd international symposium on empirical software engineering and measurement (ESEM), pp 401–404

Pfahl D (2001) An integrated approach to simulation based learning in support of strategic and project management in software organisations. Fraunhofer-IRB-Verlag, Stuttgart

Pfahl D (2014) Process simulation: a tool for software project managers? In: Software project management in a changing world. Springer, Berlin, pp 425–446

Pfahl D, Lebsanft K (1999) Integration of system dynamics modelling with descriptive process modelling and goal-oriented measurement. J Syst Softw 46(2):135–150. https://doi.org/10.1016/S0164-1212(99)00007-2

Pfahl D, Lebsanft K (2000) Knowledge acquisition and process guidance for building system dynamics simulation models: an experience report from software industry. Int J Softw Eng Knowl Eng 10(04):487–510

Pfahl D, Ruhe G (2002) IMMoS: a methodology for integrated measurement, modelling and simulation. Softw Process Improv Practice 7(3–4):189–210

Pfahl D, Stupperich M, Krivobokova T (2004) PL-SIM: a generic simulation model for studying strategic SPI in the automotive industry. In: IET conference proceedings. Citeseer, pp 149–158. https://doi.org/10.1049/ic:20040454

Raffo DM (2005) Software project management using prompt: a hybrid metrics, modeling and utility framework. Inf Softw Technol 47(15):1009–1017

Raffo DM, Kellner MI (2000) Empirical analysis in software process simulation modeling. J Syst Softw 53(1):31–41. https://doi.org/10.1016/S0164-1212(00)00006-6

Rus I, Neu H, Münch J (2003) A systematic methodology for developing discrete event simulation models of software development processes. In: Proceedings of the 4th international workshop on software process simulation and modeling (ProSim 2003), Portland, May 3–4

Sargent R (1999) Validation and verification of simulation models. In: WSC'99. 1999 Winter simulation conference proceedings. 'Simulation – a bridge to the future' (Cat. No. 99CH37038), vol 1. IEEE, Piscataway, pp 39–48

Shannon RE (1986) Intelligent simulation environments. In: Proceedings of the conference on intelligent simulation environments, pp 150–156

Travassos GH, Barros MO (2003) Contributions of in virtuo and in silico experiments for the future of empirical studies in software engineering. In: 2nd Workshop on empirical software engineering the future of empirical studies in software engineering, pp 117–130

Wohlin C, Runeson P, Höst M, Ohlsson MC, Regnell B, Wesslén A (2012) Experimentation in software engineering. Springer, New York

Wu M, Yan H (2009) Simulation in software engineering with system dynamics: a case study. J Softw 4(10):1127–1135

Zhang H (2012) Special panel: software process simulation – at a crossroads? In: Proceedings of the international conference on software and system process (ICSSP). IEEE, Piscataway, pp 215–216

Zhang H, Kitchenham B, Pfahl D (2010) Software process simulation modeling: an extended systematic review. In: Proceedings of the international conference on software process (ICSP). Springer, Berlin, pp 309–320

Zhang H, Jeffery R, Houston D, Huang L, Zhu L (2011) Impact of process simulation on software practice: an initial report. In: Proceedings of the 33rd international conference on software engineering (ICSE), pp 1046–1056

Bayesian Data Analysis
in Empirical Software Engineering:
The Case of Missing Data

Richard Torkar, Robert Feldt, and Carlo A. Furia

Abstract Bayesian data analysis (BDA) is today used by a multitude of research disciplines. These disciplines use BDA as a way to embrace uncertainty by using multilevel models and making use of all available information at hand. In this chapter, we first introduce the reader to BDA and then provide an example from empirical software engineering, where we also deal with a common issue in our field, i.e., missing data. The example we make use of presents the steps done when conducting state-of-the-art statistical analysis. First, we need to understand the problem we want to solve. Second, we conduct causal analysis. Third, we analyze non-identifiability. Fourth, we conduct missing data analysis. Finally, we do a sensitivity analysis of priors. All this before we design our statistical model. Once we have a model, we present several diagnostics one can use to conduct sanity checks. We hope that through these examples, the reader will see the advantages of using BDA. This way, we hope Bayesian statistics will become more prevalent in our field, thus partly avoiding the reproducibility crisis we have seen in other disciplines.

1 Introduction

Statistics, we argue, is one of the principal tools researchers in empirical software engineering have at their disposal to build an argument that guides them towards the ultimate objective, i.e., practical significance and (subsequent) impact of their

R. Torkar (✉) · R. Feldt
Chalmers and University of Gothenburg, Gothenburg, Sweden
e-mail: torkarr@chalmers.se; robert.feldt@chalmers.se

C. A. Furia
Università della Svizzera Italiana, Lugano, Switzerland
e-mail: furiac@usi.ch

© Springer Nature Switzerland AG 2020
M. Felderer, G. H. Travassos (eds.), *Contemporary Empirical Methods in Software Engineering*, https://doi.org/10.1007/978-3-030-32489-6_11

findings.[1] Practical significance is, as we have seen (Torkar et al. 2017), not very often explicitly discussed in software engineering research today and we argue that this is mainly out of two reasons.

The first one being that statistical maturity of empirical software engineering research is not high enough (Torkar et al. 2017), leading to difficulties with connecting statistical findings to practical significance. The second reason is a combination of issues hampering our research field, e.g., small sample sizes, failure to analyze disparate types of data in a unified framework, or lack of data availability (only 13% of publications provide a replication package and carefully describe each step to make reproduction feasible (Rodríguez-Pérez et al. 2018)).

Both of the above issues are worrisome since it could make it hard to strengthen arguments concerning practical significance, e.g., connecting effort and, conclusively, ROI[2] to the findings of a research study, if one would want so. For academic research to be more relevant and have more impact on practitioners, its practical significance and its implications need to be precise.

Furthermore, issues such as the above are also likely to lead empirical software engineering towards a replication crisis as we have seen in other disciplines, e.g., medicine (Ioannidis 2005b,a, 2016; Glick 1992), psychology (Aarts et al. 2015; John et al. 2012; Shanks et al. 2013), economics (Ioannidis et al. 2017; Camerer et al. 2016), and marketing (Hunter 2001).

In order to solve some of the above challenges researchers have proposed that we need to focus on, e.g., (1) openness, i.e., that data and manuscripts are accessible for all stakeholders, (2) preregistration, i.e., a planned study is peer-reviewed in the usual manner and accepted by a journal *before* the experiment is run, so that there is no incentive to look for significance after-the-fact (Dutilh et al. 2017), (3) increasing the sample size, (4) lowering the significance threshold from $p < 0.05$ to $p < 0.005$ (Benjamin et al. 2018), and (5) removing null hypothesis significance testing (NHST) altogether, which the journal *Basic and Applied Social Psychology* advocates (Trafimow and Marks 2015), as do McShane et al. (2017).

However, some researchers, most notably Gelman (2018), claim that even the above is not enough and argue that a unified approach for these matters should mainly evolve from three components: procedural solutions, solutions based on design and data collection, and improved statistical analysis.

Concerning procedural solutions, Gelman (2018) like others suggests publishing papers on, e.g., Arxiv, to encourage post-publication review, and to use preregistration as a tool for lowering the "file drawer" bias. For design and data collection, Gelman provides convincing arguments that we should focus on reducing measurement error (the example being that reducing the measurement error by a

---

[1]In this chapter, we focus on empirical software engineering research where quantitative data is a major component; for studies that are mainly qualitative, a different set of concerns need to be taken into account, see, for example, Lenberg et al. (2017).

[2]In literature, Return-On-Investment refers to, in various ways, the calculation one does to see the benefit (*return*) an investment (*cost*) has.

factor of two is like multiplying the sample size by a factor of four), and move to within-subject from between-subject study designs when possible.[3] Finally, concerning improved statistical analysis, Gelman advocates the use of Bayesian inference and multilevel models (MLMs),[4] as a way to discuss "...the range of applicability of a study," i.e., practical significance.

Overall, we side with these arguments and believe they are critical also for software engineering to better connect empirical research with the practice it ultimately aims to improve. We will thus introduce and exemplify the use of Bayesian statistical methods in empirical software engineering research. They are a good starting point since individual researchers can learn them and apply them in isolation without waiting for the community as a whole to take further steps needed to avoid a replication crisis and to become more practically relevant. We argue that using Bayesian methods allows us to better connect our findings to practical significance through the use of more balanced out-of-sample predictions, i.e., one of the outputs from Bayesian data analysis (this will be further elaborated on in Sect. 2). Additionally, we have yet to face data from empirical software engineering where Bayesian data analysis cannot be employed, and when having a small sample size, due to the priors employed, Bayesian data analysis, we would argue, shows its strengths.

In this chapter, we rely on three key concepts: Bayes' theorem, multilevel models, and Markov chain Monte Carlo sampling.

Bayes' theorem states that,

$$P(A|B) = \frac{P(B|A)P(A)}{P(B)} \tag{1}$$

where A and B are events, and $P(B) \neq 0$. In the theorem, we have two conditional probabilities, $P(A|B)$ and $P(B|A)$, the likelihood of event A occurring given that B is true and vice versa. The marginal probability is then observing A and B independently of each other, i.e., $P(A)$ and $P(B)$. Often the above is rewritten as, $P(A|B) \propto P(B|A) \times P(A)$, i.e., the posterior is proportional to the likelihood times the prior or, in other words, given a likelihood and a prior we will be able to approximate the posterior probability distribution; this is, of course, also applicable to MLMs. We will come back to these concepts in the next section.

Multilevel models are not a particularly new thing. However, in the last decades, they have become accessible to researchers due to the rise in computational power, and they go nicely in hand with Bayesian analysis. Bayesian MLMs have several advantages (McElreath 2015): (1) When using repeated sampling they do not underfit or overfit the data to the extent single-level models do (i.e., maximally), (2)

---

[3]In a within-subject design the same group of subjects are used in more than one treatment.

[4]Multilevel models can also be called hierarchical linear models, nested data models, mixed models, random coefficient, random-effects models, random parameter models, or split-plot designs.

the uncertainty across uneven sample sizes is handled automatically, (3) they model variation explicitly (between and within clusters of data), and (4) they preserve uncertainty and make much data transformation unnecessary. In our particular case, Bayes' theorem is the foundation for conducting inference when using MLMs, and Markov chain Monte Carlo (MCMC) is the engine that drives it.

The reason for using MCMC for sampling is simply that before MCMC was introduced, it was virtually impossible to sample large Bayesian multilevel models (Banerjee et al. 2014). Today, if one wants to sample from a complex, multidimensional, unknown, posterior probability distribution, MCMC is a widespread technique to use since we have the computational power available. (For more background on sampling algorithms, please see McElreath (2015, Ch. 8).)

Next, we first introduce the main elements of Bayesian data analysis (BDA) with a non-software engineering example. Our main contribution is then a detailed worked case study of applying BDA to an estimation problem in empirical software engineering. In particular, the example highlights that with this BDA analysis, we do not need to delete data points for which some data is missing. We conclude the chapter by discussing the methodological implications.

> Bayesian data analysis (BDA) is growing and, as such, is being used in many disparate scientific disciplines. The approach of BDA that we use in this chapter relies on designing a generative model which we then can use to do out-of-sample predictions. It will be a more involved analysis, but in the end we hope that it will also provide us with a richer understanding of the phenomena under study.

2   A Short Introduction to Bayesian Data Analysis

Lately, many tools and probabilistic programming languages have been developed to tackle some of the challenges we face when designing more powerful statistical models. In our view, several things have improved. First, probabilistic programming languages, e.g., using `Julia` with `Turing.jl`, or `Stan`, tailored for statistical programming, in combination with resampling techniques, have matured.[5] Second, resampling techniques based on MCMC have improved (Brooks et al. 2011). Third, procedures for using these techniques now exist (Talts et al. 2018; Betancourt 2018; Gabry et al. 2017; Gelman et al. 2017; Betancourt 2017) and are being improved iteratively (Vehtari et al. 2019). Together, these developments make more powerful analysis methods available to a wider audience.

---

[5]See https://julialang.org, http://turing.ml, and https://mc-stan.org.

In this section, we will provide a short introduction to model design, its tool support, and some terminology that we will use in this chapter. To keep it simple and general, we will take data and an example from everyday life, rather than an empirical software engineering example. We do not expect the reader to be an expert after this, but rather be able to follow what we present in this chapter, be better prepared for the empirical software engineering case study that then follows, and then perhaps read further into the literature we present in Sect. 4. Let us start with terminology.

In this chapter, we will design statistical models. We will use mathematical notation for precision as well as brevity. To generalize, a model will consist of a likelihood, a linear equation, and priors. The purpose of the model is ultimately to make predictions/inferences concerning the outcome by using a posterior predictive distribution. Let us introduce a simple example inspired by McElreath (2015).

We want to predict the height of human beings given their weight. A model could then look like this,

$$\text{height}_i \sim \mathcal{N}(\mu_i, \sigma)$$

$$\mu_i = \alpha + \beta_w \times \text{weight}_i$$

$$\alpha \sim \mathcal{N}(181, 20)$$

$$\beta_w \sim \mathcal{N}(0, 10)$$

$$\sigma \sim \text{Half-Cauchy}(0, 10)$$

Let us now go through this line by line. First, we claim that height has a Normal distribution with mean μ and standard deviation σ, i.e., our likelihood. The subset i in height, weight, and μ is an indication that this holds for each height we have in the data set, i.e., for every human being in the data set. But why a Normal distribution? Well, there are ontological and epistemological reasons for this (McElreath 2015), but in short: if we add together random values from the same distribution it converges to a normal distribution. Since there are many different factors that, jointly, determine the height of a person, e.g., their genetics, nutrients of the mother during pregnancy, food intake as a small child, etc., and their effects "add up," it is often a sensible assumption to assume the result will be normally distributed.

The next line encodes our main assumption about the heights, i.e., they have a linear connection to the weight (our linear equation). We have an intercept labeled α, expressing the average height of a human that has average weight, together with a slope β_w, which captures how much longer (shorter) a human can be expected to be for each added (subtracted) unit of weight they have. We want to estimate these two *parameters* using the data: height and weight. In this example, height is the *outcome* and weight is the *predictor*. We can have more than one outcome, this is known as a multivariate model (compared to univariate models as in the example above), and we can have more than one predictor, as we will see later in this chapter.

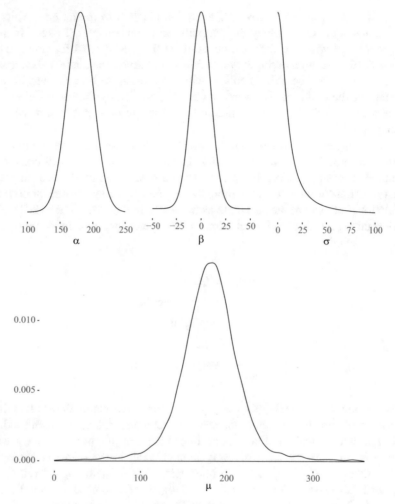

Fig. 1 Our selected prior probabilities (priors) for parameters α, β, and σ, respectively (top row). These are then combined into our prior predictive distribution for the height μ (bottom row)

Next, in a Bayesian model, we need to express our prior belief, our so-called priors. The α parameter is the intercept, and hence captures the mean height we expect (see Fig. 1 for a graphical presentation). What we are saying is that we have prior knowledge, i.e., we believe that the mean height will be 181 cm. Why 181? Well, this is the average height of the three authors of this chapter, and when writing the chapter, we had direct and reliable access to this data. Also, our prior expresses that we can expect the mean to vary with a standard deviation of 20, i.e., finding humans with a height in the range 161–201 cm would not be too uncommon even if values outside that range can also sometimes happen. For β_w, our prior indicates that the slope has a mean of 0 and a standard deviation of 10 (Fig. 1). We could also set a more specific prior here, e.g., we have a feeling that an increase in weight also leads to an increase in height, but let us use a very wide and "allowing" prior.

Finally, we have a prior on σ, which is the expected variation in actual, measured data from what our linear, "core" model predicts. We have chosen a Half-Cauchy distribution here since we know that the variation cannot be negative (Fig. 1). The Half-Cauchy is a common prior for σ and is roughly a Normal distribution cut in half, i.e., we do not allow negative values on σ.[6] It also has a higher probability for larger values than a Normal distribution, since we have less information on how much variation to expect. In the end, if we have enough evidence (data), it will dominate, also known as "swamp," the priors. This means that the priors are not as critical in situations when we collect lots of data. Before we go on and use our statistical model on actual, measured data, we should study how our model behaves based on only the priors. We can do this by sampling from our priors and "executing" the model to see which heights it predicts.

In the lower half of Fig. 1, we see the joint prior probability distribution, which is a combination of the figures on the first row. The mixtures of the priors for α, β, and σ, and the linear regression they imply could be seen as representative for our height given a weight.

So what does our prior probability distribution (Fig. 1) tell us? Well, 2.93% of the population is assumed to be more than 272 cm tall.[7] Additionally, 13.8% are less than 147 cm.[8] This seems a bit strange in our view, and even more bizarre is that 0.015% of the population is shorter than 20 cm, when the shortest human recorded was approximately 53 cm.

But there is no need to worry. The main idea when selecting priors is to delimit the volume that the sampling needs to cover. We want to get rid of obviously absurd values while ensuring that we do not rule out values that could happen. Who knows, maybe someone who is <53 cm or >272 cm will be found this year. We have just conducted a *prior* predictive analysis, which is, we claim, a compulsory part of doing Bayesian data analysis.

For actually making inferences, i.e., determining the likely ranges of the parameters given our model, we will need data. We will make use of a data set found in the `rethinking` R package and a R Markdown script of our analysis can be downloaded.[9] After sampling, we will have a *posterior* distribution, which is proportional to the likelihood and the prior distribution. In Fig. 2, we have plotted the empirical data set (circles) and the linear prediction (straight line). The narrow shaded interval is the 95% distribution of μ (i.e., the exact values for many μ from the posterior), and the wider and lighter interval is the 95% plausible region (i.e., 95% of our μ should be found within that region).

---

[6]Other priors for σ can of course also be used. Please see https://github.com/stan-dev/stan/wiki/Prior-Choice-Recommendations.

[7]The tallest man, for whom there is irrefutable evidence, was 272 cm.

[8]People of short stature are <147 cm.

[9]https://github.com/torkar/BDA_in_ESE.

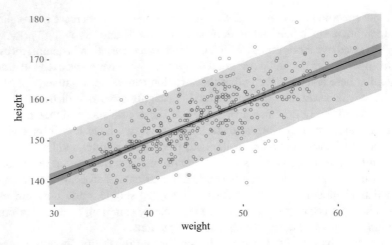

Fig. 2 Height as a function of weight. The line represents the μ, the dark shade the 95% distribution of μ, and the lighter shade the 95% plausible region

Having a posterior predictive distribution we can now start to conduct various inferences, but we will stop here for now and instead, in Sect. 3, present multiple ways we can make use of a posterior.

To summarize, the three main steps of Bayesian model design and analysis are:

1. Understand the data and the problem.
2. Design a probability model (conduct model checking and iterate if the model needs to be revised) and sample from the posterior to conduct diagnosis.
3. Conduct inference. That is, learn something about the population by using the posterior probability distribution, e.g., by conducting statistical tests or deriving estimates.

The above is an iterative process, and in the last step, we also can change the parameters to see how they affect the outcome variable, i.e., to analyze the practical implications of different scenarios and thus assessing the practical significance of the results. The above steps will next be covered in a detailed case study within empirical software engineering.

3 Case Study

Most would argue that to conduct estimations in software projects, one should not rely exclusively on expert opinion, but also on quantitative data collected in a more unbiased way. To this end, researchers have published studies making use of, among others, the International Software Benchmarking Standards Group's data repository (ISBSG).[10] (For an overview and introduction to the data sets, please see Hill et al. 2001.) Their large collection of data sets includes cost, size, and defect data from projects and sprints, which can be used for research, estimation, and prediction for and in future projects.

While the ISBSG data sets are typically cleaned and anonymized version of data sets collected from industrial projects they, like similar data sets in other collections, still exhibit many of the same characteristics that we can expect from actual projects in industry. For example, they have missing data, disparate quality in data collection procedures, and a large variety of data types. These are data quality issues we see also in empirical software engineering research in general.

As we will later see in Sect. 4, the dominant strategy to handle missing data in empirical software engineering research is to merely remove cases that have missing data (listwise deletion). We believe that this strategy is suboptimal and, generally speaking, not good for our research discipline. Even in cases when data can be classified according to the quality of the data collection procedure, as is the case with the ISBSG data sets, one sees that our community often chooses only to use a subset of data, classified to be of the highest quality (see, e.g., Keung (2008), Liebchen and Shepperd (2008) for recommendations, and Mittas et al. (2015) for an example where the authors use the recommendations). In short, we believe that data of low quality should be seen as better than no data at all, and the general rule of thumb should be never to throw away data. This is the context for our showcase and, in the following, we will both apply techniques for data imputation and conduct Bayesian data analysis on effort estimation data on the ISBSG data set collection.[11] As we will see, missing data can be naturally handled in Bayesian analysis and, thus, showcases one of the unique and pertinent strengths in an empirical software engineering context.

---

[10]http://isbsg.org.

[11]A reproducibility package, making use of brms (Bürkner 2017) (with Stan (Carpenter et al. 2017)) written in R (R Core Team 2018), can be downloaded: https://github.com/torkar/BDA_in_ESE. The raw data can, however, not be downloaded due to copyright reasons. Please see README.txt in the repository for more information and what you need to do to access the raw ISBSG data.

3.1   The Data and the Problem

We will use the ISBSG Release 10 data set and set the dependent variable to
`Effort`, i.e., the total number of person-hours to conduct a certain development
task. According to, e.g., Keung (2008), Liebchen and Shepperd (2008) and the
International Software Benchmarking Standards Group (ISBSG), the following
preprocessing steps are appropriate:

1. Only projects classified with data quality rating "A" are kept, and "B–D" are
   excluded.
2. Only projects using IFPUG (unadjusted functional size measurement) should be
   kept. However, the data description clearly states that versions ≥4.0 should not
   be compared to <4.0. Hence, we only use versions ≥4.0.
3. According to Keung (2008), some additional variables should be kept for
   compatibility with previous studies.
4. Cases with missing values should be excluded.

The above leads to variables of interests as listed in Table 1, according to Mittas
et al. (2015). If we use the variables in Table 1, and follow the advice above, we will
later see that we need to remove 3895 projects out of the total 4106 (close to 95%
of the projects). This seems wasteful but is the practice in our discipline, given the
current standards and relevant recommendations.

Imagine instead that we aim to keep as much data as possible, i.e., a data-greedy
approach. Well, first of all, we should consider including all projects no matter the
quality rating. After all, we can easily classify them differently in a statistical model
and even investigate the difference between projects depending on the data quality

Table 1 Variables of interest according to previous studies. The variable names that are underlined have been removed in this study as explained in Sects. 3.1.1 and 3.1.2. The variable name in bold was added as explained in Sect. 3.1

Name	Description
AFP	Adjusted function points
Input	Number of inputs
Output	Number of outputs
Enquiry	Number of enquiries
File	Number of files
Interface	Number of interfaces
Added	Number of added features
Changed	Number of changed features
Deleted	Number of deleted features
Effort	Actual effort (person-hours)
DQR	Data quality rating

rating. Hence, we decide to include all projects and mark them according to their data quality rating, i.e., DQR, no matter if they have missingness in them.

The next, crucial step before stating our model is to analyze causality among our variables (in Table 1). While this was not needed in the simple, height-of-humans example above, it is essential in more complex situations when multiple variables measure entities that might be causally related. Since this is almost always the case in real-world empirical software engineering research, it should be an essential step in building our statistical model. Otherwise, we risk that dependencies, e.g., correlations and collinearity, among variables might influence and could potentially weaken our analysis. Below, we will then also directly analyze correlations between predictors, through an analysis of non-identifiability before we can then decide on our model we will also discuss how to handle the missing data and the sensitivity of our priors.

3.1.1 Causal Analysis

All predictors except DQR seem to be raw and unadjusted measurements that are later used to calculate the adjusted function point (AFP).

Drawing our causal model (Fig. 3) as a directed acyclic graph (DAG) shows something generally considered to be a pipe confounder (one of the four types of relations in causal DAGs) (Pearl 2009).

In short, AFP mediates association between the other predictors and our outcome Effort, i.e., Effort⊥Input|AFP, or to put it differently, Effort is independent of Input, when conditioning on AFP.

We often worry about not having a predictor that we need for making good predictions (omitted variable bias). However, we do not often consider mistaken inferences because we rely on variables that are derived from other variables, i.e., posttreatment bias (McElreath 2015). (Rosenbaum (1984) calls this the concomitant variable bias.) In experimental studies, one would declare AFP to be a posttreatment

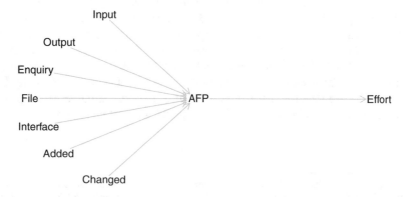

Fig. 3 A directed acyclic graph of our scientific model

variable, but the same nomenclature can be used in observational studies. To summarize, the above indicates that AFP should not be a predictor since it is derived from other, more basic, variables, so we will leave it out for now.

Note that causal analysis is not absolute in the sense that there is only one possible causal model that could be posited. Much scientific debate might be needed to argue for one or the other specific model and, thus, could lead to the exclusion of different sets of variables by different authors. As a consequence, this might lead different researchers to include or exclude different sets of variables and, thus, obtain different statistical results from separate analyses of the same data. However, in theory, this uncertainty and apparent subjectivity are still present with a traditional approach to statistical analysis, albeit hidden under the simplicity and familiarity of just applying a known statistical test.

3.1.2   Identifying Non-identifiability

Strong correlations between variables are generally speaking a challenge when building statistical models. The model will make good predictions, but it will be harder to analyze and understand since the impression will be that variables that have a strong correlation do not seem to have predictive power, while in fact, they have strong associations with the outcome (McElreath 2015, Sect. 5). As a concrete example, if you want to build a model of a person's length, using the length of both her legs as separate predictors will not help the matter, i.e., adding another leg will not add predictive power to the model since it will correlate very strongly with the length of the first included leg. This type of multicollinearity we generally want to avoid in statistical models.

Traditionally, there are two ways one can investigate this: Examining a pairs plot where all combinations of parameters and their correlations are visualized, or check if the matrix of predictor values is a full rank matrix, and thus identify non-identifiability that way.[12]

The latter, matrix-based approach consists of declaring a model $y = \beta_1 x_1 + \cdots + \beta_n x_n$, using the data, i.e., the values of the predictor variables, $x_i, \ldots, x_n$ as a matrix A, and decompose it into a product $A = QR$ of an orthogonal matrix Q, and an upper triangular matrix R. By analyzing the diagonal of the matrix R a threshold value of $|d_{ij}| < 0.1$ along the diagonal is then often used to declare a variable as unsuited for inclusion in a model. Often something like $1e^{-12}$—quasi-zero for a computer— could be used, but generally speaking anything below 1.0 has traditionally been excluded. The argument is that if it is below 1.0, then the variable would provide very little additional value to the model and should thus not be included.

---

[12]In short, different values of the parameters must generate different probability distributions of the observable variables. Otherwise we face various degrees of non-identifiability, i.e., essentially that (too) many parameter combinations could lead to the same observations.

Identifying non-identifiability for our data set from Table 1 clearly indicates that `Deleted` should be a candidate for removal ($|d_{\text{Deleted}}| = 9e^{-12}$). It might feel strange to remove predictors when our ultimate goal is to use as much data as possible. However, to build a statistical model that is sane, has good out-of-sample prediction, and is understandable, a trade-off is needed. Here we argue that the bulk of work should be done before we design our statistical model, to make use of the missing data techniques available to us.

3.1.3 Missing Data Analysis

When data is missing from cases of our data sets the most common solution is to either delete such cases or impute, i.e., "guess," based on the values we do have. Rubin (1987) has shown that very often 3–5 imputations are enough (the complete data set is imputed fully 3–5 times) and that the relative efficiency of an estimate based on m imputations is approximately:

$$\text{relative efficiency} \approx \left(1 + \frac{\gamma}{m}\right)^{-1}$$

where γ is the fraction of missing information. The relative efficiency in this case refers to using the finite m imputation estimator instead of the infinite number for the fully efficient imputation.

As an example, consider that we have 20% missing information in a variable ($\gamma = 0.2$), given $m = 5$, we have reached a relative efficiency of approximately 96%. Setting $m = 10$ we reach 98%. By doubling the computational effort, we have only a slight gain in relative efficiency. On the other hand, we have lots of computing power at our hands nowadays. However, more recently, we have seen that other recommendations for handling missing data have been presented.

Bodner (2008) and White et al. (2011) showed through simulations and by analytically deriving Monte Carlo errors, respectively, that the general rule of thumb should be $m = \gamma \times 100$, i.e., if a variable has 40% missing data ($\gamma = 0.4$) we should set $m = 40$ (using Rubin's efficiency estimate this would mean 92.6%→99.0%).

As will be evident, we will take the more conservative approach (i.e., $m = \gamma \times 100$), when we present the model implementation in Sect. 3.2.1.

Before we continue with the next section, it might be worthwhile to note that missingness in a Bayesian framework can be done in different ways. Either we conduct multiple imputations to derive uncertainty for all parameters, including our missing data. This is the path we have chosen here. The other approach would be to design a model of all data, including the missingness mechanism.

To model the missingness mechanism can be more involved and requires us to be very explicit about how our missingness occurred. At the best of times, this is a challenging task. We could instead argue that using the first approach, as we do here, shows the strengths of the Bayesian approach, since it easily can make use of various techniques, to handle missing data, in a coherent and principled way.

3.1.4 Sensitivity Analysis of Priors

Our analysis so far, to summarize, indicates that we should use seven predictors and one group variable (quality level of the project, in ISBSG terms), to predict one outcome variable (Effort). We can already now assume that we will most likely use a likelihood (i.e., our assumptions regarding the data generative process) that is based on counts (`Effort` is after all a count, the number of hours, going from zero to infinity).

Thus, we plan to use a generalized linear model, with a link function that translates between the linear predictor value and the mean of the distribution function. In the case of count distributions, such as Poisson, it is customary to use a log link function, i.e., a parameter's value is the exponentiation of the linear model. However, when setting priors for parameters and using a link function, unexpected things can happen, and the priors might not have the effect one would expect. To this end, we should always do prior predictive simulations, i.e., a sensitivity analysis of how different settings of the priors affect the predicted variable.

The description of the data set indicates that approximately 20% of the projects have more than 20 people in the team. If we assume, roughly 1700 h/year for an individual, having 60 people in a team sums up to approximately 100,000 person-hours per year. Let us now assume that this is the maximum value for our outcome variable `Effort`. Random sampling from $e^{\mathcal{N}(5,4)}$ provides us with $\bar{x} \approx 208{,}000$ (we use the exponential since we assume a log link function) indicating that this could be an acceptable prior for the intercept α.

We arrived at the values 5 and 4 above by starting from typical default values such as assuming α to be $\mathcal{N}(0, 10)$ (not uncommon as a default choice in, e.g., Poisson regressions), this would lead to $\bar{x} = 8 \times 10^{11}$ hours of work effort for an average project. This would correspond to close to half a billion people working on the project for 1 year. Thus we should use non-default priors to adapt the priors better so that they do not (often) give absurd values.

To assess the impact of very broad priors like $\mathcal{N}(0, 10)$ for our seven parameters, we thus, iteratively, compared their usage to that of other, narrower priors like $\mathcal{N}(0, 0.25)$. Furthermore, assuming a log link function, the additive effects of the seven priors for our β parameters would, on a normalized scale, correspond to $\mathcal{N}(0, (10 \times 7)^2)$ and $\mathcal{N}(0, (0.25 \times 7)^2)$, respectively. As is evident from Fig. 4a, we

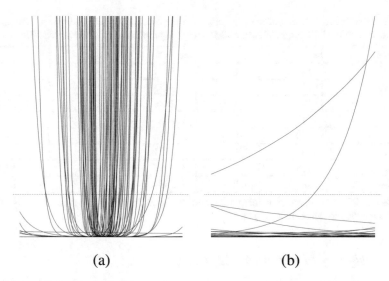

(a)   (b)

Fig. 4 Prior predictive simulation of broad and informative priors, respectively. The x-axes are z-scores, while the y-axes represent our outcome variable Effort. The dashed horizontal line corresponds to our assumed maximum value for our outcome variable and is the only value of interest in this case. We have plotted 100 simulations with the intercept $N(5, 4)$ and our seven priors for the respective β parameters. (**a**) β priors $N(0, 10)$. (**b**) β priors $N(0, 0.25)$

have a massive emphasis on extremely high y-values (we would require the world's total population to work in a project for this to happen). Now compare (a) with (b). We still allow extremely large y-values (up to 640×10^6!), but the emphasis is now a bit more realistic.

To summarize, prior predictive simulations indicate that setting $N(5, 4)$ and $N(0, 0.25)$ on α and β, respectively, allows us to delimit the multidimensional Gaussian space of possible parameter values while still not remove the probability of extreme values altogether. If we would still be uncertain, one could have conducted even more prior predictive simulations (Simpson et al. 2014). The prior knowledge we took with us when doing this analysis was that it was not likely that very many projects had billions of people involved. One could have taken a more conservative approach and claim that it is not likely that we have millions of people in our projects; however, as we will see, Hamiltonian Monte Carlo will handle these priors well given the available data.

One should always conduct prior sensitivity analysis (prior predictive simulation) before making use of the available data. There is always *some* prior knowledge one can use!

Table 2 Descriptive statistics of our predictors and the outcome variable Effort using all data available to us (i.e., 4106 projects), after conducting the preprocessing steps in Sect. 3.1

Variable	$\bar{x}$	$\tilde{x}$	max(x)	min(x)	s^2
Input	143	56	9404	0	144, 167
Output	125	47	3653	0	70, 522
Enquiry	74	27	2886	0	22, 318
File	118	43	10, 821	0	137, 172
Interface	39	10	1572	0	11, 082
Added	357	142	15, 121	0	591, 300
Changed	128	0	18, 357	0	344, 677
Effort	5384	1828	645, 694	4	391, 631, 309

From left to right: Name, mean, median, max, min, and sample variance (with removed NAs). All numbers rounded to the nearest integer

3.2 Design of Model and Diagnosis

Based on our initial analysis, we have a much clearer picture of which variables to include and the overall sensitivity of our priors. For our model one could imagine using a Poisson likelihood, that is, we have a count (Effort$_{0\rightarrow\infty}$), which we can model binomial events for when the trials N are very large and the probability p small. However, that would be a mistake.

In any analysis, it is important first to get to know the actual data. Thus, let us look at some descriptive statistics of the data (taking into account the preprocessing steps previously introduced).[13] Some issues catch the eye in Table 2. First, Effort has a max value of 645,694 (three times larger than the mean for our priors). Second, the medians are consistently lower than the means (in one case the median is zero) indicating positive skewness. Third, not visible in the table, Effort, compared to the predictors, contains no zeros (indicating that we do not need to consider zero-inflated or hurdle models (Hu et al. 2011)). Finally, the mean and the variance for our outcome variable are very different (the variance is approximately 70,000 times larger than the mean).

Concerning the latter issue, a Poisson likelihood assumes the mean and the variance be approximately equal. This allows us to use the negative binomial, known as the Gamma–Poisson (mixture) distribution, as our likelihood, i.e., a continuous mixture model where we assume each Poisson count observation has its own rate. However, since we are still using a Poisson model, in essence, one could claim that we do not need to redo analysis.

---

[13]For all data sets we use single quotes to emphasize the names, e.g., "A_clean," while we print out variable names in verbatim.

To summarize our findings so far we can now formulate our model:

$$\text{Effort}_i \sim \text{Gamma–Poisson}(\lambda_i, \phi_i)$$

$$\log(\lambda_i) \sim \alpha + \beta_{\text{Input}} \times \text{Input} + \beta_{\text{Output}} \times \text{Output} + \beta_{\text{Enquiry}} \times \text{Enquiry}$$
$$+ \beta_{\text{File}} \times \text{File} + \beta_{\text{Interface}} \times \text{Interface} + \beta_{\text{Added}} \times \text{Added}$$
$$+ \beta_{\text{Changed}} \times \text{Changed} + \alpha_{\text{DQR}[i]}$$

$$\alpha \sim \mathcal{N}(5, 4)$$

$$\beta_{1,...,7} \sim \mathcal{N}(0, 0.25)$$

$$\alpha_{\text{DQR}} \sim \mathcal{N}(0, \sigma)$$

$$\sigma \sim \text{HalfCauchy}(0, 1)$$

$$\log(\phi_i) \sim \text{Gamma}(0.5, 0.5)$$

We model each observation from a negative-binomial (Gamma–Poisson) distribution, with a failure rate λ and shape ϕ. We then use a log link for our linear model λ where we include an intercept α and parameters (β) for all predictors.

We also add varying intercepts in the form of our DQR variable. The idea is that each data quality rating should be treated uniquely by allowing us to estimate α for each rating, i.e., each DQR will have its own intercept. This will enable us to see if there is an overall difference between projects judged to have different quality ratings.

Finally, we set the aforementioned priors on our β parameters (but we use $\mathcal{N}(0, \sigma)$ for our unique intercepts, to separately estimate σ for each level of DQR). We also set HalfCauchy(0, 1) and Gamma(0.5, 0.5) for σ and ϕ, respectively. Both of these priors are regularizing priors common for these types of parameters.[14]

3.2.1 Using the Model

In the previous sections, we presented our statistical model with assumptions. In this section, we will make use of it in two ways: sampling with complete data and imputed data. However, before we begin, Table 3 describes the data sets we will use.

The data sets are divided into two categories. First, we have data sets that only take into account projects classified as having the highest quality rating ("A") and data sets where we use all four quality ratings ("AD"), taking into account the preprocessing steps in Sect. 3.1.

First, we have subsets with NAs ("A" and "AD") and, second, subsets where all original NAs are removed ("*_clean"). The logic to use these data sets is that we

---

[14]Please see here for prior choice recommendations: https://goo.gl/fx2F7V.

Table 3 Data sets used

Name	# projects	# NAs	% NAs	# zeros
"A"	501	2109	23.8	316
"A_clean"	214	0	0	316
"AD"	1689	8507	19.8	736
"AD_clean"	494	0	0	727

The "A*" and "AD*" categories are of different dimensions due to our index variable, DQR, added to the "AD*" sets. From left to right. Name of data set, number of projects (rows), number of NAs, percentage of NAs, and number of zeros

want to use as much data as possible (but we pay the price of missing data), and removing all NAs is, as we have discussed, not uncommon.

One could also imagine having subsets where all zeros are assumed to be NAs, but that would be a bit too conservative assumption in our opinion, and we leave it to the reader to try out such a scenario.

If one would like to compare our data sets with what is commonly seen in literature then, taking into account that we have a more restrictive view on which IFPUG versions are included, "A_clean" would be the most similar data set (e.g., Mittas et al. (2015) report using 501 projects, while we end up with 214, using our more restrictive subset). However, we are more interested in the cases where we have larger data sets, together with missing data, and comparing these with, e.g., "A_clean."

Missing Data Imputation

Summarizing missing data (Table 4) shows that the missingness is multivariate (there is missing data in more than one variable), connected (the second row with data indicates that we have 214 rows that are complete, i.e., no data is missing for these rows), and non-monotone (we have zeros spread out within all the ones, i.e., there is no monotonicity). Generally speaking, this indicates that data imputation is possible (in particular, connectivity is an essential part of missing data imputation).

van Buuren (2007) recommends that one calculates each variable's influx and outflux and plots them. Influx (I) is defined as the number of variable pairs with Y_j missing and Y_k observed, divided by the total number of *observed* data cells while, in the case of outflux (O), we instead divide by the total number of *incomplete* data cells. In short, a completely observed variable gives $I_j = 0$, while the opposite holds for O_j. If one has two variables with the same degree of missing data, then the variable with the highest O_j is potentially more useful for imputation purposes. Examining Fig. 5, Effort and Change have the highest O_j and I_j. To summarize, Effort will be the most influential variable for imputation, while Change will be the easiest variable to impute. This is worth keeping in mind later when we analyze the results.

To conclude, we will create multiple imputations (replacement values) for multivariate missing data, based on fully conditional specification (van Buuren 2007).

Table 4 Missingness of missing data

	Effort	Added	Input	Output	Enquiry	File	Interface	Changed	
Freq.									**# missing entries**
214	1	1	1	1	1	1	1	1	0
14	1	1	1	1	1	1	1	0	1
8	1	1	1	1	1	1	0	1	1
2	1	1	1	1	1	1	0	0	2
1	1	1	1	1	1	0	0	1	2
2	1	1	1	1	0	1	1	0	2
1	1	1	1	1	0	0	1	0	3
3	1	1	1	0	1	1	1	0	2
1	1	1	1	0	1	1	0	0	3
1	1	1	1	0	1	0	0	1	3
2	1	1	0	1	0	0	1	0	4
5	1	1	0	0	0	0	0	1	5
4	1	1	0	0	0	0	0	0	6
1	1	0	1	1	1	1	1	1	1
1	1	0	1	1	1	0	0	1	3
84	1	0	0	0	0	0	0	0	7
157	0	0	0	0	0	0	0	0	8
Missingness per variable	157	243	252	255	255	256	264	270	$\sum\sum$ **1952**

Top row lists each variable. Bottom row the number of missing entries per variable. First column, the frequency of each pattern. Last column, number of missing entries per pattern

Each incomplete variable is imputed by a separate model using predictive mean matching (numeric data), or proportional odds model/ordered logit model (factor data with >2 ordered levels) (Rubin 1986; van Buuren 2007). Concerning predictive mean matching, the assumption is that the missingness follows approximately the same distribution as the data, but the variability between the imputations over repeated draws reflects the uncertainty of the actual value.

We will approach this conservatively and follow the latest guidelines, as already discussed in Sect. 3.1.3, and hence set the number of imputations $m = 25$ (see Table 3) since we have approximately 25% missingness in certain variables.

3.2.2 Diagnostics

In this section, we will first present some diagnostics from the Hamiltonian Monte Carlo sampling we conducted.

First, the ratio of the average variance of draws within each chain to the variance of the pooled draws across chains is an estimate we can use to see how well our chains have diverged towards a common posterior. This is measured by $\widehat{R}$ and

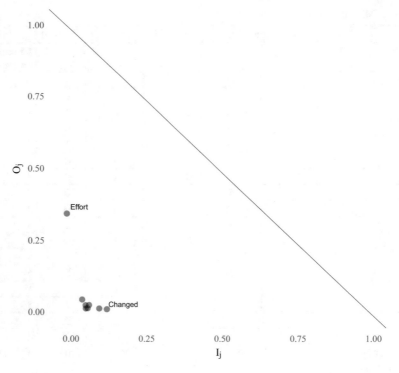

Fig. 5 Outflux versus influx of data set "A" as described in Sect. 3 (A small degree of random noise, "jitter," was added to the plot to make it more readable.)

generally speaking $\widehat{R}$ should go towards 1.00, and anything above 1.01 should be a clear warning sign of bias. In our case, for all sampling conducted, $\widehat{R}$ was consistently low (see Fig. 6a for one example where we used the "AD_clean" data set).

Second, the effective sampling was consistently high, i.e., 0.1. As an example, if we have 2000 samples from each chain, the default is then to throw away the first 1000 as warmup samples. But then we use four chains, ending up with 1000×4 samples. This means that we should not, in our example, have less than 400 samples for a parameter (see Fig. 6b).

Third, the visual inspection revealed that the chains seemed to mix well (hairy caterpillar ocular test). It should look messy, tight, and mixed (Fig. 7). If we are a bit hesitant concerning the mixture, and in particular the sampling conducted at the tails, one could also use rank plots (Vehtari et al. 2019). If we investigate Fig. 7 we see a clear difference between $\beta_{\text{Intercept}}$ and the other parameters. Using rank plots for the chains for $\beta_{\text{Intercept}}$, Fig. 8, provides a better view. We can see that there is a dip at the start of Chain 1 and the end of Chain 3, but it still indicates that the chain managed to sample quite well at the tails.

Finally, the Bayesian fraction of missing information, another diagnostic, shows a significant overlap between the energy transition density, π_E, and the marginal

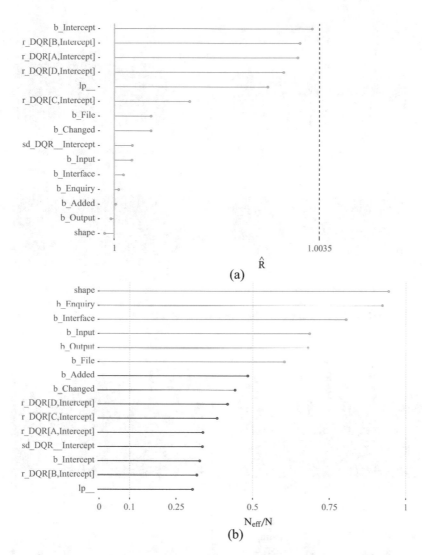

Fig. 6 $\widehat{R}$ values for each parameter (**a**) and effective sample sizes (**b**). For $\widehat{R}$ (**a**), generally speaking, any values above 1.01 are not appropriate and indicate that one or more chains are biased. Concerning effective sample sizes (**b**), anything below 0.1 is generally speaking a warning sign of a misspecified model. Here we used the "AD_clean" data set

energy distribution, $\pi_{\Delta E}$ (Fig. 9). When the two distributions are well-matched, the random walk will explore the marginal energy distribution efficiently (Betancourt 2017).

We sampled four chains, each with 2000 iterations, and the first half of the iterations were discarded as warmup iterations. For our imputed data sets this means that we have $1000 \times 4 \times 25 = 100,000$ posterior samples. Figure 10 provides a

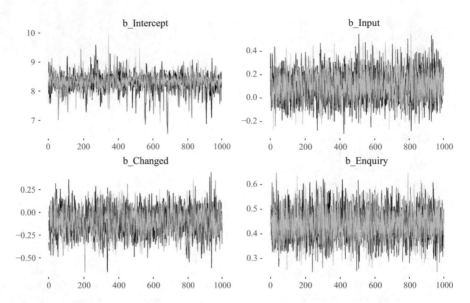

Fig. 7 Trace plots of four parameters using the "AD_clean" data set

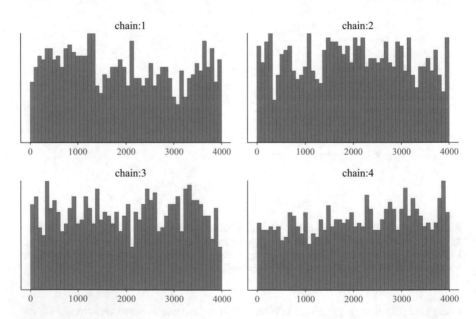

Fig. 8 Rank plots of the four chains from the $\beta_{Intercept}$ sampling. The chains should be close to uniform. Here we see a slight dip at the start of Chain 1 and the end of Chain 3. These dips can be much more exaggerated (e.g., no samples collected at all) and then there would be reasons to worry

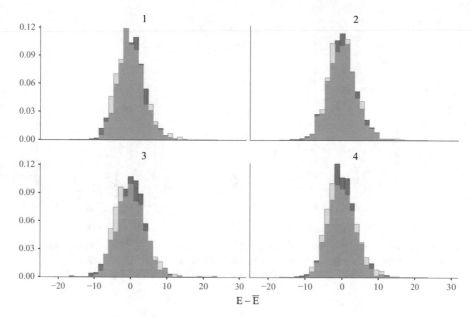

Fig. 9 Comparisons of the energy transition density, π_E, and the marginal energy distribution, $\pi_{\Delta E}$ (light and dark gray, respectively). A significant overlap is visible

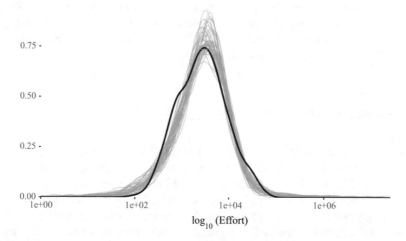

Fig. 10 Comparison of the empirical distribution of the data ("AD_clean"), to the distributions of simulated data from the posterior predictive distribution (50 samples). Note that the x-axis has been transformed

comparison of our empirical outcome y (using the data set "A_clean"), with draws from our posterior distribution; we see evidence of a fairly good match; a perfect match is not what we want since then we could just use our data as-is, i.e., the variability of each y_{rep} vis-à-vis y is what interests us.

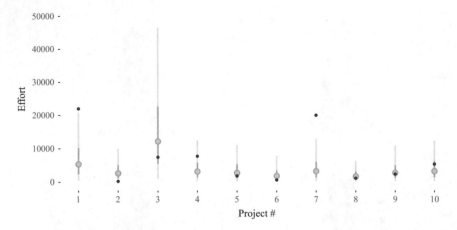

Fig. 11 Posterior predictive checks of the first 10 projects in our data set. Vertical bars with points indicate the simulated medians and darker points indicate our empirical values. Thicker and thinner lines indicate 50% and 90% central intervals, respectively. We drew 500 samples from the posterior

Another check one should do is to investigate how well the sampling (y_{rep}) matches our empirical data y for each project (row) in our data set. In Fig. 11, we have drawn 500 samples from the posterior. As we can see our empirical data, y, does not always match y_{rep}, but that is all fine actually, what we want is a model that *on average* makes better predictions. After all, if we would want perfect predictions for our data set, why not use the data set as-is?

3.3   Conduct Inference

If we turn our attention to the estimated intercepts for our group-level variable DQR (i.e., a project's rating according to the quality of data collected), we see something interesting in Fig. 12. There is a clear pattern, in both data sets, where quality rating "A" and "D" are to the left, while "B" and "C" are to the right. It is an indication that these two groups are perceived as similar to each other, which is a bit ironic since "A" and "D" are conceptually the opposite of each other in terms of data quality rating. This indicates that one should question the data quality ratings in the data set and, given enough data, DQR seems to become less critical.

Examining the estimated parameters (Fig. 13) we see that parameters perceived as "significant" differ between the data sets.[15] There are three comparisons we should make here. First, comparing imputed with cleaned data sets (within each

---

[15] Our notion of "significant" is here that the 95% highest density posterior interval does not cross zero. However, other notions do exist (Kruschke 2018).

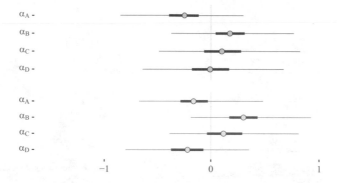

Fig. 12 Interval plots of α estimates with 50% and 95% uncertainty intervals. Upper plot is the imputed data set, below plot the cleaned data set. The uncertainty is slightly different between each category even though this is not very obvious in this plot (the cleaned data set, below, has higher uncertainty)

column). Second, comparing "A" and "AD" models (between columns). Third, compare the upper right and lower left plots (data-greedy approach vs. state of practice).

First, if we look at the left column, we see that nothing significant has changed. On the other hand, examining the right column, we see that β_{Added} is no longer significant in the imputed data set. This might make you sad. However, using all data can lead to weaker inferences and, honestly, should we not make use of all data available no matter our wishful thinking concerning inferences?

Second, if we compare our simple models with our multilevel models (between column comparisons), examining the two lower plots we see that β_{Added} has become "significant" in the model where we make use of all quality ratings (right plot). In this particular case, one would lean towards the multilevel model (right plot) since it, after all, makes use of more data and employs partial pooling to avoid overfitting.

Finally, we should compare the upper right and lower left plots (our data-greedy approach with state of practice); they are the reason for conducting this study. Two things are worth noticing here: (1) β_{Enquiry} is shifted noticeably more to the right in the imputed data set and is significant, as is $\beta_{\text{Interface}}$. (2) β_{Changed} is clearly not significant in the imputed data set, while in the cleaned data set, it is nearly so. Once again, making use of more data can lead to weaker inferences, which is a good thing.

Let us now examine what the posterior predictive distribution provides us with concerning point estimates regarding our outcome Effort. The posterior distribution allows us to set predictors at different values and generate predicted outcomes with uncertainty. In our case, we would like to examine the difference between posterior predictive distributions of "A_clean" and "AD," since "A_clean" is based on the assumptions commonly used in literature and "AD" makes use of as much data as possible, i.e., our data-greedy approach.

Plotting our two posterior distributions indicates the differences (see Fig. 14). As is clear, the median is higher when taking into account more data ("AD"), but

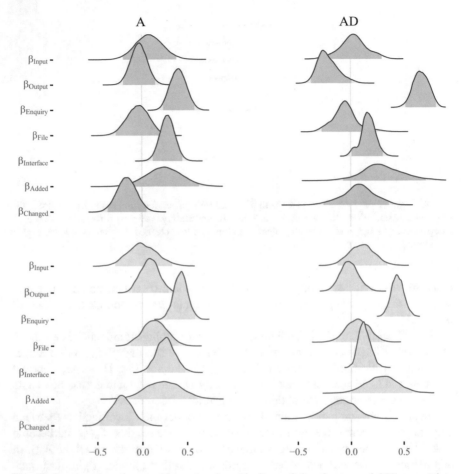

Fig. 13 Density plots drawn with overlapping ridgelines of β estimates and 95% uncertainty intervals. Left column presents data sets "A," while right column presents data sets "AD." Dark gray plots indicate imputed data sets (first row), while light gray represents cleaned sets. In particular the top right and lower left plots are of interest to us since they represent the data-greedy approach and the state of practice, respectively

the uncertainty is also slightly larger. Ultimately, comparing these types of point estimates should always go hand in hand with the purpose of the analysis, i.e., the utility function.

The posterior distribution allows us to make probabilistic statements that provide us with a deeper understanding of the phenomena we study. We could make statements for each model separately, i.e., investigating "AD" we can say that the probability that the effect is greater than 10% (a decline of $>10\%$) for the D category is 2.6%, while for the A category it is 7.2%. Alternatively, in the case of "A_clean," that the probability that the effect of Enquiry is greater than 5% (an increase of $>5\%$ in this case) is 58.6%. Of course, one could also look at the probability that

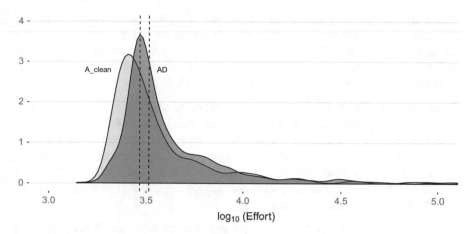

Fig. 14 Comparison of the posterior distributions of the "A_clean" and "AD" data sets ($n =$ 4000). Notice the transformation of the x-axis. The median values on natural scale, with 95% highest posterior density intervals for "A_clean" and "AD," are $\tilde{\mu}_{A\,clean} = 2937$, 95%HPDI[2069, 15441] and $\tilde{\mu}_{AD} = 3280$, 95%HPDI[1920, 17783], respectively (medians indicated by vertical lines). Highest posterior density interval (HPDI) is the tightest interval containing the specified probability mass, i.e., 95% in our case

the estimates of parameter β_{Input} are larger than 0 using the "AD_clean" and "AD" data sets, i.e., 79.8% and 60.2%, respectively.

These types of probability statements are a positive aspect of Bayesian analysis and the posterior probability distributions that accompanies it.

3.4 Threats to Validity

In this section, we will cover threats to validity from a quantitative and statistical perspective. The below threats are not the type of threats that are normally discussed in empirical software engineering (Wohlin et al. 2012) (such as threats to internal and external validity). The latter refers to a rigid experimental design (often based on statistical hypothesis testing) and is mainly qualitative; in contrast, the threats we discuss are grounded in the quantitative analysis we performed, and as such they address the very design of the analysis (which allows for much more flexibility using the tools of Bayesian data analysis). In Sect. 3.4.1 we will compare our study's design to recent guidelines concerning the design and reporting of software analytics studies.

Directed Acyclic Graphs (DAGs) Making ones scientific model explicit is dangerous since it becomes open to attack. We believe, however, that it should be compulsory in any scientific publication. We employed DAGs to this end, a concept refined by Pearl and others (Pearl 2009). Using DAGs makes things explicit. If things are explicit, they can be criticized. One threat to validity is of course that our scientific model is wrong and AFP is not a mediator (Sect. 3.1.1). This is for the reader to comment on. Of course, instead of using the graphical approach of DAGs and applying do-calculus to determine d-separation, one could walk down the road of numerical approaches according to Peters et al. (2017).

Non-identifiability Through our non-identifiability analysis we concluded that the variable Deleted should be removed. Removing this variable is a trade-off. The non-identifiability analysis showed that it should be removed, thus allowing for better understandability and better out-of-sample prediction. However, we could have taken a more prudent approach and investigated Deleted's role in predictions, but in this particular case, we believe the initial analysis provided us with a convincing argument to remove it.

Priors The sensitivity analysis of priors provided us with confidence regarding the choice of priors. We conducted prior predictive analysis and, together with recommendations regarding default priors, concluded that our selection of priors was balanced. However, our conclusions could be wrong, and further studies could indicate that our priors are too broad. The latter is, however, what one can expect when doing science.

Bayesian Data Analysis In a Bayesian context, model comparison is often divided into three categories M-open, M-complete, and M-closed (Yao et al. 2018; Navarro 2019). In the M-open world the relationship between the data generating process and our list of models $M = M_1, \ldots, M_K$ is unknown. However, what we do know is that M_t, our "true" model, is not in M, and we cannot specify the explicit form $p(\tilde{y}|y)$ due to computational or conceptual reasons. In the M-complete world, M_t is also not in M, but we use any model in M that is closest in Kullback–Leibler divergence (Yao et al. 2018; Betancourt 2015). Finally, in the case of the M-closed world, $M_t \in M$.

The bulk of statistical methodology is concerned with the latter category (M-closed) and Clarke et al. (2013) claim that,

> this class of problems is comparatively simple and well-studied.

Many problems we face are in the M-complete and not the M-closed world (this chapter is such an example). Selecting the "best" model is often done through relative comparisons of $M_1, \ldots, M_K$ using the Watanabe–Akaike information criterion (WAIC) or leave-one-out cross-validation with Pareto-smoothed importance sampling (Vehtari et al. 2017). However, to use WAIC or PSIS-LOO for out-of-sample prediction, one should use the same data set for each model (e.g., you can change the likelihood and priors, but the data set is fixed).

In this chapter, we have not done model comparison (e.g., using PSIS-LOO (Vehtari et al. 2017)), but the reason is apparent—we use different data sets—which is the purpose of this chapter. To this end we defend our choice of likelihood, i.e., the Gamma–Poisson (a.k.a. negative binomial), epistemologically: If we have counts from zero to infinity, where the variance is significantly different from the mean then, from a maximum entropy point of view, Gamma–Poisson is a rational choice. By conducting posterior predictive checks, we ultimately received yet another validation to strengthen us in our opinion that the model has predictive capabilities (Sect. 3.3).

Residuals One threat to validity is also the residuals of the model (fitting deviation). If the residuals are too large, it is an indication that the model does not fit data well. This is a trade-off since a perfect fit could imply overfitting. By conducting posterior predictive checks, we concluded that the models, as such, had a convincing fit (see, e.g., Fig. 10).

3.4.1   Common Threats in Software Analytics Papers

Finally, we believe that using the traditional threats to validity nomenclature seen in empirical software engineering research most likely does not fit the type of studies we present here. Instead we will propose something different.

Menzies and Shepperd (2019) present 12 "bad smells" in software analytics papers. Below we will now cover each "smell" and contrast it with what we did in this chapter.

1. **Not interesting.** (Research that has negligible software engineering impact.) We argue that the problem we have analyzed in this section is not only relevant, common, and interesting. To this we mainly point to Sect. 4.
2. **Not using related work.** (Unawareness of related work concerning RQs and SOA.) We point to further reading (Sect. 4) as a basis for this study, i.e., studies which throw away data and show how other state-of-the-art analytical approaches might be more suitable.
3. **Using deprecated and suspect data.** (Using data out of convenience.) The data is definitely suspect as we have shown by our analysis of data quality ratings, but it would be hard to argue that the data is deprecated. However, we used a particular version of the data set, but that was due to our intention to align with previous work.
4. **Inadequate reporting.** (Partial reporting, e.g., only means.) In this section, we have presented not only point estimates but also contrasted different distributions and derived probabilistic statements. We would have also liked to provide model comparisons but, alas, the design of this study did not allow this. To this end, we rely on posterior predictive checks.
5. **Underpowered experiments.** (Small effect sizes and little theory.) Using more data provides us with more statistical power, and we base our priors on state-of-the-art recommendations and logical conclusions, e.g., estimating that the world's population is part of a project is not appropriate.
6. **$p < 0.05$ and all that.** (Abuse of null hypothesis testing.) We mention p-values only when making a point not to use them.
7. **Assumptions of normality and equal variances.** (Impact of outliers and heteroscedasticity.) We use a Bayesian generalized linear model, which we

model using a Gamma–Poisson likelihood. Additionally, we employ multilevel
models when possible, and hence make use of partial pooling (which takes into
account the presence of outliers).

8. **Not exploring stability.** We conducted a sensitivity analysis of priors, and we
report on the differences between imputed and cleaned data sets.
9. **No data visualization.** We leave it up to the reader to decide if appropriate
levels of visualization were used. We have followed guidelines on data visualization (Gabry et al. 2017).
10. **Not tuning.** We avoid bias in comparisons mainly by clearly stating our
assumptions, conducting a sensitivity analysis, making use of multilevel models, and, generally speaking, following guidelines on how to conduct Bayesian
data analysis.
11. **Not exploring simplicity.** Using state-of-the-art missing data analysis is
needed and wanted to decrease our bias. Additionally, using a complex mixture
model was unavoidable because of epistemological reasons, as presented earlier
in this section. We used simulated data to assess the appropriateness of our
likelihood and priors independently.
12. **Not justifying choice of learner.** This concerns, ultimately, the risk of overes-
timation (or overfitting). We would argue that any usage of frequentist statistics
would potentially introduce this "smell," i.e., using uniform priors, as is the
case in a traditional frequentist setting, ensures maximum overfitting.

3.5 Discussion

We argue that one should have solid reasons to throw away data since we now have
techniques available that can provide us with the opportunity to use as much data as
possible. The example we provided showed that by using missing data techniques,
in combination with Bayesian multilevel models, we could better make use of the
data and, thus, gain higher confidence concerning our findings. The inferences
can become weaker, but ask yourself if that is not how you think your fellow
researchers should conduct their analysis. We could show two things in our analysis:
(1) Parameters' "significance" changed depending on if we used imputation or not
and (2) there was really not much of a difference between the various data quality
ratings (once again indicating that we should use as much data as possible).

However, we pay a price for this more sophisticated analysis. It is a more
involved analysis compared to a frequentist analysis where only the likelihood of
the outcome is required to be specified, and maximum likelihood estimates are not
conditioned on the observed outcome; the uncertainty is instead connected to the
sampling distribution of the estimator. The same applies to confidence intervals
in the frequentist world, i.e., one can set up a distribution of predictions, but it
entails repeating the process of random sampling on which we apply the estimator
every time to then generate point predictions. Contrast this with conditioning on the
posterior predictive distribution, which is based on the observed outcome.

Additionally, making probabilistic statements is very much more natural when having a posterior at hand, while the p-values we have made use of traditionally rely on observing a z-statistic that is so large (in magnitude) if the null hypothesis is true, i.e., not if the scientific hypothesis is true. To make the point, the term "p-value" was used in this section for the first time here in this section and in our case, where we used different data sets, one could have expected us to lean towards traditional hypothesis testing, since it was not possible to compare models explicitly, regarding out-of-sample predictions.

We will not further contrast our approach with how analyses are done in empirical software engineering today. Suffice to say, issues such as the arbitrary $\alpha = 0.05$ cutoff, the usage of null hypothesis significance testing, and the reliance on confidence intervals, have been criticized (Ioannidis 2005b; Morey et al. 2016; Nuzzo 2014; Woolston 2015), and when analyzing the arguments, we have concluded that many of the issues plaguing other scientific fields are equally relevant to come to terms within empirical software engineering.

> We believe that evidence-based interpretation is more straightforward with Bayesian data analysis, and empirical software engineering should embrace it as soon as possible. In our view, it is a natural choice to make in this particular case; to base one's inferences on more data is wise, and doing so in a Bayesian context is natural.

4 Recommended Further Reading

There are few early publications in software engineering where we see evidence of using MLMs. In Ehrlich and Cataldo (2012) the authors used multilevel models for assessing communication in global software development, while in Hassan et al. (2017) the authors applied MLMs for studying reviews in an app store. However, both studies used a frequentist approach (maximum likelihood), i.e., not a Bayesian approach.

As far as we can tell, there are only a few examples of studies in software engineering that have applied BDA with MLMs to this date (Furia 2016; Ernst 2018). Furia (2016) presents several cases of how BDA could be used in computer science and software engineering research. In particular, the aspects of including prior belief/knowledge in MLMs are emphasized, which is further elaborated on in Furia et al. (2019). Ernst (2018) on the other hand, presents a conceptual replication of an existing study where he shows that MLMs support cross-project comparisons while preserving local context, mainly through the concept of partial pooling, as used in Bayesian MLMs.[16]

Finally, much literature on BDA exist, but not all have the clarity that is needed to explain, sometimes, relatively complex concepts. If one would like to read up on the basics of probability and Bayesian statistics we recommend Jaynes (2003), for a slightly more in-depth view of Bayesian statistics we would recommend Lambert (2018). For a hands-on approach to BDA, we recommend McElreath (2015); McElreath's book *Statistical Rethinking: A Bayesian Course with Examples in R and Stan* is an example of how seemingly complex issues can be explained beautifully while at the same time help the reader improve their skills in BDA. To conclude, there is one book that every researcher should have on their shelf, *Bayesian Data Analysis* by Gelman et al. (2013), which is considered the leading text on Bayesian methods.

Missing data can be handled in two main ways. Either we delete data using one of the three main approaches (listwise or pairwise deletion and column deletion) or we impute new data. Concerning missing data, we conclude the matter is not new to the empirical software engineering community. Liebchen and Shepperd (2008) have pointed out that the community needs more research into ways of identifying and repairing noisy cases, and Mockus (2008) claims that the standard approach to handle missing data, i.e., remove cases of missing values (e.g., listwise deletion), is prevalent in empirical software engineering.

Two additional studies on missing data are, however, worthwhile pointing out. Myrtveit et al. (2001) investigated listwise deletion, mean imputation, similar response pattern imputation, and full information maximum likelihood (FIML), and concluded that FIML is the only technique appropriate when data are not missing completely at random. Finally, Cartwright et al. (2003) concluded that k-nearest neighbor and sample mean imputation are significantly better in improving model fit when dealing with imputation. However, much has happened concerning research in imputation techniques lately.

In this chapter, we focused on multivariate imputation by chained equations (MICE), sometimes called fully conditional specification or sequential regression multiple imputation, a technique that has emerged as a principled method of dealing with missing data during the last decade (van Buuren 2007). MICE specifies a multivariate imputation model on a variable-by-variable basis by a set of conditional densities (one for each incomplete variable) and draws imputations by reiterating the conditional densities. The original idea behind MICE is old, see, e.g., stochastic relaxation (Geman and Geman 1984), but the recent refinements and implementations have made the technique easily accessible.

Finally, related work concerning the ISBSG data set is worthwhile pointing out. Fernández-Diego and de Guevara (2014) present pros and cons of using the ISBSG data set. A systematic mapping review was used as the research method, which was applied to over 120 papers. The dependent variable of interest was usually

---

[16]Partial pooling takes into account variance between units.

`Effort` (more than 70% of the studies), and the most frequently used methods were regression ($\sim$60%) and machine learning ($\sim$35%), the latter a term where many techniques can hide. Worth noting is also that Release 10 was used most frequently, which provided us with a reason to also use that data set. Additionally, we also used `Effort` as the dependent variable of interest, since a majority of the studies seem to find that variable interesting to study. (The importance of the ISBSG data set, when considering replication studies in empirical software engineering, has already been pointed out by Shepperd et al. (2018).) By and large, our chapter took another approach entirely, we imputed missing data in a Bayesian context, and we see this more as complementary to some of the work mentioned above.

5 Conclusion

In this chapter, we introduced the reader to Bayesian data analysis. Before even designing the model, we took several steps, each providing us with a better understanding of the data. We did a causal analysis, analyzed non-identifiability, performed sensitivity analysis of priors, and an analysis of missing data. Additionally, we presented the reader with several diagnostics one should use for sanity checking a statistical model. Except for the missing data analysis (if no missingness is present), we would argue that this is something one should always do when conducting Bayesian data analysis.

Missing data was an additional complexity that our case presented. We recommend that one should always be conservative with throwing away data. Many state-of-the-art techniques exist today, which provides the researcher with ample of possibilities to conduct rigorous, systematic, and transparent missing data analysis. We followed a traditional imputation approach, but other approaches, i.e., purely Bayesian, do exist. In our example, we showed that inferences can become weaker, which is not a bad thing, and that the qualitative assessment of quality ratings can be biased. This further strengthens the argument never to throw data away.

By using Bayesian data analysis, we believe that researchers will be able to get a more nuanced view of the challenges they are investigating. In short, we do not need p-values for this.

References

Aarts AA, et al (2015) Estimating the reproducibility of psychological science. Science 349(6251):aac4716. https://doi.org/10.1126/science.aac4716

Banerjee S, Carlin B, Gelfand A (2014) Hierarchical modeling and analysis for spatial data, 2nd edn. Chapman and Hall/CRC monographs on statistics and applied probability. Taylor and Francis, Boca Raton

Benjamin DJ, et al (2018) Redefine statistical significance. Nat Hum Behav 2:6–10. https://doi.org/10.1038/s41562-017-0189-z

Betancourt M (2015) A unified treatment of predictive model comparison. arXiv:1506.02273

Betancourt M (2017) A conceptual introduction to Hamiltonian Monte Carlo. arXiv:1701.02434

Betancourt M (2018) Calibrating model-based inferences and decisions. arXiv:1803.08393

Bodner TE (2008) What improves with increased missing data imputations? Struct Equ Model Multidiscip J 15(4):651–675. https://doi.org/10.1080/10705510802339072

Brooks S, Gelman A, Jones G, Meng XL (2011) Handbook of Markov chain Monte Carlo. CRC, Boca Raton

Bürkner PC (2017) brms: an R package for Bayesian multilevel models using Stan. J Stat Softw 80(1):1–28. https://doi.org/10.18637/jss.v080.i01

Camerer CF, et al (2016) Evaluating replicability of laboratory experiments in economics. Science 351(6280):1433–1436. https://doi.org/10.1126/science.aaf0918

Carpenter B, Gelman A, Hoffman M, Lee D, Goodrich B, Betancourt M, Brubaker M, Guo J, Li P, Riddell A (2017) Stan: a probabilistic programming language. J Stat Softw 76(1):1–32. https://doi.org/10.18637/jss.v076.i01

Cartwright MH, Shepperd MJ, Song Q (2003) Dealing with missing software project data. In: Proceedings of 5th international workshop on enterprise networking and computing in healthcare industry (IEEE Cat. No.03EX717), pp 154–165. https://doi.org/10.1109/METRIC.2003.1232464

Clarke JL, Clarke B, Yu CW (2013) Prediction in M-complete problems with limited sample size. Bayesian Anal 8(3):647–690. https://doi.org/10.1214/13-BA826

Dutilh G, Vandekerckhove J, Ly A, Matzke D, Pedroni A, Frey R, Rieskamp J, Wagenmakers EJ (2017) A test of the diffusion model explanation for the worst performance rule using preregistration and blinding. Atten Percept Psychophys 79(3):713–725. https://doi.org/10.3758/s13414-017-1304-y

Ehrlich K, Cataldo M (2012) All-for-one and one-for-all?: a multilevel analysis of communication patterns and individual performance in geographically distributed software development. In: Proceedings of the ACM 2012 conference on computer supported cooperative work (CSCW '12). ACM, New York, pp 945–954. https://doi.org/10.1145/2145204.2145345

Ernst NA (2018) Bayesian hierarchical modelling for tailoring metric thresholds. In: Proceedings of the 15th international conference on mining software repositories (MSR '18). IEEE, Piscataway, pp 587–591. https://doi.org/10.1145/3196398.3196443

Fernández-Diego M, de Guevara FGL (2014) Potential and limitations of the ISBSG dataset in enhancing software engineering research: a mapping review. Inf Softw Technol 56(6):527–544. https://doi.org/10.1016/j.infsof.2014.01.003

Furia CA (2016) Bayesian statistics in software engineering: practical guide and case studies. arXiv:1608.06865

Furia CA, Feldt R, Torkar R (2019) Bayesian data analysis in empirical software engineering research. IEEE Trans Softw Eng. https://doi.org/10.1109/TSE.2019.2935974

Gabry J, Simpson D, Vehtari A, Betancourt M, Gelman A (2017) Visualization in Bayesian workflow. arXiv:1709.01449

Gelman A (2018) The failure of null hypothesis significance testing when studying incremental changes, and what to do about it. Personal Soc Psychol Bull 44(1):16–23. https://doi.org/10.1177/0146167217729162

Gelman A, Carlin J, Stern H, Dunson D, Vehtari A, Rubin D (2013) Bayesian data analysis, 3rd edn. Chapman and Hall/CRC texts in statistical science. Taylor and Francis, Boca Raton

Gelman A, Simpson D, Betancourt M (2017) The prior can often only be understood in the context of the likelihood. Entropy 19(10):555. https://doi.org/10.3390/e19100555

Geman S, Geman D (1984) Stochastic relaxation, Gibbs distributions, and the Bayesian restoration of images. IEEE Trans Pattern Anal Mach Intell 6(6):721–741. https://doi.org/10.1109/TPAMI.1984.4767596

Glick JL (1992) Scientific data audit—a key management tool. Account Res 2(3):153–168. https://doi.org/10.1080/08989629208573811

Hassan S, Tantithamthavorn C, Bezemer CP, Hassan AE (2017) Studying the dialogue between users and developers of free apps in the Google Play Store. Empir Softw Eng 23(3):1275–1312. https://doi.org/10.1007/s10664-017-9538-9

Hill PR, Stringer M, Lokan C, Wright T (2001) Organizational benchmarking using the ISBSG data repository. IEEE Softw 18:26–32. https://doi.org/10.1109/52.951491

Hu MC, Pavlicova M, Nunes EV (2011) Zero-inflated and hurdle models of count data with extra zeros: examples from an HIV-risk reduction intervention trial. Am J Drug Alcohol Abuse 37(5):367–375. https://doi.org/10.3109/00952990.2011.597280

Hunter JE (2001) The desperate need for replications. J Consum Res 28(1):149–158. https://doi.org/10.1086/321953

Ioannidis JPA (2005a) Contradicted and initially stronger effects in highly cited clinical research. J Am Med Assoc 294(2):218–228. https://doi.org/10.1001/jama.294.2.218

Ioannidis JPA (2005b) Why most published research findings are false. PLoS Med 2(8):e124. https://doi.org/10.1371/journal.pmed.0020124

Ioannidis JPA (2016) Why most clinical research is not useful. PLOS Med 13(6):1–10. https://doi.org/10.1371/journal.pmed.1002049

Ioannidis JPA, Stanley TD, Doucouliagos H (2017) The power of bias in economics research. Econ J 127(605):F236–F265. https://doi.org/10.1111/ecoj.12461

Jaynes ET (2003) Probability theory: the logic of science. Cambridge University Press, Cambridge

John LK, Loewenstein G, Prelec D (2012) Measuring the prevalence of questionable research practices with incentives for truth telling. Psychol Sci 23(5):524–532. https://doi.org/10.1177/0956797611430953

Keung J (2008) Empirical evaluation of Analogy-X for software cost estimation. In: Proceedings of the second ACM-IEEE international symposium on empirical software engineering and measurement (ESEM '08). ACM, New York, pp 294–296. https://doi.org/10.1145/1414004.1414057

Kruschke JK (2018) Rejecting or accepting parameter values in Bayesian estimation. Adv Methods Pract Psychol Sci 1(2):270–280. https://doi.org/10.1177/2515245918771304

Lambert B (2018) A student's guide to Bayesian statistics. SAGE, Beverly Hills

Lenberg P, Feldt R, Wallgren Tengberg LG, Tidefors I, Graziotin D (2017) Behavioral software engineering—guidelines for qualitative studies. arXiv:1712.08341

Liebchen GA, Shepperd M (2008) Data sets and data quality in software engineering. In: Proceedings of the 4th international workshop on predictor models in software engineering (PROMISE '08). ACM, New York, pp 39–44. https://doi.org/10.1145/1370788.1370799

McElreath R (2015) Statistical rethinking: a Bayesian course with examples in R and Stan. CRC, Boca Raton

McShane BB, Gal D, Gelman A, Robert C, Tackett JL (2017) Abandon statistical significance. arXiv:1709.07588

Menzies T, Shepperd M (2019) "Bad smells" in software analytics papers. Inf Softw Technol 112:35–47. https://doi.org/10.1016/j.infsof.2019.04.005

Mittas N, Papatheocharous E, Angelis L, Andreou AS (2015) Integrating non-parametric models with linear components for producing software cost estimations. J Syst Softw 99:120–134. https://doi.org/10.1016/j.jss.2014.09.025

Mockus A (2008) Missing data in software engineering. In: Shull F, Singer J, Sjøberg DIK (eds) Guide to advanced empirical software engineering. Springer, London, pp 185–200. https://doi.org/10.1007/978-1-84800-044-5_7

Morey RD, Hoekstra R, Rouder JN, Lee MD, Wagenmakers EJ (2016) The fallacy of placing confidence in confidence intervals. Psychon Bull Rev 23(1):103–123. https://doi.org/10.3758/s13423-015-0947-8

Myrtveit I, Stensrud E, Olsson UH (2001) Analyzing data sets with missing data: an empirical evaluation of imputation methods and likelihood-based methods. IEEE Trans Softw Eng 27(11):999–1013. https://doi.org/10.1109/32.965340

Navarro DJ (2019) Between the devil and the deep blue sea: tensions between scientific judgement and statistical model selection. Comput Brain Behav 2(1):28–34. https://doi.org/10.1007/s42113-018-0019-z

Nuzzo R (2014) Scientific method: statistical errors. Nature 506(7487):150–152. https://doi.org/10.1038/506150a

Pearl J (2009) Causality: models, reasoning and inference, 2nd edn. Cambridge University Press, New York

Peters J, Janzing D, Schölkopf B (2017) Elements of causal inference: foundations and learning algorithms. In: Adaptive computation and machine learning. MIT Press, Cambridge

R Core Team (2018) R: a language and environment for statistical computing. In: R foundation for statistical computing, Vienna, Austria. https://www.R-project.org/

Rodríguez-Pérez G, Robles G, González-Barahona JM (2018) Reproducibility and credibility in empirical software engineering: a case study based on a systematic literature review of the use of the SZZ algorithm. Inf Softw Technol 99:164–176. https://doi.org/10.1016/j.infsof.2018.03.009

Rosenbaum PR (1984) The consequences of adjustment for a concomitant variable that has been affected by the treatment. J R Stat Soc Ser A 147(5):656–666

Rubin DB (1986) Statistical matching using file concatenation with adjusted weights and multiple imputations. J Bus Econ Stat 4:87–94. https://doi.org/10.1080/07350015.1986.10509497

Rubin DB (1987) Multiple imputation for nonresponse in surveys. Wiley, Hoboken

Shanks DR, et al (2013) Priming intelligent behavior: an elusive phenomenon. PLOS One 8(4):1–10. https://doi.org/10.1371/journal.pone.0056515

Shepperd M, Ajienka N, Counsell S (2018) The role and value of replication in empirical software engineering results. Inf Softw Technol 99:120–132. https://doi.org/10.1016/j.infsof.2018.01.006

Simpson DP, Rue H, Martins TG, Riebler A, Sørbye SH (2014) Penalising model component complexity: a principled, practical approach to constructing priors. arXiv:1403.4630

Talts S, Betancourt M, Simpson D, Vehtari A, Gelman A (2018) Validating Bayesian inference algorithms with simulation-based calibration. arXiv:1804.06788

Torkar R, Feldt R, de Oliveira Neto FG, Gren L (2017) Statistical and practical significance of empirical software engineering research: a maturity model. CoRR abs/1706.00933

Trafimow D, Marks M (2015) Editorial. Basic Appl Soc Psychol 37(1):1–2. https://doi.org/10.1080/01973533.2015.1012991

van Buuren S (2007) Multiple imputation of discrete and continuous data by fully conditional specification. Stat Methods Med Res 16(3):219–242. https://doi.org/10.1177/0962280206074463

Vehtari A, Gelman A, Gabry J (2017) Practical Bayesian model evaluation using leave-one-out cross-validation and WAIC. Stat Comput 27:1413–1432. https://doi.org/10.1007/s11222-016-9696-4

Vehtari A, Gelman A, Simpson D, Carpenter B, Bürkner PC (2019) Rank-normalization, folding, and localization: an improved $\widehat{R}$ for assessing convergence of MCMC. arXiv:1903.08008

White IR, Royston P, Wood AM (2011) Multiple imputation using chained equations: issues and guidance for practice. Stat Med 30(4):377–399. https://doi.org/10.1002/sim.4067

Wohlin C, Runeson P, Höst M, Ohlsson MC, Regnell B, Wesslén A (2012) Experimentation in software engineering. Springer, Berlin

Woolston C (2015) Psychology journal bans P values. Nature 519(7541):9. https://doi.org/10.1038/519009f

Yao Y, Vehtari A, Simpson D, Gelman A (2018) Using stacking to average Bayesian predictive distributions (with discussion). Bayesian Anal 13(3):917–1007. https://doi.org/10.1214/17-BA1091

Part III
Knowledge Acquisition and Aggregation

Automating Systematic Literature Review

Katia R. Felizardo and Jeffrey C. Carver

Abstract Systematic literature reviews (SLRs) have become the foundation of evidence-based software engineering (EBSE). Conducting an SLR is largely a manual process. In the past decade, researchers have made major advances in automating the SLR process, aiming to reduce the workload and effort for conducting high-quality SLRs in software engineering (SE). The goal of this chapter is to provide an overview of strategies researchers have developed to automate the SLR process. We used a systematic search methodology to survey the literature about the strategies used to automate the SLR process in SE. Study selection is the most supported activity, while protocol definition, data extraction, and synthesis have only partial support. SE researchers have most frequently explored the visual text mining strategy. Visual text mining is useful from the beginning of the process (formulation of research questions) to the end of the process (extracting and summarizing data). Overall, we recommend that the SE community develop more automated strategies to reduce the manual effort required for SLRs in SE.

1 Introduction

Secondary studies, such as systematic literature reviews (SLRs), systematic mappings (SMs), and rapid reviews (RRs, see chapter "Rapid Reviews in Software Engineering") are beneficial for software engineering (SE) practice and research.

SLRs are one of the key aspects of the evidence-based software engineering (EBSE) paradigm. They play an important role by synthesizing relevant evidence about a topic of interest through transparent, auditable methods. Despite their

K. R. Felizardo (✉)
Federal University of Technology – Paraná (UTFRP), Departament of Computing,
Cornélio Procópio, PR, Brazil
e-mail: katiascannavino@utfpr.edu.br

J. C. Carver
University of Alabama, Department of Computer Science, Tuscaloosa, AL, USA
e-mail: carver@cs.ua.edu

© Springer Nature Switzerland AG 2020
M. Felderer, G. H. Travassos (eds.), *Contemporary Empirical Methods in Software Engineering*, https://doi.org/10.1007/978-3-030-32489-6_12

importance, the process of conducting an SLR is much more labor intensive than a traditional (i.e., non-systematic) narrative literature review.

SE researchers and SLR authors have highlighted a number of challenges with the SLR process. The following list describes some of the most common challenges (Carver et al. 2013; Hassler et al. 2014).

1. **Developing the Protocol** is a non-trivial activity since the authors must make important SLR planning decisions about the review question, selection criteria, search strategy, study selection, data extraction, quality assessment, and data synthesis (Staples and Niazi 2007).
2. **Searching for Evidence** can be difficult due to factors like inadequate search strategy, heterogeneity of SE terminology, and limited range of indexing terms (Brereton et al. 2007; Dybå et al. 2007; Dieste and Padua 2007; Dieste et al. 2009; Zhang and Muhammad 2011; Zhang et al. 2011; Carver et al. 2013; Wohlin 2014; Al-Zubidy et al. 2017; Kitchenham and Brereton 2013; Waiyahong and Reddy 2014; Al-Zubidy and Carver 2019; Sjøberg et al. 2007).
3. **Selecting Relevant Studies** is a difficult activity due to the large number of studies authors must analyze (Engström et al. 2008; Felizardo et al. 2017a).
4. **Extracting Data** is difficult because authors use inconsistent data formats and paper designs (Riaz et al. 2010).
5. **Synthesizing the Evidence** is especially difficult because papers may not provide all the necessary information. In addition, the differences between studies is a source of heterogeneity (Cruzes and Dybå 2010; Felizardo et al. 2011).

In this chapter, we provide an overview of the aspects of the SLR process that lend themselves to automation. Then we compile many published strategies for automating the SE SLR process.

The remainder of this chapter is organized as follows. Section 2 presents the SLR activities that are most amenable to automation. Section 3 describes the various strategies proposed for automating SLR activities. Section 4 provides a discussion of the findings. Section 5 recommends further reading. Section 6 presents the final remarks.

2 SLR Activities Amenable to Automation

Based on our experience and on published literature (Carver et al. 2013; Hassler et al. 2014), in this section we enumerate five SLR activities that have the most potential for automation: Developing the Protocol, Searching for Evidence, Selecting Relevant Studies, Extracting Data, and Synthesizing the Evidence. We organize the following discussion around these five activities.

2.1 Developing the Protocol

Creating the SLR protocol is complex and time-consuming. However, to ensure a high-quality SLR, the authors must perform this step well (Staples and Niazi 2007). The purpose of an SLR is to answer clear and focused research question(s). Therefore, well-formulated research questions are necessary to guide the review process. However, identifying a knowledge gap and translating that knowledge gap into an answerable question is difficult due to increase in volume and availability of scientific information.

Text analysis through the combinations of words within studies has the potential to identify knowledge gaps in collections of scientific studies and help define research questions in a clear, unambiguous manner prior to performing the review (Westgate et al. 2005). Even before developing the protocol, automated support can help researchers find previous SLRs related to the research question, thereby reducing the effort needed to establish whether a previous review exists (Tsafnat et al. 2014). Consequently, text analysis can reduce the number of duplicate SLRs. Even if the text analysis locates an outdated SLR, it would be preferable for a researcher to update that SLR instead of conducting a new SLR.

2.2 Searching for Evidence

Another challenge in conducting a high-quality SLR is performing the search (Zhang and Muhammad 2011). According to Dieste and Padua (2007), because the design and execution of an appropriate and effective search string is critical, the authors must be careful. The primary approach SLR authors use to identify evidence is employing search strings in the various digital libraries (DLs). For this process to be effective, authors must have an adequate method for defining the search strings, which is a time-consuming and error-prone step.

Al-Zubidy and Carver (2019) conducted an SLR of published SLRs and a survey of SLR authors to identify barriers and solutions related to the SLR search process. Based on 84 studies in the literature and 131 survey responses, they identified barriers related to the DLs, automation support, and SLR authors. The barriers specifically related to automation support are prime candidates for additional automation and tools support. These barriers include:

1. **Developing the search string**—Authors also find it difficult to define keywords, their synonyms, and their appropriate combinations for search purposes (Sjøberg et al. 2007; Carver et al. 2013; Frantzi et al. 2000; Wohlin 2014). One reason for this difficulty is the lack of standardized terminology within SE (Wohlin 2014). Therefore providing support for defining appropriate search strings could be of great benefit to SLR authors by reducing the time required for this step. Construction of the entire search string is also an option for automation. Having

defined the main terms, they could be automatically merged with an AND and synonyms could be merged with an OR.

2. **Converting the search string to the appropriate format(s) for each DL—** DLs do not provide adequate support for the type of automated search required for SLRs, i.e., the same search string does not work in all DLs without some sort of modification (Brereton et al. 2007; Dybå et al. 2007; Dieste et al. 2009; Zhang and Muhammad 2011; Zhang et al. 2011; Al-Zubidy et al. 2017; Kitchenham and Brereton 2013). Therefore, authors must modify the search string manually to obtain valid results in each of the DLs used.

3. **Importing/exporting studies in a standardized format—**Data standardization is currently a significant topic for information retrieval systems and for DLs, primarily, when used by SLR researchers to gather data from different sources. The data standardization processes aim to improve information retrieval, prevent loss of data, and provide non-duplicated data (Waiyahong and Reddy 2014).

2.3 Selecting Relevant Studies

After conducting the search, the next challenge is selecting the studies most relevant to the research questions. As reported by Felizardo et al. (2017a), the number of studies that included SLRs in the area of SE varies widely. In fact, it is possible to find SLRs that analyze tens of studies up to those that analyze thousands of studies. Working through these studies, especially when there are a very large number of them, requires significant effort from the SLR author(s). In addition, many of the studies returned by the search process are irrelevant to the underlying research question, resulting in additional wasted effort (Engström et al. 2008).

Automated support for study selection can assist by reducing the number of papers the author(s) must read, by acting as a second "reader," by increasing the speed of selection, and prioritizing which papers the author(s) should read (O'Mara-Eves et al. 2015).

2.4 Extracting Data

Extracting useful data from a collection of studies is one of the most challenging SLR activities. SLR authors have to examine each study to identify the information relevant to the research question(s). Therefore, automation of this activity can save a large amount of time. However, Jonnalagadda et al. (2015) performed an SLR to identify tools related to automating SLR data extraction. They concluded that creating a universal automatic data extraction tool is not feasible. The solution is to automatically retrieve data in specific scientific areas.

Among the many difficulties faced by automation are enormous diversity of studies, vast amount of different data, each scientific field and each research group might have its own vocabulary, and similar research goals and outcomes can be described in different ways. Moreover, because SLRs and other secondary studies are a recent practice in SE, authors of earlier papers did not write with these types of studies in mind. Therefore, a large number of SE papers (at least until recently) do not follow the type of standard structure that helps SLR authors extract appropriate information.

For a more complete discussion about threats to validity in SLR, please see chapter "Guidelines for Managing Threats to Validity of Secondary Studies in Software Engineering".

2.5 Synthesizing the Evidence

Because the overall goal of an SLR is to synthesize information presented in a disparate set of studies and present the findings to the reader in an easily understandable fashion, this step is critical to the success of an SLR. If studies are very heterogeneous it may be most appropriate to summarize the data in a narrative fashion. However, when studies refer to similar data, a statistical/graphical summary might be more appropriate.

Cruzes and Dybå (2010) found that SLR authors often report their findings in large tables containing data from individual studies (e.g., title, authors, year, outline, strengths). This type of reporting is not as useful as a tabular synthesis or other visual representations that help make the overall findings more understandable. The results of an experiment by Felizardo et al. (2011) showed SLR experts and students were able to understand SLR findings presented in graphical or tabular form with less time and the same accuracy compared with other presentations of the results. However, the process of manually producing tables and graphs could greatly benefit from automation to reduce the required amount of manual work.

Some tools that are not specific to SLRs may support the synthesis activity. For example, NVivo may produce tabulations and graphs from qualitative analysis applied to the studies.

For more information about evidence aggregation in SE, please see chapter "Research Synthesis in Software Engineering".

3 Strategies for Automating SLR Activities

This section provides an overview of some of the automation strategies proposed for the five activities described in Sect. 2.

3.1 Systematic Literature Search

We conducted a systematic search by using backward and forward snowballing to identify the current literature on SLR automation in SE. Our first step was to develop a list of relevant studies, based on our experience researching SLRs, as our starting set. We began with a list of 19 studies with which we were already familiar (Abilio et al. 2014; Felizardo et al. 2010, 2012b, 2014a, 2017b; Feng et al. 2017a; Ghafari et al. 2012; Laghrabli et al. 2015; Mergel et al. 2015; Muñoz Caro et al. 2017; Neto et al. 2000; Octaviano et al. 2016; Osborne 2018; Rasmus et al. 2017; Santos 2018; Silva 2009; Singh et al. 2018; Souza et al. 2017; Torres et al. 2012; Yu and Menzies 2019).

We applied both backward and forward snowballing to each of these 19 studies.

We performed three iterations looking at the references and citations. We extracted the citations with the help of search engines, such as Google Scholar. Table 1 details these three iterations.

The inclusion and exclusion criteria were:

(IC1) The study must be within SE **AND**
(IC2) The study must discuss a strategy for the SLR automation.

(EC1) The study is only an abstract **OR**
(EC2) The study is an older version of other study already considered **OR**.

Table 2 summarizes the results of the process and includes the references for all included studies.

Table 1 Set of included/excluded studies using backward and forward snowballing

Strategy	Round	Included	Excluded
Backward	Round 1	3 studies (Ramampiaro et al. 2010; Tomassetti et al. 2011; Fabbri et al. 2012)	583 studies
Backward	Round 2	1 study (Sun et al. 2012)	95 studies
Backward	Round 3	0	135 studies
Forward	Round 1	2 studies (Aliyu et al. 2018; Götz 2018)	45 studies
Forward	Round 2	4 studies (Abilio et al. 2014; Feng et al. 2017b; Shakeel et al. 2018; Pulsiri and Vatananan-Thesenvitz 2018)	5 studies
Forward	Round 3	0	5 studies
Total	3 rounds	10 studies	868 studies

Table 2 Snowballing rounds and their respective seed set

Round	Seed set
Round 1	19 studies (Feng et al. 2017a; Mergel et al. 2015; Souza et al. 2017; Rasmus et al. 2017; Ghafari et al. 2012; Felizardo et al. 2010, 2012b, 2014a, 2017b; Octaviano et al. 2016; Yu and Menzies 2019; Muñoz Caro et al. 2017; Singh et al. 2018; Osborne 2018; Santos 2018; Neto et al. 2000; Torres et al. 2012; Silva 2009; Laghrabli et al. 2015)
Round 2	5 studies (Ramampiaro et al. 2010; Tomassetti et al. 2011; Fabbri et al. 2012; Aliyu et al. 2018; Götz 2018)
Round 3	5 studies (Abilio et al. 2014; Feng et al. 2017b; Shakeel et al. 2018; Pulsiri and Vatananan-Thesenvitz 2018; Sun et al. 2012)

In summary, during the first round we found 47 studies that cited at least one of the 19 studies from the original seed set. These studies were candidates for inclusion. After we applied the selection criteria, only two of these 47 remained (Aliyu et al. 2018; Götz 2018). In addition, the 19 studies in the seed set referenced a total of 583 studies. After applying the inclusion criteria, we included only three of them (Fabbri et al. 2012; Ramampiaro et al. 2010; Tomassetti et al. 2011).

In Round 2, we started with the five studies identified in Round 1 (Aliyu et al. 2018; Fabbri et al. 2012; Götz 2018; Ramampiaro et al. 2010; Tomassetti et al. 2011). We found nine studies that cited at least one of these five and included four of them (Abilio et al. 2014; Feng et al. 2017b; Pulsiri and Vatananan-Thesenvitz 2018; Shakeel et al. 2018). In addition, the five studies referenced 95 studies. We included only one of these studies.

In Round 3, we found five studies that cited at least one of the studies identified in Round 2. We did not include any of them. In addition, the studies in Round 2 cited 135 other studies. None of these were relevant.

Therefore, because we found no additional studies in Round 3, we stopped the snowballing process. These three iterations resulted in a total of ten new studies (Aliyu et al. 2018; Abilio et al. 2014; Fabbri et al. 2012; Feng et al. 2017b; Götz 2018; Pulsiri and Vatananan-Thesenvitz 2018; Ramampiaro et al. 2010; Shakeel et al. 2018; Sun et al. 2012; Tomassetti et al. 2011).

In the next sections, we discuss the strategies obtained in our systematic search and how they can support SLR activities.

3.2 Developing the Protocol

The existing automation support in this area is based on visual text mining (VTM) and focuses on identifying the most appropriate research questions.

Visual Text Mining The SLR Planning Based on Suffix Tree Clustering (*SLRP-STC*) is a VTM strategy designed to identify common phrases in a collection of studies and use these phrases as the basis for creating clusters (Feng et al. 2017a). *SLRP-STC* supports decision-making activities within the SLR planning phase, such as specifying research topics.

VTM makes use of the strong visual processing abilities possessed by humans to support knowledge discovery. VTM is an extension of text mining (TM), a practice commonly used to extract patterns and non-trivial knowledge from natural language textual documents. VTM combines mining algorithms with information visualization techniques to support visualization and interactive data exploration.

The four strategies that are part of the *SLRP-STC* are (1) retrieve web studies, (2) clean irrelevant information, e.g., stopwords (the most common words in a language such as "the"), (3) identify phrases, and (4) provide a visual representation (cluster) of the relevant information extracted and analyzed from the web studies.

VTM groups the retrieved studies into clusters. It uses the classification of topics (e.g., "Tool, support") to suggest topics for research questions.

A difference between the *SLRP-STC* and other typical VTM strategies is that *SLRP-STC* retrieves online studies and clusters web search results, whereas typical strategies use off-line studies collection that has standardized format.

3.3 Searching for Evidence

Relative to the search phase, we identified two types of automation: (1) automation to help in search string generation (Mergel et al. 2015; Rasmus et al. 2017; Souza et al. 2017) and (2) automation to help during search execution (Ghafari et al. 2012; Lausberger 2017). The sections below provide information about these types of automation.

3.3.1 Visual Text Mining

VTM can also be applied to iteratively elaborate a search string by suggesting new terms (Mergel et al. 2015). Initially, VTM extracts and recommends relevant terms based on a collection of studies returned from using a preliminary search string. Then, the researcher can refine the string by inserting the suggested terms and re-running the process until the search string is suitable. The two main limitations of this approach are that it works only on IEEE Xplore and only on abstracts.

3.3.2 Artificial Intelligence (AI)

Similar to TM/VTM strategies, AI also enables the creation and calibration of search strings (Souza et al. 2017). The hill climbing (HC) algorithm runs as follows (Souza et al. 2017): a user provides a set of parameters including, terms, synonyms, number of iterations, and a list of control studies (studies that must be retrieved when searching in a given DL) to the HC algorithm to create an initial search string. From the initial search string the HC algorithm generates a set of neighbor search strings. The neighbor strings are similar to initial string with small changes in each part of the string, e.g., addition or removal of terms/synonyms previously defined by the user. If a neighbor string is better in terms of sensibility and precision (considering the control group) than the initial string, then the HC algorithm selects this new neighbor string and the process restarts interactively until the HC algorithm reaches the specified number of iterations. Generally, SLR researchers use at least three DLs as sources for primary studies in their SLRs. However, this AI strategy uses only IEEE Xplore as source (Souza et al. 2017).

3.3.3 Machine Learning

Machine learning is a strategy that semi-automates both search and selection, provides cost savings, and allows for replicability (Rasmus et al. 2017). The main goal of machine learning is to use statistical inference to learn which studies are relevant. The input to the process is a set of included and excluded studies to train a classifier. The algorithm then extends this set of studies by automated searching and snowballing. The algorithm generates the search string using a data-driven approach based on terms from title, abstract, and keyword of the currently accepted papers. The algorithm executes the string in the Scopus library and automatically downloads only the metadata. Then, the algorithm performs snowballing. Scopus has tool support for backwards snowballing. Then, the algorithm marks the results as included or excluded through the classifier. Finally, the researcher validates the classification. This validation is added to the training set for the classifier and the process is used interactively and iteratively. A weakness of this strategy is that the search string is kept fixed once the selection phase is started. Moreover, the validation is a proof of concept and uses only Scopus.

Once the authors have a search string, they can use a tool created by Ghafari et al. (2012) that unifies the search across best-known DLs in SE or a tool by Lausberger (2017) to automatically adapt search terms to different DLs during search execution. Study results show the strategy by Ghafari et al. decreased search time and increased the readability of the results compared with a manual strategy. In both cases, the SLR author still has to provide the tool with a search string to execute.

Feng et al. (2017a) also provide a unified search tool for DLs, including IEEE Xplore, the ACM Digital Library, the Web of Science, Science Direct, Scopus, and Google Scholar. However, due to the limited access to the full text of studies, the tool only retrieves title, keywords, and abstract.

3.4 Selecting Relevant Studies

Our review of the literature identified a number of automated strategies for selecting relevant studies. We group these strategies into four categories as follows.

3.4.1 Text Mining/Visual Text Mining

TM helps filter relevant studies during the first stage of selection (reading abstracts), thereby reducing the set of studies that researchers must examine in the final selection (full text). Initially, researchers indicate the most well-known and fundamental studies on the chosen topic. Then, TM identifies studies with similar content and studies that have conceptual relations to the content expressed in the already selected papers. The main advantage of this strategy is the reduction of workload to classify studies, without losing any relevant studies. The reduced workload allows researchers to manage large collection of studies. However, it is important to conduct a wider empirical validation of this strategy (Tomassetti et al. 2011).

Using VTM it is possible to generate two visualizations of the primary studies to support the selection activity: content-maps and edge bundles. *Content-maps* organize documents into clusters based on the similarity of their content. By placing similar documents physically close to each other in the visualization, this strategy helps authors identify those studies that are similar and extract appropriate information from them. *Edge bundle* is a hierarchical tree visualization containing nodes and links (i.e., relationships between nodes). Nodes represent primary studies with links representing the relationships between the primary studies.

VTM strategies can facilitate a researcher's exploration, interpretation, and decision-making about a large set of primary studies (Felizardo et al. 2010, 2012b; Octaviano et al. 2016; Malheiros et al. 2007). VTM strategies minimize efforts, accelerate the selection process, and allow authors to be more comprehensive in the selection process. Because VTM supports a larger search space, it reduces the chances of authors missing a relevant study.

Building on this initial work, Felizardo et al. (2014a) evaluated the effectiveness of the VTM strategy. The study found VTMs give solid clues about which studies the author(s) should review closely, reducing the overall number of studies manually evaluated and the total time required. They also evaluated how well such a strategy supported the evolution of SLRs through adding new evidence. The strategy increases the number of correctly chosen studies. Overall, VTM strategies improve the performance and accuracy of study selection during the update of SLRs.

One limitation of VTM approaches is that, although scalability is feasible, they have only been tested on small datasets (containing at most 261 studies). Introducing VTM in the SLR process requires additional knowledge about the visual tools.

3.4.2 Sampling

Sampling strategies save time by presenting the SLR author(s) with a subset of the studies for manual analysis. We found two strategies that used sampling:

- Using bibliometric approximation, Muñoz Caro et al. (2017) determine the sample size needed to attain a confidence level of 95% with a confidence interval of 10%. They reduced a large set of primary studies (4846) to a representative sample of 94 studies that had to be manually reviewed while still maintaining a confidence level of 95%. The 94 studies were randomly chosen from the retrieved studies.
- While conducting a tertiary study, Singh et al. (2018) ranked the distribution of the retrieved studies across DLs and then used random sampling based on this ranking to identify a sample of studies. For example, if 30% of the retrieved studies were from IEEE Xplore, then the expected percentage of studies from IEEE Xplore in the sample is 30%.

The key difficulty in using sample strategies is to allow repeatability.

3.4.3 Machine Learning

Researchers have also used both unsupervised learning (K-means) (Xiong et al. 2018) and semi-supervised learning (Timsina et al. 2016) to identify and classify relevant studies. Researchers have also shown that use of different classification models and features sets can work well with human decisions in the selection process (Bannach-Brown et al. 2019).

One specific machine learning strategy, *FASTREAD* has shown promising results. *FASTREAD* combines and parameterizes the most efficient active learning algorithms to support study selection when there are a large number of candidate studies. Results show that *FASTREAD* can find results while reviewing 20–50% fewer studies than other strategies (Yu and Menzies 2019). An automated assistant to this strategy, called *FAST*, helps further minimize researcher efforts by using keywords to identify and rank relevant studies. *FAST* helps reduce research effort by 20% (Yu and Menzies 2019). A positive aspect of *FASTREAD* is that it was validated using SE SLRs. Problems including how to assign selection task to multiple reviewers will be explored in the future. Novel methods should also be explored for parameter selection.

3.4.4 Other

We identified a few other strategies in the literature for supporting the study selection process.

- Expert-Driven Automatic Methodology *(EDAM)*, which generates an ontology using candidate studies and then classifies studies using that ontology, allowed researchers to spend their effort on analysis and discussion rather than on classification (Osborne 2018). The main advantage of EDAM is it infers the domain ontology using the set of retrieved studies, reflecting the real trends of the studies and avoiding arbitrary reviewers' decisions about keywords used to cluster similar studies. The ontology is structured hierarchically; however, subareas (e.g., software requirements, software quality, etc.) are subsumed by previous area at the upper level of the taxonomy (e.g., SE). Deeper hierarchies could allow a finer-grained ontology providing a higher precision in the clustering process.
- Concept Maps, which summarize a complex structure of textual information, help researchers identify the most relevant studies (Felizardo et al. 2017b; Santos 2018). The use of CM presents numerous advantages. They have a flexible structure and are easy to understand, allow for knowledge sharing and there is a large diversity of subareas of computer science in which CMs can be applied, including SE. However, the most important limitation in the use of CM is its scalability, i.e., how to scale a CM to thousands of nodes. A representation of a CM can lose its utility when the amount of information increases and the high number of concepts and cross-links between concepts makes it difficult to understand the represented knowledge. This strategy can be supported with natural language processing to reduce the effort required (Santos 2018).
- Another strategy is to rank studies in decreasing order of importance for an SLR with respect to the terms in the search string. The presence of a term in the title of the study has more weight than its presence in keywords. As a result, the most relevant studies appear earlier in the list. Although the strategy does not indicate a percentage of studies considered relevant, in the case study performed, relevant studies were ranked between 15% and 20% of the top ranking studies. Further validation is required to confirm the initial results (Abilio et al. 2014).

Table 3 summarizes the strategies previously described addressing study selection automation.

3.5 Extracting Data

We identified three strategies to automatically extract information from studies.

Table 3 Studies addressing study selection automation in SE

Strategy	Purpose (P)	References
VTM	P1[a]; P2[b]; P3[c]	Felizardo et al. (2010, 2012b, 2014b), Malheiros et al. (2007), Octaviano et al. (2016)
VTM	P1[a]; P2[b]	Felizardo et al. (2014a)
TM	P1[a]; P3[c]	Tomassetti et al. (2011)
Sampling	P1[a]; P4[d]	Muñoz Caro et al. (2017), Singh et al. (2018)
Machine learning (FASTREAD)	P1[a]; P4[d]	Yu and Menzies (2019)
Semi-supervised learning	P1[a]; P3[c]	Timsina et al. (2016)
Ontology (EDAM)	P1[a]; P3[c]	Osborne (2018)
Concept map	P1[a]	Felizardo et al. (2017b), Santos (2018)
Ranking	P3[c]	Abilio et al. (2014)

[a]P1: Increase the speed of selection
[b]P2: Be a second screener
[c]P3: Prioritize the list of studies for manual reading
[d]P4: Reduce number needed to read

3.5.1 Extractive Text Summarization

An extractive text summarization strategy partitions a document into a set of topics and then chooses the most relevant sentences for each topic (Neto et al. 2000). The TextTiling algorithm (Hearst 1993) is used for partitioning documents into topics. Term frequency–inverse sentence frequency (TF–ISF) (Neto et al. 2000) is the metric that classifies the relevance of each topic. The number of sentences selected from each topic is proportional to the relative importance of the topic within the document. The size of the summary is flexible, defined by the researcher. Using human judgement, the quality of three out of seven summaries created was considered as satisfactory in terms of capturing of the main ideas and understandability for researchers who did not read the full text. The results obtained are encouraging; however, there is a need for more tests to obtain more consistent results.

Another strategy, developed by Torres et al. (2012), has as its main objective to locate sentences that specifically represent study results. Initially, the strategy converts the papers into a plain text format and removes undesirable characters. Then it extracts pieces of text (sentences) that represent the results of the scientific papers. Next, it represents each sentence as attribute vector of features. Text classification strategies use a number of predefined features of importance, including keyword frequency, sentence length, paragraph and section positions, and the lexical connectivity (number of words shared between the sentences), to automatically infer the category of the sentences. Rule-based and machine learning algorithms then select the best sentences. While the performance on unstructured text, as found in research papers, was lower than on more structured texts, the result was still promising. For example, this strategy can reduce the text to be analyzed to 1/5 of the original size, decreasing the effort required to perform the data extraction activity.

3.5.2 Regular Expressions

This strategy uses a template that characterizes experimental studies in SE and uses regular expression rules to extract the template information directly from the studies (Silva 2009). While regular expressions are useful for extracting information, they have the following limitations: a limited number of extraction rules and case sensitivity.

3.5.3 Text Mining and Machine Learning

TM and machine learning identify section headings (i.e., paper structure) from research studies. This approach uses a statistical analysis of the most frequent words/phrases in the section headings to build the structure, which guides subsequent automatic extraction of data. This approach achieved an accuracy of 82%. From 1000 studies analyzed, the strategy correctly identified the section headings and their associated text in 820 documents. Obviously not all the papers will conform exactly to the structure, but researchers are developing appropriate techniques to deal with this problem (Aliyu et al. 2018).

3.6 Synthesizing the Evidence

We found the following strategies for automated support for the synthesis process.

3.6.1 Visual Text Mining

VTM, discussed earlier, can also support the categorization and classification of studies in a systematic mapping (SM). This strategy creates two visualizations: (1) a cluster view and (2) a chronological view. A cluster view presents a set of clusters and related topics. Each cluster contains a subset of studies and topics that form the basis for category definition. By analyzing the topics in a cluster, VTM suggests terms for the subset of studies in that cluster. This view makes it possible to identify evidence gaps clearly (i.e., clusters with low concentration of primary studies) and evidence groups (i.e., clusters with high concentration of primary studies). A chronological view gives a visual representation of the studies based on their publication year. This representation makes it possible to identify how much the topic of interest has been investigated throughout the years. A case study has shown that VTM reduces effort for categorizing and classifying studies (Felizardo et al. 2010), but there is a need for more studies to confirm these findings.

3.6.2 Association Rules

Laghrabli et al. (2015) developed a strategy for extracting multiple patterns using association rules analysis. Its goal is to generate relationships, associations, correlations, or frequent patterns among the attributes of a collection of studies (included studies in an SLR). Using the rules extracted, researchers can draw conclusions, e.g., whether there are strong relationships between the methods, algorithms, etc., under analysis. However, a large collection of studies is necessary for extracting interesting and reliable rules. Laghrabli et al. (2015) selected 35 studies for their illustrative example, but there is a need for a larger sample.

Tables 4, 5, and 6 summarize the strategies previously presented as well as their strengths and weaknesses.

Table 4 Strategies supporting SLR activities in SE

Strategy	Activities supported
Visual text mining	Definition of research questions (Feng et al. 2017a)
	Generation of search string (Mergel et al. 2015)
	Images to select studies (Adeva et al. 2014; Felizardo et al. 2012b, 2014a; Octaviano et al. 2016)
	Creation of initial categories for SM (Felizardo et al. 2010)
Artificial intelligence (AI)	Generation of search string (Souza et al. 2017)
Text mining	Recommendation of studies (Tomassetti et al. 2011)
	Data extraction (Aliyu et al. 2018)
Machine learning	Recommendation of studies (Yu and Menzies 2019)
	Data extraction (Aliyu et al. 2018)
Sampling	Definition of studies sample (Muñoz Caro et al. 2017; Singh et al. 2018)
Ontology	Selection of studies (Osborne 2018)
Concept map (CM)	Selection of studies (Felizardo et al. 2017b; Santos 2018)
Ranking	Selection of studies (Abilio et al. 2014)
Extractive text summarization	Summarization of topics (Neto et al. 2000; Torres et al. 2012)
Regular expressions	Summarization of topics (Silva 2009)
Association rules	Relationships between methods (Laghrabli et al. 2015)

Table 5 Strategies supporting SLR activities in SE: Strengths

Strategy	Strengths
Definition of research questions (Feng et al. 2017a)	Identify topics of research
	Retrieve online studies
	Clustering web search results
Generation of search string (Mergel et al. 2015; Souza et al. 2017; Rasmus et al. 2017)	Suggest new terms
	Extract the most significant terms
	Interactive and iterative process
	Consider a collection of studies
Unification of the search (Ghafari et al. 2012; Lausberger 2017)	Adapt search terms to different DLs
Images to select studies (Felizardo et al. 2010, 2012b, 2014a; Octaviano et al. 2016)	Avoid the missing of a relevant study
	Reduction of studies manually evaluated
	Reduction of the time to select studies
	Support the evolution of SLRs
Recommendation of studies (Yu and Menzies 2019; Abilio et al. 2014; Tomassetti et al. 2011)	Reduction of the burden of study selection (Yu and Menzies 2019; Tomassetti et al. 2011)
	Identify and rank relevant studies (Yu and Menzies 2019; Abilio et al. 2014)
	Management of large collection of studies (Tomassetti et al. 2011)
Definition of studies sample (Muñoz Caro et al. 2017; Singh et al. 2018)	Reduction of studies manually evaluated
Selection of studies (Osborne 2018; Felizardo et al. 2017b; Santos 2018)	Flexible structure (Felizardo et al. 2017b; Santos 2018)
	Knowledge sharing (Felizardo et al. 2017b; Santos 2018)
	Applicable in SE area (Felizardo et al. 2017b; Santos 2018)
	Domain is automatically inferred (Osborne 2018)
Extraction of data (Aliyu et al. 2018)	Automatic extraction of data using a structure
Creation of initial categories for SM (Felizardo et al. 2010)	Reduction of effort
	Topics "translate" the content of the studies
Relationships between methods (Laghrabli et al. 2015)	Extraction of multiple patterns
Summarization of topics (Neto et al. 2000; Torres et al. 2012; Silva 2009)	The number of sentences is proportional to the importance of the topic (Neto et al. 2000)
	Summary size defined by user (Neto et al. 2000)
	Reduction of the text to 1/5 (Torres et al. 2012)
	Useful in extracting information (Silva 2009)

Table 6 Strategies supporting SLR activities in SE: Weaknesses

Strategy	Weaknesses
Definition of research questions (Feng et al. 2017a)	Extraction based on metadata
Generation of search string (Mergel et al. 2015; Souza et al. 2017; Rasmus et al. 2017)	Extraction based on metadata
	Validated in only one DL
	Synonyms are not considered
Unification of the search (Ghafari et al. 2012; Lausberger 2017)	Need of a search string to execute
Images to select studies (Felizardo et al. 2010, 2012b, 2014a; Octaviano et al. 2016)	Validated on small datasets
	Additional knowledge on visual tools
Recommendation of studies (Abilio et al. 2014; Yu and Menzies 2019)	Restricted to having only one reviewer (Yu and Menzies 2019)
	Parameters are arbitrarily chosen (Yu and Menzies 2019)
	Wider empirical validation is needed (Abilio et al. 2014; Tomassetti et al. 2011)
Definition of studies sample (Muñoz Caro et al. 2017; Singh et al. 2018)	No repeatability of sample (random)
Selection of studies (Osborne 2018; Felizardo et al. 2017b; Santos 2018)	Scalability (Felizardo et al. 2017b; Santos 2018)
	Ontology-hierarchy refinement (Osborne 2018)
Extraction of data (Aliyu et al. 2018)	Not all the papers match to the structure
Creation of initial categories for SM (Felizardo et al. 2010)	Wider empirical validation is needed
Relationships between methods (Laghrabli et al. 2015)	>35 studies are necessary
Summarization of topics (Neto et al. 2000; Torres et al. 2012; Silva 2009)	Wider empirical validation is needed (Neto et al. 2000; Torres et al. 2012)
	Limited number of extraction rules (Silva 2009)
	Regular expressions are case sensitive (Silva 2009)

4 Discussion

Overall, we found encouraging results that researchers are investing more effort into the development of automated strategies to support the SLR process. Table 7 provides a summary of the strategies previously described in Sect. 3. An analysis of the strategies shows that some activities have full automation support (e.g., study selection), while others have only partial support (e.g., protocol definition, data extraction, and synthesis). In fact, other studies have found many SLRs

Table 7 SLR process automation in SE

SLR phase	Automated support
Planning—protocol definition	
Definition of research questions	Feng et al. (2017a)
Generation of search string	Mergel et al. (2015), Souza et al. (2017), Rasmus et al. (2017)
Execution—searching for evidence	
Unification of the search	Ghafari et al. (2012), Lausberger (2017)
Execution—selecting relevant studies	
Images to select studies	Felizardo et al. (2010, 2012b, 2014a), Octaviano et al. (2016)
Recommendation of studies	Yu and Menzies (2019), Tomassetti et al. (2011)
Definition of studies sample	Muñoz Caro et al. (2017), Singh et al. (2018)
Selection of studies	Osborne (2018), Felizardo et al. (2017b), Santos (2018), Abilio et al. (2014)
Execution—extracting data	
Summarization of topics	Neto et al. (2000), Torres et al. (2012), Silva (2009)
Data extraction	Aliyu et al. (2018)
Execution—synthesizing the evidence	
Creation of initial categories for SM	Felizardo et al. (2010)
Relationships between methods	Laghrabli et al. (2015)

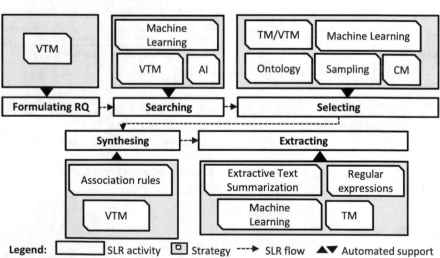

Fig. 1 Visual summary of strategies supporting SLR activities in SE

lack appropriate synthesis (Cruzes and Dybå 2010), perhaps due to the lack of automation support.

As demonstrated in Fig. 1, among the strategies previously presented, VTM is the most used to reduce the amount of time required for conducting an SLR (Feng

Table 8 Strategies validation maturity level in SE

Type of validation	References
Case study	Abilio et al. (2014), Aliyu et al. (2018), Feng et al. (2017a), Ghafari et al. (2012), Lausberger (2017), Felizardo et al. (2010, 2012b, 2014a, 2017b), Octaviano et al. (2016), Yu and Menzies (2019), Muñoz Caro et al. (2017), Osborne (2018), Santos (2018), Neto et al. (2000), Torres et al. (2012), Silva (2009), Laghrabli et al. (2015)
Preliminary study	Mergel et al. (2015)
Controlled experiment	Souza et al. (2017)
Proof of concept	Rasmus et al. (2017)
Preliminary analysis	Singh et al. (2018)

et al. 2017b). VTM is a strategy especially explored in the SE community to support the formulation of research questions (Feng et al. 2017a), searching (Mergel et al. 2015), selection of studies (Adeva et al. 2014; Felizardo et al. 2012b, 2014a; Octaviano et al. 2016), and synthesis (Felizardo et al. 2010).

Table 8 shows that the majority of strategies have only preliminary evaluations. Often the studies describe examples of the strategy in use or a small case study. Moreover, we found several limitations in the presented validations, such as the papers do not compare the strategies to other strategies published in the literature, there is no standard dataset used to validate the different strategies, and usually validation of search strategies occurs in a reduced number of sources (IEEE Xplore or Scopus). Despite the various initiatives, SLR automation is an immature research area and more validation work is essential to determine the value of "new" strategies to automate the SLR process. In addition, researchers need to perform more large-scale case studies to validate the strategies. As a summary, Table 9 highlights both the current research and the open challenges (Shakeel et al. 2018; Pulsiri and Vatananan-Thesenvitz 2018) as inspiration for future work on SLR automation.

4.1 Research Question Identification and Prioritization

Because the unexplored space for SLRs in SE is quite large, researchers may struggle to choose the "best" RQs around which to focus their SLR. New algorithms could help prioritize potential research questions based on various factors such as which ones have greater relevance to a specific area of research or which have most value to industry. Similarly, automated tools could help researchers determine when the RQ chosen for an SLR duplicates, or largely duplicates, questions already covered in an existing SLR. While there are search strings specifically designed to

Table 9 Existing strategies for SLR in SE and future research

Activity description	Current	Future research	References
Definition of research questions (RQs)			
Definition of research questions	•		Feng et al. (2017a)
Research question identification		•	
Research question prioritization		•	
Searching for evidence			
Generation of search string	•		Mergel et al. (2015), Souza et al. (2017), Rasmus et al. (2017)
Unification of the search	•		Ghafari et al. (2012), Lausberger (2017), Ramampiaro et al. (2010)
Customization of search strings for DLs		•	
Validating search string for each DL		•	
Reporting limitations from search		•	
Extracting references for snowballing		•	
Selecting relevant studies			
Images to select studies	•		Felizardo et al. (2010, 2012b, 2014a), Octaviano et al. (2016)
Recommendation of studies	•		Yu and Menzies (2019), Tomassetti et al. (2011)
Definition of studies sample	•		Muñoz Caro et al. (2017), Singh et al. (2018)
Selection of studies	•		Osborne (2018), Felizardo et al. (2017b), Santos (2018), Abilio et al. (2014)
Refining selection criteria		•	
Extracting data			
Summarization of topics	•		Neto et al. (2000), Torres et al. (2012), Silva (2009)
Data extraction	•		Aliyu et al. (2018)
Data standardization		•	
Resolving divergence of extracted data		•	
Synthesizing the evidence			
Creation of initial categories for SM	•		Felizardo et al. (2010)
Revelation of relationships	•		Laghrabli et al. (2015)
General			
Validation of automation		•	
"Plug and Play" tools		•	

find SLRs (Napoleão et al. 2019), currently, the process of identifying related SLRs and RQs is not trivial. A researcher may follow published guidelines (Mendes et al. 2019) to decide whether it is more preferable to update an existing SLR rather than conduct a new one.

4.2   Automated Searching

As a key starting point in identifying the right set of studies, the SE community needs tools to support integrated search in the DLs (Al-Zubidy and Carver 2019; Marshall et al. 2014; Ramampiaro et al. 2010). There are still a number of inconsistencies in the automated search features of the most commonly used DLSs (Singh et al. 2018), including: (1) definition and customization of search strings for each DL, (2) learning the expected behavior of each DL, (3) validating the search strings defined for each DL, and (4) reporting the validity threats and limitations that arise from the search process. In general, there is still expectations that a researcher manually develops a complete search string for each DL.

DLs (IEEE Xplore, ACM DL, etc.) are more prone to provide mechanisms to search and export papers (e.g., web services) than are Search Engines (Scopus, Google Scholar, etc.). In Search Engines researchers have to implement the search through precarious web scraping techniques. This lack of export functionality is an important discussion to be raised by the SE community in order to request changes in DLs/Search Engineers policies.

4.3   Snowballing

Although use of automatic search is the recommended strategy for identifying studies in an SLR (Webster and Watson 2002), snowballing can also prove useful in some cases. There are two types of snowballing: backward snowballing and forward snowballing. In either case, researchers first identify a set of relevant studies (the seed set). Then, for backward snowballing, they examine each of the references included in the studies in the seed set looking for other relevant studies. For forward snowballing, researchers examine the papers that cite the ones included in the seed set. In either case, when a research identifies a paper that is relevant to the SLR, the researcher adds that paper to the seed set and continues with forward or backward snowballing until she/he finds no more new references. Performing snowballing manually is a tedious and time-consuming process. This task seems amenable to tool support, at least in terms of automatically extracting references, if not helping to determine the relevancy of those references.

4.4   Data Standardization

DLs and tools have different data formats. It is often difficult to integrate the metadata from the various DLs (Shakeel et al. 2018) or the results from different tools. Data standardization can help researchers take advantage of the strengths of various tools and facilitate collaboration. As of this writing, we are not aware of any efforts to standardize SLR data in SE.

4.5   Automated Data Extraction

Fully automated data extraction is challenging due to different ways to report numerical results (e.g., tables or graphs), restricted full text access, and lack of information provided by study authors. Another challenge is obtaining high-quality, accurate extracted data. In most cases, two researchers perform data extraction independently and resolve conflicts. Tool support could be helpful to identify disagreements, serve as an arbiter on disagreements, or even take the place of one of the human reviewers (Marshall et al. 2018).

4.6   Refining the Inclusion/Exclusion Criteria

Researchers initially define inclusion and exclusion criteria during the SLR planning phase. However, because study selection is an iterative process (Zhang and Muhammad 2011), these criteria may need refinement. Automated text mining tools could help by extracting terms from candidate studies that could be useful in refining the criteria while performing SLR.

4.7   Validation of Automation

With all of the existing strategies, and any new ones developed, there is still a need for solid validation. Researchers need to ensure that the strategies are providing valid results and are actually saving effort. The evaluation can use various metrics including: workload savings, ease of use, precision, and recall.

4.8   Development of an International Collaboration

Up until now, much of the effort towards developing automated tools for SE SLRs has been performed disjointedly in various research groups around the world. Due to the independent nature of these efforts, the SE community has not had the full benefit of the work. A lack of agreement on the technical standards or data exchange rules among these tools prevents their full integration.

We would like to see greater co-operation among the different efforts along with agreed-upon standards to enable "plug and play" standardization among different tools. We propose that it would be beneficial if we could combine the strengths of existing tools (Marshall et al. 2014, 2018) and integrate them into the activities of the SLR process. For this proposal to work, these tools will have to work together and be able to exchange data/results.

Even with all these tools (properly integrated), human effort is still essential to a successful SLR. Human effort is required for various activities in specific SLRs and for providing data to "train" tools which can then automate (or semi-automate) activities of the SLR process. Thus, tools and automation must operate in a mutually beneficial manner (Thomas et al. 2017).

5   Recommended Further Reading

Researchers can save much effort and resources through partial and complete automation of SLR activities. Based on our analysis in this chapter, this section highlights some of the references on automated tools for SLR activities.

Table 10 provides a list of some existing tools (Marshall et al. 2014, 2018; Al-Zubidy and Carver 2014).

The Systematic Review Toolbox (http://systematicreviewtools.com/about.php) is a community-driven, searchable, web-based catalog of tools that support the SLR process in multiple domains, including SE. Using the search it is possible to identify SLR tools and which aspects of the SLR process they support (e.g., protocol development, automated search, study selection, quality assessment, data extraction, automated analysis, text analysis, meta-analysis, report writing, collaboration, document management).

The Toolbox presents the up-to-date list of tools. However, one caution with the information presented in the Systematic Review Toolbox is that we have no assurance of the quality of the data. For example, a separate analyses of the automated search features for SE SLR tools found that *StArt*, *SLuRp*, and *SLR-Tool* do not fully support automated search on the DLs, even though the website claims that they do (Al-Zubidy and Carver 2019).

Table 10 Tools which support researchers in conducting SLR in SE

Tool	Brief description	Future reading
Linked Data[a]	It suggests the use of text mining to semi-automate the selection activity	Tomassetti et al. (2011)
PEx/Revis[b]	It provides visual representations of studies to support selection activity	Felizardo et al. (2010, 2011, 2012a, 2014a)
Review Toolkit[c]	It supports simple literature filtering, design of a taxonomy, classification of literature, and analysis of the classification by generated diagrams	Götz (2018)
SluRp[d]	It supports the whole SLR process, the management of a large number of studies, and shares tasks among a group of researchers	Bowes et al. (2012)
SLRONT[e]	It describes common terminologies and their relationships during the SLR process	Sun et al. (2012)
SLR-Tool[f]	It supports the whole SLR process and uses text mining to refine search results	Fernández-Sáez et al. (2010)
StArt[g]	It assists SLR conduction from protocol creation to results presentation through graphics	Fabbri et al. (2012), Hernandes et al. (2012)
UNITEX[h]	It automatically extracts knowledge from studies using text mining	Torres et al. (2012)

[a]No prototype available
[b]http://vicg.icmc.usp.br/vicg/tool/1/projection-explorer-pex
[c]https://github.com/sebastiangoetz/slr-toolkit
[d]https://uhra.herts.ac.uk/handle/2299/14730
[e]No prototype available
[f]https://alarcos.esi.uclm.es/
[g]http://lapes.dc.ufscar.br/tools/start_tool
[h]https://unitexgramlab.org/pt

6 Conclusion

The SLR process consists of five basic activities; (1) developing the protocol, (2) retrieving relevant studies from the literature, (3) selecting appropriate studies for inclusion, (4) extracting data from the studies, and (5) synthesizing the evidence. Much of this process is labor intensive. However, automation can provide support for each of these activities. The objective of this chapter is to present current strategies that support the automation of SLR activities, so that researchers can produce SLRs in SE more efficiently and cost effectively. We performed a (non-exhaustive) survey of the literature to describe strategies and tools that support or automate the SLR process or its activities. We found a number of strategies for automation of the search and selection activities, but fewer about protocol definition and automation of the data extraction/synthesis activities.

Our primary conclusions are:

1. We identified strategies to automate activities across the SLR process. These strategies aim to reduce the human effort required for conducting an SLR.
2. Because an SLR requires careful search and review of the literature, which are time-consuming activities, reducing the search and selection effort will result in faster results from SLRs and potentially improve decision-making in SE industry (Kitchenham et al. 2009; Lu et al. 2009; Grigoleit et al. 2015).
3. The development of automation tools has been slow and fragmented in SE. To fully reach the potential of automating SLRs, researchers will need a sustained coordinated collaborative effort. Automation tools need to be able to work together and exchange data so SLR authors can choose the most appropriate set of tools for their review.

Each of the strategies described in this chapter has the potential to automate various activities of the SLR process. However, many of these strategies are relatively unknown in the SE SLR community. There is a need for better dissemination and use by SE researchers so we can develop an evidence base about their usage and more insight into their relative advantages. The strategies discussed are complementary and should be composed in such a way to take advantage of their strengths. This topic is worth of further investigation.

Key Chapter Takeaways

- Researchers are devoting more effort to the development of SLR automation tools.
- There is still a need for more formal evaluation of these tools as most evaluations use only case studies.
- There are still needs for automated tool support in most phases of the SLR process.
- While a large number of tools exists, the efforts have generally been fragmented and would benefit from more integration.

References

Abilio R, Vale G, Pereira D, Oliveira C, Morais F, Costa H (2014) Systematic literature review supported by information retrieval techniques: a case study. In: 40th Latin American computing conference (CLEI' 14), pp 1–11

Adeva JJG, Atxa JMP, Carrillo MU, Zengotitabengoa EA (2014) Automatic text classification to support systematic reviews in medicine. Expert Syst Appl 4(41):1498–1508

Al-Zubidy A, Carver JC (2014) Review of systematic literature review tools – technical report serg–2014-03. Technical report, University of Alabama

Al-Zubidy A, Carver JC (2019) Identification and prioritization of SLR search tool requirements: an SLR and a survey. Empir Softw Eng 1(24):139–169

Al-Zubidy A, Carver JC, Hale DP, Hassler EE (2017) Vision for SLR tooling infrastructure: prioritizing value-added requirements. Inf Softw Technol 2017(91):72–81

Aliyu MB, Iqbal R, James A (2018) The canonical model of structure for data extraction in systematic reviews of scientific research articles. In: 15th International conference on social networks analysis, management and security (SNAMS'18), pp 264–271

Bannach-Brown A, Przybyla P, Thomas J, Rice ASC, Ananiadou S, Liao J, Macleod M (2019) Machine learning algorithms for systematic review: reducing workload in a preclinical review of animal studies and reducing human screening error. Syst Rev 1(8):23

Bowes D, Hall T, Beecham S (2012) Slurp: a tool to help large complex systematic literature reviews deliver valid and rigorous results. In: 2nd International workshop on evidential assessment of software technologies (EAST'12), pp 33–36

Brereton PO, Kitchenham BA, Budgen D, Turner M, Khalil M (2007) Lessons from applying the systematic literature review process within the software engineering domain. J Syst Softw 80(4):571–583

Carver JC, Hassler E, Hernandes E, Kraft NA (2013) Identifying barriers to the systematic literature review process. In: 7th International symposium on empirical software engineering and measurement (ESEM'13), pp 203–213

Cruzes DS, Dybå T (2010) Synthesizing evidence in software engineering research. In: ACM-IEEE international symposium on empirical software engineering and measurement (ESEM'10), pp 1–10

Dieste O, Padua A (2007) Developing search strategies for detecting relevant experiments for systematic reviews. In: 1st International symposium on empirical software engineering and measurement (ESEM'07), pp 215–224

Dieste O, Grimán A, Juristo N (2009) Developing search strategies for detecting relevant experiments. Empir Softw Eng 14(5):513–539

Dybå T, Dingsøyr T, Hanssen GK (2007) Applying systematic reviews to diverse study types: an experience report. In: 1st International symposium on empirical software engineering and measurement (ESEM'07), pp 225–234

Engström E, Skoglund M, Runeson P (2008) Empirical evaluations of regression test selection techniques: a systematic review. In: 2nd International symposium on empirical software engineering and measurement (ESEM'08), pp 22–31

Fabbri SCPF, Hernandes E, Di Thommazo A, Belgamo A, Zamboni A, Silva C (2012) Using information visualization and text mining to facilitate the conduction of systematic literature reviews. In: 14th International conference on enterprise information systems (ICEIS'12), pp 243–256

Felizardo KR, Nakwgawa EY, Feitosa D, Minghim R, Maldonado JC (2010) An approach based on visual text mining to support categorization and classification in the systematic mapping. In: 14th International conference on evaluation and assessment in software engineering (EASE'10), pp 1–10

Felizardo KR, Riaz M, Sulayman M, Mendes E, MacDonell SG, Maldonado JC (2011) Analysing the use of graphs to represent the results of systematic reviews in software engineering. In: 25th Brazilian symposium on software engineering (SBES'11), pp 174–183

Felizardo KR, MacDonell SG, Mendes E, Maldonado JC (2012a) A systematic mapping on the use of visual data mining to support the conduct of systematic literature reviews. J Softw 2(7):450–461

Felizardo KR, Salleh N, Martins RM, Mendes E, MacDonell SG, Maldonado JC (2012b) Using visual text mining to support the study selection activity in systematic literature reviews. In: 5th International software engineering and measurement (ESEM'12), pp 1–10

Felizardo KR, Andery GF, Paulovich FV, Minghim R, Maldonado JC (2014a) A visual analysis approach to validate the selection review of primary studies in systematic reviews. Inf Softw Technol 10(54):1079–1091

Felizardo KR, Nakagawa EY, MacDonell SG, Maldonado JC (2014b) A visual analysis approach to update systematic reviews. In: 18th International conference on evaluation and assessment in software engineering (EASE'14), pp 1–4

Felizardo KR, Nakagawa EY, Fabbri SCPF, Ferrari FC (2017a) Systematic literature review in software engineering: theory and practice (in Portuguese), 1st edn. Elsevier Brazil, São Paulo

Felizardo KR, Takemiya SH, Souza EF (2017b) Analyzing the use of graphical abstracts to support study selection in secondary studies. In: Experimental software engineering (ESELAW'17), pp 1–10

Feng L, Chiam Y, Abdullah ERMF, Obaidellah U (2017a) Using suffix tree clustering method to support the planning phase of systematic literature review. Malays J Comput Sci 4(30):311–332

Feng L, Chiam YK, Lo SK (2017b) Text-mining techniques and tools for systematic literature reviews: a systematic literature review. In: 24th Asia-Pacific software engineering conference (APSEC' 17), pp 41–50

Fernández-Sáez AM, Genero M, Romero FP (2010) SLR-tool – a tool for performing systematic literature reviews. In: 5th International conference on software and data technologies (ICSOFT'10), pp 157–166

Frantzi K, Ananiadou S, Mima H (2000) Automatic recognition of multi-word terms. Int J Digit Libr 2(3):117–132

Ghafari M, Saleh M, Ebrahimi T (2012) A federated search approach to facilitate systematic literature review in software engineering. Int J Softw Eng Appl 2(3):1–13

Götz S (2018) Supporting systematic literature reviews in computer science: the systematic literature review toolkit. In: 21st ACM/IEEE International conference on model driven engineering languages and systems: companion proceedings (MODELS'18), pp 22–26

Grigoleit F, Vetro A, Diebold P, Mendez DF, Bohm W (2015) In quest for proper mediums for technology transfer in software engineering. In: 9th International symposium on empirical software engineering and measurement (ESEM'15), pp 1–4

Hassler E, Carver J, Kraft NA, Hale D (2014) Outcomes of a community workshop to identify and rank barriers to the systematic literature review process. In: 18th International conference on evaluation and assessment in software engineering (EASE'14), pp 1–10

Hearst MA (1993) TextTiling: a quantitative approach to discourse segmentation – technical report 93/24. Technical report, University of California

Hernandes E, Zamboni A, Thommazo A, Fabbri SCPF (2012) Using GQM and TAM to evaluate StArt – a tool that supports systematic review. CLEI Electron J 1–2012(15):1–13

Jonnalagadda S, Goyal P, Huffman M (2015) Automating data extraction in systematic reviews: a systematic review. Syst Rev 4(1):78

Kitchenham BA, Brereton PO (2013) A systematic review of systematic review process research in software engineering. Inf Softw Technol 1(55):2049–2075

Kitchenham BA, Brereton OP, Budgen D, Turner M, Bailey J, Linkman S (2009) Systematic literature reviews in software engineering – a systematic literature review. Inf Softw Technol 1(51):7–15

Laghrabli S, Benabbou L, Berrado A (2015) A new methodology for literature review analysis using association rules mining. In: 10th International conference on intelligent systems: theories and applications (SITA'15), pp 1–6

Lausberger C (2017) Konzeption von suchprozessen und suchstrategien für systematische literatur reviews (in German). Master's thesis, Otto-von-Guericke-University Magdeburg

Lu X, Liu L, Liu L (2009) Relationship research between communication activities and success indexes in small and medium software projects. In: International conference on information science and engineering (ICISE'09), pp 5022–5025

Malheiros V, Hohn E, Pinho R, Mendonça M, Maldonado J (2007) A visual text mining approach for systematic reviews. In: 1st International symposium on empirical software engineering and measurement (ESEM'07), pp 245–254

Marshall C, Brereton OP, Kitchenham BA (2014) Tools to support systematic reviews in software engineering: a feature analysis. In: 18th International conference on evaluation and assessment in software engineering (EASE'14), pp 13:1–13:10

Marshall C, Kitchenham BA, Brereton OP (2018) Tool features to support systematic reviews in software engineering – a cross domain study. e-Informatica Softw Eng J 1(12):79–115

Mendes E, Wohlin C, Felizardo KR, Kalinowski M (2019) When to update systematic literature reviews in software engineering? Inf Softw Technol (submitted manuscript, under review)

Mergel GD, Silveira MS, da Silva TS (2015) A method to support search string building in systematic literature reviews through visual text mining. In: 30th Annual ACM symposium on applied computing (SAC'15), pp 1594–1601

Muñoz Caro C, Niño A, Reyes S (2017) A bibliometric approach to systematic mapping studies: the case of the evolution and perspectives of community detection in complex networks. Preprint. arXiv: 1702.02381

Napoleão BM, Felizardo KR, de Souza EF, Petrillo F, Vijaykumar NL, Nakagawa EY (2019) Establishing a search string to detect secondary studies in software engineering. Inf Softw Technol (submitted manuscript, under review)

Neto JL, Santos AD, Kaestner CAA, Freitas A (2000) Generating text summaries through the relative importance of topics. In: Advances in artificial intelligence, IBERAMIA 2000 1952. Lecture notes in computer science

Octaviano FR, Felizardo KR, Maldonado JC, Fabbri SCPF (2016) Semi-automatic selection of primary studies in systematic literature reviews: is it reasonable? Empir Softw Eng 6(20):1898–1917

O'Mara-Eves A, Thomas J, McNaught J, Miwa M, Ananiadou S (2015) Using text mining for study identification in systematic reviews: a systematic review of current approaches. Syst Rev 1(4):1–5

Osborne F, Muccini H, Lago P, Motta E (2018) Reducing the effort for systematic reviews in software engineering. https://research.vu.nl/en/publications/reducing-the-effort-for-systematic-reviews-in-software-engineering

Pulsiri N, Vatananan-Thesenvitz R (2018) Improving systematic literature review with automation and bibliometrics. In: Portland international conference on management of engineering and technology (PICMET' 18), pp 1–8

Ramampiaro H, Cruzes D, Conradi R, Mendona R (2010) Supporting evidence-based software engineering with collaborative information retrieval. In: 6th International conference on collaborative computing: networking, applications and worksharing (CollaborateCom'10), pp 1–5

Rasmus R, Bjarnason E, Runeson P (2017) A machine learning approach for semi-automated search and selection in literature studies. In: 21st International conference on evaluation and assessment in software engineering (EASE'17), pp 1–10

Riaz M, Sulayman M, Salleh N, Mendes E (2010) Experiences conducting systematic reviews from novices' perspective. In: 14th International conference on evaluation and assessment in software engineering (EASE'10), pp 44–53

Santos V (2018) Concept maps construction using natural language processing to support studies selection. In: 33rd Annual ACM symposium on applied computing (SAC'18), pp 926–927

Shakeel Y, Krüger J, Nostitz-Wallwitz Iv, Lausberger C, Durand GC, Saake G, Leich T (2018) (Automated) literature analysis – threats and experiences. In: 13th International workshop on software engineering for science (SE4Science' 18), pp 20–27

Silva MCR (2009) Contextextractor: uma ferramenta de apoio para a extração de informações de contexto de artigos de engenharia de software experimental (in Portuguese). Master's thesis, Universidade Salvador

Singh P, Galster M, Singh K (2018) How do secondary studies in software engineering report automated searches? In: 22nd International conference on evaluation and assessment in software engineering (EASE'18), pp 145–150

Sjøberg DIK, Dybå T, Jørgensen M (2007) The future of empirical methods in software engineering research. In: Future of software engineering (FOSE'07), pp 358–378

Souza FC, Santos A, Andrade S, Durelli R, Durelli V, Oliveira R (2017) Automating search strings for secondary studies. In: Information technology – new generations. Part of the advances in intelligent systems and computing book series (AISC'17), pp 839–848

Staples M, Niazi M (2007) Experiences using systematic review guidelines. J Syst Softw 80(9):1425–1437

Sun Y, Yang Y, Zhang H, Zhang W, Wang Q (2012) Towards evidence-based ontology for supporting systematic literature review. In: 16th International conference on evaluation assessment in software engineering (EASE' 12), pp 171–175

Thomas J, Noel-Storr A, Marshall I, Wallace B, McDonald S, Mavergames C, Glasziou P, Shemilt I, Synnot A, Turner T, Elliott J (2017) Living systematic reviews: 2. Combining human and machine effort. J Clin Epidemiol 1(91):31–37

Timsina P, Liu J, Shang Y (2016) Using semi-supervised learning for the creation of medical systematic review: an exploratory analysis. In: 49th Hawaii international conference on system sciences (HICSS'16), pp 1195–1203

Tomassetti F, Rizzo G, Vetro A, Ardito L, Torchiano M, Morisio M (2011) Linked data approach for selection process automation in systematic reviews. In: 15th International conference on evaluation and assessment in software engineering (EASE'11), pp 31–35

Torres JAS, Cruzes DS, Salvador L (2012) Automatic results identification in software engineering papers. Is it possible? In: 12th International conference on computer science and its applications, pp 108–112

Tsafnat G, Glasziou P, Choong MK, Dunn A, Galgani F, Coiera E (2014) Systematic review automation technologies. Syst Rev 3(1):74

Waiyahong N, Reddy ER (2014) Technical standards for accessing information in the 21st century: Z39.50 to web gateways. In: 3rd International conference on integrated information (IC-ININFO'13), pp 26–31

Webster J, Watson R (2002) Analyzing the past to prepare for the future: writing a literature review. MIS Q 2(26):13–23

Westgate MJ, Barton PS, Pierson JC, Lindenmayer DB (2005) Text analysis tools for identification of emerging topics and research gaps in conservation science. Conserv Biol 6(29):1606–1614

Wohlin C (2014) Writing for synthesis of evidence in empirical software engineering. In: 8th International symposium on empirical software engineering and measurement (ESEM'14), pp 1–10

Xiong Z, Liu T, Tse G, Gong M, Gladding PA, Smaill BH, Stiles MK, Gillis AM, Zhao J (2018) A machine learning aided systematic review and meta-analysis of the relative risk of atrial fibrillation in patients with diabetes mellitus. Front Physiol 9:835

Yu Z, Menzies T (2019) Fast2: an intelligent assistant for finding relevant papers. Expert Syst Appl 15(120):57–71

Zhang H, Muhammad AB (2011) An empirical investigation of systematic reviews in software engineering. In: 5th International symposium on empirical software engineering and measurement (ESEM'11), pp 1–10

Zhang H, Babar MA, Tell P (2011) Identifying relevant studies in software engineering. Inf Softw Technol 6(53):625–637

Rapid Reviews in Software Engineering

Bruno Cartaxo, Gustavo Pinto, and Sergio Soares

Abstract Integrating research evidence into practice is one of the main goals of evidence-based software engineering (EBSE). Secondary studies, one of the main EBSE products, are intended to summarize the "best" research evidence and make them easily consumable by practitioners. However, recent studies show that some secondary studies lack connections with software engineering practice. In this chapter, we present the concept of Rapid Reviews, which are lightweight secondary studies focused on delivering evidence to practitioners in a timely manner. Rapid reviews support practitioners in their decision-making, and should be conducted bounded to a practical problem, inserted into a practical context. Thus, Rapid Reviews can be easily integrated in a knowledge/technology transfer initiative. After describing the basic concepts, we present the results and experiences of conducting two Rapid Reviews. We also provide guidelines to help researchers and practitioners who want to conduct Rapid Reviews, and we finally discuss topics that may concern the research community about the feasibility of Rapid Reviews as an evidence-based method. In conclusion, we believe Rapid Reviews might be of interest to researchers and practitioners working on the intersection of software engineering research and practice.

B. Cartaxo (✉)
Federal Institute of Pernambuco (IFPE), Paulista, Pernambuco, Brazil

G. Pinto
Federal University of Pará (UFPA), Belém, Pará, Brazil
e-mail: gpinto@ufpa.br

S. Soares
Federal University of Pernambuco (UFPE), Recife, Pernambuco, Brazil
e-mail: scbs@cin.ufpe.br

© Springer Nature Switzerland AG 2020
M. Felderer, G. H. Travassos (eds.), *Contemporary Empirical Methods in Software Engineering*, https://doi.org/10.1007/978-3-030-32489-6_13

1 Introduction

Evidence-based practice aims to curate the best research evidence in a given domain of expertise and integrate the findings into practice (McKibbon 1998). The medical research field was one of the pioneers embracing such a paradigm. More recently, following the promising results in medicine, many other research fields have been adopting evidence-based practice, such as psychology (Anderson 2006), nursing (DiCenso et al. 1998), crime prevention (Farrington et al. 2003), social work (Webb 2001), and education (Davies 1999). The seminal paper of Kitchenham et al. (2004) introduced the evidence-based practice in the software engineering community. According to the authors, the goal of evidence-based software engineering (EBSE) is to provide the means by which current best evidence from research can be integrated with practical experience and human values in the decision-making process regarding the development and maintenance of software. (Kitchenham et al. 2004) (bold emphasis added)

Considering this goal, it is no coincidence that secondary studies are the main products of EBSE. Some authors argue that the knowledge aggregated in secondary studies is the most appropriate to be transferred to practice (Lavis et al. 2003). This belief is rooted in years of evidence-based practice, showing that individual studies often lead to different conclusions compared to more mature and comprehensive secondary studies (Lavis et al. 2003). As an example, a study comparing the mortality rates of for-profit and nonprofit hospitals found a lower risk of death in for-profit hospitals. On the opposite direction, a secondary study, considering data from studies that summed up 26,000 hospitals and 38 millions patients, found a higher risk of death in for-profit hospitals (Devereaux et al. 2002).

Fast forwarding 15 years, EBSE is now a mature field with new studies being conducted on a regular basis (da Silva et al. 2011; Borges et al. 2014, 2015). However, despite its evolution, several researchers claim that EBSE still lacks connection with software engineering practice (Hassler et al. 2014; Santos and da Silva 2013; da Silva et al. 2011). An investigation with researchers specialized in EBSE revealed that the "lack of connection with industry" is the sixth top barrier to conduct secondary studies, from a total of 37 barriers (Hassler et al. 2014). In the same direction, the study of Santos and da Silva (2013) deployed a survey to 44 authors of 120 secondary studies; only six of them affirmed their studies had direct impact on industrial practice. In addition, a tertiary study identified that only 32 out of 120 secondary studies provide guidelines to practitioners. These findings may indicate that EBSE has not been accomplishing its main goal.

The evidence-based medicine community also faced similar problems in its early days and it is still facing them to some extent nowadays (Best et al. 1997; Tricco et al. 2015, 2017). To mitigate this lack of connection with practice, one of the most successful initiatives of the medical field is what has been called Rapid Reviews (RRs) (Tricco et al. 2015). Rapid Reviews are secondary studies aiming to provide research evidence to support decision-making in practice. RRs must be conducted taking into account the constraints inherent to practical environments, such as time and effort. RRs usually deliver evidence in a more timely manner, with lower costs, and reporting results through more appealing mediums (Cartaxo et al. 2018a). As a consequence, RRs tend to be more connected to practice when compared to Systematic Reviews (SRs).[1] To achieve these goals, RRs omit or simplify some steps of SRs. For instance, RRs can limit the search sources or use just one person to screen primary studies (Tricco et al. 2015).

Inspired by our peers from the medical field, we recently introduced the concept of RRs in software engineering contexts (Cartaxo et al. 2018a,b, 2019). The kick start of an RR is a practical problem that exists in a software project. This particular problem must motivate researchers to screen the literature looking for potential answers. As a consequence, researchers must work closely to practitioners to guarantee that the RR is close tied to a practical context. Instead of using a traditional paper-based format, the results of an RR should be incorporated in more attractive mediums, such as Evidence Briefings, which are one-page documents reporting the main findings of an RR (Cartaxo et al. 2016).

At first sight, one may argue that while RRs speed up the process by simplifying some predefined steps of SRs, they may also introduce methodological threats. To better understand this concern, several studies were conducted in medicine to evaluate the impact of RRs methodological adaptations, in comparison to SRs (Abou-Setta et al. 2016; Corabian and Harstall 2002; Best et al. 1997; Taylor-Phillips et al. 2017; Van de Velde et al. 2011). Although there is evidence reporting divergences between RRs and SRs (Van de Velde et al. 2011), there is more evidence reporting the similarity of results obtained with those two approaches (Abou-Setta et al. 2016; Corabian and Harstall 2002; Best et al. 1997; Taylor Phillips et al. 2017). While further investigations are still needed to draw more conclusive results, RRs should not be understood as a replacement for SRs. Instead, we believe that both can (and should) co-exist: while SRs are important to provide in-depth evidence, RRs are useful to easily and quickly transfer scientific knowledge to practice.

In this chapter, we present the background concepts related to RRs (Sect. 2); show results and experiences on conducting this type of studies in software engineering (Sect. 3); introduce guidelines on how to plan, perform, and report RRs (Sect. 4); further discuss topics about the feasibility of RRs that may concern the software engineering research community (Sect. 5); list recommended further reading (Sect. 6); and close with the conclusions (Sect. 7).

---

[1]By SRs we mean the more methodologically rigorous secondary studies like meta-analyses, the traditional systematic literature reviews, or systematic mapping studies (Kitchenham and Charters 2007).

2 Background

In this section we provide some background information about what an RR is; why using RRs, based on evidence of their benefits; who is using RRs; and how RRs compare to SRs in terms of their results and methodological characteristics.

2.1 What Is a Rapid Review?

Rapid Reviews are practice-oriented secondary studies (Watt et al. 2008; Haby et al. 2016; Polisena et al. 2015; Tricco et al. 2017). The main goal of an RR is to provide evidence to support decision-making towards the solution, or at least attenuation, of issues practitioners face in practice. To support this goal and to meet time constraints of practitioners, RRs have to deliver evidence in shorter time frames when compared to SRs, which often take months to years (Tricco et al. 2015). To make RRs compliant with such characteristics, some steps of SRs are deliberately omitted or simplified.

Since RRs are a recent phenomenon in evidence-based medicine, many methodological variations have been identified. This can be observed in the study of Featherstone et al. (2015), which analyzed the methods employed in many published RRs. Additionally, Tricco et al. (2016) interviewed 40 RRs producers and also observed the presence of method variability. These two studies identified high heterogeneity among RRs, from varying time frames to ambiguous definitions of what an RR is. Despite RRs high methodological variability, the majority of RRs share at least the following core aspects:

Rapid Reviews Should Be Performed in Close Collaboration with Practitioners, Bounded to Practical Problems, and Conducted Within Practitioners Context The argument to conduct lightweight secondary studies like RRs holds only in scenarios where time and costs are hard constraints. This kind of scenario is typically observed in the practice of many fields. Therefore, RRs are only conceived bounded to practical problems and conducted within their practical contexts. Thus, practitioners should be willing to devote part of their busy schedule in order to participate on RRs, although the level of participation can vary. RRs that are neither conducted with practitioners' collaboration nor related to a problem that emerged from a practical context are considered deviations, and then, should be avoided by the software engineering community.

Rapid Reviews Are Intend to Reduce Costs and Time of Heavyweight Methods To better fit in the practitioners' agenda, RRs should be conducted and reported in a timely manner. Many strategies have been applied to RRs in health-care related fields to reduce cost and time, such as limiting search strategy by date of publication and/or search source; using just one person to screen studies; not conducting quality appraisal of primary studies; presenting results with no formal synthesis, among others (Tricco et al. 2015, 2016).

Rapid Reviews Results Should Be Reported Through Mediums Appealing to Practitioners One important aspect of RRs is the way they are reported. Many authors argue that alternative mediums should be used—when practitioners are the target audience—instead of the traditional research paper format (Beecham et al. 2014; Grigoleit et al. 2015; Cartaxo et al. 2016). To substantiate this claim, Tricco et al. (2015) observed that, although RRs present several variations on their methods and terminologics, 78% present results as a narrative summary reported in mediums that better fit practitioners' needs. Examples of alternative mediums include: the Contextual Summaries of Young et al. (2014), which limit the report to a one-page document; the Briefings presented by Chambers and Wilson (2012), which summarize the main findings of a secondary study in one section; or even the Evidence Summaries by Khangura et al. (2012), which use an informative box separated from the main text to highlight the audience and nature of the report. In the context of software engineering, there are only a few approaches that can be used in this regard. We particularly recommend Evidence Briefings (Sect. 4.3.1) as a potential way to report the results of an RR.

It is important to note that RRs are neither (1) ad-hoc literature reviews nor (2) an excuse for absence of scientific rigor. RRs must be systematic, by means of following a well-defined protocol. In addition, all the methodological concessions made to an RR must be documented in its protocol. In the RR's report, there must also be a disclaimer about potential methodological limitations (although the details can go on the protocol only, aiming to make the report as concise as possible).

2.2 Why Should One Use Rapid Reviews?

The emerging character of RRs can be explained in terms of their benefits. For instance, a study observed that RRs saved approximately $3 million when implemented in a hospital (McGregor and Brophy 2005). Moreover, a survey exploring the use of 15 RRs revealed that 67% were used as reference material and 53% were used to, in fact, support decision-making in practice (Hailey 2009). Additionally, Lawani et al. (2017) reported that RRs enabled the development of clinical tools more rapidly than with SRs. Other studies have also demonstrated positive impact of RRs in practice (Taylor-Phillips et al. 2017; Hailey et al. 2000; Batten 2012; Zechmeister and Schumacher 2012; Tricco et al. 2015). Although the main targets of RRs are practitioners, some benefits to researchers and the research community as a whole can be identified. For example, RRs can support and facilitate applied research or serve as a platform to make software engineering research more relevant (Beecham et al. 2014).

2.3 Who Is Using Rapid Reviews?

Although RRs are not well-known in software engineering, there is a growing interest in RRs in health-related fields. For instance, Tricco et al. (2015) mapped 100 RRs published between 1997 and 2013 in medicine. Additionally, major medicine venues, such as the prestigious Systematic Reviews journal[2] officially recognized RRs as one of the evidence-based practice methods (Moher et al. 2015). Moreover, Cochrane—a global renowned group of researchers and practitioners specialized in evidence diffusion in health-care—announced in 2016 a group to play a leading role in guiding the production of RRs (Garritty et al. 2016; Cochrane Rapid Reviews Methods Group n.d.). Due to the increasing importance of RRs, the Canadian Agency for Drugs and Technologies in Health (CADTH) promoted the Rapid Review Summit in 2015, which focused on the evolving role and practices of RRs to support informed health care policy and clinical decision-making (Polisena et al. 2015). Even the World Health Organization (WHO) has recently published a guide presenting the importance of RRs (Tricco et al. 2017).

2.4 How Rapid Reviews Are Compared to Systematic Reviews?

Some studies were conducted to evaluate the impact of RRs methodological adaptations by comparing them with SRs. A scoping review found nine studies comparing the results of RRs and SRs. The comparision found that the results of RRs and SRs were similar (Abou-Setta et al. 2016). To illustrate, Corabian and Harstall (2002) compared six RRs with their SRs peer reviewed publications. The conclusions differed only in one case. Another example is the study of Best et al. (1997), where two of the RRs conducted by the authors were in agreement with SRs published later on the same topic. Still, Taylor-Phillips et al. (2017) conducted an RR

---

[2]https://systematicreviewsjournal.biomedcentral.com.

and an SR about the same topic in order to compare their results. The comparison shows that RRs can provide similar results compared to SRs. In that case, both RR and SR identified the same set of papers.

Although there is evidence reporting the similarity of results obtained by RRs and SRs, there is also evidence on the opposite side. For instance, the work of Van de Velde et al. (2011) compared results from their RR to an SR that was conducted by another group, on the same topic, and conflicting results were observed. Therefore, further investigations are still needed to draw more conclusive results.

> **Rapid Reviews Should Not Be Considered as Replacements for Systematic Reviews** We believe RRs should be understood as a complementary scientific product. More concretely, while SRs are important to curate in-depth knowledge, RRs are important to easily and quickly transfer established knowledge to practice.

Table 1 compares the main methodological characteristics of RRs and SRs. The RRs characteristics are based on many medicine studies and guidelines (Tricco et al. 2017; Khangura et al. 2012; Abou-Setta et al. 2016; Taylor-Phillips et al. 2017), while the SRs characteristics are based on Kitchenham's software engineering guidelines (Kitchenham and Charters 2007; Cruzes and Dybå 2011a; Santos and da Silva 2013).

3 Examples of Rapid Reviews

In this section, we describe two RRs that we conducted. The goal is to make people who want to perform an RR familiar with the approach. The real problems that the two conducted RRs were intended to provide solutions to are (1) the improvement of customer collaboration and (2) the improvment of team motivation, respectively. We will use these two RRs as example throughout this chapter.

3.1 Improving Customer Collaboration

This RR was conducted in collaboration with an innovation institute. At first, we performed an interview with the institute's representatives to identify the problems they were facing. Among various software projects, we focused on the one that was having difficulties related to low customer collaboration. The complete and detailed results of this experience are reported in Cartaxo et al. (2018a).

Table 1 Comparison of rapid reviews with systematic reviews methodological characteristics

Characteristic	Rapid reviews	Systematic reviews
Problem	Bounded to a practical problem and conducted within a practical context	Can emerge from academic and practical contexts (Kitchenham and Charters 2007). However, SRs focusing on problems emerged from practice are the exception (Santos and da Silva 2013)
Research questions	Lead to answers that help solving or at least attenuating the practitioners' problem. Exploratory questions aiming to identify which are the strategies and their effectiveness to deal with practitioners problem are one of the gold standards	SRs admit questions aiming to support practitioners decision-making, but also studies that are primarily of interest to researchers, with no practice-oriented questions (Kitchenham and Charters 2007)
Protocol	Must have a document formalizing the protocol	Must have a document formalizing the protocol
Stakeholders roles	Conducted in close collaboration with practitioners, sometimes even having practitioners responsible for executing some of the steps	Despite practitioners participation is possible, researchers usually conduct the entire process
Time frame	Days or weeks	Months or years
Search strategy	– May use few or just one search source (e.g., Scopus) – May limit search by publication year, language, and study design	– Multiple sources to search for primary studies are recommended – May also limit search by publication year, language, and study design, although more comprehensive search is recommended
Selection procedure	– Can be conducted by a single person – The inclusions/exclusion criteria can be more restrictive aiming to focus on primary studies conducted in contexts similar to the one motivating the RR. (e.g., studies with small-/medium/large companies, with companies in countries under specific laws, with open source projects only, etc.) (Tricco et al. 2017)	– Must be conducted in pairs to avoid selection bias – Usually is less restrictive regarding specificities of primary studies context, especially when it is a mapping study, broader in scope
Quality appraisal	Conducted by a single person, or not conducted at all (Tricco et al. 2017)	Conducted in pairs to avoid threats to validity due to low primary studies' quality

(continued)

Table 1 (continued)

Characteristic	Rapid reviews	Systematic reviews
Extraction procedure	Usually conducted by a single person to reduce time and effort	Conducted in pairs to avoid extraction bias
Synthesis procedure	Narrative summaries are the most common way to synthesize evidence (Tricco et al. 2015)	More systematic methods should be applied (e.g., meta-analysis, meta-ethnography, thematic analysis, etc.), although it is not always the case (Cruzes and Dybå 2011a)
Report	Alternative mediums that better fit practitioners needs (e.g., Evidence Briefings)	Traditional research paper format

This particular software project was late, and the software team needed either the approval or information from its customers to conclude many of the pending tasks. However, the team was having a hard time to establish a proper communication with their client. To illustrate this, one of the participants affirmed that "emails requesting clarification about requirements take one or two weeks for customer to reply."

In this context, we decided to conduct an RR together with the practitioners to provide evidence about strategies that would help them to deal with low customer collaboration. More concretely, each aspect of the RR protocol was discussed with the practitioners (e.g., the research questions, the inclusion/exclusion criteria, etc.). Online channels such as Skype and email were frequently used during this step. After selecting 17 primary studies, we summarized the findings in an Evidence Briefing document (Cartaxo et al. 2016). We also ran a workshop to discuss the findings and to answer additional questions. A full-time researcher (experienced in conducting secondary studies) was assigned to conduct this RR, which lasted 6 days. That time frame comprehends the first interview with the institute representatives to identify their problem, up to the workshop in the end to present and discuss the RR results.

After the workshop, we interviewed practitioners to assess their perception regarding the RR we conducted together with them. Practitioners reported many benefits regarding the use of RRs, such as the novelty of the approach, the applicability to their problem, the reliability of the content, among others. They also reported that the RR fostered the learning of new concepts. As a shortcoming, however, they found that some findings were not clear in the printed version of the Evidence Briefing—although they became clearer after discussing with researchers during the workshop (Cartaxo et al. 2018a).

We also did a follow-up with the practitioners 2 months after the workshop to assess whether they applied some of the strategies and findings reported in the RR. Interestingly, we discovered that practitioners indeed adopted some of the strategies in their daily work habits to improve customer collaboration, such as *Story Owner*, *Change Priority*, and *Risk Assessment Up Front* (Cartaxo et al. 2018a).

3.2 Improving Team Motivation

This RR was performed in collaboration with a software company that develops educational software products in Recife, Brazil. We first contacted the IT director, who is responsible for all technological aspects of the company. After presenting the goal of this research, a project manager joined us and discussed problems regarding low team motivation he faced in one of their projects. Similar to the RR on low customer collaboration, this RR was conducted in close collaboration with the practitioners from the software company (e.g., defining the research questions and the protocol). The complete and detailed results of this experience are reported in Cartaxo (2018).

Thirty five studies were selected and their evidence summarized and reported in an Evidence Briefing document. The results were also presented in a workshop. This RR took 8 days of a researcher experienced in conducting secondary studies.

When interviewing the practitioners after the workshop, they reported many benefits regarding the use of RRs, such as improvements in team confidence and the reliability on RRs findings. They also demonstrated to be willing to embrace RRs in their own process. This particular finding revealed that practitioners are willing to take the risks of using less rigorous methods, such as RRs, in exchange for evidence delivered in short time frames.

4 The Rapid Review Process

Conducting an RR involves three main phases *planning*, *performing*, and *reporting*. We describe them in detail next.

These phases are similar to the ones of an SR, as described by Kitchenham and Charters (2007). Each phase comprises various specific steps and that is where the differences between RRs and SRs become evident. While the latter adopts strategies aiming to reduce any type of research bias and to guarantee evidence quality, the former aims to deliver scientific evidence in a timely manner to support practitioners' decision-making.

4.1 Planning a Rapid Review

The planning phase of an RR comprehends the creation of a protocol to define all the decisions and procedures demanded to conduct the RR. The protocol must also make the practical problem it intends to provide evidence for explicit, as well as the roles of each stakeholder aiming to guarantee practitioners' active participation.

4.1.1 Demand for a Rapid Review

The demand for an RR can emerge from different sources under different contexts. Some possible arrangements we envision are:

- **Practitioners ask for a Rapid Review:** A decision-maker (i.e., practitioner) contacts a researcher or research institution asking for an RR aiming to make decisions based on evidence.
- **Researcher aligns her/his research agenda based on a practical problem:** A researcher contacts a software company (or an open source team) facing problems related to her/his research agenda. A researcher then proposes an RR to both provide evidence that practitioners need and to bound her/his research on a practical problem.
- **Researcher prospects a research agenda based on a practical problem:** A researcher contacts a software company (or an open source team) aiming to prospect practical problems to focus her/his research on. In this case, the RR has initially no predetermined focus. To narrow it down, the researcher could leverage interviews with practitioners to grasp the problems they are facing and then decide which one to tackle. This is how we conducted the two RRs presented in Sect. 3.

4.1.2 Defining the Problem

Close collaboration with practitioners is crucial to define the problem that will drive an RR. Since sometimes the problem is not already well-defined (or perhaps not even the practitioner is fully aware of the main problem s/he is facing), researchers can use qualitative research methods such as interviews or focus groups to better understand the context and the (eventually hidden) problems (Cartaxo et al. 2018a). Depending on how clear a problem is to practitioners, interviews could be more exploratory (e.g., to understand the whole challenges and needs), more objective (e.g., to understand missing details), or even skipped (e.g., if the problem is very well-defined). One important point to bear in mind when interviewing practitioners to define problems for RRs is that this may be an interactive process. Sometimes you identify a practical problem but there are no studies approaching such problem, so an RR will not be viable, and you may need to find another problem.

4.1.3 Defining the Research Questions

Research questions in RRs are as important as in SRs (Kitchenham and Charters 2007). Once they are defined, all effort is towards answering them. However, to provide useful answers, one has to ask meaningful questions. In RRs, answers are considered useful when they help practitioners to solve or at least attenuate their practical problem. Consequently, questions are considered meaningful only when they lead to such answers.

> **Research Questions in Rapid Reviews Should Be Defined in Close Collaboration with Practitioners** Questions aiming to identify research gaps or to provide more general insights into the research community should be avoided, and left to SRs. RRs should provide answers bounded to the practical context they are inserted into. In other words, RRs naturally have a narrower character than SRs.

Each problem will certainly demand different kinds of questions and approaches to investigate them. However, in our experience, exploratory questions aiming to identify strategies to deal with a particular problem are the cornerstone of RRs (Cartaxo et al. 2018a) since the most important thing to practitioners under time constraints is to discover strategies, supported by evidence, to solve their problems (Yourdon 1995). Examples of such questions are found in the RRs presented in Sect. 3. In the RR about customer collaboration we asked:

- What are the strategies to improve customer collaboration in software development practice?
- What are their effectiveness?

Similarly, in the RR about team motivation we asked:

- What are the strategies to improve software development teams motivation?
- What are their effectiveness?

Other research questions are possible, if answering them helps practitioners towards the solution of their problem. For instance, in the RR about customer collaboration, we also added the following two research questions:

- What are the benefits of customer collaboration in software development practice?
- What are the problems caused by low customer collaboration in software development practice?

Answers to those questions are useful because the findings were used by the development team to convince their customers about the importance of a better collaboration. On the other hand, these research questions were not necessary in the RR about team motivation, since the problem was internal to the company, and the stakeholders already agreed with the importance to improve team motivation. They just did not know how they can do it effectively.

4.1.4 Defining the Stakeholders Roles

An RR is a joint initiative between researchers and practitioners. Thus, active participation of both sides is not only important, but (as we see it) mandatory. The **researchers' role** is to guarantee the methodological consistency and transparency, while the **practitioners' role** is to make sure that the research is bounded to an actual practical problem, so the evidence will be useful.

In that context, different levels of participation are possible. Considering the extremes, it is possible for researchers to perform all activities related to an RR (e.g., defining the protocol, selecting primary studies, extracting data, synthesizing evidence, and reporting the results) as long as practitioners are involved in the entire process, validating each decision and ensuring the RR is bounded to their practical problem. We could also perceive, nevertheless, that practitioners could perform all activities of an RR, as long as researchers are involved, in particular, to validate each methodological decision. Any level of participation between these two extremes is also possible and encouraged. However, the effort of each stakeholder will be defined taking into account the time constraints and resource limitations in each specific situation.

Both, the RR about customer collaboration and team motivation were conducted near the extreme where researchers defined and executed the reviews. However, the practitioners were aware of every single step made, validating and making suggestions to it. This alignment between researchers and practitioners is crucial in order to avoid researchers losing focus, which in turn may lead to research questions that, although interesting from a pure academic perspective, are not related to a practical problem.

Since RRs and even SRs are not well-known in practice (Cartaxo et al. 2017), we believe this kind of arrangement (where researchers perform most of an RR's tasks) will happen more frequently, at least at the beginning. However, if the collective effort to link software engineering research and practice more closer unfolds, then we believe practitioners will recognize the relevance of initiatives like RRs and will be more willing to actively participate.

4.1.5 Creating the Protocol

The protocol of an RR has the same goal as the protocol of an SR: to specify all the methodological steps that undertake the review. The protocol itself is one of the most important elements that makes both RRs and SRs systematic. In this sense, it is important to highlight that RRs are not synonymous to ad-hoc literature reviews, but rather systematic. As a consequence, an RR demands a well-documented protocol.

A major difference between RRs and SRs protocols, nevertheless, is the natural inclination of the former to suffer changes throughout the review process. These changes might happen due to the flexible process that RRs allow. However, changes made after the protocol definition must be documented and justified transparently (Tricco et al. 2017).

The components of an RR protocol are similar to the ones of SRs as described by Kitchenham and Charters (2007), such as: research questions, search strategy, inclusion/exclusion criteria, selection procedure, extraction procedure, synthesis procedure, reporting, among others.

Again, we want to highlight the importance of establishing a close collaboration with practitioners when defining and conducting an RR protocol. This is crucial to make sure practitioners' needs are well-covered and the RR will be performed aiming to provide useful answers. An example of an RR protocol can be found in Cartaxo et al. (2018a).

4.2   Performing a Rapid Review

In this section we present some strategies that may be used to reduce time and cost of performing an RR. For each step, we present some suggestions on how to perform the step. However, one does not have to embrace all strategies, on the contrary, the researcher has to analyze the context and limitations where an RR is being conducted and define which strategies better conciliate given trade-offs. For instance, an RR may use more than one search source to identify primary studies if ensuring broad coverage is critical, but skip the quality appraisal. While other RRs may use just one search source and conduct a rigorous quality appraisal if the reliability on the evidence is critical.

Transparency Is the Golden Standard in Rapid Reviews Regardless of the strategies employed to reduce cost and/or time to conduct an RR, limitations and threats to validity must be reported in the protocol. Practitioners may and are willing to consume evidence based on less rigorous methods like RRs, as long as they are aware of the limitations and threats to validity (Cartaxo et al. 2018a).

4.2.1   Search Strategy

SRs usually employ multiple search strategies to guarantee exhaustive coverage such as using multiple search engines, manual search in conference proceedings and journal issues, as well as forward and backward snowballing approaches.

Adopting all these strategies simultaneously can be extremely resource consuming. An RR, on the other hand, may choose to focus on a single search strategy. For instance, instead of using several search engines, RRs may focus on a single one, more likely Scopus or Google Scholar. These search engines cover a wide spectrum of research papers and usually index papers from the major digital libraries. Complementing the results of the search engine with a snowballing approach has also shown to be a viable option (Badampudi et al. 2015). There are other approaches that, if employed, could reduce the effort placed on conducting RRs, such as:

1. Limiting the search by date;
2. Restricting the language in which the paper is written;
3. Focusing on a given geographical area, or;
4. Limiting the primary studies according to their research method (e.g., controlled experiments only, or case studies only) (Tricco et al. 2017).

It is important to note that those approaches may lead to relevant studies being not included and, as a consequence, reducing the coverage of an RR. If one of these strategies is adopted, threats to validity must be transparently reported. In both RRs, the one about customer collaboration and the one about team motivation, we used one search source only: the Scopus search engine.

4.2.2   Selection Procedure

Since RRs are bound to a practical context, one may define restrictive inclusion/exclusion criteria. The goal here is twofold: to reduce the amount of studies to screen and to provide evidence that better fit practitioners' needs.

For instance, the RR about team motivation was conducted in a small private company with collocated teams. Therefore, some of the inclusion/exclusion criteria were as follows:

• The study must not be related to large companies;
• The study must not be related to distributed teams;
• The study must not be related to crowd source software development;
• The study must not be related to open source software development;

Defining restrictive inclusion/exclusion criteria may reduce the time and effort to conduct an RR. However, this procedure does not necessarily incur in threats to validity. In fact, it may be considered good practice to consider evidence only from primary studies conducted in similar contexts to that of the performed RR. Highly contextualized studies are considered one of the best ways to have impact in practice (Dybå et al. 2012; Cartaxo et al. 2015).

Moreover, SRs usually require independent screening of studies by at least two reviewers (Kitchenham and Charters 2007; Tricco et al. 2017), which is very resource intensive. RRs, on the other hand, may have a selection procedure conducted by a single reviewer. Another option is to have a second reviewer just to pass through a reduced sample of studies. Such strategies may obviously introduce selection bias and must be reported accordingly.

Usually, SRs split the selection procedure into several substeps. In the first substep, reviewers screen primary studies' titles and abstracts, and in the second, the entire papers content. To abbreviate this process, one may split the selection procedure into three substeps, instead of two. The first substep can be dedicated to screening primary studies' titles only. This might accelerate the exclusion of papers that are clearly out of scope since it prevent one to read papers abstracts. On the other side, it may provoke false negatives. The second substep would select primary studies based on abstract only, and the third substep based on the entire content. Regarding this particular strategy, one of the practitioners that participated on the RR about customer collaboration give us the following feedback:

> Sometimes we search for solutions in just one source [...] Then we do it exactly as recommended by that source but it may not work for us. When we do it like this [the RR], we can have more possibilities [the strategies identified by the RR], even considering it was conducted faster [the RR compared to SRs], and maybe many things [papers] could be lost just because of the title [the first round of selection procedure, which we analyzed only the titles of the papers], because someone put a bad title. That is ok, who cares?

4.2.3 Quality Appraisal

In addition to inclusion/exclusion criteria, quality criteria are also usually defined in SRs in order to select high quality evidence only. In a more extreme view, RR researchers can entirely skip this step, but threats to validity associated with this decision must be transparently reported. Both RRs we presented in Sect. 3, adopted this strategy.

Another less radical strategy would be to focus only on studies published in conferences and/or journals that employ a rigorous review process. This may increase the chances of selecting high quality evidence with a low effort (e.g., no need to analyze the evidence quality of each and all papers). Although this approach can also have limitations (e.g., a potentially relevant study could have published on a less prestigious venue or on arXiv), at least we know that the primary studies being included already passed through a rigorous sieve.

If evidence quality is critical in the context where the RR is being conducted, a strategy that may reduce the time and effort is to have quality appraisal carried out by a single reviewer or using pairs to appraise just a sample of papers. This differs from SRs, where quality appraisal is recommended to be conducted fully in pairs.

4.2.4 Extraction Procedure

The data extraction procedure can be conducted by a single reviewer in RRs, as long as the inherent biases are transparently reported. Both RRs we presented in Sect. 3, adopted this strategy. Moreover, in SRs, when data is missing on the selected studies, it is usually recommended to contact the authors. Researchers who conducted RRs in medicine very infrequently indeed contacted primary studies' authors (Tricco et al. 2017). That can be a viable strategy: studies with missing data should probably be excluded from the RR and their exclusion must be reported. RRs consumers (a.k.a. practitioners) can reach those studies later if they wish to.

4.2.5 Synthesis Procedure

Knowledge synthesis is probably one of the most important steps of any secondary study, but at the same time one of the most time-consuming activities. However, a tertiary study revealed that as many as half of the SRs analyzed in software engineering do not present any kind of formal knowledge synthesis procedure (Cruzes and Dybå 2011b). They also summarized various methods for knowledge synthesis (e.g., meta-analysis, meta-ethnography, grounded theory, qualitative metasummary, among others) to encourage researchers to apply them. Furthermore, the chapter "Research Synthesis in Software Engineering" of this book summarizes the most frequently used synthesis methods in software engineering.

A possible strategy to reduce time and effort synthesizing evidence in RRs is using lightweight methods like narrative synthesis (Cruzes and Dybå 2011b; Tricco et al. 2017) in contrast to the more rigorous and time/effort consuming ones like meta-analysis (Lipsey and Wilson 2001) or grounded theory (Stol et al. 2016) methods alike. This decision brings an obvious limitation and must be reported, so practitioners consuming RRs evidence can make informed decision.

Conclusions, recommendations, and implications are particularly important in RRs since they can guide practitioners to adopt the synthesized knowledge. In medicine, they encourage researchers to dedicate time to make her/his conclusions and recommendations to practitioners and avoid presenting a report with findings only (Tricco et al. 2017). We experienced such kind of demand from practitioners on the RR about team motivation when a practitioner gave us the following feedback:

> since it [the RR] was focused on our problem, maybe if there was something saying which one [strategy identified with the RR] you recommend [...] this is what is missing [...] maybe it is missing a conclusion, the researcher's comments.

In addition, one should keep in mind that those conclusions, recommendations, and implications should be strongly bounded to the RR's context, in opposition to the ones drawn from SRs that usually aim to reach a wider audience and scope (Tricco et al. 2017).

4.3 Reporting a Rapid Review

Reporting and disseminating knowledge produced with RRs are as important as conducting the RR itself. SRs are usually conducted in academic environment and thus the report is usually focused on that audience. That means SRs are commonly reported in scientific paper format and diffused through academic journals and conferences.

RRs, however, target software practitioners. Therefore, one should consider that not all information that is crucial to researchers is also relevant to practitioners (e.g., research method, background, related work, etc.). As a consequence, RRs must be reported in a more straightforward way, focusing on results and recommendations, so practitioners can easily consume the information to support their decision-making.

There are several approaches that could be used in this regard, as presented in Sect. 2.1 (Chambers and Wilson 2012; Khangura et al. 2012; Young et al. 2014; Best et al. 1997). This section presents the concept of Evidence Briefings, which are alternative mediums to report RRs more focused on practitioners needs, and also discusses the importance of disseminating knowledge produced with RRs.

4.3.1 Evidence Briefings

Evidence Briefings are one-page documents reporting the main findings of RRs (Cartaxo et al. 2016). A template, as well as examples of such documents can be found online.[3] The Evidence Briefings template was defined based on the best practices observed in medicine as well as on Information Design (Tondreau 2011) and Gestalt Theory (Lupton and Phillips 2015) principles. Figure 1 shows an example of an Evidence Briefing. The numbers within squares denote each part of Evidence Briefing's structure, and following there are some guidelines on how to fill each of those parts:

1. The **title** of an Evidence Briefing should be as concise as possible, and comprise one or two lines only. Titles with more than two lines should be avoided since they might reduce document space to report RRs' findings.
2. To fill the Evidence Briefing's **summary**, we suggest researchers to adopt the following structure: *This briefing reports scientific evidence on* <RESEARCH GOAL>. The summary should span few lines. Following is an example of Evidence Briefing's summary: "This briefing reports scientific evidence on the challenges involved in using Scrum for global software development (GSD) projects, and strategies available to deal with them."
3. The **findings** section is the most important one. It should list the main findings of the RR. When writing the findings, we recommend to use one finding per paragraph. Bullets to highlight important points as well as charts, figures, and tables are welcome since they make the findings even easier to read. Findings should be short sentences, straight to the point. The findings section should not include information about the research method. The idea of the Evidence Briefing is to quickly communicate the main findings of an RR to practitioners. If they

---

[3]http://cin.ufpe.br/eseg/briefings.

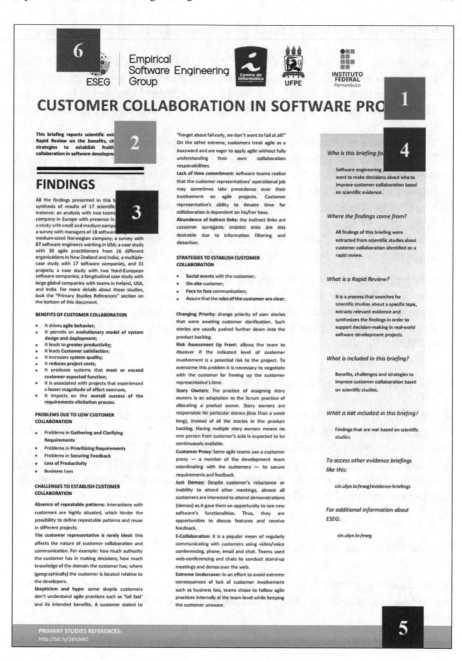

Fig. 1 Evidence Briefing structure

have interest they can refer to the complementary material reference shown in item 5.

4. The **box at the right side** of the Evidence Briefing should be filled with information about the Evidence Briefing's target audience, clarifications about what information is included, and what is not included in the Evidence Briefing. The template has a complete set of suggestions to structure information in the right box.

5. The **reference** to complementary material should be placed at the bottom of the Evidence Briefing. It may be a link to a webpage containing at least the following documents/information: the RR protocol document and a list of references to the primary studies included in the RR.

6. **Logos** of universities, software companies, and any other institutions involved in the RR initiative should be placed at the very top of the Evidence Briefing document. This publicizes the institutions producing Evidence Briefings and might make practitioners search for more RRs on institutions' websites.

Although other mediums to transfer scientific evidence exist, we recommend the use of the Evidence Briefings because, as observed in an empirical evaluation, both researchers and practitioners are positive about using Evidence Briefings as a medium to transfer scientific knowledge to software engineering practice (Cartaxo et al. 2016).

4.3.2 Dissemination of Rapid Reviews Results

Not all RRs are disseminated beyond the practitioners' scope due to sensitive information belonging to the software company involved. However, if this is not the case, we recommend researchers conducting an RR to post the resulting report (e.g., Evidence Briefing) online on the research institution's or the company's website. Sharing the report on social networks such as Twitter or ResearchGate can also increase the impact of the reviews.

5   Further Discussions on the Feasibility of Rapid Reviews

In this section we present further discussions about topics that may concern software engineering research community about the feasibility of RRs as an evidence-based method.

5.1   Research Community Viewpoints on Rapid Reviews

Although RRs are a rising research method in the medical domain, they are so far hardly recognized in the SE community. We believe our community could and should benefit from it. However, due to the lack of RR studies in software engineering, little is known about how our research community perceives the adoption of RRs.

This is particularly important because, according to Rogers (2003), the perceptions of all individuals involved in an initiative is one of the main predictors of its adoption. The importance of exploring the perceptions of practitioners—as we have done in Cartaxo et al. (2018a)—is easy to understand since practitioners are the target audience of RRs. But the perceptions of researchers should certainly not be neglected. Moreover, if the software engineering research community discards RRs, such kind of initiative can easily end even before having shown its potential. In informal discussions with EBSE specialists during conferences, we observed that their opinions about RRs seem to be highly polarized, especially when methodological concessions are made.

This feeling is now backed up with evidence from a study we conducted with 37 software engineering researchers (Cartaxo et al. 2019). We applied a Q-Methodology approach, enabling us to identify that researchers in software engineering can be classified in four groups according to their viewpoint on RRs:

Unconvinced Researchers aligned with this viewpoint are the ones that agree the most that further research comparing the methods and results of RRs and SRs is required before they decide how they think about RRs. The indecision of this viewpoint towards RRs is even more explicit when we look at the contradictory affirmations these participants provided. They think a well-conducted RR may produce better evidence than poorly conducted SRs, but on the other hand, they have more confidence in evidence produced with an SR than in evidence produced with an RR.

Enthusiastic Researchers aligned with this viewpoint are generally positive about RRs and believe RRs can provide reasonable evidence to practitioners if minimum standards to conduct and report RRs are established. They also strongly agree that a well-conducted RR may produce better evidence than a poorly conducted SR.

Picky Researchers aligned with this viewpoint are very skeptical about RRs, as well as concerned about the quality of primary studies included in RRs and how the results are reported. This negative perception can be explained by a strong belief hold by researchers aligned with this viewpoint, that knowledge users (practitioners) do not fully understand the implications of RR methodological concessions. Researchers sharing this point of view also put little faith in RRs validity. They strongly disregard the possibility that RRs can be timely and valid, especially when methodological concessions are made.

Pragmatic Researchers aligned with this viewpoint pragmatically focus on a variety of contextual information to decide if RRs are the best fit to support decision-making. They also believe practitioners are able to understand the impacts of flexible research methods adopted by RRs. Still, they believe rigid standards in RRs could reduce their usefulness to practitioners.

Although the viewpoints are quite diverse, there is a consensus that both RRs and SRs can be conducted very well or very poorly, and that time needed to conduct an evidence synthesis study is not related to its quality. The main concerns about RRs—not necessarily shared among the four viewpoints—are: the need for more evidence about the effectiveness of RRs, the importance to determine minimum standards, the relevance of quality assessment to include primary studies, and the emphasis on transparency in RRs.

With this typology in mind, one can better understand what the main concerns of researchers are and promote better understanding about RRs. As a consequence, our community can pave a road better connecting research with practice and make software engineering research more impactful and relevant.

5.2 Publishing Rapid Reviews in Scientific Peer Reviewed Venues

Since RRs are commonly reported in non-scientific paper format (i.e., Evidence Briefings), they are usually internally reviewed, but not peer reviewed (Tricco et al. 2017). This may be seem as an unpromising incentive for researchers to conduct RRs since publishing papers in peer reviewed venues is important for their career. Nevertheless, we encourage researchers who conduct RRs to also publish their results in traditional scientific venues by reporting their results in a scientific outlet too.

Rapid Reviews Can and Should Also Be Published in Academic Peer Reviewed Venues One may argue that an RR will probably not constitute enough contribution to deserve a rigorous scientific publication. However, one should note that RRs are usually inserted into broader knowledge/technology transfer initiatives (Cartaxo et al. 2018b), and such initiatives are usually very enriching and welcomed in scientific venues. The paper may report not only the RR protocol and results, but also the perceptions of practitioners participating in the entire RR initiative. One example of such a peer reviewed RR publication in software engineering is one of our works (Cartaxo et al. 2018a). Additionally, if the cooperation between researchers and practitioners goes beyond the RR itself—for instance, when researchers actively participate, together with practitioners, designing the solutions to practitioners' problems based on the evidence provided by the RR, and adopting a participatory method like action research—the paper may report how the knowledge produced with that RR was applied in practice, and to what degree it solved or at least attenuated practitioners' problems. In fact, this kind of research would probably close the entire knowledge/technology transfer cycle in a marvelous way. It puts the scientific knowledge in action with direct impact to practice.

5.3   On the Use of Grey Literature

The last point that is worth discussing is whether one could conduct an RR with grey literature. This is a positive argument along these lines, which is often related to how practitioners share and acquire knowledge (i.e., through blog posts, talks, videos, etc.). These mediums are often created by (and for) practitioners and do not necessarily pass through a rigorous revision process. Although some researchers are taking advantage of grey literature (Garousi et al. 2016, 2017) in academic studies, there are still some conservative researchers that favor the traditional peer reviewed literature. In this chapter, we do not intend to add more fire on this already heated debate. However, we also concur that eventually, a researcher conducting an RR would have to think about what kind of literature s/he will include in her/his review. To guide this researcher, our experience suggests that researchers should focus only on peer reviewed literature when conducting an RR. This is particularly due to the fact that RRs may have already several limitations and threats to validity. We believe that adding grey literature to this equation could weaken the quality of the review produced, at least in the eyes of an unconvinced researcher. Obviously, this is a hypothesis that could be tested in follow-up studies. For more detailed information about using grey literature as evidence, refer to the chapter "Benefitting from the Grey Literature in Software Engineering Research" in this book.

6   Recommended Further Reading

For a better comprehension of this chapter, we suppose the reader has experience conducting SRs, or at least has knowledge of what an SR is, as well as the steps and procedures it comprises. If that is not the case, we refer the reader to the Kitchenham and Charters (2007) guidelines as well as the Kitchenham et al. (2004) EBSE seminal paper.

Regarding RRs, one can read the first experience conducting such kind of study in software engineering in Cartaxo et al. (2018a). We also recommend reading the practical guide on RRs provided by the World Health Organization (Tricco et al. 2017). It distills most of the accumulated experience conducting RRs in medicine. For a comprehensive view on the state of practice and research about RRs in medicine, one can take a look on Tricco et al. (2015) scoping study. It analyzes 100 RRs conducted between 1997 and 2013 under various perspectives, such as RRs characteristics, terminology, citation, impact on practice, comparison with SRs, among others. For a better understanding on how RRs fit in a more comprehensive knowledge/technology transfer initiative, there is our study proposing such a model in Cartaxo et al. (2018b).

Regarding initiatives related to RR, there is a recent trend towards the use of grey literature in multivocal literature reviews (MLRs) (Garousi et al. 2016, 2017; Yasin and Hasnain 2012). Generally speaking, the use of MLRs shares the core goal of an RR, which is to make research more aligned with practice. However, there is a fundamental difference between these two approaches. On the one hand, RRs aim to provide knowledge based on scientific evidence from peer-reviewed and rigorous primary studies only, as well as deliver evidence in a timely manner. On the other hand, MLRs apply systematic methods to synthesize not only primary studies, but also grey literature. Moreover, MLRs do not necessarily emerge from a practical problem nor are they necessarily concerned about delivering evidence in a timely manner to practitioners. While RRs flexibilize the method, MLRs flexibilize the source of evidence. However, flexibilizing both aspects at the same time may produce results of low validity. Thus, RRs and MLRs are different approaches, although both can potentially contribute to reduce the gap between software engineering research and practice.

7   Conclusion

A new era of software engineering has emerged and it is changing the way we think about empirical research. In a recent series of posts at Communications of ACM blog, Meyer (2018a,b,c) precisely framed this era throughout a vision where empirical evidence and practice orientation are pivotal elements:

> As long as empirical software engineering was a young, fledgling discipline, it made good sense to start with problems that naturally landed themselves to empirical investigation. But now that the field has matured, it may be time to reverse the perspective and start from the consumer's perspective: for practitioners of software engineering, what problems, not yet satisfactorily answered by software engineering theory, could benefit, in the search for answers, from empirical studies? (Meyer 2018a)

Meyer's voice certainly is not alone. Many other researchers are starting to recognize practice orientation as the next long way ahead (Beecham et al. 2014; Duarte 2015; Laird and Yang 2015; Santos and da Silva 2013). Unfortunately, there is evidence that secondary studies in software engineering lack connection with practice (Santos and da Silva 2013; da Silva et al. 2011; Hassler et al. 2014; Cartaxo et al. 2017).

In this chapter, we introduced the concept of Rapid Reviews (RRs) in the context of knowledge transfer in software engineering. They are a type of secondary studies aiming to provide research evidence to support decision-making in practice, and in consequence, must be conducted taking into account the constraints inherent to practical environments. RRs usually deliver evidence in a more timely manner, with lower costs, reporting results through more appealing mediums, and more connected to practice, when compared to Full Systematic Reviews.

We also presented examples of experiences conducting RRs together with software engineering practitioners. They affirmed to have learned new concepts about the problem they were facing, as well as declared to trust in the findings provided by RRs. We also presented guidelines covering the entire RRs process aiming to help researchers and/or practitioners interested in conducting their own RRs.

Even looking for all the good results, to be fair, one has to highlight that RRs are not always a bed of roses. RRs have their limitations, and this must be considered carefully. They are certainly neither a silver bullet nor can they replace Systematic Reviews. Moreover, we explored and provided solutions aiming to address some concerns that researchers may have about the feasibility of RRs as a viable evidence-based research method. Such concerns are researchers perceptions (skepticism) about RRs flexible strategies, how to publish RRs in scientific rigorous peer review venues, as well as how to disseminate the results obtained by RRs.

In conclusion, we believe RRs can play an important role in promoting knowledge transfer from scientific empirical evidence to practice and reduce the gap between academic research and software engineering practice.

References

Abou-Setta AM et al (2016) Methods for developing evidence reviews in short periods of time: a scoping review. PloS One 11(12)

Anderson NB (2006) Evidence-based practice in psychology. Am Psychol 61(4):271–285

Badampudi D, Wohlin C, Petersen K (2015) Experiences from using snowballing and database searches in systematic literature studies. In: Proceedings of the 19th international conference on evaluation and assessment in software engineering, EASE '15. ACM, New York, pp 17:1–17:10. http://doi.acm.org/10.1145/2745802.2745818

Batten J (2012) Comment on editorial literature reviews as a research strategy. J Sch Nurs 28(6):409–409

Beccham S, O'Leary P, Baker S, Richardson I, Noll J (2014) Making software engineering research relevant. Computer 47(4), 80–83. http://dx.doi.org/10.1109/MC.2014.92

Best L, Stevens A, Colin-Jones D (1997) Rapid and responsive health technology assessment: the development and evaluation process in the south and west region of England. J Clin Eff 2(2):51–56

Borges A, Ferreira W, Barreiros E, Almeida A, Fonseca L, Teixeira F, Silva D, Alencar A, Soares S (2014) Support mechanisms to conduct empirical studies in software engineering. In: Proceedings of the 8th ACM/IEEE international symposium on empirical software engineering and measurement, ESEM '14. ACM, New York, pp 50:1–50:4. http://doi.acm.org/10.1145/2652524.2652572

Borges A, Ferreira W, Barreiros E, Almeida A, Fonseca L, Teixeira E, Silva D, Alencar A, Soares S (2015) Support mechanisms to conduct empirical studies in software engineering: a systematic mapping study. In: Proceedings of the 19th international conference on evaluation and assessment in software engineering, EASE '15, pp 22:1–22:14

Cartaxo B (2018) A model to transfer knowledge from research to software engineering practice based on rapid reviews and evidence briefings. PhD thesis, Center of Informatics – Federal University of Pernambuco – CIn/UFPE

Cartaxo B, Almeida A, Barreiros E, Saraiva J, Ferreira W, Soares S (2015) Mechanisms to characterize context of empirical studies in software engineering. In: Experimental software engineering Latin American workshop (ESELAW 2015), pp 1–14

Cartaxo B, Pinto G, Vieira E, Soares S (2016) Evidence briefings: towards a medium to transfer knowledge from systematic reviews to practitioners. In: Proceedings of the 10th ACM/IEEE international symposium on empirical software engineering and measurement, ESEM '16. ACM, New York, pp 57:1–57:10. http://doi.acm.org/10.1145/2961111.2962603

Cartaxo B, Pinto G, Ribeiro D, Kamei F, Santos RES, da Silva FQB, Soares S (2017) Using q&a websites as a method for assessing systematic reviews. In: 2017 IEEE/ACM 14th international conference on mining software repositories (MSR), pp 238–242

Cartaxo B, Pinto G, Soares S (2018a), The role of rapid reviews supporting decision-making in software engineering practice. In: 22nd International conference on evaluation and assessment in software engineering (EASE).

Cartaxo B, Pinto G, Soares S (2018b) Towards a model to transfer knowledge from software engineering research to practice. Inf Softw Technol 97:80–82. http://www.sciencedirect.com/science/article/pii/S0950584918300028

Cartaxo B, Pinto G, Fonseca B, Ribeiro M, Pinheiro P, Soares S, Baldassarre MT (2019) Software engineering research community viewpoints on rapid reviews. In: Proceedings of the 13th ACM/IEEE international symposium on empirical software engineering and measurement (ESEM), ESEM '19

Chambers D, Wilson P (2012) A framework for production of systematic review based briefings to support evidence-informed decision-making. Syst Rev 1:32

Cochrane Rapid Reviews Methods Group (RRMG) (n.d.) http://methods.cochrane.org/rapidreviews/. Accessed 27 Mar 2018

Corabian P, Harstall C (2002) Rapid assessments provide acceptable quality advice. In: Annu Meet Int Soc Technol Assess Health Care

Cruzes DS, Dybå T (2011a) Research synthesis in software engineering: a tertiary study. Inf Softw Technol 53(5):440–455. Special Section on Best Papers from {XP2010}. http://www.sciencedirect.com/science/article/pii/S095058491100005X

Cruzes DS, Dybå T (2011b) Research synthesis in software engineering: a tertiary study. Inf Softw Technol 53(5):440–455

da Silva FQ, Santos AL, Soares S, França, ACC, Monteiro CV, Maciel FF (2011) Six years of systematic literature reviews in software engineering: an updated tertiary study. Inf Softw Technol 53(9):899–913. Studying work practices in Global Software Engineering. http://www.sciencedirect.com/science/article/pii/S0950584911001017

Davies P (1999) What is evidence-based education? Br J Educ Stud 47(2):108–121

Devereaux P, Schünemann HJ, Ravindran N, Bhandari M, Garg AX, Choi PT-L, Grant BJ, Haines T, Lacchetti C, Weaver B et al (2002) Comparison of mortality between private for-profit and private not-for-profit hemodialysis centers: a systematic review and meta-analysis. J Am Med Assoc 288(19):2449–2457

DiCenso A, Cullum N, Ciliska D (1998) Implementing evidence-based nursing: some misconceptions. Evid Based Nurs 1(2):38–39

Duarte CHC (2015) Patterns of cooperative technology development and transfer for software-engineering-in-the-large. In: 2015 IEEE/ACM 2nd international workshop on software engineering research and industrial practice, pp 32–38

Dybå T, Sjøberg DI, Cruzes DS (2012) What works for whom, where, when, and why?: on the role of context in empirical software engineering. In: Proceedings of the ACM-IEEE international symposium on empirical software engineering and measurement, ESEM '12. ACM, New York, pp 19–28. http://doi.acm.org/10.1145/2372251.2372256

Farrington DP, MacKenzie DL, Sherman LW, Welsh BC et al (2003) Evidence-based crime prevention. Routledge, London

Featherstone RM et al (2015) Advancing knowledge of rapid reviews: an analysis of results, conclusions and recommendations from published review articles examining rapid reviews. Syst Rev 4:50

Garousi V, Felderer M, Mäntylä MV (2016) The need for multivocal literature reviews in software engineering: complementing systematic literature reviews with grey literature. In: EASE

Garousi V, Felderer M, Mäntylä MV (2017) Guidelines for including the grey literature and conducting multivocal literature reviews in software engineering. Preprint. arXiv: 1707.02553

Garritty C et al (2016) Cochrane rapid reviews methods group to play a leading role in guiding the production of informed high-quality, timely research evidence syntheses. Syst Rev 5:184

Grigoleit F, Vetro A, Fernandez DM, Bohm W, Diebold P (2015) In quest for proper mediums for technology transfer in software engineering. In: ESEM

Haby MM, Chapman E, Clark R, Barreto J, Reveiz L, Lavis JN (2016) What are the best methodologies for rapid reviews of the research evidence for evidence-informed decision making in health policy and practice: a rapid review. Health Res Policy Syst 14(1):83. https://doi.org/10.1186/s12961-016-0155-7

Hailey D (2009) A preliminary survey on the influence of rapid health technology assessments. Int J Technol Assess Health Care 25:415–418

Hailey D et al (2000) The use and impact of rapid health technology assessments. Int J Technol Assess Health Care 16:651–656

Hassler E, Carver JC, Kraft NA, Hale D (2014) Outcomes of a community workshop to identify and rank barriers to the systematic literature review process. In: Proceedings of the 18th international conference on evaluation and assessment in software engineering, EASE '14. ACM, New York, pp 31:1–31:10. http://doi.acm.org/10.1145/2601248.2601274

Khangura S, Konnyu K, Cushman R, Grimshaw J, Moher D (2012) Evidence summaries: the evolution of a rapid review approach. Syst Rev 1:10

Kitchenham B, Charters S (2007) Guidelines for performing systematic literature reviews in software engineering

Kitchenham BA, Dybå T, Jorgensen M (2004) Evidence-based software engineering. In: Proceedings of the 26th international conference on software engineering, ICSE '04. IEEE Computer Society, Washington, pp 273–281. http://dl.acm.org/citation.cfm?id=998675.999432

Laird L, Yang Y (2015) Transferring software engineering research into industry: the Stevens way. In: 2015 IEEE/ACM 2nd international workshop on software engineering research and industrial practice, pp 46–49

Lavis JN, Robertson D, Woodside JM, McLeod CB, Abelson J (2003) How can research organizations more effectively transfer research knowledge to decision makers? Milbank Q 81(2):221–248

Lawani MA et al (2017) Five shared decision-making tools in 5 months: use of rapid reviews to develop decision boxes for seniors living with dementia and their caregivers. Syst Rev 6:56

Lipsey MW, Wilson DB (2001) Practical meta-analysis. SAGE Publications, Thousand Oaks

Lupton E, Phillips JC (2015) Graphic design: the new basics, 2nd edn. Princeton Architectural Press, New York

McGregor M, Brophy JM (2005) End-user involvement in health technology assessment (HTA) development: a way to increase impact. Int J Technol Assess Health Care 21:263–267

McKibbon K (1998) Evidence-based practice. Bull Med Libr Assoc 86(3):396

Meyer B (2018a) Empirical answers to important software engineering questions (part 1 of 2). https://cacm.acm.org/blogs/blog-cacm/224351-empirical-answers-to-important-software-engineering-questions-part-1-of-2/fulltext

Meyer B (2018b) Empirical answers to important software engineering questions (part 2 of 2). https://cacm.acm.org/blogs/blog-cacm/224677-empirical-answers-to-important-software-engineering-questions-part-2-of-2/fulltext

Meyer B (2018c) The end of software engineering and the last methodologist. https://cacm.acm.org/blogs/blog-cacm/224352-the-end-of-software-engineering-and-the-last-methodologist/fulltext

Moher D et al (2015) All in the family: systematic reviews, rapid reviews, scoping reviews, realist reviews, and more. Syst Rev 4:183

Polisena J et al (2015) Rapid review summit: an overview and initiation of a research agenda. Syst Rev 4:137

Rogers E (2003) Diffusion of innovations, 5th edn. Free Press, New York. https://books.google.com.br/books?id=9U1K5LjUOwEC

Santos RES, da Silva FQB (2013) Motivation to perform systematic reviews and their impact on software engineering practice. In: 2013 ACM/IEEE international symposium on empirical software engineering and measurement, pp 292–295

Stol K-J, Ralph P, Fitzgerald B (2016) Grounded theory in software engineering research: a critical review and guidelines. In: Proceedings of the 38th international conference on software engineering, ICSE '16. ACM, New York, pp 120–131. http://doi.acm.org/10.1145/2884781.2884833

Taylor-Phillips S et al (2017) Comparison of a full systematic review versus rapid review approaches to assess a newborn screening test for tyrosinemia type 1. Res Synth Methods 8:475–484

Tondreau B (2011) Layout essentials: 100 design principles for using grids. Design essentials. Rockport Publishers, Beverly

Tricco A, Antony J, Zarin W, Strifler L, Ghassemi M, Ivory J, Perrier L, Hutton B, Moher D, Straus SE (2015) A scoping review of rapid review methods. BMC Med 13:224

Tricco AC et al (2016) An international survey and modified Delphi approach revealed numerous rapid review methods. J Clin Epidemiol 70:61–67

Tricco AC, Langlois EV, Straus SE et al (2017) Rapid reviews to strengthen health policy and systems: a practical guide. World Health Organization, Geneva

Van de Velde S et al (2011) Medicinal use of potato-derived products: conclusions of a rapid versus full systematic review. Phytother Res 25:787–788

Watt A, Cameron A, Sturm L, Lathlean T, Babidge W, Blamey S, Facey K, Hailey D, Norderhaug I, Maddern G et al (2008) Rapid reviews versus full systematic reviews: an inventory of current methods and practice in health technology assessment. Int J Technol Assess Health Care 24(2):133–139

Webb SA (2001) Some considerations on the validity of evidence-based practice in social work. Br J Soc Work 31(1):57–79

Yasin A, Hasnain MI (2012) On the quality of grey literature and its use in information synthesis during systematic literature reviews

Young I et al (2014) A guide for developing plain-language and contextual summaries of systematic reviews in agri-food public health. Foodborne Pathog Dis 11(12):930–937

Yourdon E (1995) When good enough software is best. IEEE Softw 12:79–81

Zechmeister I, Schumacher I (2012) The impact of health technology assessment reports on decision making in Austria. Int J Technol Assess Health Care 28:77–84

Benefitting from the Grey Literature
in Software Engineering Research

Vahid Garousi (iD), Michael Felderer (iD), Mika V. Mäntylä (iD),
and Austen Rainer (iD)

Abstract Researchers generally place the most trust in peer-reviewed, published information, such as journals and conference papers. By contrast, software engineering (SE) practitioners typically do not have the time, access, or expertise to review and benefit from such publications. As a result, practitioners are more likely to turn to other sources of information that they trust, e.g., trade magazines, online blog posts, survey results, or technical reports, collectively referred to as grey literature (GL). Furthermore, practitioners also share their ideas and experiences as GL, which can serve as a valuable data source for research. While GL itself is not a new topic in SE, using, benefitting, and synthesizing knowledge from the GL in SE is a contemporary topic in empirical SE research and we are seeing that researchers are increasingly benefitting from the knowledge available within GL. The goal of this chapter is to provide an overview of GL in SE, together with insights on how SE researchers can effectively use and benefit from the knowledge and evidence available in the vast amount of GL.

1 Introduction

Scientists generally place the most trust in peer-reviewed, published information, such as journals and conference papers, according to the Institute for Work &

V. Garousi (✉) · A. Rainer
Queen's University Belfast, Belfast, Northern Ireland, UK
e-mail: v.garousi@qub.ac.uk; a.rainer@qub.ac.uk

M. Felderer
Department of Computer Science, University of Innsbruck, Innsbruck, Austria

Blekinge Institute of Technology, Karlskrona, Sweden
e-mail: michael.felderer@uibk.ac.at

M. V. Mäntylä
University of Oulu, Oulu, Finland
e-mail: mika.mantyla@oulu.fi

© Springer Nature Switzerland AG 2020   385
M. Felderer, G. H. Travassos (eds.), *Contemporary Empirical Methods in Software
Engineering*, https://doi.org/10.1007/978-3-030-32489-6_14

Health (2019). By contrast, software practitioners typically do not have access to peer-reviewed publications, or the time or expertise to read such publications. As a result, practitioners are more likely to turn to other sources of information that they trust, e.g., trade magazines, online blog posts, question-answers sites, survey results, or technical reports, collectively referred to as *grey literature (GL)*, as mentioned in a technical report by the Institute for Work & Health (2019). Furthermore, practitioners also share their ideas and experiences as GL, which can serve as a valuable data source for research. Indeed, Devanbu et al. (2016) and Rainer et al. (2003) both found that practitioners most trust their peers, particularly local experts. This situation can lead to various negative outcomes for research, e.g., the limited quality and quantity of communication between researchers and practitioners as reported by Garousi et al. (2019), and the limited relevance and applicability of many research papers when applied into industrial settings.

In an online article by the University of New England (2019), it is mentioned that *"Much grey literature is of high quality. Grey literature is often the best source of up-to-date research on certain topics, such as rural poverty."* We wonder about the comparable situation in software engineering (SE). As examples, there is a book by Brooks (1995), entitled *The Mythical Man-Month*, and also another book by DeMarco and Lister (2013), entitled *Peopleware*. While both of these books formally belong to the GL, since they are books, and, yet, they are highly cited in SE research.

We and many researchers, e.g., Elliott (2019), share the opinion that *"if used with care, grey literature can open up valuable additional sources of information for researchers."* Furthermore, according to a paper by Farace (1997), the growth rate of GL was 3–4 times that of conventional peer-reviewed literature. With the major advancement of the Internet, we believe that the dissemination rate of GL would be much higher now.

While GL can offer a wealth of additional information for researchers, some of this information being much more current than research, GL should also be treated with caution and cross-checked with other sources. For example, an assessment by the Intergovernmental Panel on Climate Change (IPCC) of climate science in 2007 was subsequently criticized by the Inter-Academy Council (IAC), an umbrella council for science academies. According to Rincon (2010), the IAC reported that part of the IPCC report contained statements based on little evidence, and the use of GL in that assessment *"sparked controversy."*

> There is a great potential for benefitting from grey literature in software-engineering research.

Other papers put forward bold ideas relating to GL, e.g., Banks (2006) suggested the notions of a *"continuum of scholarship"* and *"the eventual collapse of the distinction between grey and non-grey literature,*" implying that different types of literature (peer-reviewed and grey) are, or could be, merging into each other.

Over many years, SE research has used a variety of practitioner-generated content in close collaboration with practitioners, e.g., the work by Molléri et al. (2016) on interviews, opinion surveys, and project documents and the work by Sharp et al. (2010) on ethnographies. Garousi et al. (2019) recently suggested the use of GL as a knowledge source in SE research (Garousi and Mäntylä 2016; Williams and Rainer 2017). As reported by Garousi et al. (2019), a large number of SE practitioners write and share technical writings as GL, e.g., in the form of blog-like documents, videos, and white papers. As recent work in SE has shown—e.g., Garousi et al. (2016a), Rainer (2017), Williams and Rainer (2017), and Rainer and Williams (2019)—there is great potential for benefitting from GL in SE research.

Practitioners have shared their ideas and experiences online for many years, and thus, GL itself is not a recent topic in SE. However, using, benefitting, and synthesizing knowledge from the GL in SE is a contemporary issue in SE research and in empirical SE. The goal of this chapter is to provide an overview of GL, together with insights into using and benefitting from the knowledge available in the vast amount of GL in SE research.

The remainder of this chapter is organized as follows. We first review the general concept of GL and provide further background information. We then review the state of GL in SE research, including context, types, diversity, and scale of GL in SE research and practice. We then suggest and discuss a selection of approaches for using and analyzing GL in SE research.

2 The General Concept of Grey Literature

In this section, we provide an overview of the general concept of GL, including different types of GL, and how GL has been conceived and used in other research disciplines.

2.1 What Is GL and What Are Its Types, in General?

Though there are many definitions of GL in the literature, they are quite similar. The *Cochrane Handbook for Systematic Reviews of Interventions* (Lefebvre et al. 2008) defines GL as "*literature that is not formally published in sources such as books or journal articles.*" According to the Institute for Work & Health (2019), GL is essentially any document that has *not* gone through formal peer review for publication. There is an annual conference on GL[1] and an international journal

---

[1] www.textrelease.com

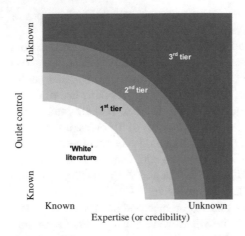

3rd **tier GL: Low outlet control/ Low credibility:** such as blogs, emails, tweets

2nd **tier GL: Moderate outlet control/ Moderate credibility:** such as annual reports, news articles, presentations, videos, Q/A sites (such as StackOverflow), Wiki articles

1st **tier GL: High outlet control/ High credibility:** such as books, magazines, government reports, white papers

Fig. 1 "Shades" of grey literatures (based on Adams et al. 2016)

on GL.[2] There is also a Grey Literature Network Service,[3] which is *"dedicated to research, publication, open access, education, and public awareness to grey literature."*

However, which types of sources are considered as GL depends to some extent on the research discipline. Therefore, models that classify source types into categories of GL are very helpful. There are many models for classifying different categories of GL and GL sources, e.g., the model by Adams et al. (2016), shown in Fig. 1, stems from the management sciences. This model has two dimensions: (1) expertise and (2) outlet control. Both dimensions run between the extremes "unknown" and "known." Expertise is the extent to which the authority and knowledge of the producer of the content can be determined. Outlet control is the extent to which content is produced, moderated, or edited in conformance with explicit and transparent knowledge-creation criteria. Rather than having discrete bands, the gradation in both dimensions is on a continuous range between known and unknown, producing the shades of GL. To emphasize: the figure is not intended to suggest discrete boundaries between the tiers.

The model presented in Fig. 1 is comparable with Table 1, developed by Giustini and Thompson (2010), which shows the spectrum of the "white," "grey," and "black." The "white" literature is visible in both Fig. 1 and Table 1 and indicates that both expertise and outlet control are fully (or at least sufficiently) known. With the examples presented in Table 1, GL corresponds mainly to the second tier in Fig. 1, with moderate outlet control and expertise.

"Black" literature is at the low end of both the outlet control and credibility spectrums. Blogs, but also emails and tweets, mainly refer to ideas, concepts, or

---

[2]http://www.greynet.org/thegreyjournal.html

[3]www.greynet.org

Table 1 Spectrum of the "white," "grey," and "black" literature

"White" literature	"Grey" literature	"Black" literature
• Published journal papers • Conference proceedings • Books	• Preprints • e-prints • Technical reports • Lectures • Datasets • Audio-video (AV) media • Blogs	• Ideas • Concepts • Thoughts

From: Giustini and Thompson (2010)

thoughts that are not peer reviewed by any "outlets." They are typically in the third tier of the model presented in Fig. 1.

We noted earlier that there are "shades" of grey in the classifications given in Fig. 1 and Table 1 and, depending on the degree of peer review during the process of creating the item of GL, a specific item of GL can be in different tiers of Fig. 1. For example, in a GL review study of microservices, Soldani et al. (2018) identified 20 blog posts for further analyses, using a quality checklist to identify the higher-quality GL. As a contrasting example that analyzed the types, frequencies, and findability of interdisciplinary GL, Marsolek et al. (2018) treated conference papers as GL. This is because, in some disciplines, conferences accept all submitted papers with no peer review. However, in SE research at least, the highly ranked conferences have established peer review processes to select submitted papers for publication in a similar process to journals. Thus, the SE research community does not in general treat conference papers as GL.

> Grey literature sources can be classified according to the two dimensions: expertise and outlet control. Expertise is the extent to which the authority and knowledge of the producer of the content can be determined. Outlet control is the extent to which content is produced, moderated, or edited in conformance with explicit and transparent knowledge-creation criteria.

As further contrasting examples, M.Sc. and Ph.D. theses are often reviewed by several examiners and therefore are also often peer reviewed. Also, in most software companies who intend to share technical reports or white papers online, such documents are almost always reviewed to some degree by peers, and therefore such publications could be considered as peer-reviewed literature. The peer review process for technical documents differs from the peer review of academic publications, however. For example, academic peer review is often done anonymously by reviewers who are independent, with less potential for conflicts of interest. The peer review process is also managed by an independent editor. By contrast, the peer review of technical documents, in practice, may often be undertaken by known colleagues. Thus, in summary, we conclude that what constitutes GL depends on the standards of the respective research discipline.

We also recognize that the rise of social media is increasing the extent of GL in SE. Storey et al. (2014) write of "The (R)Evolution of Social Media in Software Engineering." They illustrate that communication and social media produce data through different channels and this communication evolves over the years. For example, Usenet, Email List, and SourceForge used to be popular, but currently tools such as Stack Overflow, Slack, and GitHub dominate. Social media is usually third level (tier) GL, in Fig. 1, but some of content sources such as Stack Overflow or Wikipedia can be considered second level GL as there are informal controls and other people can edit and improve the content. Williams and Rainer (2017) recommend that GL materials "*need to be rigorous, relevant, well written and experience based for them to be considered credible to [SE] researchers.*" Another consideration is that as one lowers the quality threshold, i.e., move from tier 1 to 3 (in Fig. 1), the amount of available literature grows to enable large-scale quantitative analysis. The scale of this GL is further addressed in Sect. 3.5.

Due to the limited control of expertise and outlet in GL, it is important to also identify GL producers. Giustini and Thompson (2010) identified the following GL producers: (1) government departments and agencies (i.e., in municipal, provincial, or national levels); (2) nonprofit economic and trade organizations; (3) academic and research institutions; (4) societies and political parties; (5) libraries, museums, and archives; (6) businesses and corporations; and (7) freelance individuals, i.e., bloggers, consultants, and Web 2.0 enthusiasts. Marsolek et al. (2018) found that GL was present in the majority (68%) of the subject databases and almost all institutional repositories (95%).

2.2 GL in Other Research Disciplines

GL is already established in a number of other research disciplines. Marsolek et al. (2018) examined 118 subject databases used by academic researchers, together with 115 repositories held by North American institutions, which included GL. The databases and repositories covered the arts, business, education, health sciences, humanities, multidisciplinary research, natural sciences, physical sciences and engineering, and social sciences.

> Grey literature is already established, as a source of knowledge/evidence, in many other research disciplines.

Luzi (2000) identified stages in the growth of GL, from its first appearance in the post-war period to its evolution into electronic GL, and analyzes a selection of studies and conferences organized up to the 1990s. He also examines the first databases: these transformed the way in which GL was collected and distributed. Luzi's review is of course dated now by about 20 years. In contrast to Luzi's retrospective, Banks (2006) took a more prospective view and considers political and technological aspects for increasing access to valuable GL. For Banks, institutional repositories present an exciting opportunity for both the preservation and retrieval of GL.

Other relevant work includes discussions by Thompson (2001) of ways in which GL in engineering can be acquired and used, and arguments provided by McKimmie and Szurmak (2002) on how grey questions can drive research.

2.3   Usage and Analysis of GL in the CS Research

GL has also received attention in the computer science (CS) research community, e.g., computational linguistics, data and knowledge engineering, information retrieval, database, and expert systems. Studies have analyzed the GL data to answer a variety of research questions. For example, Swanson et al. (2014) focused on identifying narrative clauses in personal stories. Their study used 50 personal stories drawn from 5000 blog posts. Facca and Lanzi (2005) reported a survey on mining "interesting" knowledge from weblogs. Park et al. (2010) analyzed 588 sentences from 6000 blog posts on WordPress. Kurashima et al. (2009) analyzed 29 million blog posts collected using the BlogRanger 2.0 API. In another study, Kurashima et al. (2006) analyzed 62,396 articles from two Japanese blog hosting sites. Finally, Inui et al. (2008) analyzed 50 million posts from 150 million weblog posts (in Japanese). Bansal et al. (2007) developed *BlogScope*, a system for analyzing temporally ordered streaming text online. At the time, *BlogScope* "... *track[ed] more than 36 million blogs with more than 837 million posts in the blogosphere ... [fetching on average] 14,000 new documents every hour*," a quote from Lakshmanan and Oberhofer (2010). The service was shut down in early 2012.

3   Grey Literature in Software Engineering

In this section, we review the state of GL in SE, considering the context, types, diversity, and scale of GL.

3.1   What Is GL in SE?

Based on the two dimensions to classify GL defined in the previous section, i.e., expertise and outlet control, GL in SE can be defined as any material about SE that

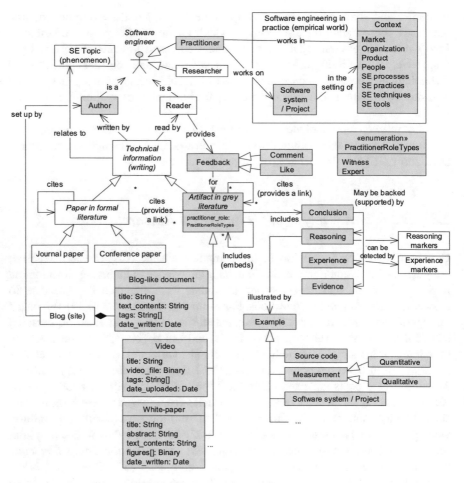

Fig. 2 A context diagram showing the context of GL in SE

is not formally peer reviewed nor formally published. We summarize the concept of GL in SE using a UML context diagram (see Fig. 2).

Grey literature in SE can be defined as any material about SE that is not formally peer reviewed nor formally published.

At the center of this diagram lies the "*Technical information (writing)*" class which has two subclasses: *Paper in academic literature* and *Artefact in grey literature*. A *technical information* piece is written by one or more *Authors* and is read by one or more *Readers*, who are themselves *Software Engineers*. A *Software*

Engineer has two subtypes: *Practitioner* and *Researcher*. An *Artefact in grey literature* could be a *Blog-like document*, or *Video*, or *White paper*, etc. According to Rainer (2017), an *Artefact in grey literature* could include *Conclusions* which in turn may be backed (supported) by *Reasoning*, *Experience*, and/or *Evidence* and illustrated by one or more *Examples*. The *Practitioner* writes an *Artefact in grey literature* using her/his professional experience of software practice (empirical world).

3.2 Scale of the Software Engineering Community: Academia Versus Industry

To further understand the role and position of GL in SE practice and SE research, we present a high-level view of the community of SE practice versus research. We look at the estimated population of the two communities.

According to a report by Evans Data Corporation (2018), there were about 23 million software developers worldwide in 2018, and that number is estimated to reach 27.7 million by 2023. According to an *IEEE Software* paper by Briand (2012), *"4000 individuals" are "actively publishing in major [SE] journals,"* which can be used as the estimated size (lower bound) of the SE research community. If we divide the two numbers, we can see that on average, there is one SE academic for every 5750 practicing software engineers, indicating that the size of the SE research community is very small compared to the size of the SE practitioner community. We visualize the two communities and the current state of collaboration in Fig. 3, which has been taken from the work of Garousi et al. (2018). The chapter "Practical Industry Co-production and Technology and Knowledge Interchange" also presents important concepts about industry–academic collaborations in software engineering.

As visualized in Fig. 3, while there exist established ways to enable knowledge flow from software industry to academia, e.g., interviews, opinion surveys, and ethnography, we believe that benefitting from GL materials is another prominent enabler for this.

3.3 Process of Generating the GL Content in SE

To better understand the nature of GL in SE, it is also important to characterize the process by which GL content is generated. We depict such a process in Fig. 4 which is a simplified version of the ideas presented in Rainer and Williams (2019). The process presented in the figure is intended only as an illustrative example, not as an accurate descriptive account or a prescription of the processes that should occur.

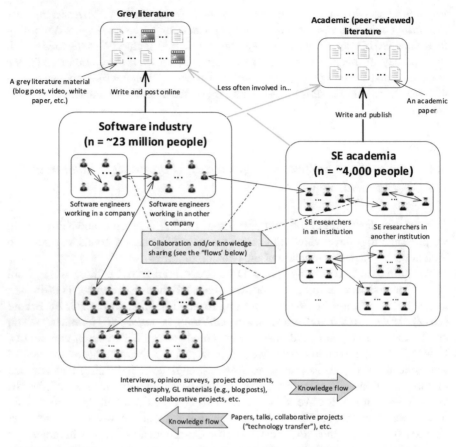

Fig. 3 Visualizing the community of software practitioners and researchers, and the knowledge flow between them (including GL); from Garousi et al. (2018)

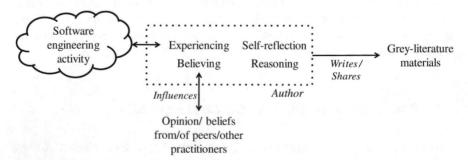

Fig. 4 Process model of the generation of GL contents; simplified from Rainer and Williams (2019)

In terms of research, we are interested in what the GL author is able to describe of real-world software engineering practice. These descriptions are obviously filtered through the processes that occur between *experiencing* and *reporting* in the model. Many of these processes are internal to the GL author. These internal processes therefore introduce threats to validity relating to subjectivity, and also challenges to research due to the invisibility of these processes. Peer review helps to counteract these threats by independently reviewing the *outputs* from the internal processes, rather than reviewing the processes themselves. The chapter "Systematic Assessment of Threats to Validity in Software Engineering Secondary Studies" presents important concepts about systematic assessment of threats to validity in software engineering secondary studies, and some of those ideas can be applied when conducting secondary studies involving GL.

In terms of the internal processes represented in Fig. 4:

- Experiencing is an active engagement between the author and the empirical world. Experiencing can take place at different levels of scope and resolution, e.g., directly experiencing programming in contrast to experiencing the "behavior" of a software organization. The formation of experience is influenced by prior beliefs and in turn influences those beliefs and is influenced by self-reflection and reasoning.
- Beliefs are defined as conceptions, personal ideologies, worldviews, and values that shape practice and orient knowledge. Passos et al. (2011) investigated the role of beliefs in software practice.
- Underpinning the processes that occur within the author, the author has the ability to self-reflect (to some degree) and to reason (to some degree) about her or his experiencing, beliefs, and reporting.

Other peoples' beliefs may influence the author. As noted earlier, Devanbu et al. (2016) and Rainer et al. (2003) have investigated the role of others' beliefs. Figure 4 indicates that, finally, the author reports information that may include some description of their experience of software practice, some expression of her or his beliefs, and some degree of reasoning relating these experiences and beliefs. It is very likely that the information reported will be incomplete in some way(s), which could also be the case for papers written by researchers.

3.4 GL as a Source of Knowledge and Evidence in SE

An emerging view in SE is that a large amount of SE-related information and experience is becoming available, much of it in the GL, and those data need to be more effectively used to solve practical issues and to push SE research forward, e.g., reported by Garousi et al. (2016a), Rainer (2017), Williams and Rainer (2017), and Rainer and Williams (2019). Lawrence and Giles (1999) observe that this situation occurs in many other disciplines. MacDonald et al. (2007) state that "*the problems of awareness [e.g., for using GL in SE research] persist, even though most of the new information is now digitally produced and arguably easier to access."* It has been recognized in other disciplines that the diffusion, use, and influence of such GL information are complex and variable processes, e.g., by Farace (1997).

GL has already been recognized as a knowledge source in other research areas, e.g., in medicine, with studies by Chavez et al. (2007) and Pappas and Williams (2011), and in earth sciences, with the study by Augusto et al. (2010).

Pappas and Williams (2011) stated that *"Because of the delay between research and publication, and because of the potential that some important research may never be published, access to innovative information is challenging. Grey literature is a tool to fill that void."*

Garousi et al. (2019) propose one approach to combine knowledge from both GL and published literature: the Multivocal Literature Reviews (MLR). An MLR is a form of a Systematic Literature Review (SLR), which includes the GL in addition to the published literature (e.g., journal and conference papers). MLRs are useful for both researchers and practitioners since they provide summaries of both the state of the art and practice in a given area.

In an MLR on when and what to automate in software testing (abbreviated ManAutoTest MLR in the following) conducted by Garousi and Mäntylä (2016), the researchers reviewed the formal and grey literature. If GL would have been excluded from the pool of papers, a significant body of experience and knowledge from practicing test engineers on the topic would have been missed. To put this in quantitative terms, we partitioned the synthesis of a major output of that MLR (factors to be considered for deciding when and what to automate in testing) by the type of source where they were mentioned in either formal or GL, as shown in Fig. 5. As we can see, out of the total of 15 factor categories, GL sources contributed a total of 219 occurrences (instances) while academic sources discussed only 67 occurrences.

Fig. 5 A main output of the MLR on ManAutoTest; from Garousi and Mäntylä (2016)

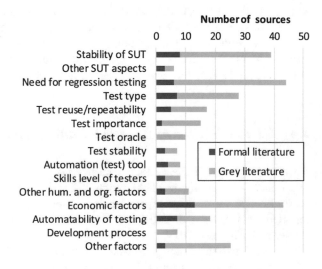

Furthermore, we can see from the figure that, if we were to not include the GL, two categories (*test oracle* and *development process*) would not have been identified in the study. The study demonstrates that GL can be a major source of knowledge and experience. In addition, we extracted in the MLR study a large number of qualitative quotes, related and in support of the factors presented in Fig. 5, e.g., a presentation by IBM engineers expressed: *"Main Application has lot of inter-dependency with other Applications which in turn cannot be automated,"* referring to the System Under Test (SUT)-related factors.

Additionally, we found in the ManAutoTest MLR that the type of evidence found in GL was generally valid viewpoints, ideas of cause–effect relationships that could be scientifically studied, as well as explanations of why and in what context certain heuristics worked while others did not. We did not, however, find any sophisticated (hardcore) empirical evidence, such as controlled experiments, in the GL. The stated findings were mostly based on claims and experience. Also, the source of evidence was difficult to identify as the reporting was of low quality. Furthermore, we observed in our study that replication of the GL results was not generally possible.

In summary, we can see that the MLR leveraged the readily available GL knowledge on the Internet to synthesize the data and answer the important RQs of the MLR study. If no GL data were to be used, the researchers had to conduct interviews and/or opinion surveys that are often costly and may lead to the same outcomes. Thus, we can see that using GL as a knowledge source can save research costs and also improve research quality.

While GL can be useful as a source of knowledge and evidence in SE research, we raise some caution about how far one can go (scientifically) with GL-based evidence. While such evidence could clearly complement empirical studies in SE, it cannot substitute conventional data gathered in traditional empirical studies. As we will discuss in one of the next subsections, there are inherent challenges when using GL in SE research, e.g., the issue of quality assurance of GL materials. Chapter "Evidence Aggregation in Software Engineering" presents concepts and approaches about evidence aggregation in software engineering, most of which can be applied for aggregation of evidence from GL.

3.5 Types of GL in SE

As noted above, there are different types of GL, for example, white papers, blog posts, and videos. Within a particular item of GL for SE, there can be considerable variety of content, e.g., a web page can contain text, formatted tables, static images (that may themselves present text or tables), animated images (e.g., GIFs), videos (that again may contain text and tables), and audio. Thus, there is a much greater diversity of types of GL and content within an item of GL compared to academic literature. We list different dimensions of variability in GL materials in Table 2.

Table 2 Dimensions of variability in GL materials; from Rainer and Williams (2019)

Dimension	Explanation and examples
Quality of written language	For example, the formality of language
Natural language	Most research appears to focus on English, but there are, of course, a very wide range of other languages to consider
Media	Video, text, static image, animated image, audio, presentations
"Encoding" of the media	Text with, for example, HTML
	(Proprietary) binary formats, e.g., Adobe PDF
Structure	Headings, subheadings
Content	Reasoning, e.g., claims, reasons, arguments
	Opinions
	Reporting of actual experience, perhaps as a "war story"
	Code-related information, e.g., source code, documentation, API
	Web links, e.g., URLs
	(Tables of) data
	Citations

3.6 Scale of GL in SE

It is hard to establish the quantity of general GL available online (without even considering variation in the quality of GL) aside from the challenge of considering the scale of SE-specific GL. Consequently, we briefly report a range of example measures for GL in general and for SE.

Statista, an online market research and business intelligence portal, reported in October 2018 that Tumblr, a popular blog platform, alone has 440 million blogs.[4] As of January 2019, WordPress self-reported[5] that "*Users produce about 136.2 million new posts and 77.7 million new comments each month.*" None of these statistics relate specifically to GL for SE, and it is unlikely that these statistics would report GL hosted on intranets.

Choi maintains a curated list[6] of blogs focusing on SE, classified by type (i.e., company, individual/group, and product/technology). Choi lists approximately 650 blogs, of which approximately 250 are written by individuals. Panji maintains a curated list of 185 software-related corporate blogs,[7] e.g., Autodesk, BBC, Dropbox, Facebook, LinkedIn, Mozilla, and Netflix. Merchant maintains a list of over 50 tech blogs.[8] Abstracta provides a list of 75 blogs and websites on software

---

[4]https://www.statista.com/statistics/256235/total-cumulative-number-of-tumblr-blogs/

[5]https://wordpress.com/activity/

[6]https://github.com/kilimchoi/engineering-blogs

[7]https://github.com/sumodirjo

[8]https://github.com/amitmerchant1990/tech-blogs

testing.[9] By contrast, Zalecki maintains a list[10] of software *podcasts*. He states that he is subscribed to over 100 podcasts, although lists 11 at his site. In their systematic GL review of microservices, Soldani et al. (2018) observed a "...
massive proliferation of grey literature [on microservices], with more than 10,000 articles on disparate sub-topics . . . ."

3.7   Benefits of Utilizing the GL in SE Research

Rainer and Williams (2019) reviewed research on the benefits, challenges, and research directions for the use of blogs in software engineering research. They identified a number of benefits to the use of blogs. Many of these benefits may apply to the use of GL more generally, but we focus here on SE. The benefits are summarized in Table 3.

3.8   Challenges of Using GL in SE Research

As well as the benefits of using blog posts (identified earlier), Rainer and Williams (2019) also identified a number of challenges to the use of blogs as a type of GL. These challenges were organized into several themes and are summarized here in Table 4.

3.9   Diversity in Quality and Degree of Evidence in GL Materials

Since processes for GL are more diverse and less controlled, compared to academic literature, the quality of GL is more diverse and often more difficult to assess. The quality of GL determines whether data from GL or conclusions raised in GL can be used and analyzed (see Sect. 4). Garousi et al. (2019) compiled a quality assessment checklist for GL shown in Table 5. It contains the criteria of authority of the producer, methodology, objectivity, date, position with respect to related sources, novelty, impact, and outlet type as well as assessment questions for each criterion.

For each type of GL, the relevant quality criteria have to be selected, adapted, and finally assessed, which can for instance be done on a two-point Likert scale with values "yes" or "no"; see for example, Garousi et al. (2019). For instance, a

---

[9]https://abstracta.us/blog/75-best-software-testing-blogs/

[10]https://michalzalecki.com/curated-list-of-podcasts-for-software-developers/

Table 3 Benefits of utilizing the GL in SE research, based on Rainer and Williams (2019)

In general, GL materials
1. Provide information on practitioners' contemporary perspectives on important topics relevant to practice and to research
2. Promote the voice of practitioners
In particular, GL materials (such as blog-like documents) provide (access to) information on the practitioner's
1. Experience and inexperience of theirs' and others' software practice
2. Motivations for that practice
3. Values relating to that practice
4. Emotions relating to that practice
5. Beliefs about software practice
6. Empirical data from their practice
7. Explanations of that practice
In providing such information, GL materials
1. Help bridge the divide between research and practice
2. Complement the research literature by "filling in gaps" in research
3. Help to counteract bias findings, as a result of publication bias in the research literature
GL materials should be considered when (Williams and Rainer 2017)
1. The topic of the research is complex
2. The topic is not "solvable" by using only the peer-reviewed research literature
3. There is a lack of quantity and/or quality of best evidence from research, or a lack of consensus in the research
4. Context is important to the study of the topic
5. The researcher intends to challenge existing assumptions and findings, either in research or practice, or both
6. A synthesis of practice and research would be valuable to either or both communities
7. The researcher intends to consider trends over time
8. The researcher seeks to better understand, assess, or demonstrate the impact of research in relation to a particular topic
Methodologically, the use of GL materials in research helps researchers to
1. Assess and address publication bias
2. Compensate for the (un)availability of other sources of evidence
3. Increase research visibility into actual software practice
4. Access harder-to-access practitioners, e.g., due to logistics, or demographics
5. Gather information for the research in a noninvasive way
6. Scale-up their research to, or with, larger samples
7. Complement and triangulate with other sources of data
8. Provide an audit trail of their research
9. Replicate each other's study through public access to original data

Table 4 Challenges of working with and using GL in SE research, based on Rainer and Williams (2019)

Challenges themes	Concrete challenges
Foundations, e.g., there are a lack of . . .	• Formal definitions of GL and GL materials • Formal models of GL materials and content, in particular – A data model of GL materials and content – A process model of the creation, review, and publication of GL materials and content • Frameworks for evaluating the quality of GL materials and content, and classifying those materials and content
Inherent nature of GL materials	There are challenges managing . . . • The very large quantity of GL materials • The variability of GL materials • The uncertain process for generating, publishing, and revising the content of GL materials
Resources	There are a lack of . . . • Central repositories of GL materials • Tools to work with GL materials and content, for example: – To select the higher-quality documents when performing a search – To select particular types of GL materials, e.g., those reporting experience, values, explanations, etc. • Datasets and corpora of GL materials
Quality assurance	While some efforts have started, e.g., Garousi et al. (2019), there is a shortage of: • Well-developed and accepted checklists for the quality assurance of various aspects of GL materials including: – The author – The document – The content of the document, e.g., claims – The readers' assessment of the credibility of the document – The readers – The readers' feedback on the document, e.g., comments, shares, up-votes
Methodology	• The evidential value of blog-like content • The appropriate research methods to use with GL materials and content

number of online comments to measure the impact only exist for source types open for comments like blog posts, news articles, or videos. A highly commented blog post may indicate popularity, but on the other hand, spam comments may bias the number of comments, thus invalidating the high popularity.

Table 5 Quality assessment checklist for GL in SE

Criteria	Questions
Authority of the producer	• Is the publishing organization reputable? For example, the Software Engineering Institute (SEI) • Is an individual author associated with a reputable organization? • Has the author published other work in the field? • Does the author have expertise in the area? (e.g., job title principal software engineer)
Methodology	• Does the source have a clearly stated aim? • Does the source have a stated methodology? • Is the source supported by authoritative, contemporary references? • Are any limits clearly stated? • Does the work cover a specific question? • Does the work refer to a particular population or case?
Objectivity	• Does the work seem to be balanced in presentation? • Is the statement in the sources as objective as possible? Or, is the statement a subjective opinion? • Is there a vested interest? For example, a tool comparison by authors that are working for a particular tool vendor • Are the conclusions supported by the data?
Date	• Does the item have a clearly stated date?
Position w.r.t. related sources	• Have key-related GL or formal sources been linked to/discussed?
Novelty	• Does it enrich or add something unique to the research? • Does it strengthen or refute a current position?
Impact	• Normalize all the following impact metrics into a single aggregated impact metric (when data are available): number of citations; number of backlinks; number of social media shares (the so-called alt-metrics); number of comments posted for a specific online entry, like a blog post or a video; number of page or paper views
Outlet type	• First tier GL (measure = 1): high outlet control/high credibility: books, magazines, theses, government reports, white papers • Second tier GL (measure = 0.5): Moderate outlet control/moderate credibility: annual reports, news articles, presentations, videos, Q/A sites (such as Stack Overflow), Wiki articles • Third tier GL (measure = 0): Low outlet control/low credibility: blogs, emails, tweets

4 How GL Can Be Used/Analyzed in SE

The SE research community has started to use the information and evidence from the GL in different ways.

4.1 Review of How GL Has Been Used/Analyzed in SE Research

Table 6 classifies the SE research community's use of GL. We distinguish in Table 6 different ways of utilizing/analyzing the GL in SE research. The first three types of study concern the use of GL in a primary study, ranging from studies with a specific

Table 6 Different ways of utilizing/analyzing the GL in SE research community so far

Study types	Type of usage/analysis	Example papers
Primary studies (from specific focus on GL to only citing GL)	Analyzing GL materials with qualitative approach	• Using argumentation theory to analyze software practitioners' defeasible evidence, inference, and belief (Rainer 2017) • An analysis of major pivots of software startups (Bajwa et al. 2017) • Analyzing the motivations and challenges of developers for blogging (Parnin ct al. 2013)
	Analyzing GL with quantitative approach	• Measuring API documentation: 1730 websites and 376 blog posts (Parnin and Treude 2011) • What are mobile developers asking about? A large-scale study using Stack Overflow (Rosen and Shihab 2016)
	Citation to GL: GL materials are cited in research papers as related works/examples	Many papers in SE cite GL materials for different reasons, e.g., to motivate the papers. Two examples of widely cited GL materials in SE are: • The economic impacts of inadequate infrastructure for software testing (Planning 2002) • Various editions of the Standish Group's "Chaos" report (The Standish Group 2019)
Secondary studies	Systematic reviews involving GL	• An MLR on iOS applications testing (Kulesovs 2015) • A GLR on choosing the right test automation tool (Raulamo et al. 2017) • An MLR on when to automate in testing (Garousi and Mäntylä 2016)

focus on GL to those studies that only cite GL. The fourth type of study concerns secondary studies, i.e., the systematic review of GL. We discuss these types in more detail in the following subsections.

4.1.1 Qualitative Analysis of GL Materials

Many SE researchers are analyzing GL material and answering GL-specific research questions even when they do not explicitly acknowledge it. The grey literature can be analyzed with both qualitative and quantitative methods (see the next section). With qualitative methods we mean analysis methods where humans read, analyze, and classify GL text in order to produce knowledge. When using a qualitative approach, one can use approaches presented in qualitative research guideline books and articles, e.g., those by Patton (2002) and Cruzes and Dybå (2011).

We can find qualitative works in this area. In some papers, humans analyze and classify the particular GL contents and explore motivations for GL production in software development. Parnin et al. (2013) analyzed why and about what the software developers write blogs. They found that the blogs covered multiple topics such as code and tool tutorials, new releases and enhancement to the products the developers were working with, and general technology discussions for example. Blogging was motivated by personal branding, evangelism, and getting feedback, and finally for personal knowledge repository. A study of similar nature was later conducted by MacLeod et al. (2015) on software developers' YouTube videos that found video content was more about technical topics such as development experience, implementation choices, and data structures. Videos were also seen as an alternative to blogging and many similar motivations for video creations existed as for blogging.

Bajwa et al. (2017) use GL of software startups and analyze their business pivots. The authors frame their study as a case study on secondary data that the authors collected from various websites. They find that software startups pivot for 14 reasons (triggers) such as negative customer reaction, unable to beat a competitor, and technological challenge. They also find evidence of ten different pivot types such as switching to a different problem and zoom-in where a particular feature becomes the whole product.

There are other studies that use a set of GL materials, but do not survey a large/r set of literature, instead adopting a kind of case study approach. As one example, Rainer (2017) used argumentation schemes to qualitatively analyze information reported by Joel Spolsky in one of his blog posts, entitled *The Language Wars*. Rainer formally modeled the integration of argumentation structures and professional experience and then showed how the arguments and experience can be related to previous research. Rainer's in-depth analyses of one blog post may be understood as a case study to complement the survey-like studies of MLRs and Grey Literature Reviews (GLRs).

4.1.2 Quantitative Analysis of GL Materials

In the quantitative analysis of GL, research methods range from simple frequency counting to advanced machine learning used for natural language processing such as Rosen and Shihab's (2016) topic modeling LDA (Latent Dirichlet Allocation) and Efstathiou et al.'s (2018) use of word embeddings. Much of the quantitative analyses of GL appears to concentrate around a small number of sources, principally Stack Overflow. This may be because the data is easy to access and relatively well structured. But in addition to Stack Overflow, one can find more analyses of blogs, e.g., by Parnin and Treude (2011), and emails, e.g., by Sharma et al. (2017), which should offer a more multivocal view. Next, we present a few examples of studies using quantitative analysis of GL.

Gruetze et al. (2016) examined topic shifts, by analyzing tags in software development QA site Stack Overflow. The authors showed declining trends in tags like Delphi and Database Design, while increasing trends were found for the programming language "R" and Node.js for example. They also show that automated tagging of posts is improved when the time of the post is considered.

As noted already, Rosen and Shihab (2016) also analyzed Stack Overflow but with respect to questions that mobile developers are asking about. They analyze 13 million posts and use LDA to cluster the data. They find that mobile developers ask about "app distribution, mobile APIs, data management, sensors and context, mobile tools, and user interface development."

Quantitative analyses of GL in Stack Overflow have also been used to create guidelines of how to create good Stack Overflow posts, e.g., by Calefato et al. (2018). The authors suggest using quantitative analysis that successful Stack Overflow questions are short, have code snippets, do not abuse uppercase letter, and have neutral emotional expressions. So the analysis of GL can be used to provide advice on how to write better GL.

Sharma et al. (2017) performed quantitative analysis on email discussion in Python language evolution. They collect a dataset of over 40,000 emails. They found that technical discussion receives clearly the highest volume of emails over social and process issues. The authors conclude that this shows that Python developers mostly care and are passionate about technical features of the language.

4.2 Citations to GL in SE Papers

Many papers in SE cite GL materials for different reasons, e.g., to motivate the papers, to use their insights/data, etc. Two example widely cited GL materials in SE are: (1) A technical report entitled "*The economic impacts of inadequate infrastructure for software testing,*" conducted by Research Triangle Institute (2002), for the American National Institute of Standards and Technology (NIST), which was cited about 700 times according to Google Scholar (October 2019) and

(2) various editions of the Standish Group's "Chaos" report, e.g., the Standish Group (2019).

We believe that by providing more citations and getting insights from GL in research papers, researchers will contribute to a stronger linkage between industry and academia, as mentioned in Garousi et al. (2016b, 2017a), since readers and follow-up research studies will be encouraged to use more real-world industrial approaches and data.

4.3 Systematic Reviews Using GL Sources

Systematic reviews systematically select, review, and synthesize knowledge in a given topic of SE. Traditionally, since the inception of evidence-based software engineering (EBSE) by Kitchenham et al. (2004), two types of review studies have been published in the SE community: Systematic Literature Reviews (SLR) and Systematic Literature Mappings (SLM or SM).

With more awareness for GL in SE, recent review studies in SE have started to include GL, e.g., Garousi et al. (2019). We first discuss the different types of systematic reviews which include GL and then discuss the guidelines to conduct such studies.

To include GL, four new types of review studies have emerged, as discussed by Garousi et al. (2019): (1) Multivocal Literature Review (MLR), (2) Multivocal Literature Mapping (MLM), (3) Grey Literature Mapping (GLM), and (4) Grey Literature Review (GLR). An MLR is a form of an SLR which includes the GL in addition to the published literature. To clearly distinguish all different types of review studies in SE, we depict the relationship among them in Fig. 6.

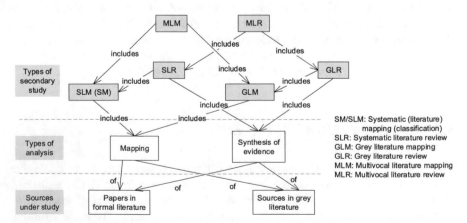

Fig. 6 Relationship among different types of systematic secondary studies (from Garousi et al. 2019)

As we see in Fig. 6, the differentiation factors of six types of systematic secondary studies are types of analysis and types of sources under study. For example, the difference between an MLR and a GLR is that, while the former reviews both GL and published literature, the latter reviews only the GL. The difference between an MLM and an MLR is that, while both analyze GL, the former reviews only the classified pool of sources, and the latter synthesizes the evidence from those sources in addition.

We looked at recent review studies in SE involving GL. We were able to find 18 such studies as shown in Table 7. Note that this list only contains the review studies involving GL focusing on SE. There have also been a recent trend on review studies involving GL in other areas of CS, e.g., an MLR on server-less computing by Sadaqat et al. (2018).

As highlighted in the table, the authors of this chapter have been involved in six (6) of these studies. As it can be seen in the table, there has been a *sharp* increase in such studies in recent years, as 9 out of 18 papers were published in 2018.

For each of the studies in Table 7, we also show the number of academic literature (AL) sources, number of GL sources, and percentage of GL sources reviewed in that study. Needless to say, the ratio would be %100 for GLR studies. The ratios, in a sense, denote the scale of AL versus GL knowledge in a given topic. For example, for the topic of involving security in DevOps (DevSecOps), the numbers of AL/ GL sources are 2/50 (a GL ratio of 96%), while in the topic of ethics in requirements engineering, the numbers of AL/GL sources are 98/34 (a GL ratio of 26%).

Grey literature and grey literature reviews inevitably have their limitations. Rainer and Williams (2019) identified several challenges with using blog posts in software engineering research. Many of these challenges apply to GL, e.g., the vast quantity of GL available, and the variability in the quality of GL. MLRs are one approach to addressing the limitations of GL, i.e., by combining GL with AL. As researchers conduct more reviews using GL so the community can develop better guidelines, checklists, and methodology for using GL in research.

5 Recommended Further Reading

The usage of grey literature (GL) in software engineering is strongly related to evidence-based methods and literature reviews in software engineering. Kitchenham et al. (2015) provided a comprehensive book on evidence-based software engineering and systematic reviews.

For the main types of systematic literature studies in software engineering, i.e., systematic literature reviews and mapping studies, there are highly referenced guideline papers, such as guidelines by Kitchenham and Charters (2007) for Systematic Literature Reviews (SLRs), which are also extensively discussed together with background information in the aforementioned book Kitchenham et al. (2015), and Petersen et al. (2015)'s guidelines for Systematic Mapping Studies (SMSs). You could perhaps include a citation to Rapid Reviews?

Table 7 A summary of the recent review studies involving GL

Review topic	Type		Year	References	# of AL sources	# of GL sources	% of GL sources
	MLR	GLR					
Technical debt	x		2013	Tom et al. (2013)	0	35	100
iOS applications testing	x		2015	Kulesovs (2015)	12	9	42
When to automate in testing	x		2016	Garousi and Mäntylä (2016)	26	52	66
Gamification of SW testing	x		2016	Mäntylä and Smolander (2016)	6	14	70
Relationship of DevOps to agile	x		2016	Lwakatare et al. (2016)	33	201	86
Characterizing DevOps	x		2016	de Franca et al. (2016)	24	19	44
Test maturity and test process improvement	x		2017	Garousi et al. (2017b)	130	51	28
Involving security in DevOps (DevSecOps)	x		2017	Myrbakken and Colomo-Palacios (2017)	2	50	96
Choosing the right test automation tool: a GLR		x	2017	Raulamo et al. (2017)	0	53	100
Smells in SW test code	x		2018	Garousi and Küçük (2018)	46	120	28
Serious games for SW process	x		2018	Calderón et al. (2018)	6	1	14
Pains and gains of microservices		x	2018	Soldani et al. (2018)	0	51	100
Relevance of software engineering research	x		2018	Garousi et al. (2018)	33	13	28
Ethics in requirements engineering	x		2018	Aberkane (2018)	98	34	26
Function-as-a-service software development		x	2018	Leitner et al. (2018)	0	50	100
Adopting the scaled agile framework (SAFe)	x		2018	Putta et al. (2018)	52	47	47
Monolithic repositories (Monorepos)	x		2018	Brito et al. (2018)	2	21	91
Use of DevOps for e-learning systems	x		2018	Sánchez-Gordón and Colomo-Palacios (2018)	3	22	88

However, none of the above guidelines explicitly discuss GL. Garousi et al. (2019) filled this gap and provided guidelines for including GL and conducting Multivocal Literature Reviews (MLRs) in software engineering. Researchers are encouraged to consult those guidelines when planning MLR or other types of studies involving GL. The guidelines for MLRs in SE cover planning, conducting, and reporting the review. The step on conducting an MLR comprises guidelines for the search process, source selection, study quality assessment, data extraction, and data synthesis.

Marsolek et al. (2018) provided an overview of the usage of GL in other fields: arts, business, education, health sciences, humanities, multidisciplinary research, natural sciences, physical sciences and engineering, and social sciences. Especially, in health sciences, GL and its analysis is well established and there is even a book by Bonato (2018) on searching the GL.

6 Conclusion

The goal of this chapter has been to provide an overview of GL in SE, together with insights on how SE researchers can effectively use and benefit from the knowledge and evidence available in the vast amount of GL. We first reviewed the general concept of GL and provided background information. We then discussed the state of GL in SE research, including the context, types, diversity, and scale of GL in SE research and practice. We then proposed and discussed five approaches for using and analyzing GL in SE research: (1) analyzing GL materials to answer GL-specific RQs; (2) using certain GL materials for qualitative studies; (3) using certain GL materials quantitative studies; (4) citing GL materials; and (5) systematic reviews involving GL.

As discussed above and also as indicated in other studies, e.g., by the University of New England (2019), the reality is that researchers mostly write for, and read from, scientific papers published in the academic, peer-reviewed literature, and by contrast, practitioners mostly write for, and read from, materials published in the GL. By reviewing how GL has been used in SE research, this chapter aims to encourage further use of GL in SE research. We recommend all SE researchers to reduce the gap between academia and industry via using GL materials in the five forms as discussed in this chapter.

References

Aberkane A (2018) Exploring ethics in requirements engineering. Master thesis, Utrecht University
Adams RJ, Smart P, Huff AS (2016) Shades of grey: guidelines for working with the grey literature in systematic reviews for management and organizational studies. Int J Manage Rev 19:432–454

Augusto L, Bakker MR, Morel C et al (2010) Is 'grey literature' a reliable source of data to characterize soils at the scale of a region? A case study in a maritime pine forest in southwestern France. Eur J Soil Sci 61(6):807–822

Bajwa SS, Wang X, Nguyen Duc A et al (2017) "Failures" to be celebrated: an analysis of major pivots of software startups. Empir Softw Eng 22(5):2373–2408

Banks MA (2006) Towards a continuum of scholarship: the eventual collapse of the distinction between grey and non-grey literature. Publ Res Q 22(1):4–11

Bansal N, Chiang F, Koudas N et al (2007) Seeking stable clusters in the blogosphere. In: Proceedings of VLDB endowment, pp 806–817

Bonato S (2018) Searching the grey literature: a handbook for searching reports, working papers, and other unpublished research. RL & Associates LLC

Briand L (2012) Embracing the engineering side of software engineering. IEEE Softw 29(4):96–96

Brito G, Terra R, Valente MT (2018) Monorepos: a multivocal literature review. arXiv preprint arXiv:1810.09477

Brooks F (1995) The mythical man-month: essays on software engineering. Pearson Education, London

Calderón A, Ruiz M, O'Connor RV (2018) A multivocal literature review on serious games for software process standards education. Comput Stand Interfaces 57:36–48

Calefato F, Lanubile F, Novielli N (2018) How to ask for technical help? Evidence-based guidelines for writing questions on Stack Overflow. Inf Softw Technol 94:186–207

Chavez TA, Perrault AH, Reehling P et al (2007) The impact of grey literature in advancing global karst research: an information needs assessment for a globally distributed interdisciplinary community. Publ Res Q 23:3

Corporation ED (2018) Global developer population and demographic study 2018. https://evansdata.com/reports/viewRelease.php?reportID=9

Cruzes DS, Dybå T (2011) Recommended steps for thematic synthesis in software engineering. In: International symposium on empirical software engineering and measurement. IEEE, pp 275–284

de Franca BBN, Helvio Jeronimo J, Travassos GH (2016) Characterizing DevOps by hearing multiple voices. In: Proceedings of the Brazilian symposium on software engineering, pp 53–62

DeMarco T, Lister T (2013) Peopleware: productive projects and teams. Addison-Wesley, Boston

Devanbu P, Zimmermann T, Bird C (2016) Belief & evidence in empirical software engineering. In: IEEE/ACM international conference on software engineering. IEEE, pp 108–119

Efstathiou V, Chatzilenas C, Spinellis D (2018) Word embeddings for the software engineering domain. In: Proceedings of the international conference on mining software repositories. ACM, pp 38–41

Elliott C (2019) Jinfo Blog: Garner additional research sources with grey literature. https://web.jinfo.com/go/blog/70203

Facca FM, Lanzi PL (2005) Mining interesting knowledge from weblogs: a survey. Data Knowl Eng 53(3):225–241

Farace DJ (1997) Rise of the phoenix: a review of new forms and exploitations of grey literature. Publ Res Q 13(2):69–76

Garousi V, Küçük B (2018) Smells in software test code: a survey of knowledge in industry and academia. J Syst Softw 138:52–81

Garousi V, Mäntylä MV (2016) When and what to automate in software testing? A multivocal literature review. Inf Softw Technol 76:92–117

Garousi V, Felderer M, Mäntylä MV (2016a) The need for multivocal literature reviews in software engineering: complementing systematic literature reviews with grey literature. In: International conference on evaluation and assessment in software engineering. Limmerick, pp 171–176

Garousi V, Petersen K, Özkan B (2016b) Challenges and best practices in industry-academia collaborations in software engineering: a systematic literature review. Inf Softw Technol 79:106–127

Garousi V, Felderer M, Fernandes JM et al (2017a) Industry-academia collaborations in software engineering: an empirical analysis of challenges, patterns and anti-patterns in research projects.

In: Proceedings of international conference on evaluation and assessment in software engineering, Karlskrona, pp 224–229

Garousi V, Felderer M, Hacaloğlu T (2017b) Software test maturity assessment and test process improvement: a multivocal literature review. Inf Softw Technol 85:16–42

Garousi V, Borg M, Oivo M (2018) Cut to the chase: revisiting the relevance of software engineering research. arXiv preprint arXiv:1812.01395

Garousi V, Felderer M, Mäntylä MV (2019) Guidelines for including grey literature and conducting multivocal literature reviews in software engineering. Inf Softw Technol 106:101–121

Giustini D, Thompson D (2010) Finding the hard to finds: searching for grey (gray) literature. https://blogs.ubc.ca/dean/2010/02/finding-the-hard-to-finds-searching-for-grey-gray-literature-2010/

Gruetze T, Krestel R, Naumann F (2016) Topic shifts in stackoverflow: ask it like Socrates. In: International conference on applications of natural language to information systems. Springer, pp 213–221

Institute for Work & Health (2019) What researchers mean by... Grey literature. https://www.iwh.on.ca/what-researchers-mean-by/grey-literature

Inui K, Abe S, Hara K et al (2008) Experience mining: building a large-scale database of personal experiences and opinions from web documents. In: IEEE Computer Society, pp 314–321

Kitchenham B, Charters S (2007) Guidelines for performing systematic literature reviews in software engineering. EBSE technical report. EBSE-2007-01

Kitchenham BA, Dybå T, Jorgensen M (2004) Evidence-based software engineering. In: Proceedings of international conference on software engineering, pp 273–281

Kitchenham B, Budgen D, Brereton P (2015) Evidence-based software engineering and systematic reviews. CRC, Boca Raton

Kulesovs I (2015) iOS applications testing. In: Proceedings of the international scientific and practical conference, pp 138–150

Kurashima T, Tezuka T, Tanaka K (2006) Mining and visualizing local experiences from blog entries. In: International conference on database and expert systems applications. Springer, pp 213–222

Kurashima T, Fujimura K, Okuda H (2009) Discovering association rules on experiences from large-scale blog entries. In: European conference on information retrieval, pp 546–553

Lakshmanan G, Oberhofer M (2010) Knowledge discovery in the blogosphere: approaches and challenges. IEEE Internet Comput 14(2):24–32

Lawrence S, Giles CL (1999) Accessibility of information on the web. Nature 400:107

Lefebvre C, Manheimer E, Glanville J (2008) Searching for studies. In: Higgins JPT, Green S (eds) Cochrane handbook for systematic reviews of interventions. Wiley-Blackwell, Chichester

Leitner P, Wittern E, Spillner J et al (2018) A mixed-method empirical study of function-as-a-service software development in industrial practice. J Syst Softw 149:340–359

Luzi D (2000) Trends and evolution in the development of grey literature: a review. Int J Grey Lit 1(3):106–117

Lwakatare LE, Kuvaja P, Oivo M (2016) Relationship of DevOps to agile, lean and continuous deployment: a multivocal literature review study. In: Proceedings of international conference on product-focused software process improvement, pp 399–415

MacDonald BH, Cordes RE, Wells PG (2007) Assessing the diffusion and impact of grey literature published by international intergovernmental scientific groups: the case of the Gulf of Maine council on the marine environment. In: Proceedings of the international conference on grey literature, pp 84–94

MacLeod L, Storey M-A, Bergen A (2015) Code, camera, action: how software developers document and share program knowledge using YouTube. In: Proceedings of the IEEE international conference on program comprehension, pp 104–114

Mäntylä MV, Smolander K (2016) Gamification of software testing – an MLR. In: International conference on product-focused software process improvement, pp 611–614

Marsolek W, Cooper K, Farrell S et al (2018) The types, frequencies, and findability of disciplinary grey literature within prominent subject databases and academic institutional repositories. J Librariansh Sch Commun 6(1)

McKimmie T, Szurmak J (2002) Beyond grey literature: how grey questions can drive research. J Agric Food Inf 4(2):71–79

Molléri JS, Petersen K, Mendes E (2016) Survey guidelines in software engineering: an annotated review. In: Proceedings of the ACM/IEEE international symposium on empirical software engineering and measurement, 58, pp 51–56

Myrbakken H, Colomo-Palacios R (2017) DevSecOps: a multivocal literature review. In: Conference on software process improvement and capability determination, pp 17–29

Pappas C, Williams I (2011) Grey literature: its emerging importance. J Hosp Librariansh 11:228

Park KC, Jeong Y, Myaeng SH (2010) Detecting experiences from weblogs. In: Proceedings of the annual meeting of the association for computational linguistics, pp 1464–1472

Parnin C, Treude C (2011) Measuring API documentation on the web. ACM, New York, pp 25–30

Parnin C, Treude C, Storey M-A (2013) Blogging developer knowledge: motivations, challenges, and future directions. In: IEEE international conference on program comprehension, pp 211–214

Passos C, Braun AP, Cruzes DS et al (2011) Analyzing the impact of beliefs in software project practices. In: International symposium on empirical software engineering and measurement. IEEE, pp 444–452

Patton MQ (2002) Qualitative research and evaluation methods. Sage, Thousand Oaks

Petersen K, Vakkalanka S, Kuzniarz L (2015) Guidelines for conducting systematic mapping studies in software engineering: an update. Inf Softw Technol 64:1–18

Planning S (2002) The economic impacts of inadequate infrastructure for software testing. National Institute of Standards and Technology

Putta A, Paasivaara M, Lassenius C (2018) Benefits and challenges of adopting the scaled agile framework (SAFe): preliminary results from a multivocal literature review. In: International conference on product-focused software process improvement. Springer, pp 334–351

Rainer A (2017) Using argumentation theory to analyse software practitioners' defeasible evidence, inference and belief. Inf Softw Technol 87:62–80

Rainer A, Williams A (2019) Using blog-like documents to investigate software practice: benefits, challenges, and research directions. J Softw Evol Process 31(11):e2197

Rainer A, Hall T, Baddoo N (2003) Persuading developers to "buy into" software process improvement: a local opinion and empirical evidence. In: International symposium on empirical software engineering. IEEE, pp 326–335

Raulamo P, Mäntylä MV, Garousi V (2017) Choosing the right test automation tool: a grey literature review. In: International conference on evaluation and assessment in software engineering. Karlskrona, pp 21–30

Research Triangle Institute (2002) The economic impacts of inadequate infrastructure for software testing. American National Institute of Standards and Technology (NIST), Technical report 7007.011

Rincon P (2010) Stricter checks for climate body. https://www.bbc.com/news/science-environment-11131897

Rosen C, Shihab E (2016) What are mobile developers asking about? A large scale study using stack overflow. Empir Softw Eng 21(3):1192–1223

Sadaqat M, Colomo-Palacios R, Knudsen LES (2018) Serverless computing: a multivocal literature review. In: Norwegian conference for organizations' use of information technology (NOKOBIT)

Sánchez-Gordón M, Colomo-Palacios R (2018) A multivocal literature review on the use of DevOps for e-learning systems. In: Proceedings of international conference on technological ecosystems for enhancing multiculturality, pp 883–888

Sharma P, Savarimuthu BTR, Stanger N et al (2017) Investigating developers' email discussions during decision-making in Python language evolution. In: Proceedings of international conference on evaluation and assessment in software engineering. Karlskrona, ACM, pp 286–291

Sharp H, deSouza C, Dittrich Y (2010) Using ethnographic methods in software engineering research. In: ACM/IEEE international conference on software engineering, pp 491–492

Soldani J, Tamburri DA, Van Den Heuvel W-J (2018) The pains and gains of microservices: a systematic grey literature review. J Syst Softw 146:215–232

Storey M-A, Singer L, Cleary B et al (2014) The (r) evolution of social media in software engineering. In: Proceedings of the on future of software engineering, ACM, pp 100–116

Swanson R, Rahimtoroghi E, Corcoran T et al (2014) Identifying narrative clause types in personal stories. In: Proceedings of the annual meeting of the special interest group on discourse and dialogue, pp 171–180

The Standish Group (2019) CHAOS report. https://www.standishgroup.com/outline

Thompson L (2001) Grey literature in engineering. Sci Technol Libr 19(3–4):57–73

Tom E, Aurum A, Vidgen R (2013) An exploration of technical debt. J Syst Softw 86(6):1498–1516

University of New England (2019) Grey literature. https://www.une.edu.au/library/support/eskills-plus/research-skills/grey-literature

Williams A, Rainer A (2017) Toward the use of blog articles as a source of evidence for software engineering research. In: Proceedings of the international conference on evaluation and assessment in software engineering, pp 280–285

Guidelines for Managing Threats to Validity of Secondary Studies in Software Engineering

Apostolos Ampatzoglou, Stamatia Bibi, Paris Avgeriou, and Alexander Chatzigeorgiou

Abstract Secondary studies review and compile data retrieved from primary studies and are vulnerable to factors that threaten their validity as any other research method. Considering that secondary studies are often used to support the evidence-based paradigm, it is crucial to properly manage their threats, i.e., identify, categorize, mitigate, and report them. In this chapter, we build upon the outcomes of a systematic review of secondary studies in software engineering, which has identified (a) the most common threats to validity and corresponding mitigation actions and (b) the categories in which threats to validity can be classified, so as to guide the authors of future secondary studies in managing the threats to validity of their work. To achieve this goal, we describe (a) a classification schema for reporting threats to validity and possible mitigation actions and (b) a checklist, which authors of secondary studies can use for identifying and categorizing threats to validity and corresponding mitigation actions, while readers of secondary studies can use the checklist for assessing the validity of the reported results.

This paper is based on Ampatzoglou et al. (2019): Identifying, categorizing and mitigating threats to validity in software engineering secondary studies, *Information and Software Technology*, Elsevier, 106 (2), pp. 201–230, February 2019.

A. Ampatzoglou · A. Chatzigeorgiou (✉)
Department of Applied Informatics, University of Macedonia, Thessaloniki, Greece
e-mail: a.ampatzoglou@uom.edu.gr; achat@uom.gr

S. Bibi
Department of Electrical and Computer Engineering, University of Western Macedonia, Kozani, Greece
e-mail: sbibi@uowm.gr

P. Avgeriou
Department of Mathematics and Computer Science, University of Groningen, Groningen, The Netherlands
e-mail: paris@cs.rug.nl

1 Introduction

Over the past decade, due to the rise of the evidence-based software engineering (EBSE) paradigm (Kitchenham and Dybå 2004), there has been a proliferation of secondary studies. In this chapter, we focus on two types of secondary studies:

- *Systematic Literature Reviews (SLRs)*, which constitute the core tool of the evidence-based paradigm and originated in clinical medicine. SLRs aim at gathering data from previously published studies, objectively and without bias, for the purpose of synthesizing existing evidence and answering research questions. Research synthesis as described more analytically in chapter "Evidence Aggregation in Software Engineering" is a collective term for a family of methods for summarizing, integrating, and, when possible, combining the findings of different studies. Such synthesis can also identify crucial areas and questions that have not been addressed adequately with past empirical research. It is built upon the observation that empirical findings from individual studies are limited to the extent that they may be generalized (Kitchenham and Charters 2007).
- *Systematic Mapping Studies (SMS)*, which use the same basic methodology as SLRs but aim to provide a more coarse-grained overview of the research that has been performed on a topic rather than answering questions about the relative merits of competing technologies. In an SMS, published results are usually mapped onto a classification schema and visualized focusing on frequencies of publications for subtopics within the schema (Petersen et al. 2015).

EBSE research relies substantially on systematic and rigorous guidelines on how to conduct and report empirical results—e.g., experiments (Wohlin et al. 2000), SLRs (Kitchenham and Charters 2007), SMSs (Petersen et al. 2015), surveys (Pfleeger and Kitchenham 2001), and case studies (Runeson and Höst 2009). These guidelines emphasize, among others, the importance of managing (identifying, managing, and reporting) relevant *threats to validity*, i.e., possible aspects of the research design that in some way compromise the credibility of results. However, we currently lack guidelines on how to manage threats to validity in secondary studies. In this chapter, we build upon the results of a tertiary study (i.e., an SLR on secondary studies in software engineering) (Ampatzoglou et al. 2019), namely a classification schema for threats to validity and corresponding mitigation actions, combined with a checklist to be used while conducting/evaluating secondary studies.

The classification schema and the checklist can assist different stakeholders with various activities as illustrated in Fig. 1. First, we expect that a critical appraisal of secondary studies can be performed by readers and reviewers, by consulting the checklist to identify possible threats in the study design, and confirm that they have been properly mitigated. Also, the reporting of the studies can be evaluated, both in terms of threats to validity and their mitigation, as well as in terms of categorization. Second, authors of secondary studies can be guided on how to set up their study

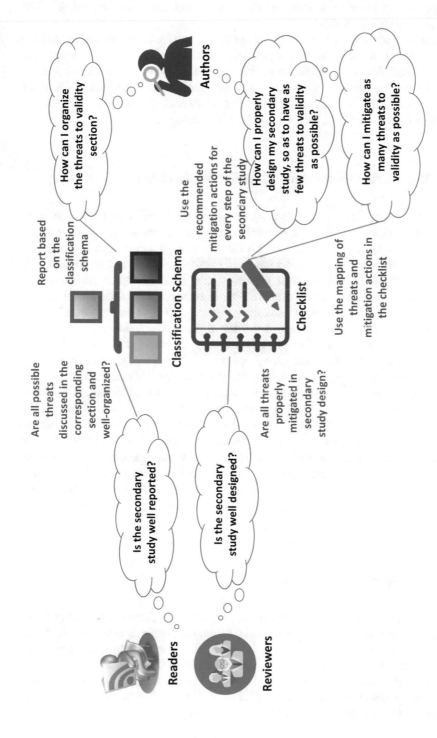

Fig. 1 Usage scenarios of threats to validity guidelines

design, so as to avoid or mitigate validity threats, while planning, conducting, and reporting secondary studies.

Section 2 presents the basis of this chapter, i.e., the classification schema and the validity checklist, proposed by Ampatzoglou et al. (2019). In Sect. 3, we present the first usage scenario, which exemplifies how the classification schema and the checklist can be used by authors of secondary studies, whereas Sect. 4 discusses the usage scenario for reviewers and readers of secondary studies. Finally, Sect. 5 discusses further readings, and Sect. 6 concludes the chapter.

2 Classification Schema and Validity Checklist

Identifying, classifying, and mitigating threats to the validity of results obtained through secondary studies are important to increase our confidence on the conclusions drawn from these results. Despite the fact that the percentage of secondary studies reporting threats to validity has been continuously increasing, considerable confusion still exists in terms of terminology, mitigation strategies, and classification (Ampatzoglou et al. 2019) often leading to erroneous classification of threats. For instance, in many secondary studies any bias that might be introduced during study selection is wrongly classified (by the authors of secondary studies) under *internal* validity almost as often as under *reliability*, pointing to inconsistencies in the classification of threats (Ampatzoglou et al. 2019). Arguably, problems in study selection can threaten both aspects of validity. On the one hand, if some studies are falsely included/excluded, the examined dataset will not be accurate, thus posing a threat to internal validity. Therefore, the investigation of any relationship will be prone to erroneous results. On the other hand, failing to include some studies in the final selection can greatly reduce the possibility that an independent replication reaches the same results posing reliability threats. While one can argue about the correctness of both classifications, multi-label classification can be confusing and does not allow for a uniform comparison of the threats. Therefore, next we present a classification schema for threats to validity and their mitigation actions, tailored for secondary studies.

2.1 Classification Schema

The classification schema consists of three levels: the first one depicting threat categories, the second, threats per se, and the third one, mitigation actions. To derive the threat categories (first level of the schema) and to facilitate the classification of any given threat, we use the planning phases of the secondary studies (i.e., search process, study filtering, data extraction and analysis—see Fig. 2). These are easily identifiable steps in the secondary study, in contrast to using the aspects of validity that are threatened (e.g., internal/external/construct validity). Moreover, we have

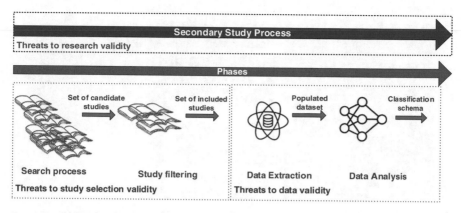

Fig. 2 Secondary studies phases and corresponding threats

added an additional category (i.e., a horizontal one) that corresponds to threats that cover the lifecycle of the secondary study:

- *Study Selection Validity*. This category involves threats that can be identified in the first two phases of secondary studies (i.e., search process and study filtering phase). Issues classified in this category threaten the validity of searching and including primary studies in the examined set. This involves threats like the *selection of digital libraries, search string construction*, etc.
- *Data Validity*. This category includes threats that can be identified in the last two phases of secondary studies (i.e., data extraction and analysis) and threaten the validity of the extracted dataset and its analysis. Examples of threats in this category are *small sample size, lack of statistical analysis*, etc.
- *Research Validity*. Threats that can be identified in all phases and concern the overall research design are classified into this category. Examples of threats in this category are *generalizability, coverage of research questions*, etc.

Although the majority of the names for threats to validity and mitigation actions can be considered self-explanatory, more details are provided in Sect. 3. We note that due to space limitations, only the most frequent mitigation actions for every threat are presented in Fig. 3a–c. The full list of mitigation actions is available online, in the accompanying technical report of Ampatzoglou et al. (2019). The three categories of validity threats along with the proposed mitigation actions are shown in Fig. 3a–c, respectively. Blue cells represent threats to validity and red cells to mitigation actions. Groups of validity threats are depicted as adjacent blue cells. When a number of mitigation actions can be used for a threat or a group of threats, they are also depicted as adjacent red cells.

The *study selection validity* category involves seven specific threats (see Fig. 3a). Five threats to validity can be grouped into a more generic one, i.e., *adequacy of initial relevant publication identification* (TV_1), whereas the rest are ungrouped. From the threats of this category, some are mutually exclusive, whereas others

Fig. 3 (**a**) Study selection validity threats and mitigation actions. (**b**) Data validity threats and mitigation actions. (**c**) Research validity threats and mitigation actions

may coexist. For example, if *selection of digital libraries* is performed, the threat *selection of publication venues* ($TV_{1.3}$) is excluded since normally only one of the two search strategies (digital libraries or venues) is selected (except if a quasi-gold standard from specific venues is used for study selection validation, then both strategies are used). The *construction of the search string* threat ($TV_{1.1}$) exists when both digital libraries and specific publication venues are selected. After the initial set of publications is derived, other aspects threaten the validity of the study: *were there enough journals and conferences for the authors to search* (TV$_2$), *what languages have the authors explored* (TV$_3$), *were all papers accessible by the authors* (TV$_4$), *how have the authors handled the duplicate articles* (TV$_5$) or *the grey literature* (TV$_6$), and is the *selection of inclusion/exclusion criteria accurate?* (TV$_7$).

The *data validity* category includes nine specific threats (see Fig. 3b), which are organized into three groups and five ungrouped threats to validity. One group includes any kind of bias that can be introduced while collecting data, namely: *data extraction bias* (TV$_{13}$), *data extraction inaccuracies, quality assessment subjectivity, unverified data extraction*, and *misclassification of primary studies* (mostly relevant for mapping studies). Another group includes limitations of the dataset (TV$_8$) that are due to the nature of the subject and not due to researchers' bias (i.e., *small sample size* and *heterogeneous primary studies*). A third group represents threats that are relevant for mapping studies and have been posed by the use of *inadequate classification schemas* or *attributes frameworks* (TV$_{15}$). Furthermore, other aspects such as the *validity of primary studies* (TV$_{12}$), *the potential lack of relationships in the dataset* (TV$_{11}$), *the publication bias* (TV$_{10}$), and *the choice of extracted variables* (TV$_9$) are classified in this category since they are prone to damaging the quality of the dataset. Other individual threats that are mapped to this category are the *researchers' bias* (TV$_{16}$) while interpreting the results and the *lack of statistical analysis* (TV$_{14}$).

Finally, the *research validity* category includes six specific threats (see Fig. 3c) that are forming two groups and include four ungrouped threats. The first group represents threats that have to do with the followed process. First, there is a possibility that the *selected research method* (i.e., mapping study vs. literature review) does not fit the goal of the study (TV$_{18}$). Second, sometimes researchers *deviate from the established review process*. The second group involves threats to *generalizability* (TV$_{22}$). The individual threats that are mapped to this category are the *lack of comparable studies* (TV$_{20}$), the *coverage of research questions* (TV$_{19}$), and the *unfamiliarity of researchers with the application domain* (TV$_{21}$). Finally, *repeatability* (TV$_{17}$) has been classified in this category since although it is threatened by data unavailability, it is also threatened by any undocumented parts of the reviewing process. Therefore, it is considered more as a horizontal threat (that pertains to the whole research process), rather than a specific threat for the data extraction or analysis phase.

Although we believe that the current classification schema improves the orthogonality among threat categories, there are still some "grey-zone" threats. Using the proposed classification schema, we address the problem of classifying a single threat to two categories: every threat is classified within one category, based on the phase of the study design, in which it was identified and the set of artifacts, whose validity is threatened. We identified five cases of threats that can be classified into more than one category:

- *Quality Assessment Subjectivity*—In the context of secondary studies, the quality of a primary study can be used either as an inclusion criterion or as a variable that is collected during data extraction (when for example, the quality of the primary studies is part of the research questions) Thus, *quality assessment subjectivity* can be classified under both study selection validity and data validity, based on the role of the quality assessment. To ease the readability of this section, *quality assessment subjectivity* is presented only as part of *data validity*.

- *Publication Bias and Validity of Primary Studies*—Although *publication bias* and *validity of primary studies* stem from the study selection phase, they threaten the validity of the extracted data, their analysis, and the subsequent interpretation. In particular *publication bias* may result in an extracted dataset that does not represent a wide research community, but only reflects the opinions of a limited number of researchers or researchers involved in a particular scientific subdiscipline. At the same time, low *validity of primary studies* also threatens the validity of the extracted dataset, since they may offer low-quality evidence. Thus, we have classified both threats in the *data validity* category.
- *Robustness of Initial Classification* and *Construction of Attribute Framework*. These two threats are highly related to data validity in the sense that if a "wrong" classification schema is selected, the complete data collection will be misguided due to the use of inaccurate classification classes and terminology. Thus, the correctness of the final dataset is threatened. Although these threats first appear in the study selection phase, their impact is mainly observed in the data analysis phase.

2.2 Checklist for Threats to Validity Identification and Mitigation

Based on the classification schema of Fig. 3, we present a checklist (as a series of questions) that authors of secondary studies should answer when performing secondary studies, so as to assess the validity of their studies. This instrument can aid both in the identification of threats (since not all threats apply in all studies) and in the suggestion of mitigation actions (what the authors can do if they identify any threat in their study design). This checklist can serve as a guide for the authors of secondary studies. The structure of the checklist is quite simple: First each top-level question is asked to understand if a specific threat exists (TV_n), and then a series of sub-questions are asked to check if a proper mitigation action MA_m has been performed. The numbering of mitigation actions is restarted for every threat to validity. Each of the three boxes below corresponds to one category of threats: study selection, data, and research validity. For example, TV_1–TV_7 correspond to the seven threats that are reported in Fig. 3a (study selection validity). The mapping between questions and threats reported in Fig. 3 is one-to-one, by considering Sect. 2.1.

Study selection validity

TV$_1$: Has your search process adequately identified all relevant primary studies?

>   **MA$_1$**: Have you used snowballing?
>   **MA$_2$**: Have you performed pilot searches to train your search string?
>   **MA$_3$**: Have you selected the most-known digital libraries *or* have you made a selection of specific publication venues *or* used broad search engines or indices (*based on the goal of your study*)?
>   **MA$_4$**: Have you compared your list of primary studies to a gold standard or to other secondary studies?
>   **MA$_5$**: Have you used a broad search process in generic search engines or indices (e.g., Google Scholar) so that you ensure the identification of all relevant publication venues?
>   **MA$_6$**: Have you used a strategy for systematic search string construction?
>   **MA$_7$**: Has an independent expert reviewed the search process?
>   **MA$_8$**: Have you used tools to facilitate the review process?
>   **MA$_9$**: Have you evaluated search results and documented the outcomes?

TV$_2$: Were primary studies relevant to the topic of the review published in several different journals and conferences?

>   **MA$_1$**: Have you used a broad search process in generic search engines or indices (e.g., Google Scholar) so that you ensure the identification of all relevant publication venues?

TV$_3$: Have you identified primary studies in multiple languages?

>   **MA$_1$**: Is their number expected to be high compared to the population?

TV$_4$: Were the full texts of all primary studies accessible from the researchers?

>   **MA$_1$**: Is the number of studies with missing full texts expected to be high compared to the population?

TV$_5$: Have you managed duplicate articles?

>   **MA$_1$**: Have you developed a consistent strategy (e.g., keep the newer one *or* keep the journal version) for selecting which study should be retained in the list of primary studies?
>   **MA$_2$**: Have you used summaries of candidate primary studies to guarantee the correct identification of all duplicate articles?

(continued)

TV$_6$: Have you included/excluded grey literature?

  MA$_1$: Does the decision to include or exclude grey literature comply with the goals of the study *and* the availability of sources?

TV$_7$: Have you adequately performed study inclusion/exclusion?

  MA$_1$: Have you used systematic voting?
  MA$_2$: Have you performed random screening of articles among authors?
  MA$_3$: Have researchers discussed the inclusion or exclusion of selected articles in case of conflict?
  MA$_4$: Have the inclusion exclusion criteria been documented explicitly in the protocol?
  MA$_5$: Have the authors discussed the inclusion/exclusion criteria *and* revised them after pilots, or by experts' suggestions after review?
  MA$_6$: Have you prescribed a set of decision rules for study inclusion/exclusion?
  MA$_7$: Have you defined quality thresholds for inclusion/exclusion?
  MA$_8$: Have you performed sensitivity analysis?
  MA$_9$: Have you quantified experts' disagreement with the kappa statistic?

Data validity

TV$_8$: Is your sample size large enough so that the obtained results can be considered valid?

  MA$_1$: Have you tried to draw conclusions based on trends?
  MA$_2$: Have you used a broad search process in generic search engines or indices (e.g., Google Scholar) so that you ensure the identification of all relevant publication venues?

TV$_9$: Have you chosen the correct variables to extract?

  MA$_1$: Has the choice of variables been discussed among authors to guarantee that the research questions can be answered?

TV$_{10}$: Are the studies in your dataset published in a limited set of venues?

  MA$_1$: Have you used snowballing?
  MA$_2$: Have you included grey literature (if this does not affect TV$_6$)?
  MA$_3$: Have you manually scanned selected venues to check if they publish articles related to your secondary study?

TV$_{11}$: Do you expect to identify relationships in your dataset?

  MA$_1$: Have you performed pilot data extraction to test the existence of relationships?

(continued)

TV$_{12}$: Does the quality of studies guarantee the validity of extracted data?

    MA$_1$: Have you focused your search process on quality venues only?

    MA$_2$: Have you used article quality assessment as inclusion criterion?

    MA$_3$: Have you assessed the validity of primary studies and their impact using statistics?

TV$_{13}$: Is there data extraction bias in your study?

    MA$_1$: Have you involved more than one researcher?

    MA$_2$: Have you identified experts' disagreement with kappa statistic?

    MA$_3$: Have you performed pilot data extraction to test agreement between researchers? (*Not applicable if MA$_1$ is no*)

    MA$_4$: Have you used experts *or* external reviewers' opinion in case of conflicts? (*Not applicable if MA$_1$ is no*)

    MA$_5$: Have you performed paper screening to cross-check data extraction?

    MA$_6$: Have you used a keywording of abstracts? (*Applicable only in mapping studies*)

TV$_{14}$: Have you performed statistical analysis?

    MA$_1$: Does your data extraction record quantitative data and, if yes, does answering your research questions imply the use of statistics?

TV$_{15}$: Have you selected a robust initial classification schema?

    MA$_1$: Have you selected an existing initial classification schema?

    MA$_2$: Have you continuously updated the schema, until it becomes stable and classifies all primary studies in one or more classes?

TV$_{16}$: Is your interpretation of the results subject to bias or is it as objective as possible?

    MA$_1$: Have you performed pilot data analysis and interpretation?

    MA$_2$: Have you conducted reliability checks (e.g., post-SLR surveys with experts)?

    MA$_3$: Have you used a formal data synthesis method?

    MA$_4$: Have you performed sensitivity analysis?

    MA$_5$: Have you used the scientific quality of primary studies when drawing conclusions?

Research validity

TV$_{17}$: Is your process reliable/repeatable?

    MA$_1$: Have more than one researcher been involved in the process?

    MA$_2$: Have you made all gathered data publicly available?

(continued)

MA₃: Have you documented in detail the review process in a protocol?

TV₁₈: Have you chosen the correct research method?

MA₁: Have the authors discussed if the selected research method (SLR or SMS) fits the goals/research questions of the study, by advocating the purpose and scope of the methods?

MA₂: Have you developed a protocol, monitored the process for deviations, and accurately reported any (if existed)?

TV₁₉: Do the answers to your research questions guarantee the accomplishment of your study goal?

MA₁: Have the authors discussed *and* brainstormed on if the research questions holistically cover the goal of the study?

MA₂: Is your study and research questions well-motivated?

MA₃: Have you consulted target audience for setting up your goals?

TV₂₀: Does your study have substantial related work, so that you can compare and discuss findings?

MA₁: Have the authors discussed *and* brainstormed to reach possible interpretations of the findings, due to the absence of related studies?

TV₂₁: Were you familiar with the research field before performing the review?

MA₁: Have the authors exhaustively searched related work so as to (a) familiarize with the field, (b) identify comparable studies, and (c) identify relevant publication venues and influential papers?

TV₂₂: Are the results of your study generalizable?

MA₁: Do your findings comply with those of existing studies?

MA₂: Have you used a broad search process w/o an initial starting date?

3 Usage Scenario 1: How Authors Can Mitigate Threats

We advise authors to use the checklist and the classification schema provided in this chapter to improve the validity of their study following a number of steps. First, the authors should create a *dedicated section for threats to validity* in both the study protocol and the study report (final manuscript). Second, this section should be *organized according to categories of threats* (e.g., by following the proposed classification schema or another established one). Third, *all threats should be checked whether they pertain to the study*. Finally, for all identified threats, either *appropriate mitigation action should be explicitly reported or an acknowledgment should be made that the threat is not (fully) mitigated.*

To facilitate the aforementioned steps, in Sects. 3.1–3.3 we present references to representative exemplary mitigation activities from the literature. Finally, in Sect. 3.4, we summarize the mitigation actions that can be applied in each phase of the secondary study execution.

3.1   Mitigating Threats to Study Selection Validity

Construction of the search string refers to problems that might occur when the researchers are building the search string. As a consequence, the search might return a large number of primary studies (including many irrelevant ones) or a very limited number (thus missing some relevant studies). A mitigation strategy that covers a wide range of activities is provided by Shahin et al. (2014), in which the authors have complemented automated searching in digital libraries (see also chapter "Automating Systematic Literature Reviews") with manual search on specific venues that are considered as important to the domain of the secondary study. In addition, the authors have used snowballing (both backward and forward) to decrease the chances of missing articles, i.e., they searched the references of the identified articles or papers that cite the identified articles for candidate articles they may have missed.

Selection of Digital Libraries refers to problems that can arise from using very specific, too broad, or not credible search engines. The consequence of this threat can be either the return of a lot irrelevant or missing of relevant studies. As a response to this threat, Garcés et al. (2017) opted to select the most adequate databases for their search. Based on the criteria discussed by Dieste and Padua (2007), they opted for using six databases: namely ACM Digital Library, IEEE Xplore, ScienceDirect, Scopus, Springer, and Web of Science. According to Kitchenham and Charters (2007), these publication databases are the most relevant sources in the computer science area.

Selection of publication venues refers to the problem that might occur, when the research team selects to explore specific venues rather than using broad search engines. The most common rationale for this decision is either the fact that a topic is too broad or that the research aims at high-quality studies only. The consequence of this threat is missing relevant studies. A rigorous process for selecting high-quality and relevant publication venues has been discussed in the recent bibliometrics study on top scholars and institutes (Karanatsiou et al. 2019). In particular, the authors have selected publication venues based on their relevance to software engineering, their specificity (e.g., architecture, maintenance), and their average number of citations per month in Google Scholar. Nevertheless, it is also crucial to pilot the searches and compare the obtained studies against a golden standard. An exemplar application of this practice is provided by Jabangwe et al. (2015), where the authors have developed the golden standard set by creating an initial validation through

Google Scholar, by identifying relevant papers to seminal works (i.e., mostly cited ones) of the secondary study domain.

The *selection of an arbitrary starting year* as a starting point for performing the search process can lead to missing studies prior to that date. In order for this decision to not be considered as a threat, it should be clear why such a choice does not influence the results. For instance, according to Li et al. (2015), after 2010 there were at least 15 studies published per year focusing on technical debt management, which is a big leap compared with the years before 2010. One reason for this could be that the MTD workshop was initiated in 2010 and this workshop raised the attention on TD and the awareness of managing TD. Therefore, future secondary studies on technical debt could use 2010 as a starting year, without considering this choice as a threat to validity. If such a justification cannot be claimed researchers should consider shifting the starting year earlier.

Problems of the search engines within digital libraries are characterized as *search engine inefficiencies* (e.g., SpringerLink cannot perform a search based only on the abstract of manuscripts). This can lead to missing studies, or deriving a large corpus of papers for filtering. A tentative mitigation action for this threat is the use of bibliography management tools (e.g., JabRef, Zotero) for further filtering the large corpus of retrieved articles, based on the desired fields. This mitigation action, although it does not reduce the amount of effort required for data collection, it ensures the consistency of data collection. A discussion on this is provided by Penzenstadler et al. (2012).

A *limited number of publication venues* in which primary studies can be published suggest a narrow scope of the secondary study. This will probably lead to obtaining a low number of primary studies. If the intended scope of the study is indeed narrow there might be no reason to mitigate this threat, as in the case of Santos et al.'s study (2016) that focuses on action research (i.e., rather young empirical method, that is still underemployed compared to more established ones, e.g., case studies, experiments) in software engineering. However, alternative strategies could be the inclusion of grey literature (see chapter "Benefitting from the Grey Literature in Software Engineering Research"), or the execution of broader searches.

Exploring studies written in a specific language (e.g., *missing non-English papers*) can lead to the omission of important studies (or number of studies) written in other languages. This threat exists in almost any secondary study that considers primary studies written in English, since most of them list it as an exclusion criterion. In our opinion this consists of a threat only in cases in which a very active community publishes high-quality papers in a domain, in languages other than English. A way to evaluate the risk that this threat poses is to assess the number of studies written in non-English languages compared to the population of the research corpus, regardless of the language.

Papers whose full text is not available cannot be processed (i.e., *papers inaccessibility*). If this number is large, the set of retrieved studies might be limited/not representative. As a mitigation action for this threat that is however questionable in terms of generalizability, Magdaleno et al. (2012) refer to asking access to the papers through email, directly from the authors. This threat is not very common, since most academic institutes have institutional access to most digital libraries. In case there is no such access, other sources (e.g., research social media, personal websites, etc.) can be used for retrieving a copy, as well as personal contact to the authors by email.

Some early versions of a study may be published in a conference and an extended one in a journal. *Duplicate studies* should be identified and handled, so that the study set does not contain duplicate information. For example, Ampatzoglou and Stamelos (2010) suggested the merging of multiple versions as one study. In the field of software engineering, a common practice among researchers is to publish their early research results in conference proceedings to get quicker feedback from the research community and as a means for evolving and maturing their work. In many cases, a publication to a software engineering journal chronologically follows and includes the results reported in the conference proceedings. In these cases, only the journal article can be added to the set of primary studies without the risk of missing relevant information.

Based on the goal of the study, *including or excluding grey literature* can pose a threat. For example, grey literature should be considered in Multivocal Literature Reviews (MLRs), in which practitioners' view should be examined. For more details on such discussions, see the paper of Montalvillo and Diaz (2016). On the other hand, if the authors are interested in focusing only on top-quality venues (e.g., Arvanitou et al. 2017; Galster et al. 2014), then grey literature should be omitted from the searching space.

Study inclusion/exclusion bias refers to problems that might occur in the study filtering phase, i.e., when applying the inclusion/exclusion criteria. Such threats are usually found in studies, in which there are conflicting inclusion/exclusion criteria, or very generic ones. As illustrative mitigation action for study inclusion/exclusion, Yang et al. (2016) suggest the following strategies: (a) set a group of inclusion and exclusion criteria for study selection, which can be provided as a basis for an objective selection process; (b) considering the possible different interpretation and understanding of selection criteria by the researchers, a pilot selection has to be conducted before the formal selection to guarantee that the researchers reached a clear and consistent understanding of the selection criteria; and (c) two researchers need to conduct the study selection independently at least in one round of selection, and discuss/resolve any conflicts between their results, to mitigate personal bias in study selection.

3.2   Mitigating Threats to Data Validity

A *small sample* threatens the validity of the dataset, since results may be (a) prone to bias (data might come from a small community), (b) not statistically significant, and (c) not safe to generalize. The small sample size can be mitigated by broadening the searching space (Ali et al. 2010), but this decision must comply with the goals of the study and the research area of interest. Additionally, according to Barreiros et al. (2011) the small sample size threat is mitigated if the quality of the obtained studies is high. Based on the findings of this study, existing secondary studies parse from less than 10 papers to more than 500 primary studies. The mean value is 90 primary studies, whereas 2.5% of our sample includes studies with less than 10 papers and 9.5% of the studies have considered more than 200 papers.

Data from primary studies that are *highly heterogeneous* are not easy/safe to synthesize, since such a process is prone to involve a high degree of subjectivity. The mitigation actions that are reported as relevant to this threat are the careful construction of the search string (Al-Baik and Miller 2015), based on the PICO strategy proposed by Kitchenham et al. (2009) that takes into account the population, intervention, comparison, and outcomes of the review. Such an approach aims at identifying only the most relevant publications, by limiting the chances for a heterogeneous dataset. Additionally, Nguyen-Duc et al. (2015) suggested the development of a data extraction form based on the research questions to ensure data homogeneity.

The *variables* that have been *chosen to be extracted* might threaten the validity of the results, since they might not fit answering the research questions. Additionally, they are prone to researchers' bias. The best practice that can be used for mitigating this threat is the extraction of variables based on the set of research questions and their beforehand mapping. An exemplary way of mapping variables to research questions is provided by Galster et al. (2014), in which the authors list the extracted variables, and inside a parenthesis they denote the corresponding research question.

Publication bias refers to cases where the majority of primary studies are identified in a specific publication venue. If the majority of primary studies stem from a single workshop, the likelihood of biasing the dataset, and thereof the results, based on the beliefs of a certain community, is rather high. To avoid publication bias, extended and broad searches (e.g., Google Scholar, Scopus) are encouraged (Lenberg et al. 2015), whereas another alternative would be the inclusion of grey literature (blogs, websites, etc.; Tiwari and Gupta 2015); see also chapter "Benefitting from the Grey Literature in Software Engineering Research." Nevertheless, we need to note that both these mitigation actions should be treated with caution, since in specific types of studies, they might hurt the quality of primary studies.

Examining *data that lack relations* might hinder reaching a conclusion. A tentative solution to this threat is the application of quality assessment as a criterion for study inclusion or exclusion. In particular, Nguyen-Duc et al. (2015) have assessed the quality of the studies in terms of rigor, credibility, and relevance by using the checklist of Dybå and Dingsøyr (2008). An alternative schema for evaluating rigor and relevance for empirical studies has been proposed by Ivarsson and Gorschek (2011). In particular, rigor is evaluated based on the description of the context, the empirical design, and the validity discussion. Relevance is assessed based on subjects, context, scale, and used research method (Kitchenham and Charters 2007).

Another type of publication bias is the *validity of the primary studies*, which suggests that the results of the secondary study might be biased from inaccurate results reported in the primary studies. A common reason for this is that studies with negative results are less probable to get accepted for publication. The two most common mitigation actions related to this threat are (a) the use of quality thresholds as an exclusion criterion (Ahmad and Babar 2016) (e.g., rigor and relevance checklist Dybå and Dingsøyr 2008; Ivarsson and Gorschek 2011) and (b) the inclusion of high-quality venues (Karanatsiou et al. 2019).

Data extraction bias refers to problems that can arise in the data extraction phase. Such problems might be caused from the use of open questions in the collected variables, whose handling is not explicitly discussed in the protocol. The specific threat to validity is one of the most common ones in software engineering. Therefore, a variety of mitigation actions have been linked to it. The most common ones are (a) the involvement of more than one researcher in the process and the continuous assessment of their level of agreement (e.g., using Fleiss's kappa, Nguyen-Duc et al. 2015), (b) the piloting through random sampling (Kabbedijk et al. 2015), and (c) the use of keywording from abstracts (Petersen et al. 2015). A special type of data extraction bias is the *quality assessment subjectivity*, i.e., the process during which the quality of the primary studies is evaluated by the authors of the secondary study. This threat is relevant only for SLRs that report the evaluation of primary studies' quality. Similarly, *data extraction inaccuracies* refer to cases when data analysis might not be carefully performed, or might not follow strict guidelines. For example, the same concept might be inconsistently classified into two primary studies. This leads to inaccuracies in the dataset. Finally, *unverified data extraction* refers to the situation in which data are not validated by external reviewers, or have not been subject to internal review. Since all the above threats fall in the generic data extraction bias threats, their mitigation can be achieved by applying the same actions.

In some designs it is *not possible to perform statistical analysis*, for example, in cases that all extracted data items are categorical. This threat can be mitigated during the selection of variables to be extracted, when the selection of numerical data can be opted (see above). Nevertheless, as noted by Engström (2008), qualitative data analysis methods are equally important to quantitative analysis. Therefore, using solid qualitative analysis methods mitigates the lack of statistical analysis.

Primary studies inconsistent classification is valid for secondary studies that aim at developing a classification schema (usually mapping studies). A similar threat is the *construction of attribute framework*. While constructing this framework, the authors define a set of possible values for the attributes (i.e., variables) that are used to characterize each primary study. If the selected values are not discrete and comprehensive, then the data extraction can result in an insufficient dataset. In case a classification schema is already in place, *robustness of initial classification* is applicable to secondary studies that rely upon it. A common mitigation while performing the classification of primary studies is to identify an existing classification schema that is tailored to fit the needs of the secondary study. The selection of this initial classification schema poses a threat to validity, since it might not be fitting for the domain, and its tailoring is not efficient. Actions that can be used for avoiding the aforementioned threat are (a) the piloting of data extraction to test the classification schema or the attribute framework—Cornelissen et al. (2009) evaluated the usefulness of the attribute framework and measured the degree to which the attributes in each facet coincide; (b) the use of an existing and established classification schema—e.g., Haselberger (2016) used the project manager competence development framework; and (c) the use of experts' opinion—Kosar et al. (2016) have relied upon the opinion of a DSL expert for obtaining a coarse-grained classification that could offer a broader picture of the field.

Researcher bias refers to potential bias that authors of the secondary studies may have while interpreting or synthesizing the extracted results. This can be a bias toward a certain topic, or because only one author worked on data synthesis. To mitigate this threat, vivid discussion among authors of the studies is encouraged, by a variety of studies. Furthermore, Nair et al. (2014) advise the execution of reliability checks; the execution of pilot interpretations is proposed by Khurum and Gorschek (2009), whereas Penzenstadler et al. (2012) compare results with existing studies.

3.3 Mitigating Threats to Research Validity

Repeatability refers to threats that deal with the replication of a secondary study. The most common reason for the existence of such threats is the lack of a detailed protocol, or the existence of researcher and data extraction bias. The key practice for boosting the repeatability of a secondary study is the development and the public sharing of a review protocol (e.g., Engström et al. 2008). Other good practices are the involvement of more than one researcher in the process (e.g., Yusifoğlu et al. 2015) and the adoption of well-known guidelines—most studies follow the guidelines of Kitchenham and Charters (2007) or of Petersen et al. (2015).

Chosen research method. Mapping studies and literature reviews are designed to serve different goals and scopes. The selection of a specific research method might not fit the goals, the scope, or the context of the performed secondary study. A discussion on the proper way for selecting the research method for a secondary study is provided by Kitchenham et al. (2010). For example, broad topics should be approached through mapping studies, whereas more specialized ones through SLRs.

Review process deviations. In some cases, researchers choose to deviate from the guidelines offered by the research method. Such deviations [e.g., not performing the keywording of abstracts step in a mapping study, despite the use of the guidelines of Petersen et al. (2015)] threaten validity, since some important aspects might be compromised. In such cases a strong argumentation should be set. For example, Galster et al. (2014) deviated from the data extraction guidelines of Kitchenham and Charters (2007) and adopted the strategy suggested by Brereton et al. (2007).

Coverage of research questions refers to the formulation of research questions that do not adequately fulfill the goal of the secondary study (i.e., setting a very generic goal, or the improper decomposition of the goal into questions). The most common best practice for resolving this threat is the use of the GQM approach that has been introduced by Basili and Selby (1991). Brainstorming among authors (Ameller et al. 2015) and the consultation of experts (Alves et al. 2016) are highly advisable.

Some secondary studies *lack comparable related work* (i.e., other secondary studies or primary studies). In this case, there is no possibility of comparing the results to existing literature. Therefore, in our opinion, the only option is the intuitive validation and discussion of the obtained results. A best practice for this is the brainstorming between the authors and possible external experts.

In some cases, secondary studies are performed by nonexpert researchers who are *unfamiliar with the research field*. The lack of knowledge in the domain can lead to undesired consequences, such as omission of well-known studies in the field, limited synthesis capacity, and inability to reason about the findings. A tentative best practice for this is the thorough studying of the literature and the detailed comparison of findings. According to MacDonnell (2019), senior researchers should be included in the data analysis and interpretation of the results of secondary studies.

Generalizability threats refer to the possibility of not being able to generalize the results of the secondary study (e.g., due to the identification of only a portion of existing primary studies). A special case of this threat that is quite frequently reported is *results not applicable to other organizations or domains*. The mitigation actions that have been linked to generalizability threats are the use of broad searches (Ding et al. 2014), and the comparison to state of the art and related studies (Staples and Niazi 2008).

3.4 Mapping Mitigation Actions to Secondary Studies Activities

To put the application of the aforementioned mitigation actions in context, we assign mitigation actions to activities of secondary studies design processes—see Fig. 4. In particular, at the first level (framed font) we present the phases for performing secondary studies as suggested by Kitchenham and Charters (2007), and then the corresponding activities (bold font). The used activities are selected as the union of the activities presented in the five studies suggesting guidelines for performing secondary studies (Ampatzoglou et al. 2019; Cruzes and Dybå 2011; Avellar et al. 2017; Kitchenham and Charters 2007; Petersen et al. 2008). Being as inclusive as possible in the selection of activities (i.e., by using the union of activities) guarantees that any author will be able to identify the activity that he intends to perform in the figure, regardless of the followed guidelines. In the third level, we list the mitigation actions that can be performed in each step. We note that the reporting phase of the secondary studies is omitted since no threats can arise at that stage. However, the step is of paramount importance, in the sense that it includes the reporting of the threats to validity per se.

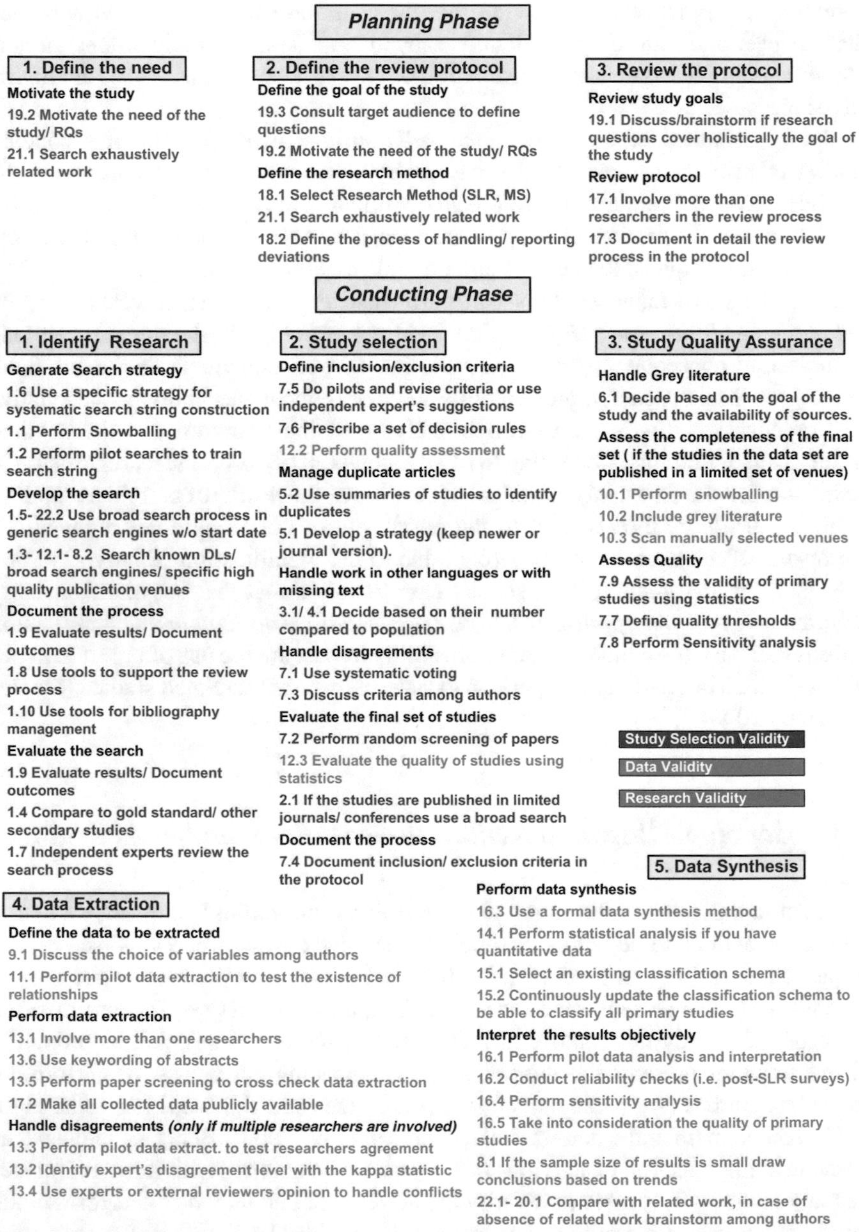

Planning Phase

1. Define the need

Motivate the study
19.2 Motivate the need of the study/ RQs
21.1 Search exhaustively related work

2. Define the review protocol

Define the goal of the study
19.3 Consult target audience to define questions
19.2 Motivate the need of the study/ RQs
Define the research method
18.1 Select Research Method (SLR, MS)
21.1 Search exhaustively related work
18.2 Define the process of handling/ reporting deviations

3. Review the protocol

Review study goals
19.1 Discuss/brainstorm if research questions cover holistically the goal of the study
Review protocol
17.1 Involve more than one researchers in the review process
17.3 Document in detail the review process in the protocol

Conducting Phase

1. Identify Research

Generate Search strategy
1.6 Use a specific strategy for systematic search string construction
1.1 Perform Snowballing
1.2 Perform pilot searches to train search string
Develop the search
1.5- 22.2 Use broad search process in generic search engines w/o start date
1.3- 12.1- 8.2 Search known DLs/ broad search engines/ specific high quality publication venues
Document the process
1.9 Evaluate results/ Document outcomes
1.8 Use tools to support the review process
1.10 Use tools for bibliography management
Evaluate the search
1.9 Evaluate results/ Document outcomes
1.4 Compare to gold standard/ other secondary studies
1.7 Independent experts review the search process

2. Study selection

Define inclusion/exclusion criteria
7.5 Do pilots and revise criteria or use independent expert's suggestions
7.6 Prescribe a set of decision rules
12.2 Perform quality assessment
Manage duplicate articles
5.2 Use summaries of studies to identify duplicates
5.1 Develop a strategy (keep newer or journal version).
Handle work in other languages or with missing text
3.1/ 4.1 Decide based on their number compared to population
Handle disagreements
7.1 Use systematic voting
7.3 Discuss criteria among authors
Evaluate the final set of studies
7.2 Perform random screening of papers
12.3 Evaluate the quality of studies using statistics
2.1 If the studies are published in limited journals/ conferences use a broad search
Document the process
7.4 Document inclusion/ exclusion criteria in the protocol

3. Study Quality Assurance

Handle Grey literature
6.1 Decide based on the goal of the study and the availability of sources.
Assess the completeness of the final set (if the studies in the data set are published in a limited set of venues)
10.1 Perform snowballing
10.2 Include grey literature
10.3 Scan manually selected venues
Assess Quality
7.9 Assess the validity of primary studies using statistics
7.7 Define quality thresholds
7.8 Perform Sensitivity analysis

Study Selection Validity

Data Validity

Research Validity

5. Data Synthesis

Perform data synthesis
16.3 Use a formal data synthesis method
14.1 Perform statistical analysis if you have quantitative data
15.1 Select an existing classification schema
15.2 Continuously update the classification schema to be able to classify all primary studies
Interpret the results objectively
16.1 Perform pilot data analysis and interpretation
16.2 Conduct reliability checks (i.e. post-SLR surveys)
16.4 Perform sensitivity analysis
16.5 Take into consideration the quality of primary studies
8.1 If the sample size of results is small draw conclusions based on trends
22.1- 20.1 Compare with related work, in case of absence of related work brainstorm among authors

4. Data Extraction

Define the data to be extracted
9.1 Discuss the choice of variables among authors
11.1 Perform pilot data extraction to test the existence of relationships
Perform data extraction
13.1 Involve more than one researchers
13.6 Use keywording of abstracts
13.5 Perform paper screening to cross check data extraction
17.2 Make all collected data publicly available
Handle disagreements *(only if multiple researchers are involved)*
13.3 Perform pilot data extract. to test researchers agreement
13.2 Identify expert's disagreement level with the kappa statistic
13.4 Use experts or external reviewers opinion to handle conflicts

Fig. 4 Mitigation actions that can be applied in each step of the secondary study design process.
* In front of each mitigation action, the code refers to the ID of the threat to validity, followed by the ID of the mitigation action in the checklist

4 Usage Scenario 2: How Reviewers Can Appraise Validity

In this section, we illustrate the scenario in which a secondary study needs to be evaluated, either by a reviewer or by a reader of the study, for the purpose of scientific review before publication or for evaluating its validity before usage, respectively. In particular, the evaluation of validity of a secondary study based on the classification schema and the checklist can be performed using two parts of the manuscript: (a) the threats to validity section and (b) the study design section. We first examine if the threats are classified/organized into sensible categories in the threats to validity section. Subsequently, we check if *all threats* to validity are discussed in the threats to validity section, or if *some of them* (or some mitigation actions) are only discussed while reporting the study design.

To illustrate this scenario, we consider a sample of five secondary studies that have been performed by the authors of this chapter (and other coauthors). We note that the evaluation provided below does not reflect upon the quality of the published studies, and the trustworthiness of the results, but only focuses on the way that the threats to validity are reported. The studies are listed in chronological order:

[S1] A. Ampatzoglou, and I. Stamelos, "Software engineering research for computer games: A systematic review," *Information and Software Technology*, Elsevier, 2010 (Ampatzoglou and Stamelos 2010).

[S2] A. Ampatzoglou, S. Charalampidou, and I. Stamelos, "Research state of the art on GoF design patterns: A mapping study," *Journal of Systems and Software*, Elsevier, 2013 (Ampatzoglou et al. 2013).

[S3] M. Galster, D. Weyns, D. Tofan, B. Michalik and P. Avgeriou, "Variability in Software Systems—A Systematic Literature Review," *Transactions on Software Engineering*, IEEE Computer Society, 2014 (Galster et al. 2014).

[S4] A. Ampatzoglou, A. Ampatzoglou, A. Chatzigeorgiou, and P. Avgeriou, "The financial aspect of managing technical debt: A systematic literature review," *Information and Software Technology*, 2015 (Ampatzoglou et al. 2015).

[S5] E. M. Arvanitou, A. Ampatzoglou, A. Chatzigeorgiou, M. Galster, and P. Avgeriou, "A mapping study on design-time quality attributes and metrics," *Journal of Systems and Software*, Elsevier, 2017 (Arvanitou et al. 2017).

In Table 1, we present the classification of threats to specific categories in the threats to validity section. From Table 1, we can observe that even for studies that come from the same group of authors (or at least overlapping ones), the classification of the threats is not uniform, or it is sometimes completely omitted. Also, we note that for the two studies that are reporting categories, the classes are similar, and quite close to the classification schema reported in Sect. 2.1. Based on this analysis, reviewers of studies [S1], [S3], and [S5] could point out to authors to either use an established classification schema or come up with their own custom schema. Authors of [S3] should be asked to include an explicit section on validity threats. Reviewers of studies who use custom classifications schemas can encourage the authors to precisely and accurately define them, if they have not done so (which

Table 1 Classification of threats into categories

Study ID	Dedicated section	Classification of threats to validity
[S1]	Yes	No categorization
[S2]	Yes	Construct validity. Defined as threats during study design Internal validity. Defined as threats occurring during data collection External validity. Referring to threats when generalizing to population Conclusion validity. Referring to possibly incorrect conclusions (e.g., missing relations, or wrongly extracted relations)
[S3]	No	No categorization
[S4]	Yes	Threats to identification of primary studies Threats to data extraction Threats to generalization of results Threats to conclusions
[S5]	Yes	No categorization

is not the case for [S2] and [S4]). Not all authors need to use an existing schema, but it is crucial that they thoroughly define the types of threats.

Proceeding to a more in-depth analysis of reported threats, Table 2 presents which of the threats to validity listed in Sect. 2.2 have been identified by the five specific studies, how they have been mitigated (the code MA_x of the mitigation action of the corresponding threat TV_y in Table 2), and where (i.e., threats or study design section) they are reported. The rows of the table correspond to a specific threat, and the columns to the five examined papers, while each cell denotes the corresponding mitigation action. A blank cell implies that either the threat is not identified or it does not apply to the specific secondary study. In case no mitigation action has been taken for a specific threat, then we mark it only as identified (ID), but not mitigated. Threats to validity that are discussed in study design (mitigated or not) but not in the "threats to validity" section are marked with italics.

From Table 2 we can observe that the selected studies are covering the majority of the possible threats to validity. Nevertheless, 80.7% of the mitigation actions of studies are only discussed as part of the study design and not the threats to validity section. Although the level of validity for the studies is high, the reporting of the threats is somehow limited. This hinders the evaluation of how threats to validity are considered and mitigated and undermines the overall validity of the studies. In very few cases a threat has been identified without applying any mitigation action, while often more than one action is applied to mitigate a given threat, which implies relatively good management of threats.

Based on this analysis, reviewers could use the proposed classification schema and checklist to encourage the authors: (a) to check whether more threats to validity pertain to their studies, preferably pointing out specific threats that the reviewers have identified; (b) suggest additional mitigation actions for the reported threats that seem more relevant to the study; (c) ensure that all identified threats are mitigated

Table 2 Identified threats to validity

Checklist question	[S1]	[S2]	[S3]	[S4]	[S5]
TV$_1$: Has your search process adequately identified all relevant primary studies?	MA$_3$ MA$_5$	MA$_3$	MA$_2$ MA$_3$ MA$_5$ MA$_6$ MA$_9$	MA$_2$ MA$_3$ MA$_4$ MA$_6$	MA$_2$ MA$_3$ MA$_4$ MA$_6$
TV$_2$: Were primary studies relevant to the topic of the review published in several different journals and conferences?	MA$_1$		MA$_1$		
TV$_3$: Have you identified primary studies in multiple languages?					
TV$_4$: Were the full texts of all identified primary studies accessible from the researchers					
TV$_5$: Have you managed duplicate articles?	MA$_1$	MA$_1$	MA$_1$	MA$_1$	MA$_1$
TV$_6$: Have you included/excluded grey literature?			MA$_1$		MA$_1$
TV$_7$: Have you adequately performed study inclusion/exclusion?	MA$_3$ MA$_4$	MA$_3$ MA$_4$	MA$_2$ MA$_3$ MA$_4$ MA$_5$	MA$_3$ MA$_4$	MA$_3$ MA$_4$
TV$_8$: Is your sample size large enough so that the obtained results can be considered valid?	MA$_1$ MA$_2$	MA$_1$	MA$_1$ MA$_2$	MA$_1$	MA$_1$
TV$_9$: Have you chosen the correct variables to extract?		MA$_1$	MA$_1$		
TV$_{10}$: Are the primary studies in your dataset published in a limited set of venues?					ID
TV$_{11}$: Do you expect to identify relationships in your dataset?					
TV$_{12}$: Does the quality of primary studies guarantee the validity of extracted data?		MA$_1$	MA$_1$		MA$_1$
TV$_{13}$: Is there data extraction bias in your study?		MA$_1$ MA$_2$	MA$_1$ MA$_5$	MA$_1$	MA$_1$
TV$_{14}$: Have you performed statistical analysis?			MA$_1$		MA$_1$
TV$_{15}$: Have you selected a robust classification schema?	MA$_1$	MA$_1$		MA$_1$	
TV$_{16}$: Is your interpretation of the results subject to bias or is it as objective as possible?		ID	MA$_1$	MA$_1$	MA$_1$
TV$_{17}$: Is your process reliable/repeatable?	MA$_1$ MA$_2$ MA$_3$	MA$_1$ MA$_3$	MA$_1$ MA$_3$	MA$_1$ MA$_3$	MA$_1$ MA$_2$ MA$_3$
TV$_{18}$: Have you chosen the correct research method?		MA$_1$	MA$_2$		
TV$_{19}$: Do the answers to your research questions guarantee the accomplishment of your study goal?	MA$_2$	MA$_2$	MA$_2$	MA$_2$	MA$_2$
TV$_{20}$: Does your study have substantial related work, so that you can compare and discuss findings?					
TV$_{21}$: Were you familiar with the research field before performing the review?	MA$_1$	MA$_1$	MA$_1$	MA$_1$	MA$_1$
TV$_{22}$: Are the results of your study generalizable?	MA$_2$	ID	MA$_2$	ID	

with at least one action; and (d) encourage them to report all the threats identified in the study design, also within the threats to validity section.

5   Recommended Further Reading

We point out three different groups of related work. First, one needs to understand how *threats to validity* are categorized in the *empirical software engineering* field, without focusing on secondary studies. The initial categorization of Cook and Campbell (1979) is a fitting starting point, and of course the seminal books by Wohlin et al. (2013), Runeson et al. (2012), and Shull et al. (2007) on experimentation, case study design, and empirical SE are also of paramount importance. Second, we advise the interested reader to refer to studies that are related to *the identification and reporting of threats to validity in medical science*, which lies at the heart of the evidence-based software engineering paradigm. This can provide valuable input for our field, since medical research is considered a more mature field in secondary study design and execution and has already inspired the guidelines for conducting secondary studies in software engineering. Indicative readings in this perspective are Avellar et al. (2017), Downs and Black (1998), Moher et al. (2015), Shea et al. (2007), and Verhagen et al. (1998). Finally, to fully comprehend the underlying concepts of this chapter, the readers can refer to the *most common guidelines for performing secondary studies* in the software engineering domain (Budgen et al. 2018; Cruzes and Dybå 2011; Kitchenham and Charters 2007; Petersen et al. 2015).

6   Conclusions

Threats to the validity of scientific results are inescapable when a particular method or experimental setup is used to collect, analyze, and interpret data. In this chapter, we have focused on factors that may jeopardize the validity of secondary studies in software engineering. In particular, based on the results of a Systematic Literature Review of secondary studies we have proposed a classification schema, depicting three threat categories (study selection, data, and research validity), threats belonging to each category, and the corresponding mitigation actions. To assist authors, reviewers, and readers in assessing the rigor of secondary studies, we provided a checklist including questions asked to understand if a specific threat is present and corresponding sub-questions to investigate if an appropriate mitigation action has been applied. Finally, we discussed guidelines for identifying and managing threats during the execution of a secondary study and actions for mitigating threats, providing examples and references to the relevant literature.

Secondary studies are a significant driver for the evidence-based software engineering and often lead to works of major significance that act as reference points in a research topic. Researchers often consult secondary studies to obtain insights to the collective knowledge in a domain and identify opportunities for further research. Ensuring a consistent classification of threats in Systematic Literature Reviews and Mapping Studies and supporting a systematic identification of appropriate mitigation actions can further increase their credibility. Eventually, the proper identification and management of threats can improve the secondary studies' process itself, solidifying the search and selection of primary studies, the extraction of data from the literature, and the applied data synthesis.

References

Ahmad A, Babar A (2016) Software architectures for robotic systems: a systematic mapping study. J Syst Softw 122:16–39

Al-Baik O, Miller J (2015) The Kanban approach, between agility and leanness: a systematic review. Empir Softw Eng 20(6):1861–1897

Ali MS, Babar A, Chen L, Stol KJ (2010) A systematic review of comparative evidence of aspect-oriented programming. Inf Softw Technol 52(9):871–887

Alves NS, Mendes TS, de Mendonsa MG, Spinola RO, Shull F, Seaman C (2016) Identification and management of technical debt: a systematic mapping study. Inf Softw Technol 70:100–121

Ameller D, Burgués X, Collell O, Costal D, Franch X, Papazoglou MP (2015) Development of service-oriented architectures using model-driven development: a mapping study. Inf Softw Technol 62:42–66

Ampatzoglou, Stamelos I (2010) Software engineering research for computer games: a systematic review. Inf Softw Technol 52(9):888–901

Ampatzoglou A, Charalampidou S, Stamelos I (2013) Research state of the art on GoF design patterns: A mapping study. J Syst Softw 86(7):1945–1964

Ampatzoglou A, Chatzigeorgiou, Avgeriou P (2015) The financial aspect of managing technical debt: a systematic literature review. Inf Softw Technol 64:52–73

Ampatzoglou S, Bibi P, Avgeriou M, Verbeek A, Chatzigeorgiou (2019) Identifying, categorizing and mitigating threats to validity in software engineering secondary studies. Inf Softw Technol 106:201–230

Arvanitou EM, Ampatzoglou A, Chatzigeorgiou A, Galster M, Avgeriou P (2017) A mapping study on design-time quality attributes and metrics. J Syst Softw 127:52–77

Avellar SA, Thomas J, Kleinman R, Sama-Miller E, Woodruff SE, Coughlin R, Westbrook TPR (2017) External validity: the next step for systematic reviews? Eval Rev 41(4):283–325

Barreiros E, Almeida A, Saraiva J, Soares S (2011) A systematic mapping study on software engineering testbeds. In: 5th International symposium on empirical software engineering and measurement, Alberta, pp 107–116

Basili VR, Selby RW (1991) Paradigms for experimentation and empirical studies in software engineering. Reliab Eng Syst Saf 32(1–2):171–191

Brereton P, Kitchenham B, Budgen D, Turner M, Khalilc M (2007) Lessons from applying the systematic literature review process within the software engineering domain. J Syst Softw 80(4):571–583

Budgen D, Brereton P, Drummond S, Williams N (2018) Reporting systematic reviews: some lessons from a tertiary study. Inf Softw Technol 95:62–74

Cook D, Campbell DT (1979) Quasi-experimentation: design & analysis issues for field settings. Houghton Mifflin, Boston

Cornelissen AZ, van Deursen A, Moonen L, Koschke R (2009) A systematic survey of program comprehension through dynamic analysis. IEEE Trans Softw Eng 35(5):684–702

Cruzes S, Dybå T (2011) Research synthesis in software engineering: a tertiary study. Inf Softw Technol 53(5):440–455

Dieste O, Padua D (2007) Developing search strategies for detecting relevant experiments for systematic reviews. In: 1st International symposium on empirical software engineering and measurement, Washington, DC, pp 215–224

Ding PL, Tang A, van Vliet H (2014) Knowledge-based approaches in software documentation: a systematic literature review. Inf Softw Technol 56(6):545–567

Downs SH, Black N (1998) The feasibility of creating a checklist for the assessment of the methodological quality both of randomised and non-randomised studies of health care interventions. J Epidemiol Community Health 52(6):377–384

Dybå T, Dingsøyr T (2008) Empirical studies of agile software development: a systematic review. Inf Softw Technol 50:833–859

Engström M, Skoglund, Runeson P (2008) Empirical evaluations of regression test selection techniques: a systematic review. In: 2nd ACM-IEEE international symposium on empirical software engineering and measurement, New York, pp 22–31

Galster M, Weyns D, Tofan D, Michalik B, Avgeriou P (2014) Variability in software systems – a systematic literature review. IEEE Trans Softw Eng 40(3):282–306

Garcés L, Ampatzoglou A, Avgeriou P, Nakagawa EY (2017) Quality attributes and quality models for ambient assisted living software systems: a systematic mapping. Inf Softw Technol 82:121–138, 2017

Haselberger D (2016) A literature-based framework of performance-related leadership interactions in ICT project teams. Inf Softw Technol 70:1–17

Ivarsson M, Gorschek T (2011) A method for evaluating rigor and industrial relevance of technology evaluations. Empir Softw Eng 16(3):365–395

Jabangwe R, Borstler J, Smite D, Wohlin C (2015) Empirical evidence on the link between object-oriented measures and external quality attributes: a systematic literature review. Empir Softw Eng 20(3):640–693

Kabbedijk J, Bezemer CP, Jansen S, Zaidman A (2015) Defining multi-tenancy: a systematic mapping study on the academic and the industrial perspective. J Syst Softw 100:139–148

Karanatsiou D, Li Y, Arvanitou EM, Misirlis N, Wong WE (2019) A bibliometric assessment of software engineering scholars and institutions (2010–2017). J Syst Softw 147:246–261

Khurum M, Gorschek T (2009) A systematic review of domain analysis solutions for product lines. J Syst Softw 82(12):1982–2003

Kitchenham, Charters S (2007) Guidelines for performing systematic literature reviews in software engineering. Technical report EBSE-2007-01, School of Computer Science and Mathematics, Keele University

Kitchenham T, Dybå MJ (2004) Evidence-based software engineering. In: Proceedings of the 26th international conference on software engineering (ICSE '04), IEEE, pp 273–281, May, 2004

Kitchenham OP, Brereton D, Budgen M, Turner J, Bailey SL (2009) Systematic literature reviews in software engineering – a systematic literature review. Inf Softw Technol, Elsevier 51(1):7–15

Kitchenham RP, Budgen D, Pearl Brereton O, Turner M, Niazi M, Linkman S (2010) Systematic literature reviews in software engineering – a tertiary study. Inf Softw Technol 52(8):792–805

Kosar T, Bohra S, Mernik M (2016) Domain-specific languages: a systematic mapping study. Inf Softw Technol 71:77–91

Lenberg P, Feldt R, Wallgren LG (2015) Behavioral software engineering: a definition and systematic literature review. J Syst Softw 107:15–37

Li Z, Avgeriou P, Liang P (2015) A systematic mapping study on technical debt and its management. J Syst Softw 101:193–220

MacDonnell SG (2019) Invited lighting talks. In: 23rd International conference on evaluation and assessment in software engineering, Copenhagen

Magdaleno AM, Werner CM, Araujo RM (2012) Reconciling software development models: a quasi-systematic review. J Syst Softw 85(2):351–369

Moher L, Shamseer M, Clarke D, Ghersi A, Liberati M, Petticrew P, Shekelle LAS (2015) Preferred reporting items for systematic review and meta-analysis protocols (PRISMA-P) 2015 statement. Syst Rev 54(1)

Montalvillo L, Diaz O (2016) Requirement-driven evolution in software product lines: a systematic mapping study. J Syst Softw 122:110–143

Nair S, de la Vara JL, Sabetzadeh M, Briand L (2014) An extended systematic literature review on provision of evidence for safety certification. Inf Softw Technol 56(7):689–717

Nguyen-Duc DS, Cruzes, Conradi R (2015) The impact of global dispersion on coordination, team performance and software quality – a systematic literature review. Inf Softw Technol 57:277–294

Penzenstadler V Bauer C, Caleroand X (2012) French, "sustainability in software engineering": a systematic literature review. In: 16th International conference on evaluation & assessment in software engineering, pp 32–41

Petersen K, Feldt R, Mujtaba S, Mattsson M (2008) Systematic mapping studies in software engineering. In: Proceedings of evaluation and assessment in software engineering, EASE, vol 8, pp 68–77

Petersen K, Vakkalanka S, Kuzniarz L (2015) Guidelines for conducting systematic mapping studies in software engineering: An update. In: Information and Software technology, vol 64, pp 1–8

Pfleeger SL, Kitchenham BA (2001) Principles of survey research: part 1: turning lemons into lemonade. SIGSOFT Softw Eng Notes 26, 6 November 2001

Runeson P, Höst M (2009) Guidelines for conducting and reporting case study research in software engineering. Empir Softw Eng 14(2):131–164

Runeson P, Höst M, Rainer A, Regnell B (2012) Case study research in software engineering: guidelines and examples. Wlley, Hoboken

Santos RE, da Silva FQ, de Magalhães CV (2016) Benefits and limitations of job rotation in software organizations: a systematic literature review. In: 20th International conference on evaluation and assessment in software engineering, p 16

Shahin M, Liang P, Babar MA (2014) A systematic review of software architecture visualization techniques. J Syst Softw 94:161–185

Shea BJ, Grimshaw JM, Wells GA, Boers M, Andersson N, Hamel C, Porter AC, Tugwell P, Moher D, Bouter LM (2007) Development of AMSTAR: a measurement tool to assess the methodological quality of systematic reviews. BMC Med Res Methodol 7(1):10

Shull F, Singer J, Sjøberg DI (2007) Guide to advanced empirical software engineering. Springer Science & Business Media, Boston

Staples M, Niazi M (2008) Systematic review of organizational motivations for adopting CMM-based SPI. Inf Softw Technol 50(7–8):605–620

Tiwari S, Gupta A (2015) A systematic literature review of use case specifications research. Inf Softw Technol 67:128–158

Verhagen P, de Vet HC, de Bie RA, Kessels AG, Boers M, Bouter LM, Knipschild PG (1998) The Delphi list: a criteria list for quality assessment of randomized clinical trials for conducting systematic reviews developed by Delphi consensus. J Clin Epidemiol 51(12):1235–1241

Wohlin C, Host M, Runeson P, Ohlsson M, Regnell B, Wesslen A (2000) Experimentation in software engineering: an introduction. Kluwer Academic, Norwell

Wohlin C, Runeson P, da Mota Silveira Neto PA, Engström E, do Carmo Machado I, Santana de Almeida E (2013) On the reliability of mapping studies in software engineering. J Syst Softw 86(10):2594–2610

Yang C, Liang P, Avgeriou P (2016) A systematic mapping study on the combination of software architecture and agile development. J Syst Softw 111:157–184

Yusifoğlu VG, Amannejad Y, Can AB (2015) Software test-code engineering: a systematic mapping. Inf Softw Technol 58:123–147

Research Synthesis in Software Engineering

Paulo Sérgio Medeiros dos Santos (iD) **and Guilherme Horta Travassos** (iD)

Abstract Research synthesis represents an essential element of the knowledge accumulation and application process, which is indispensable to any scientific field such as software engineering. In the case of the software engineering domain, the evidence is produced in both quantitative and qualitative forms, which challenges their combined analysis. Research synthesis methods, in general, follow similar processes but differ in being integrative or interpretative. This chapter intends to introduce the reader to the research synthesis theme. It discusses the most frequently used synthesis methods in software engineering. They range from the ones geared toward interpretative synthesis approaches—for instance, thematic synthesis and meta-ethnography—to those more focused on integrative approaches—e.g., case survey, qualitative comparative analysis, and statistical meta-analysis. Besides brief descriptions of these methods, the structured synthesis method is presented in detail, together with a worked example concerning the synthesis of four primary studies regarding the usage-based reading inspection technique.

1 Introduction

The scientific community is highly dependent on methodological and technological instruments to acquire, describe, and effectively disseminate its knowledge objectively. These instruments allow the researchers to interpret and exploit the available knowledge to advance the understanding of different matters.

Scientific contributions are usually built incrementally, involving some transformation, expansion, or refutation of existing conceptual and propositional knowl-

P. Santos (✉)
Federal University of the State of Rio de Janeiro, Rio de Janeiro, Brazil
e-mail: pasemes@uniriotec.br

G. H. Travassos
Department of Systems Engineering and Computer Science, COPPE, Federal University of Rio de Janeiro, Rio de Janeiro, Brazil
e-mail: ght@cos.ufrj.br

© Springer Nature Switzerland AG 2020
M. Felderer, G. H. Travassos (eds.), *Contemporary Empirical Methods in Software Engineering*, https://doi.org/10.1007/978-3-030-32489-6_16

edge. As the body of knowledge increases, scientists concentrate more effort into ensuring that new hypotheses and observations are needed and comparable with previous findings. The knowledge accumulation is mainly grounded on the organization and systematization of interrelated facts, aiming at identifying and characterizing patterns of relationships among phenomena and processes of the observed world (Overton 1991). In general, knowledge accumulation involves two main parts: its creation and application. Research synthesis plays a crucial role in the knowledge accumulation process since it organizes and summarizes the created knowledge so that it can be more conveniently applied.

Within the evidence-based practice, knowledge *creation* is directly associated with primary studies. This topic has been carefully examined in the last couple of decades, resulting in an extensive repertoire of primary study methods tailored for SE such as controlled experiment, case study, survey, ethnography, action research, and simulation (Harrison et al. 1999; Wohlin et al. 2003; Zelkowitz 2007; Easterbrook et al. 2008; Runeson and Höst 2009; Santos and Travassos 2011; de Mello et al. 2014; de França and Travassos 2016). The reading of chapter "Introduction: The Evolution of Empirical Methods in Software Engineering" can give a complete perspective on the evolution of empirical studies in software engineering (SE).

Knowledge *application*, on the other hand, concerns with how evidence produced with primary studies can reach the audience outside the academic confinement or can facilitate researchers in deriving new hypotheses. In SE, it has not yet been subjected to the same level of scrutinization as knowledge creation. A conjecture for this is that it is chronologically at the end of the knowledge accumulation progression, i.e., it occurs after knowledge creation.

Both knowledge creation and application are commonly discussed under a more extensive process known as knowledge translation. This process is fundamental to the evidence-based practice since, as the name implies, it is how knowledge can be adapted to suit other needs—i.e., besides research—usually for the practitioners in the field. By adapting the description of knowledge translation from Davis et al. (2003), who characterized the problem in medicine, Budgen et al. (2013) define knowledge translation in SE as being "*the exchange, synthesis and ethically sound application of knowledge—within a complex system of interactions between researchers and users—to accelerate the capture of the benefits of research through better quality software and software development processes.*" According to these authors, its three main concerns are (1) the outcomes of secondary studies, such as research syntheses; (2) the interpretations of what these outcomes mean in particular contexts; and (3) the appropriate forms for communicating the outcomes.

This brief description of knowledge creation and application is sufficient to draw attention to two essential issues. One is the fact that research synthesis is central to knowledge accumulation since secondary studies represent a necessary step for knowledge application. That is, the act of translating knowledge itself requires that researchers first synthesize knowledge in order to collect and discern what is essential for applying it. The other is that there is considerable heterogeneity of primary study strategies in SE. The main driver for this is primarily due to the nature of SE as, differently from most fields, it blends technical and human aspects in a balanced proportion. For instance, on the human and social side, researchers need to investigate problems such as the cognitive load of software developers (Walenstein 2003) or the software engineers' attitudes toward organizational change (Lenberg et al. 2017). On the technical side, the software product is emphasized as well as the tools supporting its development, as in the case of the adoption of programming languages and its impact on software quality (Góis Mateus and Martinez 2019). Not to mention that quantitative and qualitative perspectives are associated with particular worldviews, which influences researchers on how their investigations are conducted or interpreted (Mahoney and Goertz 2006). It leads to a situation where quantitative and qualitative findings in SE are abundantly available, resulting in considerable forms of research outcomes in the technical literature.

Therefore, this chapter presents research synthesis methods in SE, taking into account these two previously mentioned issues. It acknowledges not only the role of quantitative and qualitative findings in the knowledge translation process but also the challenges that the heterogeneity of research outcomes imposes to evidence aggregation. Thus, it aims at introducing and offering guidance for strategies and methods employed when using research synthesis methods, mainly focusing those the authors believe are most suited to address these issues. Among these methods, the chapter presents the structured synthesis method, which has been proposed explicitly for SE and can aggregate qualitative and quantitative evidence. For supporting the discussion, this chapter begins describing the basic definitions of research synthesis (Sect. 2). Then, it differentiates interpretative and integrative methods, discussing its relation with the qualitative and quantitative dichotomization (Sect. 3). The research synthesis methods commonly used in SE are presented in Sect. 4. Then, the structured synthesis method detailed in Sect. 5 is followed by a worked example in Sect. 6. The chapter ends with suggestions for further readings in Sect. 7 and a conclusion in Sect. 8.

2 Basic Definitions

The terms systematic literature review, research synthesis, and research review are often used interchangeably, but as we will see in this section, they have different meanings (Cooper and Hedges 2009).

The goal of systematic literature reviews (SLRs) is to search, identify, and collect primary studies regarding a research topic, preferably regarding a specific research question. In order to answer a research question, SLRs should provide some synthesis such that the research question at hand is addressed precisely by taking into consideration all primary studies together. Research synthesis, on the other hand, can be described as *"a collective term for a family of methods that are used to summarize, integrate, combine, and compare the findings"* (Cruzes and Dybå 2011a). It can be used as part of a systematic literature review, for synthesizing the collected primary studies, or alone provided that there is a set of primary studies as input that can be collected by, for instance, using a search strategy such as *Snowballing* (Wohlin 2016). At last, research review is associated with some quality evaluation of the current technical literature regarding a theme, although it can be easily found as a synonym for a literature review or research synthesis.

Despite the confusion around the terms, Cooper and Hedges (2009) indicate that the most definitional aspect of a research synthesis study is its primary focus and goal. According to the authors, *"research syntheses attempt to integrate empirical research to create generalizations."* To that end, like any other kind of scientific inquiry, it should follow a process or at least a set of guidelines so that the rigor of the study can be improved and its quality assessed.

The concerns regarding the rigor and quality of research synthesis studies are present since the early works regarding synthesis have flourished. For instance, Taveggia (1974) enumerates six common problems in research synthesis: selecting research; retrieving, indexing, and coding information from studies; analyzing the comparability of findings; accumulating comparable findings; analyzing distributions of results; and reporting of results. A more contemporary analysis of research synthesis methods identifies similar issues. As Sandelowski et al. (2012) state, all research synthesis studies require to define research problems, purposes, and questions; set parameters for the searching, retrieval, inclusion, and extraction of information from the technical literature; compare and translate the findings; and perform some activity of content or thematic analysis, counting, tabulating, plotting, diagramming, and narrating.

Taking these issues together, we believe that they could be used as cornerstones for a *"canonical"* research synthesis process since they represent typical circumstances that must be addressed when combining or organizing the outcomes of studies. Thus, as these issues are pervasive to any method, research synthesis methods are not differentiated by these practices per se, but rather by how, why, and when in the course of a synthesis study, these practices are executed.

In the SE realm, Ciolkowski (2009) defines an approach for quantitative aggregation whose process addresses the same concerns regarding the synthesis rigor and quality, taking into account the following steps:

1. *Definition*: Define goals, dependent and independent variables, inclusion criteria for studies
2. *Study selection*: Systematically collect primary studies, according to defined goals; assess appropriateness regarding inclusion criteria; extract data
3. *Study quality assessment*: In addition to general inclusion-exclusion criteria, it is generally considered essential to assess the "quality" of primary studies
4. *Data extraction*: Design data extraction forms to accurately record the information researchers obtain from the primary studies. In this case, extract information necessary to compute the effect size of individual studies
5. *Data synthesis*: Collate and summarize the results of the included primary studies; in this case, using meta-analysis to combine effect sizes from primary studies.

Although this approach was proposed for aggregating quantitative (primary) studies in SE, the approach's process can be thought out in other contexts. For instance, the structured synthesis method (Santos and Travassos 2013) (see Sect. 5)—a synthesis method proposed for aggregating qualitative and quantitative studies in SE—uses similar steps as a process for research synthesis, even though it represents a mixed (qualitative and quantitative) method. It shows how methods distinguish among themselves due to how they suggest performing their expected tasks and not by the steps involved in synthesizing research.

Another aspect that should be highlighted regarding the research synthesis process is the large intersection with systematic literature reviews. As it has been mentioned before, both processes are complementary. Just as an example of this intersection, the first three steps of the previously described process are more related to systematic literature reviews, in which a disciplined identification and collection of primary studies is expected, than to research synthesis itself.

Furthermore, it is essential to add that the term "systematic" is precisely associated with the idea that they can be conducted in an organized and auditable way to produce repeatable results. However, even though it seems to be achievable when independent reviewers use the same protocol, significant differences usually appear in the way the last two steps are carried out (MacDonell et al. 2010). These steps are precisely the ones that represent the procedures related to research synthesis and, as MacDonell et al. (2010) observe, are highly dependent on the researcher's individual decisions and interpretations. Nevertheless, despite this reliance on the researchers' abilities, there are two fundamental ways of performing a synthesis of research. It is the subject of the following section.

3 Synthesizing Research: Interpretation, Integration, or Both?

The typical classification used for describing primary studies, segregating the ones based on qualitative data from those based on quantitative data, gives a much less impressive view when applied for understanding secondary studies using research synthesis methods. The preferred way for describing research synthesis methods is to think about them in terms of their primary purpose, which is interpreting or integrating knowledge. Noblit and Hare (1988) are the first authors to make this distinction between research synthesis methods. The primary goal of an interpretative synthesis is to describe or develop concepts to support their organization, such as in theoretical models, taxonomical relationships, analytical arguments, or any other organizational form that allows a connection between the outcomes of the synthesized studies. An integrative synthesis, on the other hand, involves summarizing and pooling data, incorporating the results into each other. Its purpose usually involves determining the size of the combined effect when the primary studies' outcomes are considered together.

As one can suppose, a direct line can be drawn between these two classifications. Interpretative syntheses are usually associated with qualitative analysis, whereas integrative syntheses are associated with quantitative analysis. However, this link does not paint the whole picture. Even though there are authors who use these terms as synonyms (Guzmán et al. 2014), in our understanding, the arguments offered by Dixon-Woods et al. (2005) represent a more accurate description of interpretative and integrative synthesis without necessarily associating them with qualitative and qualitative analysis. For these authors, as we highlighted before, the integrative synthesis is focused on data summarization, but they add that the concepts (or variables) used to pool the data are assumed to be more secure and well specified. In contrast with an integrative synthesis, an interpretative synthesis will not be concerned with fixing the meaning of the concepts at an early stage to facilitate the summary of empirical data relating to those concepts. On the contrary, an interpretive synthesis will seek to conceptualize the available evidence guided by the research question at hand, so that the details can be abstracted away and the essential interpretations are reflected in the identified concepts usually described in the form of a theory.

Interpretative and integrative syntheses do not represent excluding alternatives. Any theory development, besides the focus on conceptual development, will involve some level of summarization in order to explain the data. Analogously, any summarization will involve some level of conceptual development, usually related to the causal relationships among variables to analyze the generalizability of aggregated outcomes. As a consequence, following this line of reasoning, interpretative and integrative methods are not restricted to qualitative and quantitative analysis, respectively. Both can use diverse forms of evidence, but this usually requires the conversion of qualitative data into a quantitative form or vice versa (Dixon-Woods et al. 2005).

When the synthesis does not use an explicit approach (interpretative or integrative) for aggregating evidence, it represents a narrative synthesis, which is an ad hoc approach that is neither traceable nor systematic. According to Guzmán et al. (2014), a narrative synthesis (or narrative summary) emphasizes a narrative description and ordering of heterogeneous evidence to produce an account of the primary studies at hand, often providing some conclusion or making new hypotheses regarding the interpretations. As one can observe in Cruzes and Dybå (2011a), most syntheses previously accomplished in SE are narrative.

3.1 Procedures for Interpreting and Integrating

This section provides a general view regarding the procedures involved in the interpretative and integrative strategies, by enumerating and presenting the actions usually taken in each type of synthesis, particularly those that best distinguish these strategies. Two aspects are discussed in this section for each type of synthesis: data *extraction* and *analysis*.

In an interpretative synthesis, the researcher must pay attention to *extract* pieces of data that support inductive interpretations, without predefined preconceptions, bias, or inclinations. For instance, a synthesis concerned with how testers use software testing tools can include one study describing whether they believe the tools are appropriate for the task at hand and another study investigating the difficulties of novice testers using the same testing tools. In terms of data analysis, one could conceptualize the former as related to the understandability and the latter as associated with the learnability. Then they realize that both are concerned with the usability of software testing tools when using the definitions regarding, for instance, the software quality properties presented in Kitchenham and Pfleeger (1996). This example shows how the inductive process supports the *analysis* in identifying concepts that can translate studies' variables or notions, which at first glance are not comparable, but when translated to the proper concept, they become comparable. In the interpretative synthesis, data *extraction* should be as open as possible, so that the *analysis* can be guided by what is discovered in the studies and not to (un)confirm an a priori hypothesis. As discussed earlier in this section, data can be of qualitative or quantitative nature. Qualitative data are usually associated with field notes or interviews, whereas quantitative data complement it with frequencies and other kinds of descriptive statistics.

In an integrative synthesis, on the other hand, the researcher is more focused on examining correlational or causal relationships. These relationships are usually defined at the beginning of the synthesis study, and they contain the concepts that are going to be investigated. As one can see, it employs deductive reasoning since the synthesis study starts with a general statement, or hypothesis, and examines the possibilities to achieve the hypothesized logical conclusion, based on the extracted data. For instance, still using the example of a synthesis related to software testing tools and taking the same concepts related to the quality properties used earlier, two hypotheses could be conceived.

One is whether there is a difference between two (or more) software testing tools regarding their learnability, using the time necessary to grasp and use the tools in a software project. The other is whether there is a relationship between the testers' experience and their understandability of the tools. These examples are sufficient to illustrate how concepts embodied the hypothesis definition itself—in this case, learnability and understandability. Thus, data *extraction* is centered on collecting information that supports or contradicts the hypotheses and relationships of interest. As data *analysis* is based on the *extracted* data, it also uses the same concepts so that all the studies can be *analyzed* together by providing some summarization of their outcomes. As in the case of interpretative synthesis, both quantitative and qualitative data can be used in the analysis. Quantitative data is usually associated with a particular property of the object under study (e.g., learnability), whereas qualitative data can add explanations to the patterns found or just incorporated in the pooling with the quantitative data by converting it.

4   Current Research Synthesis Methods

In this section, we briefly introduce some research synthesis methods that, in our understanding, are the most used in and more balanced for use in SE. The idea is to offer a list of options for taking a grasp of what is available and its applicability considering the profile of primary studies in SE.

- *Thematic synthesis*: it involves the identification of recurrent themes in technical literature, summarizing results from different studies related to each theme (Dixon-Woods et al. 2005). In the process defined in Cruzes and Dybå (2011b), five steps are indicated: data extraction, data coding, translation of codes into themes, creation of a higher-order model, and trustworthiness assessment. One of the fundamental principles driving this process is the increasing abstraction levels, starting from the text, passing through the identification of themes, and concluding with a higher-order model. It is also interesting how graphical representations are used for the model, usually a cognitive map (Cruzes and Dybå 2011b).
- *Meta-ethnography*: it seems that the most distinctive feature of meta-ethnography is the translation (reciprocal or refutational) procedure, which supports the researcher in identifying and inducing concepts and relations by considering findings in one study that is like the findings of other ones (Da Silva et al. 2013). This translation can be done literally, concept by concept, or idiomatically, preserving the text meaning. In any case, the objective is to produce new interpretations using analogies to consolidate different studies' results or by developing concepts and relations that can capture the findings together.
- *Case survey method*: conceptually more straightforward than the other methods, it consists of a closed questionnaire, which is applied to each (case) study (Yin and Heald 1975). Since the questions are closed-ended, the summarization comes from the analysis of the answers' distributions. In Yin and Heald (1975) and Larsson (1993), three methodological concerns are emphasized: (1) synthesis reliability as a parameter to assess its replicability, (2) the differentiation between weak and strong responses to estimate the confidence on each answer and on the whole synthesis, and (3) an explicit definition of criteria for excluding studies from the synthesis. See chapter "Guidelines for Case Survey Research in Software Engineering" for more details.
- *Qualitative comparative analysis*: it assumes that a given outcome can be an effect of different combinations of circumstances so that the notion of causality may be understood in terms of the sufficient and necessary conditions distinction (Dixon-Woods et al. 2005). These conditions are usually associated with the studies' dependent and independent variables, which are tabulated using dichotomous values—in the case of crisp set qualitative comparative analysis—to indicate the presence or absence of a cause, effect, or contextual aspect. The summarization is then achieved by using first-order logic to determine which descriptive inferences are supported by data, constituting the so-called explanatory model. The model

represents the sufficient and necessary conditions for the explored cause–effect relations.

- *Statistical meta-analysis*: it represents the analysis of analyses by applying statistics aiming to integrate the results of individual quantitative studies (Lipsey and Wilson 2001). It should not be confounded with secondary analysis, on which previously collected datasets are reanalyzed with more powerful statistical testing. However, it can be compared with a survey, on which the quantitative results of empirical studies (and not just individuals) characterize the participants (Schulze 2004). Due to its nature, meta-analysis only applies to quantitative results of experimental studies that are conceptually comparable (similar constructs, relationships, and the same statistical configuration). Therefore, it is not appropriate to use meta-analysis to aggregate results from different research designs even when they are dealing with the same topic of interest. Usually, the comparison of effect sizes (fixed or random) of the selected studies represents the results of a meta-analysis. However, the quality of the selected studies challenges its results (Wolf 1986). For instance, the lack of negative results reported in the technical literature can jeopardize confidence in the obtained aggregated result.

- *Theory building and statistical meta-analysis*: because it is a combination of two research strategies, its underlying idea is that theories can be developed through a statistical meta-analysis study (Yang 2002). The method is cited here to indicate the practicability of using theory-building techniques to support research synthesis. One of the main features of using theories as a tool for meta-analytical synthesis is the distinction between theory abstract constructs and observable indicators from the empirical level. Based on this idea, Yang (2002) defines three research domains: theoretical, empirical, and measurement. In the theoretical level, abstract concepts and entities are defined, which are used to define a theory. Both empirical and measurement domains are used to operationalize variables. The empirical domain contains all known existing definitions regarding how to operationalize a construct based on the definition of the theoretical domain, whereas the measurement domain contains representative samples of observations from the empirical domain for the same construct. Based on this distinction, the explicit link between theoretical and empirical levels can be formed, and meta-analytical statistic instruments are used to verify if the theoretical relationships are statistically significant according to the variables used to measure them.

- *Structured Synthesis Method (SSM)*: it is a research synthesis method that can be used to aggregate both quantitative and qualitative studies. It is a kind of integrative synthesis method, such as meta-analysis, but has several features from interpretative methods, such as meta-ethnography, particularly those concerned with conceptual development. The method is further detailed in the next section.

When choosing among these methods, we suggest considering at least two aspects: their interpretative and integrative capabilities and which type of evidence the method can synthesize (i.e., qualitative or quantitative). We created a three-level scale to describe these capabilities in the following manner:

Table 1 Classification of the research synthesis methods

Method	Interpretative level	Integrative level	Type of evidence
Thematic synthesis	Level 2	Level 1	Both qualitative and quantitative
Meta-ethnography	Level 3	Level 1	Preferably qualitative
Case survey method	Level 1	Level 2	Only evidence from case studies
Qualitative comparative analysis	Level 1	Level 2	Both qualitative and quantitative
Statistical meta-analysis	Level 1	Level 3	Only quantitative
Theory building and statistical meta-analysis	Level 2	Level 3	Only quantitative
Structured synthesis method	Level 2	Level 2	Both qualitative and quantitative

- For the interpretative scale:

  - Level 1—low concept development
  - Level 2—concepts are developed and defined, but there is no explanation of the mechanisms involving these concepts
  - Level 3—high concept development and explanation of the mechanisms involving these concepts

- For the integrative scale:

  - Level 1—some vote counting (Pickard et al. 1998) without considering the uncertainty related to each primary study included in the synthesis
  - Level 2—findings are pooled using a nominal or ordinal scale, considering the uncertainty of each primary study
  - Level 3—findings are pooled using an interval or ratio scale, considering the uncertainty of each primary study

  Table 1 uses this classification to enumerate the methods discussed in this section.

5   Integrating and Interpreting with the Structured Synthesis Method: A Small Introduction

This section depicts the structured synthesis method (SSM), which was first introduced in Santos and Travassos (2013) and used in different synthesis studies (see Sect. 7). The most salient feature of SSM is its support to combine qualitative and quantitative evidence, which is essential in SE considering the heterogeneity of primary studies in the area. This feature is a direct result of how SSM blends elements from both integrative and interpretive syntheses. Another nice feature of the method is that it was conceived for SE with specific constructs related to the software development domain (e.g., technology and software systems).

SSM uses diagrammatic models to represent essential pieces of information about primary studies and aggregate them. The central role of the models is to support the researcher in deciding whether primary studies' outcomes should be combined. In the SSM, the diagrammatic models are denominated *theoretical structures* since their representational constructs are based on theory building notions (e.g., concepts and relationships). The representation has ten constructs (eight can be seen in Sect. 6.4, Fig. 3) underlined in the following paragraphs.

There are three possible types of *structural* relationships in the representation: *is a*, *part of*, and *property of*. The *is a* and *part of* relationships use the same UML semantic of generalization and composition. Dashed connections denote *properties*. These relationships are used to link two types of concepts—*value* and *variable*.

A *value* concept represents a particular variable value, usually an independent variable. Rectangles represent *value* concepts. They are classified in *archetypes* (the root of each hierarchy), *causes* (indicated by the use of bold font and a "C1" following the name denoting that it is the "cause 1," e.g., "usage-based reading"), and *contextual aspects* (e.g., "Web system"). The four archetypes—activity, actor, system, and technology—were defined in an attempt to capture the typical scenario in SE described by an actor applying a technology to perform activities in a software system.

A *variable* concept focuses on value variations, usually associated with a dependent variable. *Variable* concepts are represented by ellipses or parallelograms symbolizing *effects* (e.g., "crucial faults") and *moderators* (not present in Fig. 3), respectively. It should be noticed that *effects* are not connected to *cause* using lines as they are implicit in the diagram. Lines are also lacking in the link between *moderators* and the (moderated) *effects*. In this case, a textual hint (e.g., "M1") is shown beside both the moderated effect and moderator (not present in Fig. 3). Both relationships *cause–effect* and *moderation* are denominated *influence* relationships.

In the theoretical structures, the notion of an effect size, used in the meta-analysis, is referred to as *effect intensity*. A seven-point *Likert* scale is used to represent the *effect intensity*. The scale ranges from strongly negative to strongly positive. It is indicated above the ellipse (e.g., $\hat{\wedge}$ indicates that "important faults" is between weakly positively and positively affected by "usage-based reading"—the number of arrows indicates the value in the scale, $\check{\vee}$ represents strongly negative and $\hat{\wedge}$ strongly positive, and half-sized arrows indicate a range such as in the case of "important faults"). Since it is used mathematically in the SSM as explained in the following paragraph, the scale is defined using a set representation {SN, NE, WN, IF, WP, PO, SP}—the set elements are abbreviations for the *Likert* scale terms, e.g., SN is "strongly negative." The other type of *variable* concepts, namely *moderators*, indicates that some positive or negative effect is moderated (i.e., reduced) when it increases or decreases, but they are not used in the examples of this chapter. The last aspect related to *variable* concepts is the association of a *belief value* (ranging from 0% to 100% or 0 to 1) to estimate the confidence in the observed *effects* and moderators. The bar under each element represents the *belief value*, e.g., "important faults" has 69% of *belief value*.

Belief values and the *intensity of the effect* (e.g., positive or negative) form the main instruments for aggregation. The SSM uses an uncertainty formalism to combine the results named mathematical theory of evidence (Shafer 1976) (also known as *Dempster–Shafer* theory, DST)—otherwise, a simple vote counting strategy would be used, which is widely regarded as inefficient and imprecise for research synthesis. The DST uses two primary inputs to combine two pieces of evidence. One is the hypotheses to which a belief value can be assigned, and the other is the *belief values* themselves. The set of possible hypotheses is called frame of discernment (or using the symbol Θ), which in the SSM is formed by the seven-point *Likert* scale used to represent the *effect* intensity.[1] That is, the set defined in the previous paragraph: $\Theta = \{SN, NE, WN, IF, WP, PO, SP\}$. In the DST, *belief values* can be assigned to both single hypotheses (e.g., $\{WP\}$) and compound hypotheses (e.g., $\{IF, WP\}$)—the latter is used when the hypothesis which is believed to be true is not clear and more than one hypothesis is chosen instead. So, a belief value assigned to a compound hypothesis $\{IF, WP\}$ should be represented as "the effect intensity is somewhere between indifferent and weakly positive." More formally, *belief values* can be assigned to any element of the powerset[2] of the frame of discernment.

Once hypotheses and *belief values* are defined for each piece of evidence, then the *Dempster's rule of combination* is applied. Equation (1) shows that the aggregated *belief value* for the hypothesis C is equal to the sum of the product of the hypotheses' *belief values* whose *intersection* between all hypotheses A_i and B_j of both evidence is C. The letters A, B, and C are sets, which are elements of the powerset, and the indexes i and j go through all the powerset elements. The function m is called the *basic probability assignment function*, which, as the name implies, is used to assign a *belief value* to the different hypotheses (i.e., sets) of the powerset.

$$m_3(C) = \frac{\displaystyle\sum_{\substack{i,j \\ A_i \cap B_j = C}} m_1(A_i)\, m_2(B_j)}{1 - K}, \text{ where} \tag{1}$$

$$K = \sum_{\substack{i,j \\ A_i \cap B_j = \varnothing}} m_1(A_i)\, m_2(B_j).$$

---

[1]The reader should note that as hypotheses are used to represent *effect* intensity in some parts of this text, the terms are used interchangeably.

[2]The powerset is a set whose elements are represented by all possible subsets of a specific set. As the frame of discernment used in the SSM is defined as $\Theta = \{SN, NE, WN, IF, WP, PO, SP\}$, the associated powerset is given by $2^\Theta = \{\{\}, \{SN\}, \{NE\}, \ldots \{SN, NE\}, \{NE, WN\}, \ldots, \{SN, NE, WN\}, \ldots, \{SN, NE, WN, IF, WP, PO, SP\}\}$.

When the intersection between two hypotheses is an empty set, it can be said that there is a conflict. A conflict is, then, redistributed to the aggregated hypotheses— that is, the function of $1 - K$ in the denominator. More details about how DST is used in SSM are available in Santos and Travassos (2013).

The next section describes a worked example using the SSM five-stage process. It is analog to the five steps presented in Sect. 2 and shares several similarities with the methods presented in Sect. 4. For comparison with those methods, the reader should check Table 2. The process briefly described below:

1. *Planning and Definition*: the study objectives are defined, including the research question and the inclusion/exclusion criteria. In some situations, a theoretical structure can be created to serve as a basis to identify what must be present in selected papers in a similar manner as extraction forms used in systematic reviews.
2. *Selection*: primary studies are collected by following a systematic procedure considering the defined criteria. Also, to help manage and organize papers, relevant information about the studies can be extracted, such as bibliographic data, research goal, or study type.
3. *Quality assessment*: the quality of primary studies is evaluated using quality assessment checklists proposed for SE. The quality assessment (combined with the type of study) is used as an input to estimate the confidence in the studies' outcomes. The SSM represents this confidence by the *belief values* that are assigned to *effects* and *moderators*.
4. *Extraction and Translation*: evidence is extracted from primary studies and translated to theoretical structures. Data extraction is performed to identify concepts and relationships following the restrictions of the diagrammatic model described above.
5. *Aggregation and Analysis*: based on the created theoretical structures, the compatible evidence is aggregated by pooling their *effects* and *moderators*. Then, the results are analyzed together.

6 A Worked Research Synthesis Example with the SSM

For this example, we have chosen the classical domain of software inspections, in particular, the usage-based reading (UBR) inspection technique. This domain was deliberately chosen because it is a well-known domain in SE, especially within the empirical software engineering community, where it has been extensively investigated and was one of the first topics to be the target of experimental studies (Basili et al. 1999). Thus, we used this in an attempt to draw attention to the application of the SSM method itself rather than to the synthesis results.

Inspection of software artifacts is a meaningful way of avoiding rework and improving software quality (Fagan 2002). The primary factors for its success are the relatively low cost of utilization and its capability in finding defects throughout

Table 2 Comparing research synthesis methods using SSM's five-stage process

Method SSM phase	Thematic synthesis	Meta-ethnography	Case survey	Qualitative comparative analysis	Theory building and meta-analysis
Planning and definition	• In general terms, these research synthesis methods do not have any particular concern about research definition and studies selection, with few minor considerations – Discussions involving meta-ethnography and qualitative comparative analysis point to the importance of prioritizing fewer studies than broad generalizations, paying *particular* attention to the studies' context				
Selection	– The case survey highlights the importance of having explicit exclusion criteria for studies				
Quality assessment	N/A	N/A	• The level of agreement between researchers is used as a parameter for results reliability	N/A	• Meta-analysis attempts to record various aspects of research methodologies for the existing studies to identify their relationship to study findings—e.g., participants' experience

Extraction and translation	• An increasing level of abstraction (text coding) is useful for concepts and relationship identification	• The method suggests using tables to enumerate most of the data used for synthesis (context, concepts, and relationships) and the synthesis itself, which contributes to the method transparency and improves the evidence comparability	• Its notion of confidence associated with survey answers, which represent evidence findings, is accommodated by D-S theory	• The logical description of (absent and present) conditions associated with dependent and independent variables is similar to the theoretical structures' value and variable concepts along with their possible relationships • Data tabulation is suggested here to describe all combinations of conditions and is similar to the role of theoretical structures in improving evidence comparability	• When modeling evidence with theoretical structures, it is essential to be aware of the differentiation between constructs, concepts, and variables since it can support researchers to identify relevant information in papers
Aggregation and analysis	• The usage of diagrammatic representation indicates its applicability as a tool for synthesis	• Translation procedure is useful to homogenize (translate) evidence models into one another	N/A	• The inductive approach is similar to the approach used in the SSM, where all theoretical structures are analyzed and refined together	N/A

the process. Moreover, software inspections can integrate the defect prevention and detection process.

The UBR is an inspection technique whose primary goal is to drive reviewers to focus on crucial parts of a software artifact from the user's point of view. In UBR, faults are not assumed to be of equal importance, and the technique aims at finding the faults that have the most negative impact on the users' perception of system quality. To that end, reviewers are given use cases in prioritized order and inspect the software artifacts following the usage scenarios defined in the ordered use cases. Therefore, UBR assumes that the set of use cases can be prioritized in a way that reflects the desired user quality perspective. If the inspection aims at finding the defects that are most critical to a particular system quality attribute, the use cases should be prioritized accordingly.

As discussed in Sect. 2, a research synthesis study usually takes a literature review (systematic or not) as input. For completeness, the five stages of the SSM process will be detailed, but it is worth mentioning that only steps 3, 4, and 5 are directly related to the synthesis. All details of this synthesis example, particularly the theoretical structures and the description of the concepts, can be found in the Evidence Factory tool.[3] A presentation of the tool features can be found in Santos et al. (2015) and dos Santos and Travassos (2017).

6.1 Planning and Definition

Using the structure suggested in SSM, the research question was defined as follows:

> What are the expected effects of the Usage-Based Reading inspection technique when it is applied for inspecting high-level design artifacts produced in the analysis phase of the software development process?

The research question incorporates aspects related to technology, activity, and system archetypes from the diagrammatic model, leaving out any consideration of the actors' characteristics. Thus, no characteristics about the organization, team, or persons, such as software development experience, are determinant for the study selection.

This phase also defines the search string to retrieve the papers based on the four archetypes of the SSM's diagrammatic representation. The only term used in the search string was "usage-based reading," which is related to the technology archetype. This simple string was sufficient because UBR is a concrete software technology and does not represent a technology category. We judged that making the search string more detailed would only add the risk of leaving out papers that did not include terms about the activity and system characteristics defined in the research question. As a result, the aspects of activity and system characteristics compose the

---

[3]http://evidencefactory.lens-ese.cos.ufrj.br/synthesis/editor/291

paper inclusion criteria. For exclusion criteria, on the other hand, the theoretical or analytical papers and articles not written in English were eliminated. The last definition for paper selection is the digital libraries to be used, which in this case was Scopus.[4]

6.2 Selection

The search was able to find 15 technical papers in Scopus with the given search string, from which four were selected following the inclusion and exclusion criteria. The selection was performed in November 2015. For the sake of exemplification and results conciseness, no updating has been executed at the time of preparing this chapter. However, the reader can use the updating opportunity as a way to experiment using the SSM before applying it in more specific and intricate aggregations. Among the excluded papers, one was a duplicate, one was classified as theoretical (analyzing the contributions of three included papers), and the others did not fulfill the inclusion criteria.

The four included studies form a family of experiments aiming at investigating UBR performance in identifying faults on software artifacts. Two researchers participated in three of them. The first experiment (Thelin et al. 2001—Study S1–27 participants) compared UBR with the ad hoc inspection. Moreover, the other three studies (Thelin et al. (2003)—Study S2–34 participants, Thelin et al. (2004)—Study S3–23 participants, and Winkler et al. (2004)—Study S4–62 participants) compared UBR against a checklist-based reading (CBR).

All the experiments used the same set of instruments. Subjects inspected a real-world high-level design document, which consisted of an overview of the software modules and communication signals that are sent to/received from the modules. The system application domain is related to taxi management, and the design document specifies the three modules composing the system: one client module used in the vehicles, one central module for the operators, and one integration module acting as a communication link between them. All faults were classified into three classes depending on the fault importance from the user's point of view. Class A or crucial faults represent faults in system functions that are crucial for a user (i.e., functions that are important for users and that are often used). Class B or important faults represent those that affect essential functions for users (i.e., functions that are either important and rarely used or not as important but often used). Class C or minor faults are those that do not prevent the system from continuing to operate. Besides the number of faults, the experiments also report the efficiency (faults/hour) and effectiveness (faults/total faults).

---

[4]http://www.scopus.com

Table 3 *Belief values* for moderation and causal relationships of theoretical structures

Study	Base *belief value*	Increase factor based on the study quality	Final *belief value*
S1	0.50	0.1858 (of 0.25)	0.6858
S2	0.50	0.2042 (of 0.25)	0.7042
S3	0.50	0.2042 (of 0.25)	0.7042
S4	0.50	0.1858 (of 0.25)	0.6858

6.3 Quality Assessment

The SSM uses the study type and quality to estimate the *belief values* for *effects* and *moderators*. Based on the study type, as all studies are *quasi*-experiments, the belief values for them have an inferior limit of 0.50. The limits for each study type are defined in Martinez-Fernandez et al. (2015), using the GRADE evidence hierarchy (Atkins et al. 2004). There are four inferior limits 0.00, 0.25, 0.50, and 0.75. Then, we add to that base value the result from the scoring scheme for systematic studies, as discussed in Martinez-Fernandez et al. (2015) with a maximum score of 0.25. These values are calculated automatically by the Evidence Factory tool (dos Santos and Travassos 2017). Table 3 presents the computed *belief values* for the four studies.

It is possible to see that *belief values* are similar. It is a direct result of the fact that the first three papers have authors in common. Thus, they tend to share the same textual structure when describing the procedures, analysis, and results. Furthermore, the fourth study is an external replication, which explains why the authors focused on reporting the same aspects to facilitate further comparison between the studies.

6.4 Extraction and Translation

The quantitative nature of the studies facilitated information extraction. Each paper enumerated dependent and independent variables, as can be seen in Fig. 1, so it was straightforward to identify theoretical structures' concepts. The context of experiments was detailed enough, which in controlled studies tend to be simpler than observational studies (Fig. 2). Moreover, translation procedures were mostly unnecessary since studies' design was similar and used the same set of variables as surrogates. Causal relationships were extracted from the statistical tests used to answer the research questions. It is essential to say that extraction and translation are solely based on what is reported. Thus, even though researchers knew important variables regarding the object of study at hand, theoretical structures only have what is in the papers' text. For instance, researchers are aware that several, if not most, studies on software inspection consider the inspector's experience as a variable. Still, researchers could not include this variable into the theoretical structures, as the four studies did not observe this aspect.

Independent variable. The independent variable is the use case order in UBR. The two experiment groups use the same use cases in different orders. One order is *prioritized* and another is *randomized*. The group with prioritized use cases is denoted *prio* group and the group with randomized use cases is denote *control* group. Notice that neither of the groups was provided with organized use cases, as would be the case if they were written in an ordinary document.

Controlled variable. The controlled variable is the *experience* of the reviewers and it is measured on an ordinal scale. The reviewers were asked to fill in a questionnaire consisting of seven different questions.

Dependent variables. The dependent variables measured are time and faults. The first four variables are direct measures. The last three are indirect measures and are calculated using the direct measures.

1. Time spent on preparation, measured in minutes.
2. Time spent on inspection, measured in minutes.
3. Clock time when each fault is found, measured in minutes.
4. Number of faults found by each reviewer.
5. Number of faults found by each experiment group.
6. Efficiency, measured as: 60 * (Number of Faults Found / (Preparation Time + Inspection Time)).
7. Effectiveness, measured as: Number of Faults Found / Total Number of Faults.

Fig. 1 Study S1 variables listing (Source: Study S1)

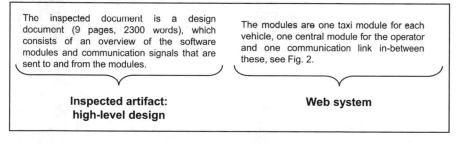

The inspected document is a design document (9 pages, 2300 words), which consists of an overview of the software modules and communication signals that are sent to and from the modules.

The modules are one taxi module for each vehicle, one central module for the operator and one communication link in-between these, see Fig. 2.

Inspected artifact: high-level design

Web system

Fig. 2 Examples of concept identification for theoretical structure modeling (Source: Study S1)

Given the similarity among the studies, the theoretical structures for the four studies share most of the concepts and relationships. Figure 3 depicts the theoretical structure modeled for the study S1 based on the information extracted. The only difference between theoretical structures from the four studies is related to the dependent variables. Two papers do not consider minor defects (class C) in their analysis. The authors do not provide any apparent justification for that, but it is

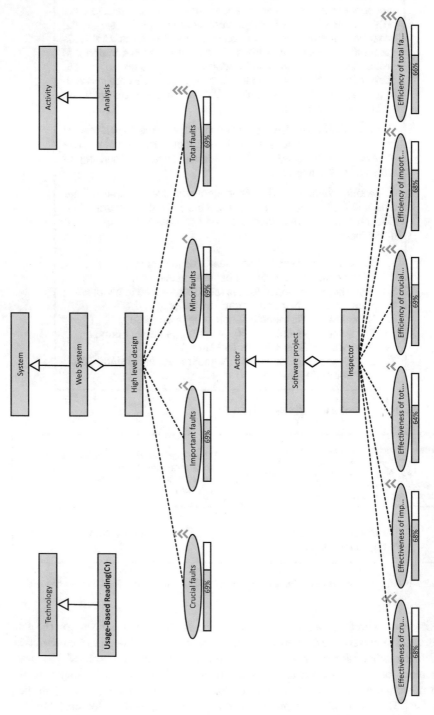

Fig. 3 Evidence model representing study S1 results (Thelin et al. 2001)

Table 4 Effects reported in UBR primary studies

Study effect	Effects showed as intensity (belief value)			
	S1	S2	S3	S4
Efficiency (total faults)	{SP} (0.66)	{SP} (0.67)	{WP, PO} (0.68)	{PO} (0.65)
Efficiency (crucial faults)	{PO, SP} (0.69)	{PO, SP} (0.70)	{WP, PO} (0.70)	{WP, PO} (0.68)
Efficiency (important faults)	{PO} (0.68)	{WP} (0.60)	{WP} (0.70)	{IF, WP} (0.69)
Efficiency (minor faults)	N/A	{WP} (0.52)	{WP} (0.70)	N/A
Effectiveness (total faults)	{WP, PO} (0.64)	{PO} (0.63)	{PO} (0.70)	{SP} (0.67)
Effectiveness (crucial faults)	{PO, SP} (0.68)	{PO, SP} (0.68)	{PO, SP} (0.70)	{SP} (0.69)
Effectiveness (important faults)	{PO} (0.68)	{WP, PO} (0.58)	{PO} (0.70)	{IF, WP} (0.69)
Effectiveness (minor faults)	N/A	{IF, WP} (0.60)	{WP} (0.70)	N/A
# Total faults	{SP} (0.69)	{PO} (0.63)	{PO} (0.70)	{SP} (0.67)
# Crucial faults	{PO, SP} (0.69)	{PO, SP} (0.68)	{PO, SP} (0.70)	{SP} (0.69)
# Important faults	{WP, PO} (0.69)	{WP, PO} (0.58)	{PO} (0.70)	{IF, WP} (0.69)
# Minor faults	{WP} (0.69)	{IF, WP} (0.60)	{WP} (0.70)	N/A

possible to conjecture that it can be associated with publication space restrictions. Table 4 enumerates all effects, along with its intensity and *belief value*. The *belief values* in Table 4 are already adjusted according to the *p-values* found in the primary studies, using the discount operation of the DST (Martinez-Fernandez et al. 2015).

It is essential to note at this point that, although we are focusing on the descriptive[5] theoretical structures for UBR, they were modeled using the dismembering operation (Santos 2015). It means that, first, similar theoretical structures (comparing UBR with ad hoc or CBR) were modeled and, then, based on the differences of the comparative cause–effect relationships, the intensity of effects for UBR was determined. This strategy was chosen, instead of extracting two

---

[5]In the SSM, there are two kinds of theoretical structures: descriptive and comparative. The difference between them is the number of causes analyzed. In descriptive theoretical structures, there is only one cause (as in Fig. 3), and the goal is to describe the *effects* (and *moderators*) of the cause. In comparative theoretical structures, two causes are compared. The *effects* and *moderators* in this case represent the difference between the two causes. Hence, an *effect* intensity instead of being considered negative or positive becomes superior or inferior to represent that one cause is superior or inferior than another regarding a given *effect*.

Table 5 Dismembering operation values for study S1

Effect	Comparative[a]	Descriptive for ad hoc	Descriptive for UBR
Efficiency (total faults)	{WS}	{PO}	{SP}
Efficiency (crucial faults)	{SU}	{WP}	{PO, SP}
Efficiency (important faults)	{WS}	{WP}	{PO}
Effectiveness (total faults)	{WS}	{WP}	{WP, PO}
Effectiveness (crucial faults)	{SU}	{WP}	{PO, SP}
Effectiveness (important faults)	{WS}	{WP}	{PO}
# Total faults	{WS}	{PO}	{SP}
# Crucial faults	{SU}	{WP}	{PO, SP}
# Important faults	{WS}	{WP}	{WP, PO}
# Minor faults	{WS}	{WP, PO}	{WP}

[a]Comparative theoretical structures use a different scale for representing the comparisons. It is a seven-point Likert scale: {SI, IN, WI, IF, WS, SU, SS}—the set elements are abbreviations for the scale terms, e.g., SI is "strongly inferior," IN is "inferior," and SS is "strongly superior"

descriptive, theoretical structures from comparative studies as recommended in SSM, because papers contained a percentage difference in most cases. Still, when individual data about each technology were present, it was used to calibrate the dismembering operation. Even secondary data, such as graphical data and boxplots, were used to that end. Table 5 lists the effects for Study S1 detailing how they were dismembered.

The conversion rules used for comparative and descriptive values are enumerated in Table 6. Both comparative and descriptive rules were defined because, in some cases, descriptive values were available. When only comparative rules are used, it can lead to some inconveniences as the rules could conflict. For instance, in the case of "efficiency (crucial faults)" in study S1, the percentage difference between the inspection techniques is 95%, as the mean values of identified faults per hour are 1.29 and 2.53 for ad hoc and UBR, respectively. Therefore, if only the percentage difference would have been considered, then the descriptive values obtained from dismembering operation should have two units of distance (e.g., WP and SP) since the 95% percentage difference is converted to {SU}. On the other hand, the approximate values of 1.29 and 2.53 map to {WP} and {PO}, respectively, according to the defined rules (Table 6), which has only one unit of difference between them. In these different cases, to make the comparative and descriptive conversion rules compatible, the precision of the converted values was reduced. As a result, in this same example, the comparative value {SU} was dismembered to {WP} and {PO, SP} instead of {WP} and {PO}.

6.5 Aggregation and Analysis

The first step involved in the aggregation phase is to analyze whether the studies can be combined. The aggregation is performed by comparing the theoretical structures'

Table 6 Conversion rules for effects quantitative values

Effect		Qualitative intensity/difference	Quantitative rule range
Comparative	Efficiency	Indifferent (IF)	[0%, 0%]
	Effectiveness	Weak difference (WI or WS)	(0%, 50%]
	# defects	Moderate difference (IN or SU)	(50%, 100%]
		Strong difference (SI or SS)	–[a]
Descriptive	Efficiency	Indifferent (IF)	0
		Weak impact (WN or WP)	(0, 2.50]
		Moderate impact (NE or PO)	(2.50, 5]
		Strong impact (SN or SP)	(5, ∞]
	Effectiveness	Indifferent (IF)	0
		Weak impact (WN or WP)	(0, 0.33]
		Moderate impact (NE or PO)	(0.33, 0.66]
		Strong impact (SN or SP)	(0.66, 1]
	# defects	Indifferent (IF)	0
		Weak impact (WN or WP)	(0, 4]
		Moderate impact (NE or PO)	(4, 8]
		Strong impact (SN or SP)	(8, 12]

[a]As we observed that the compared technologies are always able to identify defects (positive effects), we decided not to use strong difference

concepts. When they are compatible—i.e., the same concepts or synonyms—then the studies' outcomes are considered combinable. That is, they are all combined at the same time. When there are incompatibilities, then the studies have to be partitioned into sets of compatible studies, which are then combined.

Only the descriptive theoretical structures relative to UBR were analyzed to answer the research question defined for this working example. Given the similarity among the studies, it was not possible to identify any incompatibility among the theoretical structures. As mentioned above, the only difference among them was that some did not report minor faults. Still, this is not impeditive for the aggregation since, in the SSM, each *effect* is individually aggregated considering the papers in which they are present.

After analyzing the theoretical structures' compatibility and given the confidence level of each effect, the Dempster's rule of combination is used. The detailed aggregation results are listed in Table 7. The first column shows the reported effect. The second column indicates the number of papers that have reported this effect. The third column shows the aggregated UBR effect intensity. The fourth column represents the aggregated *belief* on the respective effect. The fifth column lists conflict levels computed in each combination for the respective effect. For instance, the aggregation of four pieces of evidence leads to three combinations. Conflicts are always shown in the same order ((S1⊕S3)⊕S4)⊕S2. This order was applied by the Evidence Factory tool, based on the order of the random IDs assigned to the evidence models. The sixth column registers the difference between the maximum *belief value* of individual evidence for the respective effect and the aggregated value.

Table 7 Aggregated effects of UBR

Effect	Aggregation results				
	#Papers	Intensity	Belief	Conflicts	Difference
Efficiency (total faults)	4	{SP}	0.47	0.45, 0.25, 0.49	−0.21
Efficiency (crucial faults)	4	{PO}	0.82	0.00, 0.00, 0.00	0.12
Efficiency (important faults)	4	{WP}	0.82	0.48, 0.27, 0.10	0.12
Efficiency (minor faults)	2	{WP}	0.86	0.00	0.16
Effectiveness (total faults)	4	{PO}	0.82	0.00, 0.60, 0.12	0.12
Effectiveness (crucial faults)	4	{PO, SP}	0.99	0.00, 0.00, 0.00	0.29
Effectiveness (important faults)	4	{PO}	0.75	0.00, 0.64, 0.00	0.05
Effectiveness (minor faults)	2	{WP}	0.70	0.00	0.00
# Total faults	4	{SP}	0,49	0.48, 0.28, 0.46	−0.21
# Crucial faults	4	{PO, SP}	0.99	0.00, 0.00, 0.00	0.29
# Important faults	4	{WP, PO}	0,93	0.00, 0.48, 0.00	0.23
# Minor faults	3	{WP}	0,91	0.00, 0.00	0.21

The effects that were most strengthened were the effectiveness and the number of crucial faults.

Before analyzing the aggregated results, it should first be defined how conflicts should be resolved. Although there is no incompatibility among the theoretical structures, significant conflicts between study results can be noted. There are three main factors associated with these conflicts. The first comes from the fact that results for UBR were dismembered from comparisons with both ad hoc and CBR. Therefore, some differences among results are expected. The second aspect is related to the dismembering operation itself. As defined in SSM, dismembering is imprecise and suggested to be used only in specific situations. Thus, it is a potential source of differences between results as well. The last aspect considered for explaining results is that the second combination (between S4 and the resulting aggregation from S1 and S3) has the highest frequency of conflict occurrence— half effects had conflicts in the second combination. Interestingly enough, it is the combination involving the Study S4, which is the only study that is an external experiment of UBR.

The combined *belief values* presented in Table 7 were computed using the basic conflict resolution strategy of the SSM, which ignores the conflict by redistributing it among hypotheses. However, to use this strategy, SSM establishes that all conflicts must be lower than 0.50, or the mean conflict is below $1/n$ where n is the number of combinations, which in this case is 3. Hence, it was understood that the best strategy to handle conflicts in this aggregation was incorporation—see all conflict resolution strategies in Santos (2015). Succinctly, it is a strategy that "absorbs" the conflict by making the *effect* intensity less precise. For instance, note that the *effect* intensity for "Efficiency (total faults)" changed from {SP} to {PO, SP}. Thus, it is best used when there is less interest in specific values (i.e., *effect* intensity) within the *Likert* scale and more interest in the trend. It is precisely the case in this worked example as the combined results came from comparing UBR with different techniques (ad hoc and

Table 8 Aggregated effects of UBR after conflicts resolution by incorporation

Effect	Aggregation results				
	#Papers	Intensity	Belief	Conflicts	Difference
Efficiency (total faults)	4	{PO, SP}	0.85	(Incorporated)	0.17
Efficiency (crucial faults)	4	{PO}	0.82	0.00, 0.00, 0.00	0.12
Efficiency (important faults)	4	{WP}	0.82	0.48, 0.27, 0.10	0.12
Efficiency (minor faults)	2	{WP}	0.86	0.00	0.16
Effectiveness (total faults)	4	{PO, SP}	0.87	(Incorporated)	0.17
Effectiveness (crucial faults)	4	{PO, SP}	0.99	0.00, 0.00, 0.00	0.29
Effectiveness (important faults)	4	{WP, PO}	0.77	(Incorporated)	0.07
Effectiveness (minor faults)	2	{WP}	0.70	0.00	0.00
# Total faults	4	{PO, SP}	0.99	(Incorporated)	0.29
# Crucial faults	4	{PO, SP}	0.99	0.00, 0.00, 0.00	0.29
# Important faults	4	{WP, PO}	0.93	0.00, 0.48, 0.00	0.23
# Minor faults	3	{WP}	0.91	0.00, 0.00	0.21

CBR), not to mention that the dismembering operation is imprecise by itself. Next, Table 8 presents the new *belief values* after the resolution of conflicts.

At this point, with conflicts resolved, we focus on the results themselves. The substantial agreement among the studies is noticeable, particularly the results associated with crucial faults. It can be seen in the high *belief value* of 0.99 observed in efficiency, effectiveness, and the number of crucial faults. The high *belief values* resulting from aggregation should be analyzed considering the specificities of the aggregated studies. In this case, the 0.99 *belief value* should not be necessarily interpreted as an "almost certainty" (i.e., *belief value* of 1), but rather as a virtually full agreement among four strong evidence (i.e., *quasi*-experiments). Thus, in other words, the current body of knowledge indicates that UBR seems to have a direct impact on crucial faults since it is possible to observe similar results in four different studies, which even compare different technologies (ad hoc and CBR). Nevertheless, one must take into consideration that there is a limited number of studies being considered.

Another interesting finding that can be observed in the aggregated results is the relative difference between the intensity of effects associated with crucial and minor faults. The results suggest that UBR has a more substantial impact on crucial faults than minor faults. It is precisely the most crucial aspect of UBR as it focuses inspections on the most critical type of faults. A similar pattern was observed in all dimensions explored in the studies: efficiency, effectiveness, and the number of faults. UBR has a {PO} impact over efficiency relative to crucial faults while it has {WP} for efficiency relative to minor faults. For effectiveness, {PO, SP} was found for crucial faults, and {WP} for minor faults. The same was found for the number of crucial faults. Thus, this consistency in the difference between crucial and minor faults among the studies is another significant result strengthened in the aggregation.

Based on this analysis and the overall results detailed in Table 8, there is enough input to answer this synthesis's research question. UBR inspection technique can safely be used for identifying most important (i.e., crucial) faults in high-level design, with a high level of efficiency and effectiveness. It still can be used for less critical faults, although with relatively less efficacy. These effects seem to result from the underlying mechanism behind UBR, which is the assumption that the proper prioritization of use cases can help identify relatively more critical faults.

The scope in which the aggregation findings can be claimed to be valid is explicit in the aggregated theoretical structure.[6] In all studies, the same Web system's high-level design models were inspected using UBR. Thus, it is difficult to argue any generalization beyond this context. Still, the cause of the observed effects is theoretically reproducible in other contexts with different kinds of systems and software artifacts, since the UBR working mechanism is based on use case prioritization, which is, at least theoretically, independent of the inspected software artifacts. Moreover, the studies did not explicitly consider the participation of graduate students as an essential factor influencing the findings. Arguably, this is because most subjects have experience in the SE industry. Thus, it is understandable that industry professionals can be included within the findings of external validity.

Besides external validity, considerations to other types of validity threads should be extended. In these authors' viewpoint, the most critical internal validity threat is the potential bias associated with the fact that the same researchers who authored the SSM conducted the synthesis. Thus, from the studies selection to the definition of concepts and their relationships, practically all steps were subjected to this issue. This issue was the primary motivation for choosing an inspection technique as the theme for research synthesis so that the domain aspects would not represent a confounding factor during the synthesis process. Regarding construct validity, the use of the dismembering operation represents a validity threat in itself as it increases the imprecision of effect intensity. To minimize this lack of accuracy, when apart from the percentage difference, the absolute quantitative values were available, they were used to improve the precision of the effect intensity.

6.6 Discussion

As stated at the beginning of this section, the domain of software inspections was selected for this worked example because of the substantial familiarity regarding this theme among empirical software engineering researchers since it is arguably one of the most experimentally investigated technology in SE. Thus, this familiarity was essential to focus on the SSM mechanics, not on the synthesis findings. Still, given the relative synthesis simplicity, some aspects had to be left out.

The main limitation of the worked example is the absence of qualitative studies. Therefore, although we discussed that interpretative synthesis is not restricted to the aggregation of qualitative findings, the data extraction and translation step is

---

[6]http://evidencefactory.lens-ese.cos.ufrj.br/evidenceEditor/19032

usually more abundant in this scenario. Nevertheless, it was possible to see the interpretative and integrative aspects of the SSM. The interpretations are directly related to the diagrammatic representation as it is formed by concepts, which have to be extracted or coded from the studies and translated to the theoretical structures. In the case of quantitative studies, particularly in controlled experiments, concepts are frequently taken from independent and dependent variables. It eliminated the need for text coding in our example, as it is only necessary when dealing with data from qualitative studies. The integration, on the other hand, is almost the same in the SSM regardless of whether the studies synthesized are qualitative or quantitative.

The studies included in the synthesis also have limitations of their own. Three of the four studies were conducted with at least one researcher in common. The synthesis results seem to have reflected this issue, as there were few contradictions among the studies' findings. The quality assessment also showed how the studies were similar in their planning and execution as the study type and quality are used as input for this assessment. At last, the lacking of the inspector experience among the variables considered in the studies was noticeable.

Despite these limitations, it was possible to see how the SSM works throughout its five-stage process. The first three steps define the aim of the synthesis and select the primary studies. Due to the restricted scope of the synthesis, only four studies were selected. In the fourth step, the worked example shows how the studies' findings are translated into theoretical structures. In this synthesis, it used the dependent and independent variables of the controlled experiments. Besides, in the last step, the focus was given on how the Dempster–Shafer theory was used to pool the confidence in the studies' findings.

7   Recommended Further Reading

We suggest the following further readings to complement this chapter. For those interested in a general overview of the leading research synthesis methods, Dixon-Woods et al. (2005) present several methods, ranging from those that are mostly qualitative and interpretative through the ones that are mostly quantitative and integrative. Also, Cruzes and Dybå (2011a) and Guzmán et al. (2014) show the current state of the research synthesis methods usage in SE.

Regarding the methods briefly presented in Sect. 4, they all have specific technical literature available: thematic analysis (Cruzes and Dybå 2011b), meta-ethnography (Da Silva et al. 2013), case survey method (Larsson 1993) (it is also discussed in chapter "Guidelines for Case Survey Research in Software Engineering"), qualitative comparative analysis (Yamasaki and Rihoux 2009), statistical meta-analysis (Lipsey and Wilson 2001), and theory building with meta-analysis (Yang 2002).

Additionally, for more details about SSM, some studies use the method in different domains: software reference architectures (Martinez-Fernandez et al.

2015), Kanban software process (dos Santos et al. 2018), software productivity (Chapetta 2018), and nonfunctional requirements (Buitrón et al. 2019).

At last, there are also recommendations regarding a few related themes. For instance, a computational perspective on the research synthesis theme, denominated scientific knowledge engineering, is presented in Santos and Travassos (2016). Furthermore, recently, researchers are mining treatment-outcome constructs from sequential SE data (Nayebi et al. 2019), which shares some similarities with how data is synthesized in the process of research synthesis.

8   Conclusion

This chapter discussed the relevance of research synthesis along with its central processes, methods, and procedures. Research synthesis represents an essential element of the knowledge accumulation and application process. It is indispensable to any scientific field such as SE. In fact, in the case of the SE domain, this process introduces additional challenges as evidence in the area is produced in both quantitative and qualitative forms. Research synthesis methods, in general, follow similar processes but differ in the procedures adopted to perform each of their steps. Integrative and interpretative approaches are categorizations used to differentiate these procedures. In an integrative synthesis, data is extracted from primary studies in order to confirm or refute some hypothesis. In an interpretative synthesis, data is collected to explore or provide explanations to phenomena.

The main research synthesis methods were also briefly described. The methods included here were those which are either most frequently used in SE or were evaluated as the most applicable to the SE domain. They range from the ones geared toward interpretative synthesis approaches—thematic synthesis and meta-ethnography—to those more focused on integrative approaches—case survey, qualitative comparative analysis, and statistical meta-analysis. It was also emphasized that interpretative and integrative syntheses are not synonyms to qualitative and quantitative. From the methods enumerated, for instance, both qualitative comparative analysis and statistical meta-analysis represent integrative methods, but the former primarily uses qualitative data, whereas the latter quantitative data.

Besides the brief description of these methods, the structured synthesis method was presented in detail. Its main feature is the ability to conceptualize the primary studies' context and integrate their outcomes. In SSM, interpretative synthesis aspects are concerned with the organization and development of concepts to describe contextual aspects of evidence, whereas integrative features are focused on pooling data about cause–effect or moderation relations. Because of this balanced combination of interpretative and integrative features, the SSM is also acknowledged for its ability to deal with qualitative and quantitative evidence in SE.

A worked example was used to present the SSM concerning the synthesis of four primary studies regarding the usage-based reading inspection technique. As all the four aggregated studies are quantitative, it was possible to see that SSM produces outcomes consistent with the input data. The synthesis showed that evidence was strengthened regarding the effectiveness and efficiency of UBR in identifying crucial faults, which is what is precisely intended with the inspection technique. Still, researchers must be aware that the set of studies to synthesize greatly influences the consistency and reliability of the resulting synthesis. The synthesis of poor studies will inevitably lead to poor results. In this regard, SSM has relatively fewer and more crystalline phases. The extraction and translation steps are relatively less objective than the other ones as they depend on conceptual development. On the other hand, the aggregation and analysis steps are relatively more objective since they are carried out based on the theoretical structures' formal representation.

This chapter is intended to introduce the reader to the research synthesis theme, including the application of the SSM. It is also expected that researchers can understand the challenges of conducting studies concerned with research synthesis. More importantly, it is necessary that SE advance in this theme so that the scenario where authors do not describe the form of synthesis used in their studies becomes increasingly scarce. As stated by Miller (2000), *"the good news is that we are not alone in this battle. Other disciplines also struggle with this issue, they have just been struggling longer, and hence have progressed beyond the point where we currently find ourselves."* The proposition of the SSM, specifically for SE, is an indication that the field can make progress in this realm.

References

Atkins D, Best D, Briss PA et al (2004) Grading quality of evidence and strength of recommenda-
    tions. BMJ 328:1490. https://doi.org/10.1136/bmj.328.7454.1490
Basili VR, Shull F, Lanubile F (1999) Building knowledge through families of experiments. IEEE
    Trans Softw Eng 25:456–473. https://doi.org/10.1109/32.799939
Budgen D, Kitchenham B, Brereton P (2013) The case for knowledge translation. In: 2013
    ACM/IEEE international symposium on empirical software engineering and measurement, pp
    263–266
Buitrón S, Apa C, Pino F, Travassos GH (2019) Sobre la Viabilidad de un Componente para
    Especificar Requisitos No Funcionales: Un Estudio de Síntesis Estructurada. In: XXII Ibero-
    American Conference on Software Engineering, Track: XXI Workshop on Experimental
    Software Engineering. Curran Associates, La Habana, Cuba
Chapetta WA (2018) The influence of factors on software development productivity according to a
    model of theoretical structures. Thesis, Federal University of Rio de Janeiro
Ciolkowski M (2009) What do we know about perspective-based reading? An approach for
    quantitative aggregation in software engineering. In: Proceedings of the 2009 3rd international
    symposium on empirical software engineering and measurement. IEEE Computer Society,
    Washington, DC, pp 133–144
Cooper H, Hedges LV (2009) Research synthesis as a scientific process. In: Cooper H, Hedges LV
    (eds) The handbook of research synthesis and meta-analysis, 2nd edn. Russell Sage Foundation,
    New York, pp 3–16

Cruzes DS, Dybå T (2011a) Research synthesis in software engineering: a tertiary study. Inf Softw Technol 53:440–455. https://doi.org/10.1016/j.infsof.2011.01.004

Cruzes DS, Dybå T (2011b) Recommended steps for thematic synthesis in software engineering. In: 2011 International symposium on empirical software engineering and measurement (ESEM), pp 275–284

Da Silva FQB, Cruz SSJO, Gouveia TB, Capretz LF (2013) Using meta-ethnography to synthesize research: a worked example of the relations between personality and software team processes. In: 2013 ACM/IEEE international symposium on empirical software engineering and measurement, pp 153–162

Davis D, Davis ME, Jadad A et al (2003) The case for knowledge translation: shortening the journey from evidence to effect. BMJ 327:33–35. https://doi.org/10.1136/bmj.327.7405.33

de França BBN, Travassos GH (2016) Experimentation with dynamic simulation models in software engineering: planning and reporting guidelines. Empir Softw Eng 21:1302–1345. https://doi.org/10.1007/s10664-015-9386-4

de Mello RM, da Silva PC, Runeson P, Travassos GH (2014) Towards a framework to support large scale sampling in software engineering surveys. In: Proceedings of the 8th ACM/IEEE international symposium on empirical software engineering and measurement. ACM, New York, 48, pp 1–4

Dixon-Woods M, Agarwal S, Jones D et al (2005) Synthesising qualitative and quantitative evidence: a review of possible methods. J Health Serv Res Policy 10:45–53B

dos Santos PSM, Travassos GH (2017) Structured synthesis method: the evidence factory tool. In: 2017 ACM/IEEE international symposium on empirical software engineering and measurement (ESEM), pp 480–481

dos Santos PSM, Beltrão AC, de Souza BP, Travassos GH (2018) On the benefits and challenges of using kanban in software engineering: a structured synthesis study. J Softw Eng Res Dev 6:13. https://doi.org/10.1186/s40411-018-0057-1

Easterbrook S, Singer J, Storey M-A, Damian D (2008) Selecting empirical methods for software engineering research. In: Shull F, Singer J, Sjøberg DIK (eds) Guide to advanced empirical software engineering. Springer, London, pp 285–311

Fagan M (2002) A history of software inspections. In: Broy PDM, Denert PDE (eds) Software pioneers. Springer, Berlin, pp 562–573

Góis Mateus B, Martinez M (2019) An empirical study on the quality of android applications written in Kotlin language. Empir Software Eng 24:3356. https://doi.org/10.1007/s10664-019-09727-4

Guzmán L, Lampasona C, Seaman C, Rombach D (2014) Survey on research synthesis in software engineering. In: Proceedings of the 18th international conference on evaluation and assessment in software engineering. ACM, New York, 2, pp 1–10

Harrison R, Badoo N, Barry E et al (1999) Directions and methodologies for empirical software engineering research. Empir Softw Eng 4:405–410. https://doi.org/10.1023/A:1009877923978

Kitchenham B, Pfleeger SL (1996) Software quality: the elusive target [special issues section]. IEEE Softw 13:12–21. https://doi.org/10.1109/52.476281

Larsson R (1993) Case survey methodology: quantitative analysis of patterns across case studies. Acad Manag J 36:1515–1546. https://doi.org/10.2307/256820

Lenberg P, Wallgren Tengberg LG, Feldt R (2017) An initial analysis of software engineers' attitudes towards organizational change. Empir Softw Eng 22:2179–2205. https://doi.org/10.1007/s10664-016-9482-0

Lipsey MW, Wilson DB (2001) Practical meta-analysis. Sage, Thousand Oaks

MacDonell S, Shepperd M, Kitchenham B, Mendes E (2010) How reliable are systematic reviews in empirical software engineering? IEEE Trans Softw Eng 36:676–687. https://doi.org/10.1109/TSE.2010.28

Mahoney J, Goertz G (2006) A tale of two cultures: contrasting quantitative and qualitative research. Polit Anal 14:227–249. https://doi.org/10.1093/pan/mpj017

Martinez-Fernandez S, Santos PSM, Ayala CP et al (2015) Aggregating empirical evidence about the benefits and drawbacks of software reference architectures. In: 2015 ACM/IEEE international symposium on empirical software engineering and measurement (ESEM), pp 1–10

Miller J (2000) Applying meta-analytical procedures to software engineering experiments. J Syst Softw 54:29–39. https://doi.org/10.1016/S0164-1212(00)00024-8

Nayebi M, Ruhe G, Zimmermann T (2019) Mining treatment-outcome constructs from sequential software engineering data. IEEE Trans Softw Eng:1–1. https://doi.org/10.1109/TSE.2019.2892956

Noblit GW, Hare RD (1988) Meta-ethnography: synthesizing qualitative studies. Sage, Newbury Park

Overton WF (1991) The structure of developmental theory. In: Geert P, Mos LP (eds) Annals of theoretical psychology. Springer, New York, pp 191–235

Pickard LM, Kitchenham BA, Jones PW (1998) Combining empirical results in software engineering. Inf Softw Technol 40:811–821. https://doi.org/10.1016/S0950-5849(98)00101-3

Runeson P, Höst M (2009) Guidelines for conducting and reporting case study research in software engineering. Empir Softw Eng 14:131–164. https://doi.org/10.1007/s10664-008-9102-8

Sandelowski M, Voils CI, Leeman J, Crandell JL (2012) Mapping the mixed methods–mixed research synthesis terrain. J Mixed Methods Res 6:317–331. https://doi.org/10.1177/1558689811427913

Santos PSM (2015) Evidence representation and aggregation in software engineering using theoretical structures and belief functions. Thesis, Federal University of Rio de Janeiro

Santos PSM, Travassos GH (2011) Action research can swing the balance in experimental software engineering. In: Advances in computers. Elsevier, Amsterdam, pp 205–276

Santos PSM, Travassos GH (2013) On the representation and aggregation of evidence in software engineering: a theory and belief-based perspective. Electron Notes Theor Comput Sci 292:95–118. https://doi.org/10.1016/j.entcs.2013.02.008

Santos PSM, Travassos GH (2016) Scientific knowledge engineering: a conceptual delineation and overview of the state of the art. Knowl Eng Rev 31:167–199. https://doi.org/10.1017/S0269888916000011

Santos PSM, Nascimento IE, Travassos GH (2015) A computational infrastructure for research synthesis in software engineering. In: XVIII Ibero-American conference on software engineering, track: XVII workshop on experimental software engineering. Curran Associates, Lima, pp 309–322

Schulze R (2004) Meta-analysis: a comparison of approaches. Hogrefe & Huber, Ashland

Shafer G (1976) A mathematical theory of evidence. Princeton University Press, Princeton

Taveggia TC (1974) Resolving research controversy through empirical cumulation: toward reliable sociological knowledge. Sociol Methods Res 2:395–407. https://doi.org/10.1177/004912417400200401

Thelin T, Runeson P, Regnell B (2001) Usage-based reading—an experiment to guide reviewers with use cases. Inf Softw Technol 43:925–938. https://doi.org/10.1016/S0950-5849(01)00201-4

Thelin T, Runeson P, Wohlin C (2003) An experimental comparison of usage-based and checklist-based reading. IEEE Trans Softw Eng 29:687–704. https://doi.org/10.1109/TSE.2003.1223644

Thelin T, Andersson C, Runeson P, Dzamashvili-Fogelstrom N (2004) A replicated experiment of usage-based and checklist-based reading. In: 10th International symposium on software metrics, 2004. Proceedings. IEEE, pp 246–256

Walenstein A (2003) Observing and measuring cognitive support: steps toward systematic tool evaluation and engineering. In: 11th IEEE international workshop on program comprehension, pp 185–194

Winkler D, Halling M, Biffl S (2004) Investigating the effect of expert ranking of use cases for design inspection. In: Euromicro conference, 2004. Proceedings. 30th, pp 362–371

Wohlin C (2016) Second-generation systematic literature studies using snowballing. In: Proceedings of the 20th international conference on evaluation and assessment in software engineering. ACM, New York, 15, pp 151–156

Wohlin C, Höst M, Henningsson K (2003) Empirical research methods in software engineering. In: Conradi R, Wang A (eds) Empirical methods and studies in software engineering. Springer, Berlin, pp 7–23

Wolf FM (1986) Meta-analysis: quantitative methods for research synthesis. Sage, Beverly Hills

Yamasaki S, Rihoux B (2009) A commented review of applications. In: Rihoux B, Ragin CC (eds) Configurational comparative methods. Sage, Los Angeles, pp 123–145

Yang B (2002) Meta-analysis research and theory building. Adv Dev Hum Resour 4:296–316. https://doi.org/10.1177/1523422302043005

Yin RK, Heald KA (1975) Using the case survey method to analyze policy studies. Adm Sci Q 20:371. https://doi.org/10.2307/2391997

Zelkowitz M (2007) Techniques for empirical validation. In: Basili V, Rombach D, Schneider K et al (eds) Empirical software engineering issues. Critical assessment and future directions, Springer, pp 4–9

Part IV
Knowledge Transfer

Open Science in Software Engineering

Daniel Mendez (iD), Daniel Graziotin (iD), Stefan Wagner, and Heidi Seibold

Abstract Open science describes the movement of making any research artifact available to the public and includes, but is not limited to, open access, open data, and open source. While open science is becoming generally accepted as a norm in other scientific disciplines, in software engineering, we are still struggling in adapting open science to the particularities of our discipline, rendering progress in our scientific community cumbersome. In this chapter, we reflect upon the essentials in open science for software engineering including what open science is, why we should engage in it, and how we should do it. We particularly draw from our experiences made as conference chairs implementing open science initiatives and as researchers actively engaging in open science to critically discuss challenges and pitfalls and to address more advanced topics such as how and under which conditions to share preprints, what infrastructure and licence model to cover, or how do it within the limitations of different reviewing models, such as double-blind reviewing. Our hope is to help establishing a common ground and to contribute to make open science a norm also in software engineering.

D. Mendez (✉)
Technical University of Munich, Munich, Germany

Blekinge Institute of Technology, Karlskrona, Sweden

fortiss GmbH, Munich, Germany
e-mail: mendezfe@acm.org

D. Graziotin · S. Wagner
University of Stuttgart, Stuttgart, Germany
e-mail: daniel.graziotin@iste.uni-stuttgart.de; stefan.wagner@iste.uni-stuttgart.de

H. Seibold
Ludwig-Maximilians-University Munich, Munich, Germany
e-mail: hseibold@ibe.med.uni-muenchen.de

M. Felderer, G. H. Travassos (eds.), *Contemporary Empirical Methods in Software Engineering*, https://doi.org/10.1007/978-3-030-32489-6_17

1 Introduction

In a nutshell, open science refers to the movement of making any research artifact available to the public. This ranges from the disclosure of software source code ("open source") over the actual data itself ("open data") and the material used to analyse the data (such as analysis scripts, "open material") to the manuscripts reporting on the study results ("open access").[1] Disclosing research artifacts increases transparency and, thus, reproducibility and replicability of our scientific process and our results. Open science is often seen as an important means to move forward as a scientific research community. Open data and open source—both being major principles under the common banner of open science—constitute a major hallmark in making empirical studies transparent and understandable to researchers not involved in carrying out those studies. This can be done, for example, by sharing replication packages that capture the raw data and anything necessary for their analysis and interpretation. That way, we increase the reproducibility of our research. This, in turn, strengthens the credibility of the conclusions we draw from the analysed data and it allows others to build their own work upon ours; hence, it strengthens more generally our overall body of knowledge in the research community.

Besides these more ideological views on open science and reasonable arguments in favour of engaging into it as a research community, on which any reader will probably agree, there is much more to it which we need to understand when considering open science in the context of software engineering research. There are, for example, various challenges in data disclosure—technical ones, ethical and legal ones, but also social ones—which are different to the standards and views given in other disciplines and which make open science difficult to become the norm in our own field. Consider, for example, the notion of repeatability, replicability, and reproducibility by considering the terminology as introduced by the ACM[2] (verbatim):

- **Repeatability (Same team, same experimental setup):** The measurement can be obtained with stated precision by the same team using the same measurement procedure, the same measuring system, under the same operating conditions, in the same location on multiple trials. For computational experiments, this means that a researcher can reliably repeat her own computation.
- **Replicability (Different team, same experimental setup):** The measurement can be obtained with stated precision by a different team using the same measurement procedure, the same measuring system, under the same operating

---

[1]Open science and open scholarship encompass a wide range of topics and activities, many of which are described by Tennant et al. (2019). In this chapter, we concentrate on topics we believe to be in scope of (empirical) software engineering, namely open access, open data, open materials, open source, open peer review, and registered reports.

[2]https://www.acm.org/publications/policies/artifact-review-badging.

conditions, in the same or a different location on multiple trials. For computational experiments, this means that an independent group can obtain the same result using the author's own artifacts.

- **Reproducibility (Different team, different experimental setup):** The measurement can be obtained with stated precision by a different team, a different measuring system, in a different location on multiple trials. For computational experiments, this means that an independent group can obtain the same result using artifacts which they develop completely independently.

As an engineering discipline heavily inspired by the natural sciences, we often make implicit assumptions that our focus is on quantitative and even purely computational studies (e.g., simulations). For these, existing definitions and norms hold as they are and we are able to yield replicability and reproducibility. This situation is, however, not the norm. Most studies in software engineering involve—in one form or another—humans. In the end, software is made by human beings for human beings. Human subjects, however, act purely rational in exceptional cases only, if at all (see Lambert 2006). This means that every change in an experimental context, even if strictly following the same experimental setup and procedure, will eventually yield different (context-dependent) results. Such studies would then not fit the available definition of reproducibility as used in computational studies, but it is still reasonable to argue that they would be reproducible. Further challenges in software engineering research are that much of our data emerges from sensitive (e.g., industrial) settings and finally the reliance upon qualitative data where the data analysis is less procedural when compared to quantitative data (also imposing significant integrity challenges). All this renders full disclosure often difficult and we often need to anonymise the data to act within legal and ethical constraints that most computational studies do otherwise not have. Those two facets of software engineering research alone show already that we need to adapt open science principles to the particularities of our discipline, same as it is the case in other disciplines.

How can our software engineering community of researchers adopt its own open science movement? We believe that it is a lack of proper understanding about

- what open science is (and what it is not) for software engineering,
- why we should all do our best to implement it, whether as editor, chair, or as researcher, and finally
- how we could and should do it

that often leads to a general reluctance towards implementing open science. Sometimes, it even leads to a general dismissal of the potential open science has for individual researchers and the community as a whole. All this renders our own open science movement cumbersome.

In this chapter, we cover the essentials in open science for software engineering. In particular, we establish a common ground in our discipline by elaborating on established key terms, principles, and approaches in Sect. 2—all tailored to the particularities of our discipline. We further discuss why we should engage in open science (Sect. 3) before discussing practical guidelines to implementing open science in Sect. 4. In Sect. 5, we then end with a discussion of chosen challenges and pitfalls. The latter is based on our shared experiences emerging from open science activities and lessons we learnt so far as authors and as organizers where we implemented first open science initiatives in the empirical software engineering community.

The main target audience consists of software engineering scholars interested in the general notion of open science and those interested in implementing open science in their own research practices. One hope we associate with this chapter is not only to oppose those critical voices still sceptical towards open science, but also to strengthen the voices of those supporting it out of the firm conviction that open science should soon become the norm in software engineering research, too.

2 What Is Open Science?

Open science is a movement whose aim is to render all artifacts born out of scientific research activities accessible, without any barriers, to any individual on Earth (Woelfle et al. 2011). Following Tennant et al. (2019), open science refers also to the scientific part of the broader terms of open scholarship, i.e., "the process, communication, and reuse of research as practised in any scholarly research discipline, and its inclusion and role within wider society". Open science itself is an umbrella term that encompasses several facets of openness, for example, open access, open data, open source, open government, open notebooks, or open standards (see FOSTER 2019). In the following, we discuss those concepts particularly relevant to the (empirical) software engineering research community.

2.1 Open Access

Open access is associated with publications, i.e., research articles, technical reports and papers in general. Open access occurs whenever a publication is freely available on the public Internet without any access barrier—financial, legal, or technical ones (including even not to force users to register to systems). It allows individuals to read, download, copy, distribute, print, search, or link to the full texts of publications for any lawful purpose (BOAI 2002). Minor constraints over redistribution and reuse of the publication may still apply and usually take the form of attribution. It is typical with open access publications that the authors retain the copyright of their work, and the act to render the work as open access is enabled through proper licences. The *Creative Commons* licence model is the most widely employed licence for open access (see also Sect. 2.2).

Open access can take several forms. The form depends on which version of the article is made public and at which point of the academic writing process. If authors make an own produced copy of their work openly available, they perform an act of *self-archiving*. The work is called *preprint* if it reflects a version of their manuscript that has not yet been accepted for publication at a scientific venue. If the content of the own produced work is identical to the content of the accepted publication, it is called *postprint*. The only differences between the *postprint* and the manuscript formally published by a traditional publisher like ACM, IEEE, or Springer are in typesetting differences and the location of the document. The location of pre- and postprints is typically an open repository for pre- and postprints, in contrast to the digital libraries of the publishers. One such example is given in the following while we will go more into detail in Sect. 4.

> **Self-archiving via arXiv**
>
> arXiv, pronounced as *archive* and available at https://arXiv.org, is a repository, born in 1991, of freely accessible preprints and postprints, as well as whitepapers, covering several scientific fields including physics, mathematics, and computer science (see also Ginsparg 2011). arXiv is free to access, to register to, and to submit to, but it presents two safeguards for publishing. First, authors have to be endorsed by existing members before they are allowed to register in the system. Second, every submission is moderated by volunteers who check for issues such as scope or copyright. arXiv is the de facto standard repository for mathematics and physics, and with some authors only publishing their work in there, it receives more than 10,000 submissions per month and is, at the time of writing this chapter, hosting approximately 1.5M manuscripts in a distributed archived system of multiple digital libraries all over the world.

The act of self-archiving is also known as *green open access* and it is allowed by the majority of academic publishers with some regulations.

> **Self-archiving options and publishers' regulations**
>
> Different publishers define different regulations with effect to the needs and possibilities of self-archiving, and it is imperative to strictly adhere to these rules. The SHERPA partnership, a partnership of several universities with the original goal of setting up an institutional open access repository, offers with *RoMEO*—http://www.sherpa.ac.uk/romeo—a tool summarising publishers' copyright and archiving policies. RoMEO distinguishes different categories via the following colour codes commonly adopted also in the wider sense:
>
> - **White:** Self-archiving not formally allowed
> - **Yellow:** Authors can archive preprints (i.e., pre-refereeing)

(continued)

- **Blue:** Authors can archive postprints (i.e., final draft post-refereeing) or publisher's version/PDF
- **Green:** Authors can archive preprint and postprint or publisher's version

Whenever a publisher renders an accepted publication as openly licensed and available without any restriction whatsoever, the artifact becomes open access under the *gold open access model*. This model often follows an author-pays strategy, but there exist also publishers asking for no article processing charges at all. We refer the reader to the work of Graziotin et al. (2014) for more information on open access and its publishing models.

2.2 Open Data

Open data is very similar to open access, but it is applied to any data that was produced in the course of research activities, such as the raw data obtained via a controlled experiment. Openness of data can come in various forms and at different degrees; for instance, while an abstract description of a data set (metadata) could be found and accessed online, it could still be the case that access to the full data set would only be granted upon request and only for specific research purposes carefully selected and laid out by the owners of that data set. Here, we point to the FAIR principles[3] which describe how data should ideally be made open: When data sets are Findable, Accessible, Interoperable, and Reusable, we refer to it as "FAIR data".

As pointed out by Auer et al. (2007), open (FAIR) data follows the idea that research data should be freely available to everyone to use and redistribute as they wish, without any restriction whatsoever born out of copyright and licences. As with open access, the Creative Commons deeds are commonly employed licences for open data.

Creative Commons (CC) Copyright Licences
Creative Commons copyright licences (see https://creativecommons.org/licenses/) constitute a public licence model with the aim to facilitate granting copyright permissions to published work. The two most employed Creative Commons deeds are the Public Domain (CC0, "No rights reserved") and the Attribution 4.0 (CC BY 4.0) licence. The former is a licence that implements

(continued)

---

[3]See also https://www.force11.org/group/fairgroup/fairprinciples.

true public domain, effectively acting as a renounce of any copyright on the artifacts. The latter is an open licence that allows reuse and redistribution of the artifact with the only condition of attributing the original work to the authors.

Besides the frequently used CC licence models introduced above, further ones are possible, too. One example is the Attribution-NonCommercial 4.0 (CC BY NC 4.0), which adds the clause that the original artifact and any derivation of it cannot be used for commercial purposes. While the Public Domain and the CC BY NC licences might seem more suitable for academic work, opting for them can be problematic as we explain in Sect. 5.3.

2.3 Open Source

Open source in open science is nothing different to open source software as it is commonly known by the computer science community. In fact, many argue that the open source software movement served as an inspiration for more openness in various fields going beyond software-related ones (see also the work by Boisseau et al. (2018) providing an elaborate discussion). In any case, several research endeavours in computer science and empirical software engineering, but also other disciplines as well, produce software. One such example is what is often referred to as *research software* (or scientific software), i.e., software products developed with the purpose of analyzing (empirical) data, such as Python code. In principle, the software developed can be released as open source software using known licences such as the MIT licence or the GPLv3.

2.4 Preregistration of Studies

Preregistration is a useful tool to ensure a certain level of quality of a study design, e.g., by making sure that hypotheses of a confirmatory study were actually predefined rather than being defined after having analysed the data to fit the results. Researchers define what their research questions are, why they want to pursue the research, and how exactly they will try to answer their questions. The Open Science Framework is currently one of the most common places to preregister research projects (see https://osf.io/prereg/). Some journals have reported already how preregistration avoids

- publication bias (Dickersin 1990),
- p-hacking (Head et al. 2015), and
- HARKing, i.e., hypothesising after the results are known (Kerr 1998).

These journals offer the possibility of submitting a *registered report* to their journal.[4] Such a report goes through peer review and, provided acceptance, the report is *in principle accepted* (IPA). If the researchers conduct the study as indicated in the registered report, their paper will be published in the journal regardless of the results.

2.5 Open Science Badges

For every form of open science, publishers can award *open science Badges*. Badging is a form of promoting open science activities of researchers via a specific badge that publicly recognises their open science engagement. To this end, publishers associate a specific symbol (i.e., a badge) to chosen artifacts to certify that the content is available and accessible in a persistent location.

There exist various forms of badges obeying the particularities of the various available badge systems. Some of them are publisher-specific (such as the ACM badge system[5]) and some of them are independent, such as the OSF Open Science Badges.

> **OSF Open Science Badges**
>
> A wide-spread open science badge system is the one of the Open Science Framework (OSF, https://osf.io/) and further promoted by the Center for Open Science (https://cos.io). This model distinguishes between badges in the following categories:
>
> - **Open Data:** This badge is awarded when shareable data necessary to reproduce a study are made publicly (digitally) available.
> - **Open Materials:** This badge is awarded when making available the materials of the followed research methodology necessary to reproduce or replicate that followed methodology (e.g., analysis scripts).
> - **Preregistered:** That badge is awarded when preregistering a study design including the description of the research design and study materials.

How to award which badges depends on many (often non-trivial) criteria defined by editors and following a specific reviewing model to check the eligibility to obtain the badges. Although badges are, at the time of writing this chapter, rather rare in software engineering research (such as badges for preregistered studies) and although some systems may still be perceived as difficult to implement (such as

---

[4]For a guide on writing registered reports, we refer the reader to https://osf.io/8mpji/.

[5]See https://www.acm.org/publications/policies/artifact-review-badging.

the ACM system due to the wide spectrum of often overlapping badges), badges are generally recognised to be a valuable incentive that increases the participation in open science initiatives (Rowhani-Farid et al. 2017). Hence, they are being adopted more and more by journals and conferences.

2.6 Open Peer Review

As discussed by Tennant et al. (2017), different models of peer review exist and have been experimented with lately. One of these is open peer review, for which there is, however, yet no commonly accepted and clear definition nor an agreed schema as elaborated in a secondary study by Ross-Hellauer (2017). Open peer review implementations intend to make the review process as transparent as possible and can feature factors ranging from removing the anonymity of authors and reviewers alike, over making the actual reviews public and allowing for interaction between authors and reviewers, to crowdsourcing reviews and even making manuscripts public before the review phase.

One least common denominator of open peer review focuses on the names of authors and reviewers so that both can see each other's identities. This allows for authors and reviewers to have a direct conversation rather than having to go through third parties for communication purposes (e.g., via handling editors or chairs). In the programming community, this type of review process has long been known in code reviews, but—despite the advantages recognised in the research community as shown in a recent study by Prechelt et al. (2018) on the future of peer review in software engineering—it is not yet adopted by our journals and conferences (see also Sect. 5). One exception is the Journal of Open Source Software.[6] Another definition focuses on disclosing the reviews—sometimes with the names of the reviewers. That way, reviewers can be held more accountable, but they can also serve to make the decision for acceptance more transparent to others and the reviewers can also claim the recognition they deserve. There are many fears and hopes around open peer review models, many of which are discussed in an editorial by Bolam and Foxe (2017) for the European Journal of Neuroscience after having implementing such a model. One fear (for which, however, there is no evidence yet) is the risk that early career researchers might be more reluctant to provide profound critique if their names are revealed (see also our discussion in Sect. 5.2). A partial implementation of this model where reviewer names and their reviews are made public is followed by the PeerJ Computer Science Journal, which asks the reviewers whether they wish to disclose their name and subsequently to the authors if whether they wish to disclose the peer review history in the published paper.

---

[6]For details, see https://joss.readthedocs.io/en/latest/submitting.html#the-review-process.

3 Why Do We Need Open Science?

Open science is becoming more and more accepted in scientific communities to be having many positive effects. These effects range from increased access and citation counts (Eysenbach 2006) to facilitating technology transfer with the industry and fostering collaborations through open repositories. Academic publishing and knowledge sharing is meant to become more cost-effective—German university libraries alone are estimated to be spending well beyond 200 million EUR on publication subscriptions fees per year (Schimmer et al. 2015)—and researchers and practitioners with no publisher subscriptions can freely access and build on the work of others. There are many discussions and controversies centred around publisher subscription models and how institutions (and institutional alliances) should deal with them. In this chapter, we will not even try to address these discussions to the extent they deserve, but provide a broader view on why we do need open science in general.

Imagine the following situation: A conference author submits a manuscript promising to have provided scientific and empirically informed arguments for considering Go To statements harmful; a statement previously relying on rationalist arguments of software engineering pioneers like Dijkstra (1968) only. As laid out by that author, those arguments emerge from the exploration of industrial source code—which the author does not share, maybe because of non-disclosure agreements with collaborating companies from which the data emerges, or maybe for other reasons; this statement is not made explicit in the manuscript. They have further analysed the impact of those statements based on in-depth interviews—which the author does also not share, maybe because of ethical and legal constraints. Imagine further that the reviewers find no obvious methodological flaws in the design which the author describes in great detail for both the content analysis and the interviews. The author is an experienced and recognised authority in the research community and the manuscript is written in an easy-to-follow manner. The reviewers further find the manuscript "compelling", "interesting", and the results are also "surprising" to them given the availability of contrary evidence provided by other authors who previously analysed publicly available software repositories coming to very contrary conclusions (Nagappan et al. 2015). Even if the submitting author did not discuss that other publication in detail, a presentation of that work would certainly lead to controversial and interesting discussions; something the reviewers believe to merit presentation at the prestigious conference they review for. So they recommend acceptance and the PC chairs select that publication for inclusion in the program. It is reasonable to believe that many readers of this chapter having served as co-chairs and reviewers for conferences can identify with such a situation.

Now imagine you were a young scholar analyzing the effects of software defects and you find this publication. You would certainly find this publication interesting as it could provide a useful ground for follow-up work. Ask yourself—honestly—the following questions:

- Would you trust the results? If so, based on what? The simple fact that it has been accepted by the prestigious conference? The way the manuscript is generally written? The name of the author or her or his affiliation? Maybe based on the high number of citations that this publication already has? Maybe it is a combination of all factors? Would the picture change if the author would be unknown to you and if the work would have been published at a lower ranked conference?

- Would you be able to really comprehend how the study has been carried out? Would you be able to reproduce the conclusions drawn by the author based on the insights provided in the manuscript? Would you be able to replicate the study in your own research environment?
- To what extent does that piece of work provide a good theory for your work? Would this theory be robust and reliable (i.e., scientific)? Would you consider it useful?
- How would you use the work if you could only access the abstract of the manuscript because it is hidden behind a paywall and because your institution has no subscription? Would you cite the work based on the information in the abstract? Maybe based on the statements found in other papers citing that work?
- How would you cite that work and put it in relation to your own research? Would the picture change in dependency to whether the statements in that manuscript support your own arguments or whether it contradicts them?

This very example certainly describes a fictitious situation and yet it describes in many ways the de-facto situation of software engineering research. Scientific practices need to rely on certain safeguards, such as peer review, but they are nevertheless also dictated by social and political mechanisms and many non-trivial, subjective factors in the research communities. These factors very often dictate in one form or the other which submissions eventually make it into the publication landscape and which do not, and which publications are cited and which are not. As a consequence, publication and citation regimes—although inherently rooted in scepticism—have also much to do with trust and convictions (Mendez and Passoth 2018); something which holds for most, if not all, scientific disciplines. Transparency is therefore key to break with scientific theories being grounded in common sense, taken-for-granted knowledge, hopes, convictions, and provisional beliefs.

Software Engineering still faces many challenges not found in other disciplines. Our data comprehends qualitative and quantitative data types and the theories we work on often have various disciplinary backgrounds (from mathematics over psychology to sociology). Further, our data very often emerges from highly sensitive environments making a disclosure difficult and in many cases impossible. Even if we can disclose the data, in many cases it has to be anonymised to an extent it becomes difficult to fully comprehend. All this renders building and evaluating empirically grounded theories in our field difficult. Hence, scientific practices often remain rooted in trust rather than being rooted in transparent scientific processes. Yet and as laid out by Mendez and Passoth (2018), it is theory building which constitutes a crucial foundation to our avenue towards turning our engineering discipline into a more scientific, evidence-based one, same as it was the case for many other disciplines before. Transparency, credibility, and reproducibility are cornerstones in building and evaluating robust and reliable theories for our still emerging field and open science provides a solid foundation to achieve that goal.

In essence, open science practices in general and data sharing in particular eventually allow us as a community of software engineering researchers and practitioners to effectively make contributions to our body of knowledge based upon shared data sets—making our empirical studies transparent, comprehensible, and credible—thus, we move forward as a community. As we argue, not only scientific publishing is essential in knowledge sharing and dissemination (Houghton and Oppenheim 2010), but it is an essential facet in accumulating knowledge via a variation of studies tackling the same or similar questions and building upon the same or similar settings and data sets—e.g., as part of replication studies (Gómez et al. 2012) which are rendered difficult if not impossible without clear open science principles dictating shared values and principle scientific practices.

Therefore, there is no doubt anymore *whether* open science will become the norm also in software engineering research. Ever more public and private funding bodies are implementing open access and open data policies (see, e.g., Childs et al. 2014; Van den Eynden et al. 2011). Also the research community is in tune with this movement, as we can observe: editors and conference organizers are already planning for a smooth transition to open data, and reviewers are becoming more and more sceptical towards manuscript submissions which do not disclose their data and, consequently, ask the reviewers for too much credit. It remains, however, often still a question of *how* the community should adopt open science practices and how individual researchers should open their research. We discuss this question in more detail in the next section.

4 How Do We Do Open Science?

In the following, we address the question of how to engage in open science. There are many aspects to consider when engaging as a researcher in open science. We believe that these aspects are best introduced along a simple (again, fictitious) scenario introduced next. The goal is to demonstrate opportunities along an exemplary set of practices and techniques available to engage in open science in a hands-on manner.

4.1 Exemplary Scenario

As an exemplary scenario, we consider a research project where we are researchers at European universities collaborating with project partners from other universities in the USA. Those partners are researchers in psychology. Our project aims at conducting a psychometric software engineering study and our overall goal is to collect data involving a large-scale study with human subjects. The research design is done in a joint effort. While our partners are largely responsible for the study execution and the data collection, we are largely responsible for analyzing the data and reporting on it.

To keep the example simple, we focus on the statistical analysis of quantitative data in our study, but also refer the reader to the challenges emerging from the disclosure of qualitative data in Sect. 5.

4.2 Overall Data Analysis Process

Figure 1 depicts, on the left side, the steps followed in our data analysis with a particular focus on those aspects relevant from an open science perspective. Overall, we first prepare our data and check for any errors, inconsistencies, and missing values, and we discuss these with our partners. At the same time, we start thinking about how to best answer our questions at hand. While we design our analysis procedure, we update the data structure to best fit the analysis plan. Once the analysis plan is finalised, we make it openly available. Ideally, we submit it as a *preregistered study*. This submission includes our study protocol and the material (analysis scripts) as well as a detailed sample description allowing reviewers to judge upon the potential of the study with respect to its theoretical and practical impact. After registering our study and considering the feedback received, only then, we decide to begin with the data analysis.

After discovering no clear patterns in the data, we decide to participate at a workshop where we present our ongoing work based on a previously published short paper describing the overall goal of the study and preliminary results. This work in progress presentation serves the purpose of receiving further feedback from

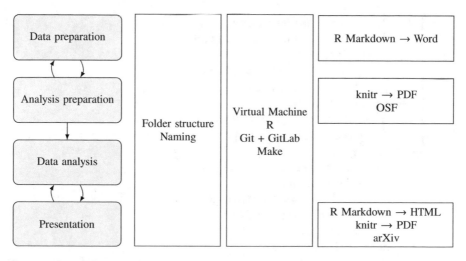

Fig. 1 Schema of an exemplary simple project

the research community and of getting useful ideas on how to improve our data visualisation techniques. After successfully finishing our data analysis, we finally write up our main publication on the project and disclose our manuscript preprint prior to submitting our manuscript for review to a journal.

In the following, we walk through that process while focusing on the infrastructure and tools. Our hope is that by presenting the process in such a pragmatic hands-on manner allows to fully reproduce the process as it should typically appear in a research setting.

4.3 Exemplary Walk-Through

There are various tools to be used to make our project open and reproducible. While we do not claim to be able to present an exhaustive list here, our aim is to give some examples which we use ourselves to make recommendations based on our own experiences. One basic issue to consider first is the folder structure and the naming convention. A good folder structure, in our view, could be like the one in Listing 1 as it captures the very essence of our process:

Listing 1 Project structure and naming convention for open science

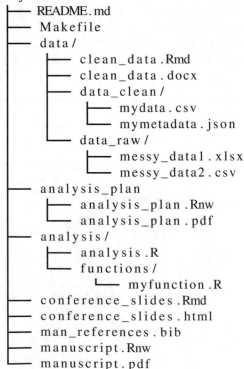

Note that the folder structure clearly defines the different steps shown in Fig. 1 and the folder and file names clearly indicate what each of them contains.

Regardless of the actual size of the project, the basic rule should be to apply that structure and naming convention concisely and consistently. We experienced it to also be important to keep the original data in a separate folder (data_raw/ in Listing 1) and to not manipulate the raw data files but to create new data files in a separate folder for the data cleaning and analysis (data_clean/ in Listing 1). In combination with a script which cleans the data (clean_data.Rmd in Listing 1), this makes the data cleaning process reproducible to others.

To keep the working environment stable in terms of software versions, we decide to use a *virtual machine* for this project. An alternative option could also be a container (Docker, Singularity, etc.). For the data cleaning and the analysis, we decide to use *R* (see also R Core Team 2018). R is an open source software environment for statistical computing. An alternative to that could be to use Python. R scripts (e.g., analysis.R in Listing 1) are text files that can be executed in the R console. In contrast to click-and-point programs (e.g., SPSS when used without syntax) or programs producing binary files (e.g., Excel), R, same as Python, allows for a reproducible workflow which can be easily version controlled.

For version control, in our project, we decide to use *Git* (Chacon and Straub 2014). We further use it in combination with the Git-repository hosting service *GitLab* (https://gitlab.com). That version control system allows us and our collaborating partners to trace the versions of all produced text documents in an organised fashion. In combination with the hosting service GitLab, these versions remain available online to all involved in our project. For automating our workflow, we use Make (Stallman et al. 2001). To this end, and we keep referring to Listing 1, we store a Makefile in our main project folder which contains the information on how different files depend on each other, for example, that data/clean_data.Rmd depends on data/data_raw/messy_data1.xlsx and data/data_raw/messy_data2.csv and produces data/data_clean/mydata.csv, data/data_clean/mymetadata.json, and data/clean_data.docx. Our Makefile also documents how the outputs can be produced (via bash commands).

Next to using R for our project, we use *R Markdown* (see Xie et al. 2018) and *knitr* (see Xie 2015). Both allow users to combine R code chunks with explanatory text snippets and, thus, allowing for literate programming (Knuth 1984). Our text is formatted with Markdown (R Markdown) and LaTeX (knitr). As our partners rely on MS Word, we regularly convert our R Markdown documents to Word documents for constant feedback by commenting directly in those documents. This simplifies the communication about the constant data checking and cleaning process. For an intermediate project report and later for the manuscript writing, we use knitr as it gives us more formatting options.

Our analysis plan is written with knitr and we upload the PDF to the open science framework (OSF, https://osf.io). This allows us to use the analysis plan for preregistration of the work we aim to do. Preregistration allows to reduce biases in the process of the data analysis (see also https://osf.io/prereg). We create the slides for the conference again using R Markdown which can produce high quality HTML slides. The manuscript is written using knitr and we make it available as open access on the preprint server arXiv (https://arXiv.org). To check whether preprint sharing is within the legal constraints of the publisher of the conference, we check for it using the search engine SHERPA RoMEO (http://sherpa.mimas.ac.uk/romeo).

As we see that the publisher follows a yellow open access model allowing to disclose the preprints but not the postprints, we choose to upload our preprint only. After that submission, we directly submit our manuscript to a peer-reviewed journal. Upon acceptance of the manuscript by that journal, we update our preprint with the DOI provided by the publisher, but do not submit the postprint, i.e., the postproduction version of the manuscript to comply with the copyright agreement. This preprint version is also the one we distribute among the community, e.g., via social media.

Since all root documents are text files (except for data/data_raw/messy_data1. xlsx) we can further put them under version control with Git. Through GitLab, we can make them easily accessible to others. This way, our project folder myproject/ can be seen as a replication package. Prior to disclosure, however, we check for parts in our data that need anonymisation to comply with the European General Data Protection Regulation (GDPR) as well as with the approval notification of the Institutional Review Board of our partners in the USA. We remove any data that might allow to trace observations back to individuals participating in the study.

For our work to be reproducible in a long-term manner, we need to further document the versions of the software used. The virtual machine does that for us, but is not very portable. The option we follow is to use the version management system *packrat* in R (see Ushey et al. 2018).

We notice that our partners are very reluctant to share the data because of its sensitivity and because they fear misuse (e.g., when taken out of its context), thus, we would not be able to follow the FAIR principles (Sect. 2.2) as anticipated. It is, however, possible for us to convince our project partners to disclose the data when implementing some safeguards. To this end, we decide to disclose our data using the service platform Zenodo (https://zenodo.org) while choosing *Restricted Access*. Other researchers interested in accessing the data can first read the extensive metadata describing the content of the data and how it was produced. If they believe that the data would fit their scope of interest, they can apply for access and our previously established *Data Use and Access Committee (DUAC)*, formed by us data owners and a member of the responsible ethics committee, so that we can decide whether to grant access to the data or not.

That very example, we hope, illustrates an open science-conform study analysis and reporting producing all artifacts relevant to an open science format adoptable to software engineering and including the disclosure of:

1. A study protocol submission and review prior to publication (preregistered study)
2. The replication package including all analysed data (open data) and all files, scripts, and codebooks necessary to comprehend the study (open materials)
3. A preprint (yellow open access)

Needless to say, the example is a simplified one neglecting some challenges we typically encounter in practice. In the following, we discuss those challenges in more detail.

5 Challenges, Pitfalls, and Guidelines

In the following, we discuss typical challenges and pitfalls in open science from the perspective of researchers engaging in open science. To this end, we draw from our experiences covering both the roles of researchers and the roles of organizers (handling editors and conference and workshop organizers).

5.1 General Issues

The major challenge that keeps researchers from following all the open science practices described above is probably the difficulty and effort required when making everything openly available. All the practices constitute additional steps that researchers have to do in addition to the non-open research process. They might be motivated to do these additional steps to support the scientific process and higher visibility of open publications. Yet, this motivation has limits. Therefore, the ease of doing open science practices is essential.

In our experience, the difficulty of being open has reduced dramatically over the years. It is easy and cost-free to handle a research project on GitHub or OSF, to permanently publish data on Zenodo or figshare, and to provide preprints on services like arXiv. Some difficulty lies in the details, such as the LaTeX requirements of arXiv, but nowadays we mostly work with modern web applications that behave as one would expect.

Another challenge that might keep researchers from employing openness in their research is the area of conflict between anonymity and confidentiality on the one side and openness on the other. In open science, we ideally would like to make everything open that helps others to understand, verify, and build on our work. When we work with companies, however, they have an understandable interest to protect their intellectual property and reputation, often reflected in signed non-disclosure agreements. Therefore, we have to reduce the data that we can make open or anonymise the data that we have. This is, again, additional effort and a risk that we accidentally make something open that should be confidential.

Similarly, when our studies involve humans, they have an interest in protecting their private data. With the EU GDPR, we now also have a strong legal basis for that. Hence, again, we have the risk to violate corresponding laws. In both cases, companies and individual humans, it is therefore imperative to publish any potentially sensitive data only with the explicit consent of the study participants. Only they themselves can decide what is sensitive and critical for them. In principle, this holds for any kind of publication and, hence, only needs to be extended to ask for consent for publishing the data as well. Anonymising company names is often enough. For anonymising sensitive data of study participants, there are also established techniques (see, e.g., Saunders et al. 2015).

The challenge of anonymity also plays into the third more general issue we would like to mention: Often, openness is merely an afterthought. After we have done all the work, we provide a preprint and make the data available. Ideally, however, the whole process should be open, for example, by using OSF or GitHub for all the documents, data, and analysis scripts. In terms of anonymity, this is difficult, as we cannot make everything open and often need a shadow repository with the original raw data. The raw data needs then to be carefully filtered when stored in an open repository. Yet, keeping everything open has the advantage that there is no way of manipulation during the analysis and publication phases of the research. We cannot make the hypothesis fit the data in hindsight because we documented the hypothesis before we did the analysis.

5.2 Sharing Preprints

For preprints, we need to consider where we want to publish the paper later on. Upon acceptance of our manuscript, we can also post a postprint. This is rarely a problem when we already have a preprint that is simply updated. Otherwise, there might be publisher-specific embargo periods that need to be adhered to.

> **Self-archiving Options for Software Engineering**
> In principle, different publishers have different criteria about what they allow at all and what licences to choose. One helpful overview of the different self-archiving options in tune with the regulations of the major publishers in Software Engineering is, as we believe, provided by van Deursen (2016).

One challenge we would like to highlight in the context of preprint sharing emerges from the trend in software engineering to push for double-blind reviewing models by also anonymising not only reviewers' identifies but also ones of the authors. While the higher goal to reduce potential biases is laudable, it complicated open science practices considerably. Conferences are increasingly adopting a double-blind model of peer review, which does not easily allow preprints to be made available because it might allow the reviewers to find out who the authors are. It has been our effort to start a trend in conferences to allow self-archiving preprints and instruct peer reviewers to not actively look for the papers under review online, but it remains nevertheless a challenge. The picture would change if open peer review would be implemented in a code review style (as discussed in Sect. 2.6). However, the downside and fear of many researchers is that open peer review will put a lot of pressure on researchers, especially early career researchers: Both as authors—the reviewers will know who made potential mistakes—and as reviewers—the authors will know who proposed the changes or even who recommended rejection of the paper.

5.3 Choosing Appropriate Licences

A common pitfall while starting to use open science practices is to assign unsuitable licences. arXiv, for example, allows to select an ad hoc non-exclusive licence (to arXiv). Granting this minimal licence is compatible with any relevant venue a researcher might want to submit to. Hence, it keeps all options open even if the paper is rejected at the initially planned venue. Adding a Creative Commons licence could reduce this flexibility considerably. In fact, arXiv itself allows to choose from various Creative Commons licences (CC BY, CC BY-SA, CC BY-NC-SA) as well as the CC0 dedication, i.e., public domain (see also Arxiv 2019a).

Many argue that CC0 is preferable because it frees people from dealing with all attributions. However, in the scientific context, attributing the source and authors of all artifacts that are used is good practice independent of the licence used. Some preprint servers might enforce the CC BY. This licence is also recommendable for postprints, provided postprint sharing is compatible with the publisher copyright agreement, as it ensures that the researchers are given credit while giving others the largest amount of freedom to share and reuse the manuscript.

In principle, choosing the proper licence is a non-trivial but important task, because certain licences for preprints might cause incompatibility issues further down a publishing chain. Certain licences, including some Creative Commons ones, prevent the work to be used in commercial settings (the -NC part of the CC) or require the redistribution of derivative works using the same licence (the -SA part of the CC). Traditional publishers are, most of the times, commercial entities that require either a full copyright transfer or exclusive rights to distribute the work in a more restricted way, i.e., selling access to papers through paywalls. Non-commercial and share-alike CC licences are, thus, in most of the cases incompatible with traditional publishing models.

Even the more liberal CC BY licence, which only requires attribution and does not enforce a share-alike clause, might pose issues with traditional publishing as it is non-revocable and allows commercial use by anyone (i.e., non-exclusive to the publisher). The CC0 dedication has also caused issues with traditional publishing in the past, as pointed out by O'Connor (2011). The default licence by arXiv is a non-exclusive licence to distribute (Arxiv 2019b), and, virtually, does solely allow arXiv to distribute and display a document (meaning that, theoretically, we are not allowed to do anything at all with arXiv submissions but reading them). This licence is perhaps the most restrictive one among the free licences, making it compatible with traditional publishing (if the copyright transfer conditions allow for it, see Sect. 2.1).

We can provide two recommendations. arXiv default non-exclusive licence to distribute should be used when there is certainty to publish a paper with a traditional publisher. A CC BY licence should be used when there is certainty to publish a paper with a gold open access journal. We do not recommend licensing any preprint, postprint, or data set using a non-commercial clause (-NC). While counter-intuitive at first sight (we wish for our work to stay free, after all), a non-commercial clause prevents the work to be used by commercial entities. The term *commercial* is, from a legal perspective much broader than it might appear at first; it might affect a large spectrum of people and entities including a simple blog if the website uses an advertisement system. There exist open companies that were born from commercial entities and that are therefore not non-profit (e.g., figshare and PeerJ), and these would not be allowed to make any use of material licensed with the -NC clause. Some of the work might include data mining of papers and data sets and aggregating results, which might still be very useful for the advancement of knowledge. For more information on these legal aspects, we direct the reader to a joint group of copyright experts and Wikimedia (2013).

5.4 Sharing Data and Materials

A common pitfall in publishing open data and open materials, e.g., as part of replication packages, is to use a personal or institutional website for quickly and easily making them available. It gives one a unique ID in the form of a URL. Yet, a challenge is that we cannot ensure that the URL stays valid and that the content stays on the website. As it has been empirically demonstrated, e.g., by Koehler (2002, 2003), web pages disappear continuously. Therefore, repositories such as Zenodo or figshare, providing a DOI and ensuring permanent archival, are much preferable.

There are small differences between the repositories, but both are recommendable. figshare is commercial but free to use, and its usability seems more polished than at Zenodo. Furthermore, figshare participates in data preservation mechanisms, while Zenodo does not. The permanency of Zenodo is ensured, because it is financed by the European Union and run by CERN.

Similarly as with preprint sharing in the context of double-blind reviewing models, the availability of open data and material would also reveal the authors' identity and, hence, is rendered complicated. While there is no easy solution to the problem of sharing preprints when following a double-blind reviewing model, open data repositories allow researchers now to publish data anonymously for review, thus, being compliant to restrictions imposed by such reviewing model. The authors of the data can then be made public after the paper is accepted. A set of instructions on how to share and archive open data and keep it compatible with double-blind review are presented by Graziotin (2019).

5.5 Preparing Qualitative Data

Achieving replicability and reproducibility of qualitative studies is particularly challenging and many might argue that it is not possible at all (see also the introductory discussion). This renders, however, the disclosure of qualitative data not less important than the disclosure of quantitative data. Even if we cannot support reproducibility of qualitative studies in the nearer sense (if interpreting those terms literally), we can at least achieve transparency of the research and support researchers not involved in the study in understanding how the researchers carrying out the study have drawn their conclusions.

Qualitative data is usually the most difficult to prepare for disclosure in a replication package, because it is most personal and most difficult to anonymise within legal and ethical constraints. A number is more abstract (and easier to open) than spoken words spoken (and transcribed) by individuals, e.g., during an interview. Ideally, we anonymise also qualitative data[7] and publish it with the explicit consent of the participants. It is important to be open about it upfront to understand whether the participants will agree. Especially for qualitative data, it might often not be the case that we get the consent. Then, it is even more important that at least the analysis material is shared. This is typically easier to share and may include a study protocol as well as the coding schema and coding rules used when coding qualitative data (e.g., as part of a Grounded Theory study). That way, reviewers and other researchers can at least check the trustworthiness of the analysis process and understand how the authors have drawn their conclusions.

6 Conclusion

Open science describes the movement to render all artifacts born out of scientific research activities accessible. Openness in our research processes is important to move forward in building reliable and robust theories, thus, turning our discipline into a more scientific one. As outlined in this chapter, we still face, however, various challenges other disciplines do not face. Despite those challenges of adapting open science to the software engineering context, we can still see that our research community is making great progress in that direction. We have ourselves either accompanied or fully implemented efforts to help the community opening up their research artifacts.

In the course of our endeavour, we have noticed very well that introducing open science into a research community is a difficult and sensitive task, because open science is still often confronted with prejudice, but also because many authors, despite their willingness to conform to such policies, do not often know how exactly

---

[7]By anomymisation of qualitative data we refer to the removal of any information that allows to reveal the individuals' identities and/or otherwise sensitive not directly related to the study.

to follow such an initiative; that is to say, it is often difficult to see what we should do and what we can do (also considering ethical and legal constraints).

This is also the reason why we, as organizers, are often constraint by a general reluctance of implementing mandatory open science principles (e.g., via open data policies), thus, rendering the transition to more openness in our discipline rugged. However, the implementations of open science policies in the recent editions of conferences and journals—even if non-mandatory ones where authors could participate on a voluntary basis with the support of dedicated open science chairs—nevertheless showed high participation ratios with more than 50% of the authors disclosing their data. Such a support by the community and the positive feedback, e.g., in Town Hall meetings, strengthen our confidence in that the research community is showing more and more awareness of the importance of open science and that open science will eventually become the norm.

One hope we associate with our ongoing efforts in implementing open science initiatives in software engineering venues is to send strong signals into the research community and to gradually increase the awareness of participating researchers to move further in that direction.

Arguably, we are still confronted with various challenges, such as:

- How to implement a uniform and transparent guideline to review disclosed artifacts covering all possible variations in the different types of study (e.g., quantitative and qualitative ones)?
- How to implement preregistered studies (which we consider especially important to tackle the problems of publication bias or p-hacking) in tune with the reviewing processes of our existing journals and conferences and how to redefine existing roles and responsibilities?
- How to properly reward authors with a clear and easy to understand (and to use) badge system which recognises the differences in the various study types and the difficulties in opening up sensitive, e.g., industrial, data?
- How to implement open peer reviews? We can nowadays observe a significant turn in the existing single-blinded reviewing regime, which we applaud, but instead of opening up reviews as well, the current trend is towards even more closeness via double-blind reviewing models, thus, rendering other open science activities difficult, too.

We are still convinced that it is not anymore a question whether open science will become the norm also for the software engineering research community, but we recognise that there is still a long way to go, also because we still need to increase the awareness for what open science is, why it is so important, and how to properly adopt such principles to software engineering.

The chapter at hands is intended to address these questions and to contribute to the movement. Our hope is to further encourage all members of our research community in joining us in this important endeavour of actively shaping an open science agenda for the software engineering community.

Acknowledgements We want to thank all the members of the empirical software engineering research community who are actively supporting the open science movement and its adoption to the software engineering community. Just to name a few: Robert Feldt and Tom Zimmermann, editors in chief of the Empirical Software Engineering Journal, are committed to support the implementation of a new Reproducibility and Open Science initiative[8]—the first one to implement an open data initiative following a holistic process including a badge system. The steering committee of the International Workshop on Cooperative and Human Aspects of Software Engineering (CHASE) supported the implementation of an open science initiative from 2016 on. Markku Oivo, general chair of the International Symposium on Empirical Software Engineering and Measurement (ESEM) 2018, has actively supported the adoption of the CHASE open science initiative with focus on data sharing for the major Empirical Software Engineering conference so that we could pave the road for a long-term change in that community. Sebastian Uchitel, general chair of the International Software Engineering Conference (ICSE) 2017, further supported an initiative to foster sharing of preprints, and Natalia Juristo, general chair of ICSE 2021, further actively supports the adoption of the broader ESEM open science initiative to our major general software engineering conference. Finally, we want to thank Per Runeson, Klaas-Jan Stol, and Breno de França for their elaborate comments on earlier versions on this manuscript.

References

Arxiv (2019a) arxiv license information. https://arxiv.org/help/license. Archived: http://web.archive.org/web/20190410151011/https://arxiv.org/help/license. Accessed 10 Apr 2019

Arxiv (2019b) arxiv license information. https://arXiv.org/licenses/nonexclusive-distrib/1.0/license.html. Archived: http://web.archive.org/web/20190410165523/https://arxiv.org/licenses/nonexclusive-distrib/1.0/license.html. Accessed 10 Apr 2019

Auer S, Bizer C, Kobilarov G, Lehmann J, Cyganiak R, Ives Z (2007) DBpedia: a nucleus for a web of open data. Springer, Berlin, pp 722–735

BOAI (2002) Budapest open access initiative. https://www.budapestopenaccessinitiative.org/read

Boisseau T, Omhover J-F, Bouchard C (2018) Open-design: a state of the art review. Des Sci 4:e3

Bolam JP, Foxe JJ (2017) Transparent review at the European journal of neuroscience: experiences one year on. Eur J Neurosci 46(11):2647–2647. https://onlinelibrary.wiley.com/doi/abs/10.1111/ejn.13762

Chacon S, Straub B (2014) Pro Git. Apress, New York

Childs S, McLeod J, Lomas E, Cook G (2014) Opening research data: issues and opportunities. Rec Manag J 24(2):142–162

Dickersin K (1990) The existence of publication bias and risk factors for its occurrence. J Am Med Assoc 263(10):1385. https://doi.org/10.1001/jama.1990.03440100097014

Dijkstra EW (1968) Go to statement considered harmful. Commun ACM 11:147–148

Eysenbach G (2006) Citation advantage of open access articles. PLoS Biol 4(5):e157

FOSTER (2019) Open science taxonomy. https://www.fosteropenscience.eu/taxonomy/term/7

Ginsparg P (2011) It was twenty years ago today… Preprint. arXiv:1108.2700

Gómez O, Juristo N, Vegas S (2012) Replication types in experimental disciplines. In: Proceedings of the 2010 ACM-IEEE international symposium on empirical software engineering and measurement, pp 1–10

Graziotin D (2019) How to disclose data for double-blind review and make it archived open data upon acceptance. https://ineed.coffee/5205/. Archived: https://web.archive.org/web/20190410141340/https://ineed.coffee/5205/. Accessed 10 Apr 2019

---

[8] See also https://github.com/emsejournal/openscience.

Graziotin D, Wang X, Abrahamsson P (2014) A framework for systematic analysis of open access journals and its application in software engineering and information systems. Scientometrics 101(3):1627–1656. Available: https://arxiv.org/abs/1308.2597

Head ML, Holman L, Lanfear R, Kahn AT, Jennions MD (2015) The extent and consequences of p-hacking in science. PLOS Biol 13(3):e1002106. https://doi.org/10.1371/journal.pbio.1002106

Houghton JW, Oppenheim C (2010) The economic implications of alternative publishing models. Prometheus 28(1):41–54

Kerr NL (1998) Harking: hypothesizing after the results are known. Personal Soc Psychol Rev 2(3):196–217

Knuth DE (1984) Literate programming. Comput J 27(2):97–111

Koehler W (2002) Web page change and persistence? A four-year longitudinal study. J Am Soc Inf Sci Technol 53(2):162–171. https://doi.org/10.1002/asi.10018

Koehler W (2003) A longitudinal study of web pages continued: a consideration of document persistence. Inf Res 9(2). http://www.informationr.net/ir/9-2/paper174.html

Lambert C (2006) The marketplace of perceptions. Harv Mag 108(4):50

Mendez D, Passoth J-H (2018) Empirical software engineering: from discipline to interdiscipline. J Syst Softw 148:170–179

Nagappan M, Robbes R, Kamei Y, Tanter É, McIntosh S, Mockus A, Hassan A (2015) An empirical study of goto in C code from GitHub repositories. In: Proceedings of the 2015 10th joint meeting on foundations of software engineering. ACM, New York

O'Connor R (2011) The ACM and me. http://r6.ca/blog/20110930T012533Z.html. Archived: http://web.archive.org/web/20190410153103/http://r6.ca/blog/20110930T012533Z.html. Accessed 10 Apr 2019

Prechelt L, Graziotin D, Méndez Fernández D (2018) A community's perspective on the status and future of peer review in software engineering. Inf Softw Technol 95:75–85

R Core Team (2018) R: A language and environment for statistical computing. R Foundation for Statistical Computing, Vienna. https://www.R-project.org/

Ross-Hellauer T (2017) What is open peer review? A systematic review [version 2; peer review: 4 approved]. F1000Research 6:588. https://doi.org/10.12688/f1000research.11369.2

Rowhani-Farid A, Allen M, Barnett AG (2017) What incentives increase data sharing in health and medical research? A systematic review. Res Integrity Peer Rev 2(1):4

Saunders B, Kitzinger J, Kitzinger C (2015) Anonymising interview data: challenges and compromise in practice. Qual Res 15(5):616–632. PMID: 26457066. https://doi.org/10.1177/1468794114550439

Schimmer R, Geschuhn KK, Vogler A (2015) Disrupting the subscription journals' business model for the necessary large-scale transformation to open access. http://pure.mpg.de/pubman/item/escidoc:2148961

Stallman RM, McGrath R, Smith P (2001) GNU make, Citeseer

Tennant JP, Dugan JM, Graziotin D, Jacques DC, Waldner F, Mietchen D, Elkhatib Y, Collister LB, Pikas CK, Crick T, Masuzzo P, Caravaggi A, Berg DR, Niemeyer KE, Ross-Hellauer T, Mannheimer S, Rigling L, Katz DS, Tzovaras BG, Pacheco-Mendoza J, Fatima N, Poblet M, Isaakidis M, Irawan DE, Renaut S, Madan CR, Matthias L, Kjær JN, O'Donnell DP, Neylon C, Kearns S, Selvaraju M, Colomb J (2017) A multi-disciplinary perspective on emergent and future innovations in peer review [version 3; peer review: 2 approved]. F1000Research 6:1151. https://doi.org/10.12688/f1000research.12037.3

Tennant J, Beamer JE, Bosman J, Brembs B, Chung NC, Clement G, Crick T, Dugan J, Dunning A, Eccles D et al (2019) Foundations for open scholarship strategy development. https://osf.io/preprints/metaarxiv/b4v8p

Ushey K, McPherson J, Cheng J, Atkins A, Allaire J (2018) packrat: a dependency management system for projects and their R package dependencies. R package version 0.5.0. https://CRAN.R-project.org/package=packrat

Van den Eynden V, Corti L, Woollard M, Bishop L, Horton L (2011) Managing and sharing data; a best practice guide for researchers. Retrieved from the University of Essex Data Archive: http://repository.essex.ac.uk/2156/1/managingsharing.pdf. Accessed 31 Mar 2020 van Deursen A (2016) Green open access FAQ. https://avandeursen.com/2016/11/06/green-open-access-faq/. Archived: https://web.archive.org/web/20190410141222/https://avandeursen.com/2016/11/06/green-open-access-faq/. Accessed 10 Apr 2019

Wikimedia (2013) Consequences, risks and side-effects of the license module "non-commercial use only". OpenGLAM. https://openglam.org/2013/01/08/consequences-risks-and-side-effects-of-the-license-module-non-commercial-use-only/

Woelfle M, Olliaro P, Todd MH (2011) Open science is a research accelerator. Nat Chem 3:745 EP

Xie Y (2015) Dynamic documents with R and knitr, 2nd edn. Chapman and Hall/CRC, Boca Raton. ISBN 978-1498716963. https://yihui.name/knitr/

Xie Y, Allaire J, Grolemund G (2018) R Markdown: the definitive guide. Chapman and Hall/CRC, Boca Raton. ISBN 9781138359338. https://bookdown.org/yihui/rmarkdown

Third Generation Industrial Co-production in Software Engineering

Tony Gorschek and Krzysztof Wnuk

Abstract Industry–academia collaboration is one of the cornerstones of empirical software engineering. The role of researchers should be developing new practices and principles that enable industry in meeting the engineering challenges today and in the future. This chapter describes the third generation of industrial co-production in software engineering that includes seven steps. The co-production model and experiences associated with its use represent deep and long-term co-production with over thirty companies, many of which are still active partners in Software Engineering Research Lab (SERL).

1 Introduction

Software is at the core of almost every product and service today. Doing your taxes, handling your bank errands, driving a car, or even booking a dentist appointment, all powered by software. Software has created unprecedented benefits for companies to be more effective, efficient, and to create smarter products to compete in the marketplace. Software also enables the creation of completely new types of business. However, as more companies transform into software intensive companies, the amoung of software and software development activities in exploding (Gorschek 2018).

Software is also increasing in size, complexity, and interactions. This puts new demands on how software is conceived, developed, evolved, and maintained; in essence software engineering. Finding the balance between quickly responding to market needs and keeping costs reasonable remains challenging.

The role of researchers can and should be developing new practices and principles that enable industry in meeting the engineering challenges of today

T. Gorschek (✉) · K. Wnuk
Department of Software Engineering, Blekinge Institute of Technology, Karlskrona, Sweden
e-mail: Tony.Gorschek@bth.se; Krzysztof.Wnuk@bth.se

© Springer Nature Switzerland AG 2020   503
M. Felderer, G. H. Travassos (eds.), *Contemporary Empirical Methods in Software Engineering*, https://doi.org/10.1007/978-3-030-32489-6_18

and the future. For clarity. The terms "new practices and principles" contain any method, model, framework, practice, tool, ways-of-working, and so on that enable the engineering, evolution, and long-term asset management of software and/or software-intensive products and services. From now on, all these practices and principles are called Solution(s).

The role of a software engineering researcher is the application of a scientifically based and valid methodology to develop, validate, and transfer said solution. In this context, defining usable and useful is critical. Usable in its base form denotes if a solution can be used for its purpose, and to what extent. Useful denotes to what degree a solution delivers value during said use, and to what extent. A significant part of "proving" that your solution is good or not involves measuring if it is usable and useful. This will become apparent later in this chapter.

One way to develop and transfer research results and solutions to industry is to use co-production as a collaboration approach. The term *co-production* refers to the collaborative work of researchers and practitioners in industry to identify challenges and devise solutions that can be used in practice (Sannö et al. 2019). Co-production has many origins and can be associated with, for example, action research (Rapoport 1970; Hult and Lennung 1980). However, co-production for the purposes of this chapter is more of a macro-framework of research methods in which many other micro-methodologies (e.g., case studies, action research, experimentation, etc.) can be used in combination to achieve co-production.

This chapter is centered around a co-production model that was devised, tried, and refined over a period of 15 years at the Software Engineering Research Lab (SERL-Sweden) at Blekinge Institute of Technology, Sweden. The co-production model and experiences associated with its use represent deep and long-term co-production with over thirty companies, many of which are still active partners in SERL (Gorschek et al. 2006; Wohlin et al. 2012). We also provide some general lessons learned on knowledge and technology transfer and publication strategy.

2   The Three Generations of Software Engineering Research

The **first** generation of software engineering research was greatly focusing on developing and establishing theoretical underpinnings of the discipline. Since software engineering originates from computer science, many early advancements originate from computer science research and offer increased understanding of challenges in developing and maintaining large software systems (Naur and Randell 1969). Later on, software engineering continued to grow and develop theories and models in many subareas, e.g., software architecture and decomposition (Parnas 1972) or management of software projects (Brooks 1995). Experimentation and lab validation dominate in the first generation of software engineering, supported by experience reports and essays about challenges and methods for managing large software projects.

The **second** generation of software engineering research broadens the research topics within software engineering and the empirical methods used to work with these topics. For example, software engineering researchers start to use interview studies and grounded theory as methods for qualitative data analysis and reasoning (Robson and McCartan 2016). Prominent authors offer guidelines on how to conduct experiments (Wohlin et al. 2012), case studies (Runeson et al. 2012), surveys (Punter et al. 2003), or even construct theories in software engineering (Sjøberg et al. 2008), see also chapters "Guidelines for Case Survey Research in Software Engineering," "Challenges in Survey Research," and "The Design Science Paradigm as a Frame for Empirical Software Engineering." Detailed guidelines on what method to use in what circumstances are offered by Lethbridge et al. (2005), supported with guidelines of using advanced statistics in software engineering (Arcuri and Briand 2011). What characterizes the second generation of software engineering research is a lack of long-term commitment from the studied company and a discrete nature of the studies. Phenomena are often studied under a limited period and proposed solutions are rarely deployed to studied organization and used without the assistance of the researchers.

3   The Model for Co-production in Software Engineering

The seven steps described below are not necessarily sequential or determinant in order or effort spent. For clarity, they are presented in a chronological manner. The focus of the chapter is also on the co-production itself and not the overall research methodology. That judicious application and use of research methodologies is assumed in every step, but not detailed more than necessary for the purpose of describing co-production, see Fig. 1.

3.1   Step 1: What Is the Problem?

Never, ever, use the word "problem." Industry partners have challenges and opportunities for improvement. The first thing to remember is that companies are people, people in groups have politics and culture. Be aware of politics, learn and respect the culture, and make allies.

Establishing contacts, selling yourself and the research collaboration, and getting access to a company that is willing to work with you can be seen as *Step 0*. *Step 0* is not really covered in this chapter focusing on the co-production. However, it can be as simple as giving an invited seminar on research and challenges overall, to spark the interest of engineers and managers listening.

One overarching thing we should never forget, and which can be utilized with great success is that a researcher is not an employee, nor a consultant. This might make access and the way into a company harder, but it also gives you the element of

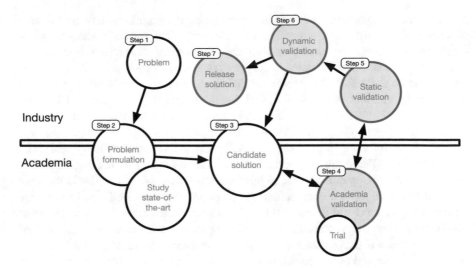

Fig. 1 The steps of the industrial co-production in software engineering

trust. A researcher can capitalize on being an external, unbiased party that focuses on solving problems and supplying solutions, rather than developing products or working at the company in question. In addition, a researcher's work follows a set of rules (ethics and methodology), and any results are scrutinized by not only the industrial partner but also peers (peer-review). Handled correctly this can give credibility that can be leveraged for attention and trust during a collaboration between you as a researcher and your industrial partner(s). The assumption for the purposes of this chapter is that you have established the relationship with your industrial partner and at least secured the commitment to start working together in a broad area.

Step 1 (see Fig. 1) is about identifying potential improvement areas (challenges) based on industry needs. In its purest form, this is done by performing a process assessment or exploratory investigation of some sort. This phase consists of four main activities.

3.1.1   Activity 1: Select an Overarching Area or Direction

It is impossible to assess an entire organization from all areas and perspectives. The size and possible findings are too great. Moreover, you as a researcher have a research focus (requirements engineering, testing, architecture, and so on). This is probably the first delimitation in area. Further refinement and narrowing can be relevant and beneficial depending on circumstances. Initial workshops with your industrial partner to discuss areas that require improvement can also be a good way forward. The challenge here is to make sure you do not select what to do at this point. The company telling you what to do exactly often leads to working on symptoms rather than actual cause/effect items. Symptoms are not the same as long-term challenges.

3.1.2   Activity 2: Plan and Execute the "Assessment"

Like all terms and concepts subject to fashion, process assessment and improvement (SPI) is by today's standards seen as old. However, the core methodology supplied by SPI frameworks like CMMI or uniREPM (Chrissis et al. 2003; Svahnberg et al. 2015), or even the original PDCA (Edwards 1986) and QIP, is still very much valid and useful. The purpose of the assessment is threefold.

1. The assessment should be planned and anchored at an appropriate level of the industry partner organization. How long will it take? What is your population and sample (what (selection) of products will you study, what roles and selection of practitioners having this role will you interact with, and so on) of your study? What methodology (see below) will you use and why? This needs to be planned and written down and agreed upon before you start. Typically, you will have a reference group or contact person at the company that opens doors and advises you. In order for this group or individual to help you, it is your job to be professional and offer all the "sales support" this person needs to get the resources and access needed for the assessment. A plan is such a thing.
2. Finding out what the challenges are (a.k.a. problems), how they manifest, their source both in origin and observation, their impact, and potential for being addressed. The process assessment models out there are often a combination of traditional methods used in exploring a phenomenon like case-study research (on an abstract level), and interviews, workshops, and document and artifact analysis on a detailed level. Further, the method used to analyze the data collected needs to be planned. Choose a combination of methodologies as appropriate. Remember, the assessment's purpose is to narrow down what to focus your research on, thus is a part of the research itself, and the results from such an assessment are research results in themselves (e.g., interview results about challenges in an area, document analysis about the currently used processes and methodologies).

   A critical part of the assessment is to use triangulation and root-cause analysis. Triangulation implies that you use more than one source to identify and describe challenges (e.g., documents and interviews and artifacts that show the same phenomena but from different perspectives and different sources). A root-cause analysis is also a good way to dig deeper and separate cause from symptom (e.g., "we have problems with bugs" can have a root cause of inadequate requirements analysis). Examples of dedicated research focused assessment frameworks and their use as well as result reporting can be found in Svahnberg et al. (2015), Pettersson et al. (2008), Pernstål et al. (2012). A good practical example of triangulation and root-cause analysis can be found here (Pernstål et al. 2015, 2019).
3. As you are performing the assessment you are getting to know your partner. You meet people, more importantly they meet you. Trust is built, especially

in the assessment stage as you listen, take notes, and try to understand. The relationship built here is crucial for a long-term relationship with the industrial partner. Relationships are always between you as a researcher and one individual at a time at the partner site. Establish and take care of these relationships, you will need them down the line.

3.1.3   Activity 3: Report and Collect

As the assessment is completing and analysis is underway (largely done) you need to report your findings in several ways and formats. Papers and technical reports can be two such forums. But this is not enough in any way. Most important is to give feedback to the ones that participated in your assessment. This can take the form of one or several seminars and/or workshops. Results, analysis, and implications are presented, root-cause analysis is clarified, and dependencies between findings are made clear. A good rule of thumb is that the audience already know what they told you. Repeating that is not relevant. Added value is in the form of your analysis and findings based on what they showed you and told you. By this stage, you as a researcher should know more about the challenges and their causes than any one of the people that participated in the assessment.

By reporting back to the same people you met in the assessment you show them that their investment has given results in the short-term (in the form of findings), and you as a researcher should also utilize this opportunity to get additional input and confirmation (or identify errors) in the assessment. A great way to do this is to ask for it explicitly as a part of the seminar/workshop. Surveys post-seminar can also be a complement.

3.1.4   Activity 4: Select

By this stage you often have a rather long list of "challenges" identified. One good practice is to ask as many as possible to prioritize the challenges identified in the assessment (perhaps as a part of Activity 3 above). This gives you and your industry partner reference group/contact(s) input as to what to focus on. Overall, there are three aspects that should dictate what challenges to focus your research around. Listed in order of importance: (1) the importance to the company or potential benefit if solved/addressed; (2) the dependencies between the challenges; (3) your interest area—the least important, but still relevant.

> *Running Example Step 1* The area for research is managing quality require-
> ments. However, this is a large area within requirements engineering research
> and body of knowledge. The important part of the assessment is to understand
> what abstraction level and what organization we should study for improving
> quality requirement. A good idea here is to start from a focus group meeting
> with several roles to discuss what is quality, what is the impact of quality on
> internal business and stakeholders, and what benefits a company may achieve
> by investing in improving both the processes and product quality.

3.2 Step 2: Is It Researchable?

One of the most difficult things to do when working in co-production with industry
is to separate consultancy and research. Industry partners will be very happy to have
you do work for them, especially since you probably are very qualified, and cheap
(your salary most likely comes from university). Overall the rule of thumb is that
you do only research. Research is what you can publish (peer-reviewed venue). This
chapter will not go into a long discussion about what does or does not constitute
research; however, it is important that you are clear towards your industrial partner
as this will come up.

The purpose of Step 2 is to delve deeper into one or several of the challenges
in Step 1. This can be done in any number of ways but generally involves three
activities.

> *Running Example Step 2 (Is It Researchable?)* When discussing the area and
> the symptoms in Step 1, you identified that a company lacks an adequate
> tool for the needs and education in managing quality requirements. The
> need to introduce a new (better) tool is highly prioritized by the company
> and You are asked to do that as a part of the research project. The answer
> is that installing and configuring a tool is no research and you should be
> clear in communicating that this is consultancy, maybe qualified work but
> not research. You should explain this to the company and move to the other
> challenge. For example, the information meta-model that the tool will use
> and the associated improvements to handing quality requirements could be a
> potential researchable area. Therefore, root-cause analysis of the challenges
> is a very important step and it helps to define what is researchable and prepare
> conducting focused state-of-the-art study.

3.2.1 Activity 1: Problem Formulation

Problem formulation involves a deepening of the root-cause analysis of the challenge(s) (see Step 1), but also breaking the challenge(s) into actual research problems. In its simplest form you want to (1) be able to describe the context of the challenge, (2) the area(s) of research/study, and (3) either identify a number of research questions or potentially refine into a hypothesis. The end result is a research direction with concrete research questions to answer.

3.2.2 Activity 2: Study State of the Art

Exploring state of the art is often done in parallel with Activity 1. However, a more detailed and systematic review of state of the art is often a part of reading up on a subject, positioning the problem formulation/research (from Activity 1) to other research and being able to explain how your research will contribute to the state of the art. An example of a systematic literature review (SLR) done in conjunction with Step 2 can be found here Pernstål et al. (2013).

The literature review helps you to systematically obtain evidence about the area of interest and formulate conclusions or recommendations based on the analysis and synthesis of the evidence found in the selected papers. The process should be transparent and traceable and decisions taken during the literature review (e.g., what papers to include) should be clearly documented. Chapters "Automating Systematic Literature Review" and "Rapid Reviews in Software Engineering" offer more details about systematic literature reviews.

A critical lesson in Step 2 is not to lose touch with your industrial partner. Doing a 1 year SLR is a very bad idea. You need to keep in touch with your industrial partner, as well as present, discuss, and validate your ideas and findings, even from this step. A rule of thumb is that Step 2 should not take more than 2–3 months of calendar time to not risk the industrial partner moving on. Another good idea is to find a recent SLR in the area of interest that contains a summary of the core papers in the area and perform snowballing on these articles.

Our experience shows that a faster systematic literature review (narrow and efficient methodology applied, see, e.g., snowballing (Wohlin 2014)) is preferable. The purpose here is not to be perfect, rather to gauge; are the challenges and subsequent problem formulation and breakdown likely to result in new research that complements what is already out there? Other chapters provide additional information around searching gray literature as so-called multivocal literature reviews chapter "Benefitting from the Grey Literature in Software Engineering Research", and rapid reviews covered in chapter "Rapid Reviews in Software Engineering".

If the answer is yes, then you move on to Step 3 of the co-production model as fast as possible. If the answer is no, on the other hand, move to the next challenge(s) on the list. An overall tip for Step 2 is that even if much of the work is reading, you can do the reading at the company partners' offices. That way you are part of the environment, can talk to people, and be seen.

Selecting and detailing a research area is the topic for whole books and will not be covered here in any detail in this chapter. However, type of contribution is relevant for the discussion. The base question that any engineering scientist has to ask is; if a research area is well established and significant research has been conducted, why does my industrial partner have challenges/problems in this very area? The answer can be that the company simply is unaware of the many "solutions" available. If this is the case, then a very good idea is that you, as a researcher, help facilitate the transfer and adaptation of one or several already existing "solutions." This can be a research contribution as you can do research on the adoption and subsequently measure the usability and usefulness of a solution, even if it is not new or yours. One of the benefits of this is presenting a solution to the partner company. However, many, if not most, solutions out there (even if well published) have rarely been extensively tried in industry. However, let us say that the solution has been validated in industry, thus it appears to scale and show utility. Even then it most likely needs modification and adaptation to fit and be a solution to your partner company's challenges. All this is very relevant and publishable engineering research in itself.

> *Running Example Step 2 (Selecting an Area)* The challenge is "misman-agement of quality requirements that lead to misunderstanding and defects later in product development". The root cause shows (among other things) (1) inadequacies in specification where quality requirements are often neglected and (2) inadequacies in communication in relation to requirements between practitioners, roles, departments, etc. You start reading up and find a lot of research in both of these fields (hundreds, if not thousands, of papers and methods/tools, etc. already published). On this level, it seems like it will be hard for you to contribute. Two choices exist. One, you can move on to another area where less research is done and it is easier to contribute, or two, you can delve deeper and see if you can contribute even if the area is well researched. Maybe the problem is in decision-making about quality requirements? If so, you should study how a requirement is decided upon since its inception (both quality and functional), what roles are involved, what artifacts are produced, and who prepares, takes, and influences the decisions made about these requirements.

Outcomes from Step 2 result often in a hybrid. There are often many potential solutions, but few are actually validated and tested in a real environment (shown to be usable, useful, and scalable). These solutions can, however, act as input and inspiration to you in your work to solve your partner company's challenges. This is all very good research practice if done correctly.

3.2.3   Activity 3: Formulate a Research Plan

Once you have an idea of what research to start with, whether it be to develop something completely new, use existing research, or a hybrid, you need to develop a plan for the next steps. These steps are basically the same as the ones described in this co-production model.

3.3   Step 3: Solution or Not Solution?

The co-production model has a rather large step between Step 2 and this Step 3. Step 3 is the "do the research" step. From Step 2 we should have an idea of research direction, area, and details on the initial parts of a plan. This research could be further empirical studies (so more investigation deeper, and not a "solution"). Studying a phenomenon in industry is relevant, valuable, and publishable.

Industry partners can be shown that further study can be directly beneficial to the company and provide direct improvements. However, even after further study, some sort of solution will be part of the research and change the nature of the research activities from descriptive (what we can observe and what are the challenges or problem associated with the phenomenon we are exploring) to prescriptive (can we develop a way to improve the current way-of-working). For the purposes of this chapter, we will focus on creating and delivering some sort of solution.

At the core of any solution is a continuous collaboration with industry partners while developing the solution. This is critical. Sitting at university for months, then visiting the company to show them what you have is most often not a good idea. What you want is to involve company practitioners in the work. This can take the form of formal workshops, work sessions, meetings, and so on (Santos and Travassos 2009). However, informal discussions are at least as beneficial and important. Sit at your partner company site. Discuss your research and ideas during a lunch break. This is a great way to get input and also build trust and acceptance of any solution you eventually come up with, as it was "made here" at the company site, with constant input and feedback. This can be seen as a type of action research (Pernstål et al. 2015).

> *Running Example Step 3* You came to a conclusion that a new way to specify and communicate quality requirements could significantly limit mis-understandings (usefulness), but at the same time not increase level work needed or formality (usability and scalability). You call this way of quality requirements specification/communication "QRImP." You are sure that the improved communication part is a way to improve decision-making about

(continued)

quality requirements since it will provide improved rationale for decisions and help decision makers to perform better work.

QRImP was developed based on challenges identified (Step 1), it was refined and formulated for research (Step 2), and you developed a solution in the form of QRImP (Step 3), in collaboration (many coffee machine discussions, workshops, and meetings) with many practitioners and also colleagues at university over months of work. Now what? Well, what you actually have developed is a candidate solution that needs to be "tested" and improved. This is described in Steps 4–6, as these steps are validation and improvement incrementally within each steps and evolutionary as the steps progress.

3.4 Lab-Based (Static) Validation and Improvement in Academia

Most of the time Step 3 (developing the candidate solution), Step 4, and Step 5 happen simultaneously or at least overlap to some extent. For reasons of clarity, we describe the steps in sequence. Step 4 is validation in academia. You devise a "solution" of some sort, whether it be a method, model, framework, way-of-working, organizational improvement, tool, or equivalent, and try it out on the so-called toy examples and/or use students as subjects to try it out. Albeit being a smart way to do initial validation of a solution, it also has many inherited flaws, inconsistencies, and scalability problems.

Many researchers critique this type of lab-based scaled-down validation as it does not represent an industrial scale, context, or application using practitioners subjected to time and resource pressure. Our experience is that utilizing scaled-down scenarios and/or students or even fellow researchers as subjects is beneficial. Any use of industry resources poses a cost and disturbs the real production environment. This should be avoided if non-production environments can be utilized to catch the same incompatibility with the candidate solution. Wohlin et al. (2012) offer a comprehensive overview and guidelines on how to plan, conduct, and report experiments in software engineering.

Doing a short experiment with colleagues, or students, in a controlled environment can not only catch items that simply do not work, but you can also measure usability and usefulness in an accurate manner as you can do, for example, a controlled experiment and compare your candidate solution to another way-of-working.

Lab-based validation is one step and not the end of validation, despite evidence to the contrary looking at peer-reviewed papers in many fields (where an experimental validation is sufficient for publishing in many top venues). However, since software engineering is an applied engineering science, ending at the lab validation stage is especially troubling. The only reason to end at the lab validation step in software engineering is if the solution fails so badly that there is no reason to carry on.

The data collected during lab validation can and should be used to improve the solution. In many cases, this implies simplification of the solution and making it less useful and more usable. This might be contrary to your training as a scientist and engineer; however, it is wise to remember that a perfect solution that no one uses is a meaningless solution from the company's point of view.

Lab validation is a perfect opportunity to try to balance usefulness and usability as well as scalability of a solution. Does it take the students 2 h to specify and coordinate one requirement? Well, if your industrial partner has a hundred require-ments to handle per year (e.g., slow system evolution, safety critical applications, for example), your solution may be acceptable. However, if your industry partner has thousands of requirements per year, which change constantly as competition and market circumstances evolve, then they will be lucky to have 5 min to spend on a single requirement during initial specification and communication.

A notable problem inherent in software engineering research is that problems can be very complex, but any solution has to be simple. This might sound obvious, but publishing "simple solutions" might not be that easy as reviewers do not see the entire evolution. The contribution of creating and refining a solution that is usable and useful in industry and used for real requires a lot of work and time and often does not result in many more publications. The point of taking the next step is working towards refining and transferring the solution to reality and measuring how well your solution works; not inventing new solutions or more advance concepts.

A good indication of when to stop/move on from the lab validation is when you cannot learn more without adding the reality of industry to the validation (realistic scale, real practitioners as subjects, industry partner context, and limitations). The limited and scaled-down nature of lab validation can, however, be used to build a case for your industry partner.

During lab validation, the solution and instrumentation are refined in continuous collaboration with the company. The interaction with the company is realized in seminars and presentations of results from the lab validations. Step 5 often overlaps with Step 4 as the focus is on building the trust of the company in the developed solution. The main potential is to build trust. Lab validation not only enables you to improve the solution but shows this to the industry partner—you are doing all you can to improve a solution that was coproduced with and by them, without wasting their time and resources. It also minimizes risk for the partner, as major problems associated with the solution can be caught before they invest in the next step.

Running Example Step 4 How well do the QRImP specification and coor-dination method work in comparison to another established way to achieve the same task? How can we measure that the effort dedicated to introducing

(continued)

QRImP would yield expected benefits? How large should be the group of participants (roles, availability) so we can objectively measure the effects of introducing QRImP. How many quality requirements should be specified and decided upon with the help fo QRImP? How to measure improved communication and narrowing some communication gaps with the help of QRImP?

When you develop the instrumentation for the lab-based validation you get a good idea on what is needed for later industrial validation in terms of training, manuals, templates, tools, etc. to support and enable the use of QRImP. For example, you can measure the quality of requirements specified with the QRImP template, the communication issues (delays, decisions that need to be reversed), or other negative effects to see the effect of introduction of QRImP.

3.5   Step 5: Static Validation in Industry

Static validation is often characterized by trying out your solution on a limited scale. The subjects are real industrial practitioners (you need to think about population and sample in relation to the future potential users of the solution); however, the time and scale of application are limited.

Static validation is often a collection of activity steps and a progression towards more realistic scenarios. Below examples of this are described based on real cases in research. Please observe that these examples should be adapted to fit your contextual characteristics and case specifics. The purpose of the static validation is to get input to refine and improve the solution to the extent that the partner company wants to try it in their real production environment. Static validation is conducted at several levels described below:

Level 1: Workshop Sessions This typically denotes dedicated work sessions where you plan and call a meeting. A handful of practitioners come, and you present your solution, give them initial training and tools (from nothing, a simple template, to an actual tool, depending on your solution), and let them try out the solution using real data (e.g., requirements in our example). Data collection here is both direct and indirect. You can measure things like task completion, defects, time to get proficient, and so on.

Direct measurement gives you absolute measures what worked and what did not, the comparison of your solution to the current way of working gives you additional relative judgement. Direct measurement gives you absolute measures what worked and what did not, the comparison of your solution to the current way of working gives you additional relative judgement. During the session, actual observation and lightweight logging (Lethbridge et al. 2005) of behavior and work can be useful as a data collection tool in addition. A tip is to have one or two supporting scientists in these sessions. The main scientist is typically the workshop leader and will have a hard time observing and taking notes.

Level 1 is often carried out with multiple groups (as large groups are hard to observe); thus you might replicate the "study" several times. Whether you choose to change the solution (and/or instrumentation) between iterations is context dependent and presents pros and cons either way. Our experience is that the validity threats introduced (or sample size reduced as if you change instrumentation or perform several smaller studies) are preferable than running studies with a solution and/or instrumentation you know should be updated.

Level 2: Lightweight Production During workshops (where you optimally got a lot of input utilizing several methodologies) the solution is refined either iterative or in batches. Once you judge that more workshops will not yield different results (this can be observed via the data collected) you can move on to static validation closer to the production environment. This involves joining an actual production team on an appropriate level that works with areas relevant to your solutions utilization. The mandate to allow this comes from the issue that some of the same people participating in the previous workshops are the same production team/practitioners you now join. They use your solution to do their job. You as a researcher are on hand to support them and to some extent compensate for the learning curve of any new way-of-working. In this environment, it is much harder to be an external "observer" and collect data in an objective manner as you become embedded into the team. However, debriefings and observations are still important and possible. It is also possible to combine post-work interviews or surveys as a complement. This is still an activity to collect data to be used as input for improving your solution.

The practitioners' goals are aligned (they have a vested interest to really see if the solution works for real), but their primary goal is to do their work. Thus, any data collection is up to you in this phase especially as generally you are not supported by other scientists. The production environment is typically sensitive to disruption, and you as a scientist should embed yourself into the term to minimize distractions and biases. Having extra scientists present is typically impractical as a larger contingent of scientists disturbs the production environment even more than one.

It should be observed that static validation is very costly for an industrial partner. Person hours of the practitioners participating is only one part, the real cost for the company is best alternative investment. That is, what they could have been doing in their production environment, and all subsequent effects of this downstream are cancelled to work with you and help validate the solution. Often researchers forget that there is almost never any slack in an industrial production environment, thus it is always a trade-off. This insight should inspire a researcher to be very well prepared and maximize every opportunity for data collection aiming to improve the solution.

A central delivery of Step 5 is significant amounts of data on the usability and usefulness of the solution, in addition to the evolution of the solution during the static validation. This is critical from a research perspective, but also for the industrial partner in preparation for the next step. Step 5 also brings significant educational value since the participants get improved understanding of the method and potential benefits when implemented in the organization.

> *Running Example Step 5* After receiving encouraging positive results from the QRImP lab validation (Step 4), you move on to static validation with industry (Step 5). Here a large part of the instrumentation developed for the lab validation can be reused, together with the description of the desired participants and their required levels of expertise and availability.
>
> You then plan and execute a workshop session and invite the roles you decided are relevant and should use or be impacted by QRImP. You give the group some initial training in the method (with many simple examples), followed by a request to take some requirements from their environment and work with them using QRImP.
>
> It is important to be at least 2 persons in the room so one can moderate and make sure it progresses according to the plan and the second person takes notes and collect any other relevant data. It is wise to run more than one workshop with two separated group and compare the results. Collect comments and improvement suggestions during the workshops to tune and improve QRImP. Ask for reasons and rationale for improvement to make sure that the improvements are harmonized with the overarching goal of the method.

3.6 Step 6: Dynamic Validation in Industry

The goal of dynamic validation is to let industry use the solution uninterrupted by researchers. In this step there should be no action research, if you need to be on board you are still in the static validation step. Dynamic validation is critical as the true success of any co-production effort and solution is if an industry partner and the practitioners use the solution after the researchers leave the organization. Dynamic validation can be divided into three parts, and you can and often have to iterate within the activities.

3.6.1 Activity 1: Sell-In, Buy-In, Finding the Right Production Instance

If you have worked closely with the industry partner throughout Steps 1–5, the move towards trying out your solution in a production instance (project, iteration, etc.) will be a natural next step. In some companies, there will still be a need for you to present your case, and to sell the usability and usefulness of your solution to middle-/senior management before they invest in dynamic validation. Again, the risk for the company at this stage is greater than in any other step. You need to train practitioners in using the solution, supply manuals, tool support, maybe even transfer data from other systems. This is a part of your preparation for dynamic validation.

Do you remember under Step 2 we had a discussion about the distinction between research and consultancy? The delivery of a tool (might be a commercial one supporting your solution), the training of using the solution (using the tool), and so on is consultancy (or at least not research). However, this is completely acceptable and mandated given that it is in preparation for dynamic validation of your solution. Thus, what is consultancy and what is not depends on the intent and context. The preparation for the dynamic validation is mostly on you, but the subsequent validation is all on the industry partner and the practitioners. Optimally you should not even be present in the environment at all.

3.6.2 Activity 2: Data Gathering

What is the research part of Step 6? Mostly preparation. You should instantiate a measurement program since you want to measure the usability and usefulness of the solution in a completely real use scenario in a real live production environment. In dynamic validation, practitioners use the solution without the researchers being there or being able to help, or do any changes in how the practitioners use the solution. The measurements you introduce need to collect as much data as possible pertaining to usability and usefulness with as little (close to zero) interference from the measurement being done. Any measurement interference in "normal" operations is a threat to validity and also constitutes a confounding factor (Wohlin et al. 2012; Feldt and Magazinius 2010).

Exactly how measurement is done varies depending on your solution, the production environment and context of use (Petersen and Wohlin 2009). For example, if there is tool support measurement on use, task completion, etc. can be collected. If artifacts are produced (e.g., in our example, requirements) they can be tagged and saved in as a granular versioning/variant manner as possible. If other artifacts (code) result from the main solution artifacts (requirement) these are saved for later analysis. Going against the no interference policy, you can do some direct measurement, especially if use and artifact-based measurements are not possible.

For example, one of the practitioners can be "responsible" for the new way-of-working (the solution). This person can then collect data as a part of this job. You can also present surveys (short and fast ones) in the use process. However, please observe that the practitioners not only have their jobs to do, but you are asking them to change how they work and learn a new way (solution) at the same time. Any additional parts are pressuring them further during the production instance. After the production instance has ended (and the dynamic validation round has ended) you can do more direct measurement in various forms.

3.6.3 Activity 3: Data Analysis and Data Reconstruction

As a validation round ends and data is collected, analysis of the impact of applying the solution is the focus. Measurements in relation to usability and usefulness are key; however, there are complementary parts. Improvement ideas and deal breakers (what was bad) are gathered through, e.g., interviews and workshops. This should be done as fast as possible with as many as possible that were using the solution in the production environment.

The data collected and analyzed can result in one of the three outcomes:

1. **The usability and usefulness are too low compared to previous ways-of-working.** If this is the case you can either abandon the solution (that does not mean that it was bad research) or you can reverse back to Step 3 and redesign your solution.
2. **The usability and usefulness are higher than the previous way-of-working.** The company decides to progress to Step 7 (covered later in more detail).
3. **The solution is promising, but needs work and improvement and more validation before it can move on to be used for real in the organization.** This third outcome is the most common. Outcome one is the least common given that you have refined and progressed with the solution using co-production, and large surprises should have been caught earlier in the lab and static validation rounds.

Step 6 is often executed several times for several reasons. One of the reasons is that after the first static validation round you have tested the solution in one production environment only. Companies are heterogeneous in terms of what they do, and how they work. Thus, the solution might need several variants (instances) at different places to be eligible for more dynamic validation rounds. Dynamic validation completion depends on two goals. First, does the company have the confidence to move on to Step 7, and second, have you as a researcher exhausted the potential for data collection in relation to the solution (short-term).

Running Example Step 6 You need to start from creating a summary presentation of the results from the static validation that you can use to find the production instance that would be interested in continuously using QRImP. It is important here to remember the goals and the challenges and associate the results from static validation as clear indication that we are on the good path towards intended improvements. At Step 6, you need to work intensively with sell-in activities but also remember what is researchable (please see Step 2 for details).

For example, as a research you should not develop a tool unless it is a step towards gathering data for dynamic validation and later handing over the tool management to the studied company. Based on the validation in academia and static validation, you should establish a measurement program

(continued)

and decide about the frequency of data collection (how often would you measure if QRImP helps with managing quality requirements), and how often the results will be shared with the management team. You should also appoint a person who can be "responsible" for introducing the new "way-of-working" and making sure it is not forgotten or neglected.

3.7   Step 7: Solution Release

A company progressing to Step 7 is committing to using the solution without the assist or influence of the researchers. Your role in the end of Step 6 is of course significant research reporting (peer-review), but also significant reporting (mostly in the form of discussions and presentations) to the company on multiple levels. This gives the decision makers decision support input as to convincing management and themselves to adopt the solution.

The institutionalization of the solution in the company is not really part of the research; however, it is in your interest to be supportive of these efforts for two main reasons. The future collaboration and research with the company is dependent to a degree, but more importantly, the ability to get access to long-term study of the solution post-release. In Step 6 we did try out the solution in a real environment; however, the long-term effects of the solution on the company (people, teams, products, and other artifacts) are largely unknown.

In our example, improving requirements communication might result in, e.g., improved team coherence (soft factor) and improved ability to test customer value (hard factor). By helping with the company with instances (not doing it all but helping) you might be able to get them to let you also instantiate some sort of measurement program alongside it. This will enable you to monitor and collect data on a complete organizational scale, continuously. This can easily be motivated to the company (input for them too) when the measurement program is reasonably non-intrusive and low cost. The ability to perform such longitudinal studies (Sjøberg et al. 2007) is as rare as it is a great opportunity. Steps 1–7 completed implies you actually start over with a new set of challenges.

Running Example Step 7 You should work mostly with packaging your research results and the artifacts created so that the person "responsible" can smoothly take over. A significant amount of effort you should also decide to creating educational material about QRImP (recording lectures with examples from the company, slides, and supplementary material). Lastly, you should present the results from dynamic validation to several roles and levels of the organization to raise awareness and enable more easy technology transfer.

4   General Lessons Learned

This chapter presents some general lessons learned and experiences from applying the presented model. We focus here on clarifying what means a delivery and how the developed solution should be treated by both the researcher and industry. We also clarify how to establish an effective publication strategy when working with the model.

A Word on Technology and Knowledge Transfer   The actual solution creation and subsequent refinement through validation is the visible delivery. However, just as much knowledge and improvement is "transferred" as an indirect effect of the co-production and collaboration work itself. The researcher learns about the industry partner's context, products, challenges, technologies, ways-of-working, and more. At the same time practitioners at the company learn more about themselves and thus can change and improve things independent of the actual solution. Practitioners also learn things associated with the work. For example, training practitioners to try the solution out will improve their knowledge in the application field (become better at specifying requirements and/or communication and coordination in our example). This effect is hard for a researcher to measure. Purists will say that this in itself constitutes a confounding factor and validity issue. Engineering scientists say, any positive influence on state-of-practice is a good thing and our job.

A Word on Publications and Papers   As you might have noticed very little has been voiced about "studies" and "papers" during the description of the co-production model. Working in real co-production and trying to base solutions on real problems and then devise solutions that eventually can and will be used in a real production environment without you as a researcher is very hard, prone to failure, and relatively speaking, harder to publish. You do not do studies and then a paper or two (a.k.a. "hit and run" research). You do not listen to industry, devise a solution that you apply on a toy example or subject students to, and then stop and write paper after paper (toy level validation). If publications are your main goal, I would stay away from co-production in any real sense. However, if you want to work with industry and earn a status as an expert "problem solver," then co-production is vastly rewarding. As a researcher, you very seldom get to see the results of your work beyond some peer-recognition and citations. Seeing something you helped create working without your assistance, being used by strangers 10 years after you released in a company is the real reward. If the practitioners using the solution have renamed it, use it in a different way than you originally intended, and do not know who you are, that is success.

All of this said, of course you can publish. Maybe you will not churn out papers at the speed of changing statistical methods on the same data set of open source data, but your papers will be much more relevant and contain real data and report on solutions you measure. We would like to avoid detailing the reporting part, but since younger researchers might read this chapter, we wanted to share examples of how you can plan out your publication parts while working in a co-production scenario.

Tips for reporting industrial co-production in software engineering

Step 1 Finding challenges is, in essence, a detailed and deep empirical study of one or several macro-cases (companies) and/or micro-cases (dept. or divisions in a comp.). Real challenges, their descriptions, and actual origin are in themselves research results. This is especially if you apply a rigorous assessment methodology.

Step 2 Investigating state of the art, doing detailed root-cause analysis, and combining this with empirical data is relevant for publication. The quality of the publication depends on the scope and rigidness of the state-of-the-art investigation.

Step 3 Formulating a candidate solution is often very interesting to convey in a position paper, spanning everything from a good workshop where your ideas can be discussed, to actual heavier publications—depending on the novelty and potential of your candidate solution. Remember, you are basing its creation on input from industry even if the solution is not validated yet.

Step 4 Lab validation can result in any number of publications, from student experiments to simulations and details on the solution. Refinement evolution based on lab validation is also interesting and relevant to base in a publication(s).

Step 5 Static validation is often very well anchored, and you collect data from actual industrial practitioners in several iterations and phases of solution evolution. You also measure real usability and usefulness in this step, all relevant for publication.

Steps 6 and 7 The data collected on the use, usability, usefulness of the solution, and impact in industry is well worth publication, often resulting in several heavier papers.

Overall As you progress through the steps you will notice that you might need to develop macro contributions so that you can move on and validate and improve the solution itself. These "macro" contributions can, for example, be: new ways of assessing a company (Steps 1–2), new tools and tool support for the solution, new ways to measure usability and usefulness of your solution, and so on. All of these are also relevant in their own right and viable for publication.

5 Recommended Further Reading

Wohlin et al. (2012) outline the success factors powering the industry–academia collaboration. The authors highlight the usefulness of 14 factors, e.g., collaboration champion on site, buy-in and support from company management, researcher's visible presence, and regular meetings.

Svahnberg et al. (2015) offer a framework for requirements engineering process assessment that is lightweight and offers comprehensive overview of the maturity level of an organization. The assessment brings practical examples of how to plan questions in various areas of software engineering, how to collect the answers and prepare the report to the companies.

Pettersson et al. (2008) offer detailed guidelines on how to perform lightweight process assessment and improvement planning. It is the initial work that led to the creation of uniREPM (Svahnberg et al. 2015) and brings practical viewpoints of process assessment and improvement.

Pernståy et al. (2012) offer a method for root-cause analysis when performing software process improvement activities. Flex-RCA method for root-cause analysis is used to delve deeper into challenges identified to find root causes as a part of the evaluation and subsequent improvement activities.

On the methodological stance, Wohlin (2014) outline how to conduct snow-balling literature studies in software engineering as an alternative to database search systematic literature reviews, while Lethbridge et al. (2005) list what data collection techniques to use in what empirical study in software engineering. They divide the techniques into the first-order techniques where the researcher has a direct context with study subjects and second and third-degree techniques where researchers study artifacts produced during software engineering activities.

Wohlin et al. (2012) offer a comprehensive overview how to plan, conduct, and report experiments in software engineering. The authors provide detailed guidelines with examples about how to plan an experiment, select dependent and independent variables, subjects, and objects as well as instrumentation.

6 Conclusion

The co-production model presented here is one way of achieving co-production. The idea is not to follow it like a blueprint, but rather use it to get inspiration and understanding of the incremental and also stepwise nature of building a solution, but also in building trust and commitment from your industrial partner. There are many downsides to working in close collaboration with industry. The academic reward systems are not really gauged to reward success that is actually defined as making a real difference in reality.

The number of publications, H-index, funds acquired, doctoral students supervised, courses thought, and peer-recognition can all be good but do not necessarily have anything to do with co-production. So why do we do it? This is a long conversation and we can only speak for ourselves. We are engineers. We love solving problems. As researchers, we get to try to solve really tricky and complex problems. As engineering scientists this means solving complex problems by devising solutions that actually work in an applied setting. Not in theory, not maybe sometime in the future.

Acknowledgements We thank current and past SERL members and collaborating companies for inspiration in writing this chapter.

References

Arcuri A, Briand L (2011) A practical guide for using statistical tests to assess randomized algorithms in software engineering. In: 2011 33rd international conference on software engineering (ICSE). IEEE, Piscataway, pp 1–10

Brooks Jr, FP (1995) The mythical man-month: essays on software engineering, anniversary edition, 2/E. Pearson Education India, Noida

Chrissis MB, Konrad M, Shrum S (2003) CMMI guidelines for process integration and product improvement. Addison-Wesley Longman Publishing Co., Inc., Boston

Edwards DW (1986) Out of the crisis. Massachusetts Institute of Technology, Center for Advanced Engineering Study, Cambridge

Feldt R, Magazinius A (2010) Validity threats in empirical software engineering research-an initial survey. In: Proceedings of the 22nd international conference on software engineering & knowledge engineering (SEKE'2010), pp 374–379

Gorschek T (2018) Evolution toward soft(er) products. Commun ACM 61(3):78–84

Gorschek T, Garre P, Larsson S, Wohlin C (2006) A model for technology transfer in practice. IEEE Softw 23(6):88–95

Hult M, Lennung S-A (1980) Towards a definition of action research: a note and bibliography. J Manag Stud 17(2):241–250

Lethbridge TC, Sim SE, Singer J (2005) Studying software engineers: data collection techniques for software field studies. Empir Softw Eng 10(3):311–341

Naur P, Randell B (1969) Software engineering: report of a conference sponsored by the NATO science committee, Garmisch, 7th–11th October 1968

Parnas DL (1972) On the criteria to be used in decomposing systems into modules. Commun ACM 15(12):1053–1058

Pernståhl J, Magazinius A, Gorschek T (2012) A study investigating challenges in the interface between product development and manufacturing in the development of software-intensive automotive systems. Int J Softw Eng Knowl Eng 22(07):965–1004

Pernståhl J, Feldt R, Gorschek T (2013) The lean gap: a review of lean approaches to large-scale software systems development. J Syst Softw 86(11):2797–2821

Pernståhl J, Gorschek T, Feldt R, Florén D (2015) Requirements communication and balancing in large-scale software-intensive product development. Inf Softw Technol 67:44–64

Pernståhl J, Feldt R, Gorschek T, Florén D (2019) FLEX-RCA: a lean-based method for root cause analysis in software process improvement. Softw Qual J 27(1):389–428

Petersen K, Wohlin C (2009) Context in industrial software engineering research. In: 2009 3rd international symposium on empirical software engineering and measurement. IEEE, Piscataway, pp 401–404

Pettersson F, Ivarsson M, Gorschek T, Öhman P (2008) A practitioner's guide to light weight software process assessment and improvement planning. J Syst Softw 81(6):972–995

Punter T, Ciolkowski M, Freimut B, John I (2003) Conducting on-line surveys in software engineering. In: Proceedings 2003 international symposium on empirical software engineering, 2003. ISESE 2003. IEEE, Piscataway, pp 80–88

Rapoport RN (1970) Three dilemmas in action research: with special reference to the Tavistock experience. Hum Relat 23(6):499–513

Robson C, McCartan K (2016) Real world research. Wiley, Hoboken

Runeson P, Host M, Rainer A, Regnell B (2012) Case study research in software engineering: guidelines and examples. Wiley, Hoboken

Sannö A, Öberg AE, Flores-Garcia E, Jackson M (2019) Increasing the impact of industry–academia collaboration through co-production. Technol Innov Manag Rev 9(4):37–47

Santos PSMD, Travassos GH (2009) Action research use in software engineering: an initial survey. In: Proceedings of the 2009 3rd international symposium on empirical software engineering and measurement. IEEE Computer Society, Washington, pp 414–417

Sjøberg DIK, Dybå T, Jorgensen M (2007) The future of empirical methods in software engineering research. In: 2007 Future of software engineering, FOSE '07, Washington. IEEE Computer Society, Washington, pp 358–378

Sjøberg DI, Dybå T, Anda BC, Hannay JE (2008) Building theories in software engineering. In: Guide to advanced empirical software engineering. Springer, Berlin, pp 312–336

Svahnberg M, Gorschek T, Nguyen TTL, Nguyen M (2015) Uni-REPM: a framework for requirements engineering process assessment. Requir Eng 20(1):91–118

Wohlin C (2014) Guidelines for snowballing in systematic literature studies and a replication in software engineering. In: Proceedings of the 18th international conference on evaluation and assessment in software engineering. Citeseer, p 38

Wohlin C, Aurum A, Angelis L, Phillips L, Dittrich Y, Gorschek T, Grahn H, Henningsson K, Kagstrom S, Low G, Rovegard P, Tomaszewski P, van Toorn C, Winter J (2012) The success factors powering industry-academia collaboration. IEEE Softw 29(2):67–73

Wohlin C, Runeson P, Höst M, Ohlsson MC, Regnell B, Wesslén A (2012) Experimentation in software engineering. Springer Science & Business Media, Berlin

Printed in the United States
by Baker & Taylor Publisher Services